PATTERNS FOR A PURPOSE

A Rhetorical Reader

PATTERNS FOR A PURPOSE

A Rhetorical Reader

Second Edition

BARBARA FINE CLOUSE

Boston   Burr Ridge, IL   Dubuque, IA   Madison, WI   New York
San Francisco   St. Louis   Bangkok   Bogotá   Caracas   Lisbon
London   Madrid   Mexico City   Milan   New Delhi   Seoul
Singapore   Sydney   Taipei   Toronto

McGraw-Hill College

A Division of The **McGraw·Hill** Companies

3 4 5 6 7 8 9 0 DOC/DOC 9 3 2 1 0 9

ISBN   0-07-011980-5

Editorial director and Publisher: *Phillip A. Butcher*
Sponsoring editor: *Sarah Moyers*
Developmental editor: *Alexis Walker*
Marketing manager: *Lesley Denton*
Project manager: *Kari Geltemeyer*
Production associate: *Debra R. Benson*
Designer: *Kiera Cunningham*
Supplement coordinator: *Linda Huenecke*
Compositor: *York Graphic Services, Inc.*
Typeface: *11/13 Berkeley*
Printer: *R.R. Donnelley & Sons Company*

Library of Congress Cataloging-in-Publication Data

Clouse, Barbara Fine.
    Patterns for a purpose : a rhetorical reader / Barbara Fine
Clouse. — 2nd ed.
        p.   cm.
    Includes index.
    ISBN 0-07-011980-5 (acid-free paper)
    1. College readers.   2. English language—Rhetoric.   I. Title.
PE1417.C6314 1998
808' .0427—dc21   98-2964

http://www.mhhe.com

For Denny, with love

CONTENTS

Chapter 4

Narration   131

---

*Selections with an asterisk are new to this edition.

Chapter 5

Exemplification   197

Chapter 6

Process Analysis   261

Chapter 7

Comparison-Contrast   325

Chapter 8

Cause-and-Effect Analysis   385

Chapter 9

Classification-Division   443

Chapter 10

Definition   501

Chapter 11

Additional Readings: A Casebook for Argumentation-Persuasion   569

Appendix

Writing Paraphrases, Quotations, Summaries, and Syntheses   677

THEMATIC CONTENTS

Health and Medicine

Memories

ESSAY PAIRS

This table of contents makes suggestions for instructors who assign pairs of essays representing similar or opposing perspectives. Assigning selections in this fashion is an excellent way to show how different writers can approach the same subject matter in vastly different ways. By no means do the pairings represent all the possibilities; instructors are likely to find many more combinations for stimulating discussion and writing.

PREFACE

ANOTHER RHETORICAL READER? WHY BOTHER?

Patterns for a Purpose is a rhetorical reader like no other. While it shares many of the features found in the best rhetorical readers, it includes a number of improvements, including these:

- **The rhetorical patterns are presented as means, not ends.** *Patterns for a Purpose* focuses on the patterns as ways to fulfill the writer's purpose. Thus, the readings are identified according to the patterns they exhibit and how those patterns help writers do the following: express feelings and relate experience, entertain, inform, and persuade.

- **The rhetorical patterns are not taught in isolation.** *Patterns for a Purpose* acknowledges that rhetorical patterns often appear in combination, so each chapter of essays includes at least two selections that illustrate how two or more patterns can be combined to achieve a variety of purposes.

- **Argumentation-persuasion is treated as both pattern and purpose.** Other rhetorical readers treat argumentation-persuasion only as a rhetorical pattern. Yet persuasion is a purpose, so in *Patterns for a Purpose* argumentation-persuasion essays appear in every chapter of readings. The chapter on cause-and-effect analysis, for example, includes a cause-and-effect analysis meant to persuade the reader; the chapter on narration shows a narrative essay meant to persuade the reader, and so forth. However, because of the importance of argumentation-persuasion, the sophistication it requires of students, and the specific conventions associated with it, argumentation-persuasion also gets exclusive attention in Chapter 11.

- **A casebook provides a unique set of instructional opportunities.** Although Chapter 11, "A Casebook on Argumentation-Persuasion," focuses on the strategies of writing

argumentation-persuasion, it also does a great deal more. Ten
high-interest readings on five timely issues give students an opportunity to grapple with and write about controversial subjects
that matter to them. Many of the readings offer different perspectives on the same issue, affording students opportunities to
engage in evaluative and other kinds of critical thinking. In addition, the casebook provides opportunities to engage in summary and synthesis writing, thus preparing students for the
higher-order writing tasks they will encounter in many of their
classes. (Explanations for writing summaries and syntheses, along
with the conventions for paraphrasing, quoting, and documenting sources according to the newest MLA guidelines are given in
the appendix, which can readily be used with Chapter 11.)

 • *Exceptional apparatus accompanies each reading.* This
apparatus, which provides the framework for a thorough analysis of the readings and which offers an unusually generous number of writing opportunities, includes these features:

— A headnote before the reading gives biographical background on the author and rhetorical information on the
selection, including the patterns used and the purposes
they serve.

— Three sets of questions ensure a thoughtful analysis:
the first set checks reading comprehension and encourages critical thinking; the second examines rhetorical features; the third focuses on language and style.

— A prompt is given for collaborative discussion or writing, for instructors who incorporate group work. If desired,
this prompt can be used for individual consideration.

— An average of six writing assignments accompany each
reading: a journal prompt; three or more "Using the Pattern"
assignments, which call for writing in the pattern under
consideration; a "Considering a Theme" assignment, which
calls for writing on a thematic point raised in the selection;
a "Connecting the Readings" assignment, which calls for responding to the selection and at least one other reading.

— Further increasing the writing opportunities, each chapter of readings closes with 20 writing assignments one of which is in a rhetorical context that specifies the situation, audience and purpose.

• *The Appendix, "Writing Paraphrases, Quotations, Summaries, and Synthesis," focuses on handling borrowed material responsibly.* This material, which also treats current MLA documentation and includes a sample summary and synthesis, can be combined with the casebook in Chapter 11 to create controlled research assignments that serve as a bridge into courses that require research writing.

ADDITIONAL FEATURES

• *Readings address a broad range of perspectives.* Every effort was made to include high-quality readings on a range of topics by diverse authors. There is a mix of traditional favorites like E.B. White's "Once More to the Lake" and never-before-anthologized pieces like Joy Williams's "The Inhumanity of the Animal People." The selections represent a range of length and difficulty, and many cultural backgrounds. Issues discussed are both timely and enduring, global and personal. While many of the selections focus on the world beyond the campus, a number of essays treat issues of particular importance to college students, including freedom of speech on college campuses, college pressures, violence on campus, drinking on campus, and college absurdities.

• *Chapter 1, "Writing an Essay," provides full, integrated coverage of the writing process and the elements of an essay.* It describes specific procedures for generating ideas; identifying audience, purpose, role, and tone; outlining; drafting; revising; and editing. In addition, it describes strategies for those who like to compose at the computer. The chapter also explains the characteristics of the various parts of an essay and links those parts to the writing process to give students an integrated understanding of process and product. Helpful features in this chapter include exercises, a revision checklist, and a student essay in progress.

+ *Chapter 2, "Critical Thinking and Active Reading," provides a foundation for approaching written texts that will prove valuable both in and beyond the composition classroom.* The chapter covers the components of critical thinking, errors in logic, and procedures for active reading and responding to a text.

+ *Each chapter of readings offers complete instructional support.* In addition to the apparatus surrounding each reading (described above), each rhetorical chapter opens with information on the characteristics of the pattern and how it can help the writer achieve a range of purposes. Of particular value to students is the section on how to use the pattern in college writing across the curriculum. Clear explanations and advice on selecting and ordering details, practical writing strategies, a revising checklist, and an annotated student essay help ensure success.

NEW TO THE SECOND EDITION

Patterns for a Purpose has a new design and size, but its appearance is not all that has changed. The second edition is a substantive revision developed in collaboration with instructors who used the book and generously shared their experiences and offered suggestions. Thus, the changes improve both the teachability of the book and its usefulness to students. These changes are among the most notable:

+ *Twenty-five new readings refresh the text.* These readings are longer and a bit more challenging than the ones they replace, so *Patterns for a Purpose* now has a broader range of selections to make it a more versatile learning resource. With a few exceptions, readings are now arranged within each chapter from the shorter, more accessible pieces to the longer, more challenging ones.

+ *The apparatus surrounding the readings has been expanded and reconfigured.* Headnotes are longer, offering more contextual information; postreading questions have been expanded and organized into three sets: "Reading Closely and Thinking Critically," "Examining Structure and Strategy," and "Considering Language and Style." The headings "Using the Pattern," "Considering a Theme," and "Connecting the Readings" now indicate the nature of each writing assignment. In addition, the writing assignments at the end of the reading chapters now include assignments in a rhetorical context that designates purpose, audience, and situation.

• *The explanations of the patterns (the introductory material opening Chapters 3 through 11) have been expanded.* Each chapter opening now includes more detailed explanations, a new discussion of using the pattern in college writing across the curriculum, and a revising checklist. In addition, several of the annotated student essays have been replaced with more analytic student models.

• *There is an increased emphasis on critical thinking.* A significant part of Chapter 2 explains the components of critical thinking and how to incorporate critical thinking into the active reading process. It also includes an expanded discussion of how to avoid errors in logic. In addition, the first set of questions after each reading requires students to engage in critical thinking.

• *The first three chapters have been combined into Chapters 1 and 2, and exercises have been added to Chapter 1.* Collapsing the first three chapters into two provides a more efficient, straightforward presentation of the writing process and essay structure; the exercises give students an opportunity to try out strategies for handling critical aspects of the writing process.

• *Chapter 1 now includes information on composing at the computer.*

• *The casebook in Chapter 11 has been thoroughly revised.* It now includes 10 argumentation-persuasion selections: one on drinking on campus, one on cohabitation versus marriage, two on affirmative action, three on free speech on campus, and three on animal rights—all with full apparatus and multiple writing assignments. Many of the writing assignments require students to consider more than one reading. In addition, the chapter includes an expanded discussion of argumentation-persuasion, an explanation of the Toulmin model, and a discussion of induction and deduction.

♦ *Current MLA sample entries of works cited, including ones for electronic sources, have been added to the appendix.*

ACKNOWLEDGMENTS

It is always a pleasure to work with the good folks at McGraw-Hill. In particular, I renew my thanks to Jean Akers and Laurie PiSierra, whose guidance and intelligence informed the first edition and, by extension, this one. For this edition, I have had the privilege of working with sponsoring editor, Sarah Moyers, development editor, Alexis Walker, and project manager, Kari Geltemeyer. Their guidance, support, and counsel contributed much to this edition, and I am most appreciative. I am especially grateful to Lesley Denton, whose early efforts got this project started.

The following reviewers offered sound advice, thoughtful criticism, and the wisdom born of their classroom experience. They helped shape this edition in important ways, and I am truly appreciative:

Patrick McMahon, Tallahassee Community College; Spencer Oleson, Mountain View College; Kirk Adams, Tarrant County Junior College—SE; Kathleen McWilliams, Cuyamaca College; Harriett S. Williams, University of South Carolina (Columbia); Sharon Nichols, Gaston College; Jane M. Kinney, Valdosta State University; John W. Crawford, Henderson State University; Deborah A. Gutschera, College of DuPage; Bradley W. Bleck, Community College of Southern Nevada; Barbara L. DeStefano, Georgia Southwestern State University; Richard Regan, Fairfield University; Stuart P. Mills, University of Denver; Bruce R. Magee, Louisiana Tech University; Alan Brown, Livingston University; Mitzi Brunsdale, Maryville State University; Marian Davis, Jacksonville State University; Mary Ann McCandless, Butler County Community College; Walden Madsen, City University of New York—Brooklyn; Carol Newell, Northern Virginia Community College;

Christopher Picard, San Juan College; Douglas Roycraft, Erie Community College; Merritt Stark, Henderson State University; Vivian Thomlinson, Cameron University; Lawrence Watson, University of Wisconsin—Stevens Point; and Gary Zacharias, Palomar College.

Finally, my heartfelt thanks goes to Denny, whose patience knows no bounds, and to Greg and Jeff, who lowered their boom boxes so I could think.

Barbara Fine Clouse

T O   T H E   S T U D E N T :
H O W   T O   B E C O M E
A   B E T T E R   W R I T E R

Are you wondering how a book of readings can help you become a better writer? In case you are, let me explain that it can help in several ways. First, the selections in this book can help you break through writer's block by giving you ideas to write about. Do you have an essay due next week on the general subject of campus problems? Then read "Free Speech on Campus" (page 149), and you may be moved to write about how to deal with hate speech; or read "College Pressures" (page 477), and you may decide to write about the effects of stress on college freshmen; or read "What Is Behind the Growth of Violence on College Campuses" (page 420), and you may decide to write about the causes of campus crime. When you need ideas for your writing, consult the tables of contents on pages vii and xxi for interesting titles, read the essays, and you may find yourself inspired.

Reading the essays in this book will also help you become a better writer by exposing you to strategies to incorporate in your own writing. You may like the way a particular author uses anecdotes as illustrations or the way another author uses description to enliven things or the way another author closes with a dramatic statement. By all means, try the approach yourself. You will increase your repertoire of strategies, and become a more versatile writer. (Just remember that it is acceptable to model a technique, but copying the words and style of another author is a form of plagiarism.)

As you read the selections in this book, you will sharpen your ability to identify main and supporting points, think critically, and evaluate the effectiveness of words, sentences, and paragraphs. Of course, you will bring these sharpened skills to your own writing, which is bound to improve as a result. Futhermore, the more you read and become sensitive to the needs of a reader, the more audience awareness you bring to your own writing—and nothing makes a writer more effective than a keen sense of audience.

Apart from the readings, other features of *Patterns for a Purpose* can help you become a better writer. Chapter 1, for example, offers detailed information on how an essay is constructed and specific techniques you can try to improve your writing process. The openings of Chapters 3 through 11 also offer you information on the characteristics of essays and strategies you can try in order to produce effective writing. Study this material and try the techniques described. Incorporate into your writing process those techniques that work well; abandon techniques that do not work well and replace them with other procedures. This trial-and-error approach will lead you to discover your own effective writing procedures.

Of course, nothing takes the place of practice and experience, so *Patterns for a Purpose* offers a wealth of writing opportunities to give you that practice and experience. After each reading and at the end of Chapters 3 through 11, you are offered a wide variety of writing assignments. Treat these assignments as opportunities to practice and improve. The journal assignments can be particularly valuable to you because they are likely to be ungraded, so they offer a stress-free opportunity to try things out, experiment, and practice.

In addition to this book, other resources are available to help you become a better writer, and you should take full advantage of them. Your classmates are a particularly valuable resource. Form a writers' group and meet regularly to share your work with each other, offering honest criticism, praise, and suggestions. Use classmates as a sounding board, ask them for help, and trade strategies. Because collaboration can be very helpful to writers, a number of collaborative activities appear in *Patterns for a Purpose* with the heading "For Group Discussion or Writing."

If your campus has a writing center, that, too, can be a valuable resource. The writing center is an excellent place to find a sensitive reader to respond to a draft so you a get a sense of reader reaction and revisions that might be necessary. The writing center is also a great place to talk about writing tasks when you are blocked. Kicking around ideas with the writing center staff can move you forward.

Your most obvious—and valuable—resource is your writing instructor. When you have problems, concerns, or questions, you should meet with your instructor for help. Anytime you do not understand an instructor's comment on a draft or final copy, you should seek clarification so you can bring that information to your next effort.

As you use your resources and work to become a better writer, you are bound to make mistakes. Mistakes are an important part of the learning process. If you study them, determine how to eliminate them, and work to avoid them next time, your mistakes will help you improve. Like this text, your classmates, the writing center, and your instructor, mistakes are a resource you can use to become a better writer.

Barbara Fine Clouse

CHAPTER

1

✿ WRITING AN ESSAY

The best way to become a better writer is to improve the procedures you follow when you write. Unfortunately, no one can tell you that certain procedures will guarantee successful writing. Instead, you must experiment a little to discover the procedures that work best for you. This chapter can help with that experimentation. It explains the areas that all writers must pay attention to:

Generating ideas (discovering what you have to say).

Ordering ideas (determining the progression of ideas).

Drafting (writing a preliminary version of the essay).

Revising (rewriting the essay to improve content, organization, and expression of ideas).

Editing (finding and correcting errors in grammar and usage).

In addition to explaining idea generation, ordering, drafting, revising, and editing, this chapter presents several procedures for working on each of these areas. Sample these procedures until you find ones that work well for you, and your writing is sure to improve. Keep in mind, however, that different writers function in different ways, and the procedures that work well for some of your classmates will not necessarily work well for you. Your goal is to find your own effective procedures.

As you develop your own process by discovering effective procedures, keep in mind that writing rarely moves in a straight line from idea generation through editing. You will frequently find yourself doubling back before going forward. For example, while you are checking your draft for spelling errors (part of editing), you may think of a better way to handle your introduction (part of generating ideas). By all means, go back and rewrite; never consider something "done" just because you first turned your attention to it during an earlier phase.

GENERATING IDEAS

Perhaps you think that writing is the product of inspiration and that it involves staring at a blank page or computer screen until a brilliant flash of insight sends your pen racing across the page or your fingers flying across the keys. If the inspiration does not strike, perhaps you assume that you cannot write, so you might as well pack it up and go play racquetball. If you think this way, you are not alone—but you are wrong.

Inspiration *does* strike writers on occasion, but most often it does not, and we must rely on other techniques to come up with ideas. Collectively, these other techniques are called *idea generation.* Successful writers use the idea generation techniques described in this chapter to pursue ideas in the absence of inspiration. They use these techniques to shape writing topics and to discover ideas for developing their writing topics.

Shaping a Writing Topic

Many times an instructor will specify your writing topic. In that case, your first priority is to be sure you understand the terms of the assignment so you meet your instructor's expectations. First of all, you must be sure you understand the *kind of paper* called for. Does your instructor want you to take a position and defend it? Summarize an author's ideas? Explain the meaning of a concept? Compare and contrast two essays? Consider, for example, this assignment that could be made in response to "American-ization Is Tough on 'Macho'" (page 61):

> In what ways do movies and television influence our views of how men or women are supposed to behave?

This topic requires you to deal with only one gender; dealing with both is not called for and would result in an unwieldy paper. The topic also requires you to provide examples of specific movies and television programs to illustrate your points.

Now consider this topic based on the same reading selection:

> Agree or disagree with Rose Del Castillo Guibault's claim that "the American *macho* is a chauvinist, a brute, uncouth, selfish, loud, abrasive, capable of inflicting pain, and sexually promiscuous."

This topic requires a different approach, for you must persuade your reader of the validity of your point of view by arguing convincingly.

In addition to understanding the kind of paper required, you must also be sure you understand the *terms of the assignment*: the length; the due date; the necessary manuscript form; the need to have a teacher conference, engage in peer review, or submit an outline; and so forth. If you have questions about the nature of an assigned topic, or if you are having difficulty fulfilling the assignment, speak to your instructor for guidance.

When you are not given a specific topic to respond to, the following idea generation techniques can help you shape a writing topic.

1. *Review the journal entries and marginal notes you made during active reading.* (See page 58 on active reading.) Your comments, questions, and areas of disagreement and agreement may suggest a topic. For example, the marginal note in response to paragraph 7 of "Americanization Is Tough on 'Macho'" (page 61) could prompt an essay about the image of males presented in action movies.

2. *Use a provocative quotation as a topic source.* For example, in paragraph 16 of "Americanization Is Tough on 'Macho'," the author says, "I believe it was the feminist movement of the early '70s that changed *macho's* meaning." This quotation could prompt an essay about the changing meaning of *macho.*

3. Pick a subject treated in a reading and brainstorm. To brainstorm, make a list of every idea that occurs to you and then examine the list for possible topics. For best results, you should not censor yourself. Just list everything that occurs to you without evaluating the worth of the ideas. For example, one student wrote the following list to brainstorm for topics about violence in sports.

fan violence	*why athletes are violent*
player violence	*Are athletes too violent?*
causes of violence	*Is it violence or aggression?*
effects of violence	*How can we make sports less*
Is the violence justified?	*violent?*
violence = part of the game	*Fans love it.*
It's expected.	*Players think it's okay.*
Is society sick if it likes	*Are players violent off the*
violence?	*field?*
players getting hurt	*fans getting hurt*

The student ultimately drew his topic from the question in his list "Are players violent off the field?" That question prompted him to write about players being violent on the playing field and nonviolent off the field.

4. Freewrite for about ten minutes on a subject found in a reading. To freewrite, write nonstop without censoring yourself. Simply record everything that occurs to you without worrying about its quality or about spelling, grammar, or neatness. Do not stop writing for any reason. If you run out of ideas, just write anything: the alphabet, names of family members—anything. Soon new ideas will occur to you and you can record those.

The following freewriting was done by a student in response to an essay that argues that female homemakers should not be financially dependent on their husbands. As you review the freewriting, notice that the author did not worry about correctness. Also notice that she allowed herself to write even silly things as she waited for better ideas to surface.

> *William Raspberry says women who are homemakers shouldn't be considered as dependant on male breadwinners. Well that's true but aren't male breadwinners dependant on the homemaker too? Could they cope if the woman walked out? I bet not, theird be hell to pay. Let's see what to write, oh the guy would have to pay sommeone to come in and clean and cook and take care of the kiddies. That would be hard and expensive. Let's see what do I think now? Maybe we should pay homemakers a salary. Could that be done? Maybe. Or maybe a giant PR campaign to upgrade the image of homemakers—yeah bring Madison Avenue into the act. I agree with Raspberry that women shouldn't be dependant financially if they are homemakers but I know a lot of women who don't mind so I doubt anything will change.*

The student's freewriting suggests at least three topics:

- The need to upgrade the image of homemakers.
- Paying homemakers for the jobs they do.
- Why some women do not mind depending on males.

Your freewriting may not yield as many topics, but it is likely to suggest at least one.

5. *Examine the subject of a reading from different angles.* Answering these questions will help:

  a. Can I describe something related to the subject?
  b. Can I compare and/or contrast the subject with something?
  c. Does the subject make me think of something else?
  d. Why is the subject important?
  e. Do I agree or disagree with the author?
  f. What interests me about the subject?
  g. Can I give the author's ideas a broader or different application?

> **h.** Can I explain the causes and effects of something in the reading?
>
> **i.** Can I relate the subject to my own experience?

6. *Use a computer.* If you like to use a computer or word processor, try these variations of freewriting and brainstorming. To freewrite, sit down at a blank screen and write whatever comes to mind without using the delete, backspace, or cursor keys. Just plow through for about 10 minutes. Print out your material and look for topic ideas. To brainstorm, list ideas as they occur to you. When you can think of nothing else, review your list, delete and add as you care to, and print out what you have.

An Essay in Progress: Shaping a Topic

To see how idea generation techniques can help you shape a writing topic, examine the following brainstorming list written by student writer, Jeff, who was working to shape a writing topic based on "Americanization Is Tough on 'Macho'" (page 61).

> *sources of American concept of "macho"*
> *why the concept is wrong (?)*
> *why Am. don't understand the Latin macho*
> *nature of concept of "ideal male"*
> *when this ideal is unreasonable*
> *nature of concept of "ideal female"*
> *how this ideal is unreasonable*
> *cultural conflict over gender roles*
> > *— world scale*
> > *— national scale*
> > *— local scale*
> *need for more realistic concept of gender roles*
> *strong silence vs. aggression*

Notice that Jeff felt free to abbreviate and place a question mark next to an idea he was unsure of. During idea generation, use any notations that stimulate your thinking and help you push forward.

After reviewing his brainstorming, Jeff decided his topic would be the nature of the concept of the ideal male.

Exercise 1.1: Shaping a Writing Topic

Select two topics from the following list and shape a writing topic from each. For one subject, use brainstorming to shape a topic. For the other subject use freewriting. Save your work to use in a later exercise.

a. MTV	*e.* The image of women in the media
b. Education	*f.* The movie rating system
c. Television	*g.* Friendship
d. Automobiles	*h.* Technology

The Writing Context

Successful writers do not plan their writing in a vacuum. Instead, they consider the following factors that make up the context for their writing: purpose, audience, and role. These factors, which are discussed next, affect idea generation and just about everything else the writer does.

   1. *Purpose.* A successful essay is written for one or more of these purposes:

- To entertain the reader.
- To relate the writer's experience and/or express the writer's feelings to the reader.
- To inform the reader about something interesting or important.
- To persuade the reader to think or act a particular way.

Purpose is an important element of the essay because it influences the writer's approach. Say, for example, that you are a single parent who wants to write about the child care problems in this country. If you want to entertain your reader, you can write a funny piece about what you went through the day you had to take final examinations and the babysitter canceled. If you want to express your feelings to your reader, you can describe how much you worry about whether your children get quality care while you are at work. If you want to inform your reader, you can explain what the child care options are for a single working parent of preschool children. If you want to persuade your reader, you can argue for a federally funded child care program. Of course, you can also combine purposes. For example, you can relate your own experiences and then go on to argue that a federally funded program would make life easier for you and others. Obviously, each of these essays would have a different character because the content would be shaped by the writer's purpose. Because each essay would be so different, the character of each must be considered during idea generation.

If you need help establishing a purpose or combination of purposes for your writing, try answering these questions:

> What ideas, feelings, or experiences can I relate to my reader?
>
> What can I inform my reader about?
>
> In what way can I entertain my reader?
>
> In what way can I persuade my reader to think or act differently?

2. Audience. The writer of a successful essay will have a clear sense of audience—that is, a clear sense of who the reader is and what that reader is like. A sense of audience is important if the writer is going to fulfill his or her purpose. Suppose you want to write an essay about the pollution in a local river. If the essay were written for your biology class, it might include a great deal of technical information about specific chemical pollutants. However, if the essay were for a letter to your local newspaper, such technical information might overwhelm the average reader. Now let's say that you are writing to convince your reader to support a school levy that would raise property taxes. If your reader has school-age children, you could argue that the quality of their education will improve if the levy passes. However, if your reader has no children, you may do better to argue that good schools will increase the value of the reader's property.

In some writing classrooms, you can establish any audience for your writing, but in others you must consider your classmates and teacher to be your audience. Regardless of the situation in your particular class, be sure you have a clear sense of who your reader is and what your audience's particular characteristics and needs are. This information will significantly affect your idea generation.

If you need help identifying an audience for your writing, try answering the following questions.

Who would enjoy reading my essay?

Who would learn something from my essay?

Who is interested in my topic?

Who should be persuaded to think or act in the way my essay recommends?

Who would find my essay important?

Who needs to hear what I have to say?

Once you have identified your audience, you should take some time to think about your reader's traits and needs. You must understand your reader's characteristics and meet the needs of your audience, or you will fail to achieve your purpose. Answering these questions can help you assess your audience.

What does my reader already know about my topic?

What information will my reader need to appreciate my view?

Does my reader have any strong feelings about my topic?

How interested is my reader in what I have to say?

Will my reader's age, gender, level of education, income, job, politics, or religion affect reaction to my topic?

3. *The writer's role.* In addition to audience and purpose, the writer's role influences the character of an essay and, hence, idea generation. For example, a student writing for a teacher will be careful to conform to all the terms of the assignment. An employee writing for a supervisor will adopt the appropriate respectful tone. A friend writing to another friend may be casual and use slang, but a student writing an essay as part of a scholarship competition will not include slang.

To appreciate the significance of the writer's role, consider a report on how to select the right college. A person in the role of a high school counselor will provide an objective set of procedures, but a person in the role of a college admissions counselor may slant detail to favor his or her school. A person in the role of a student may express the frustrations that are part of the process, but a person in the role of a parent may stress financial concerns.

If a role for your writing does not suggest itself, consider one of the following.

student	brother	husband	friend
employee	sister	wife	roommate
young adult	retiree	average, general reader	neutral party
parent	man	woman	authority

An Essay in Progress: Identifying the Writing Context
Jeff decided his purpose would be to inform the reader of the source of misconceptions about the idealized male. He established his audience as the average, general reader, and his role as that of a young, concerned male.

Exercise 1.2: Identifying the Writing Context
1. For each writing topic given, set up a possible writing context by establishing a possible purpose, audience, and role. For example, using the topic the dangers of boxing, your purpose might be to persuade the reader that boxing should be banned; your audience, boxing fans; and your role, concerned citizen.

     a. Topic: a car accident you witnessed.

     b. Topic: a report on the financial health of the local schools.

     c. Topic: the use of pesticides on food grown in the United States.

d. Topic: the causes of the high divorce rate in the United States.

2. Select one of the writing contexts you created for number 1 and change the context by altering one or more of the features (audience, purpose, and role). How do you think the change(s) will affect the final essay?

3. Establish a writing context for each of the topics you generated in response to Exercise 1.1. Save your work to use in a later exercise.

Discovering Ideas to Develop Your Topic

Once you have a topic, whether it is one you developed yourself or one that was assigned to you by your instructor, you will need to discover ideas for developing that topic. Some of the following procedures may help.

1. *Write a discovery draft.* A discovery draft is not really a first draft. It is more a preliminary effort to identify what you already know about your topic and what you can think of along the way. To write a discovery draft, simply start writing anything that comes to mind about your topic. Do not worry about anything except getting down everything you can think of. If you cannot think of much, you may not know enough about your topic, or you may need to try some other idea generation techniques.

2. *Review the journal entries and marginal notes you made during active reading.* They may include ideas for developing your topic. (See page 58 on active reading.)

3. *Write a brainstorming list that focuses on your subject.* Like brainstorming for a topic, brainstorming for ideas to develop a topic involves listing every idea that occurs to you. Remember, do not evaluate the worth of your ideas; just write down everything you can think of. Later, you can reject anything unusable. Here is an example of a brainstorming list for one of the topics that emerged from the freewriting on page 5.

Topic: the need to upgrade the image of homemakers

> *homemakers are the backbone of the family*
>
> *they work hard*
>
> *they work long hours, 7 days a week*
>
> *it would be very expensive to pay people to do everything that homemakers do*
>
> *homemakers make it possible for other family members to do things*
>
> *they often do volunteer work that helps schools and society at large*
>
> *women would feel less like they need outside jobs for fulfillment*
>
> *nothing is more important than homemaking*
>
> *we must stop assigning value according to how much money is earned*

Because brainstorming is a means of idea generation, its results are preliminary. Thus, you need not use everything on the list, and you can add to the list at any time.

   4. Consider the patterns of development. The following patterns of development are explained and illustrated throughout this text:

   Description (using words to explain what something looks, sounds, feels, smells, and/or tastes like).

   Narration (telling a story).

   Exemplification (providing examples).

   Process analysis (explaining how something works or how it is made or done).

   Comparison-contrast (explaining similarities and/or differences).

   Cause-and-effect analysis (explaining the reasons for and results of an action).

   Classification-division (breaking something down into its parts; grouping items into categories).

   Definition (explaining the meaning of a term or concept).

If you ask yourself the following questions, you can discover specific patterns and ideas for developing your topic.

   a. What can I describe about my topic?
   b. What story can I narrate about my topic?
   c. What examples illustrate my points?
   d. What process or procedures relate to my topic?
   e. What can I compare or contrast my topic to?
   f. What are the causes or effects of my topic?
   g. Is there anything about my topic that can be classified into groups?
   h. Is there anything about my topic that can be broken down into parts?
   i. Are there any terms or concepts that I can define?

To see how considering patterns of development can help with idea generation, consider the following chart.

Topic: the need to upgrade the image of homemakers

Pattern	Idea
Description	Describe the image of the homemaker that many people have
Narration	Tell the story of the time a friend felt embarrassed at a dinner party because she was the only woman who did not work outside the home
Exemplification	Give examples of advertisements that show working mothers as the ideal
Process analysis	Explain a procedure for upgrading the image of homemakers
Comparison-contrast	Contrast the perception of the homemaker with the perception of the woman working outside the home
Cause-and-effect analysis	Explain the effects the current image of the homemaker has on family life
Classification-division	Explain the components of the image of the homemaker
Definition	Provide a definition of a *homemaker*

5. *Try clustering.* Clustering helps you generate ideas and see how those ideas relate to each other. To cluster, first write your topic in the center of the page and draw a circle around it. As ideas to develop your topic occur to you, write them down, circle them, and draw lines attaching them to the circled ideas they relate to. As with all idea generation techniques, do not censor yourself. Write down everything, regardless of its quality. The sample clustering below was done as a form of idea generation for an essay about violence on the playing field.

In the final version of the essay, the writer did not use all of the ideas in his clustering; also, he used some ideas that do not appear in the clustering. That is fine because nothing about idea generation is set in stone. Also notice that the writer placed "split personality" in two spots on the clustering. That is also fine. If you are unsure what an idea relates to, jot it down in more than one spot and solve the problem later.

6. *Talk to other people about your topic.* Your classmates, in particular, can suggest ideas for developing your topic.

7. *Consult library sources and other materials for ideas on your topic.* However, check the Appendix on ways to handle material you take from other sources.

8. *Combine techniques.* Many writers like to use more than one idea generation technique. They may, for example, begin with a freewriting and then try a clustering. Or they may begin with a brainstorming list and then talk to other people. Feel free to combine idea generation strategies in any way that suits you.

9. *Use a computer.* If you like to use a computer, these variations of freewriting and writing a discovery draft may appeal to you. Try freewriting with the screen dark. Just turn the brightness dial all the way down and freewrite "blindfolded." You will have many typing errors, but the freedom that comes from not seeing what you are writing can stimulate your thinking. You can also try writing a discovery draft at the computer. Because writing goes faster this way, you may find you are spilling out ideas at a faster rate. (Be sure to save your work frequently and print out hard copies of your work.)

An Essay in Progress: Discovering Ideas to Develop Your Topic

Student-author Jeff wrote the clustering on page 16 to discover ideas to develop the topic he generated with the brainstorming list on page 6.

Exercise 1.3: Discovering Ideas to Develop Your Topic

1. Select three of the following topics. For each one, generate three ideas that could be used for development. Use a different idea generation technique for each topic.

> The causes of stress among college students.
>
> The characteristics of a leader.
>
> Your most embarrassing (or your proudest) moment.
>
> The value of final examinations.

2. Using the idea generation techniques of your choice, discover enough ideas to write a first draft on one of the topics you established a writing context for in number 3 of Exercise 1.2.

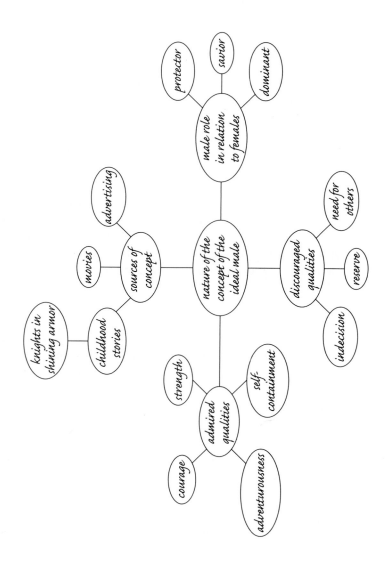

Developing a Thesis

To be successful, an essay must have a central point—a main message the writer wants to convey. This central point is the *thesis,* the idea that everything else in the essay relates to. In other words, the thesis is the controlling idea of an essay. While generating ideas, your thesis idea may occur to you early on. If not, you must ponder your idea generation material to develop a suitable thesis. As you do, remember the characteristics of an effective thesis, explained here.

Very often, the thesis has two parts. One part expresses the subject of the essay; the other part expresses the author's position on that subject.

Subject	Writer's Position on Subject	Thesis
MTV	Parents should limit their children's exposure to it.	Parents should limit their children's exposure to MTV.
practical jokers	There are three kinds.	Careful observation reveals three kinds of practical jokers.
the author's father	He was a strict disciplinarian.	My father was a strict disciplinarian.

A thesis can do more than indicate the subject and the writer's position on the subject. It can also note the main points the writer will make in the essay, like this:

subject:	MTV
writer's position:	Parents should limit their children's exposure to it.
points to be made:	MTV contains sexually explicit material. It demeans people.
thesis:	Parents should limit their children's exposure to MTV because the channel contains sexually explicit material, and it demeans people.

An essay's thesis is one or two sentences that often appear in the essay's introduction, frequently at the end of that section. However, a thesis can also be in the middle of an essay or at the end, in the conclusion. The following paragraphs illustrate different placements of the thesis, which is underlined as a study aid.

Thesis at the Beginning

<u>I am always tardy, a habit that creates difficulties for my family and friends.</u> Ever since I was a child, I have tended to get up late, show up for meals late, and leave for school late. I am not sure when I last saw the opening credits for a movie because I typically arrive 10 or 15 minutes into the film. Usually, my friends and family forgive me, but who knows how long they will tolerate my lateness when it causes them so many problems?

Thesis in the Middle

We all have personality traits that hurt us as much as they help us. It might be our sense of humor or our dedication to perfection. <u>The quality that hurts me as much as it helps me is my overdeveloped sense of responsibility.</u> Most people would see a sense of responsibility as a positive trait. However, when it is overdone, it can be harmful.

Thesis at the End

Have you ever received unwanted credit cards in the mail? Did a credit card company ever offer you such a big line of credit at such a low interest rate that you could not resist the offer? Yes, accepting the cards is tempting, but they come with risks the credit card companies never mention. <u>As a former credit card addict, I can assure you that the dangers of relying on credit are very serious.</u>

Sometimes the thesis is not stated at all. Instead, it is strongly implied by the information in the essay. However, as a student writer, you may find it easiest to state the thesis and place it at the end of the introduction, where it can stand as a reference point for everything that follows.

Regardless of where a writer places the thesis, some guidelines apply:

1. The thesis should not be a formal announcement.

   no: This paper will discuss the reasons the United States needs election reform.

   yes: The United States would benefit from election reform.

   no: The following essay will explain how to behave during a job interview.

yes: If you want to land that dream job, follow my advice during the job interview.

no: I want to tell you the characteristics of a nurturing family.

yes: All nurturing families share the same characteristics.

2. The thesis should present something arguable or in need of explanation, rather than a statement of fact.

no: Drunk drivers are a menace. (No one will disagree with this statement of fact, so why construct an essay around it?)

yes: To make the roads safer for everyone, we should suspend the driver's license of anyone convicted of drunk driving. (This thesis presents an arguable point.)

no: During the Depression my grandmother raised four children by herself. (This is a statement of fact.)

yes: I have always admired my grandmother's strength and courage during difficult times. (This thesis allows for explanation.)

3. The thesis should present a manageable topic; it should not take in too much.

no: Our system of education is in need of a complete overhaul. (An essay that discusses changes in every aspect of the educational system will be much longer than the standard college essay. If the essay is a reasonable length, the discussion will be superficial.)

yes: To be competitive with the rest of the world, we must change the way we teach mathematics. (This thesis presents a topic that can be treated in adequate detail in a manageable length.)

4. The thesis should be written in specific language; avoid using such vague words as *nice, interesting, good, bad,* and *great.*

no: Playing high school football was a great experience.

yes: Playing high school football taught me self-confidence and the importance of teamwork.

Exercise 1.4: Developing a Thesis

1. Explain what you can expect to find in an essay with each of the following thesis statements. Try to determine the pattern of development (p. 12) and purpose (p. 7) for each essay.

Example: The 12-month school year has several advantages. The essay will mention and explain the effects of the 12-month school year, perhaps to persuade the reader that it is the best academic calendar.

     a.   Professional athletes are often viewed as heroes.

     b.   Karate is an excellent sport for school-age children.

     c.   To find the right job, a person needs a strategy.

     d.   A good teacher has a sense of humor, a commitment to excellence, and the ability to be flexible.

     e.   The spring drought will create economic hardships in the Midwest.

   2.   In the following thesis statements, underline the topic once and the writer's position on the topic twice. If the main points are included, place brackets around them.

     a.   Universities should not have physical education requirements because they delay students' progress and contribute little to students' education.

     b.   I was deeply moved by the prayer service held at the war memorial.

     c.   Paul Newman's success as a film star is a result of his wise choice of roles, his sex appeal, and his acting talent.

     d.   African-American authors Toni Morrison and Maya Angelou have very different writing styles.

     e.   Oil and gas well drilling should be banned from residential areas because it is a danger to the environment and a problem for homeowners.

   3.   Indicate whether each thesis is acceptable or unacceptable. If it is unacceptable, state what is wrong with the thesis and rewrite it to make it acceptable.

     a.   Regular exercise is important to a person's physical well-being.

     b.   *I Love Lucy* is one of the most popular television comedies of all time.

     c.   Newspapers are a better source of information about current affairs than network news programs.

    d. The following paragraph will explain why all high school students should take four years of a foreign language.

    e. The current movie rating system is inadequate for a number of reasons.

    f. The entertainment available to Americans is of the poorest quality.

    g. Summer camp is a good experience for children.

    4. Return to the idea generation material and topic you developed for number 2 of Exercise 1.3. Study that material and develop a thesis from it. Save your work to use in a later exercise.

ORDERING IDEAS

Once you have generated ideas and developed a thesis, you are ready to consider in what order your ideas should appear. The order of ideas is important because a reader who cannot follow the progression of a writer's ideas will become confused and frustrated. Thus, a writer must order ideas logically to keep the reader engaged in the essay. In general, a writer has three possibilities for ordering details:

    1. Chronological order

    2. Spatial order

    3. Progressive order

    Chronological order arranges details across time. The event that occurred first is written first; the event that occurred second is written second, and so on. Obviously, this technique is useful for storytelling (narration). However, it is also helpful for giving the details of a process when it is necessary to explain what is done first, second, third, and so on.

    Spatial order arranges details as they appear across space— front to back, near to far, top to bottom, left to right. This order is often used to describe a place or scene.

Another arrangement for details is *progressive order.* With this order, you arrange details from the least to the most important, compelling, interesting, representative, surprising, and so forth. A progressive order allows for a big finish because the most significant detail comes at the end. A variation of progressive order is to begin and end with the strongest points and sandwich everything else in the middle for the strongest possible beginning and ending. Progressive order is often used in argumentation-persuasion because a strong final point helps convince a reader.

Because the pattern of development often determines the order of details, the introductions to chapters that discuss patterns of development (Chapters 3 through 10) also discuss ordering details. In addition, since you will often find yourself combining patterns, you will also combine methods of ordering ideas. An essay that combines narration and description, for example, may use both chronological and spatial orders.

Transitions

Arranging details in a logical order is not always enough. A writer may also have to signal how ideas relate to each other with devices called *transitions.*

1. *Transitional words and phrases.* A number of words and phrases can signal the relationship between ideas. The chart on p. 23 notes some of them.

2. *Repetition of words or ideas.* Repeating key words or ideas can help a writer achieve transition and improve the flow of writing. Here are two examples:

repeating a word: Chronic fatigue <u>syndrome</u> is becoming more widely recognized in the medical community and therefore more frequently diagnosed. This <u>syndrome</u> is so debilitating that its sufferers often cannot work.

repeating an idea: <u>A group of volunteer parents is now working cooperatively with school authorities</u> to introduce more extracurricular activities into the schools and to begin a drug awareness program. <u>These worthy efforts</u> will no doubt improve the quality of education in our township.

Transition Chart

Relationship	Transitions	Example
addition	also, and, too, in addition, furthermore, first, further	The apartment has all the features I want. <u>In addition,</u> the rent is low.
time	now, then, before, after, earlier, later, soon, finally, next	<u>First,</u> measure the flour. <u>Then</u> add it to the butter and eggs.
space	near, next to, away from, beside, inside, to the left, alongside, behind	Go two blocks west to the light. <u>On the right</u> is the park.
comparison	similarly, likewise, in the same way, in like manner	The mayor will recommend some layoffs. <u>Similarly,</u> she will not approve any new hirings.
contrast	however, in contrast, but, still, on the contrary, nevertheless, yet	The House will pass the jobs bill. <u>However,</u> the Senate will vote it down.
cause and effect	since, because, so, as a result, consequently, thus, therefore, hence	Half the students are sick with the flu. <u>Thus,</u> school will be closed.
emphasis	indeed, in fact, surely, certainly, without a doubt	Everyone enjoys Dr. Hill's class. <u>In fact,</u> it is always the first to close.
illustration	for example, for instance, specifically, in particular	Counting fat grams is a good way to diet. Dana, <u>for example,</u> lost a pound a week that way.
summary or clarification	in summary, in conclusion, in brief, in short, in other words, all in all	The President has vetoed the spending bill. <u>In short,</u> he will not raise taxes.

3. *Synonyms.* Another way to achieve transition is to use a synonym for a word or idea mentioned earlier, like this:

> The workers expressed their <u>dissatisfaction</u> with management's latest wage offer.
> Their <u>discontent</u> may well lead to a strike.

4. *Sentences that look backward and forward.* A good way to achieve transition between paragraphs is to begin a paragraph with a sentence that looks back to something in the previous paragraph and forward to something in the paragraph coming up. Assume, for example, that you have just written a paragraph about the fact that Dr. Garcia gives students extra help, and you are about to write a paragraph about how she makes students feel comfortable in class. You could write one of these sentences to open the new paragraph and achieve transition by looking back to the previous paragraph and forward to the one coming up:

looking back   looking forward

[In addition to giving students extra help,] [Dr. Garcia always makes them feel comfortable in class.]

looking back

[Dr. Garcia does more than provide extra help to those in need;]

looking forward

[she also makes sure that everyone feels comfortable in class.]

Outlining

Outlining can help you find the best order for your details so you do not ramble and thereby confuse your reader. Many people resist outlining because they are only familiar with the formal outline that involves numbered and lettered lists and subcategories. This kind of outline can be very helpful, but if it is not for you, alternatives are available. To learn which kind of outlining is best for you, try one or more of the techniques described in this chapter.

Regardless of the kind of outline you write, some guidelines apply. First, write a preliminary version of your thesis. Although this thesis is subject to change, it can serve as a guide for your work. As you outline, check your details against this early version of your thesis to be sure they are relevant. Also, consider your details in light of your purpose, audience, and role to be sure your points are compatible with them. Finally, as you outline, feel free to add and delete details. Idea generation is ongoing, so you should remain receptive to ideas as they occur to you.

The Scratch Outline

The scratch outline is the least detailed outline. It is simply a list of the main ideas you plan to include in your first draft, written in the order you plan to cover them. Typically, the scratch outline just covers main points with no mention of details for developing those points, so it is not well suited for complicated essays or for writers who must plan in detail before drafting. As an example, here is a scratch outline based, in part, on some of the ideas generated with the clustering on page 14.

> *Preliminary thesis: Even nonviolent people are often violent on the playing field.*
> *Violence is okay because it's part of the game.*
> *A player has to be violent to compete with other players.*
> *Sports is different from the real world, so violence is justified.*
> *Fans want the violence.*

If you like to brainstorm at the computer, you can take the next step and turn your brainstorming list into a scratch outline. To do so, first delete ideas you do not want to use and add any new ones that occur to you. Then, using your cut-and-paste functions, arrange the ideas in your list in the order you want to treat them in your draft.

The Informal Outline

The informal outline is more detailed than the scratch outline. It includes some details for developing main points and it groups related ideas together, so the writer has a sense of which details will appear together in the same paragraph. Although more detailed than the scratch outline, the informal outline may not be suitable for complex papers or writers who need a fair amount of structure before they draft. An informal outline might look like this:

Preliminary thesis: *Even nonviolent people are often violent on the playing field.*

Violence is okay because it's part of the game.
> *Use roommate as example.*
> *Coaches only play people with killer instinct.*

A player has to be violent to compete with other players.
> *Get other guys before they get you.*
> *If everyone else is violent, you have to be, too.*
> *Violence is okay if you win the game.*

Sports is different from the real world, so violence is justified.
> *It's only a game and not part of reality, so it's okay to be violent.*
> *But the injuries are real.*

Fans want the violence.
> *Fans cheer for violence.*
> *They even act violently themselves in the stands.*

The Outline Tree

An outline tree, which can be moderately to heavily detailed, allows a writer to see how ideas relate to each other. Many writers appreciate the visual representation the tree provides. To construct an outline tree, write your preliminary thesis at the top of a page and connect ideas with "branches," the way the following student example illustrates:

Even nonviolent people are often violent on the playing field.

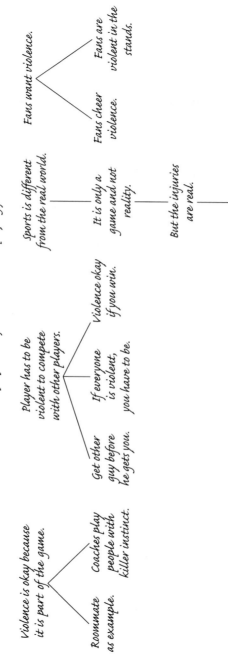

Violence is okay because it is part of the game.

Roommate as example.

Coaches play people with killer instinct.

Player has to be violent to compete with other players.

Get other guy before he gets you.

If everyone is violent, you have to be.

Violence okay if you win.

Sports is different from the real world.

It is only a game and not reality.

But the injuries are real.

Soccer example.

Fans want violence.

Fans cheer violence.

Fans are violent in the stands.

27

The Outline Worksheet

With an outline worksheet like the one that follows, you can plan your draft in detail by filling in the blanks with words and phrases that indicate the points you will make:

Paragraph 1

1. Opening comments to arouse reader's interest:_____

   _____

   _____

2. Preliminary thesis: _____

   _____

Paragraph 2

1. Main point (topic sentence idea): _____

   _____

2. Supporting details to develop main point: _____

   _____

   _____

Paragraph 3

1. Main point (topic sentence idea): _____

   _____

2. Supporting details to develop main point: _____

   _____

   _____

   [*Note:* Continue this way until all your main points are discussed.]

Final Paragraph

Ideas to bring essay to a satisfying finish: _____

_____

The Formal Outline

The formal outline allows you to plan your essay in considerable detail. To construct a formal outline, write your preliminary thesis at the top of the page. Then label your main points with roman numerals and your supporting details with capital letters. Details that explain or illustrate supporting details are given numbers. You are probably familiar with the formal outline, which looks something like this:

Preliminary thesis: _____

   I.
      A.
      B.
      C.
  II.
      A.
      B.
          1.
          2.
 III.
      A.
          1.
          2.
          3.
      B.
          1.
          2.
      C.

To see how a formal outline plots a draft, review the following formal outline for an essay with this thesis: <u>Nonviolent people can be violent on the playing field.</u>

    I. *Hurting people is part of the game.*
      A. *My roommate is gentle off the basketball court and hurtful on the court.*
      B. *If he didn't hurt others, the coach would bench him.*
    II. *Violence is necessary for winning.*
      A. *Players feel violence is okay if they win.*
        1. *In my soccer game, an opposing player intentionally hurt one of our players.*

    2. *He did it to win.*
  B. *Players injure others so they don't get hurt themselves.*
III. *Players think violence is okay because sports are games.*
  A. *But the violence is real.*
  B. *The injuries are lasting.*
    1. *Our soccer goalie missed a month of school.*
    2. *He still has effects from a violent play.*
IV. *Fans like violence.*
  A. *Fans encourage player violence.*
  B. *Fans are violent themselves.*

If you like to compose at the computer, check your word processing program to see if it has outlining capability. If it does, you can develop a formal outline by filling in the various levels.

An Essay in Progress: Outlining

Using his clustering as a guide (see page 16), student writer Jeff developed the following informal outline. You will notice that Jeff did not use all the ideas from his clustering and that he included ideas that do not appear in the clustering. Writers are always free to change things as new ideas occur to them.

Preliminary thesis: The popular concept of the ideal male is unsuitable in our society.

<u>*The sources of the ideal are ridiculous.*</u>
  movie industry
    – highly unrealistic situations
  advertising
    – deceitful industry to begin with
  folktales and childhood stories
    – originated in completely different eras and societies
<u>*The admired/discouraged qualities of the ideal are out of place.*</u>
  instinctive vs. considered action
    – increasingly complex society
  self-containment vs. need for others
    – increasingly cooperative society

The idealized male's relation to women is archaic.
protector, savior, rescuer, dominant male
    – increasing appearance of female equality in all respects

Exercise 1.5: Ordering Ideas

1. For each thesis statement, indicate whether the order of ideas is likely to be spatial, chronological, or progressive.

   a. The University should offer a study skills seminar as part of its orientation program.

   b. Once the flood waters receded, I discovered the devastation to my apartment.

   c. The movie version of *Jurassic Park* is better than the book version.

   d. I will always remember the day Julio won the state pole vault championship.

   e. You can learn to change the oil in your car and save money as a result.

   f. At sunset, the flower garden of Municipal Park offers a peaceful retreat.

2. Using the techniques of your choice, generate ideas for an essay with one of the following preliminary thesis statements:

Americans are too materialistic.
Americans are not too materialistic.

Then write an informal outline for the essay.

3. Using the techniques of your choice, generate ideas for an essay with one of the following preliminary thesis statements:

Our interest in physical fitness has gone too far.
Our interest in physical fitness has not gone too far.

Then write an outline tree for the essay.

4. Using the thesis and ideas you have as a result of completing number 4 for Exercise 1.4, write a formal outline or fill in an outline worksheet, as you prefer. Feel free to add or delete ideas as you see fit. Save your work to use in a later exercise.

DRAFTING

The first draft is nothing more than an initial attempt to get ideas down in essay form. Because it is a first attempt, it will be very rough—and that is fine. First drafts are supposed to be rough, which is why they are often called rough drafts. Later, during revising, you can make all the necessary improvements. In order to draft, you must understand the parts of an essay: the introduction, the supporting details, and the conclusion. The next section of the chapter will examine those parts.

The Introduction

Because first impressions are important, a successful essay will begin well. In general, that beginning will be a one- or two-paragraph introduction aimed at stimulating the reader's interest and presenting the thesis. A writer can approach the introduction many ways, some of which are illustrated in the examples that follow. (Notice that the thesis, underlined as a study aid, appears as the last sentence of each introduction. Student writers often find this placement convenient. However, as explained on page 18, the thesis can appear elsewhere.)

Open with an Arresting Statement

Parents do not want to be parents anymore. That is what Ann Landers discovered after asking her readers whether they would have children if they had it to do over again. An overwhelming majority responded no. <u>I can only conclude from this that too many of us become parents for the wrong reasons.</u>

Provide Background Information

Five percent of the population is afflicted with attention deficit disorder, a neurological condition that makes people distractible, hyperactive, and unable to concentrate. At one time, we thought ADD was a childhood disorder that was outgrown by the age of eighteen. Now we know differently. <u>Thus, colleges should make special provision for the significant number of students who have attention deficit disorder.</u>

Tell a Story (Use Narration)

The new kid walked into fourth-period English with his head down. He handed a slip to Mrs. Kuhlins, who announced, "Frankie is our new student, class. I trust that you will make him welcome." With that, Frankie brushed a stray hair out of his eyes and shuffled to a seat in the back. His clothes were hopelessly out of date, and his hair was a mess. But as he passed my desk, our eyes met, and I saw something there. <u>At that moment, I knew there was something special about this new kid.</u>

Establish Yourself as Someone Knowledgeable about the Subject

When I was six, I joined a T-ball league and spent a glorious summer at third base. When I was ten, I began playing intramural basketball and learned the pleasures of rebounding and making foul shots. In junior high school, I began running middle distances for the track team and learned the joy of crossing the finish line in one last burst of speed. In high school, I lettered in three sports. <u>As a result of all these years of playing team sports, I have come to realize that there are three kinds of coaches.</u>

Explain Your Purpose

If you are planning to buy a used car, you run the risk of making a very costly mistake. <u>For this reason, you should know what to look for when you examine and test drive an automobile.</u>

Describe Something

His belly swelled over his belt line and cascaded toward the bony knees that poked out between the white knee socks and navy blue polyester stretch shorts. His face was twisted into a permanent scowl, and his eyes squinted against the sun until they formed slits. To call roll, he barked each boy's name and checked it off on the clipboard that was never more than arm's reach away. <u>I was only five minutes into seventh-grade gym, but I could tell Mr. Winnikee deserved his reputation as the gym teacher from hell.</u>

Define Something

A grandmother is supposed to be a white-haired, chubby woman who rolls her stockings below the knees and spends her days knitting scarves and baking cookies for her grandchildren. <u>However, someone forgot to tell my mother's mother all this because, believe me, she is not the typical grandmother.</u>

Use an Interesting or Pertinent Quotation

Last week at his press conference, the governor said, "It is with regret that I announce a 20 percent subsidy cut to higher education. I believe, however, that this cut is the least painful way to balance the state budget." <u>The governor is wrong; these cuts will have a catastrophic effect on the people of this state.</u>

Note: Avoid quotations such as "The early bird gets the worm" or "Better late than never." These are clichés more likely to bore than interest a reader.

For additional ways to handle the introduction, you can consult the openings to Chapters 3 through 10.

Supporting Details

The supporting details are all the points made to prove or explain the thesis. It is impossible to overestimate the importance of the supporting details because they are the heart of an essay. In fact, the supporting details are so important that an essay's success or failure rests on them. To be successful, supporting details must be *adequate* and *relevant*.

Adequate Detail

Each main point you make in your essay is a generalization. To have adequate detail, you must back up every generalization with enough detail to prove or explain it to your reader's satisfaction. If, for instance, you say your roommate is a practical joker, you have made a generalization. You then must prove that generalization with examples of your roommate's practical jokes. If you say that Chez Paris is the most beautiful restaurant in town, you are making a generalization and must support it with descriptive details, showing why you find it beautiful. If you say that schoolchildren should not be grouped by ability because such grouping discourages achievement, you must explain that generalization by showing how ability grouping discourages achievement. In short, you cannot expect a reader to accept what you say just because you say it—you must explain and prove your generalizations. A good way to remember the need to provide adequate detail is to remind yourself that a writer must "show and not just tell."

You can show and not just tell by carefully moving from the general to the specific. To do this, first state a generalization; then go on to give specific points to prove or support that generalization.

To appreciate the need to show and not just tell, and to see how a writer can move from the general to the specific, contrast the following two drafts. Draft A does not support generalizations, but draft B does—by moving from the general to the specific. The specific points appear underscored as a study aid.

Draft A

Dr. Garcia is a dedicated teacher. She is concerned about students and always willing to give a struggling young scholar extra attention. In addition, she takes pains to include everyone in class discussions, even the shy students who ordinarily do not participate. Particularly impressive is the personal interest she takes in each of her students. No wonder her class is always one of the first to fill up every semester.

Draft B

Dr. Garcia is a dedicated teacher. She is concerned about students and always willing to give a struggling young scholar extra attention. <u>Last week, for example, two students were having trouble finding topics for their research papers, so Dr. Garcia met them at the library and helped them explore the possibilities.</u> In addition, she takes pains to include everyone in class discussions, even the shy students who ordinarily do not participate. <u>One way she does this is to ask people their opinions on subjects under discussion. That way, they do not have to worry about giving a wrong answer. Another way she brings students into discussions is to plan group work so students can talk to each other in more comfortable, smaller groups.</u>

   Particularly impressive is the personal interest Dr. Garcia takes in each of her students. <u>Everyone writes a journal, and from the journals Dr. Garcia learns about her students' interests, successes, problems, and family life. Because she comes to know her students so well, she can talk to them about things important to them, which creates a bond between student and teacher. As a result, all her students come to understand that Dr. Garcia cares about them.</u> No wonder her class is always one of the first to fill up every semester.

Relevant Detail

Supporting details must be relevant, which means they must be clearly related to the thesis. Most readers will grow annoyed when details are not related to the matter at hand. Thus, if you want to argue for the elimination of the physical education requirement at your school, you would not mention that it would also be a good idea to eliminate the foreign language requirement. In the following draft, one sentence presents irrelevant detail. When you read, you will notice the annoying distraction created by that sentence.

> Many universities are altering their teacher education curricula to require prospective teachers to get into the classroom as soon as possible, even in the freshman year. These future teachers observe, tutor, and in general get the feel of a teacher's responsibilities. The plan is a good one because students can decide early on if they are suited to teaching and change

> their majors if necessary. In the more traditional curriculum, an education major waits until the junior or senior year to get into the classroom, when it can be too late to change majors without serious inconvenience and expense. Many students in all programs change majors and problems are to be expected. Certainly it makes sense to move prospective teachers into the classroom as early as possible, so the plan should catch on.

You probably found the next to last sentence annoying and distracting because it is not closely enough related to the matter at hand. To avoid such irrelevant detail in your own writing, outline carefully to be sure everything is related to the thesis.

The Source and Form of Supporting Details

Now that you understand the need to provide adequate, relevant detail, you may be wondering where all these details will come from. For the most part, your supporting details will come from your own experience and observation, as well as from what you learn in the classroom and as a result of reading, watching television, or listening to the radio. If you need to go beyond these sources for supporting details, you may rely on the facts, statistics, and opinions of experts, some of which you may find in this book and some of which you can research in the library. (If you do use such borrowed material, be sure to check the appendix for information on paraphrasing, quoting, summarizing, synthesizing, and documenting source material.)

Most of the rest of this book helps you learn about the forms your supporting details can take. These forms are called *patterns of development*. Specifically, there are chapters on these patterns of development: description, narration, exemplification, process analysis, comparison-contrast, cause-and-effect analysis, definition, and classification-division. Of course, you can combine two or more of these patterns to form your supporting detail.

Each pattern of development is treated in its own chapter; however, the inside covers of this book also give a brief explanation of each pattern. Take a look now at that information on the inside covers and refer to it whenever a particular pattern is mentioned and you are unsure of its nature.

So you can see how the patterns of development can help you back up your points and achieve your purpose, here are examples of how they support the thesis used earlier in the chapter, that Dr. Garcia is a dedicated teacher.

description:	give details that show how Dr. Garcia looks and acts
narration:	tell a story about a time Dr. Garcia helped a student
exemplification:	give examples of ways Dr. Garcia shows interest in students
process analysis:	explain Dr. Garcia's process for using groups to help students learn
comparison-contrast:	compare and/or contrast Dr. Garcia with other teachers to show how good she is
cause-and-effect analysis:	explain the effects of one or more of Dr. Garcia's teaching methods
definition:	define a "good teacher" and show how Dr. Garcia conforms to that definition
classification-division:	classify all the ways Dr. Garcia helps students

Of course, you would not use all these patterns in a single essay, but they do provide options to consider as you develop your supporting details.

Tone

Speakers can use tone of voice to convey their feelings. Similarly, writers can establish a *tone* for their writing. Tone is the writer's attitude or feelings toward the reader or the subject of the writing. Thus, the tone can be angry, sarcastic, serious, preachy, argumentative, conciliatory, hurtful, playful, earnest, scornful, hostile, enthusiastic, neutral, and so forth.

Most often, tone is established by the word choice used in the supporting details. Notice, for example, how word choice creates the different tones in the following sentences on the same subject.

angry and judgmental tone:	Many so-called citizens who are too tight-fisted to invest in the future of our children refuse to vote for the school levy.
neutral tone:	A significant number of citizens hesitate to pass the school levy and thereby increase their taxes.

Organizing Supporting Details into Body Paragraphs

The supporting details of an essay are arranged in central paragraphs called *body paragraphs.* Typically, each body paragraph focuses on one aspect of the thesis and develops that aspect with adequate, relevant supporting details. (An aspect of the thesis that requires considerable explanation can be the focus of more than one body paragraph.) The focus of each body paragraph can be stated in a sentence or two known as the *topic sentence,* which can come at the beginning, in the middle, or at the end of the body paragraph. At times, the topic sentence can be strongly implied by the detail in the paragraph rather than expressly stated.

Student writers often find it easiest to compose a body paragraph that begins with a topic sentence followed by the supporting details meant to explain or prove the idea in that topic sentence. Thus, if you were writing an essay with the thesis "Dr. Garcia is a dedicated teacher," your essay might have three body paragraphs, each beginning with a version of one of these topic sentences:

Dr. Garcia makes sure every student is relaxed in class.

Dr. Garcia is always willing to give students extra help.

Dr. Garcia takes a personal interest in each of her students.

Notice that each of these topic sentences is relevant to the thesis. Similarly, the supporting detail in each body paragraph should be relevant to the topic sentence of that paragraph. Thus, the first body paragraph would include only details about helping students relax, the second only details about providing students with extra help, and the third only details about taking a personal interest in students.

When to Paragraph

Typically, writers begin a new body paragraph each time they move to a new idea to support the thesis. However, other considerations can dictate when to paragraph. For example, if you have a great deal to say about one point, you can break up the discussion into two or more paragraphs. If you have a point that deserves special emphasis, you can place it in its own paragraph, or if you have an extended example or narration (a story), you can set it off by placing it in its own paragraph.

The Conclusion

The conclusion is a very important part of a successful essay because it influences the reader's final, lasting impression. No matter how strong your introduction and body paragraphs are, if your ending is weak, your reader will come away from the essay feeling let down.

An effective conclusion can be a sentence or two, or it can be a full paragraph. Either way, many approaches are available to the writer. If your essay is long, with many ideas, you can summarize your main points as a helpful reminder to your reader. However, if your essay is brief and the ideas are easily remembered, summarizing is not a good idea because it will bore rather than help a reader.

Sometimes an effective conclusion comes from repeating the thesis or another important idea. Typically, this approach works when the repetition provides emphasis for dramatic effect. Other times, writers delay the statement of their thesis until the conclusion because they want to build up to it.

Another common technique is to introduce a new but related idea in the conclusion. The idea must be clearly related to the rest of the essay to avoid confusing the reader with something that seems unconnected to the topic. Finally, a writer often crafts an effective conclusion by combining approaches.

Other approaches to the conclusion are illustrated below. In addition, the openings to Chapters 3 through 10 suggest ways to handle conclusions.

Draw a Conclusion from the Information in the Essay (This illustration is from an essay about the effects of divorce.)
Recent evidence suggests that the children of divorced parents suffer a number of difficulties, regardless of their age at the time of the divorce. For this reason, parents who stay together "for the sake of the children" may be doing the right thing.

Present the Final, Most Important Point (This illustration is from an essay arguing against censorship.)

The most compelling reason to oppose censorship is the threat it poses to our First Amendment rights. Once we limit free speech, we establish a climate that permits the chipping away at our freedoms until our rights are severely curtailed.

Offer a Solution to a Problem Mentioned in the Essay (This illustration is from an essay that explains problems associated with college athletics.)

College athletics will remain controversial until we reform the system dramatically. Perhaps the most honest thing to do is to hire the athletes to play and pay them salaries. If they want to use their paychecks to pay for tuition, fine. If not, they can just be university employees. The fans will still turn out to see the teams, regardless of whether the players are student athletes or professional athletes.

Call Your Readers to Action (This illustration is from an essay arguing for increasing the salary of teachers.)

To improve the quality of education, we must increase teachers' salaries to make them compatible with those in business and industry. Only then will we attract the best people to the profession. Thus, we must support school levies that fund pay increases and lobby boards of education to do whatever it takes to increase teachers' salaries.

Look to the Future (This illustration is from an essay explaining the effects of the Route 8 bypass.)

Once the Route 8 bypass is built, our area will become a major crossroads. In ten years, our economy will be flourishing from the business and commerce that will result from our strategic location, and our tax base will broaden to the benefit of our schools and infrastructure.

Leave Your Reader with a Final Impression (This illustration is from an essay on discrimination against overweight people.)

Our society discriminates against overweight people, and it's a shame. Many capable people never get a chance to show what they can do because of our narrow-mindedness.

The Title

Although the title is the first thing a reader sees, many people develop it last because a good title often suggests itself after the supporting details are written. There are many ways to approach the title. Sometimes a clever or funny title is a good way to pique your reader's interest. However, not everyone can be clever or funny, so it is fine to write a title that suggests the content of the essay, like "My Backyard" or "Lists," which are in this book. Sometimes an intriguing title like "What Sort of Car-Rt-Sort Am I?" (which also appears in this book) can stimulate a reader's interest. Usually, you should avoid a title that presents your thesis. If your title is "Capital Punishment Is Inhumane," you will tip your hand too soon. Also, avoid very broad titles that do not suggest your content. "Television" is too broad, but "The Effects of Television Violence" is fine.

Tips for Writing Your First Draft

When you draft, the following tips may be helpful:

1. *Use your outline as a guide,* but do not be a slave to it. Add and delete ideas as you judge necessary. Remember, idea generation continues through all stages of writing.

2. *Push through from beginning to end* in one sitting so you maintain momentum.

3. *Skip troublesome parts.* If you cannot think of a word or a way to express something or a way to develop a point, leave a blank space and go on. If you want, leave a note about what needs to be done later: "Explain this," "Add an example," "Find word," and so on.

4. *Skip your introduction* if it is keeping you from progressing. However, write out your preliminary thesis so you do not lose sight of it.

5. *Try returning to idea generation and outlining* if a reasonable amount of time passes and you cannot get the draft down. You may not yet have enough ideas for a draft.

6. *Use a computer.* If you like to compose at the computer, the copy/paste function may prove very helpful during drafting. If you are having trouble expressing something, copy in the relevant portion of your outline as a placeholder. Later during

revising, you can shape this material as necessary. (Be sure to save
your work often and print out hard copies of *every* draft.)

An Essay in Progress: Drafting

Using his informal outline as a guide (see page 30), Jeff wrote the
first draft that appears below. You will notice that Jeff departed
from his outline at times, which is fine. Nothing is ever set in
stone. Knowing that he would polish the draft during revision,
Jeff concentrated on getting his ideas down as best he could without laboring over anything. As you read the draft, you will notice that it is rough in many ways: The introduction needs work,
specific examples are needed to support points, the paragraphing
needs to be reworked, and much of the tone and word choice
need to be revised. You will also notice that Jeff realized some of
this while drafting and wrote reminders to himself in brackets
about revisions to make.

The Not-So-Ideal Ideal Male

We, the people of the United States of America, are being bullied, tricked,
and led astray by products of our own culture. We are being fed falsehoods,
and we digest them happily, but we are being poisoned. Our own culture —
our own heritage and popular society—is feeding us misinformation; we
are being led to believe in an absurd concept of the ideal male. [fix intro.]

The root of the inappropriateness of this idealization lies in the nature of
its main perpetuators—the movie and advertising industries, and folktales
and childhood stories. The most obvious of these sources is the movie industry, which produces totally unrealistic plots typically having (perhaps
subtly, but still) superhuman males as heroes. We watch these movies and
feel that this is what our men are supposed to be like. [give examples] The
cartoonish action movies are generally the most extreme, and these are
targeted at the most vulnerable audience—teenage boys who are ready to
become men. They see these heroes on the screen and see visions of
themselves in ten years. This is tragic. An equally prevalent but less glaring source of deception is the advertising industry. They bombard us every
day with quick scenes of powerful, intimidating male atheletes endorsing
their products. [give examples] The message is this: you should buy this
product because this man should be your idol. Physical dominance is put
in the spotlight as much as the product. A third projector of this concept
comes from our heritage, and that is its problem. Folktales and childhood
stories are usually legends that have been passed down through genera-

tions of people. Nobody even remembers how long ago they were created. That is precisely the trouble. Triumphant men like Robin Hood originated in an entirely different society; they are heroes of the distant past, and they do not befit the present.

The problem these unsuitable sources of the ideal male present is that their admired and discouraged qualities are out of place. In action movies and folk tales, the hero wins the battle because his instincts are flawless. He knows just where every attacker will be in a battle, and he knows by sight which fair maiden will be faithful to him. But in the real world today, how often does a man fend off a small mob in hand-to-hand combat or choose his wife from a lineup of beautiful princesses? To apply the power of under-statement — rarely. In our highly complex, and civilized, society, the consid-ered decision is more important than the instinctive or rash one. Also, the men of advertising, movies, and legends are loners. Their great strength stems from the fact that they need no one else to help them accomplish their goals. Again, this clashes with modern society. Our world is becoming in-creasingly cooperative on all levels — from interpersonal to international. A realistic man knows that the help of others is esential in achieving his dream.

Finally, the men these sources give us often are deplorable in their re-lations to women. Many times the entire purpose of the movie, advertise-ment, or tale is for the hero to "get" the woman. He is almost invariably her protector, savior, or unrepellable lover. In a world in which possibly the characteristic of modern history is the rise of women nearer and nearer to equality, how can the ideal man have this type of relationship with women? The answer is simple: he is not the ideal man.

Exercise 1.6: Drafting

1. Refer to the thesis statements and supporting details you have as a result of completing numbers 2 and 3 of Exercise 1.5. For each thesis and set of supporting details, do the fol-lowing:

- *a.* Decide on a possible approach to the introduction and explain why the approach is a good one.
- *b.* Write two topic sentences that could open two body paragraphs.
- *c.* Decide on a possible approach to the conclusion and ex-plain why the approach is a good one.

2. Using the material you have as a result of completing number 4 of Exercise 1.5 (and adding and deleting ideas as you wish), write a first draft.

REVISING THE DRAFT

Experienced writers will tell you that the heart of any writing is revision, the process of shaping and refining the first draft until it is ready for the reader. Revision is a difficult, time-consuming process; it is *not* a matter of making a few word changes, adding a comma here and there, and correcting spellings. It is a complete rethinking of the essay to be sure everything is suited to the writer's purpose, audience, and role. Thus, revising involves changing words, reordering details, adding and deleting ideas, reshaping sentences, and so on. It does not, however, involve matters of correctness such as grammar, spelling, punctuation, and capitalization. These concerns are dealt with later, during editing. To be sure you consider all that you should when you revise, you may want to use the checklist that follows.

Revision Checklist

Thesis (see page 17)
1. Be sure your essay has a clearly stated or strongly implied thesis.
2. Be sure your thesis is not a statement of fact.
3. Be sure your thesis can be treated in a manageable length.
4. Be sure your thesis is not a formal announcement and that it is expressed in specific language.

Introduction (see page 32)
1. Be sure your introduction makes a good first impression.
2. Be sure your introduction is suited to your purpose, audience, and role.

Supporting Details (see page 34)
1. Be sure all your details are suited to your purpose, audience, and role.
2. Be sure your details are in a logical order and arranged in body paragraphs.
3. Be sure each body paragraph has a clearly stated or strongly implied topic sentence.
4. Be sure all your details are relevant to the thesis and appropriate topic sentence.

5. Be sure you have enough details to support the thesis, each topic sentence, and each generalization.
6. Be sure you use transitions to move smoothly from idea to idea and from paragraph to paragraph.
7. Avoid flaws in logic (p. 55).

Conclusion (see page 39)
1. Be sure your essay comes to a satisfying finish.
2. Be sure your conclusion is appropriate to your purpose, audience, and role.

Expression
1. Eliminate unnecessary words.
2. Be sure all your ideas are clearly expressed.
3. Substitute specific words for vague ones.
4. Change any words not compatible with your tone.
5. Rewrite tired expressions (clichés) such as "cold as ice."
6. Rewrite to eliminate choppy or sing-song prose.

Tips for Revising

1. Leave your work for at least a day to clear your head and gain objectivity about your draft. This way, you stand a better chance of identifying changes that should be made.

2. Allow plenty of time, because revising is time consuming. Plan your work to allow revising over a period of several days.

3. Revise in stages by considering one or two of the revision concerns at a time. (Use the Revision Checklist to be sure you consider everything.) As an alternative, revise one or two paragraphs at a time. Be sure to take a break whenever you get tired.

4. Read your draft aloud to hear problems you overlook visually.

5. Revise typed copy because you are less likely to overlook problems in type than in your own handwriting.

6. Trust your instincts if you have a nagging feeling that a problem exists. It probably does, even if you cannot give the problem a name or figure out a solution at the moment.

7. *Avoid editing,* which comes later. If you deal with spelling, grammar, punctuation and such, you will be distracted and not focus on revision concerns.

8. *Ask reliable readers to react to your draft,* but be sure you use people who know the qualities of effective writing and who will not hesitate to offer constructive criticism. (Praise makes a writer feel good, but it does not help with revision.) Also, evaluate your readers' reactions carefully and accept or reject them thoughtfully.

9. *Be prepared to write multiple drafts.* Writers often go from first drafts to second, third, and fourth before reaching final copy.

10. *Use a computer.* A computer can be very helpful during revising, but you must be careful. Because computer-generated material looks polished and hence trouble free, you can be fooled into overlooking problems. If you like to use a computer, however, be sure to study a print copy of your draft in addition to what you see on the screen. Identifying weaknesses is often easier when you work from a printed copy. Also, if you can split your screen, try placing a copy of the revision checklist in a window for easy reference. Of particular help will be your computer's copy, move, insert, and delete functions, which will allow you to easily move sentences, rearrange paragraphs, and add and delete words and details.

Exercise 1.7: Revising the Draft

1. Read the first draft that follows and then make four suggestions you think the author should consider during revising.

Is Today's Athlete a Good Sport

I have been playing soccer for a long time and I can see that players are playing much more violently now than they used to. Players will do anything to win, even stuff they would never consider doing off the field. I think that today's athlete is one person on the field and another person off the field.

Players think that hurting someone is okay because it's just part of the game. My roommate, for example, is a real gentle guy until he gets on the basketball court, then he's rough and ready and violent. If he didn't play that way, the coach would keep him on the bench.

Many players say they have to be violent to beat the other players. They don't feel they've done anything wrong as long as they win. In one of my soccer games, for example, an opposing player intentionally spiked the sweeper and cheated to get the goal.

A lot of times, players justify violence by saying "it's only a game" and not reality. Yes, it's a game but the injuries are real and can cause a lot of problems and pain. For example, a player on my soccer team missed a month of school as a result of an opposing player who knocked him into the goal. I'm sure the player didn't think twice about the consequences of his actions.

Unfortunately, fans love the violence. The more violence, the more cheering. They're violent in the stands, too.

The violence must stop and players should be penalized for it. Otherwise, people will get hurt more and more.

2. Revise the draft you wrote in response to number 2 of Exercise 1.6.

EDITING THE DRAFT

Before typing the essay into its final form, the successful writer carefully checks for mistakes in grammar, spelling, punctuation, capitalization, and usage. This check is editing. Editing is very important because a reader will lose confidence in the writer if the essay has many errors. When you edit, consider the following tips.

1. *Leave your draft for a day* before editing to clear your head and improve your chances of finding mistakes.

2. *Know the kinds of mistakes you typically make* and be on the lookout for them. For example, if spelling is a problem for you, pay particular attention to this feature of your draft.

3. *Edit more than once,* each time checking for one kind of mistake that you have a tendency to make.

4. *Point to each word with a pen* and linger over it for a second or two. This will prevent you from building speed and overlooking errors.

5. *Place a ruler under each line as you edit* to block out other material and prevent it from distracting you.

6. *Read your work aloud* to listen for mistakes. Be careful, though, to read exactly what is on the page, not what you intended to write.

7. *Trust your instincts.* If you have a feeling that something is wrong, the odds are good that a problem exists.

8. *Learn the rules.* You cannot edit effectively if you do not know the rules, so buy a handbook in your campus book store, check it on matters of grammar and usage, and learn any rules you are unfamiliar with.

9. *Use a computer.* If you edit at the computer, be sure to study a printed copy of your draft as well as the screen. Many writers find errors more easily on the printed page. While you may find grammar and spell checkers helpful, remember that these tools are not foolproof. For example, they will not tell you whether you have substituted <u>here</u> for <u>hear</u>. Finally, the computer's search function can help you locate certain kinds of problems you are in the habit of making. For example, if you frequently use <u>there</u> instead of <u>they're</u>, you can use the search function to find every instance of these words so you can look closely at them and make any needed corrections.

PROOFREADING THE FINAL COPY

After editing, use your typewriter or word processor to type your essay into the proper form for your reader. However, your work is not complete until you check carefully for typing errors. Read very slowly, lingering over each word and punctuation mark, so you do not build up too much speed and miss something. If your instructor permits, neatly ink in corrections; otherwise, retype the page or print out a new copy.

An Essay in Progress: The Final Copy

Below is the final version of the essay that Jeff wrote in response to "Americanization Is Tough on 'Macho'" (page 61). (The notes in the margin point out some of the key features of the essay.) You have already viewed the idea generation (pages 14 and 16), outlining (page 30), and drafting (page 42) that preceded this final copy. Between the first draft and the final version, Jeff wrote two additional drafts in the course of revising and editing.

The Not-So-Ideal Ideal Male

First there was Errol Flynn; then there was John Wayne. Now there are Arnold Schwarzenegger, Bruce Willis, and Jean-Claude Van Damme. These men of action and resolve are the celluloid depictions of the ideal male. They are the model that men strive for but never achieve. They are the men that women want but never find. They are the reason men feel inferior. However, the truth is that we are being led to believe in an absurd image of the ideal male, and the source of this image is movies, advertising, and childhood stories.

The introduction engages the reader's interest by providing background information and specific examples.

The thesis presents the subject as the image of the ideal male and the writer's position that the image, whose source is movies, advertising, and childhood stories, is absurd. The thesis also notes main points to be covered (movies, advertising, and childhood stories).

An obvious perpetrator of the falsehood is the movie industry, which produces unrealistic plots with superhuman male heroes. Arnold slams through brick walls and snatches the beautiful woman from the jaws of death; Bruce outwits six psychopaths to liberate a building from terrorists; Jean-Claude kickboxes his way past a vicious street gang to rescue the helpless hostage. We watch these movies and feel that this is what men are supposed to be like. Granted, cartoonish action movies are generally the most extreme, but they appeal to the most vulnerable audience — teenage boys. They see in these heroes on the screen visions of what they should be like when they become men. This is tragic because the goal is unattainable.

From the beginning, the tone (one of strong feeling, and concern) is clear.

The topic sentence presents the body paragraph's focus as the movie industry.

The author's informative and persuasive purposes are clear. His role (a concerned male) and his audience (the average, general reader, both males and females) are also becoming clear. The purpose seems to be to inform the reader about how the image of the ideal male is manipulated. The paragraph development includes cause-and-effect analysis.

Another source of deception is the advertising industry. Advertisers bombard us every day with powerful male athletes endorsing products. Michael Jordan, in all his athletic, superhero grandeur, makes us want Nikes, but even more, he makes males want to achieve athletic greatness — not likely for the average guy. Emmit Smith

The topic sentence presents the body paragraph's focus as the advertising industry. "Another source of deception" is a transition linking the paragraph to the introduction.

may sell a lot of Pepsi, but he also sells the notion that the ideal male has arms and legs as thick as tree trunks. Advertising sends two messages: you should buy this product because this man should be your idol, and if you want to be a "real man," you should have the athletic physique and prowess of a sports star. Thus, physical dominance is put in the spotlight as much as the product.

Supporting details are developed with cause-and-effect analysis and examples. The paragraph would benefit from more detail on how advertisers perpetuate the false image of the ideal male.

The topic sentence presents the body paragraph's focus as folktales and childhood stories. The words "a third perpetrator of the misconception" provide transition.

→A third perpetrator of the misconception is folktales and childhood stories, legends that have been passed down through generations. Triumphant men who confront danger and risk their lives for the underdog are everywhere in our myths, and they cause males to feel inadequate. The likes of Robin Hood, Sir Lancelot, and Davy Crockett originated in an entirely different time and society; they are heroes of the past who do not befit the present, yet their legendary (and impossible to emulate) feats shape the psyches of males. The tradition continues into more recent times, as Superman, Batman, and Spiderman fight injustice, rescue the weak, and generally contribute to the notion that real men are action figures.

Paragraph development includes specific examples. Some readers may feel the need for more details.

→The ideal men depicted in advertising, movies, and legends are loners. Their strength stems from the fact that they need no one to help them accomplish their goals. The Marlboro man always rides out alone; the action hero single-handedly saves the day. This fact causes problems for males who try to live up to the perceived ideal. It leads them to wall themselves off from others, depriving themselves of enjoyable, satisfying relationships. Further, our world is becoming increasingly cooperative on all levels—from interpersonal to international. A successful male knows that the help of others is essential to achieving his dream and that collaboration is increasingly valued in the workplace. The loner may not perform as well on the job.

The topic sentence presents the body paragraph's focus as the depiction of men as loners. Transition is achieved with the words "the ideal men."

Paragraph development includes cause-and-effect analysis.

The conclusion provides closure by presenting a final point and leaving the reader with a final impression. Transition is achieved with the word "finally."

Finally, the unfortunate image of the ideal male perpetrated by advertising, movies, and myth damages relations with women. Many times the point of the movie, advertisement, or tale is that the male hero "gets" the woman. He is almost invariably her protector, savior, or unre-

pellable lover. In a world whose defining characteristic is the advancement of women nearer and
nearer to equality, how can the ideal man have
such a relationship with women? The answer is
simple: he cannot. Indeed, once outside the
worlds of advertising, movies, and folktales, he is
not the ideal male.

To appreciate that Jeff's final essay is the product of many
stages of thinking and refinement, take another look at the idea
generation material (page 16), outline (page 30), and first draft
that preceded the previous final essay.

CHAPTER

2

⑤ CRITICAL THINKING AND ACTIVE READING

When you read to relax, you can grab a well-plotted novel, put your feet up, and lose yourself in the story as the words wash over you, and the tensions of the day melt away. This kind of reading is one of life's pleasures. Because your goal is to enjoy, it is okay if your mind wanders a bit, or if you feel too lazy to look up the meaning of a word.

College reading, however demands more involvement from you. It requires you to stay focused on the material, as you actively consider and evaluate it. It requires you to think of the material in light of what you already know and to judge the importance of what you read. College reading requires you to question, draw conclusions, make associations, develop opinions, and support those opinions. In short, college reading requires critical thinking and active reading—two processes taken up in the rest of this chapter.

CRITICAL THINKING

People sometimes assume that critical thinking is a process of finding fault or "criticizing," but this is not the case. More correctly, critical thinking involves going beyond what is readily apparent to look beneath the surface. It is a process of careful consideration that includes evaluating, looking for connections, drawing conclusions, and questioning. Critical thinking is a skill you will draw on repeatedly in college as your instructors ask you to do such things as judge the significance of ideas and consider the differences between theories. Critical thinking is also a skill you are likely to need on the job, as when a supervisor asks you to evaluate a sales trend or compare the findings of two research reports. Even in your private life, critical thinking can play a vital role. In an election year, for example, you will need to draw conclusions from campaign speeches to form judgments about candidates. Similarly, at some time, you may need to evaluate the conflicting opinions of two doctors and decide on a medical course of action.

As you can no doubt tell, critical thinking is a complex process. It involves several aspects, including the following.

1. *Distinguishing facts from opinions.* People often assume that anything in print is a fact, but the words on a page can represent only the writer's opinions. *Facts* can be proven or have been proven, but *opinions* are the writer's judgments, interpretations, or beliefs. For example, it is a fact that electricity can be used to power automobiles, but it is an opinion that electrically powered cars will be commonplace in 10 years. As a critical thinker, you must distinguish between facts and opinions when reading and determine whether or not the opinions are well-founded and supported.

2. *Questioning.* Critical thinking involves forming questions for further thought by asking about the significance of ideas, the meaning of assertions, the writer's purpose, the importance of the topic, and so forth. Such questioning helps you delve deeper into the reading.

3. *Making inferences.* An *inference* is a conclusion you draw from the information in a piece of writing and what that information suggests. For example, if a writer does not explicitly state the thesis of an essay, you will have to infer that thesis from the details given. When you make inferences, you get at the writer's underlying assumptions. For example, author Suzanne Britt contrasts neat and sloppy people in "Neat People vs. Sloppy People" (page 337). Because her portrait of sloppy people is so

much more flattering than her portrait of neat people, you can reasonably infer that Britt prefers sloppy people.

4. *Synthesizing information.* When you synthesize information, you connect your reading with what you have learned from experience, observation, thinking things over, and prior reading. Thus, synthesis involves fitting new information into the larger scheme of your knowledge. You can do this by noting how ideas in your reading support, refute, clarify, or call into question other ideas—or by noting how your previous experiences, observations, and reading challenge or confirm what you are currently reading. Say, for example, that you are reading a newspaper article that mentions the shortage of male teachers in elementary schools. If you heard an education professor explain that male elementary school teachers get little respect, you can synthesize this point with your reading using a cause-and-effect relationship.

5. *Evaluating the reading.* People often assume that anything in print is good quality. However, this is far from true, so the critical thinker must judge the quality of the reading material. To do so, assess such characteristics as the writing style, the amount and relevance of detail, the logic of the organization, the persuasiveness of the evidence, how the writing compares to other pieces you have read, and so forth. Then form an opinion about how good the selection is. Remember, when you evaluate, you are entitled to your opinion—but that opinion must be supported with your carefully considered evidence.

Avoiding Errors in Logic

Critical thinking and reading require careful reasoning. Thus, you must avoid errors in logic when you write, and you must be on the lookout for errors in logic in material you read. Some of the more frequently occurring logical flaws are described next.

1. *Overgeneralizing.* Very little is true all of the time, so be careful of sweeping statements.

> Example: The only reason teenagers quit school is to avoid the work. (This may be true for some, but not for all.)

2. *Oversimplifying.* Most issues worth arguing are complex, so be wary of "quick fix" explanations or solutions.

> Example: If women would just stay home to care for their children, we would have no day-care problem in this country. (The issue is not that simple. Many women must work in order to feed their children.)

3. *Begging the question.* "Begging the question" is basing an argument or conclusion on the truth of a point that has not been proven.

> Example: Immature couples who live together do not deserve spousal rights. (Where is the proof that couples who live together are "immature?" To assume they are is to beg the question.)

4. *Name calling.* This fallacy is also call *ad hominem* ("to the man") or *mudslinging.* It involves attacking the people who believe something instead of criticizing ideas or sticking with issues.

> Example: People who oppose school vouchers are bleeding-heart liberals who will destroy this country. (The pros and cons of school vouchers are unrelated to the people who favor them.)

5. *Either-or reasoning.* With complex issues, more than two alternatives usually exist.

> Example: If we do not ban hand guns, we will have a social crisis on our hands. (What about other alternatives, such as limited gun control or mandatory jail sentences?)

6. *Assuming an earlier event caused a later event.* This fallacy is also called *post hoc, ergo propter hoc,* which means "after this, therefore because of this." The fact that one event occurred before another does not prove that the first event caused the second.

> Example: After homosexual characters began to be featured in television and movies, more people began considering homosexual marriage. (The first event did not necessarily cause the second.)

7. *Attacking or defending an issue on the basis of what was believed or done in the past.* This kind of fallacy would have kept women from getting the vote.

Example: If our grandparents managed without federally subsidized health care, so can we. (Our grandparents lived in a different world.)

8. *Assuming that what is true for one person is true for everybody.*

Example: My cousin and his girlfriend live together without benefit of marriage, and they are just fine. Obviously, marriage is not that important. (What is true for the cousin may not be true for others.)

9. *Playing to general sentiments.* This fallacy is also called *ad populum,* which means "to the crowd." It involves winning people over by calling upon commonly held feelings like patriotism, fear of war, and religious fervor rather than discussing issues.

Example: I would make an excellent senator because I come from humble beginnings and know what it means to work for a living. (This argument appeals to our respect for those who work their way to better circumstances. It says nothing about my political qualifications.)

10. *Falsely indicating that one point follows conclusively from another.* This fallacy is also called *non sequitur,* which means "it does not follow."

Example: Fewer minority students are attending our university this year. Apparently, minorities are losing interest in higher education. (The conclusion does not follow from the premise. There may be many causes for the decline in enrollment, including the fact that many minority students are attending other colleges.)

11. *Using the "as any fool can see" approach.* Because this approach insults those who disagree, it can alienate readers.

Example: It is apparent to everyone that deer hunting solves many problems. (No, it is not apparent to everyone, or your essay would not be necessary.)

Example: As any reasonable person can see, prison reform is necessary. (Those who disagree are cast as "unreasonable," both unfair and likely to alienate some readers.)

12. *Alluding to but not naming authorities.* Careful readers distrust phrases like "experts agree" or "research shows"

because they suggest authority or evidence without naming that authority or evidence.

> Example: Studies show that most Americans distrust politicians. (What studies?)

ACTIVE READING

To be a mature reader, you must engage in *active reading*. Active reading requires you to bring your critical thinking skills to bear on what you read. You must separate fact from opinion, form questions, make inferences, synthesize ideas, and evaluate thoughtfully. At times, you may draw conclusions different from those of your classmates or other readers, but that is fine. You do not have to agree with others. However, you must support whatever views you have with evidence from the text.

Sometimes you will be uncertain about the meaning of all or part of an essay, and sometimes you will change your mind. If you are puzzled, say so; then question other readers, and ask questions in class. If today you think one thing about an essay, but yesterday you thought another, you need not worry. Reading is an ongoing process, so your reactions and views may change as you continue to reflect.

Active reading and critical thinking require time and energy. The longer and more complex the piece, the more time and energy you must invest. The active reading procedures described next will help you. While they are suitable for most college writing, feel free to vary them to suit your needs and the material you are reading.

Step 1: Preview the Material

Before you read, you should preview the material for clues about its content, author, purpose, audience, and tone. These five procedures can help.

1. *Consider the author and title* and what they suggest about the piece. Do you know the author's politics or usual subject matter? Is the author a newspaper columnist, a humorist, or a political commentator? Think about the title and what hints it gives you. Of course, some titles will tell you more than others. In this book, for example, the title "College Pressures" tells you much more than the title "What Sort of Car-Rt-Sort Am I?"

   2. Check out the publication information (in this book, see the acknowledgments page). When and where the essay first appeared will suggest how current the information is and who the original audience was.

   3. Read the headnote. In this text, reading selections are preceded by headnotes that tell something about the author's background and publications and something about the content of the selection. This information can help you draw conclusions and evaluate the reading.

   4. Read heading, charts, bold type, and lists for clues to content.

   5. Read the first paragraph or two and the first sentence of other paragraphs to learn a little about the tone, subject matter, and organization of the selection.

Step 2: Read the Selection in One Sitting, If Possible

After previewing the material, you will have formed some expectations about the selection. Next, you should quickly read the material through in one sitting, without pausing or laboring over anything. Just relax and get whatever you can from the piece, and do not worry about what you do not understand. If you encounter unfamiliar words, circle them to check later. (If the piece is too long to read in one sitting, read it as quickly as you can in as few sittings as possible.) As you read quickly, form whatever impressions you can about the thesis, content, purpose, intended audience, tone, organization, and quality of the piece.

Step 3: Reread and Study

After your quick reading of the selection, reread and study the material closely to discover as much as you can. Shorter, simpler selections may take only one additional reading, but longer, more complex pieces may require several more readings. You should read and study with a pen in your hand so you can make notes in the margin, in a journal, or on a separate sheet of paper. You may find the following procedures helpful as you read and study.

    *1. **Look up the words you circled earlier*** and write their meanings in the margin as a study aid.

    *2. **Identify the thesis.*** If it is stated, place brackets around it; if it is implied, write out the thesis in the margin or at the end of the piece.

    *3. **Underline the main points made to support the thesis.*** Often these can be found in the topic sentences. Be careful not to underline too much or the selection will have more sentences underlined than not.

    *4. **Make notations as you engage in critical thinking.*** As you reread and study, rely on your critical thinking skills to distinguish fact from opinion, form questions, make inferences, synthesize, and evaluate. To facilitate this process and help you keep a record of your reactions, write notes in the margins. For example, if you like a passage or strongly agree, place an exclamation point next to it. If you disagree, write "no." If a point goes unsupported, write something like "prove this," or if you do not understand something, write a question mark. Note your important responses any way that is convenient for you, using notations like "clever," "reminds me of psych lecture," "who cares?" and so forth. (For an example of a marked essay, see "Americanization Is Tough on 'Macho'," beginning on page 61.)

    As you reread the text, studying it and thinking critically, look for answers to questions like these:

> What is the source of the author's ideas: experience, observation, considered opinion, or research?
>
> Is the author expressing facts, opinion, or both?
>
> Is the author's detail adequate and convincing? Does the author support generalizations by showing and not just telling?

What is the author's purpose? Tone? Intended audience? Role? (See the discussion on purpose, audience, role, and tone beginning on page 7.)

Do you agree or disagree with the author? Do you like or dislike the selection? What does it make you think of? Does it arouse any strong feelings?

What is the significance of the selection?

(For an example of answering critical thinking questions in a journal, see page 65.)

To see what a marked essay can look like, review the following selection marked by a student. Following the essay, also look at the questions the student answered in her journal.

A Sample Marked Essay

AMERICANIZATION IS TOUGH ON "MACHO"
Rose Del Castillo Guibault

1   What is *macho?* That depends which side of the border you come from.

2   Although it's not unusual for words and expressions to lose their subtlety in translation [the negative connotations of macho in this country are troublesome to Hispanics.]————— *Closest thing to a stated thesis*

3   Take the newspaper descriptions of alleged mass murderer Ramon Salcido. That an insensitive, insanely jealous, hard-drinking, violent Latin male is referred to as *macho* makes Hispanics cringe. — *Who is this?*

4   "*Es muy macho,*" the women in my family nod approvingly, describing a man they respect. But in the United States, when women say, "He's so macho," it's with disdain.

5   The Hispanic *macho* is manly, responsible, hardworking, a man in charge, a patriarch. A man who expresses strength through silence. What the Yiddish language would call a *mensch.* — *male head of family sounds like Dad*

6   The American *macho* is a chauvinist, a brute, uncouth, selfish, loud, abrasive, capable of inflicting pain, and sexually promiscuous. — *crude* } *good description* — *pure*

7   Quintessential *macho* models in this country are Sylvester Stallone, Arnold Schwarzenegger,

and Charles Bronson. In their movies, they exude toughness, independence, masculinity. But a closer look reveals their machismo is really violence masquerading as courage, sullenness disguised as silence, and irresponsiblity camouflaged as independence.

Interesting—never thought of this before.

8   If the Hispanic ideal of *macho* were translated to American screen roles, they might be Jimmy Stewart, Sean Connery, and Laurence Olivier.

needs more detail for proof

9   <u>In Spanish, *macho* enobles Latin males. In English, it devalues them. This pattern seems consistent with the conflicts ethnic minority males experience in this country. Typically the cultural traits other societies value don't translate as desirable characteristics in America.</u>

Examples from other cultures needed.

10   I watched my own father struggle with these cultural ambiguities. He worked on a farm for twenty years. He laid down miles of irrigation pipe, carefully plowed long, neat rows in fields, hacked away at (recalcitrant) weeds and drove tractors through whirlpools of dust. He stoically worked twenty-hour days during harvest season, accepting the long hours as part of agricultural work. When the boss complained or upbraided him for minor mistakes, he kept quiet, even when it was obvious the boss had erred.

hard to handle

Is complaining a strength or a weakness?

11   He handled the most menial tasks with pride. At home he was a good provider, helped out my mother's family in Mexico without complaint, and was indulgent with me. Arguments between my mother and him generally had to do with money, or with his stubborn reluctance to share his troubles. He tried to work them out in his own silence. He didn't want to trouble my mother — a course that backfired, because the imagined is always worse than the reality.

This is my idea of macho—males never share worries & fears.

12   Americans regarded my father as decidedly un-*macho*. His character was interpreted as nonassertive, his loyalty nonambition, and his quietness ignorance. I once overheard the boss's son blame him for plowing crooked rows in a field. My father merely smiled at the lie, knowing the boy had done it, but didn't refute it, confident his good work was well known. But the boss instead ridiculed him for being "stupid" and letting a kid get away with a lie. Seeing my embarrassment,

why unions are needed!

my father dismissed the incident, saying, "They're the dumb ones. Imagine, me fighting with a kid."

13   I tried not to look at him with American eyes because sometimes the reflection hurt.

} well put

14   Listening to my aunts' clucks of approval, my vision focused on the qualities America overlooked. "He's such a hard worker. So serious, so responsible." My aunts would secretly compliment my mother. The unspoken comparison was that he was not like some of their husbands, who drank and womanized. My uncles represented the darker side of macho.

Father is meek but strong?

15   In a patriarchal society, few challenge their roles. If men drink, it's because it's the manly thing to do. If they gamble, it's because it's how men relax. And if they fool around, well, it's because a man simply can't hold back so much man! My aunts didn't exactly meekly sit back, but they put up with these transgressions because Mexican society dictated this was their lot in life.

} the thing to do, but not the macho thing.

16   <u>In the United States, I believe it was the feminist movement of the early '70s that changed *macho's* meaning.</u> Perhaps my generation of Latin women was in part responsible. I recall Chicanos complaining about the chauvinistic nature of Latin men and the notion they wanted their women barefoot, pregnant, and in the kitchen. The generalization that Latin men embodied chauvinistic traits led to this interesting twist of semantics. Suddenly a word that represented something positive in one culture became a negative (prototype) in another.

} I don't get this.

——— model

17   <u>The problem with the use of *macho* today is that it's become an accepted stereotype of the Latin male. And like all stereotypes, it distorts truth.</u>

18   The impact of language in our society is undeniable. And the misuse of *macho* hints at a deeper cultural misunderstanding that extends beyond mere word definitions.

} interesting; I wish she had explored this more.

This essay really makes me sad for all the men who show strength every day but are seen in a negative light.

Recording Responses in a Journal

You may find it convenient to record your responses to reading in a journal. If you choose to keep a journal, date each entry and indicate the reading you are responding to. Some people write in the journal in place of making marginal notes, and others record some reactions in the margins and others in the journal. In a writing class, a journal can come in handy because you can refer to your reactions to readings when you need writing ideas, and you can use the journal to write trial drafts and experiment with ideas. This text includes a journal writing assignment after each reading that gives you an opportunity to consider in writing one of the ideas in the reading selection.

If you like, you can use the journal to answer the critical thinking questions on page 60. Here, for example, are answers to these questions for "Americanization Is Tough on 'Macho'" the way they might appear in a journal.

Answers to Questions about "Americanization Is Tough on 'Macho' "

1. What is the source of the author's ideas: experience, observation, or research? *The author's ideas came from personal experience and observation.*

2. Is the author expressing facts, opinions, or both? *The points about the connotation of macho are facts, as are the examples about the father and other relatives. The rest is opinion.*

3. Is the author's detail adequate and convincing? Does the author support generalizations by showing and not just telling? *More detail is needed to prove the point in paragraph 9. At the end, the author needs to explain more about the cultural misunderstandings.*

4. What are the author's purpose, tone, intended audience, and role? *Her purpose is to correct misunderstandings about the meaning of macho and the nature of Latin males. The tone is concerned, serious, and controlled. The audience is non-Hispanics. The author assumes the role of knowledgeable person, educator, and Hispanic.*

5. Do you agree or disagree with the author? Do you like or dislike the selection? What does it make you think of? Does it arouse any strong feelings? *I don't have enough experience around Hispanic males to agree or disagree, but I see little evidence of the stereotyped Hispanic male in the media. I like the essay, especially the parts about the author's family, but I wish there were more details. It makes me sad for a group of men who are very strong but viewed as weak.*

6. What is the significance of the selection? *The essay is important because it aims to increase understanding between cultures and dispel a common misconception. The last paragraph, in part, presents this significance.*

3

⑥ DESCRIPTION

The Readings, the Patterns, and the Purposes

My Backyard   *Mary E. Mebane*
description to express feelings and relate experience

My Neighborhood   *Alfred Kazin*
description to express feelings and relate experience *and* to inform

The Deer at Providencia   *Annie Dillard*
description with narration to express feelings and relate experience

The Courage of Turtles   *Edward Hoagland*
description to inform, to persuade, *and* to entertain

Once More to the Lake   *E.B. White*
description with narration and comparison-contrast to express feelings and relate experience

The Stone Horse   *Barry Lopez*
description with narration, process analysis, contrast, and cause-and-effect analysis to inform *and* to express feelings and relate experience

THE PATTERN

Like most people, when you notice something striking, you probably want to share it with others. Thus, you find yourself saying things like, "Come see this sunset" or "You've got to hear this song." Writers have the same impulse. They want to relate their experiences and express their sensory impressions, so they describe them in such a way that their readers can also experience them in their imaginations. To appreciate how description can allow writers to convey sensory impressions, consider this sentence, taken from a newspaper description of Tennessee's Reelfoot Lake:

> Shaggy cypress trees jut from dark waters where white waterlilies as big as dinner plates bloom.

Can you picture that scene? Probably more clearly than you would with this less descriptive sentence:

> Trees grow out of the lake at the point where large waterlilies bloom.

The first sentence shows the power of words to create mental pictures, which is a primary purpose of description: using words to move your reader to mentally see, hear, smell, taste, and touch in a particular manner. In a similar way, writers can use words to convey how it feels to experience a situation or emotion, as is the case in this example from "My Neighborhood" (page 87):

> Everything beginning at Blake Avenue would always wear for me some delightful strangeness and mildness.

THE PURPOSES OF DESCRIPTION

People write description to express themselves, to entertain, to inform, and to persuade. For example, on vacation, you might write description on a postcard to *express* to someone back home the way you see and react to the breathtaking view from your hotel balcony. Newspaper columnist Russell Baker once wrote a humorous description of a local shopping mall to *entertain* his readers. Someone in the public relations department of your university might draft a description of the campus for inclusion in the school catalog in order to *inform* prospective students about what the campus is like. A travel agent can describe a Caribbean beach resort to *persuade* people to book a tour to that spot.

Although it can serve a variety of purposes, description is most often expressive, so it most often serves to help writers share their perceptions. As human beings, we have a compelling desire to connect with others, and one way we do that is by sharing our experiences with other people. Description helps us do that. In addition, because well-written description is beautiful and therefore pleasurable to read, a secondary purpose of description is often to entertain.

Since description helps the reader form mental pictures, writers often rely on it to add interest and vividness. That is, description helps writers do more than just *tell* that something is true; it allows them to *show* that something is true. For this reason, writers often combine description with other patterns of development. For example, suppose you are writing an explanation of how to make the perfect spaghetti sauce (this would be *process analysis,* an explanation of how something is made). If you tell your reader to pick only the best tomatoes, you might go on to describe how those tomatoes look, feel, and smell, so your reader knows how to select them. Now suppose you are telling a story about the time you wrecked your uncle's classic car (this would be *narration*). You might describe what the car looked like after the wreck to add vividness and to help your reader appreciate how badly the car was wrecked.

Description in College Writing

One mark of an educated person is the ability to observe closely and assess the significance of what is observed. Thus, in your college classes, you will frequently be called upon to observe, describe, and evaluate. For example, in an art history course, you might be asked to describe two paintings by Van Gogh to show their similarities and differences. In a music appreciation course, you might be asked to describe a Chopin nocturne to explain the technique. In an advertising course, you might be required to describe an ad for a particular product to learn about persuasive strategies. In your history courses, you might be asked to describe conditions after events such as wars, coups, economic reversals, and social reforms to assess their affects. In a biology lab, you might need to describe organs after dissection in order to understand their condition, and in a psychology lab, you might need to describe the behavior of a mouse following a particular experiment to learn about the effects of certain stimuli.

OBJECTIVE AND EXPRESSIVE DETAILS

Objective details give a factual, impartial, unemotional account, whereas *expressive details* present a more subjective, personal, or emotional view. A bank appraiser describing a piece of property would use objective details because his or her personal opinion about the property is not relevant. However, an advertising executive writing a description of a new car would use expressive detail to create an emotional appeal to persuade the consumer to buy the car. Notice the difference between objective and expressive details in these examples, taken from readings in this chapter.

objective details: The Rock Pile, full of weeds and tall trees, was a place of mystery. It had so many rocks and some of them were so large that it was left uncleared with just a path through it. Behind me I could overhear voices coming from the back porch and kitchen. (From "My Backyard," page 80.)

expressive details: As for the ducks, I couldn't stroll in the woods and not feel guilty, because they were crouched beside every stagnant pothole, or were slinking between the bushes with their heads tucked into their shoulders so that I wouldn't see them. If they decided I had, they beat their way up through the screen of trees, striking their wings dangerously, and wheeled about with that headlong, magnificent velocity to locate another poor puddle. ("The Courage of Turtles," page 101.)

Whether expressive or objective, descriptive details are *sensory details* (details that pertain to the senses: sight, sound, taste, smell, and touch). Sometimes a writer uses only one sense—typically sight—and other times a writer appeals to several senses.

To see how a writer can appeal to the five senses, consider the following sentences taken from essays in this chapter.

sight: She wore a smock and a beret, and was homely, short and eccentric-looking, with funny black hair, like some of the ladies who show their painting in Washington Square in May. ("The Courage of Turtles," page 101)

sound: I remember the air whistling around me as I ran, the panicky thud of my bones in my sneakers. ("My Neighborhood," page 87)

taste: A drink of cool well water from a sweet-tasting gourd when you're thirsty is the best drink in the world. ("My Backyard," page 80)

smell: I guess I remembered clearest of all the early mornings, when the lake was cool and motionless, remembered how the bedroom smelled of the lumber it was made of and the wet woods whose scent entered through the screen. ("Once More to the Lake," page 110)

touch: I felt the uneven pressure of the earth hard against my feet. ("The Stone Horse," page 119)

Descriptive Words

The writer of both objective and expressive description chooses words carefully. This does not mean you should dash to the dictionary and thesaurus to find as many big words as possible, for the unpleasant result of the word hunt can be something like this:

The pulchritudinous rose imparted delightful olfactory sensations upon me.

This sentence illustrates two problems that can occur when writers abandon their own natural styles and pile on words taken form the thesaurus and dictionary: The writing becomes stiff, pretentious, and unnatural, and the reader has a hard time understanding.

Of course, you can turn to the dictionary and thesaurus when you are stuck, but usually you can write effective description with words you already know. The key is to use *specific* nouns, verbs, and modifiers rather than general ones because specific words are more descriptive. The following list will help you see the difference between general and specific words.

General nouns	Specific nouns
car	Ford Taurus
sweater	cardigan
shoe	Nike
class	Physics 103
meat	filet mignon
magazine	*Newsweek*

General verbs	Specific verbs
walk	stroll
spoke	shouted
look	glance
went	raced

General modifiers	Specific modifiers
nice	elegant
awesome	overwhelming
terrible	frightening
bad	gaudy

The more expressive you want your description to be, the more specific your word choice should be. Consider the following sentence, which could be well suited to objective description:

> The shopper picked up an item on the sale table, looked it over carefully, and dropped it back on the table.

However, for expressive description, more specific word choice is called for:

> The wild-eyed bargain hunter seized a neatly folded sweater, scrutinized every inch, then dropped it unfolded in the middle of the table.

To develop effective descriptive language, expect to work through a series of refinements, something like this:

first draft: The house stood in the shadow of the huge tree.

revision 1:   The huge tree cast a shadow over the house.

revision 2:   The enormous poplar cast a shadow over the house.

revision 3:   The enormous poplar cast an eerie shadow over the house.

Because a little description can go a long way, do not overwhelm your reader by stringing together too many modifiers, or you will create an overburdened sentence like this:

> The emaciated, spindly, waxen old man stared vacantly into the barren, colorless hallway as his bony, arthritic, pale fingers played absently with the beige fringes of the faded blue bedspread.

When you do have highly descriptive sentences, balance them with less descriptive ones so your reader is not overwhelmed. For example, consider this passage from "The Courage of Turtles," where a highly descriptive sentence is preceded and followed by less descriptive ones:

> Baby turtles in a turtle bowl are a puzzle of geometrics. They're as decorative as pansy petals, but they are also self-directed building blocks, propping themselves on one another in different arrangements, before upending the tower. The timid individuals turn fearless, or vice versa.

Similes and Metaphors

Similes and metaphors are often part of description because they help create mental images. A simile uses the words *like* or *as* to compare two things that are not usually seen as similar. Here is an example of a simile taken from "My Backyard":

> The water below looked like quicksilver in the sun. (Water is compared to quicksilver with the word *like*.)

A metaphor also compares two things not usually seen as similar, but without *like* or *as*. Consider the metaphor in this passage from "The Courage of Turtles":

> Baby turtles in a turtle bowl are a puzzle in geometrics. (In order to give the reader a vivid mental picture, the author compares baby turtles to puzzle pieces that form different geometric shapes.)

SELECTING AND ORDERING DETAILS

If you describe something small and uncomplicated, such as a chair, you can probably describe all its features. However, if you are describing something larger or more complex, including all the features would be difficult for you and overwhelming for your reader. With more complex descriptions, writers can settle on a *dominant impression* of what they are describing, then select only those details that convey that impression. For example, say you want to describe the house you grew up in. Describing all aspects of that house is a formidable task, but one you can cut to manageable size by choosing only those details that convey how you feel about the house or how you view the house. Thus, if the house had warmth, describe only the features that show warmth and ignore everything else. If the house was cheerful, describe only the cheerful features; if the house was an architect's nightmare, then describe the architectural problems, and so on.

To shape a thesis, write a sentence that expresses what you are describing and your dominant impression. Here are some examples:

> **I was always embarrassed by the rundown house I grew up in.** (The house will be described; the dominant impression is "rundown.")
>
> **At noon, the park comes alive with businesspeople taking a midday respite from the pressures of work.** (The park at noon will be described; the dominant impression is that it is alive with the activity of businesspeople.)

To order your descriptive details, a number of arrangements are possible. Often a *spatial* arrangement makes sense. In this arrangement, you order details across space, from front to back, near to far, left to right, and so on. Sometimes a *progressive* order is effective. This way, you order details from the least to the most important or telling. For example, if you were describing your rundown house, you would begin with the least rundown features and move gradually to the most rundown, saving the most telling description for a big finish. If you are moving through a place, a *chronological* order is possible. This way, you describe what you see first, second, third, and so on across time.

SUGGESTIONS FOR WRITING DESCRIPTION

1. Describe something you can go to and observe, so selecting details is easier. If you describe something from memory, be sure the memory is fresh enough to allow for vivid, specific details.

2. If you have trouble settling on a dominant impression, make a list of all the emotions your subject arouses in you and all the reactions you have to the subject; then choose one of those feelings or reactions as your dominant impression.

3. List the details of what you are describing (observe your subject, if possible). Do not worry about being descriptive at this point. Just get down ideas the best way you can. Then review your list and circle the points you will include in your first draft.

4. When you write your first draft, be as descriptive as you comfortably can be, but do not labor over anything. Descriptive language does not come easily; choosing specific nouns, verbs, and modifiers takes time and often involves a series of revisions, so do not expect too much too soon. When you revise after writing your draft, you can get your descriptions just right.

5. If you use a dictionary or thesaurus for help, be aware of the connotations of words you take from these sources, and be sure you use words that are natural for you. Otherwise your style will be inflated, and your meaning may be unclear.

Checklist for Revising Description

1. Do all your details work together to convey a single dominant impression?

2. Have you used specific nouns, verbs, and modifiers to appeal to the appropriate senses?

3. Have you followed highly descriptive sentences with less descriptive ones?

4. Are your descriptive details suited to your objective or expressive approach?

5. Do all your details work to fulfill your purpose or combination of purposes?

6. Are your details arranged in a suitable order, indicated by topic sentences and transitions as needed?

ANNOTATED STUDENT ESSAY

Student author Ralph Mitchell uses expressive and objective detail to describe a one-of-a-kind store. As you read, notice how the simple, specific words create effective description.

The Gendarme
Ralph Mitchell

Paragraph 1
The thesis (first sentence) notes what is being described (The Gendarme) and the dominant impression (it is one of a kind). Objective description creates visual images of the store and includes a simile (the store is like Shangri-La). Mitchell creates a sense of the store's uniqueness with the ideas that it is beyond the realm of the casual traveler and tucked away in an obscure corner.

1   In an obscure corner of West Virginia, near the triangular intersection of state routes 28, 55, and 33, stands the climbing store known as The Gendarme; it is a one-of-a-kind establishment. Few of the people passing by on the nearby road are even aware of its presence. Like the mythical city of Shangri-La, it exists beyond the realm of the casual traveler; to find it takes purpose. Tucked away behind Buck Harper's General Store and the Rocks View Restaurant, its construction mimics the small barns and outbuildings of the local inhabitants. The siding consists of rough sawn boards nailed vertically; the cracks between the boards are covered with equally rough battens. The silver steel roof is the Gendarme's most prominent feature. The raised ribs running the length of it, from the spouting to the ridge, provide a sense of purpose to the structure that is lost among the rest of its components. One small window on the side and one door in front permit a meager amount of natural light into the interior. Off to the side, a sign announcing the name of the store hangs from a pole; it is faded with age and almost hidden from view behind the branches of a small tree.

Paragraph 2
The topic sentence (sentence 1) gives the paragraph's focus as the porch. Supporting details are largely objective descriptions appealing to sight. Mitchell works to support idea of uniqueness by providing rich detail. Notice the simile ("Some perch like chickens"). Specific words include *cluttered, tatters, haphazardly,* and *corroded.* Detail is in spatial order.

2   The porch is cluttered with an odd assortment of chairs and benches. An aluminum lawn chair, its nylon seat hanging in tatters, sits dejectedly next to a log bench suspended from four crooked legs of various diameters. Its top hewn flat, it appears almost as an afterthought. The porch posts are tied together with a wooden railing that, judging from the amount of wear, must be used as seating also. Ashtrays, the origin of which cannot be discerned, are strewn haphazardly about. Some perch like chickens on the railing; others hunker down among the jetsam

strewn about the floor, fighting for a space of their own. In the center, an old cable reel, battered, burned, carved, and stained, presides over the collection—the remnants of someone's snack still adorning its top. Pushed back against the wall to the left of the door sits a corroded aluminum box about six feet long, three feet deep, and two feet high. Stenciled on the front in official looking letters are the words, "For Emergency Use Only. Stokes Litter." Covering the top of the box are bundles of firewood neatly bound and labeled "$3." A large bulletin board is handily fastened to the wall above the firewood. Covering its face are a multitude of notes, advertisements, and Park Service notices. One note reads, "To whom it may concern: Wasp nest located above the crux of Soler, use caution if climbing this route." Another offers climbing shoes for sale "cheap." A third, tattered and faded, makes a person wonder if Jennifer ever did meet Steve at the base of Old Man's route. A Park Service notice, advising of cliff closures due to the Peregrine Falcon nesting season, hangs off to the right. Immediately to the right of the notice is the door.

Paragraph 3
The topic sentence (sentence 1) gives the paragraph's focus as the walls inside; it includes a transition ("Once inside") to note spatial order. The description is more expressive, with words and phrases like "revered" and "the innocence of the sport." Spatial order is signaled with transition "Towards the back of the store." The dominant impression is emphasized with "In any other sport."

3   Once inside, a person is immediately struck by the incredible amount of climbing paraphernalia clinging to the walls and counters. The sight of this immediately sets the climber salivating and probably is about as comprehensible to the nonclimber as implements used for brain surgery are to a plumber. Towards the back of the store, a collection of used and outdated equipment hangs from the wall. In any other sport, they would reside in a Hall of Fame or a museum—icons behind glass, to be revered, out of touch to all. But here they typify the innocence of the sport, where the pioneers and the legends remain accessible to even the meekest among their brethren.

Paragraph 4
The topic sentence (sentence 1) gives the focus as John Markwell and includes a transition ("behind the cash register") to signal spatial order. "Holding court" is a metaphor comparing John to royalty. Specific words include "purveyor," and "brilliant visionary." The strict relevance of this paragraph may be debated by some readers.

4   Holding court behind the cash register stands John Markwell: purveyor of fine climbing gear and finer advice. The twinkle in his eye as he talks to a customer reveals the nature of someone who truly enjoys what he is doing. A head of graying hair seems to be his only concession to the passing years, for his trim, athletic build speaks of someone years younger. He first started

his business out of the back of a Volkswagen bus in the mid-60s. He was a brilliant visionary or damned lucky, as few could have foreseen the dramatic growth of the sport in the subsequent years. He lives in a fine brick home several doors back up the road, one of the seven or eight that comprise the little community of Mouth of Seneca. After living here for over 20 years, he is still regarded with suspicion by the locals. His children, however, participate fully as members of the community, after having spent their entire lives as playmates of the local children.

Paragraph 5
The paragraph opens with a transition ("Towards dusk") signaling chronological order. Specific words to create description appealing to sight include "flattened rattlesnake," and "rebellious haircut." The paragraph emphasizes the dominant impression by describing the wide range of people who contribute to the unique quality of the store.

5   Towards dusk, the climbers begin filtering into the parking area across the street from Harper's General Store. Stepping gingerly over a flattened rattlesnake, they pause (no doubt wondering about the sanctity of their tents pitched nearby) then continue down the community's only alley onto the porch of the Gendarme, settling into whatever seating is still available. One climber, wearing brightly colored clothing and a rebellious haircut, stands talking animatedly. His arms gesticulate wildly, for he remains full of adrenaline from the day's climb. Another sits in a chair tipped back against the wall, hands folded across his chest, eyeing with apparent amusement the actions of the rest of the group. None is a permanent resident of the area. Most are from town and cities all over the eastern United States, and several have traveled from the West and from other countries as well. They are drawn here by the nearby climbing and the opportunity to renew old friendships and establish new ones.

Paragraph 6
The topic sentence (sentence 1) gives the paragraph's focus as conversation. Mitchell emphasizes the dominant impression by noting the unique range of discussion topics.

6   The conversation begins as an anarchic free-for-all then gradually forms into a common subject, with everyone offering his or her own insight. The topics could include anything: from yesterday's epic climbs to tomorrow's projects, from the terminal ballistics of the newly adopted FBI 40 caliber sidearm to the amount of iguana guano produced by a pet iguana in a week. As the night turns to early morning, the group reluctantly disbands, returning to their tents to pass the remainder of the night in relative quiet.

Paragraph 7

The conclusion provides closure by explaining the significance of The Gendarme and by highlighting its special role.

7   Previous generations each laid claim to a unique edifice to serve as a focal point for their social interaction. During the 1940s, the General Store served this purpose. Later generations used the drugstore soda fountain, the drive-up root beer stand, and fast food restaurants. In today's age of the car phone, E-mail, and fax, social boundaries no longer are defined by physical limits, such as a neighborhood or a town, but by common interests and goals. The Gendarme stands as a contemporary version of a social centerpoint for one small segment of society: the climbing community.

MY BACKYARD
Mary E. Mebane

Born in Durham, North Carolina, Mary Mebane (1933 – 1992) earned a Ph.D. in English from the University of North Carolina. She was first a public school teacher and then an English professor at the University of South Carolina. Mebane wrote mostly about the lives of Southern blacks after 1960. She is also the author of two autobiographical works: Mary *(1981) and* Mary, Wayfarer *(1983). In "My Backyard," which is taken from the earlier autobiography, Mebane describes her childhood surroundings to relate part of her Southern rural experience, an experience of poverty, hardship, and struggle. As you read, notice the early signs that Mebane was to become a writer.*

THE PATTERN	THE PURPOSE
description	*to express feelings and relate experience*

1   My name is Mary.

2   When I first opened my eyes to the world, on June 26, 1933, in the Wildwood community in Durham County, North Carolina, the world was a green Eden—and it was magic. My favorite place in the whole world was a big rock in the backyard that looked like the back of a buried elephant. I spent a lot of time squatting on that rock. I realize now that I probably selected it because it was in the *center* of our yard, and from it, by shifting ever so slightly, this way and that, I could see *everything*. I liked to look. Mama must have told me several thousand times that I was going to die with my eyes open, looking.

3   When I sat on the rock with my back to the house, the fields were in front of me. On the left was another lot that we called the Rock Pile, and to the right was an untended strip of land, strewn with rocks but cleared enough to be plowed sometimes. The Rock Pile, full of weeds and tall trees, was a place of mystery. It had so many rocks and some of them were so large that it was left uncleared with just a path through it. Behind me I could overhear voices coming from the back porch and kitchen. I could see who was chopping or picking something

in the garden and I could see who was coming through the Rock Pile.
4   The road in front of our house was a dirty strip swirling with the
thick red dust of state trucks going to and from the rock quarry. I saw
the quarry once. To me it was one of the Seven Wonders of the World—
a very wide hole, dug deep in the ground. The trucks around it looked
like little toys. It was a mountain going in the wrong direction, with me
standing at the top. Good-looking Edmund, the one with the limp from
polio, died at the rock quarry. Explosives. They didn't want anyone to
see his body. Someone said that they found only pieces. He was a grown
man and I was a child at the time, but I remember him. He came down
from Virginia to stay with his sister and find work. Like his sisters, he
was very light-skinned and had thick, curly brown hair. I used to wonder about his hair. Did they find a lock of curly brown hair after the ex-
plosion?
5   Then there was a rich white contractor who lived on the highway. His oldest son had died as a young man, in another part of the
state, backing a truck too near such an opening. The truck had started
to slide and he couldn't stop it. I saw his picture once, when I went as
a teenager to baby-sit at their house. His brother, then a grown man and
my employer for the evening, told me about the accident. In the photograph the dead heir was still a child, about nine years old, sitting on
a horse, smiling at the camera.
6   The world consisted of me at first; then, when Ruf Junior, the
baby, was big enough to walk, he joined me on the rock. My older
brother, Jesse, was a boy who came dashing by to or from some adventure, and he might say something or he might not. My mother, Non-
nie, and my father, Rufus, were the grown people who called me to dinner, to bed, or to do chores.
7   One day a car came up to the house and a lady got out, while a
man put suitcases on the porch. The lady was Aunt Jo, and she stayed
with us for several years. Sometimes other people came, but they were
visitors, and unless they had someone my age for me to play with, they
didn't affect me one way or the other.
8   I would squat on that rock, my stick legs poking through the
openings of my dirt-stained bloomers, my birdlike head turning from
side to side, my gaze, unblinking, focusing up, down, in front of me,
in back of me, now zooming in on the lower yard, then penetrating
deeper into the garden, then rising up ever so slightly to where the corn
was planted on the hill. I was in the center of life and I didn't miss a

thing; nothing slipped by unobserved or unnoted. My problems started when I began to comment on what I saw. I insisted on being accurate. But the world I was born into didn't want that. Indeed, its very survival depended on not knowing, not seeing—and, certainly, not saying anything at all about what it was really like.

9   The whole backyard slanted down. It started at the well and sloped down to the lettuce patch. When it rained, water ran in gullies clear down to a ditch Daddy had dug parallel to the flow to make the water run off. Later he decided to stop the flow up higher, and Ruf Junior and Jesse and I toted rocks and formed a little dam between the big sloping rock and the two less-big rocks that lay on either side of it.

10   The rock on the left was big, but it looked like a rock, not like the back of a buried elephant. I could see all around it, but it was big. My brothers and I couldn't move it, not even when we all pushed together. The one on the right of the big sloping rock looked like its brother. You couldn't see where it started or stopped. Its back was like the back of a smaller gray buried elephant—the younger brother of the large gray sloping elephant that was buried in the middle.

11   The little dam, built up with sticks and rocks, held fast; later, when it rained, the running dirt stopped there and backed up and covered some of the hundreds of rocks that studded the backyard and on which we stubbed innumerable bare toes in the May-to-September, school-is-out summer.

12   The well was in the upper part of the backyard, before the slope started. The wooden box that was the superstructure of the well was partly rotted; there were wide spaces between the boards, and my brothers and I had been warned not to lean too hard on them when we pulled the bucket up or we would fall in. The bucket was beaten up from banging on the rocks that lined the narrow well, and when the bucket came out, water sloshed over the side and spurted out of the little holes in it. The rocks in the well had wet green moss on them as far down as the eye could see. The well was about the width of a giant inner tube, but rough where the rocks stuck out all the way down. When you looked over the boards, the water below looked like quicksilver in the sun. I would look into the well and think deep thoughts and smell the wet moss and rotting wood.

13   Hanging on a nail on the well was a gourd to drink out of. This was full and round at one end and tubular at the other, and had tiny ridges in its mud-brown interior. A drink of cool well water from a

sweet-tasting gourd when you're thirsty is the best drink in the world.
14   Sometimes I liked to lean over the edge of the well and look past
the box where the wood had rotted and splintered from the water, past
the moss lining the bottom of the wood and the rocks paving the well.
I thought that underneath the moving water was China. I read a story
in the second grade that said that if you dig a deep, deep hole down
from where you were and put your eye down, clear through the hole
on the other side you would see China.
15   I believed stories like that. Just as once I read a story about Mexico and was struck by the bold designs on the pottery. That night I
dreamed that I was in heaven and God looked like the father of a Mexican family, dark, with black hair and a long, colorful robe, with his wife
and child by his side. They were standing in front of a clay house, and
nearby were enormous pottery jars with bright designs on them.
16   Our well wasn't as deep as it should have been, and a couple of
summers it went dry, so we would go to one of the springs. The nearest, at the bottom of a little slope, bubbled clear water up out of clean
sand. The shallow encircling wall was about three hands high and a
child could curl up and hold his feet with his hands around its cir-
cumference. The water there bubbled up endlessly, clear and sweet,
shaded by tall North Carolina pines. The other spring was farther away.
It was larger, more conventional, and not nearly so romantic.
17   In the morning the sun glistened on the long grass in the vacant
lot that was never mowed. The cow ate the grass and kept it low, all except the spot where I emptied the peepots. She wouldn't eat there unless Mama sprinkled a lot of salt on it to fool her. Then sometimes she
would eat it and sometimes she wouldn't. This grass was on the lot next
to the main yard. Daddy sometimes plowed it all up and harrowed it
and sowed it with grain and got mad when Mr. Jake's chickens came
over from next door and ate it all up. But it was dry, hard, cracked land
and never grew much of anything.
18   On the left side of the main yard was the Rock Pile, where I
picked blackberries. Aunt Jo made purple dye from the pokeberries that
also grew there, and sometimes she cooked poke salad, which I hated;
it tasted like cooked leaves. But I liked the dye. When Aunt Jo dipped
a white gunnysack in the dark water and it came up a beautiful purple,
I was filled with wonder.
19   Sometimes my brothers and I played jumping from rock to rock.
If you stepped off a rock you were "out." Sometimes snakes slid out of

the Rock Pile. My brothers and I couldn't run through it; the briars tore too bad. But we had a path and as long as I stayed in the path I felt safe. One step either to the right or the left of the patch and I felt scared. Not only of snakes and other natural dangers but of something else. I didn't know what.

20   At the bottom of the yard there was a vegetable garden with green growing things: lettuce and cabbage and cucumbers and squash. Little sticks held up the vines of tomatoes and string beans and butter beans. Beyond it, the field ran up a little hill from the garden a long way and then down to some pines. After the rows of pines, the Bottom started. It was low there and wet most of the time, but I liked it; my father worked hard there with Suki, the mule, plowing. I followed him there all the time, but I liked mainly to play near the creek in the Bottom and on the pine-straw-covered mounds, where I slid down into the gullies.

Reading Closely and Thinking Critically

1. In your own words, write a thesis that conveys the subject and dominant impression of the essay.

2. From Mebane's description of her backyard and her activities, what can you conclude about her childhood? Was she happy? How do you know?

3. Write a list of words that describe the author as a child.

4. Using the evidence in the essay as clues, tell what the early indications were that Mebane had a writer's sensibilities.

5. In paragraph 8, Mebane says, "My problems started when I began to comment on what I saw. I insisted on being accurate. But the world I was born into didn't want that. Indeed, its very survival depended on not knowing, not seeing—and, certainly, not saying anything at all about what it was really like." What do you think Mebane means? Does her essay conform to the ideas she is expressing here?

6. Do you think that Mebane feels deprived because her childhood was spent in poverty? Explain.

Examining Structure and Strategy

1. Cite three descriptive words, phrases, or sentences that you find particularly effective. Why do they work so well?

2. Mebane uses both objective and expressive description. Cite examples of each. Which does she rely on more heavily?

3. Mebane's description extends beyond her backyard. Is this a problem? Explain.

4. When Mebane says in her second sentence that "the world was a green Eden—and it was magic," she leads the reader to expect an upbeat description. Yet her essay has many dark notes: people died prematurely; her surroundings were stark; her family was poor. Given the essay's opening, are these dark notes a problem? Why do you think Mebane mentions the darker side of her life?

5. "My Backyard" is an excerpt from Mebane's autobiography. What kind of reader do you think would enjoy reading about Mebane's life?

Considering Language and Style

1. Mebane's description includes metaphors and similes (see page 73). Cite an example of each.

2. Name the Seven Wonders of the World (paragraph 4). Consult a dictionary or encyclopedia if necessary.

3. Consult a dictionary if you are unsure of the meaning of any of these words: *quarry* (paragraph 4), *toted* (paragraph 9), *quicksilver* (paragraph 12), *gourd* (paragraph 13).

For Group Discussion or Writing

As a child, Mebane had no video games, Barbie dolls, swing sets, and other expensive toys that many children have. Do you think she had less fun than children who had more toys? Do you think she had an advantage over children with more toys? Consider these questions with two or three classmates.

Writing Assignments

1. *In your journal.* In about two pages, tell about your childhood. In what ways was it similar to Mebane's, and in what ways was it different?

2. *Using the pattern.* In paragraph 3, Mebane says that the Rock Pile next door "was a place of mystery." Using expressive and/or objective detail, describe a place from your youth that "was a place of mystery."

3. *Using the pattern.* For Mebane, the rock quarry was a special place of wonderment: "it was one of the Seven Wonders of the World." Using expressive and/or objective detail, describe a place from your youth that was full of wonderment. If you like, you can also tell what you did there.

4. *Using the pattern.* Write a description of the backyard of your childhood home. Like Mebane, convey a sense of your surroundings, the people in your world, and your activities. Also like Mebane, try to convey what life was like in the world that included your backyard.

5. *Considering a theme.* Think back to some aspect of your own childhood world (your house, your backyard, your neighborhood, your school, and so forth). Explain how that part of your world influenced you then and whether its influence continues into the present.

6. *Connecting the readings.* "Shades of Black" on page 469 was also written by Mebane, but it deals with adult concerns. Read that selection and refer to "My Backyard" to explain what aspects of Mebane's thinking and personality as an adult were evident when she was a child.

MY NEIGHBORHOOD
Alfred Kazin

A prolific writer of literary criticism and autobiographical works, Alfred Kazin is a masterful wordsmith. He often writes reminiscences of the immigrant Jewish neighborhood where he grew up. He has also edited volumes of works by the important American authors Herman Melville, F. Scott Fitzgerald, Theodore Dreiser, and Nathaniel Hawthorne. In 1989, he published Our New York, *a look at New York City that he produced with photographer David Finn. "My Neighborhood," which is an excerpt from his autobiographical* A Walker in the City (1951), *is a vivid portrait of the harsh reality of the Brooklyn tenement that he grew up in. As you read, notice that Kazin does more than just relate the particulars of his childhood neighborhood; he also expresses the conflicting feelings he had about the block he grew up on and the world beyond it.*

THE PATTERN	THE PURPOSE
description	*to express feelings and relate experience*

1   The block: *my* block. It was on the Chester Street side of our house, between the grocery and the back wall of the old drugstore, that I was hammered into the shape of the streets. Everything beginning at Blake Avenue would always wear for me some delightful strangeness and mildness, simply because it was not of my block, *the* block, where the clang of your head sounded against the pavement when you fell in a fist fight, and the rows of storelights on each side were pitiless, watching you. Anything away from the block was good: even a school you never went to, two blocks away; there were vegetable gardens in the park across the street. Returning from "New York," I would take the longest routes home from the subway, get off a station ahead of our own, only for the unexpectedness of walking through Betsy Head Park and hearing gravel crunch under my feet as I went beyond the vegetable gardens, smelling the sweaty sweet dampness from the pool in summer

and the dust on the leaves as I passed under the ailanthus trees. On the block itself everything rose up only to test me.

2   We worked every inch of it, from the cellars and the backyards to the sickening space between the roofs. Any wall, any stoop, any curving metal edge on a billboard sign made a place against which to knock a ball; any bottom rung of a fire escape ladder a goal in basketball; any sewer cover a base; any crack in the pavement a "net" for the tense sharp tennis that we played by beating a soft ball back and forth with our hands between the squares. Betsy Head Park two blocks away would always feel slightly foreign, for it belonged to the Amboys and the Bristols and the Hopkinsons as much as it did to us. *Our* life every day was fought out on the pavement and in the gutter, up against the walls of the houses and the glass fronts of the drugstore and the grocery, in and out of the fresh steaming piles of horse manure, the wheels of passing carts and automobiles, along the iron spikes of the stairway to the cellar, the jagged edge of the open garbage cans, the crumbly steps of the old farmhouses still left on one side of the street.

3   As I go back to the block now, and for a moment fold my body up again in its narrow area—there, just there, between the black of the asphalt and the old women in their kerchiefs and flowered housedresses sitting on the tawny kitchen chairs—the back wall of the drugstore still rises up to test me. Every day we smashed a small black viciously hard regulation handball against it with fanatical cuts and drives and slams, beating and slashing at it almost in hatred for the blind strength of the wall itself. I was never good enough at handball, was always practicing some trick shot that might earn me esteem, and when I was weary of trying, would often bat a ball down Chester Street just to get myself to Blake Avenue. I have this memory of playing one-o'-cat by myself in the sleepy twilight, at a moment when everyone else had left the block. The sparrows floated down from the telephone wires to peck at every fresh pile of horse manure, and there was a smell of brine from the delicatessen store, of egg crates and of the milk scum left in the great metal cans outside the grocery, of the thick white paste oozing out from behind the fresh Hecker's Flour ad on the metal signboard. I would throw the ball in the air, hit it with my bat, then with perfect satisfaction drop the bat to the ground and run to the next sewer cover. Over and over I did this, from sewer cover to sewer cover, until I had worked my way to Blake Avenue and could see the park.

4   With each clean triumphant ring of my bat against the gutter leading me on, I did the whole length of our block up and down, and never knew how happy I was just watching the asphalt rise and fall, the curve of the steps up to an old farmhouse. The farmhouses themselves were streaked red on one side, brown on the other, but the steps themselves were always gray. There was a tremor of pleasure at one place; I held my breath in nausea at another. As I ran after my ball with the bat heavy in my hand, the odd successiveness of things in myself almost choked me, the world was so full as I ran—past the cobblestoned yards into the old farmhouses, where stray chickens still waddled along the stones; past the little candy store where we went only if the big one on our side of the block was out of Eskimo Pies; past the three neighboring tenements where the last of the old women sat on their kitchen chairs yawning before they went up to make supper. Then came Mrs. Rosenwasser's house, the place on the block I first identified with what was farthest from home, and strangest, because it was a "private" house; then the fences around the monument works, where black cranes rose up above the yard and you could see the smooth gray slabs that would be cut and carved into tombstone, some of them already engraved with the names and dates and family virtues of the dead.

5   Beyond Blake Avenue was the pool parlor outside which we waited all through the tense September afternoons of the World's Series to hear the latest scores called off the ticker tape—and where as we waited, banging a ball against the bottom of the wall and drinking water out of empty Coke bottles, I breathed the chalk off the cues and listened to the clocks ringing in the fire station across the street. There was an old warehouse next to the pool parlor; the oil on the barrels and the iron staves had the same rusty smell. A block away was the park, thick with the dusty gravel I liked to hear my shoes crunch in as I ran round and round the track; then a great open pavilion, the inside mysteriously dark, chill even in summer; there I would wait in the sweaty coolness before pushing on to the wading ring where they put up a shower on the hottest days.

6   Beyond the park the "fields" began, all those still unused lots where we could still play hard ball in perfect peace—first shooing away the goats and then tearing up goldenrod before laying our bases. The smell and touch of those "fields," with their wild compost under the billboards of weeds, goldenrod, bricks, goat droppings, rusty cans,

empty beer bottles, fresh new lumber, and damp cement, lives in my mind as Brownsville's great open door, the wastes that took us through to the west. I used to go round them in summer with my cousins selling near-beer to the carpenters, but always in a daze, would stare so long at the fibrous stalks of the goldenrod as I felt their harshness in my hand that I would forget to make a sale, and usually go off sick on the beer I drank up myself. Beyond! Beyond! Only to see something new, to get away from each day's narrow battleground between the grocery and the back wall of the drugstore! Even the other end of our block, when you got to Mrs. Rosenwasser's house and the monument works, was dear to me for the contrast. On summer nights, when we played Indian trail, running away from each other on prearranged signals, the greatest moment came when I could plunge into the darkness down the block for myself and hide behind the slabs in the monument works. I remember the air whistling around me as I ran, the panicky thud of my bones in my sneakers, and then the slabs rising in the light from the street lamps as I sped past the little candy store and crept under the fence.

7   In the darkness you could never see where the crane began. We liked to trap the enemy between the slabs and sometimes jumped them from great mounds of rock just in from the quarry. A boy once fell to his death that way, and they put a watchman there to keep us out. This made the slabs all the more impressive to me, and I always aimed first for that yard whenever we played follow-the-leader. Day after day the monument works became oppressively more mysterious and remote, though it was only just down the block; I stood in front of it every afternoon on my way back from school, filling it with my fears. It was not death I felt there—the slabs were usually faceless. It was the darkness itself, and the wind howling around me whenever I stood poised on the edge of a high slab waiting to jump. Then I would take in, along with the fear, some amazement of joy that I had found my way out that far.

Reading Closely and Thinking Critically

1. Kazin's feeling about his neighborhood and the territory beyond his neighborhood contrast with each other. Describe this contrast.

2. Kazin has conflicting feelings about his neighborhood. Describe those conflicting feelings. Describe Kazin's conflicting feelings about the world beyond his neighborhood.

3. As an adult returning to his old neighborhood, how does Kazin feel about the block he grew up on? Cite evidence to support your view.

4. When Kazin says, "We worked every inch of it [his block]" (paragraph 2), what do you think he means?

5. Why was Kazin so drawn to the monument works?

6. Since it is at the edge of the neighborhood, the monument works can be taken as the bridge from Kazin's neighborhood to the outside, a bridge from the known to the unknown. With this in mind, interpret the last two sentences of the selection.

Examining Structure and Strategy

1. Very early in the essay—in the first two paragraphs, in fact— Kazin conveys the idea that his neighborhood was a harsh, difficult place. Cite three or four examples of word choices that help convey this idea.

2. Kazin uses both objective and expressive description (see page 70). Cite an example of each.

3. To which of the five senses does Kazin's description appeal? Cite an example of description that appeals to each sense you name.

4. Which paragraphs begin with topic sentences? What purpose do these topic sentences serve?

5. Cite a description that you particularly like and explain why it appeals to you.

6. Do you think a reader must be familiar with urban life in order to appreciate "My Neighborhood"? Why or why not?

Considering Language and Style

1. "My Neighborhood" opens with a four-word sentence fragment. What is the effect of this beginning?

2. Consult a dictionary if you are unsure of the meaning of any of these words: *tawny* (paragraph 3), *fanatical* (paragraph 3), *brine* (paragraph 3), *ticker tape* (paragraph 5), *near-beer* (paragraph 6).

3. Are any of the words in number 2 obsolete because they are relevant to a much earlier time? Explain.

For Group Discussion or Writing

Although Kazin enjoyed aspects of his neighborhood, he found life on the block harsh, difficult, and confining; although he longed for the world beyond because he found it milder, he feared the uncertainty of the outside. How do you explain Kazin's ambivalent feelings? Are they normal? Do young people commonly experience such conflicting feelings regardless of where they are raised? With three or four classmates, consider the answers to these questions.

Writing Assignments

1. *In your journal.* Write out the most vivid memory of your childhood neighborhood and the positive and/or negative emotions this memory stirs in you. Also, try to explain why you feel the way you do.

2. *Using the pattern.* Like Kazin, share a part of your past by describing the neighborhood where you grew up. Your description should convey whether you liked the neighborhood, disliked the neighborhood, or had conflicting feelings about it. As an alternative, explain to what extent you were "hammered into the shape of the streets" (paragraph 1).

3. *Using the pattern.* Describe any place that raises conflicting emotions in you — your house or apartment, a doctor's office, a hospital, or your parents' home, for example. Select details that help you convey these conflicting emotions.

4. *Using the pattern.* Part of Kazin's description focuses on the games he played as a child. Describe a common childhood game. You can include the place where it is played and the people it is played with if you like. Try to convey what the game means to children and what they learn as a result of playing.

5. *Using the pattern.* Kazin's neighborhood had a significant impact on him. In fact, he says that he "was hammered into the shape of the streets." Select a place that had a signifcant impact on you (for example, your grandparents' farm, your best friend's house, or the Little League fields) and describe it, being sure to express how the place affected you.

6. *Considering a theme.* The monument works were a source of both fear and attraction for Kazin. Tell about something from

childhood that both attracted and frightened you. What do you think caused the conflicting emotions? As an alternative, tell about some vivid childhood memory and the emotions the memory stirs. (Consult your previous journal entry for ideas for this essay.)

7. *Connecting the readings.* Explain how Kazin viewed his childhood surroundings and how Mary Mebane viewed hers (see "My Backyard," page 80). Then go on to draw one or more conclusions about how children are affected by their surroundings.

THE DEER AT PROVIDENCIA
Annie Dillard

Both a writer and a teacher of writing, Annie Dillard was a columnist for The Living Wilderness *and a contributing editor for* Harper's *magazine. Dillard won a Pulitzer Prize in 1975 for her first book of prose,* The Pilgrim at Tinker Creek, *a collection of observations about the beauty and violence of the natural world near her Virginia home. Dillard's other works include poetry;* Encounters with Chinese Writers *(1984), a work about her visit to China as part of a United States cultural delegation;* The Writing Life *(1989), a narrative about the writing process; and a book of essays,* Teaching a Stone to Talk *(1982). "The Deer at Providencia," from* Teaching a Stone to Talk *(1982), is a description of the torment of a deer. The description is a powerful component of Dillard's narration (story) about the suffering of humans and animals. Notice the weaving of descriptive and narrative elements as Dillard relates her experience and expresses her uncertainty with readers who probably have the same question she has: "What is going on?"*

THE PATTERNS	THE PURPOSE
description and narration	*to express feelings and relate experience*

1   There were four of us North Americans in the jungle, in the Ecuadorian jungle on the banks of the Napo River in the Amazon watershed. The other three North Americans were metropolitan men. We stayed in tents in one riverside village, and visited others. At the village called Providencia we saw a sight which moved us, and which shocked the men.

2   The first thing we saw when we climbed the riverbank to the village of Providencia was the deer. It was roped to a tree on the grass clearing near the thatch shelter where we would eat lunch.

3   The deer was small, about the size of a whitetail fawn, but apparently full-grown. It had a rope around its neck and three feet caught in the rope. Someone said that the dogs had caught it that morning and the villagers were going to cook and eat it that night.

4   This clearing lay at the edge of the little thatched-hut village. We could see the villagers going about their business, scattering feed corn for hens about their houses, and wandering down paths to the river to bathe. The village headman was our host; he stood beside us as we watched the deer struggle. Several village boys were interested in the deer; they formed part of the circle we made around it in the clearing. So also did four businessmen from Quito who were attempting to guide us around the jungle. Few of the very different people standing in this circle had a common language. We watched the deer, and no one said much.

5   The deer lay on its side at the rope's very end, so the rope lacked slack to let it rest its head in the dust. It was "pretty," delicate of bone like all deer, and thin-skinned for the tropics. Its skin looked virtually hairless, in fact, and almost translucent, like a membrane. Its neck was no thicker than my wrist; it was rubbed open on the rope, and gashed. Trying to paw itself free of the rope, the deer had scratched its own neck with its hooves. The raw underside of its neck showed red stripes and some bruises bleeding inside the muscles. Now three of its feet were hooked in the rope under its jaw. It could not stand, of course, on one leg, so it could not move to slacken the rope and ease the pull on its throat and enable it to rest its head.

6   Repeatedly the deer paused, motionless, its eyes veiled, with only its rib cage in motion, and its breaths the only sound. Then, after I would think, "It has given up; now it will die," it would heave. The rope twanged; the tree leaves clattered; the deer's free foot beat the ground. We stepped back and held our breaths. It thrashed, kicking, but only one leg moved; the other three legs tightened inside the rope's loop. Its hip jerked; its spine shook. Its eyes rolled; its tongue, thick with spittle, pushed in and out. Then it would rest again. We watched this for fifteen minutes.

7   Once three young native boys charged in, released its trapped legs, and jumped back to the circle of people. But instantly the deer scratched up its neck with its hooves and snared its forelegs in the rope again. It was easy to imagine a third and then a fourth leg soon stuck, like Brer Rabbit and the Tar Baby.

8   We watched the deer from the circle, and then we drifted on to lunch. Our palm-roofed shelter stood on a grassy promontory from which we would see the deer tied to the tree, pigs and hens walking under village houses, and black-and-white cattle standing in the river. There was even a breeze.

9   Lunch, which was the second and better lunch we had that day, was hot and fried. There was a big fish called *doncella,* a kind of catfish, dipped whole in corn flour and beaten egg, then deep fried. With our fingers we pulled soft fragments of it from its sides to our plates, and ate; it was delicate fish-flesh, fresh and mild. Someone found the roe, and I ate of that too—it was fat and stronger, like egg yolk, naturally enough, and warm.

10   There was also a stew of meat in shreds with rice and pale brown gravy. I had asked what kind of deer it was tied to the tree; Pepe had answered in Spanish, *"Gama."* Now they told us this was *gama* too, stewed. I suspect the word means merely game or venison. At any rate, I heard that the village dogs had cornered another deer just yesterday, and it was this deer which we were now eating in full sight of the whole article. It was good. I was surprised at its tenderness. But it is a fact that high levels of lactic acid, which builds up in muscle tissues during exertion, tenderizes.

11   After the fish and meat we ate bananas fried in chunks and served on a tray; they were sweet and full of flavor. I felt terrific. My shirt was wet and cool from swimming; I had had a night's sleep, two decent walks, three meals, and a swim—everything tasted good. From time to time each one of us, separately, would look beyond our shaded roof to the sunny spot where the deer was still convulsing in the dust. Our meal completed, we walked around the deer and back to the boats.

12   That night I learned that while we were watching the deer, the others were watching me.

13   We four North Americans grew close in the jungle in a way that was not the usual artificial intimacy of travelers. We liked each other. We stayed up all that night talking, murmuring, as though we rocked on hammocks slung above time. The others were from big cities: New York, Washington, Boston. They all said that I had no expression on my face when I was watching the deer—or at any rate, not the expression they expected.

14   They had looked to see how I, the only woman, and the youngest, was taking the sight of the deer's struggles. I looked detached, apparently, or hard, or calm, or focused, still. I don't know. I was thinking. I remember feeling very old and energetic. I could say like Thoreau that I have traveled widely in Roanoke, Virginia. I have thought a great deal about carnivorousness; I eat meat. These things are not issues; they are mysteries.

15   Gentlemen of the city, what surprises you? That there is suffering here, or that I know it?

16   We lay in the tent and talked. "If it had been my wife," one man said with special vigor, amazed, "she wouldn't have cared *what* was going on; she would have dropped *everything* right at that moment and gone in the village from here to there to there, she would not have *stopped* until that animal was out of its suffering one way or another. She couldn't *bear* to see a creature in agony like that."

17   I nodded.

18   Now I am home. When I wake I comb my hair before the mirror above my dresser. Every morning for the past two years I have seen in that mirror, beside my sleep-softened face, the blacked face of a burnt man. It is a wire-service photograph clipped from a newspaper and taped to my mirror. The caption reads: "Alan McDonald in Miami hospital bed." All you can see in the photograph is a smudged triangle of face from his eyelids to his lower lip; the rest is bandages. You cannot see the expression in his eyes; the bandages shade them.

19   The story, headed MAN BURNED FOR SECOND TIME, begins:

> "Why does God hate me?" Alan McDonald asked from his hospital bed.
> "When the gunpowder went off, I couldn't believe it," he said. "I just
> couldn't believe it. I said, 'No, God couldn't do this to me again."

He was in a burn ward in Miami, in serious condition. I do not even know if he lived. I wrote him a letter at the time, cringing.

20   He had been burned before, thirteen years previously, by flaming gasoline. For years he had been having his body restored and his face remade in dozens of operations. He had been a boy, and then a burnt boy. He had already been stunned by what could happen, by how life could veer.

21   Once I read that people who survive bad burns tend to go crazy; they have a very high suicide rate. Medicine cannot ease their pain; drugs just leak away, soaking the sheets, because there is no skin to hold them in. The people just lie there and weep. Later they kill themselves. They had not known, before they were burned, that the world included such suffering, that life could permit them personally such pain.

22   This time a bowl of gunpowder had exploded on McDonald.

> "I didn't realize what had happened at first," he recounted. "And
> then I heard that sound from 13 years ago. I was burning. I rolled to put
> the fire out and I thought, 'Oh God, not again.'

"If my friend hadn't been there, I would have jumped into a canal with a rock around my neck."

His wife concludes the piece, "Man, it just isn't fair."

23   I read the whole clipping again every morning. This is the Big Time here, every minute of it. Will someone please explain to Alan Mc-Donald in his dignity, to the deer at Providencia in his dignity, what is going on? And mail me the carbon.

24   When we walked by the deer at Providencia for the last time, I said to Pepe, with a pitying glance at the deer, *"Pobrecito"*—"poor little thing." But I was trying out Spanish. I knew at the time it was a ridiculous thing to say.

Reading Closely and Thinking Critically

1. In your own words, write a sentence or two that expresses the thesis of "The Deer of Providencia."

2. Describe the way the men react to the deer. How is their reaction different from Dillard's? Why are the men surprised by Dillard's reaction to the deer?

3. Why does Dillard note (in paragraph 10) that high levels of lactic acid tenderize meat?

4. What view of women is referred to in paragraphs 15 and 16?

5. Do you agree with Dillard that *"Pobrecito"* ("poor little thing") was a ridiculous thing for her to say as she walked by the deer? Explain.

6. Why do you think that Dillard kept the picture and article about Alan McDonald?

Examining Structure and Strategy

1. What approach does Dillard take to her introduction (see page 32)?

2. Dillard writes of the deer at Providencia and of Alan McDonald. What do these two have in common? That is, how is it possible to discuss both in the same essay?

3. Which paragraphs are developed primarily with description? Which are developed primarily with narration (story-telling)?

4. Which of the descriptive paragraphs are developed primarily with objective detail and which with expressive detail (see page 70)?

5. What attitude toward the deer is Dillard's audience likely to have? How is the reader likely to react to the deer's plight?

Considering Language and Style

1. Dillard uses language to describe the deer as fragile. Cite two examples of such language.

2. What is particularly significant about the name of the village (Providencia)?

3. Consult a dictionary if you are unsure of the meaning of any of these words: *watershed* (paragraph 1), *thatch* (paragraph 2), *translucent* (paragraph 5), *spittle* (paragraph 6), *promontory* (paragraph 8), *carnivorousness* (paragraph 14).

For Group Discussion or Writing

With three or four classmates, consider this question: Do you see a difference between the suffering of the deer and the suffering of Alan McDonald? If so, explain what that difference is. If not, explain why.

Writing Assignments

1. *In your journal.* At one time, killing animals for food was a necessity, but many people claim that we no longer need to do so, that vegetarianism is a solution to animal killing and suffering. Attack or defend the killing of animals for food.

2. *Using the pattern.* Like Dillard, describe an animal engaged in some activity. For example, you could describe a kitten at play, a cat washing itself, a dog chasing a ball, or fish swimming in a tank. If possible, use expressive detail to convey the animal's level of comfort.

3. *Using the pattern.* If you ever experienced considerable pain, write a description of what you went through. You can describe, for instance, having a broken leg, a migraine headache, or a sports injury.

4. *Using the pattern.* Like Dillard, relate an experience by telling a story that includes description. Pick an experience that teaches something about life.

5. *Considering a theme.* Answer the question that Dillard poses in paragraph 23: What kind of world allows the suffering that the deer and McDonald endured?

6. *Connecting the readings.* Discuss the degree and kinds of suffering in the world and/or how people cope with that suffering. The information in "The Deer at Providencia," "Untouchables" (page 236), and "What Is Poverty?" (page 515), may give you some ideas.

THE COURAGE OF TURTLES
Edward Hoagland

A brilliant essayist famous for his nature writings, Edward Hoagland has published essays in Newsweek, Commentary, *the* New York Times, *and the* Village Voice. *He has also written novels, travel books, and a book of stories with Gretl Ehrlich called* City Tales/Wyoming Stories *(1986). "The Courage of Turtles" is from his collection of essays by the same name (1985). One of his acclaimed nature essays, it is a richly detailed portrait of turtles, their habits, and the vulnerability they share with all creatures of the wild. While Hoagland's lush description is entertaining, it also informs the reader about the nature of turtles and aims to persuade the reader to be wary of unchecked development.*

THE PATTERN	THE PURPOSES
description	*to inform, to entertain, and to persuade*

1   Turtles are a kind of bird with the governor turned low. With the same attitude of removal, they cock a glance at what is going on, as if they need only to fly away. Until recently they were also a case of virtue rewarded, at least in the town where I grew up, because, being humble creatures, there were plenty of them. Even when we still had a few bobcats in the woods the local snapping turtles, growing up to forty pounds, were the largest carnivores. You would see them through the amber water, as big as greeny wash basins at the bottom of the pond, until they faded into the inscrutable mud as if they hadn't existed at all.

2   When I was ten I went to Dr. Green's Pond, a two-acre pond across the road. When I was twelve I walked a mile or so to Taggart's Pond, which was lusher, had big water snakes and a waterfall; and shortly after that I was bicycling way up to the adventuresome vastness of Mud Pond, a lake-sized body of water in the reservoir system of a Connecticut city, possessed of cat-backed little islands and empty shacks and a forest of pines and hardwoods along the shore. Otters, foxes and mink left their prints on the bank; there were pike and perch. As I got older, the estates and forgotten back lots in town were parceled out and sold for nice prices, yet, though the woods had shrunk, it seemed that

fewer people walked in the woods. The new residents didn't know how to find them. Eventually, exploring, they did find them, and it required some ingenuity and doubling around on my part to go for eight miles without meeting someone. I was grown by now, I lived in New York, and that's what I wanted on the occasional weekends when I came out.

3   Since Mud Pond contained drinking water I had felt confident nothing untoward would happen there. For a long while the developers stayed away, until the drought of the mid-1960s. This event, squeezing the edges in, convinced the local water company that the pond really wasn't a necessity as a catch basin, however; so they bulldozed a hole in the earthen dam, bulldozed the banks to fill in the bottom, and landscaped the flow of water that remained to wind like an English brook and provide a domestic view for the houses which were planned. Most of the painted turtles of Mud Pond, who had been inaccessible as they sunned on their rocks, wound up in boxes in boys' closets within a matter of days. Their footsteps in the dry leaves gave them away as they wandered forlornly. The snappers and the little musk turtles, neither of whom leave the water except once a year to lay their eggs, dug into the drying mud for another siege of hot weather, which they were accustomed to doing whenever the pond got low. But this time it was low for good; the mud baked over them and slowly entombed them. As for the ducks, I couldn't stroll in the woods and not feel guilty, because they were crouched beside every stagnant pothole, or were slinking between the bushes with their heads tucked into their shoulders so that I wouldn't see them. If they decided I had, they beat their way up through the screen of trees, striking their wings dangerously, and wheeled about with that headlong, magnificent velocity to locate another poor puddle.

4   I used to catch possums and black snakes as well as turtles, and I kept dogs and goats. Some summers I worked in a menagerie with the big personalities of the animal kingdom, like elephants and rhinoceroses. I was twenty before these enthusiasms began to wane, and it was then that I picked turtles as the particular animal I wanted to keep in touch with. I was allergic to fur, for one thing, and turtles need minimal care and not much in the way of quarters. They're personable beasts. They see the same colors we do and they seem to see just as well, as one discovers in trying to sneak up on them. In the laboratory they unravel the twists of a maze with the hot-blooded rapidity of a mammal. Though they can't run as fast as a rat, they improve on their

errors just as quickly, pausing at each crossroads to look left and right. And they rock rhythmically in place, as we often do, although they are hatched from eggs, not the womb. (A common explanation psychologists give for our pleasure in rocking quietly is that it recapitulates our mother's heartbeat *in utero*.)

5   Snakes, by contrast, are dryly silent and priapic. They are smooth movers, legalistic, unblinking, and they afford the humor which the humorless do. But they make challenging captives; sometimes they don't eat for months on a point of order—if the light isn't right, for instance. Alligators are sticklers too. They're like war-horses, or German shepherds, and with their bar-shaped, vertical pupils adding emphasis, they have the *idée fixe* of eating, eating, even when they choose to refuse all food and stubbornly die. They delight in tossing a salamander up towards the sky and grabbing him in their long mouths as he comes down. They're so eager that they get the jitters, and they're too much of a proposition for a casual aquarium like mine. Frogs are depressingly defenseless: that moist, extensive back, with the bones almost sticking through. Hold a frog and you're holding its skeleton. Frogs' tasty legs are the staff of life to many animals—herons, raccoons, ribbon snakes— though they themselves are hard to feed. It's not an enviable role to be the staff of life, and after frogs you descend down the evolutionary ladder a big step to fish.

6   Turtles cough, burp, whistle, grunt and hiss, and produce social judgments. They put their heads together amicably enough, but then one drives the other back with the suddenness of two dogs who have been conversing in tones too low for an onlooker to hear. They pee in fear when they're first caught, but exercise both pluck and optimism in trying to escape, walking for hundreds of yards within the confines of their pen, carrying the weight of that cumbersome box on legs which are cruelly positioned for walking. They don't feel that the contest is unfair; they keep plugging, rolling like sailorly souls— a bobbing, infirm gait, a brave, sea-legged momentum—stopping occasionally to study the lay of the land. For me, anyway, they manage to contain the rest of the animal world. They can stretch out their necks like a giraffe, or loom underwater like an apocryphal hippo. They browse on lettuce thrown on the water like a cow moose which is partly submerged. They have a penguin's alertness, combined with a build like a Brontosaurus when they rise up on tiptoe. Then they hunch and ponderously lunge like a grizzly going forward.

7   Baby turtles in a turtle bowl are a puzzle in geometrics. They're as decorative as pansy petals, but they are also self-directed building blocks, propping themselves on one another in different arrangements, before upending the tower. The timid individuals turn fearless, or vice versa. If one gets a bit arrogant he will push the others off the rock and afterwards climb down into the water and cling to the back of one of those he has bullied, tickling him with his hind feet until he bucks like a bronco. On the other hand, when this same milder-mannered fellow isn't exerting himself, he will stare right into the face of the sun for hours. What could be more lionlike? And he's at home in or out of the water and does lots of metaphysical tilting. He sinks and rises, with an infinity of levels to choose from; or, elongating himself, he climbs out on the land again to perambulate, sits boxed in his box, and finally slides back in the water, submerging into dreams.

8   I have five of these babies in a kidney-shaped bowl. The hatchling, who is a painted turtle, is not as large as the top joint of my thumb. He eats chicken gladly. Other foods he will attempt to eat but not with sufficient perseverance to succeed because he's so little. The yellow-bellied terrapin is probably a yearling, and he eats salad voraciously, but no meat, fish or fowl. The Cumberland terrapin won't touch salad or chicken but eats fish and all of the meats except for bacon. The little snapper, with a black crenelated shell, feasts on any kind of meat, but rejects greens and fish. The fifth of the turtles is African. I acquired him only recently and don't know him well. A mottled brown, he unnerves the green turtles, dragging their food off to his lairs. He doesn't seem to want to be green—he bites the algae off his shell, hanging meanwhile at daring, steep, head-first angles.

9   The snapper was a Ferdinand until I provided him with deeper water. Now he snaps at my pencil with his downturned and fearsome mouth, his swollen face like a napalm victim's. The Cumberland has an elliptical red mark on the side of his green-and-yellow head. He is benign by nature and ought to be as elegant as his scientific name *(Pseudemys scripta elegans),* except he has contracted a disease of the air bladder which has permanently inflated it; he floats high in the water at an undignified slant and can't go under. There may have been internal bleeding, too, because his carapace is stained along its ridge. Unfortunately, like flowers, baby turtles often die. Their mouths fill up with a white fungus and their lungs with pneumonia. Their organs clog up from the rust in the water, or diet troubles, and, like a dying man's, their

eyes and heads become too prominent. Toward the end, the edge of the shell becomes flabby as felt and folds around them like a shroud.

10   While they live they're like puppies. Although they're vivacious, they would be a bore to be with all the time, so I also have an adult wood turtle about six inches long. Her shell is the equal of any seashell for sculpturing, even a Cellini shell; it's like an old, dusty, richly engraved medallion dug out of a hillside. Her legs are salmon-orange bordered with black and protected by canted, heroic scales. Her plastron—the bottom shell—is splotched like a margay cat's coat, with black ocelli on a yellow background. It is convex to make room for the female organs inside, wheras a male's would be concave to help him fit tightly on top of her. Altogether, she exhibits every camouflage color on her limbs and shells. She has a turtleneck neck, a tail like an elephant's, wise old pachydermous hind legs and the face of a turkey—except that when I carry her she gazes at the passing ground with a hawk's eyes and mouth. Her feet fit to the fingers of my hand, one to each one, and she rides looking down. She can walk on the floor in perfect silence, but usually she lets her shell knock portentously, like a footstep, so that she resembles some grand, concise, slow-moving lid. But if an earthworm is presented, she jerks swiftly ahead, poises above it and strikes like a mongoose, consuming it with wild vigor. Yet she will climb on my lap to eat bread or boiled eggs.

11   If put into a creek, she swims like a cutter, nosing forward to intercept a strange turtle and smell him. She drifts with the current to go downstream, maneuvering behind a rock when she wants to take stock, or sinking to the nether levels, while bubbles float up. Getting out, choosing her path, she will proceed a distance and dig into a pile of humus, thrusting herself to the coolest layer at the bottom. The hole closes over her until it's as small as a mouse's hole. She's not as aquatic as a musk turtle, not quite as terrestrial as the box turtles in the same woods, but because of her versatility she's marvelous, she's everywhere. And though she breathes the way we breathe, with scarcely perceptible movements of her chest, sometimes instead she pumps her throat ruminatively, like a pipe smoker sucking and puffing. She waits and blinks, pumping her throat, turning her head, then sets off like a loping tiger in slow motion, hurdling the jungly lumber, the pea vine and twigs. She estimates angles so well that when she rides over the rocks, sliding down a drop-off with her rugged front legs extended, she has the grace of a rodeo mare.

12   But she's well off to be with me rather than at Mud Pond. The other turtles have fled—those that aren't baked into the bottom. Creeping up the brooks to sad, constricted marshes, burdened as they are with that box on their backs, they're walking into a setup where all their enemies move thirty times faster than they. It's like the nightmare most of us have whimpered through, where we are weighted down disastrously while trying to flee; fleeing our home ground, we try to run.

13   I've seen turtles in still worse straits. On Broadway, in New York, there is a penny arcade which used to sell baby terrapins that were scrawled with bon mots in enamel paint, such as KISS ME BABY. The manager turned out to be a wholesaler as well, and once I asked him whether he had any larger turtles to sell. He took me upstairs to a loft room devoted to the turtle business. There were desks for the paper work and a series of racks that held shallow tin bins atop one another, each with several hundred babies crawling around in it. He was a smudgy-complexioned, serious fellow and he did have a few adult terrapins, but I was going to school and wasn't actually planning to buy; I'd only wanted to see them. They were aquatic turtles, but here they went without water, presumably for weeks, lurching about in those dry bins like handicapped citizens, living on gumption. An easel where the artist worked stood in the middle of the floor. She had a palette and a clip attachment for fastening the babies in place. She wore a smock and a beret, and was homely, short and eccentric-looking, with funny black hair, like some of the ladies who show their paintings in Washington Square in May. She had a cold, she was smoking, and her hand wasn't very steady, although she worked quickly enough. The smile that she produced for me would have looked giddy if she had been happier, or drunk. Of course the turtles' doom was sealed when she painted them, because their bodies inside would continue to grow but their shells would not. Gradually, invisibly, they would be crushed. Around us their bellies—two thousand belly shells—rubbed on the bins with a mournful, momentous hiss.

14   Somehow there were so many of them I didn't rescue one. Years later, however, I was walking on First Avenue when I noticed a basket of living turtles in front of a fish store. They were as dry as a heap of old bones in the sun; nevertheless, they were creeping over one another gimpily, doing their best to escape. I looked and was touched to discover that they appeared to be wood turtles, my favorites, so I bought one. In my apartment I looked closer and realized that in fact this was a dia-

mondback terrapin, which was bad news. Diamondbacks are tidewater turtles from brackish estuaries, and I had no sea water to keep him in. He spent his days thumping interminably against the baseboards, pushing for an opening through the wall. He drank thirstily but would not eat and had none of the hearty, accepting qualities of wood turtles. He was morose, paler in color, sleeker and more Oriental in the carved ridges and rings that formed his shell. Though I felt sorry for him, finally I found his unrelenting presence exasperating. I carried him, struggling in a paper bag, across town to the Morton Street Pier on the Hudson. It was August but gray and windy. He was very surprised when I tossed him in; for the first time in our association, I think, he was afraid. He looked afraid as he bobbed about on top of the water, looking up at me from ten feet below. Though we were both accustomed to his resistance and rigidity, seeing him still pitiful, I recognized that I must have done the wrong thing. At least the river was salty, but it was also bottomless; the waves were too rough for him, and the tide was coming in, bumping him against the pilings underneath the pier. Too late, I realized that he wouldn't be able to swim to a peaceful inlet in New Jersey, even if he could figure out which way to swim, But since, short of diving in after him, here was nothing I could do, I walked away.

Reading Closely and Thinking Critically

1. What main point is Hoagland making in "The Courage of Turtles"?

2. In paragraph 1, Hoagland says that turtles in his town were "a case of virtue rewarded." In your opinion, what does he mean?

3. Why is it that Hoagland "couldn't stroll in the woods and not feel guilty"?

4. Why does Hoagland refer to the courage of turtles when courage seems an unlikely trait to ascribe to these animals?

5. In paragraph 2, Hoagland says, "Though the woods had shrunk, it seemed that fewer people walked in the woods. The new residents didn't know how to find them." What do you think the author means? How would you describe his tone? (See page 37 for an explanation of tone.)

6. Hoagland says in paragraph 14 that there were so many turtles in the arcade that he did not rescue even one of them. Why did he not rescue any? Do you think less of Hoagland for not attempting a rescue? Explain.

7. In the end, Hoagland walks away. Explain the significance of this ending and how it relates to his main point.

Examining Structure and Strategy

1. Explain the significance of the title of the essay. Do you think the title is a good one? Why or why not?

2. Note two or three descriptions you particularly like. What makes these descriptions effective? Often the strength of Hoagland's descriptions rests on his use of specific, simple words. For example, note the specific "hot-blooded," "rapidity," and "twists" in "they unravel the twists of a maze with the hot-blooded rapidity of a mammal" (paragraph 4). Cite one example each of a simple, specific noun, verb, and modifier.

3. Hoagland often uses *personification,* which is the granting of human qualities to animals or nonliving things. For example, in paragraph 5, Hoagland says that snakes are "legalistic." Cite three other examples of personification.

4. For what purpose does Hoagland tell the story of the turtles in the penny arcade?

5. Do you think "The Courage of Turtles" is better suited for a reader who is a city-dweller or a country-dweller? Explain.

Considering Language and Style

1. Hoagland uses a great many similes and metaphors (see page 73) to describe turtles. Cite three examples. What do the similes and metaphors contribute to the essay?

2. In paragraph 5, Hoagland refers to the "staff of life." What is the meaning of this reference and why is its use an appropriate one?

3. Consult a dictionary if you are unsure of the meaning of any of these words: *carnivores* (paragraph 1), *untoward* (paragraph 3), *recapitulates* (paragraph 4), *in utero* (paragraph 4), *priapic* (paragraph 5), *idée fixe* (paragraph 5), *apocryphal* (paragraph 6), *metaphysical* (paragraph 7), *perambulate* (paragraph 7), *crenelated* (paragraph 8), *portentiously* (paragraph 10), *nether* (paragraph 11), *ruminatively* (paragraph 11), *bon mots* (paragraph 13), *gumption* (paragraph 13).

For Group Discussion or Writing
With some classmates, decide whether or not the guilt that Hoagland felt when he walked in the woods was justified. If you think that it was, explain why and what should be done to prevent similar guilt in the future. If you think that it was not, explain why not.

Writing Assignments

1. *In your journal.* Hoagland has written many essays about nature. As a result of reading "The Courage of Turtles," would you be interested in reading other of his nature essays? Why or why not?

2. *Using the pattern.* If you have a pet, write a description of the appearance, characteristics, and behavior of that pet in a way that conveys your fondness and respect for the animal. If you wish, you may use personification, similes, and metaphors, as Hoagland does.

3. *Using the pattern.* If there is an animal you particularly dislike, write a description of that animal's appearance, characteristics, and behavior in a way that conveys your dislike. If you wish, you may use personification, similes, and metaphors, as Hoagland does.

4. *Using the pattern.* Write a description of a habitat that is endangered by the development of a shopping area, highway, housing development, or some other encroachment.

5. *Considering a theme.* Do you think that wildlife and its natural habitats should be protected, even if that means a slowdown of growth of business, industry, and housing? State and defend your position. If you wish, you may limit your discussion to a specific industry and animal, such as the logging industry and the spotted owl or the oil industry and arctic caribou.

6. *Connecting the readings.* Both "The Courage of Turtles" and "The Deer at Providencia" (page 94) present views of animals and views of the relationship between people and animals. Compare and contrast the views in these selections and then explain your own view on the subject.

ONCE MORE TO THE LAKE
E. B. White

A superb essayist whose literary accomplishments won him the Presidential Medal of Freedom in 1963, Elwyn Brooks White (1899–1985) wrote for The New Yorker *for 50 years and helped establish its reputation for excellence with his "Talk of the Town" column. He also wrote the popular children's book* Charlotte's Web *(1952), and with William Strunk, Jr., he wrote the popular and enduring writer's guide,* The Elements of Style *(1959). In "Once More to the Lake," written in 1941, White uses description to relate his visits to a family vacation spot in Maine, visits made both as a child and as an adult. The spot is, at once, the same and different after the passing of years. As you read, notice that White's description leads him to a disarming conclusion.*

THE PATTERNS	THE PURPOSE
description with narration and comparison-and-contrast	*to express feelings and relate experience*

1   One summer, along about 1904, my father rented a camp on a lake in Maine and took us all there for the month of August. We all got ringworm from some kittens and had to rub Pond's Extract on our arms and legs night and morning, and my father rolled over in a canoe with all his clothes on; but outside of that the vacation was a success and from then on none of us ever thought there was any place in the world like that lake in Maine. We returned summer after summer—always on August 1 for one month. I have since become a salt-water man, but sometimes in summer there are days when the restlessness of the tides and the fearful cold of the sea water and the incessant wind that blows across the afternoon and into the evening make me wish for the placidity of a lake in the woods. A few weeks ago this feeling got so strong I bought myself a couple of bass hooks and a spinner and returned to the lake where we used to go, for a week's fishing and to revisit old haunts.

2   I took along my son, who had never had any fresh water up his nose and who had seen lily pads only from train windows. On the journey over to the lake I began to wonder what it would be like. I won-

dered how time would have marred this unique, this holy spot—the coves and streams, the hills that the sun set behind, the camps and the paths behind the camps. I was sure that the tarred road would have found it out, and I wondered in what other ways it would be desolated. It is strange how much you can remember about places like that once you allow your mind to return into the grooves that lead back. You remember one thing, and that suddenly reminds you of another thing. I guess I remembered clearest of all the early mornings, when the lake was cool and motionless, remembered how the bedroom smelled of the lumber it was made of and of the wet woods whose scent entered through the screen. The partitions in the camp were thin and did not extend clear to the top of the rooms, and as I was always the first up I would dress softly so as not to wake the others, and sneak out into the sweet outdoors and start out in the canoe, keeping close along the shore in the long shadows of the pines. I remembered being very careful never to rub my paddle against the gunwale for fear of disturbing the stillness of the cathedral.

3   The lake had never been what you would call a wild lake. There were cottages sprinkled around the shores, and it was in farming country although the shores of the lake were quite heavily wooded. Some of the cottages were owned by nearby farmers, and you would live at the shore and eat your meals at the farmhouse. That's what our family did. But although it wasn't wild, it was a fairly large and undisturbed lake and there were places in it that, to a child at least, seemed infinitely remote and primeval.

4   I was right about the tar: It led to within half a mile of the shore. But when I got back there, with my boy, and we settled into a camp near a farmhouse and into the kind of summertime I had known, I could tell that it was going to be pretty much the same as it had been before—I knew it, lying in bed the first morning smelling the bedroom and hearing the boy sneak quietly out and go off along the shore in a boat. I began to sustain the illusion that he was I, and therefore, by simple transposition, that I was my father. This sensation persisted, kept cropping up all the time we were there. It was not an entirely new feeling, but in this setting it grew much stronger. I seemed to be living a dual existence. I would be in the middle of some simple act, I would be picking up a bait box or laying down a table fork, or I would be saying something and suddenly it would be not I but my father who was saying the words or making the gesture. It gave me a creepy sensation.

5   We went fishing the first morning. I felt the same damp moss covering the worms in the bait can, and saw the dragonfly alight on the tip of my rod as it hovered a few inches from the surface of the water. It was the arrival of this fly that convinced me beyond any doubt that everything was as it always had been, that the years were a mirage and that there had been no years. The small waves were the same, chucking the rowboat under the chin as we fished at anchor, and the boat was the same boat, the same color green and the ribs broken in the same places, and under the floorboards the same fresh water leavings and debris—the dead hellgrammite, the wisps of moss, the rusty discarded fishhook, the dried blood from yesterday's catch. We stared silently at the tips of our rods, at the dragonflies that came and went. I lowered the tip of mine into the water, tentatively, pensively dislodging the fly, which darted two feet away, poised, darted two feet back, and came to rest again a little farther up the rod. There had been no years between the ducking of this dragonfly and the other one—the one that was part of memory. I looked at the boy, who was silently watching his fly, and it was my hands that held his rod, my eyes watching. I felt dizzy and didn't know which rod I was at the end of.

6   We caught two bass, hauling them in briskly as though they were mackerel, pulling them over the side of the boat in a businesslike manner without any landing net, and stunning them with a blow on the back of the head. When we got back for a swim before lunch, the lake was exactly where we had left it, the same number of inches from the dock, and there was only the merest suggestion of a breeze. This seemed an utterly enchanted sea, this lake you could leave to its own devices for a few hours and come back to, and find that it had not stirred, this constant and trustworthy body of water. In the shallows, the dark, water-soaked sticks and twigs, smooth and old, were undulating in clusters on the bottom against the clean ribbed sand, and the track of the mussel was plain. A school of minnows swam by, each minnow with its small individual shadow, doubling the attendance, so clear and sharp in the sunlight. Some of the other campers were in swimming, along the shore, one of them with a cake of soap, and the water felt thin and clear and unsubstantial. Over the years there had been this person with the cake of soap, this cultist, and here he was. There had been no years.

7   Up to the farmhouse to dinner through the teeming dusty field, the road under our sneakers was only a two-track road. The middle track was missing, the one with the marks of the hooves and the

splotches of dried, flaky manure. There had always been three tracks to choose from in choosing which track to walk in; now the choice was narrowed down to two. For a moment I missed terribly the middle alternative. But the way led past the tennis court, and something about the way it lay there in the sun reassured me; the tape had loosened along the backline, the alleys were green with plantains and other weeds, and the net (installed in June and removed in September) sagged in the dry noon, and the whole place steamed with midday heat and hunger and emptiness. There was a choice of pie for dessert, and one was blueberry and one was apple, and the waitresses were the same country girls, there having been no passage of time, only the illusion of it as in a dropped curtain—the waitresses were still fifteen; their hair had been washed, that was the only difference—they had been to the movies and seen the pretty girls with the clean hair.

8   Summertime, oh, summertime, pattern of life indelible with fade-proof lake, the wood unshatterable, the pasture with the sweetfern and the juniper forever and ever, summer without end; this was the background, and the life along the shore was the design, the cottages with their innocent and tranquil design, their tiny docks with the flagpole and the American flag floating against the white clouds in the blue sky, the little paths over the roots of the trees leading from camp to camp and the paths leading back to the outhouses and the can of lime for sprinkling, and at the souvenir counters at the store the miniature birchbark canoes and the postcards that showed things looking a little better than they looked. This was the American family at play, escaping the city heat, wondering whether the newcomers in the camp at the head of the cove were "common" or "nice," wondering whether it was true that the people who drove up for Sunday dinner at the farmhouse were turned away because there wasn't enough chicken.

9   It seemed to me, as I kept remembering all this, that those times and those summers had been infinitely precious and worth saving. There had been jollity and peace and goodness. The arriving (at the beginning of August) had been so big a business in itself, at the railway station the farm wagon drawn up, the first smell of the pine-laden air, the first glimpse of the smiling farmer, and the great importance of the trunks and your father's enormous authority in such matters, and the feel of the wagon under you for the long ten-mile haul, and at the top of the last long hill catching the first view of the lake after eleven months of not seeing this cherished body of water. The shouts and cries

of the other campers when they saw you, and the trunks to be un-
packed, to give up their rich burden. (Arriving was less exciting nowadays, when you sneaked up in your car and parked it under a tree near
the camp and took out the bags and in five minutes it was all over, no
fuss, no loud wonderful fuss about trunks.)

10   Peace and goodness and jollity. The only thing that was wrong
now, really, was the sound of the place, an unfamiliar nervous sound of
the outboard motors. This was the note that jarred, the one thing that
would sometimes break the illusion and set the years moving. In those
other summertimes all motors were inboard; and when they were at a
little distance, the noise they made was a sedative, an ingredient of summer sleep. They were one-cylinder and two-cylinder engines, and some
were make-and-break and some were jump-spark, but they all made a
sleepy sound across the lake. The one-lungers throbbed and fluttered,
and the twin-cylinder ones purred and purred, and that was a quiet
sound, too. But now the campers all had outboards. In the daytime, in
the hot mornings, these motors made a petulant, irritable sound; at
night in the still evening when the afterglow lit the water, they whined
about one's ears like mosquitoes. My boy loved our rented outboard,
and his great desire was to achieve single-handed mastery over it, and
authority, and he soon learned the trick of choking it a little (but not
too much), and the adjustment of the needle valve. Watching him I
would remember the things you could do with the old one-cylinder engine with the heavy flywheel, how you could have it eating out of your
hand if you got really close to it spiritually. Motorboats in those days
didn't have clutches, and you would make a landing by shutting off the
motor at the proper time and coasting in with a dead rudder. But there
was a way of reversing them, if you learned the trick, by cutting the
switch and putting it on again exactly on the final dying revolution of
the flywheel, so that it would kick back against compression and begin
reversing. Approaching a dock in a strong following breeze, it was difficult to slow up sufficiently by the ordinary coasting method, and if a
boy felt he had complete mastery over his motor, he was tempted to
keep it running beyond its time and then reverse it a few feet from the
dock. It took a cool nerve, because if you threw the switch a twentieth
of a second too soon you would catch the flywheel when it still had
speed enough to go up past center, and the boat would leap ahead,
charging bull-fashion at the dock.

11   We had a good week at the camp. The bass were biting well and the sun shone endlessly, day after day. We would be tired at night and lie down in the accumulated heat of the little bedrooms after the long hot day and the breeze would stir almost imperceptibly outside and the smell of the swamp drift in through the rusty screens. Sleep would come easily and in the morning the red squirrel would be on the roof, tapping out his gay routine. I kept remembering everything, lying in bed in the mornings—the small steamboat that had a long rounded stern like the lip of a Ubangi, and how quietly she ran on the moon-light sails, when the older boys played their mandolins and the girls sang and we ate doughnuts dipped in sugar, and how sweet the music was on the water in the shining night, and what it had felt like to think about girls then. After breakfast we would go up to the store and the things were in the same place—the minnows in a bottle, the plugs and spinners disarranged and pawed over by the youngsters from the boys' camp, the Fig Newtons and the Beeman's gum. Outside, the road was tarred and cars stood in front of the store. Inside, all was just as it had always been, except there was more Coca-Cola and not so much Moxie and root beer and birch beer and sarsaparilla. We would walk out with the bottle of pop apiece and sometimes the pop would backfire up our noses and hurt. We explored the streams, quietly, where the turtles slid off the sunny logs and dug their way into the soft bottom; and we lay on the town wharf and fed worms to the tame bass. Everywhere we went I had trouble making out which was I, the one walking at my side, the one walking in my pants.

12   One afternoon while we were at that lake a thunderstorm came up. It was like the revival of an old melodrama that I had seen long ago with childish awe. The second-act climax of the drama of the electrical disturbance over a lake in America had not changed in any important respect. This was the big scene, still the big scene. The whole thing was so familiar, the first feeling of oppression and heat and a general air around camp of not wanting to go very far away. In midafternoon (it was all the same) a curious darkening of the sky, and a lull in every-thing that had made life tick; and then the way the boats suddenly swung the other way at their moorings with the coming of a breeze out of the new quarter, and the premonitory rumble. Then the kettle drum, then the snare, then the bass drum and cymbals, then crackling light against the dark, and the gods grinning and licking their chops in the

hills. Afterward the calm, the rain steadily rustling in the calm lake, the return of light and hope and spirits, and the campers running out in joy and relief to go swimming in the rain, their bright cries perpetuating the deathless joke about how they were getting simply drenched, and the children screaming with delight at the new sensation of bathing in the rain, and the joke about getting drenched linking the generations in a strong indestructible chain. And the comedian who waded in carrying an umbrella.

13   When the others went swimming my son said he was going in, too. He pulled his dripping trunks from the line where they had hung all through the shower and wrung them out. Languidly, and with no thought of going in, I watched him, his hard little body, skinny and bare, saw him wince slightly as he pulled up around his vitals the small, soggy, icy garment. As he buckled the swollen belt, suddenly my groin felt the chill of death.

Reading Closely and Thinking Critically

1. Why does White return to the lake after an absence of 40 years? Do you think the reasons the author gives are the only ones? Explain.

2. What do you think White's dominant impression of the lake is as an adult?

3. What conclusion does White draw about the passage of time? Where is that conclusion best expressed?

4. White mentions several times that he has trouble distinguishing himself from his son and that he has trouble distinguishing the present from the past. Why do you think he experiences this blurring of identities and time?

5. White believes that his past summers at the lake were "infinitely precious and worth saving" (paragraph 9). Why?

6. If White had visited the lake more regularly over the past 40 years, do you think the visit described in the essay would have prompted the same feelings and realizations? Explain.

7. Do you find "Once More to the Lake" an upbeat essay or a depressing essay? Explain.

Examining Structure and Strategy

1. White appeals to the senses of smell, touch, and sound in addition to the sense of sight. Mention one example each of description that appeals to smell, touch, and sound. Underline the specific words. Cite two other descriptions that you find particularly appealing. Underline the specific words.

2. What metaphor (see page 73) does White include in paragraph 2? In paragraph 12? What do these metaphors contribute?

3. *Narration* is storytelling. What narration does White include?

4. *Comparison-contrast* shows similarities and differences. In what way does White compare and contrast?

5. White does not refer to his son by name, nor does he describe the boy very much. Why does he not give his son more identifying characteristics?

6. Can a middle-aged and youthful reader appreciate "Once More to the Lake" equally well? Explain.

Considering Language and Style

1. Look up the meaning of paen; then read paragraph 8 aloud. How is that paragraph similar to a paen?

2. Consult a dictionary if you are unsure of the meaning of any of these words: *incessant* (paragraph 1), *gunwale* (paragraph 2), *primeval* (paragraph 3), *helgrammite* (paragraph 5), *pensively* (paragraph 5), *indelible* (paragraph 8), *petulant* (paragraph 10), *Ubangi* (paragraph 11), *premonitory* (paragraph 12), *languidly* (paragraph 13).

For Group Discussion or Writing

"Once More to the Lake" deals with issues of youth and age. To what extent are we concerned with issues of youth and age in our culture? Cite specific examples to support your view.

Writing Assignments

1. *In your journal.* In paragraph 12, when he writes of the thunderstorm, White notes that "the joke about getting drenched [links] the generations in a strong indestructible chain." What events, experiences, and circumstances link the generations in your family or in your locale? Explain in a page or two.

2. Using the pattern. White says, "It is strange how much you can remember about places like [the lake] once you allow your mind to return into the grooves that lead back." Allow your mind "to return into the grooves" and lead you back to a place you enjoyed as a child. Describe that place in a way that conveys why you enjoyed it.

3. Using the pattern. If you have ever returned to a place after being away for a while, describe the ways the place changed and the ways it stayed the same. You could, for example, describe your first trip home after being away at school for several months.

4. Using the pattern. In paragraph 9, White describes the excitement of arriving at the lake. Write a description of your arrival someplace special or important. For example, you could describe your arrival at college, the site of your wedding, your graduation ceremony, an annual vacation spot, or the hospital for an operation.

5. Using the pattern. Paragraph 12 describes a thunderstorm. Write your own description of a thunderstorm or write a description of another kind of weather; a spring shower, a blizzard, an ice storm, a tornado, a hurricane, or a windstorm, for example. If you like, you can use one or more metaphors.

6. Considering a theme. In "Once More to the Lake," White comes to recognize his own mortality. Tell about some event that caused you to recognize or think about your mortality. Explain what happened, how you were affected, and why you were affected that way.

7. Connecting the readings. In "Two Views of the Mississippi" (page 349), Mark Twain, like White, considers his youthful and adult views of a significant place. Explain the conclusions each author reaches about the passage of time and to what extent the authors agree or disagree. Also, include your own view about how the passage of time affects a person's opinion of a place.

THE STONE HORSE
Barry Lopez

Born in New York in 1945, Barry Lopez is an author and naturalist who writes short stories as well as articles on the environment and natural history. His nonfiction works include Of Wolves and Men *(1978) and* Arctic Dreams: Imagination and Desire in a Northern Landscape *(1986). The latter book earned him the National Book Award. "The Stone Horse" (1989), is at once historical and personal. In it, Lopez examines an archaeological artifact called an intaglio, which is a figure carved into a hard surface. His description of the artifact (the stone horse) leads to thoughts of history and personal remiscence so that Lopez both informs the reader and expresses a bit about himself.*

THE PATTERNS	THE PURPOSE
description with narration, process analysis, contrast, and cause-and-effect analysis	*to inform and express feelings and relate experience*

1   A BLM[1] archaeologist told me, with understandable reluctance, where to find the intaglio.[2] I spread my Automobile Club of Southern California map of Imperial Country out on his desk, and he traced the route with a pink felt-tip pen. The line crossed Interstate 8 and then turned west along the Mexican border.

2   "You can't drive any farther than about here," he said, marking a small X. "There's boulders in the wash. You walk up past them."

3   On a separate piece of paper he drew a route in a smaller scale that would take me up the arroyo to a certain point where I was to cross back east, to another arroyo. At its head, on higher ground just to the north, I would find the horse.

4   "It's tough to spot unless you know it's there. Once you pick it up..." He shook his head slowly, in a gesture of wonder at its existence.

5   I waited until I held his eye. I assured him I would not tell anyone else how to get there. He looked at me with stoical despair, like a

---

1. Bureau of Land Management (part of the Department of the Interior)
2. See headnote.

man who had been robbed twice, whose belief in human beings was offered without conviction.

6   I did not go until the following day because I wanted to see it at dawn. I ate breakfast at four A.M. in El Centro and then drove south. The route was easy to follow, though the last section of road proved difficult, broken and drifted over with sand in some spots. I came to the barricade of boulders and parked. It was light enough by then to find my way over the ground with little trouble. The contours of the landscape were stark, without any masking vegetation. I worried only about rattlesnakes.

7   I traversed the stone plain as directed, but, in spite of the frankness of the land, I came on the horse unawares. In the first moment of recognition I was without feeling. I recalled later being startled, and that I held my breath. It was laid out on the ground with its head to the east, three times life size. As I took in its outline I felt a growing concentration of all my senses, as though my attentiveness to the pale rose color of the morning sky and other peripheral images had now ceased to be important. I was aware that I was straining for sound in the windless air, and I felt the uneven pressure of the earth hard against my feet. The horse, outlined in a standing profile on the dark ground, was as vivid before me as a bed of tulips.

8   I've come upon animals suddenly before, and felt a similar tension, a precipitate heightening of the senses. And I have felt the inexplicable but sharply boosted intensity of a wild moment in the bush, where it is not until some minutes later that you discover the source of electricity—the warm remains of a grizzly bear kill, or the still moist tracks of a wolverine.

9   But this was slightly different. I felt I had stepped into an unoccupied corridor. I had no familiar sense of history, the temporal structure in which to think: this horse was made by Quechan people three hundred years ago. I felt instead a headlong rush of images: people hunting wild horses with spears on the Pleistocene veld of southern California; Cortés[3] riding across the causeway into Montezuma's Tenochtitlán,[4] a short-legged Comanche, astride his horse like some sort of ferret, slashing through cavalry lines of young men who rode like

3. Hernando Cortés (1485 – 1547): a Spaniard who conquered Mexico and held Montezuma hostage.

4. Montezuma II (1480? – 1520): Aztec emperor during the time of the Spanish conquest. Tenochtitlián was his capital city.

farmers; a hoof exploding past my face one morning in a corral in Wyoming. These images had the weight and silence of stone.

10   When I released my breath, the images softened. My initial feeling, of facing a wild animal in a remote region, was replaced with a calm sense of antiquity. It was then that I became conscious, like an ordinary tourist, of what was before me, and thought: this horse was probably laid out by Quechan people. But when? I wondered. The first horses they saw, I knew, might have been those that came north from Mexico in 1692 with Father Eusebio Kino.[5] But Cocopa people, I recalled, also came this far north on occasion, to fight with their neighbors, the Quechan. And *they* could have seen horses with Melchior Díaz, at the mouth of the Colorado River in the fall of 1540. So, it could be four hundred years old. (No one in fact knows.)

11   I still had not moved. I took my eyes off the horse for a moment to look south over the desert plain into Mexico, to look east past its head at the brightening sunrise, to situate myself. Then, finally, I brought my trailing foot slowly forward and stood erect. Sunlight was running like a thin sheet of water over the stony ground and it threw the horse into relief. It looked as though no hand had ever disturbed the stones that gave it its form.

12   The horse had been brought to life on ground called desert pavement, a tight, flat matrix of small cobbles blasted smooth by sand-laden winds. The uniform, monochromatic blackness of the stones, a patina of iron and magnesium oxides called desert varnish, is caused by long-term exposure to the sun. To make this type of low-relief ground glyph,[6] or intaglio, the artist either selectively turns individual stones over to their lighter side or removes areas of stone to expose the lighter soil underneath, creating a negative image. This horse, about eighteen feet from brow to rump and eight feet from withers to hoof, had been made in the latter way, and its outline was bermed at certain points with low ridges of stone a few inches high to enhance its three-dimensional qualities. (The left side of the horse was in full profile; each leg was extended at 90 degrees to the body and fully visible, as though seen in three-quarter profile.)

13   I was not eager to move. The moment I did I would be back in the flow of time, the horse no longer quivering in the same way before

---

5. Father Eusebio Kino (1645? – 1711): Jesuit missionary.
6. A symbolic character cut into something.

me. I did not want to feel again the sequence of quotidian events—to be drawn off into deliberation and analysis. A human being, a four-footed animal, the open land. That was all that was present—and a "thoughtless" understanding of the very old desires bearing on this particular animal: to hunt it, to render it, to fathom it, to subjugate it, to honor it, to take it as a companion.

14   What finally made me move was the light. The sun now filled the shallow basin of the horse's body. The weighted line of the stone berm created the illusion of a mane and the distinctive roundness of an equine belly. The change in definition impelled me. I moved to the left, circling past its rump, to see how the light might flesh the horse out from various points of view. I circled it completely before squatting on my haunches. Ten or fifteen minutes later I chose another view. The third time I moved, to a point near the rear hooves, I spotted a stone tool at my feet. I stared at it a long while, more in awe than disbelief, before reaching out to pick it up. I turned it over in my left palm and took it between my fingers to feel its cutting edge. It is always difficult, especially with something so portable, to rechannel the desire to steal.

15   I spent several hours with the horse. As I changed positions and as the angle of the light continued to change I noticed a number of things. The angle at which the pastern carried the hoof away from the ankle was perfect. Also, stones had been placed within the image to suggest at precisely the right spot the left shoulder above the foreleg. The line that joined thigh and hock was similarly accurate. The muzzle alone seemed distorted—but perhaps these stones had been moved by a later hand. It was an admirably accurate representation, but not what a breeder would call perfect conformation. There was the suggestion of a bowed neck and an undershot jaw, and the tail, as full as a winter coyote's, did not appear to be precisely to scale.

16   The more I thought about it, the more I felt I was looking at an individual horse, a unique combination of generic and specific detail. It was easy to imagine one of Kino's horses as a model, or a horse that ran off from one of Coronado's columns. What kind of horses would these have been? I wondered. In the sixteenth century the most sought-after horses in Europe were Spanish, the offspring of Arabian stock and Barbary horses that the Moors brought to Iberia and bred to the older, eastern European strains brought in by the Romans. The model for this horse, I speculated, could easily have been a palomino, or a descendant of horses trained for lion hunting in North Africa.

17   A few generations ago, cowboys, cavalry quartermasters, and draymen would have taken this horse before me under consideration and not let up their scrutiny until they had its heritage fixed to their satisfaction. Today, the distinction between draft and harness horses is arcane knowledge, and no image may come to mind for a blue roan or a claybank horse. The loss of such refinement in everyday conversation leaves me unsettled. People praise the Eskimo's ability to distinguish among forty types of snow but forget the skill of others who routinely differentiate between overo and tobiano pintos. Such distinctions are made for the same reason. You have to do it to be able to talk clearly about the world.

18   For parts of two years I worked as a horse wrangler and packer in Wyoming. It is dim knowledge now; I would have to think to remember if a buckskin was a kind of dun horse. And I couldn't throw a double-diamond hitch over a set of panniers—the packer's basic tie-down—without guidance. As I squatted there in the desert, however, these more personal memories seemed tenuous in comparison with the sweep of this animal in human time. My memories had no depth. I thought of the Hittite cavalry riding against the Syrians 3,500 years ago. And the first of the Chinese emperors, Ch'in Shih Huang, buried in Shensi Province in 210 B.C. with thousands of life-size horses and soldiers, a terra-cotta guardian army. What could I know of what was in the mind of whoever made this horse? Was there some racial memory of it as an animal that had once fed the artist's ancestors and then disappeared from North America? And then returned in this strange alliance with another race of men?

19   Certainly, whoever it was, the artist had observed the animal very closely. Certainly the animal's speed had impressed him. Among the first things the Quechan would have learned from an encounter with Kino's horses was that their own long-distance runners—men who could run down mule deer—were no match for this animal.

20   From where I squatted I could look far out over the Mexican plain. Juan Bautista de Anza passed this way in 1774, extending El Camino Real into Alta California from Sinaloa.[7] He was followed by others, all of them astride the magical horse: *gente de razón,* the people of reason, coming into the country of *los primitivos.* The horse, like the stone animals of Egypt, urged these memories upon me. And as I drew

---

7. El Camino Real: "The Royal Road" from Mexico to northern California.

them up from some forgotten corner of my mind—huge horses carved in the white chalk downs of southern England by an Iron Age people; Spanish horses rearing and wheeling in fear before alligators in Florida—the images seemed tethered before me. With this sense of proportion, a memory of my own—the morning I almost lost my face to a horse's hoof—now had somewhere to fit.

21   I rose up and began to walk slowly around the horse again. I had taken the first long measure of it and was now looking for a way to depart, a new angle of light, a fading of the image itself before the rising sun, that would break its hold on me. A I circled, feeling both heady and serene at the encounter, I realized again how strangely vivid it was. It had been created on a barren bajada between two arroyos, as nondescript a place as one could imagine. The only plant life here was a few wands of ocotillo cactus. The ground beneath my shoes was so hard it wouldn't take the print of a heavy animal even after a rain. The only sounds I heard were the voices of quail.

22   The archaeologist had been correct. For all its forcefulness, the horse is inconspicuous. If you don't care to see it you can walk right past it. That pleases him, I think. Unmarked on this bleak shoulder of the plain, the site signals to no one; so he wants no protective fences here, no informative plaque, to act as beacons. He would rather take a chance that no motorcyclist, no aimless wanderer with a flair for violence and depth of ignorance, will ever find his way here.

23   The archaeologist had given me something before I left his office that now seemed peculiar—an aerial photograph of the horse. It is widely believed that an aerial view of an intaglio provides a fair and accurate depiction. It does not. In the photograph the horse looks somewhat crudely constructed; from the ground it appears far more deftly rendered. The photograph is of a single moment, and in that split second the horse seems vaguely impotent. I watched light pool in the intaglio at dawn; I imagine you could watch it withdraw at dusk and sense the same animation I did. In those prolonged moments its shape and so, too, its general character changed—noticeably. The living quality of the image, its immediacy to the eye, was brought out by the light-in-time, not, at least here, in the camera's frozen instant.

24   Intaglios, I thought, were never meant to be seen by gods in the sky above. They were meant to be seen by people on the ground, over a long period of shifting light. This could even be true of the huge figures on the Plain of Nazca in Peru, where people could walk for the

length of a day beside them. It is our own impatience that leads us to think otherwise.

25   This process of abstraction, almost unintentional, drew me gradually away from the horse. I came to a position of attention at the edge of the sphere of its influence. With a slight bow I paid my respects to the horse, its maker, and the history of us all, and departed.

Reading Closely and Thinking Critically

1. Overall, how would you characterize Lopez's attitude toward the stone horse? Why do you think he feels the way he does?

2. Why did the archaeologist who told Lopez how to locate the stone horse want the location of this artifact kept secret? Do you agree with his thinking? Why or why not?

3. Why does Lopez leave the stone tool where he found it? If he had placed the tool in a museum or offered it to an archaeologist for study, would it have been acceptable for him to take it? Explain.

4. What can you conclude about the role of the horse and its importance to the people who crafted the intaglio?

5. Reread paragraphs 23 and 24. What do you think Lopez is saying about art and our view of art?

6. Why does the archaeologist prefer not to place an informative plaque or protective fences around the site of the horse?

7. Paragraph 17 notes that Eskimos have words to distinguish 40 kinds of snow and that a few generations ago cowboys and soldiers in the cavalry could distinguish many different kinds of horses. Why do you think that Eskimos can name so many kinds of snow and that cowboys and soldiers could name so many kinds of horses?

8. How would you characterize Lopez's view of time?

Examining Structure and Strategy

1. Lopez uses both objective and expressive description (see page 70) in "The Stone Horse." Cite two examples of each.

2. To what extent is narration (storytelling) a part of the essay? (Narration is discussed in Chapter 4.)

3. What element of contrast appears in paragraphs 8 and 9? (Contrast discussed in Chapter 7, shows how things are different.)

4. What element of process analysis appears in paragraph 12? (Process analysis, discussed in Chapter 6, shows how something is made or done.)

5. What element of cause-and-effect analysis appears in paragraphs 17, 22, and 24? (Cause-and-effect analysis, discussed in Chapter 8, shows the causes and/or effects of something.)

6. What purpose do you think paragraphs 1 through 6 serve? Why does Lopez include these paragraphs rather than begin with his description of the horse and his reaction to it?

7. What kind of audience do you think Lopez had in mind for "The Stone Horse"?

Considering Language and Style

1. Lopez's description is enhanced by similes and metaphors (see page 73). Cite two examples of such figurative language.

2. How would you describe Lopez's tone? (see page 37 on tone.)

3. Consult a dictionary if you are unsure of the meaning of any of these words: *wash* (paragraph 2), *arroyo* (paragraph 3), *stoical* (paragraph 5), *traversed* (paragraph 7), *precipitate* (paragraph 8), *Pleistocene veld* (paragraph 9), *Tenochtitlan* (paragraph 9), *drayman* (paragraph 17), *arcane* (paragraph 17), *panniers* (paragraph 18), *tenuous* (paragraph 18).

For Group Discussion or Writing

Imagine one or two artifacts that our society might leave behind and explain exactly what they represent. For example, you could pick the VCR and explain what it represents about our culture, its values, and the way we spend our time. Or you could pick a picture of a covered wagon and explain what it says about our past desire to go West, start fresh, explore new territory, and take risks.

Writing Assignments

1. *In your journal.* Assume you have the opportunity to pick one item that you own to bury in a time capsule. The item should tell something about you and what is important to you or what kind of life you lead. Tell what that item is and what it says about you.

2. *Using the pattern.* Select an item that reflects something about you, your values, your interests, and/or your activities. Describe the object as if it were an artifact that tells something about your life, long after you are gone. (Your previous journal entry may help you with this assignment.)

3. *Using the pattern.* Select an item that represents some aspect of society or history and describe that item in a way that revels its social or historical significance. Try to use a combination of expressive and objective description. If you like, you may use several patterns of development, as Lopez does.

4. *Using the pattern.* Select an item that you own, one that has been handed down to you from the past (a grandmother's ring, a great-grandfather's ax, and so forth). Describe the item in a way that conveys its significance to you.

5. *Using the pattern.* Visit a museum and describe a sculpture or painting. Be sure to decide on a dominant impression (awe, dislike, confusion, and so forth) that expresses your reaction to the piece, and choose your descriptive details to convey that dominant impression.

6. *Considering a theme.* Lopez has an extensive knowledge of history. Judging from the clues in the essay, explain Lopez's attitude toward the past. Then explain how important you think it is for people to have a detailed knowledge of history. Based on your views, describe the history curriculum you would recommend for high school students.

7. *Connecting the readings.* Read "The Deer at Providencia" on page 94 and "Am I Blue?" on page 374. Then discuss how the authors of those essays and Barry Lopez feel about animals. Explain, as well, how the three authors' views compare to your own.

ADDITIONAL ESSAY ASSIGNMENTS

See page 75 for suggestions for writing description and a revision checklist.

1. Describe a place you go to relax and convey why the place helps you unwind.

2. Describe a favorite nightspot, someplace people go to have fun. Try to convey the sense that people are enjoying themselves.

3. Describe a view from a window, using expressive detail to convey a dominant impression.

4. Describe a store where you frequently shop, using objective detail to convey to what extent the store's features meet the needs of its customers.

5. Describe a place where you enjoy spending leisure time: a bowling alley, the student union, a shopping mall, a porch, a theater, or a basketball court, for example. Use expressive detail to convey why the place appeals to you.

6. Describe the room you liked best in the house you grew up in. Your dominant impression will be how the room made you feel.

7. Describe a place during a holiday celebration. For example, you could describe your parents' dining room at Thanksgiving, Main Street during the Christmas season, or a park on Independence Day.

8. Describe your favorite vacation spot, using expressive detail to convey why you enjoy this place.

9. Describe a winter scene, a fall scene, a spring scene, or a summer scene.

10. Describe one of your classrooms.

11. Describe your bedroom. Use expressive detail to reveal what the bedroom says about you.

12. Describe a room after a party has been held there.

13. Using objective detail, describe the place where you work to show whether or not your work environment is pleasant.

14. Describe part of an amusement park.

15. Describe your favorite restaurant to convince other people to try it.

16. Describe the neighborhood you grew up in to share a portion of your past with your reader.

17. Describe a scene that shocked you.

18. Describe a rock concert for someone who has never been to one.

19. Describe a painting you enjoy.

20. *Description in context:* Assume that you are a student employee in your campus admissions office. As part of its recruiting efforts, the Director of Admissions is putting together a large, glossy brochure that presents information about the school. You have been asked to contribute to the brochure by photographing a favorite campus spot and writing a description of it. Visit a suitable spot, decide on a dominant impression, and develop your description. Keep in mind that your purpose is to present the campus attractively so that potential students will want to attend your school.

⑥ NARRATION

THE PATTERN

Everyone likes a good story. We go to movies for good stories, we read books for good stories, and we gravitate toward people at parties who tell good stories. So taken are we by stories that we tell them to our children before they go to sleep. In writing, a story is called a narration, and this chapter will explain the techniques of effective narration.

THE PURPOSES OF NARRATION

Obviously, a narration can *entertain* because a good story can amuse us and help us lose ourselves for a time. This fact helps explain the popularity of romance novels: they provide escapist entertainment. However, narrations can do more than entertain, and the selections in this chapter demonstrate the range of narrative purpose. In "By Any Other Name," Santha Rama Rau tells a story that *informs* her audience about the nature of racial discrimination; in "Salvation," Langston Hughes narrates a story to *relate* a moment of disappointment and loss of faith; in "Lost at C," Jean Shepherd narrates a humorous story to *entertain* the reader; and in "The Hanging," George Orwell tells the story of an execution, in part to *persuade* the reader that capital punishment is wrong.

A brief narration, called an *anecdote,* is often useful as a secondary pattern in other essays. For example, in an *exemplification* essay, an anecdote can be an example. If you want to illustrate that your mother is courageous, you can include a moving anecdote about the time she fended off an attack. A *comparison-contrast* that notes the differences between two mayoral candidates can include a telling anecdote about the time you met both candidates at a League of Women Voters meeting. A *cause-and-effect analysis* that explains the effects of current juvenile law can include a powerful anecdote from the newspaper about a young criminal who killed someone and was returned to the streets. A *process analysis* that explains how to surf can tell the story of the time you broke your leg because you failed to heed a caution you mention in the essay. Thus, while narration is often a pattern that stands alone, it also appears as an anecdote within other patterns of development.

Narration in College Writing

Narration can be a frequent component of college writing. For instance, a history paper on the events leading up to the Holocaust can tell the story of "The Night of the Broken Glass," when Jewish homes and businesses were looted and destroyed. A political science paper can narrate an account of the events following the Watergate break-in. Narrations are also frequently required in writing courses when students are asked to relate their personal experiences and in journalism classes when students are asked to write newspaper-style accounts of current events or campus happenings.

Narration is particularly useful for illustrating a point. Thus, if you write a paper for an education class and argue that people with learning disabilities do not get appropriate support in the classroom, you might tell the story of the time a learning-disabled friend was ignored in a high school algebra class. In a paper for a criminal justice class, you could support your point that judges should give out harsher penalties by telling the story of an offender who was repeatedly released, only to commit more crimes.

SUPPORTING DETAILS

A narration usually includes the answers to the journalist's questions who, what, when, where, why, and how. That is, the story explains *who* was involved, *what* happened, *when* it happened, *where* it happened, *why* it happened, and *how* it happened. Of course, some answers may not be appropriate for some narrations, but they are a good starting point for generating ideas. Also, different answers may be emphasized in different narrations. Thus, in some stories *who* was involved may get a great deal of attention, but in other stories, *when* it happened may be more significant and thus treated with more detail.

In addition to the answers to the journalist's questions, narration often includes descriptive detail. When a person's appearance is important to the story, that person will be described; when locale is important, a place will be described. For example, in "Lost at C," (page 154), Jean Shepherd uses description to set the scene for his narration:

> Schwartz smiled wanly. And Helen Weathers giggled—until she saw, at the same moment I did, a tall, square man standing motionless at the blackboard. He had a grim blue jaw and short, kinky black crew-cut hair. His eyes were tiny ball bearings behind glasses with thick black rims. He wore a dark, boxy suit that looked like it was made of black sandpaper. The bell rang and the door closed behind us. I joined the crowd around his desk who were putting registration cards into a box. I did likewise.

Now would be a good time to review the information on using specific words for description on page 72.

To advance the story and add vividness, narrations often include conversation. To appreciate what conversation can add to a story, consider the difference between these two approaches:

> **1.** Katie yelled to her mother and asked if she remembered to pick them up. Louise responded that she had, as she reached for the shoebox with the new tap shoes in it.
> **2.** "Hi, Mom," Katie yelled. "Did you remember to pick them up?" "Yes, darlin'," Louise responded, reaching for the shoebox with the new tap shoes in it.

The second example is more vivid and interesting because of the use of conversation. (When you use conversation, be sure to check a handbook for correct capitalization and punctuation.)

If the reader needs additional information to appreciate the story, an author can provide background information or an explanation of something. For example, in "By Any Other Name" (page 167), the author provides this explanation to help the reader understand why she and her sister attended the school that figures significantly into the narration:

> We had been sent to that school because my father, among his responsibilities as an officer of the civil service, had a tour of duty to perform in the villages around that steamy little provincial town, where he had his headquarters at that time. He used to make his shorter inspection tours on

horseback, and a week before, in the stale heat of a typically postmonsoon day, we had waved good-by to him and a little procession. . . .

Finally, since stories are often told because they make a particular point, a narration can include a statement of significance of the story. For example, in "Salvation" (page 149), Langston Hughes tells a story about attending a revival service when he was 12. He concludes his narration with a statement of the story's significance, which reads, in part:

I didn't believe there was a Jesus any more, since he didn't come to help me.

SELECTING AND ORDERING DETAILS

If you've ever listened to someone tell a story and drone on and on, you know how important it is to select narrative details carefully to avoid boring your reader with unnecessary information. This means you must choose carefully which *who, what, when, where, why,* and *how* questions to answer. It also means you must be careful not to include insignificant details, and you must not emphasize minor points, or your reader will grow annoyed. In other words, the key to a successful narration is pacing.

Arranging narrative details usually involves placing the events in chronological order. Most often this means beginning with the first event, moving to the second, on to the third, and so on. Variations of this pattern are possible, however. For some stories, you may want to begin at the end or in the middle, then flash back to the beginning.

Say, for example, you want to narrate an account of a car accident you were involved in. You could begin with the first event and move forward to the last event, like this:

A year ago, I was on my way to pick up my girlfriend, looking forward to a pleasant dinner. As I approached the intersection at Fifth and Grove, the light turned yellow, but I figured I had plenty of time to slide through.

After this opening, you would narrate an account of the accident and then go on to tell about its aftermath.

You could also begin at the end and flash back to the beginning, like this:

> As I walked out of my last physical therapy session, I thought about how remarkable it is that I can walk at all. The accident nine months earlier had left me in critical condition with a smashed pelvis.

From here, you would flash back to the beginning and narrate an account of the accident and all the events up to the time you walked out of your last physical therapy session.

You could also begin in the middle of the chronology, like this:

> I remember waking up in the hospital with my parents and sister at my side. Mom was crying and Dad looked worried. In an instant the pain overwhelmed me and I could not remember what happened. Then all at once I remembered the accident.

From this point in the middle, you would flash back to the beginning and narrate an account of the accident. You would then move chronologically through the events until you reached the last event, walking out of your last physical therapy session.

To signal chronological order, move smoothly through your time sequence, and help your reader follow the events, you can use transitions like the following:

meanwhile	later	next
soon	at first	in the meantime
second	the next day	at the same time

If you want to explain something, do so at the point in the narration where the explanation is called for. If you want to state the point your narration makes, doing so in the conclusion or in the thesis can be effective.

Many times writers omit the introduction and thesis in a narration and begin instead with the first event in the story. However, if your reader needs background information to appreciate the story, the introduction is an excellent place to supply it. Your thesis can mention the story you will tell and the significance of that story, like this:

When my younger brother and I got lost in the woods, I learned the real meaning of responsibility. (The story is about the time the writer got lost in the woods, and the significance is that the writer learned the meaning of responsibility.)

Because a story is told in chronological order, writers often omit topic sentences. The time sequence provides a clear structure, so the reader often does not need the organizational signposts provided by topic sentences.

Formal conclusions, too, may be omitted in narrations, particularly if the last event in the narration provides sufficient closure. However, if you want to state the significance of the story and you have not already done so, the conclusion can be an excellent spot for this information.

SUGGESTIONS FOR WRITING NARRATION

1. Pick a story for a reason. Rather than just tell a story for the sake of telling a story, have a purpose in mind: to entertain your reader, to inform or persuade your audience of something, and/ or to relate an experience to your audience. If you have a purpose in mind, your story will be more interesting because it will have a point.

2. To generate ideas, make a list with the answers to the *who, what, when, where, why,* and *how* questions. Decide which of these should be emphasized.

3. Identify important features about people and places and note them as points in the narration where you may want to add descriptive details.

4. Write out a statement of the significance of your narration.

5. Write your draft in one sitting; do not worry about anything except getting all the events down and answering all the appropriate journalist's questions.

Checklist for Revising Narration

1. Have you answered all the applicable journalist's questions? Are the appropriate answers emphasized?

2. Have you described people and scene when these are important to the story?

3. Where appropriate, have you provided conversation to advance the narration and add vividness?

4. If the reader requires it, have you provided necessary background information?

5. Can your reader easily determine what point your narration makes?

6. Have you omitted extraneous details that slow the pace?

7. Are your details arranged in chronological order, with or without flashback?

8. Have you used transitions to help your reader follow the chronology?

ANNOTATED STUDENT ESSAY

Student writer Robbie Warnock shares an account of the annual family reunion and comes to see the event differently now than in the past. As you read, notice the important role description plays in this narration.

The Family Reunion, Revisited

1   Once a year, with the regularity of Old Faithful, scores of people claiming to be my kin would storm my hometown. The brood did not appear gradually, but as a veritable deluge of eccentricity, and often senility. The family's elders, in their twenty-year-old gas guzzlers, circled the town like vultures, finally "nesting" at the community center. As the rusty doors squeaked open in protest, I could almost hear John Williams's "Imperial March" blasting dirgelike through my mind. It was time for the annual family reunion, and I dreaded it as much as a trip to the dentist because to a youngster like me, everyone was as old as Methuselah and as quirky as Larry, Moe, and Curly.

Paragraph 1
The introduction provides background and tells *what* and *when*. The thesis is the last sentence; it gives the subject as the annual reunion and the writer's position that the reunion was dreaded. Note the descriptive language.

2   Every woman present was clad in a floral spring dress, each with a distinct pattern. Most of

Paragraph 2
This paragraph centers on *who* by describing the people involved.

the botanical togs reeked of mothballs. This pungent aroma was the only thing that held the bees attracted by the dress at bay. The men, on the other hand, looked like reject golfers or court jesters in their mismatched clothes of many colors. After each example of Henry Ford's worst nightmare had ejected the people crammed inside, the center's double doors where opened, and the celebration commenced.

3   Food is a major love for my family, which explains why portliness is the status quo. At the reunion, long wooden tables, like those in Hrothgar's meadhall, were laden with all types of dishes. However, an elderly matriarch of the clan became discontented with the same old food served every year. To ease the monotony, she created the "Annual Odd Recipe Contest," The goal of which was to create the most appetizing dish from the most bizarre ingredients.

Paragraph 3
Description and specific word choice add interest and vitality.

4   I was present at the inception of this contest, albeit reluctantly. Along with the down-home staples, fried chicken and chocolate layer cake, I sampled a curious-looking green and purple casserole. Immediately, I fell victim to Aunt Frankie's infamous "Eggplant and Kudzu Surprise." Upon tasting the foul abomination, I fled to the nearest McDonald's and vowed never to consume another bite even remotely connected with the old crone.

Paragraph 4
This paragraph flashes back to the more distant past.

5   After eating the wonderful meal of poultry and vegetation, the family would seek amusement. Refusing to simply converse the evening away, the motley crew would begin to square dance. Recovering from whatever odd recipe I had unwittingly subjected myself to, I would glance inside to view a plethora of octogenarians tramping and stomping in a futile attempt at dancing. Then the entertainment took a nosedive. Uncle Oliver produced a set a bagpipes and unleashed a sonic aberration akin to the sound produced when a few dozen cats are run over slowly by a bulldozer.

Paragraphs 5 and 6
Details are in chronological order, and each paragraph begins with a transitional phrase. Details emphasize *who* and *what*. The vivid description continues.

6   After the musical torture, the group underwent a schism. The men ditched their wives and each group would nestle in a separate corner and settle down enough to actually begin conversations unrelated to food. Now the talk

focused on the past. At just the right moment, Uncle Oliver presented a hundred or so bags, each sealed, labeled, and containing a piece of debris from the family homeplace. As he presented these heirlooms, he recited a stentorian lecture on the "sacred domicile." Each member of the family then received a fragment of the house.

7   Stomach churning, ears smarting, and bearing a Ziploc bag containing a burnt bit of shingle, I returned home at the end of the day, praising God for deliverance. Today, I see things differently, however. Rather than eccentricity, I see love and a memorial to past times. The would-be Scotsman Oliver wanted the kids to cherish their heritage. I now regret my impatience and impudence because I realize that the reunion was an annual link between the past and the present. I now realize that the past is a treasure and the key to the future. For one more chance to remember and relive those times, I would square dance, listen to bagpipes, and even choke down kudzu.

Paragraph 7
The conclusion presents the last event and the significance of the narration (the reunion served an important purpose). The last paragraph also answers *why*.

WHOM TO BELIEVE?
Robert Satter

Robert Satter certainly knows about the law and our judicial system. He has been a judge of the court of common pleas, a judge on the Connecticut Superior Court, a lawyer, and a Connecticut state representative. His essay, "Whom to Believe?", taken from Doing Justice *(1990), combines narration, cause-and-effect analysis, and process analysis in an account of a trial. The insights offered will likely inform you about the American judicial system, particularly the role of judges.*

THE PATTERNS	THE PURPOSE
narration with cause-and-effect analysis and process analysis	*to inform*

1   The phone rings in my chambers a few minutes after ten. The calendar judge for the civil part of Hartford Superior Court is on the line.

2   "Bob, I'm sending you a court case to try. *Romano v. Costello.* Your clerk is bringing you the file. The lawyers say it's a short trial."

3   A court case means I will hear it without a jury and I alone will determine the facts, resolve the issues of law, and render a final judgment. Determining the facts is often the most difficult.

4   The facts of the case are the conclusions drawn from the evidence. The evidence is mainly in the form of testimony, so finding the facts requires assessing not only what witnesses say on the stand, but which are telling the truth. Since people on each side of a case often give contradictory versions of the same event, the subtext of a trial is credibility—which witnesses, and to what extent, are to be believed. I suspect it will be so in the trial being sent to me.

5   Certain kinds of cases are required to be tried by a judge alone. Among them are so-called equity actions, in which one party seeks an injunction to forbid the other party from doing an illegal or harmful act or seeks to compel the other party to specifically perform a contract. Others are appeals from decisions of administrative agencies. Actually, any case can be tried to the court without a jury if the parties so desire

and they often do when they want a quicker hearing, or when the issues are complicated and they do not trust a jury to decide them. Businessmen in particular prefer to have their commercial and corporate
controversies resolved by judges.

6   The lawyers appear at my chambers. I know them both as hardworking practitioners. We chat informally for a few moments, I calling
them by their first names. I glance at the complaint in the file. It alleges
that the plaintiff has loaned the defendant $10,000; the defendant has
failed to pay on time; the plaintiff demands damages equal to the
amount of the loan plus interest and costs.

7   "Do you have a defense?" I ask the defendant's lawyer.

8   "You bet, Your Honor. My client claims—"

9   "Wait a minute," the plaintiff's lawyer interrupts, bristling, "we
can't discuss the case before the judge who's going to hear it."

10   "Take it easy, fellows. I just want to know what the issue is. Any
chance of settling the case? If so, I will send you to another judge who
can help you reach an agreement."

11   The trying judge in a court case cannot get involved in settlement
negotiations with the attorneys. He may learn facts not admissible into
evidence or learn the parties' compromise positions, which may improperly influence his ultimate decision.

12   Both lawyers shake their heads. The plaintiff's attorney says,
"We've tried to settle, Judge, but there's no chance. The case has to be
tried."

13   "Okay, let's try it," I say.

14   The next moment I am on the bench. The courtroom is small
and spare, as unpretentious as the waiting room of a rural railroad station. None of the splendor of a jury courtroom. Aside from the court
clerk and reporter, the only others present are the two lawyers and their
clients. I have just finished bantering with the lawyers and am now conducting the trial with strict formality. I am amazed at how quickly all
of us assume our roles.

15   Since this is a court case, lawyers will forgo the hammy vaude-
ville gestures they pull before jurors: the dramatic thrusting of a document at the witness as if piercing his heart; the rolling of the eyes upward and the incredulous shaking of the head at the witness's last
answer. They will also eschew hackneyed tactics, such as asking witnesses called by the other attorney whether they talked to the attorney
before testifying. They know judges understand that lawyers must speak

to witnesses in order to prepare them for trial. If the attorneys do engage in such playacting, I will say, "Counsel, please don't waste my time with this nonsense. Let's get on with the case."

16   I also try court cases differently from jury cases. For example, although the rules of evidence are supposed to be applied alike in both, I , and most judges, apply them with less rigor in court cases. The analogy can be made between the difference in adult conversation when children are in the room and when they are out of earshot. In court cases, where there is no jury, I tend to be more liberal in letting in evidence that the rules might exclude as unreliable, because, as an experienced trier, I feel capable of disregarding such evidence.

17   The plaintiff's attorney motions to his client to take the stand. The clerk asks the short, gray-haired man to raise his right hand and intones, "You solemnly swear that the evidence you shall give, concerning the case now in question, shall be the truth, the whole truth, and nothing but the truth, so help you God?"

18   "I do."

19   "Give your name and address."

20   "Frank Romano, Thirty-nine Preston Street, Hartford."

21   The witness takes his seat in the chair on the raised stand next to the bench. He sits stiffly, ceaselessly kneading his thick hands in his lap. Under questioning by his attorney, he testifies that his niece's husband wanted to start a sidewalk construction business. "That's Joe," he says, pointing to the defendant. "He asked me to loan him ten thousand dollars, and promised to pay me back in two years. I was glad to help him get going in a new business."

22   The $10,000 check to the order of Joseph Costello is introduced into evidence; it has been duly endorsed and cashed. Mr. Romano's lawyer asks:

23   "Was your agreement with Costello in writing?"

24   "No. I trusted him. He was my *paisan.*"[1]

25   Mr. Romano concludes by saying that after three years he demanded payment, and when it was not forthcoming, he started this suit.

26   I have been listening and observing the witness. I notice that he holds his head slantwise and seems to speak into a space rather than directly to his lawyer.

---

[1]*paisan:* fellow countryman (Italian).

27   The defendant's attorney begins his cross-examination of Romano by eliciting from him that he has no children and Joe's wife, Felicia, is his favorite niece. Then the lawyer asks, "Didn't you really give the money to Mr. Costello so he could provide a better living for Felicia?"

28   "Yes, I wanted to help Felicia. But the money was a loan to Joe."

29   "Yet you waited three years to ask for the money back when you said the loan was for two years, isn't that so?"

30   "I wanted to see if Joe would pay me back on his own."

31   "Isn't it a fact that you didn't demand payment until after Joe left Felicia and started the divorce?"

32   "That had nothing to do with it," Mr. Romano retorts angrily. "It was a loan, and I wanted my money back."

33   After both counsel finish with the witness, I have a question to ask him. Although in a jury case I intervene as little as possible in order to permit the attorneys to convince the jury in their own way, in court cases they have to convince me, and the decision is my responsibility. I am more interested in finding out all the information that will help me decide than I am protecting the trial strategy of the lawyers. So I ask from the bench, "Tell me, Mr. Romano, if there had not been a divorce between Joe and Felicia, would you still be asking for the money?"

34   "Well, Judge . . . I don' . . . I love Felicia. . . ." Mr. Romano looks at his attorney. "But it was a loan, Judge," he says in a rising voice. "Joe promised to pay me back, and he didn't."

35   Mr. Costello is called by his attorney to the stand. He is a muscular man of about thirty, with wavy black hair and blue eyes. The clerk recites: "You solemnly swear that the evidence you shall give, concerning the case now in question, shall be the truth, the whole truth, and nothing but the truth, so help you God?"

36   "I do."

37   He is at ease on the witness chair, but I notice he speaks slightly out of the side of his mouth. After some preliminary questions, his lawyer asks, "What was the arrangement concerning the ten thousand dollars with your uncle-in-law?"

38   "He knew I was going into the construction business and offered to help me. I said I didn't know if I could pay him back. He said, 'Don't worry about it, Joe. This is a gift. Felicia is my favorite niece. I'm glad to help her in this way.' I thanked him. A few days later he gave me the check."

39   "What happened next?" asks his lawyer.

40   "Three years later Felicia and I got divorced. Then for the first time he started pestering me for the money. I woulda paid him just to get him off my back. But the business is barely breaking even, and I just don't have the dough."

41   Cross-examination does not shake the essentials of his story. That is the case. Simple set of facts. The only thing difficult is the decision.

42   Was the money given as a loan or a gift? Whom am I to believe, the uncle or the nephew? On what basis can I decide who was telling the truth?

43   In olden days the sworn oath of a witness as a God-fearing man was thought to assure his telling the truth. Now God is not so feared. We rely on the tendency of people generally to be truthful, on the professional ethics of lawyers not to suborn perjury, and on the weapon of cross-examination. In practice, all are slender reeds.

44   Professor John Henry Wigmore, leading authority on evidence, warns of the latent errors in oral testimony of "Perception, Recollection or Narration." Witnesses may testify erroneously because they perceive an event incompletely, recall it imperfectly, or tell it inaccurately. Clues to such errors can sometimes be revealed by artful cross-examination. However, the best of cross-examination can rarely crack deliberate perjury or its next of kin, the conscious shading of the truth by a witness out of his own self-interest. Here the uncle and the nephew have equal self-interest to remember the facts in the way that favored each of them.

45   Can I decide credibility on my observations of the demeanor of the uncle and the nephew on the stand: the uncle's tenseness, his way of never looking at his lawyer; the nephew's ease, his manner of speaking out of the side of his mouth? Can I, in Shakespeare's felicitous words, "find the mind's construction in the face"? Are the external signs—squints of the eye, twitches in the cheek, nervous gestures of the hands—reliable clues of the speaker's truth or falsity?

46   I know so little about the uncle and nephew. The uncle has been on the stand about thirty minutes, the nephew twenty. A friend who served on a jury once complained about his lack of information about the background of the witnesses.

47   "What did you want to know?" I asked.

48   "For one thing, what people who know the witness think of him. People like his neighbors, his pastor, his banker. For another, what kind of person the witness is. Things like does he pay his debts, give to charities, drink to excess."

49   "But," I protested, "that would open up so many areas that the trial would never end."

50   Yet my friend was right in his essential point. Witnesses on the stand appear two-dimensional. Rarely is the third dimension of their character revealed.

51   Forced to decide in the uncle-nephew case, I choose to believe the nephew. It rings truer to me that the divorce, and not the original understanding about the money, is the real reason the uncle wants to be repaid. I do so despite the uncle's heated denial. But my decision in favor of the nephew has no solid, objective basis; it is founded not on analysis, but on a hunch.

Reading Closely and Thinking Critically

1. Why is determining the facts the most difficult part of trying a case?

2. Explain the role of credibility in a trial.

3. On what basis does Judge Satter have to make his decision? Why is his decision difficult to make?

4. Is the analogy regarding the rules of evidence in paragraph 16 a valid one? Do you think the judge acts responsibly when he uses different standards in court and jury cases? Explain.

5. The author mentions that he noticed the first witness held his head slantwise and spoke into space (paragraph 26) and that the second witness spoke out of the side of his mouth (paragraph 36). Why does Judge Satter mention these points? Does this information figure into this decision? Should it figure in? Explain.

6. Do you think it is possible to "find the mind's construction in the face" (paragraph 45)? Explain.

Examining Structure and Strategy

1. "Whom to Believe?" is written in the present tense, although the events clearly took place in the past. What is the effect of the present tense? Would anything be lost if the past tense were used?

2. Which of the *who, what, when, where, why, how* questions are emphasized?

3. What does the conversation contribute to the essay? Would anything be lost if Satter did not use conversation?

4. Which paragraphs include description? What purpose does that description serve?

5. Do you think this essay would be a good one to reprint in a high school newspaper? Why or why not?

Considering Language and Style

1. To give the conversation in the essay authenticity, Satter reproduces the witnesses' dialect. (A *dialect* is a variety of language characterized by a particular word choice, grammar, and pronunciation.) For example, in paragraph 34, "don'" is recorded rather than "don't." Cite three other examples of dialect.

2. The conversation in paragraphs 9 and 10 offers insight into the tone of the proceedings in the judge's chambers. What is that tone? How can you tell? (See page 37 on tone.)

3. Consult a dictionary if you are unsure of the meaning of any of these words: *render* (paragraph 3), *injunction* (paragraph 5), *eschew* (paragraph 15), *hackneyed* (paragraph 15), *suborn perjury* (paragraph 43), *felicitous* (paragraph 45).

For Group Discussion or Writing

If you had the opportunity to ask each witness three questions that would help you render a verdict, what would you ask? The questions can be about the case or the background of the witnesses.

Writing Assignments

1. *In your journal.* In a page or so, explain what you learned about the legal system as a result of reading "Whom to Believe?" Note whether or not anything surprised you and explain why or why not.

2. *Using the pattern.* In paragraph 43, Satter says, "We rely on the tendency of people generally to be truthful." Narrate a story that supports or disproves the notion that people are truthful. Your story should be based on your own experience or observation.

3. Using the pattern. If you have participated in the legal system as a witness, jury member, plaintiff, defendant, observer, or member of youth court, narrate a story that reflects your experience.

4. Using the pattern. Tell a story about a time you borrowed or lent something and a problem ensued. Try to explain what you learned as a result of the experience, and try to use some description and conversation.

5. Using the pattern. Tell a story with the title "Whom to Believe?", a story about a time you did not know which of two or more people to believe. Explain why you had trouble, what you ultimately decided, and why. If possible, explain the outcome of your decision.

6. Considering a theme. Much of the American public has formed impressions about the workings of the legal system from television. Explain what television says about the American system of criminal justice. If possible, show an attorney or law professor your conclusions to learn to what extent television's portrayal is accurate, and report your findings.

7. Connecting the readings. In paragraphs 43 and 44, Satter writes of the fact that people are not always truthful. Discuss to what extent lying is a part of life, what purpose lying serves, and whether lying is damaging or helpful. The information in "Whom to Believe?", "Lost at C" (page 154), and "Salvation" (page 149) may be helpful.

SALVATION
Langston Hughes

Born in Joplin, Missouri, Langston Hughes (1902-1967) was best know as a poet, but he was also a respected playwright, critic, and fiction writer. Hughes was an important figure in the 1920s blossoming of literature and music known as the Harlem Renaissance. A frequent contributor to the New York Post, *Hughes often wrote of African-American life in America. His works include* Simple Speaks His Mind *(1950), the first of four volumes of his short stories, and* Ask Your Mama: 12 Moods for Jazz *(1961), a collection of poetry inspired by the civil rights movement. The following selection is from Hughes's autobiographical* The Big Sea *(1940). In the essay Hughes relates an experience that changed his life dramatically, and he expresses the disillusionment he felt as a result. As you read, ask yourself what pressures led Hughes to take the action he did.*

THE PATTERN	THE PURPOSE
narration	*to express feelings and relate experience*

1   I was saved from sin when I was going on thirteen. But not really saved. It happened like this. There was a big revival at my Auntie Reed's church. Every night for weeks there had been much preaching, singing, praying, and shouting, and some very hardened sinners had been brought to Christ, and the membership of the church had grown by leaps and bounds. Then just before the revival ended, they held a special meeting for children, "to bring the young lambs to the fold." My aunt spoke of it for days ahead. That night, I was escorted to the front row and placed on the mourner's bench with all other young sinners, who had not yet been brought to Jesus.

2   My aunt told me that when you were saved you saw a light, and something happened to you inside! And Jesus came into your life! And God was with you from then on! She said you could see and hear and feel Jesus in your soul. I believed her. I had heard a great many old people say the same thing and it seemed to me they ought to know. So I sat there calmly in the hot, crowded church, waiting for Jesus to come to me.

3   The preacher preached a wonderful rhythmical sermon, all moans and shouts and lonely cries and dire pictures of hell, and then he sang a song about the ninety and nine safe in the fold, but one little lamb was left out in the cold. Then he said: "Won't you come? Won't you come to Jesus? Young lambs, won't you come?" and he held out his arms to all us young sinners there on the mourner's bench. And the little girls cried. And some of them jumped up and went to Jesus right away. But most of us just sat there.

4   A great many old people came and knelt around us and prayed, old women with jet-black faces and braided hair, old men with work-gnarled hands. And the church sang a song about the lower lights are burning, some poor sinners to be saved. And the whole building rocked with prayer and song.

5   Still I kept waiting to *see* Jesus.

6   Finally all the young people had gone to the altar and were saved, but one boy and me. He was a rounder's son named Westley. Westley and I were surrounded by sisters and deacons praying. It was very hot in the church, and getting late now. Finally Westley said to me in a whisper. "God damn! I'm tired o' sitting here. Let's get up and be saved." So he got up and was saved.

7   Then I was left all alone on the mourner's bench. My aunt came and knelt at my knees and cried, while prayers and songs swirled all around me in the little church. The whole congregation prayed for me alone, in a mighty wail of moans and voices. And I kept waiting serenely for Jesus, waiting, waiting—but he didn't come. I wanted to see him, but nothing happened to me. Nothing! I wanted something to happen to me, but nothing happened.

8   I heard the songs and the minister saying: "Why don't you come? My dear child, why don't you come to Jesus? Jesus is waiting for you. He wants you. Why don't you come? Sister Reed, what is this child's name?"

9   "Langston," my aunt sobbed.

10   "Langston, why don't you come? Why don't you come and be saved? Oh, Lamb of God! Why don't you come?"

11   Now it was really getting late. I began to be ashamed of myself, holding everything up so long. I began to wonder what God thought about Westley, who certainly hadn't seen Jesus either, but who was now sitting proudly on the platform, swinging his knickerbockered legs and grinning down at me, surrounded by deacons and old women on their knees praying. God had not struck Westley dead for taking his name in vain or for

lying in the temple. So I decided that maybe to save further trouble, I'd better lie, too, and say that Jesus had come, and get up and be saved.

12   So I go up.

13   Suddenly the whole room broke into a sea of shouting, as they saw me rise. Waves of rejoicing swept the place. Women leaped in the air. My aunt threw her arms around me. The minister took me by the hand and led me to the platform.

14   When things quieted down, in a hushed silence, punctuated by a few ecstatic "Amens," all the new young lambs were blessed in the name of God. Then joyous singing filled the room.

15   That night, for the last time in my life but one—for I was a big boy twelve years old—I cried. I cried, in bed alone, and couldn't stop. I buried my head under the quilts, but my aunt heard me. She woke up and told my uncle I was crying because the Holy Ghost had come into my life, and because I had seen Jesus. But I was really crying because I couldn't bear to tell her that I had lied, that I had deceived everybody in the church, that I hadn't seen Jesus, and that now I didn't believe there was a Jesus any more, since he didn't come to help me.

Reading Closely and Thinking Critically

1. What does young Langston Hughes expect to happen at the revival? What happens instead?

2. How was Hughes affected by what happened at the revival?

3. What do you think Hughes means in the first two sentences of the narration?

4. Why does young Langston pretend to see Jesus and be saved? Do you think he was right or wrong to pretend to be saved? What would you have done in his place? Explain.

5. How do you think young Langston's aunt would have reacted if he had told her the truth about why he was crying?

6. In what way is "Salvation" ironic? (Irony refers to events that occur in ways contrary to expectations.)

Examining Structure and Strategy

1. Do the first two sentences of "Salvation" make an effective opening? Explain why or why not.

2. Where does Hughes explain the significance of the narration?

3. Hughes includes description of people and events in his narration. Cite two examples of this description and explain what it contributes to the narration.

4. Which of the *who, what, when, where, why,* and *how* questions does Hughes emphasize the most?

5. To help the reader recognize and follow the chronological order, Hughes opens several of his paragraphs with transitions that signal time order (see page 22). Which paragraphs open with transitions, and what are those transitions?

6. In addition to telling his story, Hughes offers some explanation. What is explained and where does this explanation occur?

Considering Language and Style

1. What metaphor appears in paragraph 13? (see page 73 on metaphors.) What does this metaphor contribute to the description that appears in the essay?

2. Paragraph 12 is only four words. Explain the effect created by this four-word paragraph. What would be lost if the four words were moved to the end of paragraph 11?

3. Consult a dictionary if you are unsure of the meaning of any of these words: *revival* (paragraph 1), *dire* (paragraph 3), *rounder* (paragraph 6), *deacons* (paragraph 6), *knickerbockered* (paragraph 11), *ecstatic* (paragraph 14).

For Group Discussion or Writing

With two or three classmates, consider the following questions: What do you think would have happened if young Langston had not pretended to see Jesus and be saved? How would his aunt have reacted? How would Westley have reacted?

Writing Assignments

1. *In your journal.* In about a page, explain whether your own religious experiences more closely parallel the experiences of the young Langston Hughes or the experiences of his aunt. Provide an example to illustrate.

2. *Using the pattern.* In paragraph 2, Hughes explains that he believed his aunt when she described what it was like to be saved. However, his experience did not conform to his aunt's description. Tell a story about a time when you were led to expect something, but it did not happen. If you like, explain how you reacted.

3. *Using the pattern.* Like Hughes, narrate a story about some traumatic experience you had when you were young. Also like Hughes, explain the impact the event had on you.

4. *Using the pattern.* Hughes says he pretended to see Jesus "to save further trouble." Narrate an account of a time you or someone you know did something to avoid trouble or inconvenience. Explain the outcome.

5. *Using the pattern.* Hughes felt pressured to see Jesus and be saved. Narrate an account of a time you or someone you know was pressured to think or behave a particular way. Explain how you or the other person responded to the pressure.

6. *Considering a theme.* The religious community and a family member pressured 12-year-old Hughes to see Jesus and be saved. Pick one organization, institution, or group — religion, school, the family, the community, a peer group, and so on — and explain one or more of the pressures it exerts on us. Explain whether the pressure is a positive or negative influence.

7. *Connecting the readings.* Young people do not lead the carefree life many people think they do. Instead, they are often struggling to deal with a variety of pressures from many sources. Using the information in "Salvation," "Lost at C" (page 154), and "Complexion" (page 401), along with your own experience and observation, discuss the pressures young people face as a result of adult expectations.

LOST AT C
Jean Shepherd

Born in 1929, Chicago native and noted humorist Jean Shepherd has been an author, off-Broadway actor with four one-man shows to his credit, and a radio and television personality in Cincinnati, Philadelphia, and Detroit. He has also written a column for the Village Voice, *and he has contributed award-winning fiction to* Playboy. *His work usually treats growing up in America's heartland with humor and insight. In "Lost at C," taken from Shepherd's* Fistful of Fig Newtons *(1973), the author relates the indelible memory of his high school algebra class while entertaining the reader with both humor and drama. In addition, he informs by pointing to some unfortunate truths about American education. As you read, notice both how Shepherd creates his comic effects and what he says about education.*

THE PATTERN	THE PURPOSES
narration	*to inform, to entertain, and to express feelings and relate experience*

1   Miss Snyder stood at the blackboard and hurled the first harpoon of the season: "You freshmen who are with us today are already enrolled for the courses you will be required to take. Here are your program cards." She dealt out 3 x 5-inch blue cards, which were handed back to the freshmen. Each card was neatly lined into eight periods, and after each period was the name of a teacher, a subject, and a classroom. One period was labeled LUNCH, another STUDY, and so on. Every minute of my day was laid out for me. So much for my dreams of freedom.

2   "Freshmen, this is your first day in high school. You are no longer in grade school. If you work hard, you will do well. If you don't you will regret it. You are here to learn. You are not here to play. Remember this and remember it well: *What you do here will follow you all through life.*" She paused dramatically. In the hushed silence, I could hear Rukowski wheezing ahead of me. None of this, of course, affected him. Anyone who could block the way he could block would have no trouble getting through life.

3   "Your first class will begin in five minutes. Any questions?" No one raised a hand.

4   I sat there pawing in the chute, anxious to begin my glorious career of learning. No more would I fake my way. A new era was about to begin. The bell rang. The starting gate slammed open.

5   I had thundered a couple of hundred feet through the hall with the mob before it hit me that I had no idea where the hell I was supposed to go. As the crowd surged around me, I struggled to read my program card. All I could make out was Room 127. I had only a minute to make it, so I battled my way down a flight of stairs. Then: 101, 105, 109, 112, 117—127, just in time. Already the classroom was three-quarters filled. Ahead of me, running interference, was Rukowski, trying his luck at this course, I later learned, for the third time in as many semesters. Getting his shoulder into it, he bulled his way through the door, buffeting aside a herd of spindly little freshmen. It was Schwartz, good old Schwartz, and Flick and Chester and Helen Weathers. My old gang! Even poor old Zynzmeister. Whatever it was, I would not have to go through it alone.

6   "Hi, Schwartz!"

7   Schwartz smiled wanly. And Helen Weathers giggled—until she saw, at the same moment I did, a tall, square man standing motionless at the blackboard. He had a grim blue jaw and short, kinky black crew-cut hair. His eyes were tiny ball bearings behind glasses with thick black rims. He wore a dark, boxy suit that looked like it was made of black sandpaper. The bell rang and the door closed behind us. I joined the crowd around his desk who were putting registration cards into a box. I did likewise.

8   "All right. Settle down. Let's get organized." The man's voice had a cutting rasp to it, like a steel file working on concrete. "We sit alphabetically in this class. A's up here in front to my right. Get going."

9   I trudged behind Schwartz and Helen Weathers toward the dim recesses in the back of the classroom. Well, at least I'd be among friends. It was about a quarter of a mile to the front of the room, but I sat bolt upright in my seat, my iron determination intact. No more faking it.

10   "Class, my name is Mr. Pittinger." He was the first male teacher I had ever had. Warren G. Harding was peopled entirely by motherly ladies like Mrs. Bailey and Miss Shields. Mr. Pittinger was a whole new ball game. And I still had no idea what he taught. I would soon find out.

11   "If you work in this class, you'll have no trouble. If you don't, I promise you nothing."

12   I leaned forward at my desk, scribbling madly in my notebook: *class my name is mr. pittinger if you work you will have no trouble if you don't i promise you nothing . . .*

13   I figured if you wrote everything down there'd be no trouble. Every classroom of my life had been filled with girls on the Honor Roll who endlessly wrote in mysterious notebooks, even when nothing seemed to be going on. I never knew what the hell they were writing, so I took no chances. I figured I'd write everything.

14   "Braaghk." Mr. Pittinger cleared his gravelly throat.

15   *braaaghk,* I scribbled, *brummph.* You never know, I thought, it might appear on the exam.

16   He turned, picked up a piece of chalk, and began to scrawl huge block letters on the blackboard.

17   A–L—the chalk squeaked decisively—G–E–B–R–A. I copied each letter exactly as he'd written it.

18   "That is the subject of this course," he barked.

19   Algebra? What the hell is that?

20   "Algebra is the mathematics of abstract numbers."

21   I gulped as I wrote this down.

22   "I will now illustrate."

23   Pittinger printed a huge Y on the blackboard and below it an enormous X. I doggedly followed suit in my notebook. He then put equal signs next to the X and the Y.

24   "If Y equals five and X equals two, what does the following mean?"

25   He wrote out: $X + Y = ?$

26   Black fear seized my vitals. How could you add Xs and Ys? I had enough trouble with nines and sevens!

27   Already the crowd in front of the room were waving their hands to answer Pittinger's question. The class wasn't thirty seconds old and I was already six weeks behind. I sank lower in my seat, a faint buzzing in my ears. Instinctively I began to weave. I knew it was all over. Out of the corner of my eye I saw that Schwartz, next to me, had hunched lower and begun to emit a high, thin whimpering sound. Helen Weathers had flung up a thin spray of sweat. Chester's skin had changed to the color of the cupboards in the back of the room. And from behind me I could hear the faint, steady click of Zynzmeister's rosary.

28   Second by second, minute by minute, eon by eon that first algebra class droned on. I couldn't catch another word that was said, and by the time Mr. Pittinger wrote the second equation on the board, I was bobbing and weaving like a cobra and sending out high-voltage thought rays. A tiny molten knot of stark terror hissed and simmered in the pit of my stomach. I realized that for the first time in my school life, I had run into something that was completely opaque and unlearnable, and there was no way to fake it.

29   Don't call on me, Don't call on me, Don't call on me . . .

30   That night I ate my meatloaf and red cabbage in sober silence as the family yapped on, still living back in the days when I was known to all of them as the smartest little son of a bitch to ever set foot on Cleveland Street.

31   "Boy, look at the stuff kids study these days," the old man said with wonder as he hefted my algebra textbook in his bowling hand and riffled through the pages.

32   "What's all this X and Y stuff?" he asked.

33   "Yeah, well, it ain't much," I muttered as coolly as I could, trying to recapture some of the old élan.

34   "Whaddaya mean, ain't much?" His eyes glowed with pride at the idea that his kid has mastered algebra in only one day.

35   "Abstract mathematics, that's all it is."

36   The old man knew he'd been totally outclassed. Even my mother stopped stirring the gravy for a few seconds. My kid brother continued to pound away at the little bbs of Ovaltine that floated around on the top of his milk.

37   That night sleep did not come easily. In fact, it was only the first of many storm-tossed nights to come as, algebra class by algebra class, my terror grew. All my other subjects—history, English, social studies—were a total breeze. My years of experience in fakery came into full flower. In social studies, for example, the more you hoked it up, the better the grades. On those rare occasions when asked a question, I would stand slowly, with an open yet troubled look playing over my thoughtful countenance.

38   "Mr. Harris, sir," I would drawl hesitantly, as though attempting to unravel the perplexity of the ages, "I guess it depends on how you view it—objectively, which, naturally, is too simple, or subjectively, in which case many factors such as a changing environment must be taken into consideration, and . . . " I would trail off.

39   Mr. Harris, with a snort of pleasure, would bellow: "RIGHT! There are many diverse elements, which . . ." After which he was good for at least a forty-minute solo.

40   History was more of the same, and English was almost embarrassingly easy as, day after day, Miss McCullough preened and congratulated herself before our class. All she needed was a little ass-kissing and there was no limit to her applause. I often felt she regretted that an A+ was the highest grade she could hand out to one who loved her as sincerely and selflessly as I did.

41   Every morning at eight-thirty-five, however, was another story. I marched with leaden feet and quaking bowels into Mr. Pittinger's torture chamber. By the sixth week I knew, without the shadow of a doubt, that after all these years of dodging and grinning, I was going to fail. Fail! No B, no gentleman's C—Fail. F. The big one: my own Scarlet Letter. Branded on my forehead—F, for Fuckup.

42   There was no question whatever. True, Pittinger had not yet been able to catch me out in the open, since I was using every trick of the trade. But I knew that one day, inevitably, the icy hand of truth would rip off my shoddy façade and expose me for all the world to see.

43   Pittinger was of the new school, meaning he believed that kids, theoretically motivated by an insatiable thirst for knowledge, would devour algebra in large chunks, making the final examination only a formality. He graded on performance in class and total grasp of the subject, capped off at the end of the term with an exam of brain-crushing difficulty from which he had the option of excusing those who rated A+ on classroom performance. Since I had no classroom performance, my doom was sealed.

44   Schwartz, too, had noticeably shrunken. Even fat Helen had developed deep hollows under her eyes, while Chester had almost completely disappeared. And Zynzmeister had taken to nibbling Communion wafers in class.

45   Christmas came and went in tortured gaiety. My kid brother played happily with his Terry and the Pirates Dragon Lady Detector as I looked on with the sad indulgence of a withered old man whose youth had passed. As for my own presents, what good did it do to have a new first baseman's mitt when my life was over? How innocent they are, I thought as I watched my family trim the tree and scurry about wrapping packages. Before long, they will know. They will loathe me. I will be driven from this warm circle. It was about this time that I began to

fear—or perhaps hope—that I would never live to be twenty-one, that I would die of some exotic debilitating disease. Then they'd be sorry. This fantasy alternated with an even better fantasy that if I did reach twenty-one, I would be blind and hobble about with a white cane. Then they'd really be sorry.

46   Not that I'd given up without a struggle. For weeks, in the privacy of my cell at home, safe from prying eyes, I continued trying to actually learn something about algebra. After a brief mental pep rally— This is simple. If Esther Jane Alberry can understand it, any fool can do it. All you gotta do is think. THINK! Reason it out!—I would sit down and open my textbook. Within minutes, I would break out in a clammy sweat and sink into a funk of nonunderstanding, a state so naked in its despair and self-contempt that it was soon replaced by a mood of defiant truculence. Schwartz and I took to laughing contemptuously at those boobs and brown-noses up front who took it all so seriously.

47   The first hints of spring began to appear. Birds twittered, buds unfurled. But men on death row are impervious to such intimations of life quickening and reborn. The only sign of the new season that I noticed was Mr. Pittinger changing from a heavy scratchy black suit into a lighter-weight scratchy black suit.

48   "Well, it won't be long. You gonna get a job this summer?" my old man asked me one day as he bent over the hood of the Olds, giving the fourth-hand paint job its ritual spring coat of Simonize.

49   "Maybe. I dunno," I muttered. It wouldn't be long, indeed. Then he'd know. Everybody would know that I knew less about algebra than Ralph, Mrs. Gammie's big Airedale, who liked to pee on my mother's irises.

50   Mr. Pittinger had informed us that the final exam, covering a year's work in algebra, would be given on Friday of the following week. One more week of stardom on Cleveland Street. Ever since my devastating rejoinder at the dinner table about abstract mathematics, my stock had been the hottest in the neighborhood. My opinions were solicited on financial matters, world affairs, even the infield problems of the Chicago White Sox. The bigger they are, the harder they fall. Even Ralph would have more respect than I deserved. At least he didn't pretend to be anything but what he was—a copious and talented pee-er.

51   Wednesday, two days before the end, arrived like any other spring day. A faint breeze drifted from the south, bringing with it hints of long summer afternoons to come, of swung bats, of nights in the lilac bushes.

But not for such as me. I stumped into algebra class feeling distinctly like the last soul aboard the *Titanic* as she was about to plunge to the bottom. The smart-asses were already in their seats, laughing merrily, the goddamn A's and B's and C's and even the M's. I took my seat in the back, among the rest of the condemned. Schwartz sat down sullenly and began his usual moan. Helen Weathers squatted toadlike, drenched in sweat. The class began, Pittinger's chalk squeaked, hands waved. The sun filtered in through the venetian blinds. A tennis ball pocked back and forth over a net somewhere. Faintly, the high clear voices of the girls' glee club sang, "Can you bake a cherry pie, charming Billy?" Birds twittered.

52   My knot of fear, by now an old friend, sputtered in my gut. In the past week, it had grown to roughly the size of a two-dollar watermelon. True, I had avoided being called on even once the entire year, but it was a hollow victory and I knew it. Minute after minute inched slowly by as I ducked and dodged, Pittinger firing question after question at the class. Glancing at my Pluto watch, which I had been given for Christmas, I noted with deep relief that less than two minutes remained before the bell.

53   It was then that I made my fatal mistake, the mistake that all guerrilla fighters eventually make—I lost my concentration. For years, every fiber of my being, every instant in every class, had been directed solely at survival. On this fateful Wednesday, lulled by the sun, by the gentle sound of the tennis ball, by the steady drone of Pittinger's voice, by the fact that there were just two minutes to go, my mind slowly drifted off into a golden haze. A tiny mote of dust floated down through a slanting ray of sunshine. I watched it in its slow, undulating flight, like some microscopic silver bird.

54   "You're the apple of my eye, darling Billy . . . I can bake a cherry pie . . ."

55   A rich maple syrup warmth filled my being. Out of the faint distance, I heard a deadly rasp, the faint honking of disaster.

56   For a stunned split second, I thought I'd been jabbed with an electric cattle prod. Pittinger's voice, loud and commanding, was pronouncing my name. He was calling on ME! Oh, my God! With a goddamn minute to go, he had nailed me. I heard Schwartz bleat a high, quavering cry, a primal scream. I knew what it meant: If they got him, the greatest master of them all, there's no hope for ANY of us!

57   As I stood slowly at my seat, frantically bidding for time, I saw a great puddle forming around Helen Weathers. It wasn't all sweat.

Chester had sunk to the floor beneath his desk, and behind me Zynzmeister's beads were clattering so loudly I could hardly hear his Hail Marys.

58   "Come to the board, please. Give us the value of *C* in this equation."

59   In a stupor of wrenching fear, I felt my legs clumping up the aisle. On all sides the blank faces stared. At the board—totally unfamiliar territory to me—I stared at the first equation I had ever seen up close. It was well over a yard and a half long, lacerated by mysterious crooked lines and fractions in parentheses, with miniature twos and threes hovering above the whole thing like tiny barnacles. *X*s and *Y*s were jumbled in crazy abandon. At the very end of this unholy mess was a tiny equal sign. And on the other side of the equal sign was a zero. Zero! All this crap adds up to nothing! Jesus Christ! My mind reeled at the very sight of this barbed-wire entanglement of mysterious symbols.

60   Pittinger stood to one side, arms folded, wearing an expression that said, At last I've nailed the little bastard! He had been playing with me all the time. He knew!

61   I glanced back at the class. It was one of the truly educational moments of my life. The entire mob, including Schwartz, Chester, and even Zynzmeister, were grinning happily, licking their chops with joyous expectation of my imminent crucifixion. I learned then that when true disaster strikes, we have no friends. And there's nothing a phony loves more in this world than to see another phony get what's coming to him.

62   "The value of *C*, please," rapped Pittinger.

63   The equation blurred before my eyes. The value of *C*. Where the hell was it? What did a *C* look like, anyway? Or an *A* or a *B,* for that matter. I had forgotten the alphabet.

64   "*C*, please."

65   I spotted a single letter *C* buried deep in the writhing melange of *Y*s and *X*s and umlauts and plus signs, brackets, and God knows what all. One tiny *C*. A torrent of sweat raged down my spinal column. My jockey shorts were soaked and sodden with the sweat and stink of execution. Being a true guerrilla from years of the alphabetical ghetto, I showed no outward sign of panic, my face stony: unyielding. You live by the gun, you die by the gun.

66   "*C*, please." Pittinger moodily scratched at his granite chin with thumb and forefinger, his blue beard rasping nastily.

67   "Oh my darling Billy boy, you're the apple of my eye . . ."

68   Somewhere birds twittered on, tennis racquet met tennis ball. My moment had finally arrived.

69   Now, I have to explain that for years I had been the leader of the atheistic free-thinkers of Warren G. Harding School, scoffers all at the Sunday School miracles taught at the Presbyterian church: unbelievers.

70   That miracle stuff is for old ladies, all that walking on water and birds flying around with loaves of bread in their beaks. Who can believe that crap?

71   Now, I am not so sure. Ever since that day in Pittinger's algebra class I have had an uneasy suspicion that maybe something mysterious is going on somehwere.

72   As I stood and stonily gazed at the enigmatic Egyptian hieroglyphics of that fateful equation, from somewhere, someplace beyond the blue horizon, it came to me, out of the mist. I heard my voice say clearly, firmly, with decision:

73   "C . . . is equal to three."

74   Pittinger staggered back; his glasses jolted down to the tip of his nose.

75   "How the hell did you know?!" he bellowed hoarsely, his snap-on bow tie popping loose in the excitement.

76   The class was in an uproar. I caught a glimpse of Schwartz, his face pale with shock. I had caught one on the fat part of the bat. It was a true miracle. I had walked on water.

77   Instantly, the old instincts took over. In a cool, level voice I answered Pittinger's rhetorical question.

78   "Sir, I used empirical means."

79   He paled visibly and clung to the chalk trough for support. On cue, the bell rang out. The class was over. With a swiftness born of long experience, I was out of the room even before the echo of the bell had ceased. The guerrilla's code is always hit and run. A legend had been born.

80   That afternoon, as I sauntered home from school, feeling at least twelve and a half feet tall, Schwartz skulked next to me, silent, moody, kicking at passing frogs. I rubbed salt deep into his wound and sprinkled a little pepper on for good measure. Across the street, admiring clusters of girls pointed out the Algebra King as he strolled by. I heard Eileen Akers's silvery voice clearly: "There he goes. He doesn't say much in class, but when he does he makes it count." I nodded coolly toward my fans. A ripple of applause went up. I autographed a few algebra

books and walked on, tall and straight in the sun. Deep down I knew that this was but a fleeting moment of glory, that when I faced the blue book exam it would be all over, but I enjoyed it while I had it.

81   With the benign air of a baron bestowing largess upon a wretched serf, I offered to buy Schwartz a Fudgesicle at the Igloo. He refused with a snarl.

82   "Why, Schwartz, what seems to be troubling you?" I asked with irony, vigorously working the salt shaker.

83   "You phony son of a bitch. You know what you can do with your goddamn Fudgesicle."

84   "Me, a phony? Why would you say an unkind thing like that?"

85   He spat viciously into a tulip bed. "You phony bastard. You studied!"

86   Inevitably, those of us who are gifted must leave those less fortunate behind in the race of life. I knew that, and Schwartz knew it. Once again I had lapped him and was moving away from the field, if only for a moment.

87   The next morning, Thursday, I swaggered into algebra class with head high. Even Jack Morton, the biggest smart-ass in the class, said hello as I walked in. Mr. Pittinger, his eyes glowing with admiration, smiled warmly at me.

88   "Hi, Pit," I said with a casual flip of the hand. We abstract mathematicians have an unspoken bond. Naturally, I was not called on during that period. After all, I had proved myself beyond any doubt.

89   After class, beaming at me with the intimacy of a fellow quadratic equation zealot, Mr. Pittinger asked me to stay on for a few moments.

90   "All my life I have heard about the born mathematical genius. It is a well-documented thing. They come along once in a while, but I never thought I'd meet one, least of all in a class of mine. Did you always have this ability?"

91   "Well . . ." I smiled modestly.

92   "Look, it would be pointless for you to waste time on our little test tomorrow. Would you help me grade the papers instead?"

93   "Gosh, Pit, I was looking forward to taking it, but if you really need me, I'll be glad to help." It was a master stroke.

94   "I'd appreciate it. I need somebody who really knows his stuff, and most of these kids are faking it."

95   The following afternoon, together, we graded the papers of my peers. I hate to tell you what, in all honesty, I had to do to Schwartz

when I marked his pitiful travesty. I showed no mercy. After all, algebra is an absolute science and there can be no margin for kindness in matters of the mind.

Reading Closely and Thinking Critically

1. Why was Shepherd so happy to meet up with his friends in school?

2. What reason does Shepherd give for being called on the last day of class? Is that the real reason? Explain.

3. Discuss the meaning of the title, being sure to explain the word play that occurs.

4. How would you characterize the tone of "Lost at C"? (See page 37 for an explanation of tone.)

5. Make a list of words and phrases that describe the kind of student Shepherd was in his freshman year. Make another list of words and phrases, this time to describe the kind of teacher Mr. Pittinger was.

6. "Lost at C" is an amusing story, but like all good humor, it points to important truths while it amuses. Cite three humorous passages in the essay that point to truths.

7. What view of American education is presented in "Lost at C"? Is this view as relevant to today's reader as it was to the original audience of 1973? Explain.

Examining Structure and Strategy

1. How does the opening paragraph set the tone of the essay and give the reader an idea of what is in store?

2. Shepherd uses a considerable amount of description in "Lost at C." Cite three examples of description that you find effective, and underline the specific nouns, verbs, and modifiers (see page 72). Next, explain what the description contributes to the essay.

3. Shepherd often uses exaggeration for its comic effect. For example, in paragraph 50, to show that he took notes on the teacher's every utterance, Shepherd says he wrote down "Braaghk." Cite two other examples of exaggeration for comic effect.

4. Explain the irony (strange twist of events) that occurs in the conclusion.

Considering Language and Style

1. What metaphors does Shepherd create in paragraphs 4 and 5? (See page 73 on metaphors.) Do you find these metaphors appropriate? Why or why not?

2. *Proper nouns* give the names of specific people, places, and things. For example, the following are proper nouns: *Easter, Pedro, Washington, Nike.* Cite five proper nouns, other than people's names, that appear in the essay. What do the proper nouns contribute and how do they do so?

3. Consult a dictionary if you are unsure of the meaning of any of these words: *élan* (paragraph 33), *funk* (paragraph 46), *truculence* (paragraph 46), *impervious* (paragraph 47), *intimations* (paragraph 47), *simonize* (paragraph 48), *melange* (paragraph 65), *umlauts* (paragraph 65), *empirical* (paragraph 78), *largesse* (paragraph 81).

For Group Discussion or Writing
How do Shepherd and his friends compare to today's high school students? With some classmates, cite the chief similarities and differences.

Writing Assignments

1. *In your journal.* In a page or so, discuss your own experiences with high school math and whether or not those experiences have had an enduring influence on you.

2. *Using the pattern.* Write a narrative account of a time you were lost and confused in a class. Your story should say something about the nature of education. If you wish, you may use exaggeration for comic effect.

3. *Using the pattern.* Write a narrative account of a time you faked your way through a situation. Explain why you felt you had to pretend and what the consequences were. If you learned anything, explain what.

4. *Using the pattern.* In paragraph 61, Shepherd says that "when true disaster strikes, we have no friends." Write a narration that proves or disproves that statement.

5. *Using the pattern.* Write a narrative account of a time you enjoyed a "moment of glory" (paragraph 80). Be sure to explain what happened, how you reacted, and why you reacted the way that you did. If the moment had an enduring effect on you, you may explain that effect if you wish.

6. *Considering a theme.* How much of what Shepherd says about teachers, students, high school, and the education system is still true today? Cite specific examples to support your view.

7. *Connecting the readings.* Both "Salvation" (page 149) and "Lost at C" narrate an account of young people behaving as fakes. Explain what you think prompts people to be phonies. Also note how prevalent you think fakery is and what its consequences are.

BY ANY OTHER NAME
Santha Rama Rau

Born in India and educated in the United States, Santha Rama Rau is a travel writer, novelist, and essayist who writes of the Eastern experience. Her books include Home to India *(1944),* Remember the House *(1955), and* Gifts of Passage *(1961). In "By Any Other Name" (1951), which takes place during the period of British colonial rule in India, Rau tells of her first and last days as an Indian child in a British school. She relates her experience and informs the reader about the differences between English and Indian life. As you read, notice the description and try to determine what it contributes to the essay.*

THE PATTERNS	THE PURPOSES
narration with description	*to express feelings and relate experience and to inform*

1   At the Anglo-Indian day school in Zorinabad to which my sister and I were sent when she was eight and I was five and a half, they changed our names. On the first day of school, a hot, windless morning of a north Indian September, we stood in the headmistress's study and she said, "Now you're the *new* girls. What are your names?"

2   My sister answered for us. "I am Premila, and she"—nodding in my direction—"is Santha."

3   The headmistress had been in India, I suppose, fifteen years or so, but she still smiled her helpless inability to cope with Indian names. Her rimless half-glasses glittered, and the precarious bun on top of her head trembled as she shook her head. "Oh, my dears, those are much too hard for me. Suppose we give you pretty English names. Wouldn't that be more jolly? Let's see, now—Pamela for you, I think." She shrugged in a baffled way at my sister. "That's as close as I can get. And for *you*," she said to me, "how about Cynthia? Isn't that nice?"

4   My sister was always less easily intimidated than I was, and while she kept a stubborn silence, I said, "Thank you," in a very tiny voice.

5   We had been sent to that school because my father, among his responsibilities as an officer of the civil service, had a tour of duty to

perform in the villages around that steamy little provincial town, where he had his headquarters at the time. He used to make his shorter inspection tours on horseback, and a week before, in the stale heat of a typically postmonsoon day, we had waved good-by to him and a little procession—an assistant, a secretary, two bearers, and the man to look after the bedding rolls and luggage. They rode away through our large garden, still bright green from the rains, and we turned back into the twilight of the house and the sound of fans whispering in every room.

6   Up to then, my mother had refused to send Premila to school in the British-run establishments of that time, because, she used to say, "you can bury a dog's tail for seven years and it still comes out curly, and you can take a Britisher away from his home for a lifetime, and he still remains insular." The examinations and degrees from entirely Indian schools were not, in those days, considered valid. In my case, the question had never come up, and probably never would have come up if Mother's extraordinary good health had not broken down. For the first time in my life, she was not able to continue the lessons she had been giving us every morning. So our Hindi books were put away, the stories of the Lord Krishna as a little boy were left in midair, and we were sent to the Anglo-Indian school.

7   That first day at school is still, when I think of it, a remarkable one. At that age, if one's name is changed, one develops a curious form of dual personality. I remember having a certain detached and disbelieving concern in the actions of "Cynthia," but certainly no responsibility. Accordingly, I followed the thin, erect back of the headmistress down the veranda to my classroom feeling, at most, a passing interest in what was going to happen to me in this strange, new atmosphere of School.

8   The building was Indian in design, with wide verandas opening onto a central courtyard, but Indian verandas are usually whitewashed, with stone floors. These, in the tradition of British schools, were painted dark brown and had matting on the floors. It gave a feeling of extra intensity to the heat.

9   I suppose there were about a dozen Indian children in the school—which contained perhaps forty children in all—and four of them were in my class. They were all sitting at the back of the room, and I went to join them. I sat next to a small, solemn girl who didn't smile at me. She had long, glossy-black braids and wore a cotton dress, but she still kept on her Indian jewelry—a gold chain around her neck, thin gold bracelets, and tiny ruby studs in her ears. Like most Indian

children, she had a rim of black kohl around her eyes. The cotton dress should have looked strange, but all I could think of was that I should ask my mother if I couldn't wear a dress to school, too, instead of my Indian clothes.

10   I can't remember too much about the proceedings in class that day, except for the beginning. The teacher pointed to me and asked me to stand up. "Now, dear, tell the class your name."

11   I said nothing.

12   "Come along," she said frowning slightly. "What's your name, dear?"

13   "I don't know," I said finally.

14   The English children in the front of the class—there were about eight or ten of them—giggled and twisted around in their chairs to look at me. I sat down quickly, and opened my eyes very wide, hoping in that way to dry them off. The little girl with the braids put out her hand and very lightly touched my arm. She still didn't smile.

15   Most of that morning I was rather bored. I looked briefly at the children's drawings pinned to the wall, and then concentrated on a lizard clinging to the ledge of the high, barred window behind the teacher's head. Occasionally it would shoot out its long yellow tongue for a fly, and then it would rest, with its eyes closed and its belly palpitating, as though it were swallowing several times quickly. The lessons were mostly concerned with reading and writing and simple numbers—things that my mother had already taught me—and I paid very little attention. The teacher wrote on the easel blackboard words like "bat" and "cat," which seemed babyish to me; only "apple" was new and incomprehensible.

16   When it was time for the lunch recess, I followed the girl with braids out onto the veranda. There the children from the other classes were assembled. I saw Premila at once and ran over to her, as she had charge of our lunchbox. The children were all opening packages and sitting down to eat sandwiches. Premila and I were the only ones who had Indian food—thin wheat chapatties, some vegetable curry, and a bottle of buttermilk. Premila thrust half of it into my hand and whispered fiercely that I should go and sit with my class, because that was what the others seemed to be doing.

17   The enormous black eyes of the little Indian girl from my class looked at my food longingly, so I offered her some. But she only shook her head and plowed her way solemnly through her sandwiches.

18   I was very sleepy after lunch, because at home we always took a siesta. It was usually a pleasant time of day, with the bedroom darkened against the harsh afternoon sun, the drifting off into sleep with the sound of Mother's voice reading a story in one's mind, and, finally, the shrill, fussy voice of the ayah waking one for tea.

19   At school, we rested for a short time on low, folding cots on the veranda, and then we were expected to play games. During the hot part of the afternoon we played indoors, and after the shadows had begun to lengthen and the slight breeze of the evening had come up we moved outside to the wide courtyard.

20   I had never really grasped the system of competitive games. At home whenever we played tag or guessing games, I was always allowed to "win"—"because," Mother used to tell Premila, "she is the youngest, and we have to allow for that." I had often heard her say it, and it seemed quite reasonable to me, but the result was that I had no clear idea of what "winning" meant.

21   When we played twos-and-threes that afternoon at school, in accordance with my training, I let one of the small English boys catch me, but was naturally rather puzzled when the other children did not return the courtesy. I ran about for what seemed like hours without ever catching anyone, until it was time for school to close. Much later I learned that my attitude was called "not being a good sport," and I stopped allowing myself to be caught, but it was not for years that I really learned the spirit of the thing.

22   When I saw our car come up to the school gate, I broke away from my classmates and rushed toward it yelling, "Ayah! Ayah!" It seemed like an eternity since I had seen her that morning—a wizened, affectionate figure in her white cotton sari, giving me dozens of urgent and useless instructions on how to be a good girl at school. Premila followed more sedately, and she told me on the way home never to do that again in front of the other children.

23   When we got home we went straight to Mother's high, white room to have tea with her, and I immediately climbed onto the bed and bounced gently up and down on the springs. Mother asked how we had liked our first day in school. I was so pleased to be home and to have left that peculiar Cynthia behind that I had nothing whatever to say about school, except to ask what "apple" meant. But Premila told Mother about the classes, and added that in her class they had weekly tests to see if they learned their lessons well.

24   I asked, "What's a test?"

25   Premila said, "You're too small to have them. You won't have them in your class for donkey's years." She had learned the expression that day and was using it for the first time. We all laughed enormously at her wit. She also told Mother, in an aside, that we should take sandwiches to school the next day. Not, she said, that *she* minded. But they would be simpler for me to handle.

26   That whole lovely evening I didn't think about school at all. I sprinted barefoot across the lawns with my favorite playmate, the cook's son, to the stream at the end of the garden. We quarreled in our usual way, waded in the tepid water under the lime trees, and waited for the night to bring out the smell of the jasmine. I listened with fascination to his stories of ghosts and demons, until I was too frightened to cross the garden alone in the semidarkness. The ayah found me, shouted at the cook's son, scolded me, hurried me into supper—it was an entirely usual, wonderful evening.

27   It was a week later, the day of Premila's first test, that our lives changed rather abruptly. I was sitting at the back of my class, in my usual inattentive way, only half listening to the teacher. I had started a rather guarded friendship with the girl with the braids, whose name turned out to be Nalini (Nancy, in school). The three other Indian children were already fast friends. Even at that age it was apparent to all of us that friendship with the English or Anglo-Indian children was out of the question. Occasionally, during the class, my new friend and I would draw pictures and show them to each other secretly.

28   The door opened sharply and Premila marched in. At first, the teacher smiled at her in a kindly and encouraging way and said, "Now, you're little Cynthia's sister?"

29   Premila didn't even look at her. She stood with her feet planted firmly apart and her shoulders rigid, and addressed herself directly to me. "Get up," she said. "We're going home."

30   I didn't know what had happened, but I was aware that it was a crisis of some sort. I rose obediently and started to walk toward my sister.

31   "Bring your pencils and your notebook," she said.

32   I went back for them, and together we left the room. The teacher started to say something just as Premila closed the door, but we didn't wait to hear what it was.

33   In complete silence we left the school grounds and started to walk home. Then I asked Premila what the matter was. All she would say was "We're going home for good."

34   It was a very tiring walk for a child of five and a half, and I dragged along behind Premila with my pencils growing sticky in my hand. I can still remember looking at the dusty hedges, and the tangles of thorns in the ditches by the side of the road, smelling the faint fragrance from the eucalyptus trees and wondering whether we would ever reach home. Occasionally a horse-drawn tonga passed us, and the women, in their pink or green silks, stared at Premila and me trudging along on the side of the road. A few coolies and a line of women carrying baskets of vegetables on their heads smiled at us. But it was nearing the hottest time of day, and the road was almost deserted. I walked more and more slowly, and shouted to Premila, from time to time, "Wait for me!" with increasing peevishness. She spoke to me only once, and that was to tell me to carry my notebook on my head, because of the sun.

35   When we got to our house the ayah was just taking a tray of lunch into Mother's room. She immediately started a long, worried questioning about what are you children doing back here at this hour of the day.

36   Mother looked very startled and very concerned, and asked Premila what had happened.

37   Premila said, "We had our test today, and she made me and the other Indians sit at the back of the room, with a desk between each one."

38   Mother said, "Why was that, darling?"

39   "She said it was because Indians cheat," Premila added. "So I don't think we should go back to that school."

40   Mother looked very distant, and was silent a long time. At last she said, "Of course not, darling." She sounded displeased.

41   We all shared the curry she was having for lunch, and afterward I was sent off to the beautifully familiar bedroom for my siesta. I could hear Mother and Premila talking through the open door.

42   Mother said, "Do you suppose she understood all that?"

43   Premila said, "I shouldn't think so. She's a baby."

44   Mother said, "Well, I hope it won't bother her."

45   Of course, they were both wrong. I understood it perfectly, and I remember it all very clearly. But I put it happily away, because it had all happened to a girl called Cynthia, and I never was really particularly interested in her.

Reading Closely and Thinking Critically

1. Explain the significance of the narration. Where is that significance mentioned?

2. What differences in temperament and personality are there between Santha and Premila?

3. What are the cultural differences between the way the Indian and British students approach games?

4. In paragraph 13, Santha says that she did not know her name. How do you account for this lapse?

5. Explain the significance of the essay's title.

6. What does the headmistress's behavior tell you about the attitudes of some British in India?

7. Using the information in the essay, what can you conclude about how British rule affected Indian society?

8. Although about the colonial experience in India, "By Any Other Name" has a message that is relevant in all times and places. What is that message?

Examining Structure and Strategy

1. What purpose does the first sentence of the essay serve? At what point does the actual narration begin?

2. Several paragraphs give the reader background information and helpful explanations. Cite three such paragraphs. How do these paragraphs address the needs of Rau's audience?

3. Which answers to the journalist's questions (who?, what?, when?, where?, why?, how?) are emphasized the most?

4. What does the conversation contribute to the essay?

5. Paragraphs 16, 26, and 27 contain topic sentences. What are those topic sentences and what purpose do they serve?

6. What approach does Rau take to her conclusion?

Considering Language and Style

1. A considerable amount of description appears in the essay. Which paragraphs include description? Select one of the descriptive passages and tell what it contributes to the essay.

2. Consult a dictionary if you are unsure of the meaning of any of these words: *precarious* (paragraph 3), *intimidated* (paragraph 4), *insular* (paragraph 6), *veranda* (paragraph 7), *kohl* (paragraph 9), *ayah* (paragraph 18).

For Group Discussion or Writing

Santha and Premila each coped with discrimination in her own way. With three or four of your classmates, discuss how each girl dealt with discrimination at school. Then go on to consider the advantages and disadvantages of each coping strategy. Report your conclusions to the rest of the class.

Writing Assignments

1. *In your journal.* In paragraph 6, Santha mentions that her mother at first did not send Premila to British schools, saying, "You can bury a dog's tail for seven years and it still comes out curly, and you can take a Britisher away from his home for a lifetime, and he still remains insular." Explain what you think the mother's comment means.

2. *Using the pattern.* Like Rau, tell a story about a school event that had a significant impact on you. Be sure to make clear what the significance of your narration is by mentioning the impact.

3. *Using the pattern.* If you have experienced or witnessed prejudice, narrate an account of how you or others responded to the prejudice.

4. *Using the pattern.* Narrate a story about a time you saw a teacher show a lack of interest or a disregard for students. If possible, use conversation and description for vividness. As an alternative, narrate a story that shows how interested and caring a teacher can be.

5. *Using the pattern.* Was there ever a time when, like Santha and Premila, you felt isolated, as if you did not fit in? If so, narrate a story that relates the experience or informs the reader of what it is like to be isolated.

6. *Considering a theme.* The school in "By Any Other Name" is a reflection of the larger society in India at the time. Thus, the intolerance and insensitivity of the teacher reflect the same features

in the world outside the school. Look back on the school system you were in and write an essay that shows in what ways that system reflected the attitudes and values of society. Be sure to back up your points with specific examples.

7. *Connecting the readings.* Using the information in "By Any Other Name" and "Shades of Black" (page 469), along with your own experience and observation, explain what school is like for students who are different in some way from the majority of the class.

A HANGING
George Orwell

George Orwell (1903–1950), the pen name of Eric Arthur Blair, was a jour-
nalist and writer of autobiographical narratives best remembered for two
great works of fiction: Animal Farm *(1944) and* Nineteen Eighty Four
(1949). Orwell was born in India, where his father was in the British civil
service. Rather than attend college in England, Orwell elected to join the
British imperial police and was stationed in Burma. His experience provided
the substance of "A Hanging," which was written in 1931. During World War
II, Orwell was a writer for the British Broadcasting Company and a literary
editor for the London Tribune. *In "A Hanging," Orwell relates his experi-*
ence and expresses his feelings at the hanging of a prisoner. He also informs
the reader of what the hanging was like in order to persuade his audience that
capital punishment is wrong. As you read, notice the description and deter-
mine what it contributes.

THE PATTERNS	THE PURPOSES
narration with description	*to express feelings and relate experience, to inform, and to persuade*

1   It was in Burma, a sodden morning of the rains. A sickly light,
like yellow tinfoil, was slanting over the high walls into the jail yard.
We were waiting outside the condemned cells, a row of sheds fronted
with double bars, like small animal cages. Each cell measured about ten
feet by ten and was quite bare within except for a plank bed and a pot
for drinking water. In some of them brown, silent men were squatting
at the inner bars, with their blankets draped round them. These were
the condemned men, due to be hanged within the next week or two.
2   One prisoner had been brought out of his cell. He was a Hindu,
a puny wisp of a man, with a shaven head and vague liquid eyes. He
had a thick, sprouting mustache, absurdly too big for his body, rather
like the mustache of a comic man on the films. Six tall Indian warders
were guarding him and getting him ready for the gallows. Two of them
stood by with rifles and fixed bayonets, while the others handcuffed

him, passed a chain through his handcuffs and fixed it to their belts, and lashed his arms tight to his sides. They crowded very close about him, with their hands always on him in a careful, caressing grip, as though all the while feeling him to make sure he was there. It was like men handling a fish which is still alive and may jump back into the water. But he stood quite unresisting, yielding his arms limply to the ropes, as though he hardly noticed what was happening.

3   Eight o'clock struck and a bugle call, desolately thin in the wet air, floated from the distant barracks. The superintendent of the jail, who was standing apart from the rest of us, moodily prodding the gravel with his stick, raised his head at the sound. He was an army doctor, with a gray toothbrush mustache and a gruff voice. "For God's sake, hurry up, Francis," he said irritably. "The man ought to have been dead by this time. Aren't you ready yet?"

4   Francis, the head jailer, a fat Dravidian[1] in a white drill suit and gold spectacles, waved his black hand. "Yes sir, yes sir," he bubbled. "All iss satisfactorily prepared. The hangman iss waiting. We shall proceed."

5   "Well, quick march, then. The prisoners can't get their breakfast until this job's over."

6   We set out for the gallows. Two warders marched on either side of the prisoner, with their rifles at the slope; two others marched close against him, gripping him by the arm and shoulder, as though at once pushing and supporting him. The rest of us, magistrates and the like, followed behind. Suddenly, when we had gone ten yards, the procession stopped short without any order or warning. A dreadful thing had happened—a dog, come goodness knows whence, had appeared in the yard. It came bounding among us with a loud volley of barks and leapt round us wagging its whole body, wild with glee at finding so many human beings together. It was a large woolly dog, half Airedale, half pariah. For a moment it pranced around us, and then, before anyone could stop it, it had made a dash for the prisoner, and jumping up tried to lick his face. Everybody stood aghast, too taken aback even to grab the dog.

7   "Who let that bloody brute in here?" said the superintendent angrily. "Catch it, someone!"

8   A warder detached from the escort, charged clumsily after the dog, but it danced and gamboled just out of his reach, taking

---

[1]A native speaker of one of the southern Indian languages.

everything as part of the game. A young Eurasian jailer picked up a handful of gravel and tried to stone the dog away, but it dodged the stones and came after us again. Its yaps echoed from the jail walls. The prisoner, in the grasp of the two warders, looked on incuriously, as though this was another formality of the hanging. It was several minutes before someone managed to catch the dog. Then we put my handkerchief through its collar and moved off once more, with the dog still straining and whimpering.

9   It was about forty yards to the gallows. I watched the bare brown back of the prisoner marching in front of me. He walked clumsily with his bound arms, but quite steadily, with that bobbing gait of the Indian who never straightens his knees. At each step his muscles slid neatly into place, the lock of hair on his scalp danced up and down, his feet printed themselves on the wet gravel. And once, in spite of the men who gripped him by each shoulder, he stepped lightly aside to avoid a puddle on the path.

10   It is curious; but till that moment I had never realized what it means to destroy a healthy, conscious man. When I saw the prisoner step aside to avoid the puddle, I saw the mystery, the unspeakable wrongness, of cutting a life short when it is in full tide. This man was not dying, he was alive just as we are alive. All the organs of his body were working—bowels digesting food, skin renewing itself, nails growing, tissues forming—all toiling away in solemn foolery. His nails would still be growing when he stood on the drop, when he was falling through the air with a tenth-of-a-second to live. His eyes saw the yellow gravel and the gray walls, and his brain still remembered, foresaw, reasoned—even about puddles. He and we were a party of men walking together, seeing, hearing, feeling, understanding the same world; and in two minutes, with a sudden snap, one of us would be gone—one mind less, one world less.

11   The gallows stood in a small yard, separate from the main grounds of the prison, and overgrown with tall prickly weeds. It was a brick erection like three sides of a shed, with planking on top, and above that two beams and a crossbar with the rope dangling. The hangman, a gray-haired convict in the white uniform of the prison, was waiting beside his machine. He greeted us with a servile crouch as we entered. At a word from Francis the two warders, gripping the prisoner more closely than ever, half led, half pushed him to the gallows and helped him clumsily up the ladder. Then the hangman climbed up and fixed the rope round the prisoner's neck.

12   We stood waiting, five yards away. The warders had formed in a rough circle round the gallows. And then, when the noose was fixed, the prisoner began crying out to his god. It was a high, reiterated cry of "Ram! Ram! Ram! Ram!"[2] not urgent and fearful like a prayer or cry for help, but steady, rhythmical, almost like the tolling of a bell. The dog answered the sound with a whine. The hangman, still standing on the gallows, produced a small cotton bag like a flour bag and drew it down over the prisoner's face. But the sound, muffled by the cloth, still persisted, over and over again: "Ram! Ram! Ram! Ram! Ram!"

13   The hangman climbed down and stood ready, holding the lever. Minutes seemed to pass. The steady, muffled crying from the prisoner went on and on, "Ram! Ram! Ram!" never faltering for an instant. The superintendent, his head on his chest, was slowly poking the ground with his stick; perhaps he was counting the cries, allowing the prisoner a fixed number—fifty, perhaps, or a hundred. Everyone had changed color. The Indians had gone gray like bad coffee, and one or two of the bayonets were wavering. We looked at the lashed, hooded man on the drop, and listened to his cries—each cry another second of life; the same thought was in all our minds; oh, kill him quickly, get it over, stop that abominable noise!

14   Suddenly the superintendent made up his mind. Throwing up his head he made a swift motion with his stick "Chalo!"[3] he shouted almost fiercely.

15   There was a clanking noise, and then dead silence. The prisoner had vanished, and the rope was twisting on itself. I let go of the dog, and it galloped immediately to the back of the gallows; but when it got there it stopped short, barked, and then retreated into a corner of the yard, where it stood among the weeds, looking timorously out at us. We went round the gallows to inspect the prisoner's body. He was dangling with his toes pointed straight downwards, very slowly revolving, as dead as a stone.

16   The superintendent reached out with his stick and poked the bare brown body; it oscillated slightly. "*He's* all right," said the superintendent. He backed out from under the gallows, and blew out a deep breath. The moody look had gone out of his face quite suddenly. He

---

[2]The prisoner calls upon Rama, Hindu god who sustains and preserves.
[3](Hindi) "Hurry up!"

glanced at his wristwatch. "Eight minutes past eight. Well, that's all for this morning, thank God."

17   The warders unfixed bayonets and marched away. The dog, sobered and conscious of having misbehaved itself, slipped after them. We walked out of the gallows yard, past the condemned cells with their waiting prisoners, into the big central yard of the prison. The convicts, under the command of warders armed with lathis,[4] were already receiving their breakfast. They squatted in long rows, each man holding a tin pannikin,[5] while two warders with buckets marched around ladling out rice; it seemed quite a homely, jolly scene, after the hanging. An enormous relief had come upon us now that the job was done. One felt an impulse to sing, to break into a run, to snigger. All at once everyone began chattering gaily.

18   The Eurasian boy walking beside me nodded toward the way we had come, with a knowing smile: "Do you know, sir, our friend" (he meant the dead man) "when he heard his appeal had been dismissed, he pissed on the floor of his cell. From fright. Kindly take one of my cigarettes, sir. Do you not admire my new silver case, sir? From the boxwallah, two rupees eight annas. Classy European style."

19   Several people laughed—at what, nobody seemed certain.

20   Francis was walking by the superintendent, talking garrulously; "Well, sir, all has passed off with the utmost satisfactoriness. It was all finished—flick! Like that. It iss not always so—oah, no! I have known cases where the doctor wass obliged to go beneath the gallows and pull the prisoner's legs to ensure decease. Most disagreeable!"

21   "Wriggling about, eh? That's bad," said the superintendent.

22   "Ach, sir, it iss worse when they become refractory! One man, I recall, clung to the bars of his cage when we went to take him out. You will scarcely credit, sir, that it took six warders to dislodge him, three pulling at each leg. We reasoned with him, 'My dear fellow,' we said, 'think of all the pain and trouble you are causing to us!' But no, he would not listen! Ach, he wass very troublesome!"

23   I found that I was laughing quite loudly. Everyone was laughing. Even the superintendent grinned in a tolerant way. "You'd better all come out and have a drink," he said quite genially. "I've got a bottle of whiskey in the car. We could do with it."

---

[4]Policemen's wooden clubs.
[5]Small pan.

24   We went through the big double gates of the prison into the road. "Pulling at his legs!" exclaimed a Burmese magistrate suddenly, and burst into a loud chuckling. We all began laughing again. At that moment Francis' anecdote seemed extraordinarily funny. We all had a drink together, native and European alike, quite amicably. The dead man was a hundred yards away.

Reading Closely and Thinking Critically

1. What is Orwell's attitude toward capital punishment? What is his attitude toward the condemned prisoners? How can you tell what these attitudes are?

2. Why does the superintendent say that he wants Francis and the other guards to hurry and get the prisoner to the gallows? Do you think the reason he gives is the real one? Explain.

3. Why do you think Orwell calls the appearance of the dog "a dreadful thing"?

4. What is the significance of the condemned man stepping aside "to avoid the puddle" (paragraph 10)?

5. Why are the spectators so unnerved by the prisoner's repeated calls to his God?

6. How would you describe the superintendent's attitude toward the prisoner and the execution?

7. Of what significance is the fact that the natives and Europeans had a drink together after the hanging (paragraph 24)?

8. What do you see as the significance of the narration?

Examining Structure and Strategy

1. Orwell uses a considerable amount of description in the essay. Cite an example and explain what the description contributes.

2. Orwell often uses conversation in the essay. What purpose does this conversation serve?

3. How would you describe the tone of "A Hanging"? (See page 37 on tone.)

4. What is the effect of the last two sentences of the essay? Do you think they help Orwell fulfill his persuasive purpose? Explain.

5. Would the narration have been more effective—that is, would Orwell have better achieved his persuasive purpose—if he had said what crime the prisoner had committed? Explain.

Considering Language and Style

1. Paragraph 1 includes two similes (see page 73 on similes). What are they and what do they contribute?

2. Consult a dictionary if you are unsure of the meaning of any of these words: *sodden* (paragraph 1), *pariah* (paragraph 6), *gamboled* (paragraph 8), *incuriously* (paragraph 8), *timorously* (paragraph 15), *oscillated* (paragraph 16), *garrulously* (paragraph 20), *refractory* (paragraph 22).

For Group Discussion or Writing

How does "A Hanging" present an argument against capital punishment? Cite the specific features of the essay that help Orwell make his case and then go on to explain how readers are likely to respond to those strategies.

Writing Assignments

1. *In your journal.* Do you believe in the death penalty? Explain why or why not in a page of your journal. As an alternative, explain whether your opinion about the death penalty has changed as a result of reading "A Hanging."

2. *Using the pattern.* "A Hanging" is a narration meant to persuade the reader that capital punishment is wrong. Tell a story of your own to persuade the reader of the injustice of something: cheating, grades, final exams, college admission procedures, Little League tryouts, student council elections, hazing, and so on.

3. *Using the pattern.* In "A Hanging," Orwell recognizes that capital punishment is wrong. Narrate an account of a time you came to realize something important.

4. *Using the pattern.* The men who witnessed and supervised the hanging were clearly uncomfortable, which helps explain their behavior before, during, and after the execution. Tell a story about an event to which witnesses had a strong reaction (an accident, a death, an embarrassing moment, an argument, for example) and show how the people witnessing the event behaved.

5. *Using the pattern.* Orwell's narration tells of oppression. If you have witnessed or experienced oppression or discrimination, tell a story that relates what you witnessed or experienced.

6. *Considering a theme.* Using the evidence in the essay, explain Orwell's attitude toward capital punishment. Then go on to agree or disagree with him, making clear why you hold your view. (Your preceding journal entry may give you ideas.)

7. *Connecting the readings.* What do "A Hanging" and "By Any Other Name" (page 167) reveal about the attitude of the British toward the native populations they ruled? Why do you think the British felt and behaved the way they did? Have you seen a similar attitude in anyone you know? Explain and tell what can be done to eliminate these attitudes.

THE WATER-FAUCET VISION
Gish Jen

Gish Jen was born in 1956. In 1990, the Atlantic Monthly *honored Jen by naming her one of the new generation's most prominent writers. She is also the recipient of the National Book Critics Circle Award. In 1991, she published her novel* Typical American, *which was followed by* Mona in the Promised Land *in 1996. In "The Water-Faucet Vision," a short story which was published in 1987, Jen narrates several childhood memories centered on family and religion. It is a story that both entertains and informs. As you read, consider how your own religious beliefs (or lack of them) have influenced you.*

THE PATTERN	THE PURPOSES
narration	*to entertain and to inform*

1   To protect my sister Mona and me from the pains—or, as they pronounced it, the "pins"—of life, my parents did their fighting in Shanghai dialect, which we didn't understand; and when my father one day pitched a brass vase through the kitchen window, my mother told us he had done it by accident.

2   "By accident?" said Mona.

3   My mother chopped the foot off a mushroom.

4   "By accident?" said Mona. "By *accident?*"

5   Later I tried to explain to her that she shouldn't have persisted like that, but it was hopeless.

6   "What's the matter with throwing things?" She shrugged. "He was *mad.*"

7   That was the difference between Mona and me: fighting was just fighting to her. If she worried about anything, it was only that she might turn out too short to become a ballerina, in which case she was going to be a piano player.

8   I, on the other hand, was going to be a martyr. I was in fifth grade then, and the hyperimaginative sort—the kind of girl who grows morbid in Catholic school, who longs to be chopped or frozen to death but then has nightmares about it from which she wakes up screaming and clutching a stuffed bear. It was not a bear that I clutched, though,

but a string of three malachite beads that I had found in the marsh by the old aqueduct one day. Apparently once part of a necklace, they were each wonderfully striated and swirled, and slightly humped toward the center, like a jellyfish; so that if I squeezed one it would slip smoothly away, with a grace that altogether enthralled and—on those dream-harrowed nights—soothed me, soothed me as nothing had before or has since. Not that I've lacked occasion for soothing: though it's been four months since my mother died, there are still nights when sleep stands away from me, stiff as a well-paid sentry. But that is another story. Back then I had my malachite beads, and if I worried them long and patiently enough, I was sure to start feeling better, more awake, even a little special—imagining, as I liked to, that my nightmares were communications from the Almighty Himself, preparation for my painful destiny. Discussing them with Patty Creamer, who had also promised her life to God, I called them "almost visions"; and Patty, her mouth wadded with the three or four sticks of Doublemint she always seemed to have going at once, said, "I bet you'll be doin' miracleth by seventh grade."

9   Miracles. Today Patty laughs to think she ever spent good time stewing on such matters, her attention having long turned to rugs, and artwork, and antique Japanese bureaus—things she believes in.

10   "A good bureau's more than just a bureau," she explained last time we had lunch. "It's a hedge against life. I tell you: if there's one thing I believe, it's that cheap stuff's just money out the window. Nice stuff, on the other hand—now that you can always cash out, if life gets rough. *That* you can count on."

11   In fifth grade, though, she counted on different things.

12   "You'll be doing miracles too," I told her, but she shook her shaggy head and looked doleful.

13   "Na' me," she chomped. "Buzzit's okay. The kin' things I like, prayers work okay on."

14   "Like?"

15   "Like you 'member the dreth I liked?"

16   She meant the yellow one, with the crisscross straps.

17   "Well gueth what."

18   "Your mom got it for you."

19   She smiled. "And I only jutht prayed for it for a week," she said.

20   As for myself, though, I definitely wanted to be able to perform a wonder or two. Miracle-working! It was the carrot of carrots: it kept me doing my homework, taking the sacraments; it kept me mournfully

on key in music hour, while my classmates hiccuped and squealed their carefree hearts away. Yet I couldn't have said what I wanted such powers *for,* exactly. That is, I thought of them the way one might think of, say, an ornamental sword—as a kind of collectible, which also happened to be a means of defense.

21   But then Patty's father walked out on her mother, and for the first time, there was a miracle I wanted to do. I wanted it so much I could see it: Mr. Creamer made into a spitball; Mr. Creamer shot through a straw into the sky; Mr. Creamer unrolled and replumped, plop back on Patty's doorstep. I would've cleaned out his mind and given him a shave en route. I would've given him a box of peanut fudge, tied up with a ribbon, to present to Patty with a kiss.

22   But instead all I could do was try to tell her he'd come back.

23   "He will not, he will not!" she sobbed. "He went on a boat to Rio Deniro. To Rio Deniro!"

24   I tried to offer her a stick of gum, but she wouldn't take it.

25   "He said he would rather look at water than at my mom's fat face. He said he would rather look at water than at me." Now she was really wailing, and holding her ribs so tightly that she almost seemed to be hurting herself—so tightly that just looking at her arms wound around her like snakes made my heart feel squeezed.

26   I patted her on the arm. A one-winged pigeon waddled by.

27   "He said I wasn't even his kid, he said I came from Uncle Johnny. He said I was garbage, just like my mom and Uncle Johnny. He said I wasn't even his kid, he said I wasn't his Patty, he said I came from Uncle Johnny!"

28   "From your Uncle Johnny?" I asked stupidly.

29   "From Uncle Johnny," she cried, "From Uncle Johnny!"

30   "He said that?" I said. Then, wanting to go on, to say *something,* I said, "Oh Patty, don't cry."

31   She kept crying.

32   I tried again. "Oh Patty, don't cry," I said. Then I said, "Your dad was a jerk anyway."

33   The pigeon produced a large runny dropping.

34   It was a good twenty minutes before Patty was calm enough for me just to run to the girls' room to get her some toilet paper; and by the time I came back she was sobbing again, saying "to Rio Deniro, to Rio Deniro" over and over again, as though the words had stuck in her and couldn't be gotten out. As we had missed the regular bus home and

the late bus too, I had to leave her a second time to go call my mother, who was mad only until she heard what had happened. Then she came and picked us up, and bought us each a Fudgsicle.

35   Some days later, Patty and I started a program to work on getting her father home. It was a serious business. We said extra prayers, and lit votive candles; I tied my malachite beads to my uniform belt, fondling them as though they were a rosary, I a nun. We even took to walking about the school halls with our hands folded—a sight so ludicrous that our wheeze of a principal personally took us aside one day.

36   "I must tell you," she said, using her nose as a speaking tube, "that there is really no need for such peee-ity."

37   But we persisted, promising to marry God and praying to every saint we could think of. We gave up gum, then gum and Slim Jims both, then gum and Slim Jims and ice cream—and when even that didn't work, we started on more innovative things. The first was looking at flowers. We held our hands beside our eyes like blinders as we hurried by the violets by the flagpole, the window box full of tulips outside the nurse's office. Next it was looking at boys: Patty gave up angel-eyed Jamie Halloran and I, gymnastic Anthony Rossi. It was hard, but in the end our efforts paid off. Mr. Creamer came back a month later, and though he brought with him nothing but dysentery, he was at least too sick to have all that much to say.

38   Then, in the course of a fight with my father, my mother somehow fell out of their bedroom window.

39   Recently—thinking a mountain vacation might cheer me—I sublet my apartment to a handsome but somber newlywed couple, who turned out to be every bit as responsible as I'd hoped. They cleaned out even the eggshell chips I'd sprinkled around the base of my plants as fertilizer, leaving behind only a shiny silverplate cake server and a list of their hopes and goals for the summer. The list, tacked precariously to the back of the kitchen door, began with a fervent appeal to God to help them get their wedding thank-yous written in three weeks or less. (You could see they had originally written "two weeks" but scratched it out—no miracles being demanded here.) It went on:

> Please help us, Almighty Father in Heaven Above, to get Ann a teaching job within a half-hour drive of here in a nice neighborhood.
> Please help us, Almighty Father in Heaven Above, to get John a job doing anything where he won't strain his back and that is within a half-hour drive of here.

Please help us, Almighty Father in Heaven, Above, to get us a car.
Please help us, A.F. in H.A., to learn French.

Please help us, A.F. in H.A., to find seven dinner recipes that cost less than 60 cents a serving and can be made in a half-hour. And that don't have tomatoes, since You in Your Heavenly Wisdom made John allergic.

Please help us, A.F. in H.A., to avoid books in this apartment such as You in Your Heavenly Wisdom allowed John, for Your Heavenly Reasons, to find three nights ago (June 2nd).

Et cetera. In the left-hand margin they kept score of how they had fared with their requests, and it was heartening to see that nearly all of them were marked "Yes! Praise the Lord" (sometimes shortened to PTL), with the sole exception of learning French, which was mysteriously marked "No! PTL to the Highest."

40   That note touched me. Strange and familiar both, it seemed like it had been written by some cousin of mine—some cousin who had stayed home to grow up, say, while I went abroad and learned what I had to, though the learning was painful. This, of course, is just a manner of speaking; in fact I did my growing up at home, like anybody else.

41   But the learning *was* painful: I never knew exactly how it happened that my mother went hurtling through the air that night years ago, only that the wind had been chopping at the house, and that the argument had started about the state of the roof. Someone had been up to fix it the year before, but it wasn't a roofer, it was some man my father insisted could do just as good a job for a quarter of the price. And maybe he could have, had he not somehow managed to step through a knot in the wood under the shingles and break his uninsured ankle. Now the shingles were coming loose again, and the attic insulation was mildewing besides, and my father was wanting to sell the house altogether, which he said my mother had wanted to buy so she could send pictures of it home to her family in China.

42   "The Americans have a saying," he said. "They saying, 'You have to keep up with the Jones family,' I'm saying if Jones family in Shanghai, you can send any picture you want, *an-y* picture. Go take picture of those rich guys' house. You want to act like rich guys, right? Go take picture of those rich guys' house."

43   At that point my mother sent Mona and me to wash up, and started speaking Shanghaiese. They argued for some time in the kitchen while we listened from the top of the stairs, our faces wedged between the bumpy Spanish scrolls of the wrought-iron railing. First my mother

ranted, then my father, then they both ranted at once until finally there was a thump, followed by a long quiet.

44   "Do you think they're kissing now?" said Mona. "I bet they're kissing, like this." She pursed her lips like a fish and was about to put them to the railing when we heard my mother locking the back door. We hightailed it into bed; my parents creaked up the stairs. Everything at that point seemed fine. Once in their bedroom, though, they started up again, first softly, then louder and louder, until my mother turned on a radio to try to disguise the noise. A door slammed; they began shouting at one another; another door slammed; a shoe or something banged the wall behind Mona's bed.

45   "How're we supposed to *sleep?*" said Mona, sitting up.

46   There was another thud, more yelling in Shanghaiese, and then my mother's voice pierced the wall, in English. "So what you want I should do? Go to work like Theresa Lee?"

47   My father rumbled something back.

48   "You think you're big shot because you have job, right? You're big shot, but you never get promotion, you never get raise. All I do is spend money, right? So what do you do, you tell me. So what do you do!"

49   Something hit the floor so hard that our room shook.

50   "So kill me," screamed my mother. "You know what you are? You are failure. Failure! You are failure!"

51   Then there was a sudden, terrific bursting crash—and after it, as if on a bungled cue, the serene blare of an a capella soprano, picking her way down a scale.

52   By the time Mona and I knew to look out the window, a neighbor's pet beagle was already on the scene, sniffing and barking at my mother's body, his tail crazy with excitement; then he was barking at my stunned and trembling father, at the shrieking ambulance, the police, at crying Mona in her bunnyfooted pajamas, and at me, barefoot in the cold grass, squeezing her shoulder with one hand and clutching my malachite beads with the other.

53   My mother wasn't dead, only unconscious, the paramedics figured that out right away, but there was blood everywhere, and though they were reassuring about her head wounds as they strapped her to the stretcher, commenting also on how small she was, how delicate, how light, my father kept saying, "I killed her, I killed her" as the ambulance screeched and screeched headlong, forever, to the hospital. I

was afraid to touch her, and glad of the metal rail between us, even though its sturdiness made her seem even frailer than she was; I wished she was bigger, somehow, and noticed, with a pang, that the new red slippers we had given her for Mother's Day had been lost somewhere along the way. How much she seemed to be leaving behind as we careened along—still not there, still not there—Mona and Dad and the medic and I taking up the whole ambulance, all the room, so there was no room for anything else; no room even for my mother's real self, the one who should have been pinching the color back to my father's grey face, the one who should have been calming Mona's cowlick—the one who should have been bending over us, to help us to be strong, to help us get through, even as we bent over her.

54   Then suddenly we were there, the glowing square of the emergency room entrance opening like the gates of heaven; and immediately the talk of miracles began. Alive, a miracle. No bones broken, a miracle. A miracle that the hemlocks cushioned her fall, a miracle that they hadn't been trimmed in a year and a half. It was a miracle that all that blood, the blood that had seemed that night to be everywhere, was from one shard of glass, a single shard, can you imagine, and as for the gash in her head, the scar would be covered by hair. The next day my mother cheerfully described just how she would part it so that nothing would show at all.

55   "You're a lucky duck-duck," agreed Mona, helping herself, with a little *pirouette,* to the cherry atop my mother's chocolate pudding.

56   That wasn't enough for me, though. I was relieved, yes, but what I wanted by then was a real miracle, not for her simply to have survived, but for the whole thing never to have happened—for my mother's head never to have had to be shaved and bandaged like that, for her high, proud forehead never to have been swollen down over her eyes, for her face and neck and hands never to have been painted so many shades of blue-black, and violet, and chartreuse. I still want those things—for my parents not to have had to live with this affair like a prickle bush between them, for my father to have been able to look my mother in her swollen eyes and curse the madman, the monster that could have dared do this to the woman he loved. I wanted to be able to touch my mother without shuddering, to be able to console my father, to be able to get that crash out of my head, the sound of that soprano—so many things that I didn't know how to pray for them, that I wouldn't have known where to start even if I had the power to work miracles, right there, right then.

57   A week later, when my mother was home, and her head beginning to bristle with new hairs, I lost my malachite beads. I had been carrying them in a white cloth pouch that Patty had given me, and was swinging the pouch on my pinkie on my way home from school, when I swung just a bit too hard, and it went sailing in a long arc though the air, whooshing like a perfectly thrown basketball through one of the holes of a nearby sewer. There was no chance of fishing it out: I looked and looked, crouching on the sticky pavement until the asphalt had grazed the skin of my hands and knees, but all I could discern was an evil-smelling musk, glassy and smug and impenetrable.

58   My loss didn't quite hit me until I was home, but then it produced an agony all out of proportion to my string of pretty beads. I hadn't cried at all during my mother's accident, and now I was crying all afternoon, all through dinner, and then after dinner too, crying past the point where I knew what I was crying for, wishing dimly that I had my beads to hold, wishing dimly that I could pray but refusing, refusing, I didn't know why, until I finally fell into an exhausted sleep on the couch, where my parents left me for the night—glad, no doubt, that one of the more tedious of my childhood crises seemed to be finally winding off the reel of life, onto the reel of memory. They covered me, and somehow grew a pillow under my head, and with uncharacteristic disregard for the living room rug, left some milk and pecan sandies on the coffee table, in case I woke up hungry. Their thoughtfulness was prescient: I did wake up in the early part of the night; and it was then, amid the unfamiliar sounds and shadows of the living room, that I had what I was sure was a true vision.

59   Even now what I saw retains an odd clarity; the requisite strange light flooding the room, first orange, and then a bright yellow-green, then a crackling bright burst like a Roman candle going off near the piano. There was a distinct smell of coffee, and a long silence. The room seemed to be getting colder. Nothing. A creak; the light starting to wane, then waxing again, brilliant pink now. Still nothing. Then, as the pink started to go a little purple, a perfectly normal middle-aged man's voice, speaking something very like pig Latin, told me quietly not to despair, not to despair, my beads would be returned to me.

60   That was all. I sat a moment in the dark, then turned on the light, gobbled down the cookies—and in a happy flash understood I was so good, really, so near to being a saint that my malachite beads would come back through the town water system. All I had to do was

turn on all the faucets in the house, which I did, one by one, stealing quietly into the bathroom and kitchen and basement. The old spigot by the washing machine was too gunked up to be coaxed very far open, but that didn't matter. The water didn't have to be full blast, I understood that. Then I gathered together my pillow and blanket and trundled up to my bed to sleep.

61   By the time I woke up in the morning I knew that my beads hadn't shown up, but when I knew it for certain, I was still disappointed; and as if that weren't enough, I had to face my parents and sister, who were all abuzz with the mystery of the faucets. Not knowing what else to do, I like a puddlebrain, told them the truth. The results were predictably painful.

62   "Callie had a *vision*," Mona told everyone at the bus stop. "A vision with lights, and sinks in it!"

63   Sinks, visions. I got it all day, from my parents, from my classmates, even some sixth and seventh graders. Someone drew a cartoon of me with a halo over my head in one of the girls' room stalls; Anthony Rossi made gurgling noises as he walked on his hands at recess. Only Patty tried not to laugh, though even she was something less than unalloyed understanding.

64   "I don' think miracles are thupposed to happen in *thewers*," she said.

65   Such was the end of my saintly ambitions. It wasn't the end of all holiness; the ideas of purity and goodness still tippled my brain, and over the years I came slowly to grasp of what grit true faith was made. Last night, though, when my father called to say that he couldn't go on living in our old house, that he was going to move to a smaller place, another place, maybe a condo—he didn't know how, or where—I found myself still wistful for the time religion seemed all I wanted it to be. Back then the world was a place that could be set right: one had only to direct the hand of the Almighty and say, just here, Lord, we hurt here—and here, and here, and here.

Reading Closely and Thinking Critically

1. As a child, how was Callie affected by her religion and Catholic school education? How did her religious attitudes as an adult differ from her attitudes as a child?

2. What view of family life is depicted in "The Water-Faucet Vision"?

3. In paragraph 41, Callie says that "learning *was* painful." What did she learn that caused her pain?

4. In paragraph 64, Patty says, "I don' think miracles are thupposed to happen in *thewers.*" Explain what she means. What view of religion does Patty's comment reflect?

5. What does the list of requests on the refrigerator door tell you about the view of God held by the tenants?

6. A number of religious attitudes are represented in "The Water-Faucet Vision," including Callie's before and after her "vision," Patty's, and the tenants'. Who do you believe has the most mature or admirable view of God and religion? Explain.

7. What is the relationship between the account of the marital problems of the narrator's parents and the loss of the beads? That is, why does Jen narrate these stories together?

8. In addition to Callie's Catholic education, what may have contributed to her youthful piety?

Examining Structure and Strategy

1. How many narrations does Jen include in "The Water-Faucet Vision"? What are those narrations?

2. Jen describes people, scenes, and events. Cite two examples and explain what the descriptions contribute to the piece.

3. What do you judge to be the significance of the story? In which paragraph does Jen provide the most information about the significance?

4. Jen uses a flashback technique (see page 135). What does this technique contribute?

5. A number of paragraphs open with transitions that help the reader follow the time sequence. (See page 22 on transitions). Identify four such paragraphs.

Considering Language and Style

1. "The Water-Faucet Vision" includes *dialect,* which is the reproduction of the grammar and pronunciation of a particular variety of language. For example, paragraph 15 includes this piece of dialect: "Like you 'member the dreth I liked?" Cite three other examples of dialect in the story and explain what Jen's use of dialect contributes.

2. Consult a dictionary if you are unsure of the meaning of any of these words: *morbid* (paragraph 8), *malachite* (paragraph 8), *striated* (paragraph 8), *doleful* (paragraph 12), *votive candles* (paragraph 35), *a capella* (paragraph 51), *prescient* (paragraph 58), *trundled* (paragraph 60), *wistful* (paragraph 65).

For Group Discussion or Writing

In the last paragraph, Jen says that Callie came "to grasp of what grit true faith was made." Decide what you think that statement means and then give some examples of the "grit" of true faith.

Writing Assignments

1. *In your journal.* Religious belief is an important part of Callie's life. Explain what role religious belief plays in your life and whether that role has changed over the years.

2. *Using the pattern.* Tell a story about a time when your parents or other caregivers had a fight that you overheard. Use conversation to provide some or all of what was said. If appropriate, explain how the argument affected you.

3. *Using the pattern.* The children in "The Water-Faucet Vision" learn that parents are far from perfect. Tell a story about a time you learned a parent or some other adult important to you was not perfect. As an alternative, tell about a time when a parent or other adult disappointed you.

4. *Using the pattern.* Tell a story about a time you lost something important to you, as when Callie lost her malachite beads. Tell how you lost the item and what happened afterwards. Also, be sure to explain why the item was important to you.

5. *Considering a theme.* Religion can serve many purposes for both the individual and society. Describe the most important of these roles and speculate what would happen if religion did not fulfill that role or roles.

6. *Connecting the readings.* As we mature, changes occur in our thinking, in our emotions, in our relationships, and in our circumstances. Often changes mean that we gain something but lose something else. For example, when Callie lost her belief in a God who finds beads, some would say that she gained a more realistic view of miracles. Give examples of change as a series of gains and losses. If you wish, you may use ideas from "The Water-Faucet Vision," "Two Views of the Mississippi" (page 349) and "The View from 80" (page 353).

ADDITIONAL ESSAY ASSIGNMENTS

See pages 137 and 138 for suggestions for writing narration and for a revision checklist.

1. Narrate an account of an event that caused you to change your view of someone or something.

2. Narrate an account of an embarrassing moment that you or someone you know suffered. If you wish, make the narration humorous.

3. Narrate an account of a childhood memory. If possible, include description and conversation.

4. Tell the story of a time when things did not go as you expected them to. Be sure to indicate the significance of the narration.

5. Tell the story of an event that marked a turning point in your life. Be sure to indicate how you were affected by this event.

6. Narrate an account of a happy birthday or holiday celebration. Try to include conversation and description.

7. Tell the story of a time when you displayed or witnessed courage.

8. Tell the story of an athletic event in which you were involved. Be sure to indicate the significance of the narration.

9. Tell the story of a disappointment someone you know experienced. Be sure to indicate the significance of the narration.

10. Tell a story that shows that people can be cruel (or kind).

11. Tell a story that shows that ignorance is bliss.

12. Tell the story of a time that you or someone you know overcame an obstacle. Be sure to indicate the significance of the narration.

13. Tell the story of a time when hard work did (or did not) pay off.

14. Tell a story to persuade your reader that the public school system is in better shape than many people think it is.

15. Tell a story that reveals a personality trait of someone. For example, if you have a friend who is reckless, tell a story that illustrates that recklessness. Try to use description and conversation.

16. Tell a story that shows that things are not always what they seem.

17. Tell a story that shows that some modern device (the car, the VCR, the computer, the microwave, for example) is more trouble than it is worth. If you like, you can make the narration humorous.

18. Tell a story that shows we should be careful of what we wish for because we may get it.

19. Narrate an account of a difficult decision that you had to make. Be sure to indicate the effect the decision had on you.

20. *Narration in context.* Assume that you are contributing a piece for a "My Life" column in your campus newspaper. The piece will be a narration about a first-time experience: the first time you drove a car, a first kiss, your first day of college, your first job, your first time away from home, and so on. Your column should indicate the effect the experience had on you. If you want, you can make the narration humorous. To come up with ideas, list all the "firsts" you can think of. Pick one from your list and speak the story into a tape recorder before putting a draft on paper.

5

☺ EXEMPLIFICATION

The Readings, the Patterns, and the Purposes

On Holidays and How to Make Them Work
Nikki Giovanni
exemplification to persuade

University Days   *James Thurber*
exemplification to entertain *and* to inform

On Being the Target of Discrimination
Ralph Ellison
exemplification to express feelings and
relate experience *and* to inform

What I've Learned from Men: Lessons for a Full-
Grown Feminist   *Barbara Ehrenreich*
**exemplification with cause-and-effect
analysis, definition, and contrast** to inform
and to persuade

Untouchables   *Jonathan Kozol*
**exemplification with cause-and-effect
analysis** to inform *and* to persuade

Maintenance   *Naomi Shihab Nye*
**exemplification with cause-and-effect
analysis, narration, and contrast** to inform
and to express feelings and relate experience

THE PATTERN

How many times have you said, "Can you give me an example?" Like most of us, you probably ask for examples often—and for good reason, because nothing clarifies better. Usually, examples clarify by making the general more specific or by showing that something is true. To understand how examples work to clarify, consider this statement:

> Living in a high-tech society has its drawbacks.

To clarify that general statement, examples can be added for specificity, like this:

> Living in a high-tech society has its drawbacks. For example, our devices have become so complicated that many people can no longer operate them. I don't know anyone who can program a VCR or figure out how to get the message light to stop blinking on an answering machine after a power outage.

Now consider this statement:

> There is more to do in Las Vegas than gamble.

To clarify the statement, examples can be added to show that the statement is true, like this:

> There is more to do in Las Vegas than gamble. On my last trip, I visited Hoover Dam, which was an exciting excursion. In the past, I have also experienced the beauty of the desert, visited the Ethel M chocolate factory, enjoyed a cactus garden, seen the Liberace Museum, gone to a huge water park, and played golf on championship courses.

THE PURPOSES OF EXEMPLIFICATION

Because examples are so important for clarification, writers rely on them all the time, even when they use other patterns of development. Thus, you will see examples in essays developed largely with cause-and-effect analysis, process analysis, comparison-contrast, and any other patterns or combination of patterns. Say, for instance, that you are explaining why sexually active teenagers often do not use birth control. (This is cause-and-effect analysis.) Once you note that teenagers do not always understand when and how pregnancy can occur, you can illustrate with the example you read of a 15-year-old who became pregnant because she thought she was "safe" since it was her first sexual experience.

Although examples are often a part of essays developed with any pattern or combination of patterns, exemplification also can form the primary pattern of development to help the writer entertain, relate experience and express feelings, inform, and persuade. In this chapter, James Thurber gives humorous examples of his college mishaps in "University Days" in order to *entertain* his reader. Ralph Ellison gives examples of discrimination he has endured in part to *express* the pain of those experiences. Jonathan Kozol gives examples of what the homeless experience in order to *inform* the reader of the plight of the homeless. Finally, Nikki Giovanni offers examples of how Americans celebrate holidays to *persuade* the reader that we really do not celebrate them very well.

Exemplification in College Writing

So important are examples that you are likely to use them in most of your academic writing, including essay examinations and required papers. Thus, you will often be directed to do such things as "explain and illustrate . . . ," "define and provide examples of . . . ," and "cite illustrations to show that. . . . " In a world history class, for example, you may be asked to explain and illustrate the role of women in ancient Egypt. In a political science class, you may argue for or against gun control legislation, and to do so you may cite examples of murder rates in countries that either have or lack such legislation. In an education class, you might be called upon to argue against proficiency exams by citing examples of problems or benefits such tests provide. In a marketing class, you might be asked to define and illustrate target marketing, and in a biology class, you might be asked to define and illustrate natural selection.

SUPPORTING DETAILS

Examples can take many forms. Sometimes an example is a simple explanation. For example, Jonathan Kozol makes this statement in "Untouchables":

> Several cities have devised unusual measures to assure that homeless people will learn quickly that they are not welcome.

His clarifying examples, which follow the statement, are simple explanations:

> Several cities have devised unusual measures to assure that homeless people will learn quickly that they are not welcome. In Laramie, Wyoming, they are given one night's shelter. On the next morning, an organization called "The Good Samaritan Fund" gives them one-way tickets to another town. The college town of Lancaster, Ohio, offers homeless families one-way tickets to Columbus.

An example can also take the form of a narration. In "Untouchables," Jonathan Kozol tells the story of how financially secure Richard Lazarus became homeless. This story serves to illustrate that even middle-class people can suffer reversals that lead to the loss of their homes.

Sometimes examples take the form of description. For example, if you wanted to illustrate that people do not care about cleaning up the planet, you could describe the litter in a public park and the pollution of a local river.

The length of examples can vary from brief to extended. In general, the longer each example is, the fewer you need. For instance, in "On Being the Target of Discrimination," Ellison provides only three examples, but each one is richly detailed. Had he supplied six examples, he could have developed each one in considerably less detail. Sometimes writers combine highly detailed examples with less-detailed ones. The important thing is not how many examples you provide; it is that you provide enough examples in enough detail to clarify adequately and make your point.

SELECTING AND ORDERING DETAILS

Your examples can come from a variety of sources: personal experience, observation, general knowledge, class lectures, reading, research, and so forth. In "Untouchables," for instance, Kozol's examples of the trials of the homeless come from research—he interviewed many homeless people to get his information. In "University Days," James Thurber's examples of college misadventures come from his own experiences at Ohio State University. In "On Holidays and How to Make Them Work," Nikki Giovanni's examples of the inappropriate ways we celebrate holidays are taken from her observation of what we do on holidays. If you wanted to illustrate that people lie about unimportant things, you could do so with examples taken from a recent psychology lecture you attended.

Sometimes writers use *hypothetical examples*. These are not drawn from any single observation or experience of the writer but are created from what the writer knows *could* happen, based on common knowledge, past experience, past observation, and logic. To be effective, hypothetical examples must be plausible, and they must not be overused. For example, say that you wanted to illustrate that advertisements make drinking beer look cool. Rather than point to specific advertisements, you could say something like this:

> Beer advertisements make it seem that beer drinkers have more fun. The ads show beautiful people frolicking on the beach, playing volleyball, sitting by a campfire, and laughing away the hours. Other ads show beautiful people bundled in ski clothes, nestled by the fire, listening to jazz.

The examples in the above passage are not from specific beer ads. They are hypothetical. However, they are sufficiently like real advertisements to be effective.

In an essay developed primarily with exemplification, the thesis can embody the generalization that your examples will prove or clarify. To see this, consider the thesis of "What I've Learned from Men":

> After more than a decade of consciousness-raising, assertiveness training, and hand-to-hand combat in the battle of the sexes, we're [women] still too ladylike.

The rest of the essay provides examples of ways women are too ladylike; that is, it provides examples of ladylike behaviors that cause problems. Many times, the clarifying examples can be introduced with topic sentences, like this one from "What I've Learned from Men":

The essence of ladylikeness is a persistent servility masked as "niceness."

Following this topic sentence, Ehrenreich notes several instances of women's ladylike niceness casting them in servile roles.

Sometimes it does not matter in what order you arrange your examples, but more often the order should be carefully considered. For a progressive order, arrange your examples from the least to the most compelling. As an effective alternative, place your two strongest examples first and last, with the others in between. Progressive order is particularly effective for a persuasive purpose because it provides a strong final impression with its convincing example at the end.

Sometimes chronological (time) order is effective. For example, if you want to illustrate that a particular politician's record is unsavory, you could do so with examples arranged in chronological order from the time the politician took office up to the present.

On occasion, a spatial order is also possible. If, for example, you want to demonstrate that your campus presents obstacles for the physically disabled, you could move across campus space (maybe north to south) giving examples of physical barriers.

SUGGESTIONS FOR WRITING EXEMPLIFICATION

1. If you have trouble finding a generalization to clarify with examples, fill in the blanks in one of these sentences:

_____ is the best (worst) _____ I know.

_____ is the most (least) _____ I know.

You may end up with generalizations like these:

Lee is the wackiest person I know.

Television advertising is the most manipulative form of communication I know.

Nurses are the least appreciated professionals I know.

These sentences provide generalizations you can clarify with examples: you can give examples of Lee's wacky behavior, examples of manipulative television ads, and examples of ways nurses are underappreciated.

2. Decide early on whether you want to express feelings, relate experience, inform, entertain, and/or persuade your reader, because your purpose will influence the examples you use.

3. To generate examples for supporting details, you can ask yourself these questions:

a. What have I experienced that illustrates my generalization?

b. What have I observed that illustrates my generalization?

c. What have I read that illustrates my generalization?

d. What have I learned in school that illustrates my generalization?

e. What stories can I tell to illustrate my generalization?

f. What can I describe to illustrate my generalization?

4. List all the examples you will use and number them in the order you will present them.

5. Write your draft using your numbered list as a scratch outline. Do not worry about polished prose now. Just get your ideas down any way you can; you can refine later.

Checklist for Revising Exemplification

1. Do you have a generalization that is clearly stated (perhaps in a thesis) or strongly implied?

2. Do your examples clarify the generalization and/or show that it is true?

3. Do you have enough examples developed in enough detail? (Remember, the fewer the number of examples, the more detail you need for each.)

4. Are examples introduced with topic sentences where appropriate?

5. Are examples arranged in a progressive or other suitable order?

ANNOTATED STUDENT ESSAY

In the following piece, the student author uses exemplification to persuade the reader of the value of certain kinds of lies. The piece is interesting because despite its entertaining, light-hearted tone, it has a serious purpose.

Would I Lie to You?

1   There is no question about it; lying is wrong. Everyone who has been to Sunday School knows that the stone tablets admonish, "Thou shalt not lie." Every three-year-old knows that lying is bad—it's one of the first things parents impress on their kids, right after that bit about not following Johnny if he jumps off the bridge. There are even laws against lying. Tell a lie under oath and go immediately to jail without passing Go—you committed perjury. There is no question about it, I repeat. Lying is wrong. Or is it? The fact is, there are times when a lie is preferable to the truth.

2   The easiest lie to justify is the lie told to spare a person's feelings. For example, if the host

Paragraph 1
The introduction engages interest by stating the opposite of what the thesis will prove and with humor. The thesis (the last sentence) presents the generalization to be proven.

Paragraph 2
The first sentence is the topic sentence. It gives the focus as lies to spare feelings. The examples are hypothetical. The tone is light-hearted and casual. One of the writer's purposes is to entertain.

of a wedding reception asks you how you are enjoying the party (which, by the way, is costing the
host about $10,000), why tell the truth and an-
nounce that the band is playing too many polkas,
the chicken is undercooked, and the champagne
is warm and flat? What could possibly be gained?
In this case, a little fib won't hurt: "I'm having a
wonderful time. Thanks for inviting me. I think you
did the right thing selling your kidney to pay for
this." Similarly, you can tell your prom date that
her hideous dress is lovely, just as you can tell a
new parent that the newborn with distinct simian
traits is gorgeous.

3   Some people maintain that lying to spare
a person's feelings is not justifiable. They say that
a well-intentioned lie may seem to spare a person's feelings, but it can backfire. For example, if
you tell someone you like his bad haircut, he may
continue to get that unflattering style rather than
try a new barber. In this case, telling the truth can
cause a person to take action to correct something. I agree. However, when nothing can be
done, it serves no purpose to hurt someone when
a small lie can sustain a harmless illusion.

4   Sometimes a lie is necessary for the liar's
own good. For instance, when the boss asks you
if you mind working overtime, assure this master
of your financial well-being that nothing would
please you more and forget about those theater
tickets in your wallet. After all, there are promotions at stake, raises to consider, and a corner office to aim for. More basically, lying about your
desire to work overtime is infinitely preferable to
being fired.

5   Sometimes a lie just makes life easier, as
when dealing with a pesky telemarketer. You try
to get off the phone gracefully, but the caller
seems indefatigable in her efforts to sell you a
lifetime membership in the chia pet-of-the-month
club. You have only two choices. You could hang
up in the person's ear, but that's rude. Better to
tell a harmless lie, like this particularly effective
one: "I have to go; Billy is spin cycling himself in
the washer again." Or you could try one of these
that I found posted on the Internet: "I have to go
study for my blood test"; "I have to rotate my
crops"; "I'm busy checking the freshness dates

Paragraph 3
The first two sentences form
the topic sentence. They give
the focus as one argument
against the writer's view. The
paragraph works to dispel that
argument using hypothetical
examples. The author's persuasive purpose becomes clear.

Paragraph 4
Sentence 1 is the topic sentence.
Transition is achieved with repetition of key word *lie*. Examples are hypothetical, and the
tone remains light-hearted.
Transitions include *for instance,
after all, more basically.*

Paragraph 5
The topic sentence (the first)
gives the focus as lies making
life easier. Most of the examples
come from the Internet. Transition of emphasis is *of course.*

on my dairy products." Of course, you could just tell the solicitor to take your name off the list, but then what fun would that be?

6   Insensitive, self-centered acquaintances and relatives who call at inopportune times present a different challenge. With these people, the truth just does not work. You say, "I'm sorry; I'm busy and cannot talk right now," and the clods just carry on: "Oh, I'll just keep you a minute"— and an hour goes by. You simply have no choice but to offer a plausible lie, perhaps by stating that the baby is crying or the bathtub is about to overflow or the doorbell is ringing. Then state that you will call back later. Oh, okay, so that's another lie, but insensitive people leave you little choice.

Paragraph 6
Sentence 1 is the topic sentence. The light-hearted tone continues, but it remains clear that the author has a serious point. The example is hypothetical.

7   Finally, at times it is advisable to lie to children. For example, do you *really* want your five-year-old to be the only kid in kindergarten who knows the truth about Santa Claus and the Easter Bunny? If so, you better start saving for the extensive therapy now. Lying to children about death can also be a good idea. If little Daisy loved recently deceased Uncle Mortimer, it's okay to reassure her that he is in Heaven, even though the guy cheated on his wife, stole his children's inheritance, and was wanted in three states for grand theft auto.

Paragraph 7
Sentence 1 is the topic sentence; it opens with the transition *finally*. The examples come from the common experience of many parents.

8   Of course, lying is most often wrong, sinful, or illegal. However, small fibs have their place too. In fact, at times they are even better than the truth because they do less harm.

Paragraph 8
The conclusion reaffirms the author's position.

ON HOLIDAYS AND HOW TO MAKE THEM WORK
Nikki Giovanni

Born in Knoxville, Tennessee in 1943 and raised in Cincinnati, Ohio, Nikki Giovanni attended Fisk University, where both writing and politics became important parts of her life through her membership in the Writers' Workshop and the Student Non-Violent Coordinating Committee. Politics and writing continued to connect in her politically charged poetry and essays. An English professor at Virginia Tech, Giovanni was named Woman of the Year by Ebony *magazine. In "On Holidays and How to Make Them Work," which was published in her 1988 collection* Sacred Cows and Other Edibles, *Giovanni has a persuasive purpose. Written at the time of the first Martin Luther King Day observance, the essay argues that Americans do not know the appropriate way to celebrate their holidays. As a result, King's day could become as commercial and meaningless as other U.S. holidays. As you read, try to determine why Giovanni takes exception to these celebrations.*

THE PATTERN	THE PURPOSE
exemplification	*to persuade*

1   A proper holiday, coming from the medieval "holy day," is supposed to be a time of reflection on great men, great deeds, great people. Things like that. Somehow in America this didn't quite catch on. Take Labor Day. On Labor Day you take the day off, then go to the Labor Day sales and spend your devalued money with a clerk who is working. And organized labor doesn't understand why it suffers declining membership? Pshaw. Who wants to join an organization that makes you work on the day it designates as a day off? Plus, no matter how hidden the agenda, who wants a day off if they make you march in a parade and listen to some politicians talk on and on about nothing.

2   Hey. I'm a laborer. I used to work in Walgreen's on Linn Street. We were open every holiday and I, being among the junior people,

always "got" to work the time-and-a-half holidays. I hated those people who came in. Every fool in the Western world, and probably in this universe, knows that Christmas is December 25. Has been that way for over a thousand years, yet there they'd be, standing outside the door, cold, bleary-eyed, waiting for us to open so they could purchase a present. Memorial Day, which used to be Armistice Day until we got into this situation of continuous war, was the official start of summer. We would want to be out with our boyfriends barbecuing . . . or something, but there we were behind the counter waiting to see who forgot that in order to barbecue you need: (1) a grill, (2) charcoal, (3) charcoal starter. My heart goes out to the twenty-four-hour grocery people, who are probably selling meat!

3   But hey. It's the American way. The big Fourth of July sales probably reduced the number of fatal injuries as people spent the entire day sober in malls, fighting over markdowns. Minor cuts and bruises were way up, though, I'll bet. And forget the great nonholiday, Presidents' Day. The damned thing could at least have a real name. What does that mean—Presidents' Day? Mostly that we don't care enough to take the time to say to Washington and Lincoln: Well done. But for sure, as a Black American I've got to go for it. Martin Luther King, Jr.'s birthday has come up for the first time as a national holiday. If we are serious about celebrating it, Steinberg's will be our first indication: GHETTO BLASTERS 30% OFF! FREE TAPE OF "I HAVE A DREAM" WITH EVERY VCR PURCHASED AT THE ALL-NEW GIGANTIC MARTY'S BIRTHDAY SALE. Then Wendy's will, just maybe, for Black patrons (and their liberal sympathizers) Burn-A-Burger to celebrate the special day. Procter & Gamble will withhold Clorox for the day, respectfully requesting that those Black spots be examined for their liberating influence. But what we really want, where we can know we have succeeded, is that every Federated department store offers 50 percent off to every colored patron who can prove he or she is Black in recognition of the days when colored citizens who were Black were not accorded all the privileges of other shoppers. That will be a big help because everybody will want to be Black for a Day. Sun tanneries will make fortunes during the week preceding MLK Day. Wig salons will reap great benefits. Dentists will have to hire extra help to put that distinctive gap between the middle front teeth. MLK Day will be accepted. And isn't that the heart of the American dream?

4   I really love a good holiday—it takes the people off the streets and puts them safely in the shopping malls. Now think about it. Aren't you proud to be with Uncle Sam?

Reading Closely and Thinking Critically

1. Which paragraph contains Giovanni's thesis idea? That is, which paragraph includes the generalization that the author will clarify? In your own words, write a sentence that expresses this thesis/generalization.

2. What is Giovanni's chief objection to the way Americans celebrate holidays?

3. In paragraph 1, the author makes a pointed comment about the reason for the decline of organized labor. Cite another example of a critical comment that makes a point about something other than working on holidays.

4. What is the significance of the essay's title? Explain the wordplay.

5. Giovanni's description of potential Martin Luther King Day celebrations is the most extensive and the most satiric example in the essay. Why do you think this is so?

6. Giovanni probably does not expect to change the way Americans celebrate holidays. What, then, is her goal? Do you think she is writing for an audience of any particular race? Explain.

Examining Structure and Strategy

1. Do Giovanni's examples clarify by showing that something is true, by making the general specific, or both?

2. What examples does Giovanni provide to clarify her generalization? Are these examples brief or extended?

3. What is the source of Giovanni's examples?

4. What approach does Giovanni take to her conclusion?

Considering Language and Style

1. "On Holidays and How to Make Them Work" was published in 1988. As a result, it includes a number of dated usages. For example, in paragraph 1, the author uses men in the generic sense and excludes women. What other examples of dated usages appear? Do they create a problem for the reader and detract from Giovanni's ideas? Explain.

2. How would you describe the tone of the essay? (See page 37 on tone.)

3. Consult a dictionary if you are unsure of the meaning of this word: *pshaw* (paragraph 1).

For Group Discussion and Writing
With two or three classmates, choose a holiday celebrated in this country (Martin Luther King Day, Memorial Day, Labor Day, Thanksgiving, Presidents' Day) and decide how the holiday should be celebrated. How different is that from the way the holiday actually is celebrated?

Writing Assignments

1. *In your journal.* In paragraph 3, Giovanni mentions the American dream and the American way. Reread that paragraph, then write a page or two that explains what you think Giovanni means by one of these terms. Provide your own explanation of the same term if your meaning differs from Giovanni's.

2. *Using the pattern.* Select a holiday observed in the United States and provide your own examples to explain to the reader why you think it is celebrated in either an appropriate or an inappropriate fashion.

3. *Using the pattern.* Use examples to show how a particular holiday should be celebrated so that it is, according to Giovanni, "a time of reflection on great men, great deeds, great people" (paragraph 1). The previous group activity may give you ideas for this essay.

4. *Using the pattern.* Provide examples to show how a particular holiday is celebrated in your family.

5. *Using the pattern.* If you have ever worked on a holiday, write a generalization to describe what it was like. Then provide examples to clarify the generalization.

6. *Considering a theme.* If you agree with Nikki Giovanni that Americans do not know how to celebrate their holidays, explain why you think Americans have this problem and what the effects of it are. If you disagree with Giovanni, argue that there is nothing wrong with the way Americans celebrate their holidays.

7. *Connecting the readings.* Read "The Ways of Meeting Oppression" (page 463), "On Being the Target of Discrimination" (page 219), and "Just Walk on By" (page 413). Then describe the activities that you think should take place in schools to observe Martin Luther King Day.

UNIVERSITY DAYS
James Thurber

Ohio native and graduate of Ohio State University, beloved American humorist James Thurber (1894 – 1961) wrote essays and drew cartoons for The New Yorker. *Plagued by vision problems, he wrote more and drew less as his vision deteriorated. Thurber wrote several humorous books, including* My World and Welcome to It *(1942), which contains the famous story, "The Secret Life of Walter Mitty." He also wrote* My Life and Hard Times *(1933), from which "University Days" is taken. In this essay, which includes five extended examples of the absurdity and frustration of college life during the World War I era, Thurber entertains the reader. As you read, ask yourself whether his examples, although exaggerated, point to truths still in evidence today.*

THE PATTERN	THE PURPOSE
exemplification	*to entertain and to inform*

1   I passed all the other courses that I took at my university, but I could never pass botany. This was because all botany students had to spend several hours a week in a laboratory looking through a microscope at plant cells, and I could never see through a microscope. I never once saw a cell through a microscope. This used to enrage my instructor. He would wander around the laboratory pleased with the progress all the students were making in drawing the involved and, so I am told, interesting structure of flower cells, until he came to me. I would just be standing there. "I can't see anything," I would say. He would begin patiently enough, explaining how anybody can see through a microscope, but he would always end up in a fury, claiming that I could *too* see through a microscope but just pretended that I couldn't. "It takes away from the beauty of flowers anyway," I used to tell him. "We are not concerned with beauty in this course," he would say. "We are concerned solely with what I may call the *mechanics* of flars." "Well," I'd say, "I can't see anything." "Try it just once again," he'd say, and I would put my eye to the microscope and see nothing at all, except now and again

a nebulous milky substance—a phenomenon of maladjustment. You were supposed to see a vivid, restless clockwork of sharply defined plant cells. "I see what looks like a lot of milk," I would tell him. This, he claimed, was the result of my not having adjusted the microscope properly, so he would readjust it for me, or rather, for himself. And I would look again and see milk.

2   I finally took a deferred pass, as they called it, and waited a year and tried again. (You had to pass one of the biological sciences or you couldn't graduate.) The professor had come back from vacation brown as a berry, bright-eyed, and eager to explain cell-structure again to his classes. "Well," he said to me, cheerily, when we met in the first laboratory hour of the semester, "we're going to see cells this time, aren't we?" "Yes, sir," I said. Students to right of me and to left of me and in front of me were seeing cells; what's more, they were quietly drawing pictures of them in their notebooks. Of course, I didn't see anything.

3   "We'll try it," the professor said to me, grimly, "with every adjustment of the microscope known to man. As God is my witness, I'll arrange this glass so that you see cells through it or I'll give up teaching. In twenty-two years of botany, I—" He cut off abruptly for he was beginning to quiver all over, like Lionel Barrymore, and he genuinely wished to hold onto his temper: his scenes with me had taken a great deal out of him.

4   So we tried it with every adjustment of the microscope known to man. With only one of them did I see anything but blackness or the familiar lacteal opacity, and that time I saw, to my pleasure and amazement, a variegated constellation of flecks, specks, and dots. These I hastily drew. The instructor, noting my activity, came back from an adjoining desk, a smile on his lips and his eyebrows high in hope. He looked at my cell drawing. "What's that?" he demanded, with a hint of a squeal in his voice. "That's what I saw," I said. "You didn't, you didn't, you *didn't!*" he screamed, losing control of his temper instantly, and he bent over and squinted into the microscope. His head snapped up. "That's your eye!" he shouted. "You've fixed the lens so that it reflects! You've drawn your eye!"

5   Another course that I didn't like, but somehow managed to pass, was economics. I went to that class straight from the botany class, which didn't help me any in understanding either subject. I used to get them mixed up. But not as mixed up as another student in my economics class who came there direct from a physics laboratory. He was

a tackle on the football team, named Bolenciecwcz. At that time Ohio State University had one of the best football teams in the country, and Bolenciecwcz was one of its outstanding stars. In order to be eligible to play it was necessary for him to keep up in his studies, a very difficult matter, for while he was not dumber than an ox he was not any smarter. Most of his professors were lenient and helped him along. None gave him more hints in answering questions or asked him simpler ones than the economics professor, a thin, timid man named Bassum. One day when we were on the subject of transportation and distribution, it came Bolenciecwcz's turn to answer a question. "Name one means of transportation," the professor said to him. No light came into the big tackle's eyes. "Just any means of transportation," said the professor. Bolenciecwcz sat staring at him. "That is," pursued the professor, "any medium, agency, or method of going from one place to another." Bolenciecwcz had the look of a man who is being led into a trap. "You may choose among steam, horse-drawn, or electrically propelled vehicles," said the instructor. "I might suggest the one which we commonly take in making long journeys across land." There was a profound silence in which everybody stirred uneasily, including Bolenciecwcz and Mr. Bassum. Mr. Bassum abruptly broke this silence in an amazing manner. "Choo-choo-choo," he said, in a low voice, and turned instantly scarlet. He glanced appealingly around the room. All of us, of course, shared Mr. Bassum's desire that Bolenciecwcz should stay abreast of the class in economics, for the Illinois game, one of the hardest and most important of the season, was only a week off. "Toot, toot, too-toooooot!" some student with a deep voice moaned, and we all looked encouragingly at Bolenciecwcz. Somebody else gave a fine imitation of a locomotive letting off steam. Mr. Bassum himself rounded off the little show. "Ding, dong, ding, dong," he said, hopefully. Bolenciecwcz was staring at the floor now, trying to think, his great brow furrowed, his huge hands rubbing together, his face red.

6   "How did you come to college this year, Mr. Bolenciecwcz?" asked the professor. "*Chuffa* chuffa, *chuffa* chuffa."

7   "M'father sent me," said the football player.

8   "What on?" asked Bassum.

9   "I git an 'lowance," said the tackle, in a low, husky voice, obviously embarrassed.

10   "No, no," said Bassum. "Name a means of transportation. What did you *ride* here on?"

11   "Train," said Bolenciecwcz.

12   "Quite right," said the professor. "Now, Mr. Nugent, will you tell us—"

13   If I went through anguish in botany and economics—for different reasons—gymnasium work was even worse. I don't even like to think about it. They wouldn't let you play games or join in the exercises with your glasses on and I couldn't see with mine off. I bumped into professors, horizontal bars, agricultural students, and swinging iron rings. Not being able to see, I could take it but I couldn't dish it out. Also, in order to pass gymnasium (and you had to pass it to graduate) you had to learn to swim if you didn't know how. I didn't like the swimming pool, I didn't like swimming, and I didn't like the swimming instructor, and after all these years I still don't. I never swam but I passed my gym work anyway, by having another student give my gymnasium number (978) and swim across the pool in my place. He was a quiet, amiable blond youth, number 473, and he would have seen through a microscope for me if we could have got away with it, but we couldn't get away with it. Another thing I didn't like about gymnasium work was that they made you strip the day you registered. It is impossible for me to be happy when I am stripped and being asked a lot of questions. Still, I did better than a lanky agricultural student who was cross-examined just before I was. They asked each student what college he was in—that is, whether Arts, Engineering, Commerce, or Agriculture. "What college are you in?" the instructor snapped at the youth in front of me. "Ohio State University," he said promptly.

14   It wasn't that agricultural student but it was another a whole lot like him who decided to take up journalism, possibly on the ground that when farming went to hell he could fall back on newspaper work. He didn't realize, of course, that that would be very much like falling back full-length on a kit of carpenter's tools. Haskins didn't seem cut out for journalism, being too embarrassed to talk to anybody and unable to use a typewriter, but the editor of the college paper assigned him to the cow barns, the sheep house, the horse pavilion, and the animal husbandry department generally. This was a genuinely big "beat," for it took up five times as much ground and got ten times as great a legislative appropriation as the College of Liberal Arts. The agricultural student knew animals, but nevertheless his stories were dull and colorlessly written. He took all afternoon on each of them, on account of having to hunt for each letter on the typewriter. Once in a while he had

to ask somebody to help him hunt. "C" and "L," in particular, were hard letters for him to find. His editor finally got pretty much annoyed at the farmer-journalist because his pieces were so uninteresting. "See here, Haskins," he snapped at him one day, "why is it we never have anything hot from you on the horse pavilion?" Here we have two hundred head of horses on this campus—more than any other university in the Western Conference except Purdue—and yet you never get any real low-down on them. Now shoot over to the horse barns and dig up something lively." Haskins shambled out and came back in about an hour; he said he had something. "Well, start it off snappily," said the editor. "Something people will read." Haskins set to work and in a couple of hours brought a sheet of typewritten paper to the desk; it was a two-hundred-word story about some disease that had broken out among the horses. Its opening sentence was simple but arresting. It read: "Who has noticed the sores on the tops of the horses in the animal husbandry building?"

15   Ohio State was a land grant university and therefore two years of military drill was compulsory. We drilled with old Springfield rifles and studied the tactics of the Civil War even though the World War was going on at the time. At 11 o'clock each morning thousands of freshmen and sophomores used to deploy over the campus, moodily creeping up on the old chemistry building. It was good training for the kind of warfare that was waged at Shiloh but it had no connection with what was going on in Europe. Some people used to think there was German money behind it, but they didn't dare say so or they would have been thrown in jail as German spies. It was a period of muddy thought and marked, I believe, the decline of higher education in the Middle West.

16   As a soldier I was never any good at all. Most of the cadets were glumly indifferent soldiers, but I was no good at all. Once General Littlefield, who was commandant of the cadet corps, popped up in front of me during regimental drill and snapped, "You are the main trouble with this university!" I think he meant that my type was the main trouble with the university but he may have meant me individually. I was mediocre at drill, certainly—that is, until my senior year. By that time I had drilled longer than anybody else in the Western Conference, having failed at military at the end of each preceding year so that I had to do it all over again. I was the only senior still in uniform. The uniform which, when new, had made me look like an interurban railway conductor, now that it had become faded and too tight made me look like

Bert Williams in his bellboy act. This had a definitely bad effect on my morale. Even so, I had become by sheer practice little short of wonderful at squad maneuvers.

17   One day General Littlefield picked our company out of the whole regiment and tried to get it mixed up by putting it through one movement after another as fast as we could execute them: squads right, squads left, squads on right into line, squads right about, squads left front into line, etc. In about three minutes one hundred and nine men were marching in one direction and I was marching away from them at an angle of forty degrees, all alone. "Company, halt!" shouted General Littlefield. "That man is the only man who has it right!" I was made a corporal for my achievement.

18   The next day General Littlefield summoned me to his office. He was swatting flies when I went in. I was swatting flies when I went in. I was silent and he was silent too, for a long time. I don't think he remembered me or why he had sent for me, but he didn't want to admit it. He swatted some more flies, keeping his eyes on them narrowly before he let go with the swatter. "Button up your coat!" he snapped. Looking back on it now I can see that he meant me although he was looking at a fly, but I just stood there. Another fly came to rest on a paper in front of the general and began rubbing its hind legs together. The general lifted the swatter cautiously. I moved restlessly and the fly flew away. "You startled him!" barked General Littlefield, looking at me severely. I said I was sorry. "That won't help the situation!" snapped the General, with cold military logic. I didn't see what I could do except offer to chase some more flies toward his desk, but I didn't say anything. He stared out the window at the faraway figures of co-eds crossing the campus toward the library. Finally, he told me I could go. So I went. He either didn't know which cadet I was or else he forgot what he wanted to see me about. It may have been that he wished to apologize for having called me the main trouble with the university; or maybe he had decided to compliment me on my brilliant drilling of the day before and then at the last minute decided not to. I don't know. I don't think about it much any more.

Reading Closely and Thinking Critically

1. Thurber's thesis—and hence the generalization that his examples clarify—is unstated. In your own words, write out Thurber's thesis/generalization.

2. What absurdities and frustrations of college life does Thurber point out with his examples?

3. What kind of student does Thurber portray himself to be? What kind of teachers does Thurber portray?

4. Note two or three passages that you find amusing. Why are these passages funny? If you do not find anything amusing, explain why not.

5. Thurber stretches the truth in his examples. Does the fact that the examples are not strictly factual create a problem for you? Explain why or why not.

6. "University Days" is about college life during World War I. Is his essay still relevant to today's reader? Explain.

Examining Structure and Strategy

1. Are Thurber's examples brief or extended? What pattern of development is used for the examples?

2. Thurber's examples are introduced with topic sentences. What are those topic sentences?

3. Cite three examples of specific word choice.

4. How does Thurber use exaggeration?

5. Do you think Thurber's closing sentence makes a suitable conclusion for the essay? Explain.

Considering Language and Style

1. Paragraph 15 says that Ohio State University was a land grant university. What is a land grant university?

2. Consult a dictionary if you are unsure of the meaning of any of these words: *nebulous* (paragraph 1), *Lionel Barrymore* (paragraph 3), *lacteal opacity* (paragraph 4), *variegated* (paragraph 4).

For Group Discussion or Writing

Are the instructors and students in Thurber's examples unfair stereotypes, or are their characters rooted in fact? Back up your view with examples of your own.

Writing Assignments

1. *In your journal.* In two or three pages, write about your own "university days." You can consider your chief high and low points, your best and worst instructors and classes, frustrations and absurdities you have faced, and joys you have known.

2. *Using the pattern.* Use your own examples—extended or brief—to illustrate the frustrations of life on your college campus. (Your journal entry may give you some ideas.)

3. *Using the pattern.* Write a generalization about instructors you have had (use fictional names) and illustrate that generalization with two or three extended, narrative examples. If possible, use exaggeration for humorous effect.

4. *Using the pattern.* Use examples to illustrate a generalization about some past experience: membership in a scouting troop, a job, your elementary school days, marching band, religious school, sports, and so on.

5. *Considering a theme.* Present and describe the characteristics of higher education as Thurber sees them in "University Days." Then explain which aspect(s) of Thurber's view you agree with, disagree with, or both and why.

6. *Connecting the readings.* In "College Pressures" (page 477), William Zinsser classifies the causes of pressure on college students. Identify the sources of pressure apparent both in "University Days" and in your life as a student. Note which, if any, of Zinsser's groupings these pressures fall into.

ON BEING THE TARGET OF DISCRIMINATION
Ralph Ellison

Well known for his 1952 novel Invisible Man, *which explores racial stereo-types, Ralph Ellison (1914 – 1994) was born in Oklahoma. He studied music at Tuskegee Institute but left before graduation because of lack of funds. After leaving college, he joined the Federal Writers' Project in New York City. Later he taught at New York University, Rutgers, Yale, and other universities. His essays have been collected in* Shadow and Act *(1964),* Going to the Territory *(1986), and* Collected Essays *(1995). "On Being the Target of Discrimination" appeared in a special* New York Times Magazine *supplement in 1989. In the essay, Ellison relates examples of the discrimination he endured as a child. The examples also inform the reader of the nature of life in the United States during the time of so-called separate-but-equal laws.*

THE PATTERN	THE PURPOSE
exemplification	*to express feelings and relate experience and to inform*

1   It got to you first at the age of six, and through your own curiosity. With kindergarten completed and the first grade ahead, you were eagerly anticipating your first day of public school. For months you had been imagining your new experience and the children, known and unknown, with whom you would study and play. But the physical framework on your imagining, an elementary school in the process of construction, lay close at hand on the block-square site across the street from your home. For over a year you had watched it rise and spread in the air to become a handsome structure of brick and stone, then seen its broad encircling grounds arrayed with seesaws, swings, and baseball diamonds. You had imagined this picture-book setting as the scene of your new experience, and when enrollment day arrived, with its grounds astir with bright colors and voices of kids like yourself, it did, indeed, become the site of your very first lesson in public schooling—though not within its classrooms, as you had imagined, but well outside its

walls. For while located within a fairly mixed neighborhood this new public school was exclusively for whites.

2   It was then you learned that you would attend a school located far to the south of your neighborhood, and that reaching it involved a journey which took you over, either directly or by way of a viaduct which arched head-spinning high above, a broad expanse of railroad tracks along which a constant traffic of freight-cars, switch engines, and passenger trains made it dangerous for a child to cross. And that once the tracks were safely negotiated you continued past warehouses, factories, and loading docks, and then through a notorious red-light district where black prostitutes in brightly colored housecoats and Mary Jane shoes supplied the fantasies and needs of a white clientele. Considering the fact that you couldn't attend school with white kids this made for a confusion that was further confounded by the giggling jokes which older boys whispered about the district's peculiar form of integration. For you it was a grown-up's mystery, but streets being no less schools than routes to schools, the district would soon add a few forbidden words to your vocabulary.

3   It took a bit of time to forget the sense of incongruity aroused by your having to walk *past* a school to get *to* a school, but soon you came to like your school, your teachers, and most of your schoolmates. Indeed, you soon enjoyed the long walks and anticipated the sights you might see, the adventures you might encounter, and the many things not taught in school that could be learned along the way. Your school was not nearly so fine as that which faced your home but it had its attractions. Among them its nearness to a park, now abandoned by whites, in which you picnicked and played. And there were the two tall cylindrical fire escapes on either wing of its main building down which it was a joy to lie full-length and slide, spiraling down and around three stories to the ground—providing no outraged teacher was waiting to strap your legs once you sailed out of its chute like a shot off a fireman's shovel. Besides, in your childish way you were learning that it was better to take self-selected risks and pay the price than be denied the joy or pain of risk-taking by those who begrudged your existence.

4   Beginning when you were four or five you had known the joy of trips to the city's zoo, but one day you would ask your mother to take you there and have her sigh and explain that it was now against the law for Negro kids to view the animals. Had someone done something bad

to the animals? No. Had someone tried to steal them or feed them poison? No. Could white kids still go? Yes! So why? Quit asking questions, it's the law and only because some white folks are out to turn this state into a part of the South.

5   This sudden and puzzling denial of a Saturday's pleasure was disappointing and so angered your mother that later, after the zoo was moved north of the city, she decided to do something about it. Thus one warm Saturday afternoon with you and your baby brother dressed in your best she took you on a long streetcar ride which ended at a strange lakeside park, in which you found a crowd of noisy white people. Having assumed that you were on your way to the integrated cemetery where at the age of three you had been horrified beyond all tears or forgetting when you saw your father's coffin placed in the ground, you were bewildered. But now as your mother herded you and your brother in to the park you discovered that you'd come to the zoo and were so delighted that soon you were laughing and babbling as excitedly as the kids around you.

6   Your mother was pleased and as you moved through the crowd of white parents and children she held your brother's hand and allowed as much time for staring at the cages of rare animals as either of you desired. But once your brother began to tire she herded you out of the park and toward the streetcar line. And then it happened.

7   Just as you reached the gate through which crowds of whites were coming and going you had a memorable lesson in the strange ways of segregated-democracy as instructed by a guard in civilian clothes. He was a white man dressed in a black suit and a white straw hat, and when he looked at the fashion in which your mother was dressed, then down to you and your brother, he stiffened, turned red in the face, and stared as though at something dangerous.

8   "Girl," he shouted, "where are your *white* folks!"

9   "*White* folks," your mother said, "What white folks? I don't *have* any white folks, I'm a Negro!"

10   "Now don't you get smart with me, colored gal," the white man said, "I mean where are the white folks you come *out* here with!"

11   "But I just told you that I didn't come here with any white people," your mother said, "I came here with my boys . . . "

12   "Then what are you doing in this park," the white man said.

13   And now when your mother answered you could hear the familiar sound of anger in her voice.

14   "I'm here," she said, "because I'm a *taxpayer,* and I thought it was about time that my boys have a look at those animals. And for that I didn't *need* any *white* folks to show me the way!"

15   "Well," the white man said, "*I'm* here to tell you that you're breaking the law! So now you'll have to leave. Both you and your chillun too. The rule says no niggers is allowed in the zoo. That's the law and I'm enforcing it!"

16   "Very well," your mother said, "we've seen the animals anyway and were on our way to the streetcar line when you stopped us."

17   "That's fine," the white man said, "and when that car comes you be sure that you get on it, you hear? You and your chillun too!"

18   So it was quite a day. You had enjoyed the animals with your baby brother and had another lesson in the sudden ways good times could be turned into bad when white people looked at your color instead of *you.* But better still, you had learned something of your mother's courage and were proud that she had broken an unfair law and stood up for her right to do so. For while the white man kept staring until the streetcar arrived she ignored him and answered your brother's questions about the various animals. Then the car came with its crowd of white parents and children, and when you were entrained and rumbling home past the fine lawns and houses your mother gave way to a gale of laughter; in which, hesitantly at first, and then with assurance and pride, you joined. And from that day the incident became the source of a family joke that was sparked by accidents, faux pas, or obvious lies. Then one of you was sure to frown and say, "Well, I think you'll have to go now, both you and your chillun too!" And the family would laugh hilariously. Discrimination teaches one to discriminate between discriminators while countering absurdity with black (Negro? Afro-American? African-American?) comedy.

19   When you were eight you would move to one of the white sections through which you often passed on the way to your father's grave and your truly last trip to the zoo. For now your mother was the custodian of several apartments located in a building which housed on its street floor a drug store, a tailor shop, a Piggly Wiggly market, and a branch post office. Built on a downward slope, the building had at its rear a long driveway which led from the side street past an empty lot to a group of garages in which the apartments' tenants stored their cars. Built at an angle with wings facing north and east, the structure supported a servant's quarters which sat above its angle like a mock watchtower atop a battlement, and it was there that you now lived.

20   Reached by a flight of outside stairs, it consisted of four small rooms, a bath, and a kitchen. Windows on three of its sides provided a view across the empty frontage to the street, of the back yards behind it, and of the back wall and windows of the building in which your mother worked. It was quite comfortable but you secretly disliked the idea of your mother living in service and missed your friends who now lived far away. Nevertheless, the neighborhood was pleasant, served by a sub-station of the street-car line, and marked by a variety of activities which challenged your curiosity. Even its affluent alleys were more exciting to explore than those of your old neighborhood, and the one white friend you were to acquire in the area lived nearby.

21   This friend was a brilliant but sickly boy who was tutored at home, and with him you shared your new interest in building radios, a hobby at which he was quite skilled. Your friendship eased your loneliness and helped dispel some of the mystery and resentment imposed by segregation. Through access to his family, headed by an important Episcopalian minister, you learned more about whites and thus about yourself. With him you could make comparisons that were not so distorted by the racial myths which obstructed your thrust toward self-perception; compare their differences in taste, discipline, and manners with those of Negro families of comparable status and income; observe variations between your friend's boyish lore and your own, and measure his intelligence, knowledge, and ambitions against your own. For you this was a most important experience and a rare privilege, because up to now the prevailing separation of the races had made it impossible to learn how you and your Negro friends compared with boys who lived on the white side of the color line. It was said by word of mouth, proclaimed in newsprint, and dramatized by acts of discriminatory law that you were inferior. You were barred from vying with them in sports and games, competing in the classroom or the world of art. Yet what you saw, heard, and smelled of them left irrepressible doubts. So you ached for objective proof, for a fair field of testing.

22   Even your school's proud marching band was denied participation in the statewide music contests so popular at the time, as though so airy and earth-transcending an art as music would be contaminated if performed by musicians of different races.

23   Which was especially disturbing because after the father of a friend who lived next door in your old neighborhood had taught you the beginner's techniques required to play valved instruments you had

decided to become a musician. Then shortly before moving among whites your mother had given you a brass cornet, which in the isolation of the servant's quarters you practiced hours on end. But you yearned to play with other musicians and found none available. Now you lived less than a block from a white school with a famous band, but there was no one in the neighborhood with whom to explore the mysteries of the horn. You could hear the school band's music and watch their marching, but joining in making the thrilling sounds was impossible. Nor did it help that you owned the scores to a few of their marches and could play with a certain facility and fairly good tone. So there, surrounded by sounds but unable to share a sound, you went it alone. You turned yourself into a one-man band.

24   You played along as best you could with the phonograph, read the score to *The Carnival of Venice* while listening to Del Steigers executing triple-tongue variations on its themes; played the trumpet parts of your bandbook's marches while humming in your head the supporting voices of horns and reeds. And since your city was a seedbed of Southwestern jazz you played Kansas City riffs, bugle calls, and wha-wha-muted imitations of blues singer's pleas. But none of this made up for your lack of fellow musicians. And then, late one Saturday afternoon when your mother and brother were away, and when you had dozed off while reading, you awoke to the nearby sound of live music. At first you thought you were dreaming, and then that you were listening to the high school band, but that couldn't be the source because, instead of floating over building tops and bouncing off wall and windowpane, the sounds you heard rose up, somewhat muffled, from below.

25   With that you ran to a window which faced the driveway, and looking down through the high windowpane of the lighted post office you could see the metal glint of instruments. Then you were on your feet and down the stairs, keeping to the shadows as you drew close and peeped below. And there you looked down upon a room full of men and women postal workers who were playing away at a familiar march. It was like the answer to a silent prayer because you cold tell by the sound that they were beginners like yourself and the covers of the thicket of bandbooks revealed that they were of the same set as yours. For a while you listened and hummed along, unseen but shaking with excitement in the dimming twilight. And then, hardly before the idea

formed in your head, you were skipping up the stairs to grab your cornet, lyre, and bandbook and hurtling down again to the drive.

26   For a while you listened, hearing the music come to a pause and the sound of the conductor's voice. Then came a rap on a music stand and once again the music. And now turning to the march by the light from the window, you snapped score to lyre, raised horn to lip, and began to play; at first silently tonguing the notes through the mouthpiece and then, carried away with the thrill of stealing a part of the music, you tensed your diaphragm and blew. And as you played, keeping time with your foot on the concrete drive, you realized that you were a better cornetist than some in the band and grew bold in the pride of your sound. Now in your mind you were marching along a downtown street to the flying of flats, the tramping of feet, and the cheering of excited crowds. For at least by an isolated act of brassy cunning you had become a member of the band.

27   Yes, but unfortunately you then let yourself become so carried away that you forgot to listen for the conductor's instructions which you were too high and hidden to see. Suddenly the music faded and you opened your ears to the fact that you were now rendering a lonely solo in the startled quietness. And before you could fully return to reality there came the sound of table legs across a floor and a rustle of movement ending in the appearance of a white startled face in the opened window. Then you heard a man's voice exclaim, "I'll be damn, it's a little nigger!" whereupon you took off like a quail at the sound of sudden shotgun fire.

28   Next thing you knew, you were up the stairs and on your bed, crying away in the dark your guilt and embarrassment. You cried and cried, asking yourself how could you have been so lacking in pride as to shame yourself and your entire race by butting in where you weren't wanted. And this just to make some amateur music. To this you had no answers but then and there you made a vow that it would never happen again. And then, slowly, slowly, as you lay in the dark, your earlier lessons in the absurd nature of racial relations came to your aid. And suddenly you found yourself laughing, both at the way you'd run away and the shock you'd caused by joining unasked in the music.

29   Then you could hear yourself intoning in your eight-year-old's imitation of a white Southern accent. "Well boy, you broke the law, so you have to go, and that means you and your chillun too!"

Reading Closely and Thinking Critically

1. In paragraph 1, the author says that the new school was the site of his "first lesson in public schooling." What was that lesson?

2. What is the "peculiar form of integration" that Ellison mentions in paragraph 2? What other "peculiar form[s] of integration" can you think of?

3. After his move to a new house, Ellison made friends with a white boy. Why was that friendship important to Ellison?

4. Although the incident at the zoo was a painful one, it became an ongoing joke for Ellison's family. Explain why.

5. What do you think the author means when he writes, "Discrimination teaches one to discriminate between discriminators" (paragraph 18)?

6. By the end of the essay, Ellison has come to have definite views on race relations and definite reactions to being the target of discrimination. What are those views and reactions?

7. How do you think a racially biased person might react to "On Being the Target of Discrimination?" Why?

Examining Structure and Strategy

1. In paragraph 2, Ellison offers a detailed description of the journey black students took to their school. What does this description contribute?

2. How many examples does Ellison use? With what pattern does he develop these examples? Do you think he uses enough examples? Explain.

3. In what order does Ellison arrange his examples?

4. Ellison does not directly refer to himself. Rather than use "I," he uses "you," even though the essay is clearly autobiographical. Why do you think the author uses "you" instead of "I"?

Considering Language and Style

1. In paragraph 18, Ellison refers to "black comedy." What is "black comedy" (sometimes called "black humor")? Explain the word play involving the term "black comedy" at the end of the paragraph.

2. Consult a dictionary if you are unsure of the meaning of any of these words: *viaduct* (paragraph 2), *red-light district* (paragraph 2), *Mary Jane shoes* (paragraph 2), *incongruity* (paragraph 3), *faux pas* (paragraph 18), *affluent* (paragraph 20), *irrepressible* (paragraph 21).

For Group Discussion or Writing

In paragraph 21, Ellison explains that he learned more about himself by learning more about his white friend and his family. Consider to what extent our knowledge of ourselves is a function of what we know about other people.

Writing Assignments

1. *In your journal.* If you have experienced or observed an incident of discrimination, write about it in your journal. Otherwise, write an assessment of the current state of race relations in the United States.

2. *Using the pattern.* When Ellison writes that "streets [are] no less schools than routes to schools" (paragraph 2), he is observing that much education occurs outside of schoolroom walls. Use examples of your own educational experiences outside of school to support Ellison's observation. Be sure to explain both what you learned and how you learned it.

3. *Using the pattern.* Use examples from your own experience and observation to illustrate "the sudden ways good times can be turned to bad" (paragraph 18).

4. *Using the pattern.* Ellison notes that those who face discrimination routinely learn to counter absurdity with black comedy (paragraph 18). Explain what Ellison means and go on to give examples of ways humor—black comedy or other forms of humor—help people cope with difficult situations.

5. *Using the pattern.* Write an essay with the title "On Being _____." (Fill in the blank with some circumstance of your life— being tall or short, a single parent, an adult learner, an only child, a student athlete, and so forth.) Then use narrative examples to illustrate what life is or was like for you. Like Ellison, try to use some description and conversation.

6. *Considering a theme*. Despite his fierce desire to do so, circumstance denied Ellison the opportunity to play in a band. Tell about a time you were unable to do something that you yearned to do. Be sure to note how you were affected by your inability to participate.

7. *Connecting the readings*. In "The Ways of Meeting Oppression" (page 463), Martin Luther King, Jr. classifies and describes three methods for dealing with racial discrimination. One method King does not discuss is the method used by Ellison's family: humor. Read King's essay and evaluate whether or not humor is an effective way to meet oppression.

WHAT I'VE LEARNED FROM MEN: LESSONS FOR A FULL-GROWN FEMINIST
Barbara Ehrenreich

A social activist who has lent her support to many causes, including the women's movement, Barbara Ehrenreich earned her Ph.D. in biology from Rockefeller University. She is the author of several books, including a recent collection of essays, The Snarling Citizen *(1995). She has also been a college professor, reporter, and magazine editor. In addition to being a regular contributor to* Ms. *and* Mother Jones, *Ehrenreich has also published in a range of periodicals, including* Atlantic Monthly, New York Times Magazine, Esquire, *and* TV Guide. *She currently writes a column for* Time *magazine. In the following essay, which first appeared in* Ms. *in 1985, Ehrenreich combines several patterns of development with exemplification to inform the reader of a problem she thinks women have: they are too ladylike. She goes on to argue that women should become assertive. As you read, notice where in the essay this persuasive purpose becomes apparent.*

THE PATTERNS	THE PURPOSES
exemplification with cause-and-effect analysis, definition, and contrast	*to inform and to persuade*

1   For many years I believed that women had only one thing to learn from men: how to get the attention of a waiter by some means short of kicking over the table and shrieking. Never in my life have I gotten the attention of a waiter, unless it was an off-duty waiter whose car I'd accidentally scraped in a parking lot somewhere. Men, however, can summon a maître d' just by thinking the word "coffee," and this is a power women would be well-advised to study. What else would we possibly want to learn from them? How to interrupt someone in mid-sentence as if you were performing an act of conversational euthanasia? How to drop a pair of socks three feet from an open hamper and keep right on walking? How to make those weird guttural gargling sounds in the bathroom?

2   But now, at mid-life, I am willing to admit that there are some
real and useful things to learn from men. Not from all men—in fact,
we may have the most to learn from some of the men we like the least.
This realization does not mean that my feminist principles have gone
soft with age: what I think women could learn from men is how to get
tough. After more than a decade of consciousness-raising, assertiveness
training, and hand-to-hand combat in the battle of the sexes, we're still
too ladylike. Let me try that again—we're just too *damn* ladylike.

3   Here is an example from my own experience, a story that I blush
to recount. A few years ago, at an international conference held in an
exotic and luxurious setting, a prestigious professor invited me to his
room for what he said would be an intellectual discussion on matters
of theoretical importance. So far, so good. I showed up promptly. But
only minutes into the conversation—held in all-too-adjacent chairs—it
emerged that he was interested in something more substantial than a
meeting of minds. I was disgusted, but not enough to overcome 30-odd
years of programming in ladylikeness. Every time his comments took a
lecherous turn, I chattered distractingly; every time his hand found its
way to my knee, I returned it as if it were something he had misplaced.
This went on for an unconscionable period (as much as 20 minutes);
then there was a minor scuffle, a dash for the door, and I was out—
with nothing violated but my self-esteem. I, a full-grown feminist, con-
versant with such matters as rape crisis counseling and sexual harassment at the workplace, had behaved like a ninny—or, as I now understand it, like a lady.

4   The essence of ladylikeness is a persistent servility masked as
"niceness." For example, we (women) tend to assume that it is our responsibility to keep everything "nice" even when the person we are with
is rude, aggressive, or emotionally AWOL. (In the above example, I was
so busy taking responsibility for preserving the veneer of "niceness" that
I almost forgot to take responsibility for myself.) In conversations with
men, we do almost all the work: sociologists have observed that in
male-female social interactions it's the woman who throws out leading
questions and verbal encouragements ("So how did you *feel* about that?"
and so on) while the man, typically, says "Hmmmm." Wherever we go,
we're perpetually smiling—the on-cue smile, like the now-outmoded
curtsy, being one of our culture's little rituals of submission. We're
trained to feel embarrassed if we're praised, but if we see a criticism
coming at us from miles down the road, we rush to acknowledge it.

And when we're feeling aggressive or angry or resentful, we just tighten up our smiles or turn them into rueful little moues. In short, we spend a great deal of time acting like wimps.

5   For contrast, think of the macho stars we love to watch. Think, for example, of Mel Gibson facing down punk marauders in "The Road Warrior" . . . John Travolta swaggering his way through the early scenes of "Saturday Night Fever" . . . or Marlon Brando shrugging off the local law in "The Wild One." Would they simper their way through tight spots? Chatter aimlessly to keep the conversation going? Get all clutched up whenever they think they might—just might—have hurt someone's feelings? No, of course not, and therein, I think, lies their fascination for us.

6   The attraction of the "tough guy" is that he has—or at least seems to have—what most of us lack, and that is an aura of power and control. In an article, feminist psychiatrist Jean Baker Miller writes that "a woman's using self-determined power for herself is equivalent to selfishness [and] destructiveness—an equation that makes us want to avoid even the appearance of power. Miller cites cases of women who get depressed just when they're on the verge of success—and of women who do succeed and then bury their achievement in self-deprecation. As an example, she describes one company's periodic meetings to recognize outstanding salespeople: when a woman is asked to say a few words about her achievement, she tends to say something like, "Well, I really don't know how it happened. I guess I was just lucky this time." In contrast, the men will cheerfully own up to the hard work, intelligence, and so on, to which they owe their success. By putting herself down, a woman avoids feeling brazenly powerful and potentially "selfish"; she also does the traditional lady's work of trying to make everyone else feel better ("She's not really so smart, after all, just lucky").

7   So we might as well get a little tougher. And a good place to start is by cutting back on the small acts of deference that we've been programmed to perform since girlhood. Like unnecessary smiling. For many women—waitresses, flight attendants, receptionists—smiling is an occupational requirement, but there's no reason for anyone to go around grinning when she's not being paid for it. I'd suggest that we save our off-duty smiles for when we truly feel like sharing them, and if you're not sure what to do with your face in the meantime, study Clint Eastwood's expressions—both of them.

8   Along the same lines, I think women should stop taking responsibility for every human interaction we engage in. In a social encounter

with a woman, the average man can go 25 minutes saying nothing more than "You don't say?" "Izzat so?" and, of course, "Hmmmm." Why should we do all the work? By taking so much responsibility for making conversations go well, we act as if we had much more at stake in the encounter than the other party—and that gives him (or her) the power advantage. Every now and then, we deserve to get more out of a conversation than we put into it: I'd suggest not offering information you'd rather not share ("I'm really terrified that my sales plan won't work") and not, out of sheer politeness, soliciting information you don't really want ("Wherever did you get that lovely tie?"). There will be pauses, but they don't have to be awkward for *you*.

9   It is true that some, perhaps most, men will interpret any decrease in female deference as a deliberate act of hostility. Omit the free smiles and perky conversation-boosters and someone is bound to ask, "Well, what's come over *you* today?" For most of us, the first impulse is to stare at our feet and make vague references to a terminally ill aunt in Atlanta, but we should have as much right to be taciturn as the average (male) taxi driver. If you're taking a vacation from smiles and small talk and some fellow is moved to inquire about what's "bothering" you, just stare back levelly and say, the international debt crisis, the arms race, or the death of God.

10   There are all kinds of ways to toughen up—and potentially move up—at work, and I leave the details to the purveyors of assertiveness training. But Jean Baker Miller's study underscores a fundamental principle that anyone can master on her own. We can stop acting less capable than we actually are. For example, in the matter of taking credit when credit is due, there's a key difference between saying "I was just lucky" and saying "I had a plan and it worked." If you take the credit you deserve, you're letting people know that you were confident you'd succeed all along, and that you fully intend to do so again.

11   Finally, we may be able to learn something from men about what to do with anger. As a general rule, women get irritated; men get *mad*. We make tight little smiles of ladylike exasperation; they pound on desks and roar. I wouldn't recommend emulating the full basso profundo male tantrum, but women do need ways of expressing justified anger clearly, colorfully, and, when necessary, crudely. If you're not just irritated, but *pissed off*, it might help to say so.

12   I, for example, have rerun the scene with the prestigious professor many times in my mind. And in my mind, I play it like Bogart. I

start by moving my chair over to where I can look the professor full in the face. I let him do the chattering, and when it becomes evident that he has nothing serious to say, I lean back and cross my arms, just to let him know that he's wasting my time. I do not smile, neither do I nod encouragement. Nor, of course, do I respond to his blandishments with apologetic shrugs and blushes. Then, at the first flicker of lechery, I stand up and announce coolly, "All right, I've had enough of this crap." Then I walk out—slowly, deliberately, confidently. Just like a man.

13   Or—now that I think of it—just like a woman.

Reading Closely and Thinking Critically

1. What three things has Barbara Ehrenreich learned from men?

2. Why do you think that Ehrenreich "blush[es] to recount" the story of her encounter at the conference? Do you think she has good reason to blush? Explain.

3. Why did Ehrenreich behave as she did in the company of the lecherous professor?

4. Why do you think some women get depressed when "they're on the verge of success," and why do others "bury their achievement in self-deprecation" (see paragraph 6)?

5. Using the evidence in the essay, write a one- or two-sentence definition of lady or ladylike that reflects Ehrenreich's meaning of one of these terms.

6. Ehrenreich's essay was first published in 1985. Is her message still timely? Explain.

Examining Structure and Strategy

1. Ehrenreich delays her thesis until paragraph 2. Which sentence presents that thesis? The material before the thesis is humorous. What purpose does the humor serve? Do you think that the author was wise to begin her discussion of a serious topic in an amusing way?

2. What is the function of the narrative example in paragraph 3? Does this example clarify by showing that something is true, by making the general specific, or both? What contrast does the example set up? (Contrast, discussed in Chapter 7, points out differences.) What other paragraphs include contrast?

3. Brief examples appear in paragraphs 4, 5, 6, 7, 8, and 10. What purposes do these examples serve?

4. Which paragraph provides a definition of *ladylikeness* and *lady?* What is the purpose of that definition? (Definition, which explains the meaning of something, is discussed in Chapter 10.)

5. Paragraphs 6, 9, and 10 include cause-and-effect analysis. (Cause-and-effect analysis, which explains the causes and/or effects of something, is explained in Chapter 8.) What purpose does this analysis serve?

6. What paragraph marks Ehrenreich's move from an informative to a persuasive purpose?

7. The last two paragraphs form the essay's conclusion. What approach does Ehrenreich take to this conclusion?

Considering Language and Style

1. What connotations does the word *lady* have for most people? What connotations does it have in "What I've Learned from Men"?

2. Consult a dictionary if you are unsure of the meaning of any of these words: *maître d'* (paragraph 1), *euthanasia* (paragraph 1), *guttural* (paragraph 1), *lecherous* (paragraph 3), *unconscionable* (paragraph 3), *veneer* (paragraph 4), *rueful* (paragraph 4), *taciturn* (paragraph 9), *purveyors* (paragraph 10).

For Group Discussion and Writing

In paragraph 12, Ehrenreich writes a narration to illustrate what she should have done when she was in the company of the lecherous professor. With two or three classmates, compose your own narration to illustrate behavior that Ehrenreich could or should have displayed.

Writing Assignments

1. *In your journal.* Do you agree or disagree with Ehrenreich? How do you think women should behave? Should men be assertive while women are passive? Respond to these questions, being sure to explain why you believe as you do.

2. *Using the pattern.* Spend some time observing the way male and female students behave in the classroom. Pay attention to how often they speak, what they say, how many questions they ask, where they sit, how they interact with the instructor, how they interact with other students, and so on. If you notice a difference, explain and illustrate that difference. As an alternative, write an essay about what female students can learn from male students or about what male students can learn from female students.

3. *Using the pattern.* Write an essay with the title "What I've Learned from _____." Fill in the blank with the name of a teacher, a boss, a coach, a clergyperson, a relative, or anyone you like. Give examples to illustrate the person's desirable behavior.

4. *Using the pattern.* Do you agree with Ehrenreich? Write an essay to persuade your reader that Ehrenreich is right (or wrong). Use examples to help prove your point. (Your journal entry may give you ideas.)

5. *Considering a theme.* Ehrenreich recommends that women "get a little tougher" (paragraph 7). If women followed this advice, how do you think their behavior would change? How do you think the changes would affect men and how *they* behave?

6. *Connecting the Readings.* In "Talk in the Intimate Relationship: His and Hers" (page 354), Deborah Tannen notes the differences between the communication styles of men and women. Using the information in that essay, in "What I've Learned from Men," and your own thinking, explain whether or not women should change the way they communicate. If so, explain why and how. If not, explain why not.

UNTOUCHABLES
Jonathan Kozol

Born in 1936, Harvard University graduate Jonathan Kozol has taught in both college and public schools. He writes extensively about social issues, particularly about problems in education and the effects of poverty. In 1967, he championed education reform when he published Death at an Early Age: The Destruction of the Hearts and Minds of Negro Children in Boston Public Schools, *for which he won the first of his two National Book Awards. "Untouchables" is an excerpt from* Rachel and Her Children (1988), *a book based on Kozol's interviews with the homeless. In this excerpt, Kozol combines graphic examples with an explanation of the causes and effects of homelessness to inform his reader about the plight of the homeless. In addition, Kozol works to persuade the reader that government officials and the general public are part of the problem. As you read, try to determine why.*

THE PATTERNS	THE PURPOSES
exemplification with cause-and-effect analysis	*to inform and to persuade*

1   Richard Lazarus, an educated, thirty-six-year-old Vietnam veteran I met two days after Thanksgiving in the subway underneath [New York's] Grand Central station, tells me he had never been without a job until the recent summer. In July he underwent the loss of job, children and wife, all in a single stroke. As in almost all these situations, it was the simultaneous occurrence of a number of emergencies, any of which he might sustain alone but not all at the same time, that suddenly removed him from his home.

2   "Always, up until last summer, I have found a job that paid at least $300. Now I couldn't find a job that paid $200. When I found an opening at a department store they said that I was overqualified. If someone had asked me a year ago who are the homeless, I would not have known what to reply. Now I know the answer. They are people like myself. I went to Catholic elementary school. I had my secondary education in a private military school. I joined the service and was sent

to Thailand as an airman." He has a trade. It's known as "inventory data processing." He had held a single job in data processing for seven years until last summer when the company shut down, without a warning, and moved out of state.

3   "When the company left I could find nothing. I looked every-where. I got one job for two months in the summer. Part-time, as a se-curity guard in one of the hotels for homeless families."

4   When I ask which one it was, he says the Martinique. "I clocked the floors for fire check. From the top floor to the lobby I swore to my-self: rat infested, roach infested, drug infested, filth infested, garbage everywhere, and little children playing in the stairs. Innocent people, women, children, boxed in by their misery. Most people are permitted to make more than one mistake. Not when you're poor."

5   In September he was sick. "I was guarding homeless people and I didn't have a home. I slept in Washington Square and Central Park." He's living now in a run-down hotel operated in conjunction with the Third Street Shelter on the Bowery. "When you come in at night the guards wear gloves. They check you with a metal detector. They're afraid to touch me."

6   While we talk we watch an old man nearby who is standing flat and motionless against the wall, surrounded by two dozen bright red shopping bags from Macy's. Every so often, someone stops to put a coin into his hand. I notice the care with which the people drop their coins, in order that their hands do not touch his. When I pass that spot some hours later he will still be there. I'll do the same. I'll look at his hand—the fingers worn and swollen and the nails curled in like claws—and I will drop a quarter and extract my hand and move off quickly. . . .

7   Many homeless people, unable to get into shelters, frightened of disease or violence, or else intimidated by the regulations, look for refuge in such public places as train stations and church doorways.

8   Scores of people sleep in the active subway tunnels of Manhat-tan, inches from 600-volt live rails. Many more sleep on the ramps and station platforms. Go into the subway station under Herald Square on a December night at twelve o'clock and you will see what scarce ac-commodations mean at the rockbottom. Emerging from the subway, walk on Thirty-second Street to Penn station. There you will see an-other form of scarce accommodations: Hot-air grates in the area are highly prized. Homeless people who arrive late often find there is no vacancy, even in a cardboard box over a grate.

9   A man who's taken shelter from the wind that sweeps Fifth Avenue by sleeping beneath the outstretched arms of Jesus on the bronze doors of St. Patrick's Cathedral tells a reporter he can't sleep there anymore because shopkeepers feel that he is hurting business. He moves to the south side of the church where he will be less visible.

10   Stories like these are heard in every state and city of the nation. A twenty-year-old man in Florida tells me that he ran away when he was nine years old from a juvenile detention home in Michigan. He found that he was small enough to slip his body through the deposit slot of a Good Will box. Getting in was easy, he explains, and it was warm because of the clothes and quilts and other gifts that people dropped into the box. "Getting out," he says, "was not so easy. I had to reach my arms above my head, grab hold of the metal edge, twist my body into an S, and pull myself out slowly through the slot. When I was fourteen I was too big to fit into the slot. I believe I am the only person in America who has lived for five years in a Good Will box."

11   Thousands of American people live in dumpsters behind restaurants, hotels, and groceries. A woman describes the unimaginable experience of being awakened in the middle of a winter's night by several late-arriving garbage trucks. She nearly drowned beneath two tons of rotting vegetables and fruit.

12   A thirty-four-year-old man in Chicago found his sanctuary in a broken trash compactor. This offered perhaps the ultimate concealment, and the rotting food which generated heat may have protected him against the freezing weather of Chicago. One night, not knowing that the trash compactor had in his absence been repaired, he fell asleep. When the engine was turned on, he was compressed into a cube of refuse.

13   People in many cities speak of spending nights in phone booths. I have seen this only in New York. Public telephones in Grand Central Station are aligned in recessed areas outside the main concourse. On almost any night before one-thirty, visitors will see a score of people stuffed into these booths with their belongings. Even phone-booth vacancies are scarce in New York City. As in public housing, people are sometimes obliged to double up. One night I stood for an hour and observed three people—man, woman, and child—jammed into a single booth. All three were asleep.

14   Officials have tried a number of times to drive the homeless from Grand Central Station. In order to make conditions less attractive,

benches have been removed throughout the terminal. One set of benches has been left there, I am told, because they have been judged "historic landmarks." The terminal's 300 lockers, used in former times by homeless people to secure their few belongings, were removed in 1986. Authorities were forced to justify this action by declaring them, in the words of the city council, "a threat to public safety." Shaving, cleaning of clothes, and other forms of hygiene are prohibited in the men's room of Grand Central. A fast-food chain that wanted to distribute unsold donuts in the terminal was denied the right to do so on the grounds that this would draw more hungry people.

15   At one-thirty every morning, homeless people are ejected from Grand Central. Many have attempted to take refuge on the ramp that leads to Forty-second Street. The ramp initially provided a degree of warmth because it was protected from the street by wooden doors. The station management responded to this challenge in two ways. First, the ramp was mopped with a strong mixture of ammonia to produce a noxious smell. When the people sleeping there brought cardboard boxes and newspapers to protect them from the fumes, the entrance doors were chained wide open. Temperatures dropped some nights to ten degrees.

16   In a case that won brief press attention in December 1985, an elderly woman who had been living in Grand Central on one of the few remaining benches was removed night after night during the weeks preceding Christmas. On Christmas Eve she became ill. No ambulance was called. At one-thirty the police compelled her to move to the ramp outside. At dawn she came inside, climbed back on bench number 9 to sleep, and died that morning of pneumonia.

17   At Penn Station, fifteen blocks away, homeless women are denied use of the bathroom. Amtrak police come by and herd them off each hour on the hour. In June of 1985, Amtrak officials issued this directive to police: "It is the policy of Amtrak to not allow the homeless and undesirables to remain. . . . Officers are encouraged to eject all undesirables. . . . Now is the time to train and educate them that their presence will not be tolerated as cold weather sets in." In an internal memo, according to CBS, an Amtrak official later went beyond this language and asked flatly: "Can't we get rid of this trash?"

18   In a surprising action, the union representing the police resisted this directive and brought suit against Penn Station's management in 1986. Nonetheless, as temperatures plunged during the nights after

Thanksgiving, homeless men and women were ejected from the station. At 2:00 A.M. I watched a man about my age carry his cardboard box outside the station and try to construct a barricade against the wind that tore across Eighth Avenue. The man was so cold his fingers shook and, when I spoke to him, he tried but could not answer.

19   Driving women from the toilets in a railroad station raises questions that go far beyond the issue of "deterrence." It may surprise the readers to be told that many of these women are quite young. Few are dressed in the familiar rags that are suggested by the term "bag ladies." Some are dressed so neatly and conceal their packages and bags so skillfully that one finds it hard to differentiate them from commuters waiting for a train. Given the denial of hygienic opportunities, it is difficult to know how they are able to remain presentable. The sight of clusters of police officials, mostly male, guarding a women's toilet from its use by homeless females does not speak well for the public conscience of New York.

20   Where do these women defecate? How do they bathe? What will we do when, in her physical distress, a woman finally disrobes in public and begins to urinate right on the floor? We may regard her as an animal. She may by then begin to view herself in the same way.

21   Several cities have devised unusual measures to assure that homeless people will learn quickly that they are not welcome. In Laramie, Wyoming, they are given one night's shelter. On the next morning, an organization called "The Good Samaritan Fund" gives them one-way tickets to another town. The college town of Lancaster, Ohio, offers homeless families one-way tickets to Columbus.

22   In a number of states and cities, homeless people have been murdered, knifed, or set on fire. Two high school students in California have been tried for the knife murder of a homeless man whom they found sleeping in a park. The man, an unemployed house painter, was stabbed seventeen times before his throat was slashed.

23   In Chicago a man was set ablaze while sleeping on a bench in early morning, opposite a popular restaurant. Rush-hour commuters passed him and his charred possessions for four hours before someone called police at noon. A man who watched him burning from a third-floor room above the bench refused to notify police. The purpose was "to get him out," according to a local record-store employee. A resident told reporters that the problem of the homeless was akin to that of "nuclear waste."

24   In Tucson, where police use German shepherds to hunt for the homeless in the skid-row neighborhoods, a mayor was recently elected on the promise that he'd drive the homeless out of town. "We're tired of it. Tired of feeling guilty about these people," said an anti-homeless activist in Phoenix.

25   In several cities it is a crime to sleep in public; in some, armrests have been inserted in the middle of park benches to make it impossible for homeless people to lie down. In others, trash has been defined as "public property," making it a felony to forage in the rotted food.

26   Grocers in Santa Barbara sprinkled bleach on food discarded in their dumpsters. In Portland, Oregon, owners of some shops in redeveloped Old Town have designed slow-dripping gutters (they are known as "drip lines") to prevent the homeless from attempting to take shelter underneath their awnings.

27   Harsher tactics have been recommended in Fort Lauderdale. A city council member offered a proposal to spray trash containers with rat poison to discourage foraging by homeless families. The way to "get rid of vermin," he observed, is to cut their food supply. Some of these policies have been defeated, but the inclination to sequester, punish and conceal the homeless has attracted wide support.

28   "We are the rejected waste of the society," said Lazarus. "They use us, if they think we have some use, maybe for sweeping leaves or scrubbing off graffiti in the subway stations. They don't object if we donate our blood. I've given plasma. That's one way that even worthless people can do something for democracy. We may serve another function too. Perhaps we help to scare the people who still have a home—even a place that's got no heat, that's rat infested, filthy. If they see us in the streets, maybe they are scared enough so they will learn not to complain. If they were thinking about asking for a better heater or a better stove, they're going to think twice. It's like farmers posting scarecrows in the fields. People see these terrifying figures in Penn Station and they know, with one false step, that they could be here too. They think: 'I better not complain.'

29   "The problem comes, however, when they try to find a place to hide us. So it comes to be an engineering question: waste disposal. Store owners certainly regard us in that way. We ruin business and lower the value of good buildings. People fear that we are carriers of illness. Many times we are. So they wear those plastic gloves if they are forced to touch us. It reminds me of the workers in the nuclear reactors. They

have to wear protective clothing if they come in contact with the waste. Then you have state governors all over the United States refusing to allow this stuff to be deposited within their borders. Now you hear them talking about dumping toxic waste into the ocean in steel cans. Could they find an island someplace for the homeless?"

30   His question brings back a strange memory for me. In Boston, for years before the homeless were identified as a distinguishable category of the dispossessed, a de facto caste of homeless people dwelt in a vast public housing project built on a virtual island made, in part, of landfill and linked only by one access road to the United States. Columbia Point, adjacent to a camp for prisoners of war in World War II, was so crowded, violent and ugly that social workers were reluctant to pay visits there, few shop owners would operate a business, and even activists and organizers were afraid to venture there at night. From the highway to Cape Cod, one could see the distant profile of those high-rise structures. A friend from California asked me if it was a prison. He told me that it looked like Alcatraz. I answered that it was a housing project. The notion of shoving these people as far out into the ocean as we can does bring to mind the way that waste-disposal problems sometimes are resolved.

31   New York has many habitable islands. One of those islands has already earned a place in history as the initial stopping point for millions of European refugees who came to the United States in search of freedom. One reason for their temporary isolation was the fear that they might carry dangerous infection. New York's permanent refugees are carriers of every possible infection; most, moreover, have no prospering relatives to vouch for them, as earlier generations sometimes did, in order to assure that they will not become a burden to the state. They are already regarded as a burden. An island that served once as quarantine for aliens who crowded to our shore might serve this time as quarantine for those who huddle in train stations and in Herald Square.

32   Lazarus may not be paranoid in speaking of himself as human waste; he may simply read the headlines in the press. "I just can't accommodate them," says the owner of a building in midtown Manhattan. The mayor of Newark, where a number of homeless families have been sent from New York City, speaks of his fear that displaced families from New York might be "permanently dumped in Newark." He announces a deadline after which they will presumably be dumped back in New York.

33   New Yorkers, according to the *New York Times,* "are increasingly opposing [city] attempts to open jails, shelters for the homeless, garbage incinerators" in their neighborhoods. The *Times* reports the city has begun to "compensate communities" that will accept "homeless shelters and garbage-burning generating plants."

34   Do homeless children have some sense of this equation?

35   "Be not forgetful to entertain strangers," wrote Saint Paul, "for thereby some have entertained angels unawares." But the demonology that now accrues to homeless people, and the filth with which their bodies soon become encrusted, seem to reassure us that few of these strangers will turn out to have been angels in disguise.

36   When homeless infants die in New York City, some are buried not in New York itself but on an island in an unmarked grave. Homeless mothers therefore live with realistic fears that they may lose their infants to anonymous interment. Another fear is that their child may be taken from them at the hour of birth if they should be homeless at the time. Hundreds of babies taken by the state for this and other reasons— often they are very ill and sometimes drug addicted—remain in hospitals, sometimes for months or even years, before a foster home is found. Some of these "boarder babies," as they are described, have been kept so long that they have learned to walk and, for this reason, must be tethered in their cribs. Infants held in hospitals so long, physicians tell us, are likely to grow retarded. Some, even after many months, have not been given names. Like their homeless parents in the city's shelters, they remain bed numbers.

37   Many of these children do in time find homes, though most end up in dismal institutions where conditions are no better and often a great deal worse than those they would have faced had they been left with their own parents. Mayor Koch attempted in 1986 to establish a group home for six or seven of these babies in a small house on a quiet street in Queens. Unknown vandals set the house on fire. "Afraid of Babies in Queens," the *New York Times* headlined its editorial response.

38   It seems we *are* afraid of homeless children, not only in Queens but everywhere in the United States. It is hard to know exactly what it is we fear (the children themselves, the sickness they may carry, the adolescents they will soon become if they survive, or the goad to our own conscience that they represent when they are visible, nearby); but the fear is very real. Our treatment of these children reaffirms the distancing that now has taken place. They are not of us. They are "the Other."

39   What startles most observers is not simply that such tragedies persist in the United States, but that almost all have been well documented and that even the most solid documentation does not bring about corrective action. Instead of action, a common response in New York, as elsewhere, is the forming of a "task force" to investigate. This is frequently the last we hear of it. Another substitute for action is a press event at which a city official seems to overleap immediate concerns by the unveiling of a plan to build a thousand, or a hundred thousand, homes over the course of ten or twenty years at an expense of several billion dollars. The sweep of these announcements tends to dwarf the urgency of the initial issue. When, after a year or so, we learn that little has been done and that the problem has grown worse, we tend to feel not outrage but exhaustion. Exhaustion, however, as we have seen, turns easily to a less generous reaction.

40   "I am about to be heartless," wrote a columnist in *Newsweek* in December 1986. "There are people living on the streets . . . turning sidewalks into dormitories. They are called the homeless. . . . Often they are called worse. They are America's living nightmare. . . . They have got to go."

41   The author notes that it is his taxes which pay for the paving and the cleaning of the streets they call their home. "That makes me their landlord. I want to evict them."

42   A senior at Boston University sees homeless people on the streets not far from where he goes to class. He complains that measures taken recently to drive them from the area have not been sufficiently aggressive: "I would very much like to see actions more severe. . . . " Perhaps, he admits, it isn't possible to have them all arrested, though this notion seems to hold appeal for him; perhaps "a more suitable middle ground" may be arrived at to prevent this "nauseating . . . element" from being permitted to "run free so close to my home."

43   "Our response," says one Bostonian, "has gone from indifference to pitying . . . to hatred." I think this is coming to be true and that it marks an incremental stage in our capacity to view the frail, the ill, the disposed, the unsuccessful not as people who have certain human qualities we share but as an outcast entity. From harsh deterrence to punitive incarceration to the willful cutting off of life supports is an increasingly short journey. "I am proposing triage of a sort, triage by self-selection," writes Charles Murray. "The patient always has the right to fail. Society always has the right to let him."

44   Why is it that writings which present these hardened attitudes seem to prevail so easily in public policy? It may be that kindly voices are more easily derided. Callous attitudes are never subject to the charge of being sentimental. It is a recurrent theme in *King Lear,* writes Ignatieff[1] that "there is a truth in the brutal simplicities of the merciless which the more complicated truth of the merciful is helpless to refute." A rich man, he observes, "never lacks for arguments to deny the poor his charity. 'Basest beggars' can always be found to be 'in the poorest things superfluous.' "

45   "They are a nightmare. I evict them. They will have to go."

46   So from pity we graduate to weariness; from weariness to impatience; from impatience to annoyance; from annoyance to dislike and sometimes to contempt.

Reading Closely and Thinking Critically

1. According to Kozol, what are the prevailing attitudes toward the homeless?

2. To what extent are government officials and the general public part of the problem of homelessness?

3. In paragraph 38, Kozol says that we are afraid of homeless children. What do you think we are afraid of?

4. Do you find any examples particularly moving? Which ones? Why do you think they affect you the way they do?

5. Has your perception of the homeless changed as a result of reading "Untouchables"? Explain.

Examining Structure and Strategy

1. "Untouchables" lacks a stated thesis, but you can still identify the central point of the piece. In your own words, write out that central point.

2. The opening five paragraphs are an extended example. What pattern of development is used for the example? What purposes does the example serve?

---

[1]A noted scholar who has written on the homeless.

3. In addition to the opening paragraphs, much of the essay illustrates the plight of the homeless. Cite at least five paragraphs that serve this purpose.

4.   Which paragraphs illustrate government indifference to the homeless?

5.   Which paragraphs illustrate the public's indifference or fear of the homeless?

6.   From paragraph 17 to the end of the essay, examples appear with cause-and-effect analysis. (Cause-and-effect analysis explains the causes or effects of something; see Chapter 8.) According to these paragraphs, what causes people to treat the homeless the way they do?

Considering Language and Style

1. The title of the essay is a reference to one aspect of Indian class structure. Find out where the untouchables fit into the Indian caste system and then explain why Kozol's reference to this caste is fitting.

2. Kozol tells the story of Richard Lazarus; however, in the introduction to his book, he notes that he has changed the names of those he writes of. Why do you think Kozol chose the name "Lazarus"? Do you find the name appropriate? Explain.

3. Consult a dictionary if you are unsure of the meaning of any of these words: *Bowery* (paragraph 5), *sanctuary* (paragraph 12), *refuse* (paragraph 12), *noxious* (paragraph 15), *skid-row* (paragraph 24), *foraging* (paragraph 27), *vermin* (paragraph 27), *de facto* (paragraph 30), *Alcatraz* (paragraph 30), *demonology* (paragraph 35), *interment* (paragraph 36), *goad* (paragraph 38), *triage* (paragraph 43).

For Group Discussion or Writing

After reading "Untouchables," draw some conclusions with three or four classmates about the kind of people we are as a society. What do homelessness and our reaction to the homeless say about us? Why do we fear and scorn the homeless?

Writing Assignments

1. *In your journal.* Lazarus says that the homeless are "the rejected waste of the society" (paragraph 28). In a page or so, explain what you think Lazarus means and go on to note whether you think his assessment is correct.

2. *Using the pattern.* Pick a particular group of people on campus (for example, athletes, international students, adult learners, or minorities) and use examples to illustrate what life is like for that group. If you like, explain why that group's situation is what it is. (If you need information, do what Kozol did: interview people.)

3. *Using the pattern.* Some of Kozol's examples illustrate government indifference to the homeless, and others illustrate the general public's indifference. Kozol also explains the effect the indifference has on the homeless. In a similar fashion, write an essay that gives examples of perceived government and public indifference to another group, AIDS victims for example. Then explain the effects of this indifference. If necessary, you can check newspaper and magazine articles in your campus library for information. Be sure to check the appendix on how to document material you take from sources.

4. *Using the pattern.* The homeless are not the only "untouchables" in our society. Pick another group that is often feared or scorned and give examples to illustrate our treatment of this group. If you like, explain why the group is treated the way it is and the effects of the treatment.

5. *Using the pattern.* Were there any "untouchables" in your high school (any people feared or scorned)? If so, pick one of these groups or one of these people and use examples to illustrate how they were treated. If you like, explain why the person or people were treated a particular way and the effects of that treatment.

6. *Considering a theme.* Solving the problem of homelessness will require creative thinking. Consider the problem as you understand it from reading "Untouchables" and from any other reading, television viewing, and classwork you have done. Explain a step or steps society can take to begin addressing the problem. Think about what government, private business, individual citizens, or schools can do.

7. *Connecting the readings.* Using "What Is Poverty?" (page 515) and "Untouchables" to stimulate your thinking, describe our attitudes toward the poor and explain how our attitudes contribute to the growing problem of poverty and homelessness.

MAINTENANCE
Naomi Shihab Nye

Naomi Shihab Nye is an award-winning poet who also writes short stories.
She has taught poetry as a visiting writer at schools nationwide. She has also
edited several anthologies of poetry for children, including with Paul B.
Janeczko, I Feel a Little Jumpy Around You: A Book of Her Poems & His
Poems Collected in Pairs. *"Maintenance," which originally appeared in the*
Georgia Review *in 1990, was selected for inclusion in the 1991 edition of*
Best American Essays. *In the essay, Nye combines examples with other pat-*
terns to inform the reader about the variety of ways we tend to those tasks
necessary for maintaining order. Along the way, however, she relates some-
thing of her own approach to maintenance, and she makes a point or two
about life. As you read, think about your own maintenance tasks and how
you perform them.

THE PATTERNS	THE PURPOSES
exemplification with cause-and-	*to inform and to express feelings*
effect analysis, narration, and	*and relate experience*
contrast	

---

1   The only maid I ever had left messages throughout our house:
Lady as I was cleaning your room I heard a mouse and all the clothes in your
closet fell down to the floor there is too many dresses in there take a few off.
Your friend Marta Alejandro. Sometimes I'd find notes stuck into the
couch with straight pins. *I cannot do this room today bec. St. Jude came to*
me in a dream and say it is not safe. Our darkroom was never safe because the devil liked dark places and also the enlarger had an eye that
picked up light and threw it on Marta. She got sick and had to go to a
doctor who gave her green medicine that tasted like leaves.
2   Sometimes I'd come home to find her lounging in the bamboo
chair on the back porch, eating melon, or lying on the couch with a
bowl of half-melted ice cream balanced on her chest. She seemed depressed by my house. She didn't like the noise the vacuum made. Once
she waxed the bathtub with floor wax. I think she was experimenting.

3   Each Wednesday I paid Marta ten dollars—that's what she asked for. When I raised it to eleven, then thirteen, she held the single dollars away from the ten as if they might contaminate it. She did not seem happy to get raises, and my friends (who paid her ten dollars each for the other days of the week) were clearly unhappy to hear about it. After a while I had less work of my own and less need for help, so I found her a position with two gay men who lived in the neighborhood. She called once to say she liked them very much because mostly what they wanted her to do was shine. Shine?

4   "You know, silver. They have a lot of bowls. They have real beautiful spoons not like your spoons. They have a big circle tray that shines like the moon."

5   My friend Kathy had no maid and wanted none. She ran ten miles a day and lived an organized life. Once I brought her a gift—a blue weaving from Guatemala, diagonal patterns of thread on sticks—and she looked at it dubiously. "Give it to someone else," she said. "I really appreciate your thinking of me, but I try not to keep things around here." Then I realized how bare her mantel was. Who among us would fail to place *something* on a mantel? A few shelves in her kitchen also stood empty, and not the highest ones either.

6   Kathy had very definite methods of housekeeping. When we'd eat dinner with her she'd rise quickly, before dessert, to scrape each plate and place it in one side of her sink to soak. She had Tupperware containers already lined up for leftovers and a soup pan with suds ready for the silverware. If I tried to help she'd slap at my hand. "Take care of your own kitchen," she'd say, not at all harshly. After dessert she'd fold up the card table we'd just eaten on and place it against the wall. Dining rooms needed to be swept after meals, and a stationary table just made sweeping more difficult.

7   Kathy could listen to any conversation and ask meaningful questions. She always seemed to remember what anybody said—maybe because she'd left space for it. One day she described having grown up in west Texas in a house of twelve children, the air jammed with voices, crosscurrents, the floors piled with grocery bags, mountains of tossed-off clothes, toys, blankets, the clutter of her sisters' shoes. That's when she decided to have only one pair of shoes at any time, running shoes, though she later revised this to include a pair of sandals.

8   Somehow I understood her better then, her tank tops and wiry arms . . . She ran to shake off dust. She ran to leave it all behind.

9   Another friend, Barbara, lived in an apartment but wanted to live in a house. Secretly I loved her spacious domain, perched high above the city with a wide sweep of view, but I could understand the wish to plant one's feet more firmly on the ground. Barbara has the best taste of any person I've ever known—the best khaki-colored linen clothing, the best books, the name of the best masseuse. When I'm with her I feel uplifted, excited by life; there's so much to know about that I haven't heard of yet, and Barbara probably has. So I agreed to help her look.

10   We saw one house where walls and windows had been sheathed in various patterns of gloomy brocade. We visited another where the kitchen had been removed because the owners only ate in restaurants. They had a tiny office refrigerator next to their bed which I peeked into after they'd left the room: orange juice in a carton, coffee beans. A Krups coffee maker on the sink in their bathroom. They seemed unashamed, shrugging, "You could put a new kitchen wherever you like."

11   Then we entered a house that felt unusually vivid, airy, and hard-to-define until the realtor mentioned, "Have you noticed there's not a stick of wood anywhere in this place? No wood furniture, not even a wooden salad bowl, I'd bet. These people, very hip, you'd like them, want wood to stay in forests. The man says wood makes him feel heavy."

12   Barbara and her husband bought that house—complete with pear-shaped swimming pool, terraces of pansies, plum trees, white limestone rock gardens lush with succulents—but they brought wood into it. Never before had I been so conscious of things like wooden cutting boards. I helped them unpack and stroked the sanded ebony backs of African animals.

13   Then, after about a year and a half, Barbara called to tell me they were selling the house. "You won't believe this," she said, "but we've decided. It's the maintenance—the yardmen, little things always breaking—I'm so busy assigning chores I hardly have time for my own work anymore. A house really seems ridiculous to me now. If I want earth I can go walk in a park."

14   I had a new baby at the time and everything surprised me. My mouth dropped open, oh yes. I was living between a mound of fresh cloth diapers and a bucket of soiled ones, but I agreed to participate in the huge garage sale Barbara was having.

15   "That day," Barbara said later, "humanity sank to a new lowest level." We had made signs declaring the sale would start at 9 A.M., but

by 8, middle-aged women and men were already ripping our boxes open, lunging into the back of my loaded pickup truck to see what I had. Two women argued in front of me over my stained dish drainer. I sold a kerosene heater which we'd never lit and a stack of my great-uncle's rumpled tablecloths, so large they completely engulfed an ironing board. One woman flashed a charm with my initial on it under my nose, saying, "I'd think twice about selling this, sweetheart—don't you realize it's ten carat?"

16   Afterwards we counted our wads of small bills and felt drained, diluted. We had spent the whole day bartering in a driveway, releasing ourselves from the burden of things we did not need. We even felt disgusted by the thought of eating—yet another means of accumulation—and would derive no pleasure from shopping, or catalogues, for at least a month.

17   While their new apartment was being refurbished, Barbara and her husband lived in a grand hotel downtown. She said it felt marvelous to use all the towels and have fresh ones appear on the racks within hours. Life seemed to regain its old recklessness. Soon they moved back to the same windswept apartment building they'd left, but to a higher floor. Sometimes I stood in their living room staring out at the horizon, which always seemed flawlessly clean.

18   My mother liked to sing along to records while she did housework—Mahalia Jackson, the Hallelujah Chorus. Sometimes we would sing duets, "Tell Me Why" and "Nobody Knows the Trouble I've Seen." I felt lucky my mother was such a clear soprano. We also sang while preparing for the big dinners my parents often gave, while folding the napkins or decorating little plates of hummus with olives and radishes.

19   I hungrily savored the tales told by the guests, the wild immigrant fables and metaphysical links. My mother's favorite friend, a rail-thin vegetarian who had once been secretary to Aldous Huxley, conversed passionately with a Syrian who was translating the Bible from Aramaic, then scolded me for leaving a mound of carrots on my plate.

20   "I'm not going to waste them!" I said. "I always save carrots for last because I love them best."

21   I thought this would please her, but she frowned. "Never save what you love, dear. You know what might happen? You may lose it while you are waiting."

22   It was difficult to imagine losing the carrots—what were they going to do, leap off my plate?—but she continued.

23   "Long ago I loved a man very much. He had gone on a far journey—our relationship had been delicate—and I waited anxiously for word from him. Finally a letter arrived and I stuffed it into my bag, trembling, thinking I would read it later on the train. Would rejoice in every word, was what I thought, but you know what happened? My purse was snatched away from me—stolen!—before I boarded the train. Things like that didn't even happen much in those days. I never saw the letter again—and I never saw my friend again either."

24   A pause swallowed the room. My mother rose to clear the dishes. Meaningful glances passed. I knew this woman had never married. When I asked why she hadn't written him to say she lost the letter, she said, "Don't you see, I also lost the only address I had for him."

25   I thought about this for days. Couldn't she have tracked him down? Didn't she know anyone else who might have known him and forwarded a message? I asked my mother, who replied that love was not easy.

26   Later my mother told me about a man who had carried a briefcase of important papers on a hike because he was afraid they might get stolen from the car. The trail wove high up the side of a mountain, between stands of majestic piñon. As he leaned over a rocky gorge to breathe the fragrant air, his fingers slipped and the briefcase dropped down into a narrow crevasse. They heard it far below, clunking into a deep underground pool. My mother said the man fell to the ground and sobbed.

27   The forest ranger whistled when they brought him up to the spot. "Hell of an aim!" He said there were some lost things you just had to say goodbye to, "like a wedding ring down a commode." My parents took the man to Western Union so he could telegraph about the lost papers, and the clerk said, "Don't feel bad, every woman drops an earring down a drain once in her life." The man glared. "This was not an earring—*I am not a woman!*"

28   I thought of the carrots, and the letter, when I heard his story. And of my American grandmother's vintage furniture, sold to indifferent buyers when I was still a child, too young even to think of antique wardrobes or bed frames. And I also thought of another friend of my parents, Peace Pilgrim, who walked across America for years, lecturing about inner peace and world peace. A single, broad pocket in her tunic contained all her worldly possessions: a toothbrush, a few postage stamps, a ballpoint pen. She had no bank account behind her and noth-

ing in storage. Her motto was "I walk till given shelter, I fast till given food." My father used to call her a freeloader behind her back, but my mother recognized a prophet when she saw one. I grappled with the details. How would it help humanity if I slept in a cardboard box under a bridge?

29   Peace Pilgrim told a story about a woman who worked hard so she could afford a certain style of furniture—French provincial, I think. She struggled to pay for insurance to protect it and rooms large enough to house it. She worked so much she hardly ever got to sit on it. "Then her life was over. And what kind of a life was that?"

30   Peace Pilgrim lived so deliberately she didn't even have colds. Shortly before her death in a car accident—for years she hadn't even ridden in cars—she sat on the fold-out bed in our living room, hugging her knees. I was grown by then, but all our furniture was still from thrift stores. She invited me to play the piano and sing for her, which I did, as she stared calmly around the room. "I loved to sing as a child," she said. "It is nice to have a piano."

31   In my grandmother's Palestinian village, the family has accumulated vast mounds and heaps of woolly comforters, stacking them in great wooden cupboards along the walls. The blankets smell pleasantly like sheep and wear coverings of cheerful gingham, but no family—not even our huge one on the coldest night—could possibly use that many blankets. My grandmother smiled when I asked her about them. She said people should have many blankets and head scarves to feel secure.

32   I took a photograph of her modern refrigerator, bought by one of the emigrant sons on a visit home from America, unplugged in a corner and stuffed with extra yardages of cloth and old magazines. I felt like one of those governmental watchdogs who asks how do you feel knowing your money is being used this way? My grandmother seemed nervous whenever we sat near the refrigerator, as if a stranger who refused to say his name had entered the room.

33   I never felt women were more doomed to housework than men; I thought women were lucky. Men had to maintain questionably pleasurable associations with less tangible elements—mortgage payments, fan belts and alternators, the IRS. I preferred sinks, and the way people who washed dishes immediately became exempt from after-dinner conversation. I loved to plunge my hands into tubs of scalding bubbles. Once my father reached in to retrieve something and reeled back, yelling, "Do you always make it this hot?" My parents got a dishwasher

as soon as they could, but luckily I was out of college by then and never had to touch it. To me it only seemed to extend the task. You rinse, you bend and arrange, you measure soap—and it hasn't even started yet. How many other gratifications were as instant as the old method of washing dishes?

34   But it's hard to determine how much pleasure someone else gets from an addiction to a task. The neighbor woman who spends hours pinching off dead roses and browned lilies, wearing her housecoat and dragging a hose, may be as close as she comes to bliss, or she may be feeling utterly miserable. I weigh her sighs, her monosyllables about weather. Endlessly I compliment her yard. She shakes her head—"It's a lot of work." For more than a year she tries to get her husband to dig out an old stump at one corner but finally gives up and plants bougainvillea in it. The vibrant splash of pink seems to make her happier than anything else has in a long time.

35   Certain bylaws: If you have it, you will have to clean it. Nothing stays clean long. No one else notices your messy house as much as you do; they don't know where things are supposed to go anyway. It takes much longer to clean a house than to mess it up. Be suspicious of any cleaning agent (often designated with a single alphabetical letter, like *C* or *M*) that claims to clean everything from floors to dogs. Never install white floor tiles in the bathroom if your family members have brown hair. Cloth diapers eventually make the best rags—another reason beyond ecology. Other people's homes have charisma, charm, because you don't have to know them inside out. If you want high ceilings you may have to give up closets. (Still, as a neighbor once insisted to me, "high ceilings make you a better person.") Be wary of vacuums with headlights; they burn out in a month. A broom, as one of my starry-eyed newlywed sisters-in-law once said, *does a lot.* So does a dustpan. Whatever you haven't touched, worn, or eaten off of in a year should be passed on; something will pop up immediately to take its place.

36   I can't help thinking about these things—I live in the same town where Heloise[1] lives. And down the street, in a shed behind his house, a man produces orange-scented wood moisturizer containing beeswax. You rub it on three times, let it set, then buff it off. Your house smells like a hive in an orchard for twenty-four hours.

---

[1]Heloise: a woman who writes books and a newspaper column with household hints.

37   I'd like to say a word, just a short one, for the background hum of lesser, unexpected maintenances that can devour a day or days—or a life, if one is not careful. The scrubbing of the little ledge above the doorway belongs in this category, along with the thin lines of dust that quietly gather on bookshelves in front of the books. It took me an hour working with a bent wire to unplug the bird feeder, which had become clogged with fuzzy damp seed—no dove could get a beak in. And who would ever notice? The doves would notice. I am reminded of Buddhism whenever I undertake one of these invisible tasks: one acts, without any thought of reward or foolish notion of glory.

38   Perhaps all cleaning products should be labeled with additional warnings, as some natural-soap companies have taken to philosophizing right above the price tag. Bottles of guitar polish might read: "If you polish your guitar, it will not play any better. People who close their eyes to listen to your song will not see the gleaming wood. But you may feel more intimate with the instrument you are holding."

39   Sometimes I like the preparation for maintenance, the motions of preface, better than the developed story. I like to move all the chairs off the back porch many hours before I sweep it. I drag the mop and bucket into the house in the morning even if I don't intend to mop until dusk. This is related to addressing envelopes months before I write the letters to go inside.

40   Such extended prefacing drives my husband wild. He comes home and can read the house like a mystery story—small half-baked clues in every room. I get out the bowl for the birthday cake two days early. I like the sense of house as still life, on the road to becoming. Why rush to finish? You will only have to do it over again, sooner. I keep a proverb from Thailand above my towel rack: "Life is so short/we must move very slowly." I believe what it says.

41   My Palestinian father was furious with me when, as a teenager, I impulsively answered a newspaper ad and took a job as a maid. A woman, bedfast with a difficult pregnancy, ordered me to scrub, rearrange, and cook—for a dollar an hour. She sat propped on pillows, clicking her remote control, glaring suspiciously whenever I passed her doorway. She said her husband liked green Jell-O with fresh fruit. I was slicing peaches when the oven next to me exploded, filling the house with heavy black smoke. My meat loaf was only half baked. She shrieked and cried, blaming it on me, but how was I responsible for her oven?

42   It took me a long time to get over my negative feelings about pregnant women. I found a job scooping ice cream and had to wrap my swollen wrists in heavy elastic bands because they hurt so much. I had never considered what ice cream servers went through.

43   These days I wake up with good intentions. I pretend to be my own maid. I know the secret of travelers: each time you leave your home with a few suitcases, books, and note pads, your maintenance shrinks to a lovely tiny size. All you need to take care of is your own body and a few changes of clothes. Now and then, if you're driving, you brush the pistachio shells off the seat. I love ice chests and miniature bottles of shampoo. Note the expansive breath veteran travelers take when they feel the road spinning open beneath them again.

44   Somewhere close behind me the outline of Thoreau's[2] small cabin plods along, a ghost set on haunting. It even has the same rueful eyes Henry David had in the portrait in his book. A wealthy woman with a floral breakfast nook once told me I would "get over him" but I have not—documented here, I have not.

45   Marta Alejandro, my former maid, now lives in a green out-building at the corner of Beauregard and Madison. I saw her recently, walking a skinny wisp of a dog and wearing a bandanna twisted and tied around her waist. I called to her from my car. Maybe I only imagined she approached me reluctantly. Maybe she couldn't see who I was.

46   But then she started talking as if we had paused only a second ago. "Oh hi I was very sick were you? The doctor said it has to come to everybody. Don't think you can escape! Is your house still as big as it used to be?"

Reading Closely and Thinking Critically

1. What does Nye mean by *maintenance?* Does *maintenance* mean the same thing to everyone? Explain.

2. Explain how each of the following feels about or handles maintenance: Marta, Kathy, Barbara, and Peace Pilgrim. Whose view of maintenance appeals to you the most? Why?

3. Why was the author more inclined to have a maid than Kathy was?

---

[2]Thoreau, Henry David (1817–1862): a U.S. naturalist and author who lived simply.

4. How would you describe the author's attitude toward Marta? Why do you think she has this attitude?

5. What point do the stories about saving the carrots, the stolen love letter, and the lost briefcase make?

6. What is the moral of the story Peace Pilgrim tells in paragraph 29?

7. Why does Nye think that women are luckier than men when it comes to maintenance? Do you agree with her?

8. Why do you think the author is haunted by Thoreau?

Examining Structure and Strategy

1. Nye opens and closes her essay with references to Marta. Why do you think she does so?

2. How does Nye make use of examples?

3. How does Nye make use of narration?

4. What cause-and-effect relationship is established in paragraphs 37–38? (Cause-and-effect analysis, explained in Chapter 8, explains the causes and/or the effects of something.)

5. What is the purpose of the contrast (explanation of differences) in paragraph 33?

6. Why do you think Nye tells about the garage sale she and Barbara had?

Considering Language and Style

1. Nye's father called Peace Pilgrim a freeloader, but Nye's mother called her a prophet. What is a *freeloader*? A *prophet*? Which do you think Peace Pilgrim is?

2. Consult a dictionary if you are unsure of the meaning of any of these words: *dubiously* (paragraph 5), *domain* (paragraph 9), *masseuse* (paragraph 9), *sheathed* (paragraph 10), *brocade* (paragraph 10), *succulents* (paragraph 12), *hummus* (paragraph 18), *metaphysical* (paragraph 19), *vintage* (paragraph 28), *rueful* (paragraph 44).

For Group Discussion or Writing

The essay provides clues about why the people mentioned have the maintenance styles that they do. For example, Kathy is structured because her childhood was chaotic. With three or four classmates, explain why each of the following has the maintenance styles that she does: the author, Barbara, Peace Pilgrim, the Palestinian grandmother. What needs do the various maintenance styles fulfill for each of these women?

Writing Assignments

1. *In your journal.* In a page or so, describe your own maintenance style and why you think you have that style.

2. *Using the pattern.* In paragraph 16, Nye says of the garage sale: "We had spent the whole day bartering in a driveway, releasing ourselves from the burden of things we did not need." Explain how the things we own can be a burden and illustrate your view with examples of burdensome things.

3. *Using the pattern.* In paragraph 40, Nye refers to a proverb from Thailand: "Life is so short/ we must move very slowly." Explain what this proverb means and then give examples of ways we can move more slowly. How do you think lives will be affected by these slower movements?

4. *Using the pattern.* If you live (or have lived) in an apartment house or in a residence hall, write an essay that describes and illustrates the range of maintenance styles among those who live in these places.

5. *Using the pattern.* Use people you know as examples to illustrate different study techniques, problem-solving techniques, or attitudes toward life. If you like, you can also use narration to illustrate and cause-and-effect analysis to explain the effects of the different approaches.

6. *Considering a theme.* In paragraph 16, Nye notes that our possessions can be a burden. However, she makes it clear that sometimes we need possessions "to feel secure." Explain how possessions can be both a burden and a source of security.

7. *Connecting the Readings.* Read "What Is Poverty?" on page 515 and explain how you think Jo Goodwin Parker would define maintenance and why you think she would define the word that way.

ADDITIONAL ESSAY ASSIGNMENTS

See pages 202 and 204 for suggestions for writing exemplification and for a revision checklist.

1. Use extended and/or brief examples to show that the life of a teenager is not an easy one.

2. Use brief examples to prove that advertisements cause people to want things that they do not really need.

3. Use extended examples to show that life has its surprising moments.

4. Use humorous examples to show that people often make fools of themselves.

5. Use examples to illustrate the benefits or drawbacks of computers.

6. Form a generalization about the way some group is depicted on television (women, police officers, the elderly, teenagers, or fathers, for instance) and provide examples to illustrate that generalization.

7. Provide two or three extended examples to illustrate the fact that appearances can be deceiving.

8. Form a generalization about your relationship with one of your parents or caregivers and illustrate that generalization with examples.

9. Use illustrations to persuade your reader that sometimes a lie is better than the truth. (The student essay on page 204 fulfills this assignment.)

10. Provide humorous examples to illustrate Murphy's First Law ("What *can* go wrong, *will* go wrong").

11. Provide examples to show that people are at their worst when they are behind the wheels of their cars.

12. Use examples to persuade your reader that athletics have (or have not) assumed excessive importance in this country.

13. Use examples to persuade your reader that a student athlete is not a "dumb jock."

14. Use examples to persuade your reader that the U.S. education system is in need of a major overhaul.

15. Use examples to illustrate the best characteristics of your favorite teacher.

16 Use examples to illustrate the fact that sometimes people can surprise you.

17. To share with your reader, use examples to illustrate some aspect of the relationship you had with your best friend when you were growing up.

18. Provide brief and/or extended examples to illustrate the fact that jealousy is a destructive emotion.

19. Provide examples to illustrate the fact that people make their own luck.

20. *Exemplification in context:* Assume that your local Parents-Teachers Association (PTA) has asked families and schools to consider a month-long ban on television viewing for school-age children. The organization's goal is to get children away from their television sets and engaged in "more worthwhile" activities, such as reading, interacting with family members, studying, playing sports, enjoying hobbies, and so forth. A public forum is being held to look at the advantages and disadvantages of the proposal. Write a position paper to be distributed at the forum, a paper in which you support or attack the moratorium by offering illustrations to convince people that television has negative (or positive) effects on children.

6

⑥ PROCESS ANALYSIS

The Readings, the Patterns, and the Purposes

THE PATTERN

A process analysis explains how something is made or done. A *directional process analysis* gives the steps in a process the reader may want to perform. You encounter directional process analysis all the time. For example, when you buy a digital watch, the accompanying instruction booklet explains how to set the time, how to change the battery, how to work the alarm, and so on. Each of these explanations is a directional process analysis. When you use a recipe to prepare a new dish, you are reading and following a directional process analysis. Similarly, if you apply for a scholarship, you read the instructions for completing the application, which are a directional process analysis.

An *explanatory process analysis* tells how something works or how something is made or done, but the process explained will not be carried out by the reader. Explanatory process analyses are also common. For example, your biology textbook will explain how plants convert carbon dioxide to oxygen with the process of photosynthesis. Since the reader will not engage in photosynthesis, the process analysis is purely explanatory. Similarly, explanations of how an internal combustion engine works, how natural selection occurs, and how rivers become polluted are explanatory process analyses.

THE PURPOSES OF PROCESS ANALYSIS

A process analysis can inform the reader in a number of ways. First, it can tell how something is made or done so the reader can perform the process. For example, a process analysis that explains how to program a VCR serves this informational purpose. A process analysis can also inform the reader of a better way to do something. For example, you already know how to study, but you still might be interested in a process analysis with the title "Six Steps to More Efficient Studying" because the essay may save you time and improve your grades by showing you a better way to do something.

An explanatory process analysis informs by telling how something is made or done, even when the author knows that the reader will never perform the process. This is the case with "Behind the Formaldehyde Curtain" (page 296), which explains how a body is prepared for burial. The author knows you are not reading her essay because you want to go out and embalm a body. You are reading it because you are curious about how this process is performed and you want to learn about it.

Finally, a process analysis can inform a reader about the beauty, difficulty, or complexity of a process so the reader can better appreciate it. For example, say that you are a distance runner. If you want your reader to appreciate the rigor and discipline that go into running a cross-country race, you can describe the process of running that race to impress the reader with its difficulty.

In addition to informing a reader, a process analysis can entertain. In "Attitude," (page 271), for example, Garrison Keillor entertains with a humorous and loving account of how softball should be played.

A process analysis can also be a vehicle for expressing feelings and relating experience. For example, a writer who wants to relate a portion of his childhood could describe a process whereby he and his grandfather prepared for their annual fishing trips.

Finally, a process analysis can be written to persuade a reader. If you want to convince your reader that your way of performing a process is the best way, you will have to tell how your process is performed. If you want to convince your reader that a particular process is harmful, you will need to detail that process. In "What Sort of Car-Rt-Sort Am I?" (page 308), for example, Erik Larson explains how companies compile information about us. Larson's purpose is to show that this process is dangerous because it invades our privacy.

Process Analysis in College Writing

You are likely to use both directional and explanatory process analyses in much of your college writing. An obvious use of directional process analysis is for biology, chemistry, and physics lab reports, where you must explain the process you followed to complete various experiments. In a marketing class, an examination question might ask you to explain how to conduct a consumer survey, which will involve you in writing a directional process analysis, as will a report you write for a computer science class that explains how to develop a certain kind of computer program. In an art class, you would write a directional process analysis if you were to explain how to mix paints to achieve a desired effect.

Similarly, you will often be called upon to write explanatory process analyses. For example, for a geology midterm exam you may need to explain how erosion occurs; for a political science exam you may need to explain how the electoral college works; for a psychology class, you may need to write a research paper that tells how children acquire language.

SUPPORTING DETAILS

Because a process analysis explains how something is made or done, the primary detail will be the steps in the process. Sometimes, you will find it necessary to go on to explain *how* a particular step is performed. For example, in "Don't Just Stand There" (page 288), Diane Cole describes how to deal with racial, ethnic, and sexist remarks. At one point she tells what to do when the remark occurs at a large meeting or public talk, and then she goes on to explain how to perform the step:

> At a large meeting or public talk, you might consider passing the speaker a note . . . You could write, "You may not realize it, but your remarks were offensive because . . . "

At times, you may want to explain *why* a step is performed so your reader appreciates the importance of the step. For example, assume you are explaining the best job application procedure, and you mention that you should follow every interview with a letter of thanks that also reaffirms your interest in the position. To help your reader appreciate the importance of this step, you can explain that the letter marks you as someone who is courteous and as someone who follows through—two qualities that can help you land the job.

If you need to clarify a step to be sure your reader understands, an example may be in order. In this excerpt from "Don't Just Stand There," notice how the author uses an example to clarify how the host of a gathering can control the behavior of guests:

> If you, yourself, are the host, you can exercise more control; you are, after all, the one who sets the rules and the tone of behavior in your home. Once, when Professor Kahn's party guests began singing offensive, racist songs, for instance, he kicked them all out, saying "You don't sing songs like that in my house!" And, he adds, "they never did again."

If you think your reader might perform a step incorrectly or might perform an unnecessary step, you can explain what not to do and why. For example, in "Don't Just Stand There," the author cautions the reader not to deal with offensive remarks by embarrassing a person publicly:

> But in general, psychologists say, shaming a person in public may have the opposite effect of the one you want: The speaker may deny his offense all the more strongly in order to save face.

If a particular part of the process can be troublesome, you can point that out to the reader, as Jessica Mitford does in "Behind the Formaldehyde Curtain":

> Proper placement of the body requires a delicate sense of balance. It should lie as high as possible in the casket, yet not so high that the lid, when lowered, will hit the nose. On the other hand, we are cautioned, placing the body too low creates the impression that the body is in a box.

If you use any specialized vocabulary in your process analysis, your reader may need a definition. Notice how Erik Larson handles this in "What Sort of Car-Rt-Sort Am I?":

> Next time you see "car-rt-sort" on your bulk-rate mail, know this: Whoever sent it got a postal discount by sorting it by carrier route, a hunk of postal geography smaller than a zipcode zone.

If completing the process requires particular materials, make note of that fact early on, perhaps even in the first paragraph. If, for example, you are explaining how to build a bookcase, note the lumber sizes, tools, and other materials needed.

Finally, description is often part of a process analysis, particularly if you want to help your reader appreciate the beauty or complexity of the process. Notice, for example, how Larry Woiwode uses description in "Wanting an Orange" (page 277) when he explains the process of eating an orange that is cut in half:

> If you prefer to have your orange sliced in half, as some people do, the edges of the peel will abrade the corners of your mouth, making them feel raw, as you eat down into the white of the rind (which is the only way to do it) until you can see daylight through the orangy bubbles composing the outside . . . Close your eyes to be on the safe side, and for the eruption in your mouth of the slivers of watery meat, which should be broken and rolled fine over your tongue for the essence of orange.

SELECTING AND ORDERING SUPPORTING DETAILS

The thesis for a process analysis can mention the process to be explained, something like this:

> **A person should take great care when choosing a personal physician.** (Thesis indicates that the essay will explain how to choose a personal physician.)

In addition to mentioning the process, the thesis can also explain why it is important to understand the process:

> **To avoid making a costly mistake, follow this procedure when you shop for a car.** (Thesis indicates that the process is important because it can save the reader money.)

If you do not mention the importance of the process in the thesis, you can do so elsewhere in the essay, perhaps in your introduction or conclusion. In "Don't Just Stand There," Diane Cole uses her fourth paragraph to explain why it is important to know a process for dealing with racial and ethnic insults:

But left unchecked, racial slurs and offensive ethnic jokes "can poison the atmosphere," says Michael McQuillan, adviser for racial/ethnic affairs for the Brooklyn borough president's office. "Hearing these remarks conditions us to accept them; and if we accept these, we can become accepting of other acts."

If it is important to explain why you are qualified to describe the process, you can do so in your introduction. For example, if you are explaining an efficient note-taking system you have devised, you can explain that you have made the dean's list every term since you started using the system.

When the steps in the process must be performed in a particular order, details are arranged in a chronological (or time) order. To help your reader follow the chronological order, transitions like these can help:

First, you must . . .

Next, be careful to . . .

Now, you can . . .

After that, try . . .

Finally, you should . . .

If you need to mention what *not* to do so your reader does not make a mistake or misunderstand a step, include this information at the point in the process when the confusion can occur. If you need to define a term, do so the first time the term is used. Finally, if you need to explain why a step is performed, do so when the step is given.

SUGGESTIONS FOR WRITING A PROCESS ANALYSIS

1. Select a process you know well so you are not struggling for detail or presenting the process incompletely. However, avoid giving directions on how to cook something, how to travel to a particular destination, or how to build something. Your readers can research these things easily on their own and do not need your essay for this information.

2. Decide whether you are writing a directional or explanatory process analysis. For the former, readers must be able to follow your instructions on their own. For the latter, they need only be able to understand the process.

3. List every step in the process in the order it is performed.

4. Write a statement that explains the importance of the process.

5. With your list of steps as a guide, write out the process in one sitting without worrying about grammar, punctuation, or anything else. You can revise later. Try to include a statement that indicates the importance of understanding the process. If you wish, this statement can be your thesis.

Checklist for Revising a Process Analysis

1. Do you need to explain how any steps are performed?
2. Do you need to mention what not to do?
3. Do you need to explain why any steps are performed?
4. Do you need any clarifying examples?
5. Do you need to describe anything?
6. Do you need to define any terms?
7. Do you need to point out any troublesome aspects?
8. Have you indicated the importance of understanding the process?

ANNOTATED STUDENT ESSAY

The following student essay combines both explanatory and directional process analysis in an informative essay with the potential to save lives.

When Lightning Strikes

1   Lightning is the most dangerous, the most destructive force in nature. Each year in the United States alone, it destroys property worth hundreds of millions of dollars, and it kills more

Paragraph 1

The introduction gives background information. The thesis (the last sentence) gives the process and why it is important.

people than any other natural disaster. Yet both property and lives could be saved if people took the appropriate precautions during a thunderstorm.

2   Lightning is an electrical occurrence whose main charge flashes from the earth to a cloud, not from cloud to earth as is commonly believed. During a storm, turbulence inside clouds separates electrical charges so that negative charges accumulate in the lower part of the cloud, and positive charges build up in the earth and in the upper part of the cloud. Lightning occurs when the attraction between these opposite charges becomes strong enough to bridge the gap between them. An invisible stroke "leader" advances from the cloud toward the ground, establishing the path the lightning stroke will take. When the stroke leader nears the ground, electrical charges rush up through the conducting path to reunite the positive and negative charges. It is this return stroke that causes the bright flash and the thunder clap. Intensely powerful, the lightning stroke may contain over 100 million volts.

Paragraph 2

Before explaining the main process, paragraph 2 explains a secondary process: how lightning occurs. This provides an informative context for the rest of the essay.

3   Although most lightning deaths occur outside, people inside are not out of danger, and, therefore, must know what to do. Lightning can enter houses through chimneys, plumbing, wiring, TV antennas, or the roof. In one tragic case, lightning hit a tree beside a house, moved down the trunk to an attached wire clothesline, followed the line to a metal fitting that fastened it to the house, and reached a television set that touched that wall of the house. A young woman, attempting to unplug the set, was killed instantly.

Paragraph 3

The topic sentence (first sentence) gives the focus as people inside. Paragraph's example explains why knowing the process is important.

4   Clearly, those indoors must know how to protect themselves because lightning can enter a house a number of ways. For example, a common lightning target is a chimney with attached antenna that is not grounded with a large enough conductor. A charge striking it may jump down the chimney or find a better conductor on the way down, such as a metal fixture around the fireplace. If the new conductor is not grounded, the charge leaps out to the next-nearest conductor, and anyone in the path will feel the jolt. Therefore, during an electrical storm, it is wise to stay away from metal objects such as stoves, sinks, and

Paragraph 4

The topic sentence (first sentence) notes focus is still on those inside. Paragraph explains by what process lightning enters a house, and it gives instructions for what to do. It also explains how to perform the process and what not to do.

tubs. The safest spot is generally the center of a room, but be sure this spot is not between one conductor leading down from the roof and another leading to the ground. For example, a seat between a fireplace and a metallic heating or plumbing fixture could become an "electric chair." Obviously, an important protection is a properly installed and designed lightning-rod system that will intercept a strike and channel it harmlessly deep into the ground. This protection is not expensive; however, use a competent, experienced installer. This is definitely not a do-it-yourself project. Also, since phone wires are often hit during an electrical storm, you are wise to stay off the telephone until the storm passes.

5   If you are caught outdoors during an electrical storm, you must be particularly careful to protect yourself. The safest place to be is in a *closed* automobile. Under no circumstances should you seek shelter under isolated trees or in small groves. Try instead to find a cave, ravine, or ditch to crouch down in. Otherwise, crouch down in the open. Avoid hills, utility poles, golf courses, and anything that can attract a charge—wire fences, for example. Stay out of water, particularly out of small boats. Because rocky ground offers poor conductivity for lightning current, causing it to dissipate over a wide area, avoid such sites. Also, groups of people in the open provide more attraction than individuals, so it is wise to scatter during a thunderstorm.

6   If despite these precautions a storm strikes so close that the flash of lightning and the sound of thunder are almost simultaneous and the air has the pungent smell of ozone, you could be in big trouble. If you are in such a storm and feel your hair stand on end, you could be getting set up as a lightning target. The only thing you can do is drop to a kneeling position with only your feet and knees touching the ground and with your head down. This position will minimize your strike zone. And since you are already in a kneeling posture, I suggest you pray.

7   During thunderstorm season, we should all be aware of local weather forecasts, and when lightning is a threat, take precautions. It is a killer like no other.

Paragraph 5

The topic sentence (first sentence) gives focus as people outside. The paragraph gives the steps in the process, what not to do, and why some steps are performed.

Paragraph 6

The topic sentence (first sentence) gives the focus as what to do if the storm is close. The paragraph gives the steps in the process and why they are performed.

Paragraph 7

The conclusion reaffirms the point in the introduction, that lightning poses a serious threat.

ATTITUDE
Garrison E. Keillor

Born in Minnesota in 1942, humorist Garrison Keillor has been a staff writer for The New Yorker, *a radio entertainer, an essayist who has published in many magazines, and a novelist. His books include* Happy to Be Here *(1982), from which "Attitude" is taken,* Leaving Home *(1987),* We Are Still Married *(1989), and his best-known* Lake Wobegon Days *(1985). Keillor was the creator of and performer in National Public Radio's immensely popular "A Prairie Home Companion," which won the Peabody award for distinguished broadcasting. In "Attitude," Keillor takes a stand for proper behavior while playing softball. However, his points are probably applicable off the field as well. The essay entertains with its wit, but it also works to persuade the reader of the importance of proper behavior.*

THE PATTERN	THE PURPOSES
process analysis	*to entertain, to express feelings and relate experience, and to persuade*

1   Long ago I passed the point in life when major-league ballplayers begin to be younger than yourself. Now all of them are, except for a few aging trigenarians and a couple of quadros who don't get around the fastball as well as they used to and who sit out the second games of doubleheaders. However, despite my age (thirty-nine), I am still active and have a lot of interests. One of them is slow-pitch softball, a game that lets me go through the motions of baseball without getting beaned or having to run too hard. I play on a pretty casual team, one that drinks beer on the bench and substitutes freely. If a player's wife or girlfriend wants to play, we give her a glove and send her out to right field, no questions asked, and if she lets a pop fly drop six feet in front of her, nobody agonizes over it.

2   Except me. This year. For the first time in my life, just as I am entering the dark twilight of my slow-pitch career, I find myself taking the game seriously. It isn't the bonehead play that bothers me

especially—the pop fly that drops untouched, the slow roller juggled and the ball then heaved ten feet over the first baseman's head and into the next diamond, the routine singles that go through outfielders' legs for doubles and triples with gloves flung after them. No, it isn't our stone-glove fielding or pussyfoot base-running or limp-wristed hitting that gives me fits, though these have put us on the short end of some mighty ridiculous scores this summer. It's our attitude.

3   Bottom of the ninth, down 18–3, two outs, a man on first and a woman on third, and our third baseman strikes out. *Strikes out!* In slow-pitch, not even your grandmother strikes out, but this guy does, and after his third strike—a wild swing at a ball that bounces on the plate— he topples over in the dirt and lies flat on his back, laughing. *Laughing!*

4   Same game, earlier. They have the bases loaded. A weak grounder is hit toward our second baseperson. The runners are running. She picks up the ball, and she looks at them. She looks at first, at second, at home. We yell, "Throw it! Throw it!" and she throws it, underhand, at the pitcher, who has turned and run to back up the catcher. The ball rolls across the third-base line and under the bench. Three runs score. The batter, a fatso, chugs into second. The other team hoots and hollers, and what does she do? She shrugs and smiles ("Oh, silly me"); after all, it's only a game. Like the aforementioned strikeout artist, she treats her error as a joke. They have forgiven themselves instantly, which is un-forgivable. It is *we* who should forgive them, who can say, "It's all right, it's only a game." They are supposed to throw up their hands and kick the dirt and hang their heads, as if this boner, even if it is their sixteenth of the afternoon—*this* is the one that really and truly breaks their hearts.

5   That attitude sweetens the game for everyone. The sinner feels sweet remorse. The fatso feels some sense of accomplishment; this is no bunch of rumdums he forced into an error but a team with some class. We, the sinner's teammates, feel momentary anger at her—dumb! dumb play!—but then, seeing her grief, we sympathize with her in our hearts (any one of us might have made that mistake or one worse), and we yell encouragement, including the shortstop, who, moments before, dropped an easy throw for a force at second. "That's all right! Come on! We got 'em!" we yell. "Shake it off! These turkeys can't hit!" This makes us feel good, even though the turkeys now lead us by ten runs. We're getting clobbered, but we have a winning attitude.

6   Let me say this about attitude: Each player is responsible for his or her own attitude, and to a considerable degree you can *create* a good attitude by doing certain little things on the field. These are certain little things that ballplayers do in the Bigs, and we ought to be doing them in the Slows.

7   1. When going up to bat, don't step right into the batter's box as if it were an elevator. The box is your turf, your stage. Take possession of it slowly and deliberately, starting with a lot of back-bending, knee-stretching, and torso-revolving in the on-deck circle. Then, approaching the box, stop outside it and tap the dirt off your spikes with your bat. You don't have spikes, you have sneakers, of course, but the significance of the tapping is the same. Then, upon entering the box, spit on the ground. It's a way of saying, "This here is mine. This is where I get my hits."

8   2. Spit frequently. Spit at all crucial moments. Spit correctly. Spit should be *blown,* not ptuied weakly with the lips, which often results in dribble. Spitting should convey forcefulness of purpose, concentration, pride. Spit down, not in the direction of others. Spit in the glove and on the fingers, especially after making a real knucklehead play; it's a way of saying, "I dropped the ball because my glove was dry."

9   3. At bat and in the field, pick up dirt. Rub dirt in the fingers (especially after spitting on them). Toss dirt, as if testing the wind for velocity and direction. Smooth the dirt. Be involved with dirt. If no dirt is available (e.g., in the outfield), pluck tufts of grass. Fielders should be grooming their areas constantly between plays, flicking away tiny sticks and bits of gravel.

10   4. Take your time. Tie your laces. Confer with your teammates about possible situations that may arise and conceivable options in dealing with them. Extend the game. Three errors on three consecutive plays can be humiliating if the plays occur within the space of a couple of minutes, but if each error is separated from the next by extensive conferences on the mound, lace-tying, glove adjustments, and arguing close calls (if any), the effect on morale is minimized.

11   5. Talk. Not just an occasional "Let's get a hit now" but continuous rhythmic chatter, a flow of syllables: "Hey babe hey babe c'mon babe good stick now hey babe long tater take him downtown babe . . . hey good eye good eye."

12   Infield chatter is harder to maintain. Since the slow-pitch pitch is required to be a soft underhand lob, infielders hesitate to say, "Smoke him babe hey low heat hey throw it on the black babe chuck it in there back him up babe no hit no hit." Say it anyway.

13   6. One final rule, perhaps the most important of all: When your team is up and has made the third out, the batter and the players who were left on base do not come back to the bench for their gloves. *They remain on the field, and their teammates bring their gloves out to them.* This requires some organization and discipline, but it pays off big in morale. It says, "Although we're getting our pants knocked off, still we must conserve our energy."

14   Imagine that you have bobbled two fly balls in this rout and now you have just tried to stretch a single into a double and have been easily thrown out sliding into second base, where the base runner ahead of you had stopped. It was the third out and a dumb play, and your opponents smirk at you as they run off the field. You are the goat, a lonely and tragic figure sitting in the dirt. You curse yourself, jerking your head sharply forward. You stand up and kick the base. How miserable! How degrading! Your utter shame, though brief, bears silent testimony to the worthiness of your teammates, whom you have let down, and they appreciate it. They call out to you now as they take the field, and as the second baseman runs to his position he says, "Let's get 'em now," and tosses you your glove. Lowering your head, you trot slowly out to right. There you do some deep knee bends. You pick grass. You find a pebble and fling it into foul territory. As the first batter comes to the plate, you check the sun. You get set in your stance, poised to fly. Feet spread, hands on hips, you bend slightly at the waist and spit the expert spit of a veteran ballplayer—a player who has known the agony of defeat but who always bounces back, a player who has lost a stride on the base paths but can still make the big play.

15   This is *ball*, ladies and gentlemen. This is what it's all about.

Reading Closely and Thinking Critically

1. What does Keillor find upsetting about the attitude of the player who strikes out and the second baseperson who throws the ball badly?

2. Why does Keillor explain how to behave on a softball field? That is, why does he feel it is important to understand the process he explains?

3. How does Keillor feel about softball?

4. In paragraph 15, Keillor concludes by saying "This is *ball,* ladies and gentlemen. This is what it's all about." What do you think the author means?

5. Can the points the author makes about softball be applied beyond the playing field in life outside of sports? Explain.

Examining Structure and Strategy

1. How would you describe Keillor's tone in "Attitude"? (See page 37 on tone.)

2. Is "Attitude" a directional or explanatory process analysis?

3. For which steps in the process does Keillor explain *how* something should be done?

4. For which steps in the process does Keillor explain what *not* to do?

5. For which steps in the process does Keillor explain *why* something is done?

6. Where does Keillor discuss a troublesome aspect of the process?

Considering Language and Style

1. Keillor's word choice is relaxed and informal. For example, in paragraph 2, he says that "pussyfoot base-running . . . gives [him] fits" and in paragraph 4 he refers to a person who "chugs into second." Cite three other examples of relaxed, informal word choice. Why does Keillor use this informal diction?

2. Keillor combines his informal language with the mock-serious tone of his instructions in paragraphs 7–13. What affect does the combination create?

3. Consult a dictionary if you are unsure of the meaning of any of these words: *beaned* (paragraph 1), *bonehead* (paragraph 2), *boner* (paragraph 4).

For Group Discussion or Writing

Explain the importance of attitude in our lives and give examples of ways that attitude can make a difference.

Writing Assignments

1. *In your journal.* How would you describe Keillor's view of sports? Do you agree or disagree with that view? Explain.

2. *Using the pattern.* In paragraph 6, Keillor explains that a player can create a good attitude on the softball field. Explain a process for creating a good attitude somewhere other than on a ball field—on the job, while studying, while taking an exam, around unpleasant people, at the dentist's office, and so forth.

3. *Using the pattern.* Write a set of instructions for correct behavior for spectators at baseball games or some other sporting event. Try to adopt the humorous, mock-serious tone evident in "Attitude."

4. *Using the pattern.* Write a set of instructions for those who coach softball, baseball, football, or some other sport.

5. *Considering a theme.* Discuss a role that sports play in American society and explain whether or not you think the role is a positive or negative factor.

6. *Connecting the readings.* Both Garrison Keillor in "Attitude" and Nikki Giovanni in "On Holidays and How to Make Them Work" (page 207) concern themselves with correct behavior, although in different contexts. Explain the view of correct behavior that these authors share, and go on to agree or disagree with this view.

WANTING AN ORANGE
Larry Woiwode

Larry Woiwode is a freelance writer who has won both the National Book Award and the Critic's Circle Award. He has written two novels, What I'm Going to Do, I Think *(1969) and* Beyond the Bedroom Wall: A Family Album *(1975), and a book of poetry. Born in 1941, he is a native of the small farming town of Carrington, North Dakota. His writings, including the selection that appears here, often reflect his Midwestern sensibilities. "Wanting an Orange" originally appeared in* Paris Review *in 1984. It is part process analysis and part reminiscence that pays tribute to the orange that brightened winters in the author's boyhood North Dakota. In the selection, Woiwode entertains the reader at the same time he expresses feelings and relates his experience. Be sure to notice the important role description plays in the essay.*

THE PATTERNS	THE PURPOSES
process analysis with	*to entertain and to express*
description	*feelings and relate experience*

1   Oh, those oranges arriving in the midst of the North Dakota winters of the forties—the mere color of them, carried through the door in a net bag or a crate from out of the white winter landscape. Their appearance was enough to set my brother and me to thinking that it might be about time to develop an illness, which was the surest way of receiving a steady supply of them.

2   "Mom, we think we're getting a cold."

3   "*We?* You mean, you two want an orange?"

4   This was difficult for us to answer or dispute; the matter seemed moved beyond our mere wanting.

5   "If you want an orange," she would say, "why don't you ask for one?"

6   "We want an orange."

7   " 'We' again. '*We want an orange.*' "

8   "May we have an orange, please."

9   "That's the way you know I like you to ask for one. Now, why don't each of you ask for one in that same way, but separately?"

10   "Mom . . . " And so on. There was no depth of degradation that we wouldn't descend to in order to get one. If the oranges hadn't wended their way northward by Thanksgiving, they were sure to arrive before the Christmas season, stacked first in crates at the depot, filling that musty place, where pews sat back to back, with a springtime acidity, as if the building had been rinsed with a renewing elixir that set it right for yet another year. Then the crates would appear at the local grocery store, often with the top slats pried back on a few of them, so that we were aware of a resinous smell of fresh wood in addition to the already orangy atmosphere that foretold the season more explicitly than any calendar.

11   And in the broken-open crates (as if burst by the power of the oranges themselves), one or two of the lovely spheres would lie free of the tissue they came wrapped in—always purple tissue, as if that were the only color that could contain the populations of them in their nestled positions. The crates bore paper labels at one end—of an orange against a blue background, or of a blue goose against an orange background—signifying the colorful otherworld (unlike our wintry one) that these phenomena had arisen from. Each orange, stripped of its protective wrapping, as vivid in your vision as a pebbled sun, encouraged you to picture a whole pyramid of them in a bowl on your dining room table, glowing in the light, as if giving off the warmth that came through the windows from the real winter sun. And all of them came stamped with a blue-purple name as foreign as the otherworld that you might imagine as their place of origin, so that on Christmas day you would find yourself digging past everything else in your Christmas stocking, as if tunneling down to the country of China, in order to reach the rounded bulge at the tip of the toe which meant that you had received a personal reminder of another state of existence, wholly separate from your own.

12   The packed heft and texture, finally, of an orange in your hand—this is it!—and the eruption of smell and the watery fireworks as a knife, in the hand of someone skilled, like our mother, goes slicing through the skin so perfect for slicing. This gaseous spray can form a mist like smoke, which can then be lit with a match to create actual fireworks if there is a chance to hide alone with a match (matches being forbidden) and the peel from one. Sputtery ignitions can also be

produced by squeezing a peel near a candle (at least one candle is generally always going at Christmastime), and the leftover peels are set on the stove top to scent the house.

13   And the ingenious way in which oranges come packed into their globes! The green nib at the top, like a detonator, can be bitten off, as if disarming the orange, in order to clear a place for you to sink a tooth under the peel. This is the beset way to start. If you bite at the peel too much, your front teeth will feel scraped, like dry bone, and your lips will begin to burn from the bitter oil. Better to sink a tooth into this greenish or creamy depression, and then pick at that point with the nail of your thumb, removing a little piece of the peel at a time. Later, you might want to practice to see how large a piece you can remove intact. The peel can also be undone in one continuous ribbon, a feat which maybe your father is able to perform, so that after the orange is freed, looking yellowish, the peel, rewound, will stand in its original shape, although empty.

14   The yellowish whole of the orange can now be divided into sections, usually about a dozen, by beginning with a division down the middle; after this, each section, enclosed in its papery skin, will be able to be lifted and torn loose more easily. There is a stem up the center of the sections like a mushroom stalk, but tougher; this can be eaten. A special variety of orange, without any pits, has an extra growth, or nubbin, like half of a tiny orange, tucked into its bottom. This nubbin is nearly as bitter as the peel, but it can be eaten, too; don't worry. Some of the sections will have miniature sections embedded in them and clinging as if for life, giving the impression that babies are being hatched, and should you happen to find some of these you've found the sweetest morsels of any.

15   If you prefer to have your orange sliced in half, as some people do, the edges of the peel will abrade the corners of your mouth, making them feel raw, as you eat down into the white of the rind (which is the only way to do it) until you can see daylight through the orangy bubbles composing its outside. Your eyes might burn; there is no proper way to eat an orange. If there are pits, they can get in the way, and the slower you eat an orange, the more you'll find your fingers sticking together. And no matter how carefully you eat one, or bite into a quarter, juice can always fly or slip from a corner of your mouth; this happens to everyone. Close your eyes to be on the safe side, and for the eruption in your mouth of the slivers of watery meat, which should be

broken and rolled fine over your tongue for the essence of orange. And if indeed you have sensed yourself coming down with a cold, there is a chance that you will feel it driven from your head—your nose and sinuses suddenly opening—in the midst of the scent of a peel and eating an orange.

16   And oranges can also be eaten whole—rolled into a spongy mass and punctured with a pencil (if you don't find this offensive) or a knife, and then sucked upon. Then, once the juice is gone, you can disembowel the orange as you wish and eat away its pulpy remains, and eat once more into the whitish interior of the peel, which scours the coating from your teeth and makes your numbing lips and the tip of your tongue start to tingle and swell up from behind, until, in the light from the windows (shining through an empty glass bowl), you see orange again from the inside. Oh, oranges, solid *o*'s, light from afar in the midst of the freeze, and not unlike that unspherical fruit which first went from Eve to Adam and from there (to abbreviate matters) to my brother and me.

17   "Mom, we think we're getting a cold."

18   "You mean, you want an orange?"

19   This is difficult to answer or dispute or even to acknowledge, finally, with the fullness that the subject deserves, and that each orange bears, within its own makeup, into this hard-edged yet insubstantial, incomplete, cold, wintry world.

Reading Closely and Thinking Critically

1. Why do you think that oranges meant so much to Woiwode when he was a child?

2. What is the significance of oranges to Woiwode now that he is an adult? Why do you think that Woiwode chose to write about oranges?

3. Do you think "How to Peel and Eat an Orange" would make a better title for the essay than "Wanting an Orange"? Explain your view.

4. How many ways to eat an orange does Woiwode describe? What are those ways?

5. Is Woiwode making too much of a simple piece of fruit? Explain your view.

Examining Structure and Strategy

1. Why does Woiwode open the essay with the conversation with his mother?

2. Is "Wanting an Orange" a directional or an explanatory process analysis? The author probably realizes that the reader knows how to eat an orange. Why, then, do you think he describes the process?

3. Which paragraph explains what *not* to do and why a step is performed?

4. Which paragraph presents troublesome aspects of the process?

5. What approach does the author take to his conclusion?

Considering Language and Style

1. What recurring metaphor appears in paragraphs 12 and 13? (See page 73 for an explanation of metaphors.) Is this metaphor a good one? Explain why or why not.

2. A considerable amount of description appears in the essay, particularly in paragraphs 10 – 16. What does the description contribute? Cite two descriptions that you find particularly effective.

3. Consult a dictionary if you are unsure of the meaning of any of these words: *wended* (paragraph 10), *elixir* (paragraph 10), *abrade* (paragraph 15), *disembowel* (paragraph 16).

For Group Discussion or Writing

A number of foods are important to Americans: turkey at Thanksgiving, hot dogs at ball games, champagne on New Year's Eve, and so forth. Select a food that is important to Americans. Explain the importance of the food, including what it says about American culture.

Writing Assignments

1. *In your journal.* "Wanting an Orange" was reprinted in *Harper's* with the title "Ode to an Orange." Discuss the difference between these two titles, including whether or not the reader is likely to react differently to them. Do you think one title is better than the other? Explain.

2. Using the pattern. Woiwode explains three ways to eat an orange (in sections, sliced in half, and whole). Pick a process that can be performed in more than one way and explain the various ways to perform it. If appropriate, explain the advantages or disadvantages of each process.

3. Using the pattern. Like Woiwode, share a part of your past by explaining a process that was an important part of your childhood (catching fireflies, preparing for Halloween, decorating the Christmas tree, planting a garden with your parents, and so forth). Try to use description to convey part of the reminiscence.

4. Using the pattern. Write an essay with the title "Wanting _____." (Fill in the blank with a food that was an important part of your childhood or that is an important part of your cultural heritage.) Use process analysis to explain how to eat the food. If possible, explain the importance the food has for you and/or why you enjoy it.

5. Using the pattern. Explain a process for eating a food or performing a chore that does not appeal to you. Try to convey your distaste for the food or the chore.

6. Considering a theme. Because food can be an important part of our celebrations, eating holiday meals with family and enjoying special holiday foods may loom large in your memories of childhood. Write about one or more of your holiday memories. At least part of your focus should be on the foods or meal associated with the holiday celebration.

7. Connecting the readings. "Wanting an Orange," "Salvation" (page 149), "Once More to the Lake" (page 110), "My Backyard" (page 80), and "My Neighborhood" (page 86) all include reminiscences of childhood. How important are childhood memories to us as adults? Discuss and illustrate the role of childhood memories, drawing on two or more of the essays mentioned as well as your own experience.

HOW I'LL BECOME AN AMERICAN
Miklós Vámos

Born and educated in Hungary, Miklós Vámos writes short stories, novels, and screenplays. He has also been a contributor to Harper's, *the* Atlantic, *and the* New York Times, *as well as the East European correspondent for* The Nation. *He has taught screenwriting, playwriting, and theater at several American universities, including Yale, and Connecticut College. In "How I'll Become an American," which originally appeared in the* New York Times *in 1989, Vámos uses process analysis to take an ironic look at Americans, and the resulting portrait is not very flattering. Although entertaining, the essay also informs the reader about the character of Americans, and it works to persuade the reader that Americans should change their ways. As you read, think about how much of Vámos's characterization you agree with.*

THE PATTERN	THE PURPOSES
process analysis	*to inform, to entertain, and to persuade*

---

1   I have been Hungarian for 38 years. I'll try something else for the next 38. I'll try to be American, for instance. North American, I mean. As an American, I'll speak English fluently. I'll make American mistakes instead of Hungarian mistakes and I'll call them slang.

2   As an American, I'll have a credit card. Or two. I'll use and misuse them and have to pay the fees. I'll apply for other cards right away. Golden Visa. Golden American. Golden Gate. And I'll buy a car, a great American car. Then I'll sell my car and buy a smaller West German car because it's reliable and doesn't use so much gasoline. Later, I'll sell it and buy a smaller Japanese car with a computer aboard. Then I'll sell it and buy a camper. When I sell the camper I'll buy a bicycle.

3   As an American, I'll buy a dog. And a cat. And a goat. And a white whale. And also some big stones as pets.[1]

---

1. A reference to pet rocks, which were novelty items popular for a time in the 1980s.

4   I'll live in my own house. It will be mine, except for the 99 percent mortgage. I'll sell my house and buy a condo. I'll sell my condo and buy a mobile home. I'll sell my mobile home and buy an igloo. I'll sell my igloo and buy a tent. As an American, I'll be clever: I'll sell my igloo and buy a tent when I move to Florida from Alaska.

5   Anyway, I'll move a lot. And I'll buy the best dishwasher, microwave, dryer and hi-fi in the world—that is, the U.S.A. I'll have warranty for all—or my money back. I'll use automatic toothbrushes, egg boilers and garage doors. I'll call every single phone number starting 1-800.

6   I'll buy the fastest food I can get and I'll eat it very slowly because I'll watch TV during the meals. Of course, I'll buy a VCR. I'll watch the taped programs and then retape. Sometimes I'll retape first.

7   As an American, I'll have an answering machine, too. The outgoing message will promise that I'll call you back as soon as possible, but it won't be possible soon.

8   If I answer the phone as an exception, I'll tell you that I can't talk now because I have a long-distance call on the other line, but I'll call you back as soon as possible (see above).

9   And I'll get a job. I'll always be looking for a better job, but I won't get the job I want. I'll work really hard since as an American I wanna be rich. I'll be always in a hurry: Time Is Money. Unfortunately, my time won't be worth as much money as my bosses' time. Sometimes I will have some time and I still won't have enough money. Then I'll start to hate the wisdom of this saying.

10   As an American, sometimes I'll be badly depressed. I'll be the patient of 12 psychiatrists, and I'll be disappointed with all of them. I'll try to change my life a little bit. I'll try to exchange my wives, my cars, my lovers, my houses, my children, my jobs and my pets.

11   Sometimes, I'll exchange a few dollars into other currencies and I'll travel to Europe, Hawaii, Tunisia, Martinique and Japan. I'll be happy to see that people all over the world are jealous of us Americans.

12   I'll take at least 2,000 snapshots on each trip. I'll also buy a video camera and shoot everywhere. I'll look at the tapes, photos and slides, and I'll try to remember my experiences when I have time and am in the mood. But I won't have time or be in the mood because I'll get depressed again and again.

13   I'll smoke cigarettes. Then I'll be afraid of cancer and I'll stop. I'll smoke cigars. And opium. I'll take a breather and then try LSD and

heroin and cocaine and marijuana. To top it all off: crack. I'll try to stop then but I won't be able.

14   I'll call 1-800-222-HELP. If nothing helps, I'll have some gay experiences. And swing. And if I am still unhappy I'll make a final effort: I'll try to read a book. I'll buy some best sellers. I'll prefer James A. Michener. My second favorite will be the "How to Be Rich in Seven Weeks." I'll try to follow this advice in seven years.

15   I'll always be concerned about my health as an American. I won't eat anything but health food until I get ill. From time to time, I'll read in the paper that I should stop eating meat, sugar, bread, fiber, grains, iron, toothpaste, and that I should stop drinking milk, soda, water, acid rain. I'll try to follow this advice, but then I'll read in the paper that I should do it the other way around.

16   I'll be puzzled. "Hey, I don't even know what cholesterol is!" Yet I'll stick to decaf coffee, sugar-free cookies, salt-free butter and lead-free gasoline. I'll believe that proper diet and exercise make life longer. I'll go jogging every day until I am mugged twice and knocked down three times. Then I'll just exercise in my room, but it will also increase my appetite. I'll go on several diets, and little by little I'll reach 200 pounds.

17   As an American, I'll buy a new TV every time a larger screen appears on the market. In the end, the screen will be larger than the room. It will be difficult to put this enormous TV into my living room; thus, I will put my living room into the TV. Anyway, my living room will look very much like the living rooms you can see on the screen. My life won't differ from the lives you can see in the soaps: nobody will complain. I won't complain either. I'll always smile.

18   After all, we are Americans, aren't we?

Reading Closely and Thinking Critically

1. The thesis of "How I'll Become an American" is implied rather than stated. In your own words, write out the thesis. Why do you think the author chooses not to write a thesis early on in the essay?

2. What do you think Vámos is saying about the American attitude toward possessions?

3. Does Vámos believe that Americans are typically content with their lot? Explain.

4. How does Vámos evaluate the mental health of Americans?

5. What do you think the author is saying about the American attitude toward fitness?

6. Make a list of words that describe Americans as Vámos sees them.

Examining Structure and Strategy

1. In what way is the tone of "How I'll Become an American" ironic? (*Irony* occurs when the author says one thing but really means the opposite.)

2. Why doesn't Vámos present the steps in the process in chronological order?

3. At what points does Vámos tell why a step is performed?

4. At what points does Vámos tell how a step is performed?

5. Vámos uses a great deal of exaggeration in the essay. Cite an example of that exaggeration. What purpose does it serve?

Considering Language and Style

1. Vámos uses many short sentences, some sentence fragments, contractions, and slang. Why does he use such constructions and diction? What effect is created as a result?

2. What effect does Vámos create with the repetition of "As an American"?

3. Consult a dictionary if you are unsure of the meaning of these words: *LSD* (paragraph 13), *acid rain* (paragraph 15).

For Group Discussion or Writing

Explain how much of Vámos's characterization is accurate and how much is inaccurate, being sure to note why you believe as you do. Do you think Vámos is fair to Americans? Why or why not?

Writing Assignments

1. *In your journal.* "How I'll Become an American" originally appeared in the *New York Times*. In a page or so, consider whether or not the author's audience was likely to be offended by a foreign-born writer criticizing Americans.

2. *Using the pattern.* Write a process analysis with the title "How to Become an American," but make your portrait of the American a flattering one. If you like, you can create emphasis by repeating "As an American . . . "

3. *Using the pattern.* Write an essay that explains the process for becoming a student, an instructor, an athlete, a sorority woman, a fraternity man, or some other campus "type." Your purpose should be to entertain your reader.

4. *Using the pattern.* Write an essay with the title "How to Become a/an _____" (You fill in the blank.) Use an ironic tone to inform your reader of the process involved.

5. *Using the pattern.* Explain the process a newcomer to the Untied States can follow in order to begin fitting in as quickly as possible. If you like, you can limit your discussion to how to fit in to a particular context, such as school, a shopping mall, a grocery store, a football game, and so forth. Your tone may be ironic if you wish.

6. *Considering a theme.* Answer Vámos's attack by discussing what is *good* about Americans. Try to illustrate Americans' positive characteristics with examples.

7. *Connecting the readings.* Explain how the characteristics of Americans pointed out in "How I'll Become an American" account for the celebrations of holidays as they are described in "On Holidays and How to Make Them Work" (page 207).

DON'T JUST STAND THERE
Diane Cole

Diane Cole was born in Baltimore in 1952 and educated at Radcliffe College and Johns Hopkins University. In addition to serving as a contributing editor to Psychology Today, *she has written for* The Wall Street Journal, *the* Washington Post, *the* New York Times, Newsweek, Ms., *and* Glamour *as a freelance journalist. Her topics are often psychology and women's careers. "Don't Just Stand There" was first published in a* New York Times *supplement called* A World of Difference *(April 16, 1989), which was part of a campaign against bigotry sponsored by the Anti-Defamation League of B'nai B'rith. In her essay, Cole tells the reader how to respond to bigoted remarks and jokes. In addition, she makes the reader more sensitive to the hurtful nature of such slurs. As you read, notice Cole's liberal use of quotations, and ask yourself what they contribute.*

THE PATTERN	THE PURPOSE
process analysis	*to inform*

1   It was my office farewell party, and colleagues at the job I was about to leave were wishing me well. My mood was one of ebullience tinged with regret, and it was in this spirit that I spoke to the office neighbor to whom I had waved hello every morning for the past two years. He smiled broadly as he launched into a long, rambling story, pausing only after he delivered the punch line. It was a very long pause because, although he laughed, I did not: This joke was unmistakably anti-Semitic.

2   I froze. Everyone in the office knew I was Jewish; what could he have possibly meant? Shaken and hurt, not knowing what else to do, I turned in stunned silence to the next well-wisher. Later, still angry, I wondered, what else should I—could I—have done?

3   Prejudice can make its presence felt in any setting, but hearing its nasty voice in this way can be particularly unnerving. We do not know what to do and often we feel another form of paralysis as well: We think, "Nothing I say or do will change this person's attitude, so why bother?"

4   But left unchecked, racial slurs and offensive ethnic jokes "can poison the atmosphere," says Michael McQuillan, adviser for racial/ethnic affairs for the Brooklyn borough president's office. "Hearing these remarks conditions us to accept them; and if we accept these, we can become accepting of other acts."

5   Speaking up may not magically change a biased attitude, but it can change a person's behavior by putting a strong message across. And the more messages there are, the more likely a person is to change that behavior, says Arnold Kahn, professor of psychology at James Madison University, Harrisonburg, Va., who makes this analogy: "You can't keep people from smoking in *their* house, but you can ask them not to smoke in *your* house."

6   At the same time, "Even if the other party ignores or discounts what you say, people always reflect on how others perceive them. Speaking up always counts," says LeNorman Strong, director of campus life at George Washington University, Washington, D.C.

7   Finally, learning to respond effectively also helps people feel better about themselves, asserts Cherie Brown, executive director of the National Coalition Building Institute, a Boston-based training organization. "We've found that, when people felt they could at least in this small way make a difference, that made them more eager to take on other activities on a larger scale," she says. Although there is no "cookbook approach" to confronting such remarks—every situation is different, experts stress—there are some effective strategies.

8   *When the "joke" turns on who you are—as a member of an ethnic or religious group, a person of color, a woman, a gay or lesbian, an elderly person, or someone with a physical handicap—shocked paralysis is often the first response. Then, wounded and vulnerable, on some level you want to strike back.*

9   Lashing out or responding in kind is seldom the most effective response, however. "That can give you momentary satisfaction, but you also feel as if you've lowered yourself to that other person's level," Mr. McQuillan explains. Such a response may further label you in the speaker's mind as thin-skinned, someone not to be taken seriously. Or it may up the ante, making the speaker, and then you, reach for new insults—or physical blows.

10   "If you don't laugh at the joke, or fight, or respond in kind to the slur," says Mr. McQuillan, "that will take the person by surprise, and

that can give you more control over the situation." Therefore, in situations like the one in which I found myself—a private conversation in which I knew the person making the remark—he suggests voicing your anger calmly but pointedly: "I don't know if you realize what that sounded like to me. If that's what you meant, it really hurt me."

11   State how *you* feel, rather than making an abstract statement like, "Not everyone who hears that joke might find it funny." Counsels Mr. Strong: "Personalize the sense of 'this his how I feel when you say this.' That makes it very concrete"—and harder to dismiss.

12   Make sure you heard the words and their intent correctly by repeating or rephrasing the statement: "This is what I heard you say. Is that what you meant?" It's important to give the other person the benefit of the doubt because, in fact, he may *not* have realized that the comment was offensive and, if you had not spoken up, would have had no idea of its impact on you.

13   For instance, Professor Kahn relates that he used to include in his exams multiple-choice questions that occasionally contained "incorrect funny answers." After one exam, a student came up to him in private and said, "I don't think you intended this, but I found a number of those jokes offensive to me as a woman." She explained why. "What she said made immediate sense to me," he says. "I apologized at the next class, and I never did it again."

14   But what if the speaker dismisses your objection, saying, "Oh, you're just being sensitive. Can't you take a joke?" In that case, you might say, "I'm not so sure about that, let's talk about that a little more." The key, Mr. Strong says, is to continue the dialogue, hear the other person's concerns, and point out your own. "There are times when you're just going to have to admit defeat and end it," he adds, "but I have to feel that I did the best I could."

15   When the offending remark is made in the presence of others— at a staff meeting, for example—it can be even more distressing than an insult made privately.

16   "You have two options," says William Newlin, director of field services for the Community Relations division of the New York City Commission on Human Rights. "You can respond immediately at the meeting, or you can delay your response until afterward in private. But a response has to come."

17   Some remarks or actions may be so outrageous that they cannot go unnoted at the moment, regardless of the speaker or the setting. But

in general, psychologists say, shaming a person in public may have the opposite effect of the one you want: The speaker will deny his offense all the more strongly in order to save face. Further, few people enjoy being put on the spot, and if the remark really was not intended to be offensive, publicly embarrassing the person who made it may cause an unnecessary rift or further misunderstanding. Finally, most people just don't react as well or thoughtfully under a public spotlight as they would in private.

18   Keeping that in mind, an excellent alternative is to take the offender aside afterward: "Could we talk for a minute in private?" Then use the strategies suggested above for calmly stating how you feel, giving the speaker the benefit of the doubt, and proceeding from there.

19   At a large meeting or public talk, you might consider passing the speaker a note, says David Wertheimer, executive director of the New York City Gay and Lesbian Anti-Violence Project: You could write, "You may not realize it, but your remarks were offensive because. . . . "

20   "Think of your role as that of an educator," suggests James M. Jones, Ph.D., executive director for public interest at the American Psychological Association. "You have to be controlled."

21   Regardless of the setting or situation, speaking up always raises the risk of rocking the boat. If the person who made the offending remark is your boss, there may be an even bigger risk to consider: How will this affect my job? Several things can help minimize the risk, however. First, know what other resources you may have at work, suggests Caryl Stern, director of the A World of Difference—New York City campaign: Does your personnel office handle discrimination complaints? Are other grievance procedures in place?

22   You won't necessarily need to use any of these procedures, Ms. Stern stresses. In fact, she advises, "It's usually better to try a one-on-one approach first." But simply knowing a formal system exists can make you feel secure enough to set up that meeting.

23   You can also raise the issue with other colleagues who heard the remark: Did they feel the same way you did? The more support you have, the less alone you will feel. Your point will also carry more validity and be more difficult to shrug off. Finally, give your boss credit—and the benefit of the doubt: "I know you've worked hard for the company's affirmative action programs, so I'm sure you didn't realize what those remarks sounded like to me as well as the others at the meeting last week. . . . "

24   If, even after this discussion, the problem persists, go back for another meeting, Ms. Stern advises. And if that, too, fails, you'll know what other options are available to you.

25   *It's a spirited dinner party, and everyone's having a good time, until one guest starts reciting a racist joke. Everyone at the table is white, including you. The others are still laughing, as you wonder what to say or do.*

26   No one likes being seen as a party-pooper, but before deciding that you'd prefer not to take on this role, you might remember that the person who told the offensive joke has already ruined your good time.
27   If it's a group that you feel comfortable in—a family gathering, for instance—you will feel freer to speak up. Still, shaming the person by shouting, "You're wrong" or "That's not funny!" probably won't get your point across as effectively as other strategies. "If you interrupt people to condemn them, it just makes it harder," says Cherie Brown. She suggests trying instead to get at the resentments that lie beneath the joke by asking open-ended questions: "Grandpa, I know you always treat everyone with such respect. Why do people in our family talk that way about black people?" The key, Ms. Brown says, "is to listen to them first, so they will be more likely to listen to you."
28   If you don't know your fellow guests well, before speaking up you could turn discreetly to your neighbors (or excuse yourself to help the host or hostess in the kitchen) to get a reading on how they felt, and whether or not you'll find support for speaking up: "I know you probably didn't mean anything by that joke, Jim, but it really offended me. . . ." "It's important to say that *you* were offended—not state how the group that is the butt of the joke would feel. "Otherwise," LeNorman Strong says, "you risk coming off as a goody-two-shoes."
29   If you yourself are the host, you can exercise more control; you are, after all, the one who sets the rules and the tone of behavior in your home. Once, when Professor Kahn's party guests began singing offensive, racist songs, for instance, he kicked them all out, saying, "You don't sing songs like that in my house!" And, he adds, "they never did again."

30   *At school one day, a friend comes over and says, "Who do you think you are, hanging out with Joe? If you can be friends with those people, I'm through with you!"*

31   Peer pressure can weigh heavily on kids. They feel vulnerable and, because they are kids, they aren't as able to control the urge to fight. "But if you learn to handle these situations as kids, you'll be better able to handle them as an adult," William Newlin points out.

32   Begin by redefining to yourself what a friend is and examining what friendship means, advises Amy Lee, a human relations specialist at Panel of Americans, an intergroup-relations training and educational organization. If that person from a different group fits your requirement for a friend, ask, "Why shouldn't I be friends with Joe? We have a lot in common." Try to get more information about whatever stereotypes or resentments lie beneath your friend's statement. Ms. Lee suggests: "What makes you think they're so different from us? Where did you get that information?" She explains: "People are learning these stereotypes from somewhere, and they cannot be blamed for that. So examine where these ideas come from." Then talk about how your own experience rebuts them.

33   Kids, like adults, should also be aware of other resources to back them up: Does the school offer special programs for fighting prejudice? How supportive will the principal, the teachers, or other students be? If the school atmosphere is volatile, experts warn, make sure that taking a stand at that moment won't put you in physical danger. If that is the case, it's better to look for other alternatives.

34   These can include programs or organizations that bring kids from different backgrounds together. "When kids work together across race lines, that is how you break down the barriers and see that the stereotypes are not true," says Laurie Meadoff, president of CityKids Foundation, a nonprofit group whose programs attempt to do just that. Such programs can also provide what Cherie Brown calls a "safe place" to express the anger and pain that slurs and other offenses cause, whether the bigotry is directed against you or others.

35   In learning to speak up, everyone will develop a different style and a slightly different message to get across, experts agree. But it would be hard to do better than these two messages suggested by teenagers at CityKids: "Everyone on the face of the earth has the same intestines," said one. Another added, "Cross over the bridge. There's a lot of love on the streets."

Reading Closely and Thinking Critically

   1. According to Cole, why is it important to respond to racial, ethnic, and sexist slurs?

2. Why does Cole think it is best not to laugh at racial slurs and offensive ethnic jokes?

3. When a person makes an offensive remark, why does Cole think it is best not to shame that person publicly?

4. Cole offers procedures to help children deal with bigotry. Why do you think she includes information for children?

5. Did you learn anything as a result of reading "Don't Just Stand There"? If so, explain what you learned.

Examining Structure and Strategy

1. Which sentence is Cole's thesis because it presents the process under consideration?

2. What does the narration in paragraphs 1 and 2 contribute?

3. Cole makes frequent use of examples. Cite at least three such examples and explain their purpose in the essay.

4. Cite three paragraphs that explain what not to do and why. Which paragraph presents a troublesome aspect of the process?

5. Cole includes a considerable number of quotations. What do you think these quotations contribute?

Considering Language and Style

1. Cole uses first- and second-person pronouns (I, we, you, me, us). Why does she use these pronouns rather than third-person pronouns (he, she, they)?

2. Consult a dictionary if you are unsure of the meaning of any of these word: *ebullience* (paragraph 1), *tinged* (paragraph 1), *anti-Semitic* (paragraph 1), *rift* (paragraph 17), *volatile* (paragraph 33).

For Group Discussion or Writing

People tell insulting jokes all the time, even when they know the jokes can be hurtful. Discuss why you think people tell these jokes.

Writing Assignments

1. *In your journal.* Write about one or more times when you have overheard a racial, sexist, or ethnic slur. How did you respond and why did you respond that way? After reading Cole's essay, do you think you should have handled yourself differently? Explain. As an alternative, write about a time when you made an insulting remark or told an insulting joke. Explain your motivation and how the people around you responded.

2. *Using the pattern.* Like Cole, select a hurtful behavior (for example, classroom cheating, lying, or teenage drinking) and describe a process for dealing with it. Also, like Cole, briefly explain why the behavior is a problem. If possible, explain what not to do, and provide a narration that illustrates the problem.

3. *Using the pattern.* Select a bothersome behavior that is not hurtful (for example, talking in theaters, rudeness by salespeople, channel-switching by the person with the remote control, or inattentive table servers) and describe a process for dealing with it. Like Cole, try to explain what not to do, and try to illustrate the steps in the process.

4. *Using the pattern.* Research your university's procedure and policy for handling discrimination and harassment on campus. Then write a process analysis that explains what students or employees should do if they are victims of discrimination or harassment.

5. *Using the pattern.* If you think Cole's process for dealing with insulting remarks can be improved upon, write your own procedure for dealing with ethnic, sexist, and racial slurs. Like Cole, use examples to illustrate the steps in the process.

6. *Considering a theme.* Racial, ethnic, gender, and sexual bias are current facts of life. Explain how you think bias originates in people, what it is about people and society that allows the bias to persist, and what you think can be done to address the problem.

7. *Connecting the readings.* Using whatever information in "Don't Just Stand There" and "The Ways of Meeting Oppression" (page 463) that you care to use, along with your own ideas, write an article to be printed in a junior high school newspaper. The article should inform students of ways they can deal with discriminatory speech and behavior.

BEHIND THE FORMALDEHYDE CURTAIN
Jessica Mitford

Born in England to aristocratic parents, Jessica Mitford (1917–1997) never took to the aristocratic way of life. She moved to the United States, became a citizen, and worked at a number of jobs. She ultimately achieved fame as an investigative journalist who exposed corruption and excess in such American institutions as the funeral, television, prison, and diet industries. For her efforts, Time *magazine dubbed her the "Queen of the Muckrakers." Mitford's works include* Kind and Unusual Punishment: The Prison Business *(1973);* Poison Penmanship: The Gentle Art of Muckraking *(1979), a collection of her articles from the* Atlantic, Harpers, *and other magazines; and two volumes of autobiography. "Behind the Formaldehyde Curtain" is taken from Mitford's 1963 exposé of the funeral business,* The American Way of Death. *In this excerpt, Mitford argues that the funeral industry extracts money for unnecessary services. She also informs the reader by explaining the process of embalming. As you read, notice how the author reveals her attitude toward her subject.*

THE PATTERN	THE PURPOSES
process analysis	*to persuade and to inform*

1   The drama begins to unfold with the arrival of the corpse at the mortuary.

2   Alas, poor Yorick.[1] How surprised he would be to see how his counterpart of today is whisked off to a funeral parlor and is in short order sprayed, sliced, pierced, pickled, trussed, trimmed, creamed, waxed, painted, rouged, and neatly dressed—transformed from a common corpse into a Beautiful Memory Picture. This process is known in the trade as embalming and restorative art, and is so universally employed in the United States and Canada that the funeral director does it routinely, without consulting corpse or kin.[2] He regards as eccentric

---

1. The reference is to Hamlet's graveyard speech to Horatio about Yorick, who was buried but not embalmed.
2. The Federal Trade Commission now requires that families be informed that embalming is optional.

those few who are hardy enough to suggest that it might be dispensed with. Yet no law requires embalming, no religious doctrine commends it, nor is it dictated by considerations of health, sanitation, or even of personal daintiness. In no part of the world but in Northern America is it widely used. The purpose of embalming is to make the corpse presentable for viewing in a suitably costly container; and here too the funeral director routinely, without first consulting the family, prepares the body for public display.

3   Is all this legal? The processes to which a dead body may be subjected are after all to some extent circumscribed by law. In most states, for instance, the signature of next of kin must be obtained before an autopsy may be performed, before the deceased may be cremated, before the body may be turned over to a medical school for research purposes; or such provision must be made in the decedent's will. In the case of embalming, no such permission is required nor is it ever sought. A textbook, *The Principles and Practices of Embalming,* comments on this: "There is some question regarding the legality of much that is done within the preparation room." The author points out that it would be most unusual for a responsible member of a bereaved family to instruct the mortician, in so many words, to "embalm" the body of a deceased relative. The very term *embalming* is so seldom used that the mortician must rely upon custom in the matter. The author concludes that unless the family specifies otherwise, the act of entrusting the body to the care of a funeral establishment carries with it an implied permission to go ahead and embalm.

4   Embalming is indeed a most extraordinary procedure, and one must wonder at the docility of Americans who each year pay hundreds of millions of dollars for its perpetuation, blissfully ignorant of what it is all about, what is done, how it is done. Not one in ten thousand has any idea of what actually takes place. Books on the subject are extremely hard to come by. They are not to be found in most libraries or bookshops.

5   In an era when huge television audiences watch surgical operations in the comfort of their living rooms, when, thanks to the animated cartoon, the geography of the digestive system has become familiar territory even to the nursery school set, in a land where the satisfaction of curiosity about almost all matters is a national pastime, the secrecy surrounding embalming can, surely, hardly be attributed to the inherent gruesomeness of the subject. Custom in this regard has within this

century suffered a complete reversal. In the early days of American embalming, when it was performed in the home of the deceased, it was almost mandatory for some relative to stay by the embalmer's side and witness the procedure. Today, family members who might wish to be in attendance would certainly be dissuaded by the funeral director. All others, except apprentices, are excluded by law from the preparation room.

6   A close look at what does actually take place may explain in large measure the undertaker's intractable reticence concerning a procedure that has become his major *raison d'être.* Is it possible he fears that public information about embalming might lead patrons to wonder if they really want this service? If the funeral men are loath to discuss the subject outside the trade, the reader may, understandably, be equally loath to go on reading at this point. For those who have the stomach for it, let us part the formaldehyde curtain. . . .

7   The body is first laid out in the undertaker's morgue—or rather, Mr. Jones is reposing in the preparation room—to be readied to bid the world farewell.

8   The preparation room in any of the better funeral establishments has the tiled and sterile look of a surgery, and indeed the embalmer-restorative artist who does his chores there is beginning to adopt the term *dermasurgeon* (appropriately corrupted by some mortician-writers as "demi-surgeon") to describe his calling. His equipment, consisting of scalpels, scissors, augers, forceps, clamps, needles, pumps, tubes, bowls, and basins, is crudely imitative of the surgeon's, as is his technique, acquired in a nine- or twelve-month post-high-school course in an embalming school. He is supplied by an advanced chemical industry with a bewildering array of fluids, sprays, pastes, oils, powders, creams, to fix or soften tissue, shrink or distend it as needed, dry it here, restore the moisture there. There are cosmetics, waxes, and paints to fill and cover features, even plaster of Paris to replace entire limbs. There are ingenious aids to prop and stabilize the cadaver: a Vari-Pose Head Rest, the Edwards Arm and Hand Positioner, the Repose Block (to support the shoulders during the embalming), and the Throop Foot Positioner, which resembles an old-fashioned stocks.

9   Mr. John H. Eckels, president of the Eckels College of Mortuary Science, thus describes the first part of the embalming procedure: "In the hands of a skilled practitioner, this work may be done in a comparatively short time and without mutilating the body other than by

slight incision—so slight that it scarcely would cause serious inconvenience if made upon a living person. It is necessary to remove the blood, and doing this not only helps in the disinfecting, but removes the principal cause of disfigurements due to discoloration."

10   Another textbook discusses the all-important time element: "The earlier this is done, the better, for every hour that elapses between death and embalming will add to the problems and complications encountered. . . ." Just how soon should one get going on the embalming? The author tells us, "On the basis of such scanty information made available to this profession through its rudimentary and haphazard system of technical research, we must conclude that the best results are to be obtained if the subject is embalmed before life is completely extinct—that is, before cellular death has occurred. In the average case, this would mean within an hour after somatic death." For those who feel that there is something a little rudimentary, not to say haphazard, about this advice, a comforting thought is offered by another writer. Speaking of fears entertained in early days of premature burial, he points out, "One of the effects of embalming by chemical injection, however, has been to dispel fears of live burial." How true; once the blood is removed, chances of live burial are indeed remote.

11   To return to Mr. Jones, the blood is drained out through the veins and replaced by embalming fluid pumped in through the arteries. As noted in *The Principles and Practices of Embalming,* "every operator has a favorite injection and drainage point—a fact which becomes a handicap only if he fails or refuses to forsake his favorites when conditions demand it." Typical favorites are the carotid artery, femoral artery, jugular vein, subclavian vein. There are various choices of embalming fluid. If Flextone is used, it will produce a "mild, flexibility rigidity. The skin retains a velvety softness, the tissues are rubbery and pliable. Ideal for women and children." It may be blended with B. and G. Products Company's Lyf-Lyk tint, which is guaranteed to reproduce "nature's own skin texture . . . the velvety appearance of living tissue." Suntone comes in three separate tints: Suntan; Special Cosmetic Tint, a pink shade "especially indicated for female subjects"; and Regular Cosmetic Tint, moderately pink.

12   About three to six gallons of a dyed and perfumed solution of formaldehyde, glycerin, borax, phenol, alcohol, and water is soon circulated through Mr. Jones, whose mouth has been sewn together with a "needle directed upward between the upper lip and gum and brought

out through the left nostril," with the corners raised slightly "for a more pleasant expression." If he should be bucktoothed, his teeth are cleaned with Bon Ami and coated with colorless nail polish. His eyes, meanwhile, are closed with flesh-tinted eye caps and eye cement.

13   The next step is to have at Mr. Jones with a thing called a trocar. This is a long, hollow needle attached to a tube. It is jabbed into the abdomen, poked around the entrails and chest cavity, the contents of which are pumped out and replaced with "cavity fluid." This done, and the hole in the abdomen sewn up, Mr. Jones's face is heavily creamed (to protect the skin from burns which may be caused by leakage of the chemicals), and he is covered with a sheet and left unmolested for a while. But not for long—there is more, much more, in store for him. He has been embalmed, but not yet restored, and the best time to start the restorative work is eight to ten hours after embalming, when the tissues have become firm and dry.

14   The object of all this attention to the corpse, it must be remembered, is to make it presentable for viewing in an attitude of healthy repose. "Our customs require the presentation of our dead in the semblance of normality . . . unmarred by the ravages of illness, disease, or mutilation," says Mr. J. Sheridan Mayer in his *Restorative Art*. This is rather a large order since few people die in the full bloom of health, unravaged by illness and unmarked by some disfigurement. The funeral industry is equal to the challenge: "In some cases the gruesome appearance of a mutilated or disease-ridden subject may be quite discouraging. The task of restoration may seem impossible and shake the confidence of the embalmer. This is the time for intestinal fortitude and determination. Once the formative work is begun and affected tissues are cleaned or removed, all doubts of success vanish. It is surprising and gratifying to discover the results which may be obtained."

15   The embalmer, having allowed an appropriate interval to elapse, returns to the attack, but now he brings into play the skill and equipment of sculptor and cosmetician. Is a hand missing? Casting one in plaster of Paris is a simple matter. "For replacement purposes, only a cast of the back of the hand is necessary; this is within the ability of the average operator and is quite adequate." If a lip or two, a nose, or an ear should be missing, the embalmer has at hand a variety of restorative waxes with which to model replacements. Pores and skin textures are simulated by stippling with a little brush, and over this cosmetics are laid on. Head off? Decapitation cases are rather routinely handled.

Ragged edges are trimmed, and head joined to torso with a series of splints, wires, and sutures. It is a good idea to have a little something at the neck—a scarf or a high collar—when time for viewing comes. Swollen mouth? Cut out tissue as needed from inside the lips. If too much is removed, the surface contour can easily be restored by padding with cotton. Swollen necks and cheeks are reduced by removing tissue through vertical incisions made down each side of the neck. "When the deceased is casketed, the pillow will hide the suture incisions . . . as an extra precaution against leakage, the suture may be painted with liquid sealer."

16   The opposite condition is more likely to present itself—that of emaciation. His hypodermic syringe now loaded with massage cream, the embalmer seeks out and fills the hollowed and sunken areas by injection. In this procedure the backs of the hands and fingers and the under-chin area should not be neglected.

17   Positioning the lips is a problem that recurrently challenges the ingenuity of the embalmer. Closed too tightly, they tend to give a stern, even disapproving expression. Ideally, embalmers feel, the lips should give the impression of being ever so slightly parted, the upper lip protruding slightly for a more youthful appearance. This takes some engineering, however, as the lips tend to drift apart. Lip drift can sometimes be remedied by pushing one or two straight pins through the inner margin of the lower lip and then inserting them between the two front upper teeth. If Mr. Jones happens to have no teeth, the pins can just as easily be anchored in his Armstrong Face Former and Denture Replacer. Another method to maintain lip closure is to dislocate the lower jaw, which is then held in its new position by a wire run through holes which have been drilled through the upper and lower jaws at the midline. As the French are fond of saying, *il faut souffrir pour être belle.*[3]

18   If Mr. Jones has died of jaundice, the embalming fluid will very likely turn him green. Does this deter the embalmer? Not if he has intestinal fortitude. Masking pastes and cosmetics are heavily laid on, burial garments and casket interiors are color-correlated with particular care, and Jones is displayed beneath rose-colored lights. Friends will say "How *well* he looks." Death by carbon monoxide, on the other hand, can be rather a good thing from the embalmer's viewpoint: "One advantage is the fact that this type of discoloration is an exaggerated form

---

3. You have to suffer to be beautiful.

of a natural pink coloration." This is nice because the healthy glow is already present and needs but little attention.

19   The patching and filling completed, Mr. Jones is now shaved, washed, and dressed. Cream-based cosmetic, available in pink, flesh, suntan, brunette, and blond, is applied to his hands and face, his hair is shampooed and combed (and, in the case of Mrs. Jones, set), his hands manicured. For the horny-handed son of toil special care must be taken; cream should be applied to remove ingrained grime, and the nails cleaned. "If he were not in the habit of having them manicured in life, trimming and shaping is advised for better appearance—never questioned by kin."

20   Jones is now ready for casketing (this is the present participle of the verb "to casket"). In this operation his right shoulder should be depressed slightly "to turn the body a bit to the right and soften the appearance of lying flat on the back." Positioning the hands is a matter of importance, and special rubber positioning blocks may be used. The hands should be cupped slightly for a more lifelike, relaxed appearance. Proper placement of the body requires a delicate sense of balance. It should lie as high as possible in the casket, yet not so high that the lid, when lowered, will hit the nose. On the other hand, we are cautioned, placing the body too low "creates the impression that the body is in a box."

21   Jones is next wheeled into the appointed slumber room where a few last touches may be added—his favorite pipe placed in his hand or, if he was a great reader, a book propped into position. (In the case of little Master Jones a Teddy bear may be clutched.) Here he will hold open house for a few days, visiting hours 10 A.M. to 9 P.M.

22   All now being in readiness, the funeral director calls a staff conference to make sure that each assistant knows his precise duties. Mr. Wilber Kriege writes: "This makes your staff feel that they are a part of the team, with a definite assignment that must be properly carried out if the whole plan is to succeed. You never heard of a football coach who failed to talk to his entire team before they go on the field. They have drilled on the plays they are to execute for hours and days, and yet the successful coach knows the importance of making even the bench-warming third-string substitute feel that he is important if the game is to be won." The winning of *this* game is predicated upon glass-smooth handling of the logistics. The funeral director has notified the pallbearers whose names were furnished by the family, has arranged for the

presence of clergyman, organist, and soloist, has provided transportation for everybody, has organized and listed the flowers sent by friends. In *Psychology of Funeral Service* Mr. Edward A. Martin points out, "He may not always do as much as the family thinks he is doing, but it is his helpful guidance that they appreciate in knowing they are proceeding as they should. . . . The important thing is how well his services can be used to make the family believe they are giving unlimited expression to their own sentiment."

23   The religious service may be held in a church or in a chapel of the funeral home; the funeral director vastly prefers the latter arrangement, for not only is it more convenient for him but it affords him the opportunity to show off his beautiful facilities to the gathered mourners. After the clergyman has had his say, the mourners queue up to file past the casket for a last look at the deceased. The family is *never* asked whether they want an open-casket ceremony; in the absence of their instruction to the contrary, this is taken for granted. Consequently well over 90 percent of all American funerals feature the open casket—a custom unknown in other parts of the world. Foreigners are astonished by it. An English woman living in San Francisco described her reaction in a letter to the writer:

> I myself have attended only one funeral here—that of an elderly fellow worker of mine. After the service I could not understand why everyone was walking towards the coffin (sorry, I mean casket), but thought I had better follow the crowd. It shook me rigid to get there and find the casket open and poor old Oscar lying there in his brown tweed suit, wearing a suntan makeup and just the wrong shade of lipstick. If I had not been extremely fond of the old boy, I have a horrible feeling that I might have giggled. Then and there I decided that I could never face another American funeral—even dead.

24   The casket (which has been resting throughout the service on a Classic Beauty Ultra Metal Casket Bier) is now transferred by a hydraulically operated device called Porto-Life to a balloon-tired, Glide Easy casket carriage which will wheel it to yet another conveyance, the Cadillac Funeral Coach. This may be lavender, cream, light green—anything but black. Interiors, of course, are color-correlated, "for the man who cannot stop short of perfection."

25   At graveside, the casket is lowered into the earth. This office, once the prerogative of friends of the deceased, is now performed by a

patented mechanical lowering device. A "Lifetime Green" artificial grass mat is at the ready to conceal the sere earth, and overhead, to conceal the sky, is a portable Steril Chapel Tent ("resists the intense heat and humidity of summer and the terrific storms of winter . . . available in Silver Gray, Rose, or Evergreen"). Now is the time for the ritual scattering of earth over the coffin, as the solemn words "earth to earth, ashes to ashes, dust to dust" are pronounced by the officiating cleric. This can today be accomplished "with a mere flick of the wrist with the Gordon Leak-Proof Earth Dispenser. No grasping of a handful of dirt, no soiled fingers. Simple, dignified, beautiful, reverent! The modern way!" The Gordon Earth Dispenser (at $5) is of nickel-plated brass construction. It is not only "attractive to the eye and long wearing"; it is also "one of the 'tools' for building better public relations" if presented as "an appropriate non-commercial gift" to the clergyman. It is shaped something like a saltshaker.

26   Untouched by human hand, the coffin and the earth are now united.

27   It is in the function of directing the participants through this maze of gadgetry that the funeral director has assigned to himself his relatively new role of "grief therapist." He has relieved the family of every detail, he has revamped the corpse to look like a living doll, he has arranged for it to nap for a few days in a slumber room, he has put on a well-oiled performance in which the concept of *death* has played no part whatsoever—unless it was inconsiderately mentioned by the clergyman who conducted the religious service. He has done everything in his power to make the funeral a real pleasure for everybody concerned. He and his team have given their all to score an upset victory over death.

Reading Closely and Thinking Critically

1. In paragraph 6, Mitford says that her essay will "part the formaldehyde curtain." What do you think she means? Is the phrase a good one? Explain.

2. According to Mitford, what is the real purpose of embalming? What is the ostensible purpose?

3. What are the steps in the embalming process?

4. Why do you think Mitford names the corpse "Mr. Jones"?

5. How would you describe Mitford's attitude toward the mortuary business?

6. Who would you judge to be the original, intended audience for Mitford's exposé?

7. According to Mitford, why do morticians keep the embalming process secret?

Examining Structure and Strategy

1. What is the thesis of "Behind the Formaldehyde Curtain"?

2. What process does Mitford explain?

3. Mitford begins her explanation of a process in paragraph 7. What is the purpose of the first six paragraphs?

4. Mitford employs a considerable amount of verbal irony (saying one thing but suggesting another). For example, in paragraph 2 she refers to the casket as "a suitably costly container," but she does not really think the cost appropriate. Cite two or three other examples of verbal irony. What purpose does the irony serve?

5. The description in "Behind the Formaldehyde Curtain" is graphic and, at times, shocking. What purpose does this graphic description serve?

Considering Language and Style

1. How would you describe the tone of "Behind the Formaldehyde Curtain"? (See page 37 on tone.) Cite examples to support your view.

2. Mitford opens with a reference to burial and its preparation as "drama." In what ways is the metaphor of the drama sustained in the essay? (See page 73 on metaphors.)

3. Consult a dictionary if you are unsure of the meaning of any of these words: *bereaved* (paragraph 3), *docility* (paragraph 4), *perpetuation* (paragraph 4), *intractable* (paragraph 6), *raison d'être* (paragraph 6), *augers* (paragraph 8), *entrails* (paragraph 13), *stippling* (paragraph 15), *queue* (paragraph 23), *hydraulically* (paragraph 24).

For Group Discussion or Writing

A *euphemism* is a polite or indirect substitute for an unpleasant expression. Mitford notes a number of euphemisms employed by the funeral industry. For example, in paragraph 7, she refers to a body "reposing in the preparation room" rather than "dead on a slab in the embalming chamber." With some classmates, cite other euphemisms that appear. Explain what effect these euphemisms have on an individual's perception of the realities of death and burial.

Writing Assignments

1. ***In your journal.*** Have your views of death and the funeral industry changed after reading "Behind the Formaldehyde Curtain"? Were your views influenced at all by the graphic description in the essay? Explain in a page or two.

2. ***Using the pattern.*** Explain the funeral process for a particular religion or culture. If possible, explain the reasons for the various steps in the process. (You may research funeral rituals in your campus library to complete this assignment.)

3. ***Using the pattern.*** Select a process that you think is unnecessary or faulty and explain how that process works. Like Mitford, use verbal irony and description to convey your attitude toward the process.

4. ***Using the pattern.*** Like Mitford, write a graphic description of a grisly process (for example, baiting a fishing hook, cleaning a fish, dissecting a frog or other animal, and so on).

5. ***Using the pattern.*** Devise and describe a funeral and burial process that you think is better than anything currently followed in the United States. As you explain the steps in the process, note why they are superior to existing rituals.

6. ***Considering a theme.*** If you have experienced some of the rituals surrounding death because someone you know died, describe the rituals and your reaction to them. Explain whether you found them comforting, depressing, confusing, frightening, and so on. Also, explain why you think you reacted the way you did. If you like, you can also describe the reactions of other people. As an alternative, describe the rituals that you think should surround funerals and burials. Explain why you recommend these rituals.

7. *Connecting the readings.* A euphemism tries to make a harsh reality less distressing by substituting a more pleasant expression for an unpleasant one. Consider the euphemisms in the selection and any others you can think of. (For example, *a waiting room* in a doctor's office is a *reception area;* a dentist does not *pull* a tooth but *performs an extraction.*) Then, decide whether Sissela Bok should add the category of euphemisms to her classification of white lies in "White Lies" on page 458. Explain why or why not. (The previous group activity may give you some ideas.)

WHAT SORT OF CAR-RT-SORT AM I?
Erik Larson

A Long Island native and graduate of Columbia University School of Jour-
nalism, Erik Larson is a senior writer for Time *magazine and a recognized*
authority on the United States's gun culture. He published a series of ground-
breaking articles on guns in America for The Wall Street Journal, *and he*
wrote the acclaimed book Lethal Passage: The Journey of a Gun *(1995). In*
the following essay, which appeared in Harper's *(1989), Larson examines the*
relationship between privacy and technology. He explains several processes to
inform the reader about how companies use computers to compile and sell in-
formation about us. He combines this process analysis with examples and an
explanation of the effects of data compilation. Part of his purpose is to per-
suade the reader to be wary because data compilation can be harmful. How-
ever, as you read, notice that there are also elements of humor to entertain
the reader.

THE PATTERNS	THE PURPOSES
process analysis with exemplifi-cation and cause-and-effect analysis	*to inform, to persuade, and to entertain*

1   I get a lot of junk mail. Like most of my friends, I throw most of
the letters away unopened. I do save the catalogs, however: I pass them
to my wife, who no doubt is one of the mainstays of the $21 billion
junk-mail industry—"direct mail," as its practitioners prefer. My wife
brings catalogs to bed with her at night. She is also a doctor, and people with causes to advance and gadgets to sell like doctors. For every
piece of mail I get, she gets ten. Somewhere, I imagine a mountain has
been deforested just for her.

2   Together, she and I have been rented, matched, merged, purged,
"deduped," stockpiled, downloaded, parsed, and sorted—by zip, carrier route, carrier walk, and zip-plus-four. (Next time you see "car-rt-
sort" on your bulk-rate mail, know this: Whoever sent it got a postal
discount by sorting it by carrier route, a hunk of postal geography
smaller than a zipcode zone.) We've been scavenged by data pickers

who sifted through our driving records and auto registrations, our deed and our mortgage, in search of what direct mailers see as the keys to our identities: our sexes, ages, the ages of our cars, the equity we hold in our home. The scavengers record this data in central computers, which, in turn, merge it with other streams of revelatory data collected from other sources—the types of magazines we subscribe to, the organizations we support, how much credit we've got left—and then spit it all out (for a price) to virtually anyone who wants it. The information eventually makes its way to the country's dozen or so largest data banks, electromagnetic colossi maintained by companies that serve the direct-mail industry.

3   I feel so cheap, so used.

4   The direct-mail industry in America has quietly built itself an immense, private intelligence network in which nearly each and every one of us now resides. The biggest companies know a lot about us, and they're getting to know us even better. Lists are the raw materials. There are "compiled" lists built of records bought wholesale from state governments or built piece by piece by the scavengers. There are "response" lists created whenever people subscribe to magazines, order products through the mail, or answer consumer surveys. Advertisers can rent lists that tell what car you bought, whether you like dried fruit and nuts, whether you have a kid, whether you or your wife is pregnant.

5   Individually, these lists are mostly harmless. So what if strangers know I subscribe to *Country Living?* Within the last five years, however, advanced "merge/purge" software has given the data collectors the power to layer list upon list, cheaply and quickly, and thereby—if they wish—to turn lists into thick dossiers. Suppose my name appears on 100 lists (a conservative estimate, by the way). The data on these lists, if merged, would form a kind of "me," a character with opinions, traits, an entire personality defined by what I've registered, signed—and especially what I've purchased.

6   Moreover, a recent surge of mergers among data companies and their databases is yielding still richer profiles of consumers. Last summer, for example, R. L. Polk & Co., a huge data compiler in Detroit, acquired National Demographics & Lifestyles of Denver—a company that, with the help of the brief questionnaires that come along with the warranty materials in new radios, TVs, and other so-called consumer durables, has built a database listing the hobbies and passions of 20 million American consumers. More disquieting, however, is the entry of

TRW and Equifax, the nation's largest credit bureaus, into direct mail. They provide the mailers with lists derived from credit files—files previously available only for purposes of evaluating a consumer's creditworthiness.

7   The number of people now collected and processed is staggering. TRW keeps monthly tabs on 143 million consumers, or roughly 80 percent of all consumers over the age of eighteen. Donnelley Marketing of Stamford, Connecticut, tracks 80 million households—90 percent of all households in the country. Donnelley enriches this database by mailing marketing surveys to 30 million households at a time, ten times a year. The survey questions can get personal. One example from a recent mailing: "How many times, if any, did you medicate for diarrhea in the past year?"

8   The keepers of big data say they do it for the consumer's benefit. But data have a way of being used for purposes other than originally intended. In 1984—I mean, really, of all years—the Selective Service System used a Farrell's Ice Cream list it had rented to contact young men as they came of draft age. (The list was made up of the names of children who, in registering for an ice cream promotion, had written down their birth dates.) Also in 1984, the IRS tried using mailing lists to track down tax evaders. It approached Donnelley Marketing and two other data giants, but they refused, arguing such use would invade people's privacy. (An IRS official, however, told me one loyal American list broker, Dunhill of Washington, did supply the names and whereabouts of 2 million people.)

9   Could darker scenarios develop? Or could I just be paranoid? Did you know that advertisers can rent lists of names of men who are gay? That there are lists that single out blacks and Hispanics? And what is your first reaction when I tell you that A. B. Data Ltd., in Milwaukee, specializes in collecting the names of Jews? Two or three times a year it runs the entire population through a program it devised that selects the surnames of people statistically most likely to be Jews. Anyone named Aaroni has a 100 percent chance of being Jewish; anyone named Ronald Reagan, only a 1 percent chance. A. B. does a brisk commerce in Jewish names. Avram Lyon, A. B.'s vice president, noted when I spoke with him that Jews read books; have tended to be generous to charitable causes; and, he added, "they're well-to-do, highly assimilated. They have a lot of disposable cash." I asked if A. B. had ever received inquiries from fundamentalist types bent on direct-mail evangelism. Yes,

Lyon said, there have been inquiries, but the company turned them down.

10   My uneasiness about the magnitude of information collected by direct mailers led me to this question: Who wants *me?* On whose lists do I reside? I set out recently to find out, to collect the tiles of my personal mosaic from far-flung computers, trace my direct mail to its sources, have myself profiled, mapped, and clustered. Just who—out there, in the universe of direct mail—do they think I am?

11   I began the search for my direct-mail self on the top floor of the Clarence Mitchell, Jr., Courthouse, in Baltimore. Here, in a mundane room of ochre walls and brown tile, my mail life begins. In microfilm files 1611–278 and 1611–281, there are details stored that I would not tell a friend, let alone a stranger—what I paid for my house, the amount I borrowed to buy it, and how much I was able to scrape together for the down payment. If this information simply remained at the courthouse, it would be one thing. It doesn't. Anyone can collect it and sell it. One day last year data prospectors from Rufus S. Lusk & Son got their hands on it.

12   Lusk operates primarily in Maryland, Virginia, and Washington, D.C., collecting exact home-equity and property-tax information, indexing it, then selling it to realtors, landscapers, interior decorators— anyone who stands to profit when someone buys a home. If you work for Lusk, you spend lots of time in rooms with ochre walls.

13   "It's all public information," Carol Stewart assured me. She is vice president in charge of Lusk's branch in Timonium, Maryland, where I visited her (her office happens to have ochre walls). To test her conviction, I asked to see the real estate records of Kurt L. Schmoke, Baltimore's mayor. No doubt it would have taken me hours of prodding to get the mayor's address from his press office, let alone the amount of his mortgage. But there it all was, right on the screen of Stewart's microfiche viewer: 3320 Sequoia Avenue, zip 21215. Owner-occupied. Single-family dwelling. Acquired November 1983 for $125,000, with a $112,500 mortgage from Yorkridge-Calvert Savings and Loan. He pays $3,553.36 in annual state and local property taxes.

14   My heart leapt.

15   I asked to see the records on my own home, and these too appeared. Of far more interest to me, however, were the adjacent entries, the homes of my neighbors. Ah, Richard and Carol, Fred and Betsy,

Nancy, Margaret! I know a few things you don't know I know.

16   Seeing my name there, toiling in its own small way to help Lusk make a profit, gave me an odd feeling. My affairs were being monitored, yet I knew nothing about it. Who else was watching?

17   That afternoon, I called the Maryland Motor Vehicle Administration, to see what it might have on me. I was steered to Ed Seidel, a public-information officer who was happy to be of help, and who is himself fed up with the amount of information one has to give up these days. (When paying with a credit card, he won't give out his phone number!) The state keeps two "headers" on me, he said: one containing my registration and title information, the other my license and driving record. Both are available to anyone who wants to see them, and both are collected routinely in national sweeps by private companies (for example, by R. L. Polk). Both headers, of course, were available to me as well. Seidel told me to give him my license number. As I read each digit, he called it out to a woman somewhere nearby. A printer whined at me through the earpiece of my phone. "I hope there's nothing embarrassing there," I said.

18   "Embarrassing?" Seidel said. He chuckled. "You don't know embarrassing. Sometimes the list is as tall as my boss."

19   What can be gleaned from this? My address, of course. And the vital statistics of me and my car; I am thirty-five years old, stand six one, and weigh 185 pounds. I drive a 1984—that year again!—Honda Civic Sedan, plate number WGN103. My car weighs 3,700 pounds.

20   "It also includes an indication if anything's been flagged," Seidel said. "Which yours has."

21   He paused for effect. "You've got a little parking ticket for 12/15/88, city of Baltimore."

22   "I paid that," I said, perhaps too quickly.

23   Not only am I on file, of course; I'm on lists, countless lists. So are you. These lists, in turn, are sold or swapped to others who want to reach you through the mail. You subscribe, give, buy—and your name is put on the lists of those you've subscribed to, given to, bought from. These lists can tell worlds about your hopes and fears. An outfit called the Bureau of Protective Analysis markets the names of its 22,000 members. These people pay an annual fee, send off their urine, and in return get quarterly urinalysis reports so they can keep tabs on what the bureau calls the "eighteen potential trouble spots."

24   No one is spared a list life, not even subscribers to *The New Yorker.* The magazine began marketing its readers for the first time last year. Catalog companies, magazines, causes, and concerns can rent the list for $90 per 1,000 names. The magazine expressly bars its use, however, for such crass endeavors as sweepstakes, real estate offers, politics, and fund-raising. (*Harper's* magazine, too, rents its subscriber list.)

25   We get listed at earlier and earlier ages. *Sesame Street* magazine rents its subscriber list. So do *Snoopy Magazine* and *Mickey Mouse* magazine. Hasbro Toys peddles the 454,427 names of individuals who sent in proof-of-purchase labels to get a rebate on My Little Pony games, Jem Doll cassettes, and G. I. Joe Figurines. Recently, the mail brought the Right Start Catalog, a kind of Sharper Image for babies. It beat the baby home by a month.

26   Often list owners are reluctant to say how they acquired the names on their lists. I phoned Globe Life and Accident Insurance Co., in Oklahoma City, and asked Cynthia Cooke, list manager there, how she got my name—and, for that matter, how she knew I was a father. (I had received one of the 50 million direct-mail solicitations Globe posts every year.)

27   "I can't give that to you," she said.

28   I was ready with an argument of awesome, primitive power. "Why not?" I asked. "It's my name."

29   She laughed. "We have agreements with other people that we won't disclose that. And even if we didn't, we look upon that as proprietary information. We paid for the use of it, and—it's hard to be delicate about this—it's our business."

30   I was able to piece together a few trails, however. Here's my favorite—involving not me but my wife. Although she's a voracious consumer, she generally shuns politics. Little did she know she'd wind up in the thick of it—just by ordering, by mail, a package of frozen beef from Omaha Steaks. Omaha Steaks rented her to the G.O.P. Victory Fund of the National Republican Congressional Committee and on a separate occasion to the National Security Political Action Committee. Each committee tapped the list on its own, without first trading notes. Is there some affinity then between Republicans and red meat? "I think that's an absurd statement," said Elizabeth Fediay, chair of the National Security PAC, when I phoned her. "At some point someone probably assessed that this list has been successful with political fund-raising and political activism."

31   "The moment of truth," Doug Anderson, a vice president of Claritas Corporation, in Alexandria, Virginia, was saying. Anderson and I were sitting at a computer in a glass-enclosed room just off the company's sleek blue-gray lobby. Claritas, Latin for "clarity," is a target-marketing company, and Anderson had just entered my current zip code into the computer. I also entrusted him with two other chunks of my life—the zip I had when I lived in San Francisco and the zip I grew up with on Long Island. I was about to learn what kind of guy I am, what kind of guy I've been.

32   Claritas was founded by Jonathan Robbin, a man who delights in discovering correlations between seemingly unrelated behaviors—for example, he now knows that people who listen to religious radio don't eat salted nuts. Robbin pioneered the technique of blending census data, market research, and millions of other survey and statistical records, and then analyzing the result to predict consumer behavior. Claritas broke the country into forty neighborhood types, gave each a catchy, evocative name ("Blue-Blood Estates," "Shotguns and Pickups," and "Tobacco Roads"), ranked them in order of affluence, and dubbed the system PRIZM, for Potential Rating Index for Zip Markets. The theory is that the Blue Bloods of California behave much like the Blue Bloods of New Jersey, although the former may have better tans.

33   "The whole idea is that you can now assign every neighborhood in the United States to one of these forty types," Robbin said. "There are enclaves where people live at one phase of their lives, or are living because they share the same interests and needs as everybody else." In theory, a direct-mail company can divide a list of its best customers into PRISM clusters, determine which clusters yield the best response rates, and then target those clusters throughout the country.

34   Other companies have followed Claritas's lead. Donnelley, for example, offers ClusterPLUS. CACI International, a defense contractor and information-services company based in Arlington, Virginia, offers ACORN: A Classification of Residential Neighborhoods. ACORN can provide the longitude and latitude of a given residential area. Mine is latitude 39°20′15″ and longitude 76°35′40″. Now even the Soviets can target my neighborhood.

35   But back to Doug Anderson at his terminal.

36   "All right," he said. My current zip had bared itself on the screen. "You've got a big mix of people here." The cluster most heavily represented in my zip is "Downtown Dixie-Style," downscale souls ranked

fifth from last in terms of affluence. About 15 percent occupy cluster 32, "Public Assistance." The bottom rung. (The number assigned to each cluster does not correspond to its affluence rank.)

37   This was just the first step. For target markets, the zip is obsolete. Too broad. Indeed, my zip showed elements of thirteen different clusters. We needed to get closer, so Anderson types in the number of my block group, the smallest census division, consisting of an average of 340 households. Not every household in America gets assigned to a block group. In more rural areas, the Census Bureau tucks people into "minor civil divisions."

38   In census-speak, I live in state 24, county 510, census tract 902, block group 4. In PRIZM, that makes me a member of cluster 27, "Levittown, U.S.A."

39   The thrill of self-discovery. There are things here I never knew about myself: *I am an ice-hockey fan. I buy a lottery ticket one or more times each week. I went bowling more than twenty-five times last year. I belong to a union, install my own faucets, most often frequent pancake houses and doughnut shops. I am not at all likely to chew tobacco or buy comedy tapes and records.*

40   Anderson now began to type in the block groups of my past. How far I've fallen! In San Francisco, I belonged to cluster 37, "Bohemian Mix," one notch higher on the affluence scale than Levittown. Those were heady times: *I traveled by railroad and bought disco tapes. I drank malt liquor and imported brandy. I visited Europe and went to four or more movies every ninety days. I drank Pepsi Light. I did not own a chain saw, drive a pickup, or panel my own walls.*

41   Now, to the deep past—Take me back, Doug! State 36, county 59, census tract 4143.02, block group 5, Freeport, Long Island.

42   Cluster 27. Again. Levittown redux.

43   "You've really come full circle," Robbin said. "From a family back to a family, I mean, that's what I would suppose. Are you married with children?"

44   "Yes."

45   "That's it. You want your kids to live in a house. Do you live in a house?"

46   "Yes."

47   "But when you were in 'Bohemian Mix' you probably lived in an apartment, right?"

48   "Yes."

49   "I mean, look," Robbin said. "Is that easy to say, or is it not? I went through the same damn thing. I hated suburbia. I was brought up in a suburban area of New Jersey, a nice manicured little town called Summit. I *hated* it. I think I was assigned *Madame Bovary* about twenty times. I couldn't even find that book in a bookstore in Summit, New Jersey. Now, of course, it's different. It's upscale. Back then everybody was a troglodyte. And it was *dull*. It's odd that I now live in something very similar. I live in *Bethesda*. I've come full circle back to suburbia. I've never been able to escape it."

50   Here, set out in print for the first time, because I just made it up, is the First Law of Data Coalescence: Data must seek out and merge with other data. The shrinking cost of electronic computing and the advent of powerful list-enhancement software has triggered a wave of electromagnetic mergers. Data companies, and the data they collect, have merged in unprecedented volume over the past several years. The really momentous change, however, has been the entry of TRW and Equifax into target marketing. In 1985, both companies set up formal marketing divisions. Since then, both have aggressively acquired data and data companies, thereby enriching their already robust files. They've brought a powerful new tool to marketing—the ability to track monthly changes in virtually every consumer's financial behavior. But in transforming themselves from simple reporters to avid marketers, they've shaken a fragile compact between themselves and consumers.

51   I acquired my credit report from TRW for $5. I'd always imagined my report to be some kind of Deathstar in high elliptical orbit, periodically casting its shadow over my life.

52   What a letdown.

53   My report was a bland printout of credit lines, credit limits, and account balances, with columns of coded information telling whether I've paid my bills on time. The report did, however, give me a sense of the unfolding of my consumer life—there was my John Wanamaker's department store account from my two-year stay in Philadelphia; my account at Emporium Capwell in my "Bohemian Mix" days; and my account at Granat Brothers' San Francisco branch, the jewelry store where I paced the soft carpets for hours, agonizing over the right diamond for my wife's engagement ring.

54   Innocuous enough. But misleadingly innocuous. It's *how* the credit bureaus now use this information that gives it life, and gives one pause.

55   Neither TRW nor Equifax directly provides a marketer with credit reports. They instead compile lists of consumer names that reflect the credit data. L. L. Bean, for example, could request a list of all consumers who possess a bank card with $5,000 or more of available credit. (Neither company allows a search by specific brand of card.) TRW then searches its files and pulls a few million names. The company, however, won't return that list directly to Bean, but rather to a third-party printer, ostensibly to protect the privacy of consumers who fit the search criteria.

56   TRW also uses its credit files to build statistical models of consumers. Say L. L. Bean wants to know if those who do not respond to its catalogs have something in common. Bean gives TRW a list of those who did not respond; TRW finds those people in its files, pulls up all the credit, demographic, and auto-registration information it can on each one, and then tries to find the common thread that makes these people so recalcitrant.

57   TRW and Equifax don't need to scavenge for their credit data. It comes to them in a monthly monsoon, unbeckoned, from creditors who by agreement report to them every thirty days. This in turn allows the bureaus to detect when a consumer gets more credit, a new mortgage, or experiences some other changes in status—change being the stuff of marketer's dreams. Change rejuvenates us consumers. The new house we purchase needs down comforters from the Company Store, an armoire from Conran's, a set of chairs from Williams-Sonoma. Word that some lucky soul just got a new credit card can set the direct-mail world aflame. A newsletter sent to me by Listworld, a broker of credit-related lists in Huntsville, Alabama, put it this way: "The holder of a new credit card is a perfect target for just about everything."

58   When my mortgage company searched deep into my past, I resented the intrusion but considered it the company's right. No law required that the company lend me $100,000. My wife and I allowed ourselves to be evaluated because we stood to get something valuable in return.

59   Now, however, without any agreement from me, marketing companies can gain access to my credit history—not to provide me with credit, but to sell me something. TRW, for example, turned my wife and me over to CPC Associates, a list company in Bala Cynwyd, Pennsylvania, which in turn rented us to American Mailing Co-op in Plymouth, Minnesota, which decided we were a "special" family and offered us a

peek at Wilderness Resort, fifty-four miles outside Washington, D.C. This special family didn't want a peek at Wilderness Resort. We threw the mail out.

60   Is that what it all comes down to: I simply don't like to open junk mail? I hear some of you: Hey, you don't like it, you throw it away. What's the harm? And you might even find something you want to buy, or subscribe to, or support.

61   Well, then, if all this is so good for us consumers, why don't Equifax, TRW, and the other data keepers drop us a little note candidly explaining the true extent to which they use our names: "We and a thousand other companies are going to appropriate your name, match it, store it, rent it, swap it; we'll evaluate your geo-demographic profile, determine your ethnic heritage, calculate your propensity to consume. We'll track you for the rest of your consuming life—pitch you baby toys when you're pregnant, condos when you're fifty."

62   Perhaps we could demand they get our permission first, and insist on royalties tied to the number of names in a given database. We could negotiate exclusive licensing agreements and insist on lifelong retainers. Think of it: Some of these envelopes with checks peeking from those little plastic windows would actually contain real checks, not worthless look-alikes designed only to lure us inside.

63   The data keepers say we have nothing to fear, that they are scrupulous about protecting our records. They insist, too, that they have no use for dossiers on individuals, and use the detail available only to help target broad markets and to know the "hot buttons" that make those markets respond.

64   Yes. But the world changes. Events occur and movements swell that cause people to sacrifice the rights of their peers. "The true danger," Edmund Burke wrote, "is when liberty is nibbled away, for expedience and by parts." It is an interesting exercise to imagine the big marketing databases put to use in other times, other places, by less trustworthy souls. What, for instance, might health insurers do with the subscription lists of gay publications such as *The Advocate* and the *New York Native*?

65   If I am only uneasy, and not panicked, it is because I continue to harbor faith that the direct mailers and name harvesters don't really know what they're doing—at least not yet. Some still can't tell that my wife, who goes by her maiden name, Gleason, is indeed my wife—we get two copies of most of our direct mail. And there is an ever growing

list of catalog companies that insist that one of us is Gleason Larson. I take comfort, too, in knowing that *Mother Jones* and the conservative National Security PAC *both* seemed to feel my wife was worthy of their attention.

66   What delights me most, however, is that the folks at Victoria's Secret still send me their catalogue, that zesty album of gorgeous babes in skimpy lingerie; they still believe I'm a woman named Laura Lange.

Reading Closely and Thinking Critically

1. Larson says, "Individually, [mailing] lists are harmless." What, then, does he see that is so dangerous?

2. Those who compile mailing lists say that the data they amass is for "the consumer's benefit." How does Larson respond to that claim?

3. What particular danger is Larson pointing out in paragraph 9?

4. In the course of describing what information was compiled on him, and who compiled it, Larson asks, "Who else was watching?" What is the significance of this question?

5. Just how concerned is Larson? How can you tell?

6. Is Larson serious when he suggests in paragraph 62 that we should be paid for the use of our names?

Examining Structure and Strategy

1. Larson does not begin making his case until paragraph 5. What purpose do paragraphs 1 through 4 serve?

2. Where does the author begin developing his point with process analysis?

3. Larson really explains several processes in his essay. What are those processes?

4. In general, Larson's process analyses show the nature and extent of the information compiled about us, how this information is gathered, and the uses to which it is put. Why does Larson present all this information?

5. The author uses examples to support his points. For instance, in paragraph 6, he cites R. L. Polk & Co.'s acquisition of National Demographics & Lifestyles of Denver as an example of the merger of data companies and databases. Cite three other examples in the essay and indicate what purpose each example serves.

6. In addition to describing a process and providing examples, Larson explains the effects of something. What effects does he explain? (Cause-and-effect analysis is discussed in Chapter 8.)

7. Describe the audience you think is appropriate for "What Kind of Car-Rt-Sort Am I?"

Considering Language and Style

1. Larson often uses words and phrases for the connotations (emotional associations or content) they bring to the essay. For example, in paragraph 4, he refers to the direct-mail industry's "intelligence network," a phrase that attributes the direct-mail industry with the secrecy and sophisticated information-collection techniques of the CIA. Cite three examples of emotionally charged language in the first two paragraphs.

2. Consult a dictionary if you are unsure of the meaning of any of these words: *colossi* (paragraph 2), *dossiers* (paragraph 5), *disquieting* (paragraph 6), *mundane* (paragraph 11), *ochre* (paragraph 11), *proprietary* (paragraph 29), *troglodyte* (paragraph 49), *coalescence* (paragraph 50), *innocuous* (paragraph 54), *propensity* (paragraph 61).

For Group Discussion or Writing

Do you feel threatened by the compilation of databases and mailing lists? If so, explain what you think the danger is. If you do not feel threatened, explain why not. Do you think that the threat to privacy will increase in the future? Why or why not?

Writing Assignments

1. *In your journal.* Larson deals with a serious issue: the threat to privacy. However, throughout the essay, elements of humor give the piece a lighthearted tone. Cite the instances of humor in the essay. Then discuss whether or not this humor undermines Larson's serious purpose.

2. *Using the pattern.* Identify a process you perform on your campus that is troublesome (for example, registering, buying books, securing financial aid, or selecting an advisor) and write an essay to convince the appropriate administrator that the process is a problem. Like Larson, explain the process and use examples to persuade your reader that it is troublesome.

3. Using the pattern. Identify a troublesome process that is not part of academic life (for example, renewing your driver's license, correcting an incorrect bank card statement, or getting an insurance company to pay a medical bill). Write an essay that explains the process and use examples to show how troublesome the process is. If you like, you can employ humor and a lighthearted tone.

4. Using the pattern. Pick a process you have been involved in, one that affects people's lives significantly (for example, applying for college admission, trying out for an athletic team, or applying for a job). Describe the process and use examples to show the effects it has on people.

5. Using the pattern. Explain a process related to any aspect of using computers: how to select the best computer, how to select a word processing program, how to install a modem, how E-mail works, and so forth. Assume your reader knows very little about computers and explain the process in a way your audience will understand.

6. Considering a theme. Write a piece of legislation meant to protect the general public by restricting the extent to which information can be collected, stored, shared, and sold. Explain the details of the legislation, including specifically what it will and will not allow, and argue for its passage. As an alternative, argue that there is no need to fear the collection, storage, and dissemination of data by means of technology.

7. Connecting the readings. If Miklós Vámos does everything he mentions in "How I'll Become an American" (page 283), the computers in this country will have volumes of information on him to compile, store, and share. Based on what you learned from "What Sort of Car-Rt-Sort Am I?" and "How I'll Become an American," explain what information companies will compile on Vámos, how they will get it, with whom they will share it, and how Vámos will be affected as a result.

ADDITIONAL ESSAY ASSIGNMENTS

See pages 267 and 268 for suggestions for writing process analysis and for a revision checklist.

1. Explain a process that people should know so they can cope with an emergency: how to administer CPR, how to administer first aid to someone badly cut, what to do if a tornado strikes, what to do if fire breaks out in the home, or how to rescue a drowning person, for instance. Your purpose is to inform your reader.

2. Select a process you perform well (for example, making pizza, wrapping gifts, throwing a surprise party, or planting a garden) and describe it so that your reader can learn how to do it.

3. Explain a successful process for quitting smoking, losing weight, or giving up a particular bad habit so your reader can try it as part of a self-improvement program.

4. Explain a process that will help your reader save money: how to buy a used car, how to save money on groceries, how to buy clothes at a thrift shop, how to find bargains at flea markets, how to buy presents for less, and so on.

5. If you have a hobby, explain some process associated with that hobby: evaluating the worth of a baseball card, putting together a tropical fish tank, and so on. Let your pleasure at performing the process show.

6. If you play a sport well, explain some process associated with that sport: shooting a foul shot, sliding into home plate, and so on. Let your pleasure at performing the process show.

7. To inform your reader, explain some scientific or natural process: photosynthesis, nuclear fission, nuclear fusion, a lightning strike, hurricane formation, or cell division, for instance.

8. To entertain your reader, write a humorous explanation of a process: how to flunk a test, how to make a bad impression on a date, how to irritate a teacher, how to make a bad impression on a job interview, or how to be a slob, for instance.

9. Explain how some mechanical device works: a VCR, a cordless telephone, a compact disc, a computer, and so on.

10. To inform your reader, explain how something is made: paper, decaffeinated coffee, a baseball, and so on. If necessary, do some

research to learn about the process. (Consult the appendix on how to handle material taken from sources.)

11. To convince your reader that women suffer unfairly, explain a process they go through to conform to society's concept of beauty.

12. To relate your experience, and inform, explain the wedding ritual for the religious, ethnic, or cultural group you belong to. Try to use description to make aspects of the process as vivid as possible. As an alternative, explain the ritual for some other life cycle event.

13. Explain some process for improving relationships between people: how to fight fairly, how to communicate better, how to respect differences, how to offer constructive criticism, and so on.

14. To entertain your reader, write a humorous explanation of how to procrastinate.

15. To help a student who is away from home for the first time, explain how to do laundry. Use examples and keep the tone lighthearted.

16. Explain a way to perform a process to convince your reader that your procedures are better. For example, you can explain a better way to study, a better way to clean a room, a better way to shop, a better way to choose an adviser, or a better way to plan a party.

17. To inform college students, explain a process for coping with stress. As an alternative, explain how to relax.

18. To entertain your reader, explain how to survive adolescence. You may write from a parent's or child's point of view.

19. If you believe the system for electing a president in the United States should be changed, explain the current process and what is wrong with it to convince your reader that change is needed.

20. *Process Analysis in Context:* Assume that your college is putting together a handbook for new freshmen to help these students adjust to school and be successful. As an experienced student, you have been asked to contribute to the handbook by describing an important academic survival skill: taking notes, taking an examination, getting along with a difficult roommate, reading a textbook, studying for finals, and so on. Be sure your process analysis is written in such a way that it is genuinely useful to a new student.

ᘓ COMPARISON-CONTRAST

The Readings, the Patterns, and the Purposes

THE PATTERN

Comparison points out similarities; contrast points out differences; comparison-contrast points out both similarities and differences. Because comparison-contrast allows us to examine the features of two or more subjects, it is often used in decision making. For example, if you want to buy a CD player, you may visit several stores to compare and contrast the features of a number of models. When you chose a college, you probably compared and contrasted two or more schools before deciding on the best one for you. Comparison-contrast is so much a part of routine decision making that you probably engage in it several times a day.

THE PURPOSES OF COMPARISON-CONTRAST

As noted, comparison-contrast can help us make decisions because when we set things side by side and look at their similarities and differences, we are better able to choose between the items. However, comparison-contrast can serve a range of other purposes as well.

A writer can inform a reader about the nature of something that is not very well understood by comparing and contrasting it with something that is better understood. For example, to explain how rugby is played, you could compare and contrast it with the better-known football. Comparison-contrast can also clarify the nature of one or both subjects under consideration. For example to help the reader better understand how men and women communicate, Deborah Tannen contrasts the communication styles of both genders in "Talk in the Intimate Relationship: His and Hers" (page 354). Similarly, to help your reader better understand the changing role of women, you can compare and contrast that role today with the role women played a generation ago.

Another way comparison-contrast can inform a reader is by providing a fresh insight into something already familiar. In this case, the comparison-contrast serves to sharpen the reader's awareness or appreciation. For example, you already know a fair amount about both horses and people, but after reading Alice Walker's comparison-contrast in "Am I Blue?" (page 374), you are likely to have fresh insight into the nature of both.

In addition to informing, comparison-contrast can allow the writer to express feelings and relate experience. To relate the effects of your parents' divorce and express your feelings about it, for example, you could contrast your life before and after the divorce to reveal the impact the event had on you.

Finally, by showing that one subject is superior to the other, comparison-contrast can work to persuade a reader to think or act a particular way. For instance, to convince a reader to vote for a particular candidate, you could contrast that candidate with the opposition to show that your choice is better.

Comparison-Contrast in College Writing

Comparison-contrast has many uses in the classroom. Often you will use it to clarify and evaluate the nature of two subjects. In a political science class, you may be asked to compare and contrast two political ideologies such as socialism and communism. In a music appreciation class, you may be asked to compare and contrast the techniques of two composers; in a literature class, you may be asked to compare and contrast the symbolism in two poems; in a computer science class, you may be asked to compare and contrast the way brains and computers work; and in a cultural anthropology class, you may be asked to compare and contrast the marriage rituals in two cultures.

You are also likely to use comparison-contrast to show the superiority of one of the subjects. For example, in a clinical psychology class, you may compare and contrast two treatments for depression to show which one is better; in an advertising class, you may compare and contrast two advertising campaigns to determine which one is more effective; and in a history class, you may compare and contrast two Civil War generals to determine who was the better strategist.

CHOOSING SUBJECTS

In general, the subjects you choose to compare and contrast should be from the same category. Thus, you can compare and contrast two kinds of computers, two weight-loss programs, two poems, two mayors, and so forth. Avoid comparing and contrasting subjects so different from one another that the similarities you cite are more clever than valid. Thus, while you might be able to compare Ronald McDonald to a former President of the United States, what would be the point? You might be able to compare studying to preparing for war, but what can be learned from the side-by-side comparison of such different subjects?

Sometimes subjects from different categories can be compared using a special form of comparison known as *analogy*. With analogy, you can compare subjects from different categories if they have compelling similarities or ones that shed light on one or both subjects. For example, author Robert Jastrow once compared the human brain with a computer because the two subjects, although from different categories, function similarly in a number of ways. The analogy helped the reader to better understand how both subjects work. Other analogies might be comparing the human eye to a camera or comparing an ant colony to New York City.

Be sure to choose subjects that allow you to cite comparisons and contrasts that go beyond statements of the obvious. Do not compare and contrast the bicycle and automobile, for example, if you can note only such obvious points as number of wheels and speed of travel. However, you can use these subjects if you have a fresh approach, perhaps comparing and contrasting the lifestyles inherent in using each vehicle as a principal mode of transportation.

SUPPORTING DETAILS

Comparison-contrast may include other patterns of development. For example, if you wanted to compare and contrast the techniques of two artists, you would probably describe the styles of each person. Examples are also a frequent component of comparison-contrast, particularly when a point of comparison or contrast requires clarification. For instance, if you were comparing two political candidates, and you stated that they both favored progressive legislation, you could clarify and support that point of comparison with an example. You could note that both candidates voted for a bill that would provide tax credits for working parents with children in day care centers.

Because a story can serve as an example, narration can be a part of comparison-contrast. For example, say that you want to compare and contrast your relationship with two friends. To show the differences in the way you interact with each person, you can tell the story of the time the three of you went away for the weekend.

Process analysis, too, can form part of comparison-contrast. For example, to contrast the styles of two baseball coaches, you could explain the process each one follows to motivate players.

SELECTING DETAILS

Because mentioning every possible point of comparison and contrast is undesirable—if not impossible—you must select your details with regard to your purpose for writing. Say, for instance, that you are comparing and contrasting public and private schools. If your purpose is to convince your reader that public schools are better, then you might mention that the ethnic diversity often found in these schools can teach students more about people and their cultural heritage. If your purpose is to relate your experiences in these schools, you can tell which school you were happier in and why. If your purpose is to inform, you might tell about the academic programs in each kind of school so parents can make up their own minds about which is better for their children. If your purpose is to entertain, you can give humorous portraits of the students and teachers in each kind of school.

In addition to purpose, a sense of balance will influence your detail selection. Most times, any point you make about one of your subjects should also be made about the other subject. Thus, if you are comparing and contrasting public and private schools and you discuss the teachers in public school, you should also discuss the teachers in private school; if you discuss course offerings in public school, you should also discuss course offerings in private school, and so on. (You may notice that the authors in this chapter do not always adhere to this principle of balance. An author can depart from this principle only if the essay does not become a random collection of points about the subjects.)

Although you are likely to discuss the same points about each of your subjects, you need not do so in equal detail. A point can be discussed in more detail for one subject than for the other. For example, assume you are contrasting the way you celebrated your birthday as a child and the way you celebrate it now. If you used to have a big birthday dinner with lots of relatives, you could describe the dinner in a full paragraph or more. If you do not have such a dinner now, then you might mention in just a sentence or two that you have dinner just as if it were any other day.

ORDERING DETAILS

The thesis for a comparision-contrast essay can present the subjects under consideration and indicate whether these subjects will be compared, contrasted, or both compared and contrasted. Consider, for example, this thesis from "Neat People vs. Sloppy People":

> I've finally figured out the difference between neat people and sloppy people.

This thesis notes that the subjects under consideration are neat people and sloppy people, and it also indicates that the subjects will be contrasted. Now consider these two thesis statements:

> Although you might not expect it, optimists and pessimists do have a number of things in common.

> Smith and Jones have different political philosophies, but they implement those philosophies with similar styles.

The first thesis indicates that the essay will compare optimists and pessimists. The second thesis indicates that politicians Smith and Jones will be both compared and contrasted.

The ordering of detail in a comparison-contrast essay requires some thought. One possible arrangement is the *block method,* whereby all the points about one subject are made (in a block), then all the points about the other subject are made (in a second block.) To appreciate how the block arrangement works, look at the following outline for an essay contrasting political candidates Smith and Jones. Notice that balance is achieved by discussing the same points for both subjects.

    I. Smith
       A. Believes in states funding their own health care plans
       B. Believes in supporting education with a state income tax
       C. Wants to form a task force to study lake pollution
   II. Jones
       A. Believes the federal government should fund health care
       B. Believes in supporting education with a property tax
       C. Believes lake pollution is not a priority

A second possible arrangement for comparison-contrast detail is the *alternating pattern,* whereby a point is made for one subject, then for the other. A second point is made for the first subject, then for the other. This alternating pattern continues until all the points are made for both subjects. An outline for an essay contrasting Smith and Jones could look like this if the alternating pattern were used:

    I. View on financing health care
       A. Smith believes states should fund their own plans
       B. Jones believes the federal government should fund a plan
   II. View on financing education
       A. Smith believes in a state income tax
       B. Jones believes in a property tax
  III. View on lake pollution
       A. Smith wants to form a task force to study pollution
       B. Jones believes pollution is not a priority

In general, the block method works better for shorter essays with fewer points because the reader is not forced to remember many ideas about the first subject while reading about the second. If your essay is long or if the ideas are complex, the alternating method may be better. The alternating pattern is also the only choice if you treat more than two subjects.

If you are both comparing and contrasting, you can organize by treating similarities first and differences next. Or you can reverse this order.

To move smoothly from point to point, the following transitions are helpful:

To show similarity: similarly, likewise, in similar fashion, in like manner, in the same way

Smith believes in tax reform. *Similarly,* Jones wants to close tax loopholes.

To show contrast: however, on the other hand, conversely, in contrast

Smith favors tax reform. *However,* Jones believes current tax laws are adequate.

As you can tell, ordering detail for comparison and contrast requires careful planning. For this reason, you may want to outline, even if you do not typically do so for other kinds of essays.

SUGGESTIONS FOR WRITING COMPARISON-CONTRAST

1. If you need help with a topic, try explaining the similarities between two things usually considered different, or try noting the differences between two things thought of as alike. For example, love and hate are often thought of as opposites, but you could point out key similarities; or you could point out the differences between getting married and having a wedding—two things often thought of as the same.

2. To generate ideas, make two lists—one of every similarity you can think of and one of every difference you can think of. Study your lists and circle the most significant comparisons and contrasts. Then decide if you want to compare, contrast, or both.

   3. If you need more ideas, ask yourself these questions:
   - **a.** Do I want to express feelings, relate experience, inform, entertain, and/or persuade? What details will help me achieve my purpose?
   - **b.** Can I describe anything?
   - **c.** Can I tell a story?
   - **d.** Can I explain a process?
   - **e.** Can I use examples to illustrate anything?

4. Draw up an outline using either the block or alternating method. If you are unsure which is better, try outlining both ways before deciding.

5. Write your draft from your outline the best way you can without laboring over anything.

Checklist for Revising Comparison-Contrast

1. Is there a sound basis for considering your subjects side-by-side?

2. Do you have a thesis that presents your subjects and notes whether they will be compared, contrasted, or both?

3. Have you discussed the same points for both subjects? If not, is this a problem?

4. Have you avoided stating obvious comparisons and contrasts?

5. Have you used a block or alternating pattern to best advantage?

6. Have you used transitions to help your reader move from point to point and subject to subject?

ANNOTATED STUDENT ESSAY

Student author Danielle Witherspoon uses contrast to relate the differences between the students in her original California hometown and those in the Ohio town to which she moved.

A Matter of Geography

1   One of the first things I discovered when I moved to Ohio from California was that the carbonated beverages I had always called "soda" were only appropriately referred to as "pop." However, this small difference in lingo was the least of my problems when I first arrived because I soon discovered that teenagers in Ohio were completely different from my peers in California.

2   My first impression was that high school students in Ohio had little sense of personal style. Standard dress for boys was a flannel shirt and jeans with sneakers or brown deck shoes. The flannel shirt was almost always from a mall store called American Eagle or from the L.L. Bean catalog; the jeans were Levis or Gap; the sneakers were Nike—always; the deck shoes were Docksiders. Girls had their uniform too: blue jeans from the Gap, sweaters from The Limited, and penny loafers—I never learned their origin. Although my Ohio school was not as multicultural as my California school, I was still surprised to find kids of different ethnic backgrounds dressing almost identically. Blacks, whites, Hispanics, Asians all dressed alike. In California, diversity was even more of a given than sunny skies, and individuality was prized. In stark contrast to Ohio students, California students wore an array of styles ranging from Mom's closet vintage to mall chic to cheerleader preppy. Members of various ethnic groups wore their cultural garb proudly as badges of their unique identity. Everyone was trying to stand out from the crowd, and everyone used clothing as an index to personality. Conformity in dress was, very simply, the mark of an unimaginative wimp. And no one except the athletically inclined wore sneakers. On my first day of school in Ohio, I wore a paisley print shirt, garment dyed pants, and soft black shoes. Needless to say, I did not come close to blending in. Frankly, in typical California manner, I was pleased that I stood out. My Ohio counterparts, however, confided in me later that they thought my flamboyance made me weird.

3   I found the weekend habits of Ohio students even more astonishing than their dress.

Paragraph 1
The introduction gives one example of the contrast between Ohio and California students. The thesis (the last sentence) gives the subjects as Ohio and California students and notes that differences will be treated.

The pattern is alternating.

Paragraph 2
The first sentence is the topic sentence. It presents the first point of contrast (personal style). Note the specific detail and objective description: The points discussed for one subject are discussed for the other.

Paragraph 3
The first sentence is the topic sentence. It presents the second point of contrast (weekend habits). "Even more astonishing" suggests a progressive order. Some students may think this paragraph could use more detail.

There was not a good coffee house or bookstore bistro to be found, so I was curious to see how my new friends spent their evenings out. They shied away from informal get-togethers and film fests at home, the activities my friends and I were fond of in California. It turned out that Ohio teenagers liked restaurants. My new school chums enjoyed eating dinner and dessert out, drinking coffee with cream and sugar for hours on end. It was common for Ohio teens to spend the better parts of both Friday and Saturday nights at a local pancake house doing nothing but drinking coffee. Oh how I missed the California nights I spent watching rented movies like *Birdy* and *The Princess Bride* with my friends.

4   In California, my friends and I engaged in a variety of activities for recreation. We would roller blade, skateboard, surf, walk the beach, and generally exercise our bodies to stay fit and have fun. In Ohio, recreation seemed to revolve around trying to feel grown up by staying up late and partying with alcohol and drugs. My theory is that if Ohio teens engaged in more of the activities that California teens engaged in, they would be less likely to party so much.

5   What surprised me most of all was the apparent difference in intellectual attitude. In my new school, teenagers were so serious about their grades. Most people carried around little packs of flash cards, and lunch table talk was always part of a study group. I was accustomed to an academic routine of studying moderately and understanding what was being covered, but not obsessing about grades. However, in Ohio, the academic competition was intense. My friends fretted over percentage points and scowled for a week if they received a grade less than 95 percent. They overcompensated and stressed themselves out without concentrating on what they were actually learning. At first, it seemed odd to me that ninth graders focused on their grades so strongly. Then I realized that families in this part of the country tended to view a good education, and therefore good grades, as the only unfailing measure of success. In California, a solid education was also considered important, but so were life experiences, having fun, and personal growth.

Paragraph 4

The first sentence is the topic sentence. It presents the third point of contrast (recreation). Transition between subjects is achieved with "in Ohio" and "in California." Some students may want more detail in this paragraph.

Paragraph 5

The first sentence is the topic sentence. It presents the fourth point of contrast (intellectual attitude). The points discussed for one subject are discussed for the other, although not in equal detail. "Most of all" is a transition that notes the progressive order.

As a result of this difference, I found it very hard not to laugh when my classmates sobbed over a missed algebra problem or argued with a teacher to secure one extra point.

6   While I felt like a stranger in a strange land those first few months in Ohio, I eventually adapted and became genuinely fond of my new home and friends. We introduced each other to different ways of thinking about life, and I even started wearing a sweater every now and then. However, I still draw the line at wearing penny loafers.

Paragraph 6
The conclusion looks beyond the time discussed in the essay.

NEAT PEOPLE VS. SLOPPY PEOPLE
Suzanne Britt

Suzanne Britt graduated from Salem Academy and College with majors in English and Latin and earned her master's degree in English from Washington University in St. Louis. She has taught at North Carolina State University, Peace College, and Duke Divinity School and is now teaching at Meredith College. Her poems have appeared in literary magazines such as Denver Quarterly, Lake Superior Review, Greensboro Review, *and* Southern Poetry Review. *Her essays and articles have appeared in various newspapers and magazines, including the* Cleveland Plain Dealer, *the* Charlotte Observer, Newsweek, *the* New York Times, Books & Religion, *the* Boston Globe, Newsday, *and the* Miami Herald. *She is the author of several books, including* Skinny People Are Dull and Crunchy Like Carrots *(now out of print),* Show and Tell *(Morning Owl Press),* A Writer's Rhetoric *(Harcourt Brace Jovanovich), and* Images: A Centennial Journey *(Meredith College Press). Her essays have been widely reprinted in college textbooks both in the United States and Canada. She now writes regularly for the* Authors Ink *and is at work on a novel.*

In "Neat People vs. Sloppy People," an entertaining contrast piece taken from Show and Tell, *she describes neat people as "Lazier and meaner than sloppy people." Is there any truth to what she says, or does she play it all for laughs?*

THE PATTERN	THE PURPOSE
contrast	*to entertain*

1   I've finally figured out the difference between neat people and sloppy people. The distinction is, as always, moral. Neat people are lazier and meaner than sloppy people.

2   Sloppy people, you see, are not really sloppy. Their sloppiness is merely the unfortunate consequence of their extreme moral rectitude. Sloppy people carry in their mind's eye a heavenly vision, a precise plan, that is so stupendous, so perfect, it can't be achieved in this world or the next.

3   Sloppy people live in Never-Never Land. Someday is their métier. Someday they are planning to alphabetize all their books and set up home catalogs. Someday they will go through their wardrobes and mark certain items for tentative mending and certain items for passing on to relatives of similar shape and size. Someday sloppy people will make family scrapbooks into which they will put newspaper clippings, post-cards, locks of hair, and the dried corsage from their senior prom. Someday they will file everything on the surface of their desks, including the cash receipts from coffee purchases at the snack shop. Someday they will sit down and read all the back issues of *The New Yorker.*

4   For all these noble reasons and more, sloppy people never get neat. They aim too high and wide. They save everything, planning someday to file, order, and straighten out the world. But while these ambitious plans take clearer and clearer shape in their heads, the books spill from the shelves onto the floor, the clothes pile up in the hamper and closet, the family mementos accumulate in every drawer, the surface of the desk is buried under mounds of paper and the unread magazines threaten to reach the ceiling.

5   Sloppy people can't bear to part with anything. They give loving attention to every detail. When sloppy people say they're going to tackle the surface of the desk, they really mean it. Not a paper will go unturned; not a rubber band will go unboxed. Four hours or two weeks into the excavation, the desk looks exactly the same, primarily because the sloppy person is meticulously creating new piles of papers with new headings and scrupulously stopping to read all the old book catalogs before he throws them away. A neat person would just bulldoze the desk.

6   Neat people are bums and clods at heart. They have cavalier attitudes toward possessions, including family heirlooms. Everything is just another dustcatcher to them. If anything collects dust, its got to go and that's that. Neat people will toy with the idea of throwing the children out of the house just to cut down on the clutter.

7   Neat people don't care about process. They like results. What they want to do is get the whole thing over with so they can sit down and watch the rasslin' on TV. Neat people operate on two unvarying principles: Never handle any item twice, and throw everything away.

8   The only thing messy in a neat person's house is the trash can. The minute something comes to a neat person's hand, he will look at it, try to decide if it has immediate use and, finding none, throw it in the trash.

9   Neat people are especially vicious with mail. They never go through their mail unless they are standing directly over a trash can. If the trash can is beside the mailbox, even better. All ads, catalogs, pleas for charitable contributions, church bulletins and money-saving coupons go straight into the trash can without being opened. All letters from home, postcards from Europe, bills and paychecks are opened, immediately responded to, then dropped in the trash can. Neat people keep their receipts only for tax purposes. That's it. No sentimental salvaging of birthday cards or the last letter a dying relative ever wrote. Into the trash it goes.

10   Neat people place neatness above everything, even economics. They are incredibly wasteful. Neat people throw away several toys every time they walk through the den. I knew a neat person once who threw away a perfectly good dish drainer because it had mold on it. The drainer was too much trouble to wash. And neat people sell their furniture when they move. They will sell a La-Z-Boy recliner while you are reclining in it.

11   Neat people are no good to borrow from. Neat people buy everything in expensive little single portions. They get their flour and sugar in two-pound bags. They wouldn't consider clipping a coupon, saving a leftover, reusing plastic nondairy whipped cream containers or rinsing off tin foil and draping it over the unmoldy dish drainer. You can never borrow a neat person's newspaper to see what's playing at the movies. Neat people have the paper all wadded up and in the trash by 7:05 A.M.

12   Neat people cut a clean swath through the organic as well as the inorganic world. People, animals, and things are all one to them. They are so insensitive. After they've finished with the pantry, the medicine cabinet, and the attic, they will throw out the red geranium (too many leaves), sell the dog (too many fleas), and send the children off to boarding school (too many scuffmarks on the hardwood floors).

Reading Closely and Thinking Critically

1. Is Britt serious when she claims, in paragraph 1, that the distinction between neat and sloppy people is a moral one? Explain.

2. Britt says that neat people are insensitive, that they are bums and clods. How serious is she in this assessment? If she cannot be taken literally, then how would you describe her attitude toward neat people?

3. Cite two or three humorous passages that appeal to you. Why do you find them funny?

4. Do you think that Britt is being fair to neat people? To sloppy people? Explain.

Examining Structure and Strategy

1. Which sentence functions as the thesis because it indicates the subjects under consideration and the fact that the subjects will be contrasted?

2. In which paragraphs does Britt use examples to clarify a point of contrast?

3. Does Britt use an alternating or block pattern to organize her details?

4. Does Britt achieve balance by treating the same points about both of her subjects? If not, is the lack of balance a problem? Explain.

5. Three paragraphs describe sloppy people and seven paragraphs describe neat people. Why is there more detail about neat people?

6. Why do you think Britt waits until the end of her essay to discuss how neat people treat living things?

Considering Language and Style

1. How does Britt's tone contribute to the humor of the essay? (Tone is discussed on page 37). Cite at least two examples to illustrate your view.

2. Consult a dictionary if you are unsure of the meaning of any of these words: *rectitude* (paragraph 2), *métier* (paragraph 3), *meticulously* (paragraph 5), *scrupulously* (paragraph 5), *cavalier* (paragraph 6), *swath* (paragraph 12).

For Group Discussion or Writing

Analyze the humor in "Neat People vs. Sloppy People." Look at word choice, use of examples, detail selection, tone, and so forth, and then explain how Britt achieves her humorous effects. Be sure to provide examples to illustrate the techniques you mention.

Writing Assignments

1. *In your journal.* Are you a neat person or a sloppy person? Identify yourself as one or the other and go on to explain whether any of Britt's characterizations are true of you. Also, note to what extent you are happy to be either neat or sloppy.

2. *Using the pattern.* Turn the tables on Britt and write a humorous contrast essay that proclaims the superiority of neat people.

3. *Using the pattern.* Using humor if you wish, contrast one of the following: those who plan ahead and those who are impulsive, those who procrastinate and those who do not put things off, sports fans and those who pay little attention to sports, the athletic and the nonathletic, the lazy and the energetic, or optimists and pessimists.

4. *Using the pattern.* Write a humorous contrast of any of these campus types:

   a. students and teachers.
   b. professors and deans.
   c. older college students and younger college students.
   d. commuter students and residential students.
   e. brainy students and average students.
   f. jocks and nonathletes.

5. *Considering a theme.* Explain whether or not Britt's sentiments about neat and sloppy people are rooted in fact. To support your view, use the neat and sloppy people you know as examples, including yourself, if you wish. If you like, you may also indicate whether or not you share Britt's belief that sloppy people are better than neat people.

6. *Connecting the readings.* In "Maintenance" (page 248), the author discusses ways people take care of their possessions and what their approaches say about them and their feelings about their belongings. After reading that selection, explain the maintenance styles of the neat and sloppy people Britt refers to and what their styles say about their feelings and about their possessions.

A FARMER'S DAUGHTER
Kim Ode

Kim Ode grew up on a small farm near Sioux Falls, South Dakota, where she came to love farm life. She earned degrees in English and journalism and went to work as a newspaper reporter. When she married and moved to upstate New York, she found that she missed the Great Plains, so she moved to Minneapolis, where she is a feature writer for the Star Tribune. *In "A Farmer's Daughter," which first appeared in* Minnesota Monthly *in 1990, Ode informs the reader by comparing and contrasting farm life today with the farm life of her childhood. She also relates a bit of her family life by looking at the similarities and differences between the members of her mother's generation and herself. To inform the reader of the reasons for the changes in farm life and the effects of those changes, Ode relies on cause-and-effect analysis.*

THE PATTERNS	THE PURPOSES
comparison-contrast with	*to inform and to express feelings*
cause-and-effect analysis	*and relate experience*

1   I am a farmer's daughter, but I live in the city now, harvesting paychecks from the acres of asphalt around me. Still I think I'd make a heckuva farm wife. On rare occasions, I say that out loud to friends. Usually, there's a gentle but firm reminder that it's not possible and a firm but gentle rebuke about romantic notions. But sometimes I say it to a close friend who is another farmer's daughter and the skein of conversation unravels a bit further before it is again, inevitably, tied off. She knows what I mean about yearning for horizons, about eating sweet corn 20 minutes off the stalk, about dishing up casserole in the shade of the combine, about playing in the hayloft. We both had the same role models, women who spent a lot of time over the stove, in front of the sewing machine, and behind the wheel—and who always seemed happy. Yet we both ended up seeking other role models, encouraged more often than not by our mothers, who after all were the best judges of their happiness.

2   Every generation, another group of farmers' daughters faces the question of moving on or staying put. Yet theirs today is a different

world from the one I encountered 18 years ago in the Brandon, South Dakota, high school gymnasium as I shifted my graduation tassel from left to right. The farm crisis of the past decade is responsible for much of the change, but there also has been a shift toward acknowledging a broader range of career options for women.

3   I once asked Mom if she'd ever thought she'd end up where she was. She'd grown up on a small farm near my dad's family farm. Well, she said, she never thought she'd end up anywhere else, and her reply was in a tone that hid no regret, no undertone of missed opportunity.

4   Oh, there had been a chance, shortly after they married and were living near San Diego, where Dad was stationed as a Marine during the Korean conflict. He'd toyed with the notion of being an architect, and they'd even gone so far as to investigate some schools he could attend after his tour of duty was up. But Grandpa said he'd always counted on Dad coming back to the farm, and then Mom got pregnant (with me) and the future fell into place.

5   After answering my question, Mom turned the tables on me, asking if I ever felt—she groped for a term—if I had ever felt second-class growing up on a farm. I could truthfully answer that I never had, but what bothers me is the reaction I sometimes get, like from the woman in Rochester, New York, where my husband and I lived in the early 1980s. She confided in words clearly meant to comfort and compliment, "You don't look like a farm girl."

6   I knew what she was thinking: I didn't scrape my shoes out of habit when walking into a restaurant. I didn't wear bright blue eye shadow or order polyester suits from the Sears catalog. There wasn't a telltale crease on my lower lip from years of chewing wheatstraws. In short, I seemed to be someone like her. I decided not to declare that I once was runner-up for state dairy princess.

7   Mom said she also felt herself being measured against a stereotype at times, on infrequent occasions when she was with wives of doctors or professors or lawyers and the subject turned to what their husbands did. "I never felt bad about being married to a farmer," she said. "But I felt strange that they thought it was something I might feel bad about."

8   The farm woman I hark back to doesn't exist anymore. Although the worst of the farm crisis has passed, it's not unusual for farm women to have at least a part-time job in town. And there are many who enjoy this new life.

9   Mom has a job in the nearby city of Sioux Falls now, partly because all of us kids are grown, partly because the extra income doesn't hurt. She takes orders over the phone for cable television programs and talks to people from all over the country, which she likes, although she frets at times that the house doesn't get the care it used to, nor the community the time she once volunteered.

10   She still considers herself very much a farm wife, but life is nothing like it used to be, and thank goodness, she says. When I ask her about what her life as a young farm wife was like, Mom leans against the doorpost and gets that sort of tired look in her eyes that meets halfway down her face with a smile she's trying to raise. I realize it's a look I've seen many times before. "It was so busy," she says quietly. She tells of coming home from the hospital with my brother, their third child, on the same sweltering August day that work began on a new milkhouse. That meant fixing food for midmorning break, dinner, and midafternoon break for a crew of workmen until the first of the year. Then the silo builders arrived. All this in addition to caring for two preschoolers and a baby with a stomach ailment who required frequent feedings and didn't sleep through the night for months. Nowadays, such a crew wouldn't expect to be fed by the farm family; they'd bring lunches or drive into town.

11   I never saw that side of her life, and even had I married a farmer, I couldn't have drawn on that experience. Technology has changed so many things: The days of cooking for baling crews—mostly ravenous high school boys who smelled of sweat and alfalfa and Lava soap—are rare now with machines that shape the hay into loaves and cylinders. Air-conditioned tractor cabs eliminate the need for bringing an afternoon cold drink to the fields, and farmers can stow brownies without worrying that the frosting will melt.

12   But more to the point, had I married a farmer, there's no guarantee we'd still be farming.

13   My parents tried to dissuade my brother, now 31, from going into farming, even while they were proud that he wanted to. They saw the farm crisis looming on the horizon and suggested that he could remain close to agriculture as an extension agent or implement salesman or who knows what. But he was determined, and though he's often tired and strapped for extra money and has a wife who works in town, he doesn't regret his decision. He and my husband canoed in the Bound-

ary Waters of northern Minnesota last summer, one of his few breaks from the farm, and they came back a day early. My husband still shakes his head: "He just said he missed his animals."

14   I'll never live on a farm again. I know that. Still, that doesn't stop me and a girlhood friend from regularly mourning the fact that we aren't living our mothers' lives—that we're rushing off to jobs instead of canning peaches, or making after-school treats, or sharing a second cup of coffee with our husbands on weekday mornings.

15   She went to college, too, getting a degree as a dental hygienist. When we got together, it was as two career girls. Yet eventually there was that afternoon, maybe a half-dozen years ago, when we were sitting around her kitchen table. I don't remember which of us made the first admission, but we agreed that we never foresaw this life we were now living and that we had this great yearning to live our mothers' lives. We both regarded farm life as a high calling, regarded our mothers as happy women.

16   Our mothers, of course, laugh. They say they envy us. Where we see complications, they see diversity. Where we see a simpler life, they see less security. Where we see job stress, they see skills that offer independence.

17   The ironic thing is that my girlfriend is a farmer's wife. But she, like many farmers' partners, will never have the life her mother led because times are so different. These days, her income is consequential to the farm, so she adds doing her job in town to what her mother always did: running the oldest daughter to ball games and swimming lessons, the youngest to day-care, doing the housework and cooking the meals. And I realize that had I married a farmer, or remained on the farm in any other capacity, I'd likely still be sitting before some computer screen.

Yet I still dream of living in the country even while I'm tethered to my job in downtown Minneapolis. I wonder how spending perhaps two hours in the car every day, time that could be spent at home with my family, would balance against being able to hear rain approach across a cornfield. I wonder how much of my ruralness I'm suppressing when I talk to people, while at the same time wondering how many stereotypes I can dash. I wonder if I would have felt betrayed by the times had I remained on the farm, or if the times are conspiring to keep me away.

Reading Closely and Thinking Critically

1. Why is it no longer possible for Ode to be the kind of farmer's wife her mother was?

2. What stereotype of rural men and women does Ode refer to? How prevalent do you think this stereotype is?

3. How does the author feel about the fact that she is not the farmer's wife her mother used to be? How does Ode's mother feel about her own changed life?

4. What contrast does Ode set up in paragraphs 14 and 15?

5. Using the information Ode provides, describe the chief similarities and differences of the farmer's wife today and a generation ago.

Examining Structure and Strategy

1. What comparison does Ode make in paragraph 1? How does that comparison set the tone for the essay?

2. In what pattern does Ode arrange her comparisons and contrasts, block or alternating?

3. In paragraph 10, Ode explains what happened when her mother came home from the hospital with Ode's brother. What purpose does this explanation serve? How does it fit into the comparison-contrast pattern?

4. Which paragraphs include cause-and-effect analysis? What causes and effects are discussed? (See Chapter 8.)

5. Ode compares and contrasts several subjects: farm life today and a generation ago, her mother's role and her own, her life as it is and how she expected it to be, the stereotype of the rural person and the reality. Do you think she would have done better to treat fewer subjects in more depth? Explain.

Considering Language and Style

1. What metaphors appear in paragraph 1? (Metaphors are explained on page 73.)

2. Ode's style is informal. What elements contribute to that informal style?

3. Consult a dictionary if you are unsure of the meaning of any of these words: *silo* (paragraph 10), *strapped for* (paragraph 13), *tethered* (paragraph 18).

For Group Discussion or Writing

Ode compares and contrasts farm life today, particularly the role of the farm wife, with that of a generation ago. Select another role, occupation, or activity (dating, motherhood, teaching, choosing a college, nursing, and so forth) and compare and contrast it today with a generation ago. If you like, explain what accounts for the chief contrasts.

Writing Assignments

1. *In your journal.* In paragraph 2, Ode says, "Every generation, another group of farmers' daughters faces the question of moving on or staying put." Have you ever had to decide whether to move on or stay put? If so, explain the circumstances and what you decided and why. If not, explain why you have not faced that decision and what you would do if you did face it soon.

2. *Using the pattern.* Compare and/or contrast one aspect of the environment you grew up in (your house, your neighborhood, your place of worship, your school, and so forth) as it is today and as it was while you were growing up. If you wish, you can also discuss the causes and/or the effects of the changes.

3. *Using the pattern.* Compare and/or contrast your life today with what you thought your life would be like today. If there are striking contrasts, try to explain what accounts for those contrasts.

4. *Using the pattern.* In paragraph 6, Ode refers to the stereotype of people who live in rural areas. Compare and/or contrast the stereotype of some group of people (jocks, working mothers, teenagers, police officers, elderly people, and so forth) with the way this group of people is in reality.

5. *Using the pattern.* Compare and/or contrast your life or the life you aspire to with the life of one of your parents when he or she was your age. If there are striking contrasts, explain the reasons for those contrasts.

6. *Considering a theme.* Describe the images of rural people portrayed in the media, and explain whether these images are positive or negative. Illustrate those images with examples from television, movies, and print media.

7. *Connecting the readings.* Explain how people are affected by whether they grow up in an urban area or on a farm. The information in "My Neighborhood" (page 87) and "A Farmer's Daughter" may help you.

TWO VIEWS OF THE MISSISSIPPI
Mark Twain

Samuel Longhorn Clemens, better known as Mark Twain (1835–1910), is one of the most significant figures in American literature. Raised in Hannibal, Missouri, Twain spent his youth watching the steamboats navigate the Mississippi—boats he would later pilot himself. He was the first important American author to come from "beyond the Mississippi." Known for his humor and Western local color, Twain was also an astute social commentator. His most famous work is The Adventures of Huckleberry Finn *(1884), which Ernest Hemingway called "the best book we've ever had." It narrates the travels and adventures down the Mississippi of a white boy and a black slave. "Two Views of the Mississippi" is from Twain's autobiographical book* Life on the Mississippi *(1883). In this excerpt, he expresses contrasting views of the Mississippi River—that of a young apprentice riverboat pilot and that of a seasoned pilot. In addition, he informs the reader that when we gain knowledge, we also lose something. As you read, notice Twain's descriptive language and how that language changes with each view.*

THE PATTERN	THE PURPOSES
contrast	*to express feelings and relate experience and to inform*

1   Now when I had mastered the language of this water, and had come to know every trifling feature that bordered the great river as familiarly as I knew the letters of the alphabet, I had made a valuable acquisition. But I had lost something, too, I had lost something which could never be restored to me while I lived. All the grace, the beauty, the poetry, had gone out of the majestic river! I still keep in mind a certain wonderful sunset which I witnessed when steamboating was new to me. A broad expanse of the river was turned to blood; in the middle distance the red hue brightened into gold, through which a solitary log came floating black and conspicuous; in one place a long, slanting mark lay sparkling upon the water; in another the surface was broken by boiling, tumbling rings, that were as many-tinted as an opal; where the ruddy flush was faintest, was a smooth spot that was covered with

graceful circles and radiating lines, ever so delicately traced; the shore on our left was densely wooded, and the somber shadow that fell from this forest was broken in one place by a long, ruffled trail that shone like silver; and high above the forest wall a clean-stemmed dead tree waved a single leafy bough that glowed like a flame in the unobstructed splendor that was flowing from the sun. There were graceful curves, re-flected images, woody heights, soft distances; and over the whole scene, far and near, the dissolving lights drifted steadily, enriching it every passing moment with new marvels of coloring.

2   I stood like one bewitched. I drank it in, in a speechless rapture. The world was new to me, and I had never seen anything like this at home. But as I have said, a day came when I began to cease from not-ing the glories and the charms which the moon and the sun and the twilight wrought upon the river's face; another day came when I ceased altogether to note them. Then, if that sunset scene had been repeated, I should have looked upon it without rapture, and should have com-mented upon it, inwardly, after this fashion: "This sun means that we are going to have wind to-morrow; that floating log means that the river is rising, small thanks to it; that slanting mark on the water refers to a bluff reef which is going to kill somebody's steamboat one of these nights, if it keeps on stretching out like that; those tumbling "boils" show a dissolving bar and a changing channel there; the lines and cir-cles in the slick water over yonder are the warning that that trouble-some place is shoaling up dangerously; that silver streak in the shadow of the forest is the break from a new snag, and he has located himself in the very best place he could have found to fish for steamboats; that tall dead tree, with a single living branch, is not going to last long, and then how is a body ever going to get through this blind place at night without the friendly old landmark?"

3   No, the romance and beauty were all gone from the river. All the value any feature of it had for me now was the amount of usefulness it could furnish toward compassing the safe piloting of a steamboat. Since those days, I have pitied doctors from my heart. What does the lovely flush in a beauty's cheek mean to a doctor but a "break" that ripples above some deadly disease? Are not all her visible charms sown thick with what are to him the signs and symbols of hidden decay? Does he ever see her beauty at all, or doesn't he simple view her professionally, and comment upon her unwholesome condition all to himself? And

doesn't he sometimes wonder whether he has gained most or lost most by learning his trade?

Reading Closely and Thinking Critically

1. What subjects is Twain contrasting?

2. What are Twain's two views of the Mississippi River? What influenced each of these views?

3. As a result of mastering the river, Twain has gained something, but he has lost something as well. What has he gained and lost?

4. Although essentially a contrast piece, the selection also includes the comparison of two subjects. What subjects are compared? What are the similarities between these subjects?

5. What point do you think Twain is making about maturity? Do you agree with that point?

6. What kind of reader do you think would make the best audience for the piece? Explain your view.

Examining Structure and Strategy

1. From which sentences can the thesis be taken?

2. Are the contrasts arranged in a block or alternating pattern?

3. Are Twain's supporting details balanced? Explain.

4. Cite two or three descriptions that you find particularly appealing. Why do you like them?

5. Why does Twain close by mentioning doctors? How is this discussion relevant to the rest of the piece?

Considering Language and Style

1. What is the main difference between the word choice in paragraph 1 and paragraph 2? (The discussion of description in Chapter 3 may help you here.)

2. How does the word choice in each paragraph help Twain achieve his purpose?

3. Consult a dictionary if you are unsure of the meaning of any of these words: *trifling* (paragraph 1), *acquisition* (paragraph 1), *wrought* (paragraph 2), *sown* (paragraph 3).

For Group Discussion or Writing

Twain closes by asking whether the doctor "has gained most or lost most by learning his trade." With two or three classmates, consider this question and decide what the doctor gains and loses. As an alternative, consider the same issues for another professional: the journalist, the television star, the rock musician, the pilot, or the teacher, for example.

Writing Assignments

1. *In your journal.* Tell about a time when becoming more knowledgeable changed your view of something or someone. Overall, do you think you won more than you lost? Explain.

2. *Using the pattern.* Contrast how you viewed a person or event when you were innocent and lacking in knowledge with how you viewed the person or event when you were more experienced and knowledgeable. For example, you could contrast your views of a parent, a holiday, a teacher, or your parents' divorce. Indicate whether you lost something as a result of gaining more knowledge about the person or event. (Your journal entry may help you with ideas.)

3. *Using the pattern.* Drawing heavily on description, compare and/or contrast your current view of a particular place and the view you held as a child. For example, you could compare and/or contrast your views of your elementary school, a family vacation spot, your old bedroom, or your old neighborhood.

4. *Using the pattern.* Compare and/or contrast the attitudes of youth and maturity. Use examples to clarify your points. Also indicate which of the attitudes is better and why.

5. *Considering a theme.* Twain makes the point that with maturity and knowledge comes a loss of romanticism. As a result, we view things more in terms of their usefulness and their significance than in terms of their beauty and capacity to inspire joy. Explain how this phenomenon contributes to conflicts between young people and their parents.

6. *Connecting the readings.* Sometimes people agree on what is beautiful, and sometimes they do not. Explain what factors influence our perception of beauty and note whether or not you think those factors are good ones. The ideas in the following essays may help you: "Two Views of the Mississippi," "Am I Blue?" (page 374), "Complexion" (page 401), and "Shades of Black" (page 469).

TALK IN THE INTIMATE RELATIONSHIP:
HIS AND HERS
Deborah Tannen

Born in 1945 and raised in Brooklyn, New York, Deborah Tannen is a lin-guistics professor at Georgetown University. She has also taught at the Hel-lenic American Union in Athens, Greece, and at the City University of New York. Tannen has researched communication between the sexes and reported her findings in many scholarly publications, on television shows (including Today, CBS News, *and* Sally Jessy Raphael), *in numerous newspaper and magazine articles, and in books such as the best-selling* You Just Don't Un-derstand: Men and Women in Conversation (1990) *and* Gender and Dis-course (1994). *"Talk in the Intimate Relationship: His and Hers" is taken from Tannen's first book,* That's Not What I Meant: How Conversational Style Makes or Breaks Relationships (1986). *The excerpt explains how dif-ferences between men and women affect the way we communicate. Tannen says that the sexes have "different expectations about the role of talk in rela-tionships." As you read, ask yourself whether or not your experience bears out the points Tannen makes.*

THE PATTERNS	THE PURPOSE
contrast with exemplification, and cause-and-effect analysis	*to inform*

---

1   Male-female conversation is cross-cultural communication. Cul-ture is simply a network of habits and patterns gleaned from past ex-perience, and women and men have different past experiences. From the time they're born, they're treated differently, talked to differently, and talk differently as a result. Boys and girls grow up in different worlds, even if they grow up in the same house. And as adults they travel in different worlds, reinforcing patterns established in childhood. These cultural differences include different expectations about the role of talk in relationships and how it fulfills that role . . .

2   **He Said/She Said: His and Her Conversational Styles.** Every-one knows that as a relationship becomes long-term, its terms change.

But women and men often differ in how they expect them to change. Many women feel, "After all this time, you show know what I want without my telling you." Many men feel, "After all this time, we should be able to tell each other what we want."

3   These incongruent expectations capture one of the key differences between men and women . . . . Communication is always a matter of balancing conflicting needs for involvement and independence. Though everyone has both these needs, women often have a relatively greater need for involvement, and men a relatively greater need for independence. Being understood without saying what you mean gives a payoff in involvement, and that is why women value it so highly.

4   If you want to be understood without saying what you mean explicitly in words, you must convey meaning somewhere else—in how words are spoken, or by metamessages. Thus it stands to reason that women are often more attuned than men to the metamessages of talk. When women surmise meaning in this way, it seems mysterious to men, who call it "women's intuition" (if they think it's right) or "reading things in" (if they think its wrong). Indeed, it could be wrong, since metamessages are not on record. And even if it is right, there is still the question of scale: How significant are the metamessages that are there?

5   . . . Metamessages are a form of indirectness. Women are more likely to be indirect, and to try to reach agreement by negotiation. Another way to understand this preference is that negotiation allows a display of solidarity, which women prefer to the display of power (even though . . . the aim may be the same—getting what you want). Unfortunately, power and solidarity are bought with the same currency: Ways of talking intended to create solidarity have the simultaneous effect of framing power differences. When they think they're being nice, women often end up appearing deferential and unsure of themselves or of what they want.

6   When styles differ, misunderstandings are always rife. As their differing styles create misunderstandings, women and men try to clear them up by talking things out. These pitfalls are compounded in talks between men and women because they have different ways of going about talking things out, and different assumptions about the significance of going about it.

7   The rest of this [*discussion*] illustrates these differences, explains their origins in children's patterns of play, and shows the effects when

women and men talk to each other in the context of intimate relationships in our culture.

8   **Women Listen for Metamessages.** Sylvia and Harry celebrated their fiftieth wedding anniversary at a mountain resort. Some of the guests were at the resort for the whole weekend, others just for the evening of the celebration: a cocktail party followed by a sitdown dinner. The manager of the dining room approached Sylvia during dinner. "Since there's so much food tonight," he said, "and the hotel prepared a fancy dessert and everyone already ate at the cocktail party anyway, how about cutting and serving the anniversary cake at lunch tomorrow?" Sylvia asked the advice of the others at her table. All the men agreed: "Sure, that makes sense. Save the cake for tomorrow." All the women disagreed: "No, the party is tonight. Serve the cake tonight." The men were focusing on the message: the cake as food. The women were thinking of the metamesage: Serving a special cake frames an occasion as a celebration.

9   Why are women more attuned to metamessages? Because they are more focused on involvement, that is, on relationships among people, and it is through metamessages that relationships among people are established and maintained. If you want to take the temperature and check the vital signs of a relationship, the barometers to check are its metamessages: what is said and how.

10   Everyone can see these signals, but whether or not we pay attention to them is another matter—a matter of being sensitized. Once you are sensitized, you can't roll your antennae back in; they're stuck in the extended position.

11   When interpreting meaning, it is possible to pick up signals that weren't intentionally sent out, like an innocent flock of birds on a radar screen. The birds are there—and the signals women pick up are there—but they may not mean what the interpreter thinks they mean. For example, Maryellen looks at Larry and asks, "What's wrong?" because his brow is furrowed. Since he was only thinking about lunch, her expression of concern makes him feel under scrutiny.

12   The difference in focus on messages and metamessages can give men and women different points of view on almost any comment. Harriet complains to Morton, "Why don't you ask me how my day was?" He replies, "If you have something to tell me, tell me. Why do you have to be invited?" The reason is that she wants the metamessage of inter-

est: evidence that he cares how her day was, regardless of whether or not she has something to tell.

13   A lot of trouble is caused between women and men by, of all things, pronouns. Women often feel hurt when their partners use "I" or "me" in a situation in which they would use "we" or "us." When Morton announces, "I think I'll go for a walk," Harriet feels specifically uninvited, though Morton later claims she would have been welcome to join him. She felt locked out by his use of "I" and his omission of an invitation: "Would you like to come?" Metamessages can be seen in what is not said as well as what is said.

14   It's difficult to straighten out such misunderstandings because each one feels convinced of the logic of his or her position and the illogic—or irresponsibility—of the other's. Harriet knows that she always asks Morton how his day was, and that she'd never announce, "I'm going for a walk," without inviting him to join her. If he talks differently to her, it must be that he feels differently. But Morton wouldn't feel unloved if Harriet didn't ask about his day, and he would feel free to ask, "Can I come along?" if she announced she was taking a walk. So he can't believe she is justified in feeling responses he knows he wouldn't have.

15   **Messages and Metamessages in Talk between . . . Grown Ups?**
These processes are dramatized with chilling yet absurdly amusing authenticity in Jules Feiffer's play *Grown Ups.* To get a closer look at what happens when men and women focus on different levels of talk in talking things out, let's look at what happens in this play.

16   Jake criticizes Louise for not responding when their daughter, Edie, called her. His comment leads to a fight even though they're both aware that this one incident is not in itself important.

17   JAKE: Look, I don't care if it's important or not, when a kid calls its mother the mother should answer.

LOUISE: Now I'm a bad mother.

JAKE: I didn't say that.

LOUISE: It's in your stare.

JAKE: Is that another thing you know? My stare?

Louise ignores Jake's message—the question of whether or not she responded when Edie called—and goes for the metamessage: his implication that she's a bad mother, which Jake insistently disclaims. When Louise explains the signals she's reacting to, Jake not only discounts them but is angered at being held accountable not for what he said but for how he looked—his stare.

18   As the play goes on, Jake and Louise replay and intensify these patterns:

> LOUISE: If I'm such a terrible mother, do you want a divorce?
>
> JAKE: I do not think you're a terrible mother and no, thank you, I do not want a divorce. Why is it that whenever I bring up any difference between us you ask me if I want a divorce?

The more he denies any meaning beyond the message, the more she blows it up, the more adamantly he denies it, and so on:

> JAKE: I have brought up one thing that you do with Edie that I don't think you notice that I have noticed for some time but which I have deliberately not brought up before because I had hoped you would notice it for yourself and stop doing it and also—frankly, baby, I have to say this—I knew if I brought it up we'd get into exactly the kind of circular argument we're in right now. And I wanted to avoid it. But I haven't and we're in it, so now, with your permission, I'd like to talk about it.
>
> LOUISE: You don't see how that puts me down?
>
> JAKE: What?
>
> LOUISE: If you think I'm so stupid why do you go on living with me?
>
> JAKE: *Dammit! Why can't anything ever be simple around here?!*

It can't be simple because Louise and Jake are responding to different levels of communication. As in Bateson's example of the dual-control electric blanket with crossed wires, each one intensifies the energy going to a different aspect of the problem. Jake tries to clarify his point by overelaborating it, which gives Louise further evidence that he's condescending to her, making it even less likely that she will address his point rather than his condescension.

19   What pushes Jake and Louise beyond anger to rage is their different perspectives on metamessages. His refusal to admit that his state-

ments have implications and overtones denies her authority over her own feelings. Her attempts to interpret what he didn't say and put the metamesssage into the message make him feel she's putting words into his mouth—denying his authority over his own meaning.

20   The same thing happens when Louise tells Jake that he is being manipulated by Edie:

> LOUISE: Why don't you ever make her come to see you? Why do you always go to her?
>
> JAKE: You want me to play power games with a nine year old? I want her to know I'm interested in her. Someone around here has to show interest in her.
>
> LOUISE: You love her more than I do.
>
> JAKE: I didn't say that.
>
> LOUISE: Yes, you did.
>
> JAKE: You don't know how to listen. You have never learned how to listen. It's as if listening to you is a foreign language.

Again, Louise responds to his implication—this time, that he loves Edie more because he runs when she calls. And yet again, Jake cries literal meaning, denying he meant any more than he said.

21   Throughout their argument, the point to Louise is her feelings—that Jake makes her feel put down—but to him the point is her actions—that she doesn't always respond when Edie calls:

> LOUISE: You talk about what I do to Edie, what do you think you do to me?
>
> JAKE: This is not the time to go into what we do to each other.

Since she will talk only about the metamessage, and he will talk only about the message, neither can get satisfaction from their talk, and they end up where they started—only angrier:

> JAKE: That's not the point!
>
> LOUISE: It's *my* point.
>
> JAKE: It's hopeless!
>
> LOUISE: Then get a divorce.

American conventional wisdom (and many of our parents and English teachers) tell us that meaning is conveyed by words, so men who tend to be literal about words are supported by conventional wisdom. They may not simply deny but actually miss the cues that are sent by how words are spoken. If they sense something about it, they may nonetheless discount what they sense. After all, it wasn't said. Sometimes that's a dodge—a plausible defense rather than a gut feeling. But sometimes it is a sincere conviction. Women are also likely to doubt the reality of what they sense. If they don't doubt it in their guts, they nonetheless may lack the arguments to support their position and thus are reduced to repeating, "You said it. You did so." Knowing that metamessages are a real and fundamental part of communication makes it easier to understand and justify what they feel.

22   **"Talk to Me."** An article in a popular newspaper reports that one of the five most common complaints of wives about their husbands is "He doesn't listen to me anymore." Another is "He doesn't talk to me anymore." Political scientist Andrew Hacker noted that lack of communication, while high on women's lists of reasons for divorce, is much less often mentioned by men. Since couples are parties to the same conversations, why are women more dissatisfied with them than men? Because what they expect is different, as well as what they see as the significance of talk itself.

23   First, let's consider the complaint "He doesn't talk to me."

24   **The Strong Silent Type.** One of the most common stereotypes of American men is the strong silent type. Jack Kroll, writing about Henry Fonda on the occasion of his death, used the phrases "quiet power," "abashed silences," "combustible catatonia," and "sense of power held in check." He explained that Fonda's goal was not to let anyone see "the wheels go around," not to let the "machinery" show. According to Kroll, the resulting silence was effective on stage but devastating to Fonda's family.

25   ⸝ The image of a silent father is common and is often the model for the lover or husband. But what attracts us can become flypaper to which we are unhappily stuck. Many women find the strong silent type to be a lure as a lover but a lug as a husband. Nancy Schoenberger begins a poem with the lines "It was your silence that hooked me,/ so like my father's." Adrienne Rich refers in a poem to the "husband who is frustratingly mute." Despite the initial attraction of such quintessentially

male silence, it may begin to feel, to a woman in a long-term relationship, like a brick wall against which she is banging her head.

26   In addition to these images of male and female behavior—both the result and the cause of them—are differences in how women and men view the role of talk in relationships as well as how talk accomplishes its purpose. These differences have their roots in the settings in which men and women learn to have conversations: among their peers, growing up.

27   **Growing up Male and Female.** Children whose parents have foreign accents don't speak with accents. They learn to talk like their peers. Little girls and little boys learn how to have conversations as they learn how to pronounce words: from their playmates. Between the ages of five and fifteen, when children are learning to have conversations, they play mostly with friends of their own sex. So it's not surprising that they learn different ways of having and using conversations.

28   Anthropologists Daniel Maltz and Ruth Borker point out that boys and girls socialize differently. Little girls tend to play in small groups or, even more common, in pairs. Their social life usually centers around a best friend, and friendships are made, maintained, and broken by talk—especially "secrets." If a little girl tells her friend's secret to another little girl, she may find herself with a new best friend. The secrets themselves may or may not be important, but the fact of telling them is all-important. It's hard for newcomers to get into these tight groups, but anyone who is admitted is treated as an equal. Girls like to play cooperatively; if they can't cooperate, the group breaks up.

29   Little boys tend to play in larger groups, often outdoors, and they spend more time doing things than talking. It's easy for boys to get into the group, but not everyone is accepted as an equal. Once in the group, boys must jockey for their status in it. One of the most important ways they do this is through talk: verbal display such as telling stories and jokes, challenging and sidetracking the verbal displays of other boys, and withstanding other boys' challenges in order to maintain their own story—and status. Their talk is often competitive talk about who is best at what.

30   **From Children to Grown Ups.** Feiffer's play is ironically named *Grown Ups* because adult men and women struggling to communicate

often sound like children: "You said so!" "I did not!" The reason is that when they grow up, women and men keep the divergent attitudes and habits they learned as children—which they don't recognize as attitudes and habits but simply take for granted as ways of talking.

31   Women want their partners to be a new and improved version of a best friend. This gives them a soft spot for men who tell them secrets. As Jack Nicholson once advised a guy in a movie: "Tell her about your troubled childhood—that always gets 'em." Men expect to *do* things together and don't feel anything is missing if they don't have heart-to-heart talks all the time.

32   If they do have heart-to-heart talks, the meaning of those talks may be opposite for men and women. To many women, the relationship is working as long as they can talk things out. To many men, the relationship isn't working out if they have to keep working it over. If she keeps trying to get talks going to save the relationship, and he keeps trying to avoid them because he sees them as weakening it, then each one's efforts to preserve the relationship appear to the other as reckless endangerment.

Reading Closely and Thinking Critically

1. In a sentence of your own, state the thesis of "Talk in the Intimate Relationship: His and Hers."

2. Why does Tannen believe that men and women are from different cultures?

3. Tannen says that cultural differences mean that men and women in long-term relationships each have a different expectation for talk. What are those different expectations?

4. What are "metamessages"? Tannen says that women are more attuned to them than men. Why? Do you agree with Tannen?

5. According to Tannen, how do their different styles of talking affect communication between men and women?

6. In general, how do you think the communication style of women affects them in the workplace?

7. How do women often react to "the strong silent type"?

8. According to the author, why do men and women communicate differently?

Examining Structure and Strategy

1. How do paragraphs 1 through 7 function in the essay? You may have found these paragraphs more difficult to read than the rest of the essay. Why are they more difficult?

2. What purpose do the examples in paragraphs 8 though 14 serve? The ones in paragraphs 15 through 21? The ones in paragraph 24?

3. Where does cause-and-effect analysis appear in the essay? (Cause-and-effect analysis, discussed in Chapter 8, explains the causes and/or effects of something.) What purpose does the analysis serve?

4. Tannen's essay has no formal conclusion. Instead, the author ends with her last point. Is this a problem for the reader? Explain.

Language and Style

1. In paragraph 7, Tannen formally announces her intent by stating what will come in the rest of the selection: "The rest of this [*discussion*] illustrates these differences, explains their origins in children's patterns of play, and shows the effects when women and men talk to each other in the context of intimate relationships in our culture." In general, such announcements are avoided in papers written for English classes, but they are common in writing for the social sciences (writing like Tannen's), for business, and for science. Why do you think the announcement is considered a helpful device in these disciplines but not in language and literature essays?

2. Consult a dictionary if you are unsure of the meaning of any of these words: *incongruent* (paragraph 3), *attuned* (paragraph 4), *deferential* (paragraph 5), *rife* (paragraph 6), *adamantly* (paragraph 18), *plausible* (paragraph 21), *abashed* (paragraph 24), *catatonia* (paragraph 24), *lug* (paragraph 25), *quintessentially* (paragraph 25).

For Group Discussion or Writing

Tannen's essay includes a number of generalizations about women and men. For example, in paragraph 9, she says that women are more at-tuned to metamessages than men. With three or four classmates, cite two or three more of these generalizations and discuss whether or not you agree with them. Also discuss whether different communication styles can be attributed solely to sex, or whether other factors (age, economic status, ethnic background, and level of education, for instance) are contributing factors.

Writing Assignments

1. *In your journal.* How much of what Tannen says is confirmed by your own experience? How much of it is not? Does Tannen say anything that surprises you? Does she say anything that bothers you? Does she say anything that makes sense? Respond to one or more of the questions in about two pages.

2. *Using the pattern.* Like Tannen, select two groups of people and contrast their communication styles. Your subjects could be teens and adults, physicians and patients, teachers and students, advertisers and the general public, Northerners and Southerners, and so forth. Use examples to illustrate the different styles, and, if possible, explain why the groups communicate the way they do and/or the effects of the communication styles.

3. *Using the pattern.* Contrast the behavior of men and women, using something other than their communication styles as subjects. For example, you can contrast their dating behavior, their behavior with friends, their behavior in competitive situations, or their management styles.

4. *Using the pattern.* Compare and/or contrast ways men are portrayed on television with the ways women are portrayed. Use specific examples from shows and commercials to clarify and support your points. If possible, explain the effects these portrayals have on the viewer.

5. *Using the pattern.* For three or four days, observe the communication styles of men and women as you go about your routine. Take note of any similarities and differences you observe. Then write your own essay that compares and/or contrasts the way men and women talk. Use examples from your observation to clarify and support your points. If you wish, explain the reasons for the similarities or differences and/or explain the effects of these similarities or differences.

6. *Considering a theme.* Tannen says, "Boys and girls grow up in different worlds, even if they grow up in the same house. And as adults they travel in different worlds, reinforcing patterns established in childhood." Explain to what extent you agree or disagree with this assessment, citing your own experience and observation to support your view.

7. *Connecting the readings.* Using the information in "Talk in the Intimate Relationship" and "What I've Learned from Men" (page 229), along with your own experience and observation, offer at least two reasons why men and women are sometimes in conflict with each other. Then go on to suggest ways that both sexes can contribute to resolving the conflict.

ANGLO VS. CHICANO: WHY?
Arthur L. Campa

Arthur L. Campa (1905–1978) was born in Mexico to American missionary parents. He was the chair of the Department of Modern Languages at the University of Denver, the director of the Center of Latin American Studies, and a cultural attaché at several U.S. embassies. Additionally, he wrote a number of books on Hispanic-American culture. In "Anglo vs. Chicano: Why?" (1972) Campa informs the reader of several differences between two cultures that meet—and sometimes conflict—in the southwestern United States. He does not stop there, for he also explains the historical and geographic origins of these differences.

THE PATTERNS	THE PURPOSE
contrast with cause-and-effect analysis	*to inform*

1   The cultural differences between Hispanic and Anglo-American people have been dwelt upon by so many writers that we should all be well informed about the values of both. But audiences are usually of the same persuasion as the speakers, and those who consult published works are for the most part specialists looking for affirmation of what they believe. So, let us consider the same subject, exploring briefly some of the basic cultural differences that cause conflict in the Southwest, where Hispanic and Anglo-American cultures meet.

2   Cultural differences are implicit in the conceptual content of the languages of these two civilizations, and their value systems stem from a long series of historical circumstances. Therefore, it may be well to consider some of the English and Spanish cultural configurations before these Europeans set foot on American soil. English culture was basically insular, geographically and ideologically; was more integrated on the whole, except for some strong theological differences; and was particularly zealous of its racial purity. Spanish culture was peninsular, a geographical circumstance that made it a catchall of Mediterranean, central European and north African peoples. The composite nature of the population produced a marked regionalism that prevented close integra-

tion, except for religion, and led to a strong sense of individualism. These differences were reflected in the colonizing enterprise of the two cultures. The English isolated themselves from the Indians physically and culturally; the Spanish, who had strong notions about *pureza de sangre* [purity of blood] among the nobility, were not collectively averse to adding one more strain to their racial cocktail. Cortés led the way by siring the first *mestizo* in North America, and the rest of the conquistadores followed suit. The ultimate products of these two orientations meet today in the Southwest.

3   Anglo-American culture was absolutist at the onset; that is, all the dominant values were considered identical for all, regardless of time and place. Such values as justice, charity, honesty were considered the superior social order for all men and were later embodied in the American Constitution. The Spaniard brought with him a relativistic viewpoint and saw fewer moral implications in man's actions. Values were looked upon as the result of social and economic conditions.

4   The motives that brought Spaniards and Englishmen to America also differed. The former came on an enterprise of discovery, searching for a new route to India initially, and later for new lands to conquer, the fountain of youth, minerals, the Seven Cities of Cíbola and, in the case of the missionaries, new souls to win for the Kingdom of Heaven. The English came to escape religious persecution, and once having found a haven, they settled down to cultivate the soil and establish their homes. Since the Spaniards were not seeking a refuge or running away from anything, they continued their explorations and circled the globe 25 years after the discovery of the New World.

5   This peripatetic tendency of the Spaniard may be accounted for in part by the fact that he was the product of an equestrian culture. Men on foot do not venture far into the unknown. It was almost a century after the landing on Plymouth Rock that Governor Alexander Spotswood of Virginia crossed the Blue Ridge Mountains, and it was not until the nineteenth century that the Anglo-Americans began to move west of the Mississippi.

6   The Spaniard's equestrian role meant that he was not close to the soil, as was the Anglo-American pioneer, who tilled the land and built the greatest agricultural industry in history. The Spaniard cultivated the land only when he had Indians available to do it for him. The uses to which the horse was put also varied. The Spanish horse was essentially a mount, while the more robust English horse was used in cultivating

the soil. It is therefore not surprising that the viewpoints of these two cultures should differ when we consider that the pioneer is looking at the world at the level of his eyes while the *caballero* [horseman] is looking beyond and down at the rest of the world.

7   One of the most commonly quoted, and often misinterpreted, characteristics of Hispanic peoples is the deeply ingrained individualism in all walks of life. Hispanic individualism is a revolt against the incursion of collectivity, strongly asserted when it is felt that the ego is being fenced in. This attitude leads to a deficiency in those social qualities based on collective standards, an attitude that Hispanos do not consider negative because it manifests a measure of resistance to standardization in order to achieve a measure of individual freedom. Naturally, such an attitude has no *reglas fijas* [fixed rules].

8   Anglo-Americans who achieve a measure of success and security through institutional guidance not only do not mind a few fixed rules but demand them. The lack of a concerted plan of action, whether in business or in politics, appears unreasonable to Anglo-Americans. They have a sense of individualism, but they achieve it through action and self-determination. Spanish individualism is based on feeling, on something that is the result not of rules and collective standards but of a person's momentary, emotional reaction. And it is subject to change when the mood changes. In contrast to Spanish emotional individualism, the Anglo-American strives for objectivity when choosing a course of action or making a decision.

9   The Southwestern Hispanos voiced strong objections to the lack of courtesy of the Anglo-Americans when they first met them in the early days of the Santa Fe trade. The same accusation is leveled at the *Americanos* today in many quarters of the Hispanic world. Some of this results from their different conceptions of polite behavior. Here too one can say that the Spanish have no *reglas fijas* because for them courtesy is simply an expression of the way one person feels toward another. To some they extend the hand, to some they bow and for the more *intimos* there is the well-known *abrazo*. The concepts of "good or bad" or "right and wrong" in polite behavior are moral considerations of an absolutist culture.

10   Another cultural contrast appears in the way both cultures share part of their material substance with others. The pragmatic Anglo-American contributes regularly to such institutions as the Red Cross, the United Fund and a myriad of associations. He also establishes foundations and quite often leaves millions to such institutions. The His-

pano prefers to give his contribution directly to the recipient so he can see the person he is helping.

11   A century of association has inevitably acculturated both Hispanos and Anglo-Americans to some extent, but there still persist a number of culture traits that neither group has relinquished altogether. Nothing is more disquieting to an Anglo-American who believes that time is money than the time perspective of Hispanos. They usually refer to this attitude as the "*mañana* psychology." Actually, it is more of a "today psychology," because Hispanos cultivate the present to the exclusion of the future; because the latter has not arrived yet, it is not a reality. They are reluctant to relinquish the present, so they hold on to it until it becomes the past. To an Hispano, nine is nine until it is ten, so when he arrives at nine-thirty, he jubilantly exclaims: "*¡Justo!*" [right on time]. This may be why the clock is slowed down to a walk in Spanish while in English it runs. In the United States, our future-oriented civilization plans our lives so far in advance the present loses its meaning. January magazine issues are out in December; 1973 cars have been out since October; cemetery plots and even funeral arrangements are bought on the installment plan. To a person engrossed in living today the very idea of planning his funeral sounds like the tolling of the bells.

12   It is a natural corollary that a person who is present oriented should be compensated by being good at improvising. An Anglo-American is told in advance to prepare for an "impromptu speech," but an Hispano usually can improvise a speech because "*Nosotros la improvisamos todo*" [we improvise everything].

13   Another source of cultural conflict arises from the difference between *being* and *doing*. Even when trying to be individualistic, the Anglo-American achieves it by what he does. Today's young generation decided to be themselves, to get away from standardization, so they let their hair grow, wore ragged clothes and even went barefoot in order to be different from the Establishment. As a result they all ended up doing the same things and created another stereotype. The freedom enjoyed by the individuality of *being* makes it unnecessary for Hispanos to strive to be different.

14   In 1963 a team of psychologists from the University of Guadalajara in Mexico and the University of Michigan compared 74 upper-middle-class students from each university. Individualism and personalism were found to be central values for the Mexican students. This was explained by saying that a Mexican's value as a person lies in his

being rather than, as is the case of the Anglo-Americans, in concrete accomplishments. Efficiency and accomplishments are derived characteristics that do not affect worthiness in the Mexican, whereas in the American it is equated with success, a value of highest priority in American culture. Hispanic people disassociate themselves from material things or from actions that may impugn a person's sense of being, but the Anglo-American shows great concern for material things and assumes responsibility for his actions. This is expressed in the language of each culture. In Spanish one says, *"Se me cayó la taza"* [the cup fell away from me] instead of "I dropped the cup."

15   In English, one speaks of money, cash and all related transactions with frankness because material things of this high order do not trouble Anglo-Americans. In Spanish such materialistic concepts are circumvented by referring to cash as *efectivo* [effective] and when buying or selling as something *al contado* [counted out], and when without it by saying *No tengo fondos* [I have no funds]. This disassociation from material things is what produces *sobriedad* [sobriety] in the Spaniard according to Miguel de Unamuno, but in the Southwest the disassociation from materialism leads to *dejadez* [lassitude] and *desprendimiento* [disinterestedness]. A man may lose his life defending his honor but is unconcerned about the lack of material things. *Desprendimiento* causes a man to spend his last cent on a friend, which when added to lack of concern for the future may mean that tomorrow he will eat beans as a result of today's binge.

16   The implicit differences in words that appear to be identical in meaning are astonishing. Versatile is a compliment in English and an insult in Spanish. An Hispano student who is told to apologize cannot do it, because the word doesn't exist in Spanish. *Apología* means words in praise of a person. The Anglo-American either apologizes, which is a form of retraction abhorrent in Spanish, or compromises, another concept foreign to Hispanic culture. *Compromiso* means a date, not a compromise. In colonial Mexico City, two hidalgos once entered a narrow street from opposite sides, and when they could not go around, they sat in their coaches for three days until the viceroy ordered them to back out. All this because they could not work out a compromise.

17   It was that way then and to some extent now. Many of today's conflicts in the Southwest have their roots in polarized cultural differences, which need not be irreconcilable when approached with mutual respect and understanding.

Reading Closely and Thinking Critically

1. In your own words write out the thesis idea of "Anglo vs. Chicano: Why?"

2. Campa says that ideologically the English were insular, while the Spanish were peninsular. Explain what Campa means. What are the effects of the different orientations?

3. A number of times, Campa discusses historical backgrounds. Why do you think he does this? That is, how does the historical information help Campa fulfill his purpose?

4. Explain a possible relationship between Hispanic individualism and the "Spaniard's equestrian role" (paragraph 6). How did the horse contribute to the cultural differences between Chicanos and Anglo-Americans?

5. Explain the different views of courtesy held by Hispanics and Anglo-Americans. How does the view of courtesy relate to concepts of individualism?

6. What values are important to Hispanics? To Anglo-Americans?

Examining Structure and Strategy

1. In what pattern does Campa arrange his contrasts, alternating or block?

2. Explain how Campa uses topic sentences, and provide an example to illustrate each use.

3. Does Campa maintain balance among his supporting details? Explain.

4. How does Campa use cause-and-effect analysis in his essay? (Cause-and-effect analysis, discussed in Chapter 8, explains the reasons for and/or results of an event.)

5. What approach does Campa take to his conclusion? What do you think of his conclusion?

Considering Language and Style

1. What can you learn about the relationship between language and culture from "Anglo vs. Chicano: Why?"

2. In paragraph 9, Campa calls Anglo culture "absolutist." What does he mean?

3. Consult a dictionary if you are unsure of the meaning of any of these words: *implicit* (paragraphs 2, 16) *configurations* (paragraph 2) *insular* (paragraph 2), *equestrian* (paragraph 5), *incursion* (paragraph 7), *pragmatic* (paragraph 10), *myriad* (paragraph 10), *acculturated* (paragraph 11), *impugn* (paragraph 14).

For Group Discussion or Writing

Campa concludes by saying that cultural differences "need not be ir-reconcilable when approached with mutual respect and understanding" (paragraph 17). Discuss one or more ways people can come to resolve conflict through increased understanding.

Writing Assignments

1. *In your journal.* Campa explains that Anglo-Americans are future-oriented, while Chicanos are now-oriented. Discuss the advantages and disadvantages of each orientation.   •

2. *Using the pattern.* Contrast your values or beliefs with those of a friend or acquaintance who has different values or beliefs. Try to explain the differences by examining your ethnic backgrounds, family situations, religious upbringings, schooling, and so forth.

3. *Using the pattern.* Contrast your view of money and your spending practices with those of a friend, relative, or acquaintance. Try to explain the reasons for the differences.

4. *Using the pattern.* If you and someone you know behave differently because one of you is future-oriented and one of you is focused on the present, contrast your different behaviors and attitudes. If you think one approach is better than the other, explain why.

5. *Using the pattern.* If you are from a different culture or know someone who is, contrast some of the behaviors, values, and beliefs of people from the United States and people from the other culture.

6. *Considering a theme.* Explain which of the values mentioned in "Anglo vs. Chicano: Why?" are your values, and go on to explain how those values affect your behavior and worldview.

7. ***Connecting the readings.*** "Anglo vs. Chicano: Why?" and "By Any Other Name" (page 167) both tell about cultures in conflict. Review those selections and then devise a grade school, middle school, or high school program that could help foster respect and understanding for different cultures. Write a paper that describes the program and explains why it might work.

AM I BLUE?
Alice Walker

Born to sharecroppers in Georgia in 1944, Alice Walker is the youngest of eight children. A graduate of Sarah Lawrence College, she began her formal education in rural schools. Walker was active in the civil rights movement and registered voters in Georgia, taught in the Head Start program in Mississippi, and worked in the welfare department in New York City. She is a poet, essayist, and novelist who won a Pulitzer Prize and the American Book Award for fiction for her most famous novel, The Color Purple *(1982). In "Am I Blue?" which first appeared in* Ms. *(July 1986), Walker tells a story that includes both description and comparison-contrast to relate a bit of her experience, to inform the reader about the oneness of animals and humans, and to convince the reader to treat animals well. The title of the piece is the same as a great, old blues song. As you read, ask yourself why that title is particularly appropriate.*

THE PATTERNS	THE PURPOSES
comparison-contrast with	*to inform, to express feelings and*
narration and description	*relate experience, and to persuade*

> *"Ain't these tears in these*
> *eyes tellin' you?"*[1]

2   For about three years my companion and I rented a small house in the country that stood on the edge of a large meadow that appeared to run from the end of our deck straight into the mountains. The mountains, however, were quite far away, and between us and them there was, in fact, a town. It was one of the many pleasant aspects of the house that you never really were aware of this.

3   It was a house of many windows, low, wide, nearly floor to ceiling in the living room, which faced the meadow, and it was from one of these that I first saw our closest neighbor, a large white horse, crop-

ping grass, flipping its mane, and ambling about—not over the entire meadow, which stretched well out of sight of the house, but over the five or so fenced-in acres that were next to the twenty-odd that we had rented. I soon learned that the horse, whose name was Blue, belonged to a man who lived in another town, but was boarded by our neighbors next door. Occasionally, one of the children, usually a stocky teenager, but sometimes a much younger girl or boy, could be seen riding Blue. They would appear in the meadow, climb up on his back, ride furiously for ten or fifteen minutes, then get off, slap Blue on the flanks, and not be seen again for a month or more.

4   There were many apple trees in our yard, and one by the fence that Blue could almost reach. We were soon in the habit of feeding him apples, which he relished, especially because by the middle of summer the meadow grasses—so green and succulent since January—had dried out from lack of rain, and Blue stumbled about munching the dried stalks halfheartedly. Sometimes he would stand very still just by the apple tree, and when one of us came out he would whinny, snort loudly, or stamp the ground. This meant, of course: I want an apple.

5   It was quite wonderful to pick a few apples, or collect those that had fallen to the ground overnight, and patiently hold them, one by one, up to his large, toothy mouth. I remained as thrilled as a child by his flexible dark lips, huge, cubelike teeth that crunched the apples, core and all, with such finality, and his high, broad-breasted *enormity;* beside which, I felt small indeed. When I was a child, I used to ride horses, and was especially friendly with one named Nan until the day I was riding and my brother deliberately spooked her and I was thrown, head first, against the trunk of a tree. When I came to, I was in bed and my mother was bending worriedly over me; we silently agreed that perhaps horseback riding was not the safest sport for me. Since then I have walked, and prefer walking to horseback riding—but I had forgotten the depth of feeling one could see in horses' eyes.

6   I was therefore unprepared for the expression in Blue's. Blue was lonely. Blue was horribly lonely and bored. I was not shocked that this should be the case; five acres to tramp by yourself, endlessly, even in the most beautiful of meadows—and his was—cannot provide many interesting events, and once rainy season turned to dry that was about it. No, I was shocked that I had forgotten that human animals and non-human animals can communicate quite well; if we are brought up around animals as children we take this for granted. By the time we are

adults we no longer remember. However, the animals have not changed. They are in fact *completed* creations (at least they seem to be, so much more than we) who are not likely *to* change; it is their nature to express themselves. What else are they going to express? And they do. And, generally speaking, they are ignored.

7   After giving Blue the apples, I would wander back to the house, aware that he was observing me. Were more apples not forthcoming then? Was that to be his sole entertainment for the day? My partner's small son had decided he wanted to learn how to piece a quilt; we worked in silence on our respective squares as I thought . . .

8   Well, about slavery: about white children, who were raised by black people, who knew their first all-accepting love from black women, and then, when they were twelve or so, were told they must "forget" the deep levels of communication between themselves and "mammy" that they knew. Later they would be able to relate quite calmly, "My old mammy was sold to another good family." "My old mammy was _____." Fill in the blank. Many more years later a white woman would say: "I can't understand these Negroes, these blacks. What do they want? They're so different from us."

9   And about the Indians, considered to be "like animals" by the "settlers" (a very benign euphemism for what they actually were), who did not understand their description as a compliment.

10   And about the thousands of American men who marry Japanese, Korean, Filipina, and other non-English-speaking women and of how happy they report they are, *"blissfully,"* until their brides learn to speak English, at which point the marriages tend to fall apart. What then did the men see, when they looked into the eyes of the women they married, before they could speak English? Apparently only their own reflections.

11   I thought of society's impatience with the young. "Why are they playing the music so loud?" Perhaps the children have listened to much of the music of oppressed people their parents danced to before they were born, with its passionate but soft cries for acceptance and love, and they have wondered why their parents failed to hear.

12   I do not know how long Blue had inhabited his five beautiful, boring acres before we moved into our house; a year after we had arrived—and had also traveled to other valleys, other cities, other worlds—he was still there.

13   But then, in our second year at the house, something happened in Blue's life. One morning, looking out the window at the fog that lay

like a ribbon over the meadow, I saw another horse, a brown one, at the other end of Blue's field. Blue appeared to be afraid of it, and for several days made no attempt to go near. We went away for a week. When we returned, Blue had decided to make friends and the two horses ambled or galloped along together, and Blue did not come nearly as often to the fence underneath the apple tree.

14   When he did, bringing his new friend with him, there was a different look in his eyes. A look of independence, of self-possession, of inalienable *horse*ness. His friend eventually became pregnant. For months and months there was, it seemed to me, a mutual feeling between me and the horses of justice, of peace. I fed apples to them both. The look in Blue's eyes was one of unabashed "this is *it*ness."

15   It did not, however, last forever. One day, after a visit to the city, I went out to give Blue some apples. He stood waiting, or so I thought, though not beneath the tree. When I shook the tree and jumped back from the shower of apples, he made no move. I carried some over to him. He managed to half-crunch one. The rest he let fall to the ground. I dreaded looking into his eyes—because I had of course noticed that Brown, his partner, had gone—but I did look. If I had been born into slavery, and my partner had been sold or killed, my eyes would have looked like that. The children next door explained that Blue's partner had been "put with him" (the same expression that old people used, I had noticed, when speaking of an ancestor during slavery who had been impregnated by her owner) so that they would mate and she conceive. Since that was accomplished, she had been taken back by her owner, who lived somewhere else.

16   Will she be back? I asked.

17   They didn't know.

18   Blue was like a crazed person. Blue *was,* to me, a crazed person. He galloped furiously, as if he were being ridden, around and around his five beautiful acres. He whinnied until he couldn't. He tore at the ground with his hooves. He butted himself against his single shade tree. He looked always and always toward the road down which his partner had gone. And then, occasionally, when he came up for apples, or I took apples to him, he looked at me. It was a look so piercing, so full of grief, a look so *human,* I almost laughed (I felt too sad to cry) to think there are people who do not know that animals suffer. People like me who have forgotten, and daily forget, all that animals try to tell us. "Everything you do to us will happen to you; we are your teachers, as you are

ours. We are one lesson" is essentially it, I think. There are those who
never once have even considered animals' rights: those who have been
taught that animals actually want to be used and abused by us, as small
children "love" to be frightened, or women "love" to be mutilated and
raped . . . They are the great-grandchildren of those who honestly
thought, because someone taught them this: "Women can't think," and
"niggers can't faint." But most disturbing of all, in Blue's large brown
eyes was a new look, more painful than the look of despair: the look of
disgust with human beings, with life; the look of hatred. And it was odd
what the look of hatred did. It gave him, for the first time, the look of
a beast. And what that meant was that he had put up a barrier within
to protect himself from further violence; all the apples in the world
wouldn't change that fact.

19   And so Blue remained, a beautiful part of our landscape, very
peaceful to look at from the window, white against the grass. Once a
friend came to visit and said, looking out on the soothing view: "And
it *would* have to be a *white* horse; the very image of freedom." And I
thought, yes, the animals are forced to become for us merely "images"
of what they once so beautifully expressed. And we are used to drinking milk from containers showing "contented" cows, whose real lives we
want to hear nothing about, eating eggs and drumsticks from "happy"
hens, and munching hamburgers advertised by bulls of integrity who
seem to command their fate.

20   As we talked of freedom and justice one day for all, we sat down
to steaks. I am eating misery, I thought, as I took the first bite. And spit
it out.

Reading Closely and Thinking Critically

1. Walker compares Blue to a human being. In what ways are the
horse and a person similar?

2. In paragraphs 8 through 11, Blue's relationship with people is
compared to a number of other human relationships. What are
those relationships? What is the common element in each of these
comparisons?

3. Specifically, what messages do you think Walker is trying to
communicate to her reader?

4. Blue is given human qualities throughtout most of the essay.
However, in paragraph 18, he becomes a "beast." Why? When he

becomes beastlike, is he less like a human and more like an animal? Explain.

5. Walker says that Blue has feelings and the ability to communicate those feelings. Do you agree? Explain.

Examining Structure and Strategy

1. Which paragraph best presents Walker's focus and the ideas she wants to convey to her reader? Why does she wait so long to present her focus?

2. Which paragraphs include description? What purpose does the description serve?

3. To what extent is "Am I Blue?" a narrative essay (an essay that tells a story)?

4. Do you think Walker's title is a good one? Why or why not?

5. "Am I Blue?" appeared in *Ms.* in 1986. What kind of audience was Walker reaching? Is the essay suited to that kind of audience? Explain.

6. Walker has a persuasive purpose to some extent. Of what is she trying to persuade her reader?

Considering Language and Style

1. *Verbal irony* occurs when a speaker or writer says one thing but clearly means the opposite or nearly the opposite. Explain the irony of the images of "'contented' cows," "'happy' hens," and bulls "who seem to command their fate" (paragraph 19).

2. Walker opens paragraph 18 with this simile: "Blue was like a crazed person." (Similes are explained on page 73.) Then she follows with the more literal "Blue was, to me a crazed person." Explain this movement from a simile to a more literal statement.

3. Consult a dictionary if you are unsure of the meaning of either of these words: *inalienable* (paragraph 14) and *unabashed* (paragraph 14).

For Group Discussion or Writing

In paragraph 18, Walker notes that animals say to people, "Everything you do to us will happen to you; we are your teachers, as you are ours.

We are one lesson." Discuss what this quote means and indicate whether you agree or disagree with it.

Writing Assignments

1. *In your journal.* What do you think of vegetarianism? Should people show respect for animals by not eating meat? What about wearing leather and fur? Should people wear only material not made from animals? Explore your feelings on these matters.

2. *Using the pattern.* Walker compares Blue to a human being because he can feel and express his emotions. If you have a pet and believe that the pet shares something in common with humans, write a comparison of the pet and human beings. If possible, use some narration and description with your comparison. (Be careful to avoid obvious statements, such as "My cat, like people, must eat and drink every day.")

3. *Using the pattern.* In paragraph 19, Walker contrasts the images of animals in advertising with the reality of these animals' existence. Expand the idea in paragraph 19 into a full essay that contrasts our images of happy animals (in advertising, in children's stories, in movies, and on television, for example) and the real existence of these animals. For example, you could contrast the image of Elsie, the Borden cow, with the reality of life for dairy cows that are kept as "milking machines."

4. *Using the pattern.* Compare our treatment of animals (as pets, as parts of lab experiments, as sources of income, as helpers, as companions, as beasts of burden, and as sources of entertainment) to our treatment of each other. Your purpose is to persuade your reader that we treat animals the same way we treat human beings.

5. *Using the pattern.* Compare and contrast your view of animals before and after reading "Am I Blue?" to explain the impact of the essay on you.

6. *Considering a theme.* Summarize Walker's view of how humans treat animals, and then argue that we should or should not alter our treatment of them. (See the appendix on how to write a summary.)

7. *Connecting the readings.* Describe the view of human nature that is presented in "Am I Blue?," "By Any Other Name" (page

167), and "Untouchables" (page 236). Do you subscribe to that view of human nature? Explain why or why not, drawing on examples to illustrate your view.

ADDITIONAL ESSAY ASSIGNMENTS

See pages 332 and 333 for suggestions for writing comparison-contrast and for a revision checklist.

1. Compare and/or contrast some place on campus at two different times of the day. For example, you can compare and/or contrast a campus eating spot at the noon rush hour and again at the 3:00 lull, the football stadium during and after a game, or the library before and after finals week. Use description for vividness.

2. Compare and contrast two people who play the same sport: two basketball players, two runners, two football players, and so on. Your purpose is to help your reader appreciate the playing style of each athlete or to persuade your reader that one athlete is better than the other.

3. Compare and/or contrast two close friends, illustrating their traits with example or narration.

4. Compare and/or contrast two similar television shows (two situation comedies, two news broadcasts, two police dramas, and so on) to persuade your reader that one is better than the other.

5. Contrast two celebrations of the same holiday: Christmas before and after children, Independence Day as a child and as an adult, Thanksgiving at different grandparents' houses, and so on.

6. Contrast the way some group of people (for example, mothers, police officers, fathers, or teens) are portrayed on television with the way they are in real life.

7. Contrast two ways to do something (for example, diet, study, give a dinner party, discipline children, or ask for a date) to persuade your reader that one way is better than the other.

8. Consider your circumstances before and after some change in your life: getting married, having children, going to college, getting a job, or joining an athletic team, for example. If you wish, make your details humorous and entertain your reader.

9. In your campus library, look up advertisements in *Life* and *Look* magazines from the 1950s and compare and contrast one or two of these ads with ones in contemporary magazines to inform your reader of the changes. Use cause-and-effect analysis to explain the cause and/or the effects of the changes. (See Chapter 8.)

10. Contrast two similar restaurants in your area to persuade your reader that one is better than the other. Use description for vividness.

11. Compare and contrast the movie and book versions of the same story (*Gone with the Wind, The Firm, Jurassic Park, Presumed Innocent, The Prince of Tides,* and so on) to persuade your reader that one version is better than the other.

12. Contrast the right and wrong ways to do something (for example choose a major, study for an exam, write an essay, select an adviser, buy a car, or plan a first date). Make your details humorous and entertain your reader.

13. Compare and contrast the styles of two comedians, actors, or musicians to inform your reader about the characteristics of each one.

14. Compare and contrast the chief arguments on both sides of a controversial issue (for example, abortion, capital punishment, euthanasia, animal rights, distributing condoms in schools, or bilingual education) to inform your reader of the thinking on both sides. If necessary, research the issue in your campus library.

15. Compare and contrast two fictional characters: Batman and Superman, Captain Kirk and Captain Picard, Indiana Jones and Han Solo, and so on.

16. Contrast two kinds of students, teachers, coaches, parents, or clergy.

17. Compare and/or contrast the toys of your youth with those that are popular today. Try to draw a conclusion about what those similarities and/or differences mean.

18. If you have lived in more than one place, compare and contrast life in two of those places.

19. If you or someone close to you has lived with chronic illness, contrast life as a healthy and sick person to heighten your reader's awareness of what it is like to be ill.

20. *Comparison-contrast in context.* For an article for your student newspaper, compare and contrast two magazine advertisements for the same kind of product typically marketed to college students. You may select advertisements for two kinds of CD players, two kinds of phone cards, two brands of beer, two brands of cosmetics, two different movies, and so forth. Your purpose is to inform students of some of the techniques advertisers use to persuade them to buy their products.

---

⑥ CAUSE-AND-EFFECT ANALYSIS

THE PATTERN

Cause-and-effect analysis can examine causes, effects, or both. When you explore causes, you identify the reasons for an event; when you explore effects, you identify the results of an event; when you look at both causes and effects, you examine reasons *and* results. Cause-and-effect analysis is a frequent component of writing because we often strive to make sense of the world by understanding why events occur and how they affect us. Thus, we examine the causes of earthquakes, try to determine how a presidential candidate's victory will change the economy, work to figure out why the car does not get the gas mileage it should, struggle to understand why our best friend suddenly seems distant, and so on. An understanding of causes and effects is so important to our sense of security and our feeling that we can deal with forces in our environment that it is no surprise writing often examines the causes of something, the effects of something, or both.

THE PURPOSES OF CAUSE-AND-EFFECT ANALYSIS

Cause-and-effect analysis can work to entertain, inform, or persuade a reader. It can also allow a writer to express feelings and relate experience. In "America Has Gone on a Trip Out of Tune" (page 395), for example, Dave Barry *entertains* his reader with a funny account of the causes and effects of American's inability to sing. If you were to explain the causes of inflation, you would *inform* a reader about an economic force, or if you explained the effects of computers on reading instruction, you would *inform* your reader about a trend in education. Similarly, if you explained the causes of math anxiety, you could do so to *persuade* your reader that women are often conditioned by our culture to avoid math, and if you explained the possible effects of failure to pass a school levy, you might do so to *persuade* your reader to vote for the levy. Cause-and-effect analysis can also allow you to *express feelings* and *relate experience*, as when you explain the causes and effects of your decision to leave home and move to another state.

While an essay is often developed solely with cause-and-effect analysis, the pattern can also form part of an essay developed primarily with another pattern. For example, if you wrote a process analysis to explain how heat lightning works, part of the essay might include a discussion of the effects of heat lightning. Similarly, if you told the story of the time you were involved in a serious car accident, the narration could also include a discussion of what caused the accident.

Cause-and-Effect Analysis in College Writing

Cause-and-effect analysis is a frequent component of writing in many college classes. For instance, in a mathematics class, you might be asked to write a journal entry explaining how math affects our lives. In history and political science classes, you will often be asked to explain the causes and effects of important events. For example, you might be asked on an essay exam to explain the causes of the Teapot Dome scandal, or you might be asked to write a report evaluating the causes and effects of manifest destiny. In a sociology class, you could be asked to explain the effects of the AIDS crisis on dating practices, and in a physics, chemistry, or biology class you will likely be asked to write lab reports explaining the effects of experiments. In an education class, you may need to detail the causes of teacher burnout or the effects of whole language instruction, and in a marketing class, you could be asked to write a paper on the effects of telemarketing.

SUPPORTING DETAILS

To clarify causes and effects, many patterns can be helpful, particularly narration, exemplification, description, and process analysis. For example, say you mention that you broke up with your best friend because he or she could not keep a secret. You can establish this point by telling the story of the time your friend betrayed a confidence. You could also give several examples of times your friend shared your secrets with others. Description can also contribute to cause-and-effect analysis. For example, if you want to explain the effects of littering, you can clarify by describing a section of roadside that has been heavily littered. Sometimes, process analysis helps make a point. For example, if you want to explain the effects of tax reduction, you can note the process whereby lower taxes means more disposable income, which leads to increased spending, which spurs manufacturing, which creates jobs, and so forth.

Sometimes cause-and-effect detail includes an explanation of causal chains. In a *causal chain*, a cause leads to an effect; that effect becomes a cause that leads to another effect; then that effect becomes a cause, and so on. For example, if you wanted to explain the effects of being very tall, you might reproduce a causal chain that looks like this: being tall made you feel awkward (effect); feeling awkward (cause) reduced your self-confidence (effect); your reduced self-confidence (cause) made it hard for you to date (effect); not dating (cause) made you depressed (effect).

In addition to reproducing causal chains, you may want to point out something that is *not* a cause or an effect, especially if you need to correct your reader's understanding. For example, assume that you are explaining the effects of sex education in the schools, and you think your reader mistakenly believes that sex education leads to increased sexual activity. You may want to note that increased sexual activity has not been proven to be an effect of sex education.

Often an event has more than one cause, in which case you may need to distinguish between causes that are *immediate* and those that are *remote*. Say, for example, that you are explaining why AIDS has reached epidemic proportions. Obviously, there are many reasons, but you may cite one *immediate* cause as the laws prohibiting notification of those exposed to the disease through their HIV-positive partners without the consent of those partners. To explain the lack of laws, you can cite a more *remote* cause: Gay and HIV activists successfully lobbied against such legislation because they feared discrimination against those publicly identified as gay and/or infected. Usually, you need not identify all remote causes, so be sensitive to how far back to go. You need not, for example, cite the reasons people discriminate against homosexuals and those who are HIV positive as a remote cause of the discrimination.

Finally, be on guard against two errors in logic that can occur when you write a cause-and-effect analysis. The first error is *oversimplifying* (see page 56). Most cause-and-effect relationships are complex. Thus, to state that violence against women is solely the result of pornography is to ignore an array of other factors that likely contribute to the problem.

The second error in logic is *post hoc, ergo propter hoc,* which is automatically assuming that an earlier event caused a later one (see page 56). Thus, you cannot assume that an increase in traffic accidents at a street corner that occurred after a traffic light was installed is necessarily a result of that traffic light. Other factors must be considered, such as a change in the speed limit and an increase in the number of cars along the route.

SELECTING AND ORDERING DETAILS

To develop detail, you can ask the questions "Why?" and "Then what?" For example, say you are explaining the causes of your shyness, and you give one reason as the fact that you do not feel comfortable around people. If you ask why you do not feel comfortable, you may get the answer that your family moved so frequently that you never got to know anyone very well—that gives you another cause. Now say that you are explaining the effects of your parents' divorce on you, and you indicate that the divorce meant you saw less of your father. Ask "Then what?" and you might answer that you and your father drifted apart, so you never got to know him well—that is another effect you can write about.

When you organize your cause-and-effect analysis, a particular order may be called for. If your purpose is persuasive, you may want a progressive order so you can save your most dramatic, compelling, or significant cause or effect for the end. If you are reproducing causal chains, chronological order is needed, so you can cite the causes and effects in the order they occur. Chronological order is also called for when you are discussing causes and effects as they occurred across time. For example, a discussion of the effects of your musical talent could deal with your childhood, then your adolescence, then your adulthood. At times, you may want to arrange your details in categories. If, for example, you are explaining the effects of the passage of a school levy, you can discuss together all the effects on teachers, then the effects on students, and finally the effects on curriculum.

To focus the essay, the thesis usually indicates the topic and whether causes, effects, or both will be discussed. Topic sentences, then, can introduce your discussion of each cause or effect. Here are a sample thesis and topic sentences that could be used for an essay about the causes of drug abuse among athletes.

thesis: It is certainly wrong for athletes to use drugs, but the reasons they do so are understandable. (Thesis notes the essay will explain the causes of drug use among athletes.)

topic sentence: The pressure for professional athletes to justify their huge salaries is so great that they often see performance-enhancing drugs as the answer. (Topic sentence presents the first cause: pressure on professional athletes.)

topic sentence: Furthermore, athletes may feel that they must take the drugs in order to be competitive, since so many other athletes are taking them. (Topic sentence presents second cause: others take drugs.)

topic sentence: Finally, some athletes get hooked on drugs because their coaches and trainers administer them. (Topic sentence presents third reason: coaches and trainers give out the drugs.)

Two kinds of transitions can help you signal cause-and-effect relationships to your reader. First, these transitions signal that one thing is the effect of another: *as a result, consequently, thus, hence, therefore,* and *for this reason.* Here are two examples:

> The midterm grades were very low. *For this reason,* Professor Werner reviewed the material with the class.

> The storm damage was extensive. *As a result,* the tourist trade in the coastal town declined.

Transitions of addition (*also, in addition, additionally, furthermore,* and *another*) can also signal cause-and-effect analysis, like this:

> *Another* effect of MTV is. . .

> *In addition,* stress fractures can be caused by. . .

SUGGESTIONS FOR WRITING CAUSE-AND-EFFECT ANALYSIS

1. If you need help with a topic, try writing about the causes and/or effects of some aspect of your life or personality: shyness, math anxiety, being tall or short, being the first or last born, playing football, fearing heights, your parents' divorce, the loss of a loved one, a special talent or ability, and so on.

2. To generate ideas, list every cause and/or effect that you can think of, without pausing to evaluate whether your ideas are good or not.

3. Ask "Why?" and/or "Then what?" of every item on your list to explore additional causes and effects.

4. Study your ideas and determine which you will use. Then, for each idea note whether you can tell a story, provide an example, describe, or explain a process to help clarify.

5. Add to your list anything you should mention that is not a cause or effect.

6. Number your ideas in the order you will treat them; then write your first draft from this numbered list. At this point, just write things out as best you can without worrying about grammar, spelling, punctuation, or anything else. You can revise later.

Checklist for Revising Cause-and-Effect Analysis

1. Does your thesis indicate whether you are explaining causes, effects, or both?

2. Do topic sentences introduce your discussion of each cause, and effect?

3. Have you clarified all causes and effects with explanation, description, narration, examples, and process analysis, as needed?

4. Have you reproduced causal chains where appropriate?

5. Have you accounted for both immediate and remote causes, without going further back than necessary?

6. Have you avoided oversimplifying and *post hoc, ergo propter hoc* errors in logic?

7. Have you used transitions as appropriate to introduce causes and effects?

ANNOTATED STUDENT ESSAY

Student-author Carl Benedict informs his reader by explaining the causes of steroid use among athletes. As you read, notice how carefully each cause is presented and explained.

Why Athletes Use Steroids

1   One of the most heated controversies in athletics centers on the use of anabolic steroids. Behind the dispute is the evidence that steroids pose a health hazard. They are linked to cardio-vascular disease, liver disorders, and cancerous tumors. In addition, there is evidence that they cause personality aberrations. Still, an alarming number of athletes are willing to risk their health for the enhanced performance steroids provide— and it is not hard to understand why.

Paragraph 1
The introduction gives background information. The thesis (the last sentence) indicates that the subject is steroid use and the essay will present causes.

2   First of all, many athletes are so blinded by the obvious benefits of steroid use that they fail to note their adverse effects. They are so fo-

Paragraph 2
Sentence 1 is the topic sentence. It begins with a transition of addition and presents the first cause under consideration.

cused on the increased strength, stamina, and size that result from steroid use, they may overlook the abuse their bodies are sustaining—often until it is too late. That is, athletes who are delighting in turning in the best performance of their lives are not likely to think about future deleterious effects. This is the same psychology that keeps the nicotine addict smoking three packs a day, until the x-ray shows the lung cancer is so advanced that nothing can be done.

3   Some athletes rationalize steroid use another way. They claim that anabolic steroids pose no greater health hazard than participation in such contact sports as football, boxing, and wrestling. However, these athletes fail to understand that in addition to harming the body, steroids also heighten the danger of contact sports by making the participants larger and stronger, thereby increasing their momentum and impact.

Paragraph 3
The second cause is presented in the first two sentences. The paragraph also presents an effect: Contact sports become more dangerous.

4   Some people think steroid use continues despite the life-threatening effects because athletes are just "dumb jocks" who are not smart enough to appreciate the risks. I don't accept that explanation. Instead, I suspect that steroid use continues partly because most athletes are young, and young people never feel threatened. Part of being young is feeling invulnerable. That is why young people drive too fast, drink too much, and bungee jump. They just do not believe that anything can happen to them. The same psychology is at work with athletes. They are young people who feel they will live forever.

Paragraph 4
This paragraph explains something that is not a cause, then goes on to give a real cause. Note the transition *in addition.*

5   In addition, athletes assume that because their bodies are so physically conditioned they can withstand more punishment than the average person, so they feel even less at risk by steroid use. They think, "The average person should not do this, but I can because my body is finely tuned."

Paragraph 5
The first sentence is the topic sentence. It begins with a transition and presents the next cause. Some readers will want more detail in this paragraph.

6   Perhaps the biggest reason athletes use steroids can be explained by the spirit that lies at the heart of all athletes: competition. Once a handful of athletes enhance their performance artificially, then others follow in order to stay competitive. Eventually, steroid users dominate a sport, and anyone who wants to compete at the highest levels is forced to use steroids or lose

Paragraph 6
The first sentence is the topic sentence. "The biggest reason" notes that detail is in a progressive order. The paragraph presents a causal chain.

out. This fact explains why unscrupulous coaches and trainers who want to win at any cost have contributed to the problem by offering steroids to their players and urging them to use them. Sadly, this practice has even filtered down to the high school level in some cases.

7   Competition for the thrill of winning is only part of the explanation, however. Big-time athletics means big-time money. As the financial rewards rise in a given sport, so does the pressure to win at any cost. Huge salaries, enormous purses, big bonuses, and incredibly lucrative commercial endorsements all tempt athletes to enhance their performances any way they can.

Paragraph 7
This paragraph presents a cause that is an extension of the one given in the previous paragraph.

8   Despite drug testing before competition and dissemination of information about the dangers of anabolic steroids, athletes still use steroids because the pressures to do so are so compelling. The truth is, too many athletes think steroids only hurt the other person, or else they think using steroids is worth the risk.

Paragraph 8
The conclusion summarizes the main causes.

AMERICA HAS GONE ON A TRIP OUT OF TUNE
Dave Barry

*Born in 1947 in New York, humorist Dave Barry has been dubbed "the fun-
niest man in America" by the* New York Times. *He writes a humor column
for the* Miami Herald *that is syndicated in over a hundred newspapers. In
1988, Barry won the Pulitzer Prize for distinguished commentary. His columns
have been collected in a number of successful books, including* Bad Habits:
A 100% Fact-Free Book *(1985),* The World According to Dave Barry
(1994), and Dave Barry Is Not Making This Up *(1994). In "America Has
Gone on a Trip Out of Tune," which first appeared as a newspaper column in
1991, Barry uses cause-and-effect analysis to entertain his audience. As you
read, try to identify the specific techniques he employs to amuse the reader.*

THE PATTERN	THE PURPOSE
cause-and-effect analysis	*to entertain*

1   Recently, there was a story in *The New York Times* (motto: "Our
Motto Alone Is Longer Than An Entire Edition Of *USA Today*") reporting
that Americans are no longer any good at singing. This is the latest in a
series of alarming news stories about things that Americans are no longer
any good at, including reading, writing, arithmetic, and manufacturing
any consumer product more technologically sophisticated than pizza.

2   According to the *Times*, Americans used to do a lot of group
singing, dating back to the days when hardy pioneers crossing the
prairie would entertain themselves by sitting around the campfire and
singing folk songs such as:

      "Home, home on the range

      Where the deer

      and the antelope plAAAAACK"

3   "AAAACK" was the musical sound that the hardy pioneers made
when their larynxes were punctured by arrows shot by prairie-dwelling
Native Americans, who couldn't *stand* that song. Another one they
hated was "Mister Froggy Went A-Courting," which inspired them to in-
vent the Ant Hill Torture.

4   **Problems.** Nevertheless, public group singing remained popular until modern times, when it has been hurt by two factors:

5   **The Elimination of Religion from Public Schools.** At one time, most public schools held Christmas Programs, wherein the children sang Christmas carols. Eventually this was viewed, correctly, as unfair to other religious groups, so the schools started holding Winter Programs and including songs from other religions, starting with Judaism and gradually expanding, as society got more sensitive, to include Islam, Buddhism, Confucianism, Scientology and The Cult Of The Big Lizard.

6   Finally, to avoid offending anybody, the schools dropped religion altogether and started singing about the weather. At my son's school, they now hold the Winter Program in February and sing increasingly nonmemorable songs such as "Winter Wonderland," "Frosty the Snowman," and—this is a real song—"Suzy Snowflake," all of which is pretty funny, because we live in Miami. A visitor from another planet would assume that the children belonged to the Church of Meteorology.

7   **The Rise of Rock and Roll.** Let's face it, this is not the ideal music for group singing. The family is not going to gather 'round the old upright piano and belt out a hearty chorus of "Shake Your Groove Thing."

8   The result is that fewer and fewer Americans can sing. I have seen stark evidence of this in my own office. One of my co-workers, John Dorschner, has a song stuck in his head and can't get it out. You've probably had this happen to you. Your brain, which is easily the most overrated organ in your body when it comes to intelligence, suddenly decides to devote an entire lobe to a certain song. Sometimes it's a song you don't even like, but your brain plays it over and over and over, especially when you're trying to sleep. You're lying in bed, thinking to yourself, "Big day tomorrow! Got to make a major presentation to top management. Got to get some shut-eye." And just as you're about to lose consciousness, your brain shrieks.

> "It's my party, and I'll cry if I want to!
> CRY if I want to! CRY if I want to!"

9   You try reasoning with your brain, then speaking sternly to it, then pounding on its door and threatening to strangle it, but it continues shrieking this song until 4:30 a.m., when you finally fall into a fitful sleep, marred by a recurring nightmare wherein you inform the en-

tire board of directors, using audiovisual aids, that they would cry, too, if it happened to them.

10   **Get It Out.** Leading physicians agree that the only way to cure this condition is to go up to another person and say: "I can't get this darned song out of my head!" Then you sing the song, and suddenly, boom, it's gone from your head, because *now it's stuck in the other person's head.*

11   John has been trying to infect me with his song for several months, but, like an increasing number of Americans, he can't sing. About once a week be sticks his head into my office and says: "Are you sure you don't know this song?" And then he makes a series of noises that, if you didn't know they were supposed to be a song, you would assume were the desperate moans of a woodland creature that has somehow become lodged in John's trachea.

12   "Unnhh unnh unhh," moans the creature.

13   "The chorus goes 'Keep a-rolling'," adds John, looking at me hopefully.

14   "Don't know it!" I say, "Sorry!" Although of course I am actually happy. Shoulders slumped, John wanders off, looking for another potential victim to infect. According to *The New York Times,* we're going to see more and more unfortunate victims like John unless we, as a nation, start singing together again. So come on! Put your ear next to the newspaper and join in with me now!

"Oh I come from Alabama
With a banjo on my knAAAACK"

Reading Closely and Thinking Critically

1. Dave Barry pokes fun at aspects of American life. For example, in paragraph 1, he makes fun of the frequently appearing news articles that claim Americans cannot do things. What else does Barry poke fun at?

2. According to Barry, what has caused the decline in public singing?

3. What does Barry say are the effects of people not singing together?

4. Writers often use humor to make serious points. Do you think that Barry is making a serious point? Explain.

Examining Structure and Strategy

1. Much of Barry's humor comes from positioning something silly next to something plausible. Look, for example, at the list at the end of paragraph 1, where Barry positions the silly "manufacturing any consumer product more technologically sophisticated than pizza" after the plausible "reading, writing, arithmetic." Cite two other examples of such positioning for humorous effect.

2. Barry's specific detail adds humor and interest. For example in paragraph 3, he refers to a specific song title, "Mister Froggy Went A-Courting." Cite two other examples of specific detail.

3. In which paragraph does Barry use exemplification to help explain his cause-and-effect relationship?

4. What approach does Barry take to his introduction?

5. What causal chain does Barry reproduce in his essay?

6. Is "America Has Gone on a Trip Out of Tune" well suited to its audience, the readers of daily newspapers? Explain.

Considering Language and Style

1. Explain the effect of made-up names like "The Cult Of The Big Lizard" (paragraph 5) and "Church of Meteorology" (paragraph 6).

2. Part of Barry's humor comes from the mock serious tone achieved by citing authority. For example, in paragraph 1, he cites *The New York Times* as his source. Note two other examples of this technique.

3. Consult a dictionary if you are unsure of the meaning of *Scientology* (paragraph 5).

For Group Discussion or Writing

Dave Barry's syndicated humor column appears in newspapers across the country, and the collections of his essays are very popular books. Why do you think people find Barry so funny?

Writing Assignments

1. *In your journal.* Does Barry perform a service by writing humorous newspaper columns about the little things of life, such as the decline of group singing and the irritation of having a song stuck in one's head? Or is his column pointless? Explain your view.

2. *Using the pattern.* Like Barry, select something inconsequential that "Americans are no longer any good at" (cooking without a microwave, walking places, changing channels without a remote control, and so on). Then write a humorous account of the causes and effects of the "problem."

3. *Using the pattern.* Take a serious problem (unemployment, urban sprawl, declining knowledge of geography, rising tuition costs, and so on) and write about its humorous effects. For example, if you write about declining math skills, you could include a humorous description of the congestion in grocery store aisles as people stand around trying to figure out how much they can save if they buy the big can of soup rather than the small one.

4. *Using the pattern.* In paragraphs 5 and 6, Barry explains the causes and effects of the elimination of religion from public schools. Select some other change in our education system (inclusion, busing, dress codes, collaborative learning, team teaching, and so on), and explain the causes and/or effects of that change. Your essay can be humorous or not, as you prefer.

5. *Using the pattern.* Barry pokes fun at a harmless human characteristic (the inability to get a song out of one's head). Pick another harmless human characteristic or behavior (for example, checking the alarm even though we know it is set, habitually choosing the wrong bank or supermarket line, losing car keys, and so on). Then write a humorous essay that explains the causes and/or effects of this behavior or characteristic.

6. *Considering a theme.* In paragraph 5, Barry notes that because the Constitution calls for the separation of church and state, many public schools have eliminated school programs that refer to or celebrate religious holidays. The reasoning is that celebrating any religious holiday violates the separation because public schools are funded by the government to a large extent. Agree or disagree with the policy of eliminating holiday celebrations from public schools, being sure to supply reasons for your stand.

7. *Connecting the readings.* Barry refers to "things that Americans are no longer good at, including reading, writing, arithmetic . . ." (paragraph 1). In truth, the U.S. education system has been repeatedly criticized for not teaching the basics effectively. Based on what you know and the facts presented in "College Pressures" (page 477), argue that schools do or do not do a good job of preparing students for college.

COMPLEXION
Richard Rodriguez

Born in 1944 in San Francisco, Richard Rodriguez is a first-generation Mexican-American who spoke only Spanish until he was six years old. An editor at Pacific News Service, Rodriguez is also an author who writes frequently of his heritage. He has written several books, including two autobiographical works: Hunger of Memory *(1981) and* Days of Obligation: An Argument with My Mexican Father *(1992). He has also written articles for such magazines as* Harper's *and* The American Scholar. *In the following excerpt from* Hunger of Memory, *Rodriguez combines contrast, narration, and description to relate the effects his skin color had on his self-concept and to inform the reader about the Mexican-American experience. As you read, you may be reminded of your own adolescent struggle to feel at ease with your physical appearance.*

THE PATTERNS	THE PURPOSES
analysis of effects with contrast,	*to inform and to express feelings*
narration, and description	*and relate experience*

1   Complexion. My first conscious experience of sexual excitement concerns my complexion. One summer weekend, when I was around seven years old, I was at a public swimming pool with the whole family. I remember sitting on the damp pavement next to the pool and seeing my mother, in the spectator's bleachers, holding my younger sister on her lap. My mother, I noticed, was watching my father as he stood on a diving board, waving to her. I watched her wave back. Then saw her radiant, bashful, astonishing smile. In that second I sensed that my mother and father had a relationship I knew nothing about. A nervous excitement encircled my stomach as I saw my mother's eyes follow my father's figure curving into the water. A second or two later, he emerged. I heard him call out. Smiling, his voice sounded, buoyant, calling me to swim to him. But turning to see him, I caught my mother's eye. I heard her shout over to me. In Spanish she called through the crowd: "Put a towel on over your shoulders." In public, she didn't want to say why. I knew.

2   That incident anticipates the shame and sexual inferiority I was to feel in later years because of my dark complexion. I was to grow up an ugly child. Or one who thought himself ugly. (*Feo.*) One night when I was eleven or twelve years old, I locked myself in the bathroom and carefully regarded my reflection in the mirror over the sink. Without any pleasure I studied my skin. I turned on the faucet. (In my mind I heard the swirling voices of aunts, and even my mother's voice, whispering, whispering incessantly about lemon juice solutions and dark, *feo* children.) With a bar of soap, I fashioned a thick ball of lather. I began soaping my arms. I took my father's straight razor out of the medicine cabinet. Slowly, with steady deliberateness, I put the blade against my flesh, pressed it as close as I could without cutting, and moved it up and down across my skin to see if I could get out, somehow lessen, the dark. All I succeeded in doing, however, was in shaving my arms bare of their hair. For as I noted with disappointment, the dark would not come out. It remained. Trapped. Deep in the cells of my skin.

3   Throughout adolescence, I felt myself mysteriously marked. Nothing else about my appearance would concern me so much as the fact that my complexion was dark. My mother would say how sorry she was that there was not money enough to get braces to straighten my teeth. But I never bothered about my teeth. In three-way mirrors at department stores, I'd see my profile dramatically defined by a long nose, but it was really only the color of my skin that caught my attention.

4   I wasn't afraid that I would become a menial laborer because of my skin. Nor did my complexion make me feel especially vulnerable to racial abuse. (I didn't really consider my dark skin to be a racial characteristic. I would have been only too happy to look as Mexican as my light-skinned older brother.) Simply, I judged myself ugly. And, since the women in my family had been the ones who discussed it in such worried tones, I felt my dark skin made me unattractive to women.

5   Thirteen years old. Fourteen. In a grammar school art class, when the assignment was to draw a self-portrait, I tried but could not bring myself to shade in the face on the paper to anything like my actual tone. With disgust then I would come face to face with myself in mirrors. With disappointment I located myself in class photographs— my dark face undefined by the camera which had clearly described the white faces of classmates. Or I'd see my dark wrist against my long-sleeved white shirt.

6   I grew divorced from my body. Insecure, overweight, listless. On hot summer days when my rubber-soled shoes soaked up the heat from the sidewalk, I kept my head down. Or walked in the shade. My mother didn't need anymore to tell me to watch out for the sun. I denied myself a sensational life. The normal, extraordinary, animal excitement of feeling my body alive—riding shirtless on a bicycle in the warm wind created by furious self-propelled motion—the sensations that first had excited in me a sense of my maleness, I denied. I was too ashamed of my body. I wanted to forget that I had a body because I had a brown body. I was grateful that none of my classmates ever mentioned the fact.

7   I continued to see the *braceros,*[1] those men I resembled in one way and, in another way, didn't resemble at all. On the watery horizon of a Valley afternoon, I'd see them. And though I feared looking like them, it was with silent envy that I regarded them still. I envied them their physical lives, their freedom to violate the taboo of the sun. Closer to home I would notice the shirtless construction workers, the roofers, the sweating men tarring the street in front of the house. And I'd see the Mexican gardeners. I was unwilling to admit the attraction of their lives. I tried to deny it by looking away. But what was denied became strongly desired.

8   In high school physical education classes, I withdrew, in the regular company of five or six classmates, to a distant corner of a football field where we smoked and talked. Our company was composed of bodies too short or too tall, all graceless and all—except mine—pale. Our conversation was usually witty. (In fact we were intelligent.) If we referred to the athletic contests around us, it was with sarcasm. With savage scorn I'd refer to the "animals" playing football or baseball. It would have been important for me to have joined them. Or for me to have taken off my shirt, to have let the sun burn dark on my skin, and to have run barefoot on the warm wet grass. It would have been very important. Too important. It would have been too telling a gesture—to admit the desire for sensation, the body, my body.

9   Fifteen, sixteen. I was a teenager shy in the presence of girls. Never dated. Barely could talk to a girl without stammering. In high school I went to several dances, but I never managed to ask a girl to dance. So I stopped going. I cannot remember high school years now

---

[1]Mexican laborers admitted into the country temporarily to do seasonal work, such as harvesting crops.

with the parade of typical images: bright drive-ins or gliding blue shadows of a Junior Prom. At home most weekend nights, I would pass evenings reading. Like those hidden, precocious adolescents who have no real-life sexual experiences, I read a great deal of romantic fiction. "You won't find it in your books," my brother would playfully taunt me as he prepared to go to a party by freezing the crest of the wave in his hair with sticky pomade. Through my reading, however, I developed a fabulous and sophisticated sexual imagination. At seventeen, I may not have known how to engage a girl in small talk, but I had read *Lady Chatterley's Lover.*

10   It annoyed me to hear my father's teasing: that I would never know what "real work" is: that my hands were so soft. I think I knew it was his way of admitting pleasure and pride in my academic success. But I didn't smile. My mother said she was glad her children were getting their educations and would not be pushed around like *los pobres.*[2] I heard the remark ironically as a reminder of my separation from *los braceros.* At such times I suspected that education was making me effeminate. The odd thing, however, was that I did not judge my classmates so harshly. Nor did I consider my male teachers in high school effeminate. It was only myself I judged against some shadowy, mythical Mexican laborer—dark like me, yet very different.

Reading Closely and Thinking Critically

1. What effects did the color of Rodriguez's complexion have on him?

2. In what ways did the women in Rodriguez's family make him feel self-conscious and inferior?

3. Why do you think that Rodriguez was so attracted to the lives of the Mexican gardeners and construction workers?

4. Why did Rodriguez read so much? Why do you think he was afraid that reading and education would make him effeminate?

5. Using the information in the essay for clues, explain the author's idea of masculinity.

---

[2]The poor ones.

6. "Complexion" came from Rodriguez's autobiographical book. What kind of reader do you think would benefit most from reading about his life?

Examining Structure and Strategy

1. In which paragraphs does Rodriguez use narration to help develop the cause-and-effect relationship?

2. In which paragraph does Rodriguez indicate what is *not* an effect of his reaction to his complexion?

3. With what people does Rodriguez contrast himself? What does that element of contrast contribute to the essay?

4. Cite an example of descriptive language and explain what the description contributes.

5. In what order are the effects arranged? What are the clues to this arrangement?

Considering Language and Style

1. Rodriguez uses sentence fragments intentionally in paragraphs 1, 2, 5, 6, 8, and 9. Ordinarily, sentence fragments are an editing error. Is this the case, or do the fragments serve a purpose? Explain.

2. Rodriguez uses three Spanish words: *feo, braceros,* and *los pobres.* Does this use of Spanish contribute anything? Explain.

3. Consult a dictionary if you are unsure of the meaning of any of these words: *buoyant* (paragraph 1), *menial* (paragraph 4), *listless* (paragraph 6), *taboo* (paragraph 7), *precocious* (paragraph 9), *pomade* (paragraph 9).

For Group Discussion or Writing

With some classmates, consider the things that shape a person's self-concept. Discuss the influence of family, friends, teachers, coaches, television, advertisements, and anything else you can think of.

Writing Assignments

1. *In your journal.* Rodriguez tells about feeling very self-conscious because of his skin color. Write about some aspect of

your physical appearance that makes or made you self-conscious and explain the reason for your feeling. As an alternative, write about some feature of your appearance that you are proud of.

2. *Using the pattern.* Pick one aspect of your physical appearance (your height, weight, nose, skin color, hair, and so on) and explain what effect or effects that feature has had on you. (The previous journal writing may give you some ideas.)

3. *Using the pattern.* In paragraph 1, Rodriguez tells about his realization that his parents had a sexual relationship. Tell about a time when you came to understand something about one or both of your parents (or other caregiver) that you did not realize before. Explain what caused the insight and how that awareness affected you. As an alternative, use another adult who figured significantly in your life (for example, a coach, clergy member, teacher, or grandparent).

4. *Using the pattern.* Things that happen to us in childhood and adolescence have the power to influence us long into adulthood. Tell about something that happened in your youth that has an effect on you today. Explain why you think the event continues to affect you.

5. *Using the pattern.* Think about your high school years and settle on one experience (band, football, dating, grades, exams, homecoming, and so on). Then write an essay that explains the effects this experience had on you.

6. *Considering a theme.* Rodriguez writes a bit about what high school was like for him. Consider your high school experience and discuss how it affected you then and now.

7. *Connecting the readings.* School has a great impact on the self-concepts of young people. Explain school's potential to affect the way we view ourselves. The ideas in "Complexion," "The Water-Faucet Vision" (page 184), and "By Any Other Name" (page 167) may give you some ideas.

EXCUUUSE ME
David Segal

Born in Boston in 1964, David Segal has studied on both sides of the Atlantic, having earned a bachelor's degree from Harvard University and a master's degree from Oxford University. A journalist and writer, Segal's work has appeared in the New Republic, Harper's, *the* Washington Post, *and* The Wall Street Journal. *In addition, he has been a speech writer for the Israeli ambassador to the United States. "Excuuuse Me" first appeared in the* New Republic *(May 1992). Its title is a reference to a tag line used by Steve Martin when he was performing stand-up comedy in the 1970s. The essay analyzes effects to argue that ethnic humor serves valuable purposes and its use should not be hindered by efforts to be politically correct ("P.C." in the essay).*

THE PATTERN	THE PURPOSE
analysis of effects	*to persuade*

1   It was inevitable that the chill of sensitivity now felt in public discourse and academic life would eventually come to comedy. But P.C. humor has arrived more swiftly—and completely—than even ardent activists could have hoped. Take three films written and directed by David and Jerry Zucker and Jim Abrahams. *Airplane,* released in 1980, has a slew of gay bits, two black men speaking indecipherable jive over subtitles, close to a minyan of Jewish jokes, drug gags, references to bestiality, nun jokes, five obscenities, and one gratuitous front shot of a naked women. *Naked Gun,* released in 1989, contains only one drug joke, one obscenity, no nudity, not a single Jewish joke, and three gay lines. In 1991 and *Naked Gun 2 1/2,* there were no obscenities, no frontal nudity, just two ethnic slurs, three tentative gay jokes, and one muttered "mazel-tov." Moreover, an earnest stripe of environmentalism is painted down the movie's middle. At the end of the film the protagonist says, "Love is like the ozone layer: you only miss it once it's gone" without a hint of irony.

2   It's been a long slide downhill. Like the deficit, off-color humor touches everyone but has no constituency, and neither politicians nor pundits will be clamoring for its return anytime soon. But there are good reasons to lament its passing. Let me count the ways.

3   *Risqué humor defuses tensions.* Lenny Bruce used to do a stand-up routine in which he'd gesture to each ethnic minority in the room and call them the most offensive names in the book: "I got a nigger here, two spics there. . . ." When his audience was ready to assault him, he'd reveal his point: that epithets get at least part of their sting precisely by being placed off-limits. By spreading the abuse about, you take the sting out of it. (The caveat, of course, is that is you're going to use ethnic humor, you should avoid singling out any particular group for derision.) Today's puritans, in contrast, are a drag on our culture, impeding frank talk about race, sex, class, and sexuality, and deadening our public wit at the same time. It's no coincidence that in the 1980s, before multiculturalism killed racial jokes, productive discussions of race were more common.

4   *Risqué humor educates.* The experience of American Jews in this country may be the best example of how this works. For decades the capacity of Jewish comedians to poke fun at the peculiar tics of their people helped make Jewish otherness, a quality that aroused suspicion and hatred in bygone eras, something disarming. It's a safe bet that the films of Mel Brooks and Woody Allen did more to stymie anti-Semitism in the past twenty years than all the wide-eyed vigilance and arm-waving of the Anti-Defamation League. When a quick cut-away shot in *Annie Hall* reveals that the grandmother of Allen's WASPy girlfriend sees him as a bearded and yarmulked rabbi, we laugh even as we empathize with his discomfort. Gays have used the humor the same way. You'd be hard-pressed to watch *La Cage Aux Folles,* a musical about a troupe of mincing gay entertainers, and have your homophobia strengthened. *Airplane* had a character—John, an air traffic controller—whose jokes, improvised by gay actor and activist Steve Stucco, made fun of gay sensibility without attacking it. When someone hands him a piece of paper and asks what he can make of it, Stucco begins folding it and says, "Oh a brooch, or a hat, or a pterodactyl."

5   *Risqué humor disarms.* A classic—and rare—modern example is *In Living Color,* which showcases merciless skits about black culture. (The reason it survives the P.C. police is that it's largely written and acted by blacks.) Witness a *Star Trek* spoof, "The Wrath of Farrakhan," a vicious lampoon of the black Muslim leader; or a sketch making fun of West Indians' hard-work habits. The feature "Men on Films," starring Damon Wayans and David Alan Grier (a.k.a. Antoine and Blaine), breaks taboos and wows both gay and straight audiences—while enraging the humorless activists. One regular skit centers on "Handi Man,"

a caped, spastic superhero who foils villains with his dwarf sidekick. To believe this hardens prejudice against people with disabilities is to believe that people are fundamentally barbaric; and assuming the handicapped are too tender a subject for humor is more patronizing than outright disdain. Indeed, there may be no better way to perpetrate a myth of disabled otherness than coming up with euphemisms like "the differently abled" and making irreverent utterances off-limits.

6   *Risqué humor undermines prejudices.* A black comic I recently saw had the right idea: He said he got so mad when a grocery clerk snickered about his purchase of frozen fried chicken that "I just grabbed my watermelon and tap danced on out of there." The joke both played with stereotypes and ridiculed them: Sometimes the best offense is offense. The major problem with ethnic humor—that it is often deployed by the powerful against the powerless—is best answered not by silencing the powerful (that hardly takes away their power) but by unleashing the humorous abilities of the powerless. Allowing ethnic humor means that blacks are allowed to make fun of whites (Eddie Murphy), gays are allowed to make fun of straights (Harvey Fierstein), and women are allowed to make fun of men (Roseanne Barr). In today's more ethnically and sexually diverse media, little of this opportunity for humor is being realized. Diversity is being achieved; and the result, ironically, is more piety. This is not only a bore, but an insult to the rich traditions of gay, black, Jewish, female, fat, ugly, disabled humor—and a boon to society's wealthy, powerful, and largely unfunny elites.

7   *Risqué humor is funny.* Ethnic humor's final defense is that it makes people laugh. In a free society, this is an irrepressible—and admirable—activity, and one I suspect we did more of some years back. Ask yourself: Were you laughing harder a decade ago? When Buck Henry hosted *Saturday Night Live* in the 1970s he'd do a skit in which he played a pedophilic baby sitter who got his jollies by playing games with his two nieces, like "find the pocket with the treat" and "show me your dirty laundry." In 1967 Mel Brooks won a best screenplay Academy Award for *The Producers,* which was full of Jewish, gay, and Nazi jokes and is now a confirmed classic. Brooks's 1991 offering was *Life Stinks,* which was bereft of anything off-color and was rightly panned.

8   As we've pushed the risqué off-stage, we've brought violent slapstick back on as a means of keeping the audience's attention. *Saturday Night Live* has abandoned racy material in favor of skits like "Horrible Headwound Harry," which features Dana Carvey as a party guest bleed-

ing from the head. And last year *Home Alone,* the story of a little boy, played by Macaulay Culkin, who fends off two burglars from his house by, among other things, dropping a hot iron on their heads, became the most lucrative comedy of movie history, grossing more than $285 million. The violence was far more explicit than anything the Three Stooges ever came up with, and all of it was done by a 12-year-old. Compare this with *Animal House,* which used to be the top-grossing comedy; it was filled with sexist—and hilarious—moments like the one in which the conscience of Tom Hulce's character advises him to take advantage of his passed-out, underage date.

9   In a multicultural society like ours, humor is not a threat, it's critical support. It keeps us sane, and it's a useful safety valve. If we can't be cruel about each other in jest, we might end up being cruel to each other in deadly seriousness. The politically correct war against insensitive humor might end up generating the very social and racial tension it is trying to defuse.

Reading Closely and Thinking Critically

1. Segal opens by referring to a "chill of sensitivity" that he says is apparent in public discourse, academic life, and humor. What does Segal mean? Do you agree that such a chill exists? Explain.

2. What cause-and-effect relationship does Segal identify between the death of racial jokes and the demise of "productive discussions of race" (paragraph 3)? Do you share Segal's view? Explain.

3. Explain the cause-and-effect relationship Segal sees between off-color humor and education.

4. What does Segal mean when he says that one effect of risqué humor is that is "disarms"? What does he mean when he says that it undermines prejudices?

5. What does Segal see as the ultimate effects of the "politically correct" attack on ethnic humor? In what paragraph does he best express those effects?

Examining Structure and Strategy

1. What purpose does paragraph 1 serve?

2. Do you think the title is a good one? Why or why not? (Hint: Refer to the headnote for information on the title.)

3. Why does Segal draw so heavily on media examples like *Airplane* and *In Living Color* to prove and explain his points?

4. Segal uses topic sentences to present the effects under consideration. What are those topic sentences?

5. How would you describe Segal's intended audience?

Considering Language and Style

1. What contradiction is apparent in the phrase "the chill of sensitivity" (paragraph 1)?

2. Explain the metaphor in the statement, "An earnest stripe of environmentalism is painted down the movie's middle" (paragraph 1). (See page 73 on metaphors.)

3. Consult a dictionary if you are unsure of the meaning of any of these words: *jive* (paragraph 1), *minyan* (paragraph 1), *mazel tov* (paragraph 1), *protagonist* (paragraph 1), *pundits* (paragraph 2), *risqué* (paragraph 3), *epithets* (paragraph 3), *caveat* (paragraph 3), *Anti-Defamation League* (paragraph 4), *WASPy* (paragraph 4), *yarmulked* (paragraph 4), *pedophilic* (paragraph 7).

For Group Discussion or Writing

Do you think your campus should have guidelines for the humor in campus plays and other productions? If so, write those guidelines to distinguish between humor that is healthy and hurtful, funny and offensive. If you think your campus should not have guidelines, explain why.

Writing Assignments

1. *In your journal.* In about a page, write a definition of *political correctness.*

2. *Using the pattern.* Write an essay that explains and illustrates the effects of political correctness on something other than comedy: language, education, politics, advertising, and so forth.

3. *Using the pattern.* Select a popular comedian, funny movie, or funny television show. Explain how the public responds to the humor and why it responds the way it does.

4. Using the pattern. If you disagree with Segal, analyze the negative effects of risqué humor to persuade the reader that it should not be encouraged.

5. Considering a theme. Do you think political correctness has gone too far? Explain why or why not.

6. Connecting the readings. Summarize the positions of David Segal and Diane Cole ("Don't Just Stand There," page 288) on ethnic humor. Then indicate which author you agree with and why.

JUST WALK ON BY: A BLACK MAN PONDERS HIS POWER TO ALTER PUBLIC SPACE
Brent Staples

Born in Chester, Pennsylvania, Brent Staples earned his Ph.D. in psychology from the University of Chicago in 1982. A member of the New York Times *editorial board, Staples was previously a reporter for the* Chicago Sun-Times *before becoming an editor on the* New York Times Book Review. *He has written for the* New York Times Magazine, Harper's, *and* New York Woman. *His memoir,* Parallel Time: Growing Up in Black and White *(1994), recalls his childhood in Chester and the death of his younger brother, a drug dealer who was shot to death at age 22. The following essay appeared in* Ms. *(September 1986) and in a revised form in* Harper's *(December 1987) as "Black Men and Public Space." In the essay here, Staples uses cause-and-effect analysis to inform the reader about why some people view black men as threats. He also explains the effects this perception has on him by relating his own experience, and he informs the reader that "being perceived as dangerous" puts the black man at risk. As you read, think about how you react to the appearance of people.*

THE PATTERN	THE PURPOSES
cause-and-effect analysis	*to inform and to share feelings and relate experience*

1   My first victim was a woman—white, well dressed, probably in her early twenties. I came upon her late one evening on a deserted street in Hyde Park, a relatively affluent neighborhood in an otherwise mean, impoverished section of Chicago. As I swung onto the avenue behind her, there seemed to be a discreet uninflammatory distance between us. Not so. She cast back a worried glance. To her, the youngish black man—a broad six feet two inches with a beard and billowing hair, both hands shoved into the pockets of a bulky military jacket— seemed menacingly close. After a few more quick glimpses, she picked up her pace and was soon running in earnest. Within seconds she disappeared into a cross street.

2   That was more than a decade ago. I was 22 years old, a graduate student newly arrived at the University of Chicago. It was in the

echo of that terrified woman's footfalls that I first began to know the unwieldy inheritance I'd come into—the ability to alter public space in ugly ways. It was clear that she thought herself the quarry of a mugger, a rapist, or worse. Suffering a bout of insomnia, however, I was stalking sleep, not defenseless wayfarers. As a softy who is scarcely able to take a knife to a raw chicken—let alone hold it to a person's throat—I was surprised, embarrassed, and dismayed all at once. Her flight made me feel like an accomplice in tyranny. It also made it clear that I was indistinguishable from the muggers who occasionally seeped into the area from the surrounding ghetto. That first encounter, and those that followed, signified that a vast, unnerving gulf lay between nighttime pedestrians—particularly women—and me. And I soon gathered that being perceived as dangerous is a hazard in itself. I only needed to turn a corner into a dicey situation, or crowd some frightened, armed person in a foyer somewhere, or make an errant move after being pulled over by policeman. Where fear and weapons meet—and they often do in urban America—there is always the possibility of death.

3   In that first year, my first away from my hometown, I was to become thoroughly familiar with the language of fear. At dark, shadowy intersections in Chicago, I could cross in front of a car stopped at a traffic light and elicit the *thunk, thunk, thunk, thunk* of the driver—black, white, male, or female—hammering down the door locks. On less traveled streets after dark, I grew accustomed to but never comfortable with people who crossed to the other side of the street rather than pass me. Then there were the standard unpleasantries with police, doormen, bouncers, cab drivers, and others whose business it is to screen out troublesome individuals *before* there is any nastiness.

4   I moved to New York nearly two years ago and I have remained an avid night walker. In central Manhattan, the near-constant crowd cover minimizes tense one-on-one street encounters. Elsewhere—visiting friends in SoHo, where sidewalks are narrow and tightly spaced buildings shut out the sky—things can get very taut indeed.

5   Black men have a firm place in New York mugging literature. Norman Podhoretz in his famed (or infamous) 1963 essay, "My Negro Problem—And Ours," recalls growing up in terror of black males; they "were tougher than we were, more ruthless," he writes—and as an adult on the Upper West Side of Manhattan, he continues, he cannot constrain his nervousness when he meets black men on certain streets. Similarly, a decade later, the essayist and novelist Edward Hoagland extols

a New York where once "Negro bitterness bore down mainly on other Negroes." Where some see mere panhandlers, Hoagland sees "a mugger who is clearly screwing up his nerve to do more than just *ask* for money." But Hoagland has "the New Yorker's quick-hunch posture for broken-field maneuvering," and the bad guy swerves away.

6   I often witness that "hunch posture," from women after dark on the warrenlike streets of Brooklyn where I live. They seem to set their faces on neutral and, with their purse straps strung across their chests bandolier style, they forge ahead as though bracing themselves against being tackled. I understand, of course, that the danger they perceive is not a hallucination. Women are particularly vulnerable to street violence, and young black males are drastically overrepresented among the perpetrators of that violence. Yet these truths are no solace against the kind of alienation that comes of being ever the suspect, against being set apart, a fearsome entity with whom pedestrians avoid making eye contact.

7   It is not altogether clear to me how I reached the ripe old age of 22 without being conscious of the lethality nighttime pedestrians attributed to me. Perhaps it was because in Chester, Pennsylvania, the small angry industrial town where I came of age in the 1960s, I was scarcely noticeable against a backdrop of gang warfare, street knifings, and murders. I grew up one of the good boys, had perhaps a half-dozen fist fights. In retrospect, my shyness of combat has clear sources.

8   Many things go into the making of a young thug. One of those things is the consummation of the male romance with the power to intimidate. An infant discovers that random flailings send the baby bottle flying out of the crib and crashing to the floor. Delighted, the joyful babe repeats those motions again and again, seeking to duplicate the feat. Just so, I recall the points at which some of my boyhood friends were finally seduced by the perception of themselves as tough guys. When a mark cowered and surrendered his money without resistance, myth and reality merged—and paid off. It is, after all, only manly to embrace the power to frighten and intimidate. We, as men, are not supposed to give an inch of our lane on the highway; we are to seize the fighter's edge in work and in play and even in love; we are to be valiant in the face of hostile forces.

9   Unfortunately, poor and powerless young men seem to take all this nonsense literally. As a boy, I saw countless tough guys locked away; I have since buried several, too. They were babies, really—a teenage cousin, a brother of 22, a childhood friend in his mid-twen-

ties—all gone down in episodes of bravado played out in the streets. I came to doubt the virtues of intimidation early on. I chose, perhaps even unconsciously, to remain a shadow—timid, but a survivor.

10   The fearsomeness mistakenly attributed to me in public places often has a perilous flavor. The most frightening of these confusions occurred in the late 1970s and early 1980s when I worked as a journalist in Chicago. One day, rushing into the office of a magazine I was writing for with a deadline story in hand, I was mistaken for a burglar. The office manager called security and, with an ad hoc posse, pursued me through the labyrinthine halls, nearly to my editor's door. I had no way of proving who I was. I could only move briskly toward the company of someone who knew me.

11   Another time I was on assignment for a local paper and killing time before an interview. I entered a jewelry store on the city's affluent Near North Side. The proprietor excused herself and returned with an enormous red Doberman pinscher straining at the end of a leash. She stood, the dog extended toward me, silent to my questions, her eyes bulging nearly out of her head. I took a cursory look around, nodded, and bade her good night. Relatively speaking, however, I never fared as badly as another black male journalist. He went to nearby Waukegan, Illinois, a couple of summers ago to work on a story about a murderer who was born there. Mistaking the reporter for the killer, police hauled him from his car at gunpoint and but for his press credentials would probably have tried to book him. Such episodes are not uncommon. Black men trade tales like this all the time.

12   In "My Negro Problem—And Ours," Podhoretz writes that the hatred he feels for blacks makes itself known to him through a variety of avenues—one being his discomfort with that "special brand of paranoid touchiness" to which he says blacks are prone. No doubt he is speaking here of black men. In time, I learned to smother the rage I felt at so often being taken for a criminal. Not to do so would surely have led to madness—via that special "paranoid touchiness" that so annoyed Podhoretz at the time he wrote the essay.

13   I began to take precautions to make myself less threatening. I move about with care, particularly late in the evening. I give a wide berth to nervous people on subway platforms during the wee hours, particularly when I have exchanged business clothes for jeans. If I happen to be entering a building behind some people who appear skittish, I may walk by, letting them clear the lobby before I return, so as not to

seem to be following them. I have been calm and extremely congenial on those rare occasions when I've been pulled over by the police.

14   And on late-evening constitutionals along streets less traveled by, I employ what has proved to be an excellent tension-reducing measure: I whistle melodies from Beethoven and Vivaldi and the more popular classical composers. Even steely New Yorkers hunching toward night-time destinations seem to relax, and occasionally they even join in the tune. Virtually everybody seems to sense that a mugger wouldn't be warbling bright, sunny selections from Vivaldi's *Four Seasons*. It is my equivalent of the cowbell that hikers wear when they know they are in bear country.

Reading Closely and Thinking Critically

1. When Staples walks at night, what effect does he have on people? What do people do when they see him?

2. Although Staples is often viewed as a threat, he is the one at risk. Why?

3. Staples explains that his effect on people—particularly women—is understandable. Why does he think so?

4. According to Staples, what causes a young man to become a thug? What do you think prompts a black male to become a thug? How did Staples escape becoming a thug?

5. In paragraphs 5 and 12, Staples refers to essays by Norman Podhoretz and Edward Hoagland. What point do you think Staples is trying to make with these references?

6. Staple's essay first appeared in *Ms.* and *Harper's*. Do you think the readers of these magazines make the best audience for the piece? Explain.

Examining Structure and Strategy

1. What approach does Staples take to his introduction? Does the introduction engage your interest? Explain.

2. The essay is not about what the opening sentences lead you to believe it will be about. Is that a problem? Explain.

3. In your own words, write out the thesis of "Just Walk on By." Which sentence in the essay comes closest to expressing that idea?

4. Which paragraphs include brief narrations? What do they contribute to the essay?

5. What approach does Staples take to his conclusion? Do you think the conclusion brings the essay to a satisfying close? Why or why not?

Considering Language and Style

1. What is "public space"? What does it mean to possess the power to alter public space? Name groups of people that have the power to alter public space.

2. Consult a dictionary if you are unsure of the meaning of any of these words: *quarry* (paragraph 2), *wayfarers* (paragraph 2), *errant* (paragraph 2), *extols* (paragraph 5), *warrenlike* (paragraph 6), *bandolier* (paragraph 6), *bravado* (paragraph 9), *ad hoc* (paragraph 10), *labyrinthine* (paragraph 10), *cursory* (paragraph 11), *constitutionals* (paragraph 14).

For Group Discussion or Writing

With some classmates, discuss whether your experience confirms or contradicts Staples's thesis that young, black males are perceived as threats.

Writing Assignments

1. *In your journal.* Although we admit that appearances can be deceiving, we often are influenced by the way others look. To what extent are you influenced by the way people look? How do appearances affect who you speak to and interact with? How do appearances affect the judgments you make about people?

2. *Using the pattern.* How safe do you feel walking alone on your campus or in your neighborhood? Explain why you feel the way you do and the effects of your feeling of security or insecurity.

3. *Using the pattern.* Describe how you think you are perceived by others and explain why you think you are perceived that way. Consider how one or more factors such as your size, gender, skin color, age, manner of dress, and degree of attractiveness affect how people judge your social class, economic level, degree of intelligence, occupation, and such. Then go on to explain how you are affected by the way you are perceived.

4. *Using the pattern.* If you have ever been perceived as a threat or if you have perceived someone else as a threat, explain what caused the perception and what its effects were.

5. *Using the pattern.* Pick one of the following and explain how the person is typically perceived, as well as the effect the perception has on the person. If you do not have firsthand knowledge, you can interview the appropriate people to get your information.

a very attractive person	a very tall person
a male with long hair	a very short person
a male with an earring	a very muscular person
a physically disabled person	an elderly person

6. *Consider a theme.* In paragraph 8, Staples comments on men and power: "It is, after all, only manly to embrace the power to frighten and intimidate." Do you agree that our concept of manliness is linked to the sense of power and the ability to intimidate? If so, explain how men and women are affected by this concept of manliness. If not, explain why you disagree.

7. *Connecting the readings.* Explain how people react to those they perceive as "different." Also explain why you think people react the way they do. The ideas in "Just Walk on By" and "Untouchables" (page 236) may give you some ideas.

WHAT IS BEHIND THE GROWTH OF VIOLENCE ON COLLEGE CAMPUSES?

Dorothy Siegel

Dorothy Siegel is vice president for student services at Towson State University, Towson, Maryland, and executive director and founder of the Campus Violence Prevention Center at Towson, which has carried out significant research on issues related to campus violence. An authority on campus crime, Siegel has testified before Congress on the subject. She also lectures and leads workshops about student services and campus violence and is a consultant to the U.S. Department of Justice and Education. "What Is Behind the Growth of Violence on College Campuses" first appeared in USA Today *magazine in 1994. It examines the causes of campus violence to inform the reader. To make her points, Siegel draws heavily on statistics, some of which may surprise you.*

THE PATTERN	THE PURPOSE
analysis of causes	*to inform*

1   America's college campuses are not the war zones newspaper and magazine articles would lead the public to believe. Those crimes committed against students get major attention from the media probably because campuses are expected to be serene and safe. What is perhaps most troubling about campus crime is that the majority of the incidents, excluding theft, but including rape and other sexual assaults, are impulsive acts committed by students themselves, according to nationwide studies conducted by Towson State University's Campus Violence Prevention Center. Students are responsible for 80 percent of campus crime, although rarely with weapons.

2   It is an uphill battle to ensure student safety. Schools provide escort services, tamper-proof windows, and continually upgraded state-of-the-art exterior lighting and electronic alarm systems. These institutional efforts frequently are undone by the immortal feelings of college-age men and women. That "it-can't-happen-to-me" attitude leads to lax security behaviors that literally leave the door open for an outside threat. Universities are challenged to help students develop and

keep that awareness, except for the two weeks following an on-campus assault, when caution prevails.

3   The same students who sponsor night walks to check the lighting and grounds to increase safety will hold the door open for a stranger entering their residence hall. Despite frequent warnings, students—and even faculty, administrators, and other campus personnel—act less judiciously than they would elsewhere.

4   The mind-set of the students and probably of most of us is that crime is going to happen at night. Following a daylight abduction at one school, students demanded better lighting and evening patrols. They are loathe to follow the cautions about garages and out-of-the-way places during the day. They have trouble acknowledging, as we all probably do, that current criminal acts require new precautions, more appropriate to what is happening now.

5   Today, as part of the orientation programs at campuses across the nation, most administrators welcome students with information about crime on campus and ways they better can ensure their own safety. Because The Higher Education Security Act requires schools to report their previous year's crime statistics to the campus [community], colleges greet many new students and their parents with the previous year's count of violations and wise warnings. They are united in their efforts to command students' attention and enlist them as active partners in prevention. They use theater, video, discussions, posters, and circulars to inform students. Police statistics and reports are disseminated widely.

6   Despite this, if a stranger is seen entering a building, it is unlikely that any observers will notify the police, even if the potential assailant is dressed strangely and/or behaving oddly. If that stranger attacks someone the community will demand more protection. A series of seminars will produce good ideas and vigilant behavior for about two weeks, after which much of the more casual behavior about safety reappears.

7   When students discuss safety, it always is about dangers from outside the campus. Students are both the perpetrators and victims of most campus crime, yet it still is protection from trespassers that motivates most safety programs and is most in demand. It is an arduous and mostly unsuccessful process to convince students that they are more likely to be a victim of crime perpetrated by a member of their class or athletic team than by a stranger. It appears unthinkable that they them-

selves may become assailants. Although this message is included in many orientation programs for new students, it is nearly impossible to alert them to the potential danger from people they trust simply because they are members of the same community. Yet, eight percent of students report that they have been perpetrators and approximately 12 percent say they have been victims of assault.

8   Visitors to a campus during the day will see a reasonably civil society. Students will congregate in various common areas and study, talk, laugh, or even sleep. The homeless may gather on the campus benches while a non-student stands and shouts what he or she maintains is God's will. Literally thousands of people will pass without incident. If campus police are writing citations, it is likely to be for parking violations.

9   Yet, on any night from Thursday to Saturday on the same campus, the majority of students will be drinking, some excessively, and fights will erupt over seemingly trivial issues—who can have the bedroom, the keys, the boyfriend or girlfriend, the Nintendo. Small differences may escalate into brawls when combined with drug and alcohol abuse. Student assistants in residence halls may write up hundreds of classmates for violation of the campus alcohol policy. These reports are forwarded for administrative action. Few, if any, students will be arrested. Other drunk students will be returning from town where similar incidents may have occurred. Police rarely are called for fear of endangering the bar's liquor license. Still other students are on their way to parties, where recreational drinking is the featured attraction.

10   My first experience with campus violence came after I had spent two years in my current position as vice president for student services at Towson State University. One Friday evening, a drunk student trying to enter a residence hall to visit a friend beat the student worker who denied him access. The employee was hospitalized overnight. Although the student was criminally charged, the university immediately had to create procedures for an on-campus hearing to determine how the institution should respond. He was the first student suspended from the university because of assault charges stemming from a campus incident.

11   In the late 1970s, some students on campuses around the country reported being victims of assaults by fellow students. Residence directors observed increases in vandalism. Personnel at different schools thought they were experiencing situations unique to their own campuses. Rural and urban, large and small schools noted the existence of violent incidents, quantified in Towson State's surveys of over 1,000 col-

leges. Those studies became the nation's first national data on student-perpetrated violence. It documented that students were both victims and perpetrators of rape, other sexual violence, and physical assault.

UNITED STATES OF VIOLENCE

12   When sexual assaults and rapes are reported, an interviewer most frequently will learn that the two students have known each other, sometimes meeting at a party earlier that evening. Typically, they both will have been drinking. One may have accepted the other's invitation to share a room because a roommate was entertaining someone. He may make advances. She says she only will accept the offer of the room (or extend the offer) if it is a non-sexual relationship. He accepts the terms, but believes her accompanying him means she is willing. She thinks she has communicated effectively. He thinks he has understood. Such misunderstandings make one appreciate the clear consent to sex that Antioch College demands of its students as set forth in its most recent handbook.

13   One percent of students reported more physically brutal rapes. Four percent of female students stated that they had been raped, predominantly by other students. Researchers report that 74 percent of sexually related crimes were committed by fellow students. More than 30 percent of these sexual crimes were committed by fraternity members, while 14 percent were committed by athletes, some by friends of friends.

14   The majority of perpetrators indicated that they were drunk, high, or in need of drugs when the crimes were committed. Substance abuse is a direct correlate of violent campus behavior. Researchers from Towson State's Campus Violence Prevention Center reported in a study of responses from 1,800 college students nationwide that abuse of alcohol was heavier among victims and perpetrators than the rest of the campus population. A later study of more than 13,000 students corroborated those results, adding that students who used drugs were likely to be among the perpetrators and the victims. Perpetrators reported using intoxicants more often than did victims. In turn, the victims reported heavier drinking habits than those who were neither victims nor assailants. Whether drunk or not, a substantial majority of victims and perpetrators said that, on the day of the crime, they had been drinking and/or using drugs. It is a logical conclusion that students usually will not become victims or perpetrators in student-to-student violence if they do not use drugs or abuse alcohol.

15   In spite of all the messages of abstinence that are drilled into the nation's youth from elementary school years on, many students come to higher education with histories of excessive drinking. Against the backdrop of violence that exists in American society, the loss of control heightened by substance abuse, including alcohol, often is accompanied by violent outbursts. The various preventive efforts such as mediation and conflict resolution offered by some schools are not effective techniques for preventing the acts fueled by the presence of alcohol.

16   Universities formerly had acted *in loco parentis*. When the national age of majority was lowered to 18, college administrators had to alter their relationship with students because institutions no longer could behave as substitute parents for youths who now could vote, drink, and go to war. While it is not documented how effective such supervision of students was, it is clear that those who wished to violate the rules had to work harder to do so. The current relationship is adult-to-adult, even though the institutions recognize that many students are not fully mature. That poses a continuing dilemma for campus personnel in helping students to develop control over their behavior, thus assuring their own safety and that of their peers.

17   Although the legal drinking age has been raised to 21 in each state, the national community of 18- to 20-year-olds simply does not accept this constraint. Some estimates are that as many as 80 percent of underage students carry fake proof-of-age identification. Drinking has become a standard pastime, and binge drinking—five or more drinks at a sitting—is condoned by 85 percent of college freshmen. The number of students who report excessive drinking is less in the sophomore year and decreases in each of the subsequent years. It has not been determined if the excessive drinkers have dropped out or changed their ways. It probably is some of both. The people who have been most responsive to the substance abuse education programs are the casual users who reportedly are abstaining totally now. The laws are not effective despite substantial efforts. No way has been found to govern a population by laws they do not accept.

SEEKING UNDERSTANDING

18   College students are among the nation's brightest and most successful people. In general, they come from higher socioeconomic backgrounds than the non-college-attending members of their age group. Al-

though there has been no formal study of their behavior after university attendance, it is unlikely that perpetrators of college incidents will commit other violent crimes later. Most do not repeat offenses on campus. A contributing factor may be that many schools require those responsible to attend substance abuse intervention programs as a condition of returning to or continuing to attend the university.

19   Administrators are at a loss to understand why such an increase in student violence has emerged in the past two decades. They have tried to study the problem from several approaches, but the only factor that remains the same in the majority of cases is alcohol abuse. It is not known if as many students in the past drank as much as current ones do. Research shows, though, that almost 50 percent of freshmen had been drunk within two weeks preceding the study.

20   Behaviors that lead to violence usually are tolerated by students. Resident students are reluctant to complain, even in cases where their rights and their living space are violated by the conduct of others. They may ask for alternate housing, but are not apt to make a formal complaint. Only victims report crimes. Most actions that lead to assaultive behaviors are tolerated by the student community. Students who dislike the rowdiness are more apt to move away than to assert their rights to a more appropriate living environment.

21   On more and more campuses, housing options available to students include alcohol-free residence halls. Those who choose them have quieter and less disruptive lives. Such an option is not successful when someone other than the students themselves makes those choices.

22   It is easy to prevent violence if each student is kept under lock and key. It is a more challenging problem in a society that values freedom. The message to students is that a safe community requires their participation. The role of police is to facilitate safety, not assure it. It is a challenge to have an environment appropriate for growth and learning and safety in today's society.

23   Student society evolves and changes. For instance, women increasingly are the assaulters. Though still in the single-digit numbers and not nearly as high as the amount of incidents with male perpetrators, the total is going up. More students are participating in communal efforts to help others, which may indicate that they are assuming more membership in the campus community. They increasingly are riding the escort vans that for so long were available, but appeared inconvenient. More are working actively for a civil environment. Although

they continue to prop open doors for the pizza man, we are seeing some effort to make the school safer. More are complaining about the amount of drinking on campus, but they still are not willing to say that a room-mate drinks too much. Many student governments, fraternities, and sororities have supported the efforts, but continue alcohol-dominated parties. Students at many colleges no longer sponsor dances because of the enforcement of alcohol laws by the institutions. More students are walking with others at night. Nevertheless, the struggle remains to help students pursue safer ways.

24   In our community of 10,000 full-time students, we held admin-istrative hearings for 11 cases of physical assault in 1992. No sexual as-saults were reported. Other years, the number of assaults was as high as 35, and the highest number of sexual assaults in any year was six. When colleges were required by the 1992 National Higher Education Security Act to inform their faculty, staff, and students about crime sta-tistics on campuses, several reporters were sure that the colleges were hiding numbers. However, the amount of crimes on campuses never has been large. Still, even a single violent act requires that everyone be-come more discerning.

Reading Closely and Thinking Critically

1. Throughout the essay, Siegel presents causes of campus violence. What are those causes?

2. One cause of campus violence, according to Siegel, is the fact that students fail to report suspicious people and behavior. How do you explain this failure?

3. Why do students assume that the source of danger is outside campus, rather than within?

4. Explain the cause-and-effect relationship between sexual assaults, including rapes, and ineffective communication.

5. Do you think that a return to *in loco parentis* would reduce the amount of crime on campus? Explain.

6. As a college student, how do you react to Siegel's message? Do you think most college students would react the way you do? Would they be surprised by any of the information or moved to alter their behavior in any way? Explain.

Examining Structure and Strategy

1. Why does Siegel mention her position as vice president for student services at Towson State University?

2. What are the sources of Siegel's details (personal experience, observation, research, television, etc.)?

3. Which paragraphs include statistics? What do those statistics contribute to the essay?

4. Evaluate the effectiveness of the concluding paragraphs (paragraphs 23 and 24).

Considering Language and Style

1. In paragraph 16, Siegel says, "Universities formerly acted *in loco parentis.*" What does *in loco parentis* mean?

2. Consult a dictionary if you are unsure of the meaning of any of these words: *perpetrators* (paragraph 7), *arduous* (paragraph 7), *corroborated* (paragraph 14).

For Group Discussion or Writing

With some classmates, visit the appropriate offices on your campus to learn how much and what kind of crime exists at your school. Also learn what measures are being taken to make your campus as safe as possible. Report your findings and whether or not you think more needs to be done. If so, state what. If not, explain why not.

Writing Assignments

1. *In your journal.* In a page or so, explain whether or not you feel safe on your campus and why you feel the way you do. Also note whether or not you plan to change your behavior as a result of reading the essay. If so, explain how; if not, explain why not.

2. *Using the pattern.* Write a set of guidelines for student behavior that you think will reduce the occurrences of rape and other sexual assaults on your campus. Be sure to explain how you think each guideline will affect students and their interactions.

3. *Using the pattern.* Siegel says that "students usually will not become victims or perpetrators in student-to-student violence if they do not use drugs or abuse alcohol" (paragraph 14). With that in mind, explain what would happen if your school initiated a policy (with strict enforcement provisions) making the college and the surrounding area completely substance-free.

4. *Using the pattern.* Explain why "many students come to higher education with histories of excessive drinking" (paragraph 5). If you wish, you may also offer solutions to the problem.

5. *Using the pattern.* Explain the causes of another campus problem: cheating, declining enrollment, failure to graduate, student apathy, and so forth. As an alternative, explain the effects of the problem.

6. *Considering a theme.* In your library, find out about Antioch College's handbook guidelines referred to in paragraph 13 and discuss what you think of them.

7. *Connecting the readings.* Discuss to what extent miscommunication between women and men is responsible for sexual harassment and sexual assault. The ideas in "What Is Behind the Growth of Violence on College Campuses?" "What I've Learned from Men" (page 229), and "Talk in the Intimate Relationship" (page 354) may help you.

IT'S JUST TOO LATE
Calvin Trillin

A journalist and prolific author, Calvin Trillin was born in 1935 in Kansas City, Missouri. He graduated from Yale University in 1957 and went on to write investigative pieces, humor columns, short stories, novels, and commentary for a number of magazines, including the New Yorker. *Trillin's books include* U.S. Journals *(1971), a collection of some of his pieces from the* New Yorker; Third Helpings *(1983), writings on American food;* Killings *(1984), a look at the ways Americans get killed; and* Enough's Enough (And Other Rules of Life) *(1990), a collection of his humor columns. Trillin's book* Remembering Denny *(1993) is a memoir that attempts to explain the 1991 suicide of one of his college friends. "It's Just Too Late," taken from* Killings, *uses cause-and-effect analysis and narration to tell the reader about the events surrounding the death of a teenager. As you read, notice the elegance of Trillin's journalistic style.*

THE PATTERNS	THE PURPOSE
cause-and-effect analysis with narration	*to inform*

Knoxville, Tennessee
March 1979

1   Until she was sixteen, FaNee Cooper was what her parents sometimes called an ideal child. "You'd never have to correct her," FaNee's mother has said. In sixth grade, FaNee won a spelling contest. She played the piano and the flute. She seemed to believe what she heard every Sunday at the Beaver Dam Baptist Church about good and evil and the hereafter. FaNee was not an outgoing child. Even as a baby, she was uncomfortable when she was held and cuddled. She found it easy to tell her parents she loved them but difficult to confide in them. Particularly compared to her sister, Kristy, a cheerful, open little girl two and a half years younger, she was reserved and introspective. The thoughts she kept to herself, though, were apparently happy thoughts. Her eighth-grade essay on Christmas—written in a remarkably neat

hand—talked of the joys of helping put together toys for her little
brother, Leo, Jr., and the importance of her parents' reminder that
Christmas is the birthday of Jesus. Her parents were the sort of people
who might have been expected to have an ideal child. As a boy, Leo
Cooper had been called "one of the greatest high-school basketball
players ever developed in Knox County." He went on to play basketball at East Tennessee State, and he married the homecoming queen,
JoAnn Henson. After college, Cooper became a high-school basketball
coach and teacher and, eventually, an administrator. By the time FaNee
turned thirteen, in 1973, he was in his third year as the principal of
Gresham Junior High School, in Fountain City—a small Knox County
town that had been swallowed up by Knoxville when the suburbs began to move north. A tall man with curly black hair going on gray, Leo
Cooper has an elaborate way of talking ("Unless I'm very badly mistaken, he has never related to me totally the content of his conversation") and a manner that may come from years of trying to leave errant junior-high-school students with the impression that a responsible
adult is magnanimous, even humble, about invariably being in the
right. His wife, a high-school art teacher, paints and does batik, and
created the name FaNee because she liked the way it looked and
sounded—it sounds like "Fawn*ee*" when the Coopers say it—but the
impression she gives is not artiness but of soft-spoken small-town gen-
tility. When she found, in the course of cleaning up FaNee's room, that
her ideal thirteen-year-old had been smoking cigarettes, she was, in her
words, crushed. "FaNee was such a perfect child before that," JoAnn
Cooper said some time later. "She was angry that we found out. She
knew we knew that she had done something we didn't approve of, and
then the rebellion started. I was hurt. I was very hurt. I guess it came
through as disappointment."

2   Several months later, FaNee's grandmother died. FaNee had been
devoted to her grandmother. She wrote a poem in her memory—an almost joyous poem, filled with Christian faith in the afterlife ("Please
don't grieve over my happiness/Rejoice with me in the presence of the
Angels of Heaven"). She also took some keepsakes from her grandmother's house, and was apparently mortified when her parents found
them and explained that they would have to be returned. By then, the
Coopers were aware that FaNee was going to have a difficult time as a
teenager. They thought she might be self-conscious about the double af-
fliction of glasses and braces. They thought she might be uncomfortable

in the role of the principal's daughter at Gresham. In ninth grade, she entered Halls High School, where JoAnn Cooper was teaching art. Fa-Nee was a loner at first. Then she fell in with what could only be considered a bad crowd.

3   Halls, a few miles to the north of Fountain City, used to be known as Halls Crossroads. It is what Knoxville people call "over the ridge"—on the side of Black Oak Ridge that has always been thought of as rural. When FaNee entered Halls High, the Coopers were already in the process of building a house on several acres of land they had bought in Halls, in a sparsely settled area along Brown Gap road. Like two or three other houses along the road, it was to be constructed basically of huge logs taken from old buildings—a house that Leo Cooper describes as being, like the name FaNee, "just a little bit different." Ten years ago, Halls Crossroads was literally a crossroads. Then some of the Knoxville expansion that had swollen Fountain City spilled over the ridge, planting subdivisions here and there on roads that still went for long stretches with nothing but an occasional house with a cow or two next to it. The increase in population did not create a town. Halls has no center. Its commercial area is a series of two or three shopping centers strung together on the Maynardville Highway, the four-lane that leads north into Union County—a place almost synonymous in east Tennessee with mountain poverty. Its restaurant is the Halls Freezo Drive-In. The gathering place for the group FaNee Cooper eventually found herself in was the Maynardville Highway Exxon station.

4   At Halls High School, the social poles were represented by the Jocks and the Freaks. FaNee found her friends among the Freaks. "I am truly enlighted upon irregular trains of thought aimed at strange depots of mental wards," she wrote when she was fifteen. "Yes! Crazed farms for the mental off—Oh! I walked through the halls screams & loud laughter fill my ears—Orderlys try to reason with me—but I am unreasonable! The joys of being a FREAK in a circus of imagination." The little crowd of eight or ten young people that FaNee joined has been referred to by her mother as "the Union County group." A couple of the girls were from backgrounds similar to FaNee's, but all the boys had the characteristics, if not the precise addresses, that Knoxville people associate with the poor whites of Union County. They were the sort of boys who didn't bother to finish high school, or finished it in a special program for slow learners, or get ejected from it for taking a swing at the principal.

5   "I guess you can say they more or less dragged us down to their level with the drugs," a girl who was in the group—a girl who can be called Marcia—said recently. "And somehow we settled for it. It seems like we had to get ourselves in the pit before we could look out." People in the group used marijuana and Valium and LSD. They sneered at the Jocks and the "prim and proper little ladies" who went with Jocks. "We set ourselves aside," Marcia now says. "We put ourselves above everyone. How we did that I don't know." In a Knox County high school, teenagers who want to get themselves in the pit need not mainline heroin. The Jocks they mean to be compared to do not merely show up regularly for classes and practice football and wear clean clothes; they watch their language and preach temperance and go to prayer meetings on Wednesday nights and talk about having a real good Christian witness. Around Knoxville, people who speak of well-behaved high-school kids often seem to use words like "perfect," or even "angels." For FaNee's group, the opposite was not difficult to figure out. "We were into wicked things, strange things," Marcia says. "It was like we were on some kind of devil trip." FaNee wrote about demons and vultures and rats. "Slithering serpents eat my sanity and bite my ass," she wrote in an essay called "The Lovely Road of Life," just after she turned sixteen, "while tornadoes derail and ever so swiftly destroy every car in my train of thought." She wrote a lot about death.

6   FaNee's girl friends spoke of her as "super-intelligent." Her English teacher found some of her writing profound—and disturbing. She was thought to be not just super-intelligent but super-mysterious, and even, at times, super-weird—an introverted girl who stared straight ahead with deep-brown, nearly black eyes and seemed to have thoughts she couldn't share. Nobody really knew why she had chosen to run with the Freaks—whether it was loneliness or rebellion or simple boredom. Marcia thought it might have had something to do with a feeling that her parents had settled on Kristy as their perfect child. "I guess she figured she couldn't be the best," Marcia said recently. "So she decided she might as well be the worst."

7   Toward the spring of FaNee's junior year at Halls, her problems seemed to deepen. Despite her intelligence, her grades were sliding. She was what her mother called "a mental dropout." Leo Cooper had to visit Halls twice because of minor suspensions. Once, FaNee had been caught smoking. Once, having ducked out of a required assembly, she was spotted by a favorite teacher, who turned her in. At home, she ex-

changed little more than short, strained formalities with Kristy, who shared their parent's opinion of FaNee's choice of friends. The Coopers had finished their house—a large house, its size accentuated by the huge old logs and a great stone fireplace and outsize "Paul Bunyan"-style furniture—but FaNee spent most of her time there in her own room, sleeping or listening to rock music through earphones. One night, there was a terrible scene when FaNee returned from a concert in a condition that Leo Cooper knew had to be the result of marijuana. JoAnn Cooper, who ordinarily strikes people as too gentle to raise her voice, found herself losing her temper regularly. Finally, Leo Cooper asked a counsellor he knew, Jim Griffin, to stop in at Halls High School and have a talk with FaNee—unofficially.

8   Griffin—a young man with a warm, informal manner—worked for the Juvenile Court of Knox County. He had a reputation for being able to reach teenagers who wouldn't talk to their parents or to school administrators. One Friday in March of 1977, he spent an hour and a half talking to FaNee Cooper. As Griffin recalls the interview, FaNee didn't seem alarmed by his presence. She seemed to him calm and controlled—Griffin thought it was something like talking to another adult—and, unlike most of the teenagers he dealt with, she looked him in the eye the entire time. Griffin, like some of FaNee's friends, found her eyes unsettling—"the coldest, most distant, but, at the same time, the most knowing eyes I'd ever seen." She expressed affection for her parents, but she didn't seem interested in exploring ways of getting along better with them. The impression she gave Griffin was that they were who they were, and she was who she was, and there didn't happen to be any connection. Several times, she made the same response to Griffin's suggestions: "It's too late."

9   That weekend, neither FaNee nor her parents brought up the subject of Griffin's visit. Leo Cooper has spoken of the weekend as being particularly happy; a friend of FaNee's who stayed over remembers it as particularly strained. FaNee stayed home from school on Monday because of a bad headache—she often had bad headaches—but felt well enough on Monday evening to drive to the library. She was to be home at nine. When she wasn't, Mrs. Cooper began to phone her friends. Finally, around ten, Leo Cooper got into his other car and took a swing around Halls—past the teenage hangouts like the Exxon station and the Pizza Hut and the Smoky Mountain Market. Then he took a second swing. At eleven, FaNee was still not home.

10   She hadn't gone to the library. She had picked up two girl friends and driven to the home of a third, where everyone took five Valium tablets. Then the four girls drove over to the Exxon station, where they met four boys from the crowd. After a while, the group bought some beer and some marijuana and reassembled at Charlie Stevens's trailer. Charlie Stevens was five or six years older than everyone else in the group—a skinny, slow-thinking young man with long black hair and a sparse beard. He was married and had a child, but he and his wife had separated; she was back in Union County with the baby. Stevens had remained in their trailer—parked in the yard near his mother's house, in a back-road area of Knox County dominated by decrepit, unpainted sheds and run-down trailers and rusted-out automobiles. Stevens had picked up FaNee at home once or twice—apparently, more as a driver for the group than as a date—and the Coopers, having learned that his unsuitability extended to being married, had asked her not to see him.

11   In Charlie's trailer, which had no heat or electricity, the group drank beer and passed around joints, keeping warm with blankets. By eleven or so, FaNee was what one of her friends has called "super-mess-up." Her speech was slurred. She was having trouble keeping her balance. She had decided not to go home. She had apparently persuaded herself that her parents intended to send her away to some sort of home for incorrigibles. "It's too late," she said to one of her friends. "It's just too late." It was decided that one of the boys, David Munsey, who was more or less the leader of the group, would drive the Coopers' car to FaNee's house, where FaNee and Charlie Stevens would pick him up in Steven's car—a worn Pinto with four bald tires, one light, and a dragging muffler. FaNee wrote a note to her parents, and then, perhaps because her handwriting was suffering the effects of beer and marijuana and Valium, asked Stevens to rewrite it on a large piece of paper, which would be left on the seat of the Coopers' car. The Stevens version was just about the same as FaNee's, except that Stevens left out a couple of sentences about trying to work things out ("I'm willing to try") and, not having won any spelling championship himself, he misspelled a few words, like "tomorrow." The note said, "Dear Mom and Dad. Sorry I'm late. Very late. I left your car because I thought you might need it tomorrow. I love you all, but this is something I just had to do, but don't worry. I'm with a very good friend. Love you all. FaNee. P.S. Please try to understand I love you all very much, really I do. Love me if you have a chance."

12   At eleven-thirty or so, Leo Cooper was sitting in his living room, looking out the window at his driveway—a long gravel road that runs almost four hundred feet from the house to Brown Gap Road. He saw the car that FaNee had been driving pull into the driveway. "She's home," he called to his wife, who had just left the room. Cooper walked out on the deck over the garage. The car had stopped at the end of the driveway, and the lights had gone out. He got into his other car and drove to the end of the driveway. David Munsey had already joined Charlie Stevens and FaNee, and the Pinto was just leaving, travelling at a normal rate of speed. Leo Cooper pulled out on the road behind them.

13   Stevens turned left on Crippen Road, a road that has a field on one side and two or three small houses on the other, and there Cooper pulled his car in front of the Pinto and stopped, blocking the way. He got out and walked toward the Pinto. Suddenly, Stevens put the car in reverse, backed into a driveway a hundred yards behind him, and sped off. Cooper jumped in his car and gave chase. Stevens raced back to Brown Gap Road, ran a stop sign there, ran another stop sign at Maynardville Highway, turned north, veered off onto the old Andersonville Pike, a nearly abandoned road that runs parallel to the highway, and then crossed back over the highway to the narrow, dark country roads on the other side. Stevens sometimes drove with his lights out. He took some of the corners by suddenly applying his hand brake to make the car swerve around in a ninety-degree turn. He was in familiar territory—he actually passed his trailer—and Cooper had difficulty keeping up. Past the trailer, Stevens swept down a hill into a sharp left turn that took him onto Foust Hollow Road, a winding, hilly road not much wider than one car.

14   At a fork, Cooper thought he had lost the Pinto. He started to go right and then saw what seemed to be a spark from Stevens's dragging muffler off to the left, in the darkness. Cooper took the left fork, down Salem Church Road. He went down a hill and then up a long, curving hill to a crest, where he saw the Stevens car ahead. "I saw the car airborne. Up in the air," he later testified. "It was up in the air. And then it completely rolled over one more time. It started to make another flip forward, and just as it started to flip to the other side it flipped back this way, and my daughter's body came out."

15   Cooper slammed on his brakes and skidded to a stop up against the Pinto. "Book!" Stevens shouted—the group's equivalent of "Scram!" Stevens and Munsey disappeared into the darkness. "It was dark, no

one around, and so I started yelling for FaNee," Cooper had testified. "I thought it was an eternity before I could find her body, wedged under the back end of that car. . . . I tried everything I could, and saw that I couldn't get her loose. So I ran to a trailer back up to the top of the hill back up there to try to get that lady to call to get me some help, and then apparently she didn't think that I was serious. . . . I took the jack out of my car and got under, and it was dark, still couldn't see too much what was going on . . . and started prying and got her loose, and I don't know how. And then I dragged her over to the side, and, of course, at the time I felt reasonably assured that she was gone, because her head was completely—on one side just as if you had taken a sledgehammer and just hit it and bashed it in. And I did have the pleasure of one thing. I had the pleasure of listening to her breathe about the last three times she ever breathed in her life."

16   David Munsey did not return to the wreck that night, but Charlie Stevens did. Leo Cooper was kneeling next to his daughter's body. Cooper insisted that Stevens come close enough to see FaNee. "He was kneeling down next to her," Stevens later testified. "And he said, 'Do you know what you've done? Do you really know what you've done?' Like that. And I just looked at her, and I said, 'Yes,' and just stood there. Because I couldn't say nothing." There was, of course, a legal decision to be made about who was responsible for FaNee Cooper's death. In a deposition, Stevens said he had been fleeing for his life. He testified that when Leo Cooper blocked Crippen Road, FaNee had said that her father had a gun and intended to hurt them. Stevens was bound over and eventually indicted for involuntary manslaughter. Leo Cooper testified that when he approached the Pinto on Crippen Road, FaNee had a strange expression that he had never seen before. "It wasn't like FaNee, and I knew something was wrong," he said. "My concern was to get FaNee out of the car." The district attorney's office asked that Cooper be bound over for reckless driving, but the judge declined to do so. "Any father would have done what he did," the judge said. "I can see no criminal act on the part of Mr. Cooper."

17   Almost two years passed before Charlie Stevens was brought to trial. Part of the problem was assuring the presence of David Munsey, who had joined the Navy but seemed inclined to assign his own leaves. In the meantime, the Coopers went to court with a civil suit—they had

"uninsured-motorist coverage," which requires their insurance company to cover any defendant who has no insurance of his own—and they won a judgment. There were ways of assigning responsibility, of course, which had nothing to do with the law, civil or criminal. A lot of people in Knoxville thought that Leo Cooper had, in the words of his lawyer, "done what any daddy worth his salt would have done." There were others who believed that FaNee Cooper had lost her life because Leo Cooper had lost his temper. Leo Cooper was not among those who expressed any doubts about his actions. Unlike his wife, whose eyes filled with tears at almost any mention of FaNee, Cooper seemed able, even eager to go over the details of the accident again and again. With the help of a school-board security man, he conducted his own investigation. He drove over the route dozens of times. "I've thought about it every day, and I guess I will the rest of my life," he said as he and his lawyer and the prosecuting attorney went over the route again the day before Charlie Stevens's trial finally began. "But I can't tell any alternative for a father. I simply wanted her out of that car. I'd have done the same thing again, even at the risk of losing her."

18   Tennessee law permits the family of a victim to hire a special prosecutor to assist the district attorney. The lawyer who acted for the Coopers in the civil case helped prosecute Charlie Stevens. Both he and the district attorney assured the jurors that the presence of a special prosecutor was not to be construed to mean that the Coopers were vindictive. Outside the courtroom, Leo Cooper said that the verdict was of no importance to him—that he felt sorry, in a way, for Charlie Stevens. But there were people in Knoxville who thought Cooper had a lot riding on the prosecution of Charlie Stevens. If Stevens was not guilty of FaNee Cooper's death—found so by twelve of his peers—who was?

19   At the trial, Cooper testified emotionally and remarkably graphically about pulling FaNee out from under the car and watching her die in his arms. Charlie Stevens had shaved his beard and cut his hair, but the effort did not transform him into an impressive witness. His lawyer— trying to argue that it would have been impossible for Stevens to concoct the story about FaNee's having mentioned a gun, as the prosecution strongly implied—said, "His mind is such that if you ask him a question you can hear his mind go around, like an old mill creaking."

Stevens did not deny the recklessness of his driving or the sorry condition of his car. It happened to be the only car he had available to flee in, he said, and he had fled in fear for his life.

20   The prosecution said that Stevens could have let FaNee out of the car when her father stopped them, or could have gone to the commercial strip on the Maynardville Highway for protection. The prosecution said that Leo Cooper had done what he might have been expected to do under the circumstances—alone, late at night, his daughter in danger. The defense said precisely the same about Stevens: he had done what he might have been expected to do when being pursued by a man he had reason to be afraid of. "I don't fault Mr. Cooper for what he did, but I'm sorry he did it," the defense attorney said. "I'm sorry the girl said what she said." The jury deliberated for eighteen minutes. Charlie Stevens was found guilty. The jury recommended a sentence of from two to five years in the state penitentiary. At the announcement, Leo Cooper broke down and cried, JoAnn Cooper's eyes filled with tears; she blinked them back and continued to stare straight ahead.

21   In a way, the Coopers might still strike a casual visitor as an ideal family—handsome parents, a bright and bubbly teenage daughter, a little boy learning the hook shot from his father, a warm house with some land around it. FaNee's presence is there, of course. A picture of her, with a small bouquet of flowers over it, hangs in the living room. One of her poems is displayed in a frame on a table. Even if Leo Cooper continues to think about that night for the rest of his life, there are questions he can never answer. Was there a way that Leo and JoAnn Cooper could have prevented FaNee from choosing the path she chose? Would she still be alive if Leo Cooper had not jumped into his car and driven to the end of the driveway to investigate? Did she in fact tell Charlie Stevens that her father would hurt them—or even that her father had a gun? Did she want to get away from her family even at the risk of tearing around dark country roads in Charlie Stevens's dismal Pinto? Or did she welcome the risk? The poem of FaNee's that the Coopers have displayed is one she wrote a week before her death.

> I think I'm going to die
> And I really don't know why.
> But look in my eye
> When I tell you good-bye.
> I think I'm going to die.

Reading Closely and Thinking Critically

1. What does Trillin note are effects of being a Freak?

2. Was the fact that FaNee was a Freak a remote or an immediate cause of her death?

3. In what ways were FaNee's parents a factor in her downward spiral? Were her parents a remote or an immediate cause of FaNee's death?

4. FaNee remarks twice, "It's too late" (paragraph 4 and 8). Explain the significance of this remark.

5. Why does Cooper consider it a "pleasure" that he heard FanNee breathe her final breaths?

6. In paragraph 17, Trillin says, "There were ways of assigning responsibility, of course, which had nothing to do with the law, civil or criminal." What does Trillin mean?

Examining Structure and Strategy

1. What do you think of the opening paragraph? How does it create interest? In addition to creating interest, the paragraph suggests that FaNee was really not the ideal child mentioned in the first sentence. How does Trillin suggest that? How does Trillin use irony as part of the suggestion?

2. In what order does Trillin arrange his details?

3. Evaluate the effectiveness of the title.

4. Trillin's purpose is to inform. Why do you think Trillin wants the reader to know the details of FaNee's death?

5. How does Trillin convey his own opinion about who is responsible for FaNee's death?

Considering Language and Style

1. How would you describe Trillin's writing style? Is that style well suited to his purpose? Explain.

2. Consult a dictionary if you are unsure of the meaning of any of these words: *magnanimous* (paragraph 1), *batik* (paragraph 1), *Valium* (paragraph 10), *decrepit* (paragraph 10), *incorrigible* (paragraph 11), *deposition* (paragraph 16).

For Group Discussion or Writing
Stevens was found guilty of involuntary manslaughter. With some class-mates, consider whether or not you agree with the verdict. Also, discuss whether or not FaNee's father and mother are responsible in any way.

Writing Assignments

1. *In your journal.* Explain the meaning of the note that FaNee wrote and left in the car (paragraph 11). For example, what do you think she meant when she said, "Love me if you have a chance"?

2. *Using the pattern.* At FaNee's high school, the social poles were the Jocks and the Freaks. Describe the social poles at your high school and explain the effect membership in one of these groups had on a person.

3. *Using the pattern.* Explain the causes of a particular self-destructive behavior: using drugs, drinking excessively, smoking cigarettes, having an eating disorder, driving recklessly, drinking and driving, and so forth.

4. *Using the pattern.* If you knew a teenager who died, discuss the effects of the death on those left behind.

5. *Considering a theme.* Many teenagers are seriously troubled, some so much that they consider suicide. Devise a program for high school personnel that would help them identify and deal with troubled teens.

6. *Connecting the readings.* Read "Whom to Believe?" (page 141) and then write a three- to five-page account of a portion of Charlie Stevens's trial. Like Satter does in "Whom to Believe?" emphasize the fundamental uncertainty about the truth — in this case, whether Stevens was right to feel threatened or whether Cooper was right to feel that his daughter was at risk. Also like Satter, incorporate dialogue into your account.

ADDITIONAL ESSAY ASSIGNMENTS

See pages 391 and 392 for suggestions for writing cause-and-effect analysis and for a revision checklist.

1. If you have been the victim of sexual harassment, or if you have witnessed sexual harassment, write about the causes and/or effects of this problem. If you have not been a victim or witness, gather information by interviewing people who have been victims or witnesses or by visiting your campus affirmative action office or human resources office.

2. Analyze the causes or effects of stress in college or high school students.

3. If you have difficulty with a particular subject (English, math, science, etc.), explain why the subject causes you problems and/or the effect of having difficulty with that subject.

4. Explain the effects of an illness or disability on you or someone you know.

5. Explain the techniques television commercials (or magazine ads) use to influence us. As an alternative, explain the effects of commercials (or magazine ads) on us.

6. Select a bad habit you have (for example, procrastinating, smoking, overeating, or nail biting) and explain its causes and effects.

7. Tell about the effects of something that happened to you in school (for example, getting cut from the basketball team, being elected class president, becoming homecoming queen, or failing a course).

8. Discuss the effects of a technological advance (for example, the Internet, the compact disc, the VCR, the camcorder, or the microwave oven).

9. Select a problem on your campus (for example, poor student housing, high tuition, or degree requirements) and analyze the effects on students to persuade those in authority to remedy the problem.

10. Analyze how the neighborhood in which you grew up affected you.

11. Explain why students cheat and the effects cheating has on students.

12. If you have a particular fear (of heights, of math, of failure, and so on), explain the causes and/or effects of that fear.

13. If you ever moved to a new town, explain how the move affected you.

14. If you have children, explain the effects of becoming a parent. If you want, you can make this essay humorous.

15. If you are an international student, explain how you have been affected by living and attending school in this country.

16. Explain why football (or baseball or basketball) is so popular in this country and how the sport affects American culture.

17. Explain the effects of the movement to achieve gender equality (or desegregation, or gay rights, or affirmative action).

18. People in the United States value youth. Analyze the effects of this youth orientation.

19. Select a person who has had a significant impact on you (for example, a coach, a minister, a teacher, or a friend) and explain the effects this individual has had on you.

20. *Cause-and-effect analysis in context:* Assume you are a member of a consumer affairs panel that has secured a grant to study violence in the media. Write a report that explains why people enjoy violent movies. Your audience is other members of the panel, and your purpose is to provide them with information.

⑥ CLASSIFICATION-DIVISION

THE PATTERN

Both classification and division are methods of grouping and ordering. *Classification* takes a number of items and groups them into categories, and *division* takes one entity and breaks it down into its parts. Consider your college, for example. It orders courses in the catalog by placing them into groups according to the departments that offer those courses (English, biology, mathematics, and so on); this is *classifying*. In addition, your college organizes itself by breaking into components (the School of Education, the School of Arts and Sciences, the School of Engineering, and so on); this is *division*.

Sometimes division and classification are each performed by itself, but more often they are companion operations performed together for a specific purpose. For example, say that you are the manager of a video store and you want to organize all the tapes so customers can locate titles easily. First, you would use *division* to establish a breakdown into groupings, such as westerns, musicals, science fiction, romance, horror films, and adventure movies. Then you would use *classification* to sort the videos into the appropriate categories—*Star Wars* into the science fiction area, *Friday the 13th* into the horror movie area, and so on. Similarly, when you write, you will often find yourself dividing and then classifying.

Classification and division are so much a part of our lives that you do not have to look very far to find examples of them: the yellow pages of your phone book groups telephone numbers according to kinds of businesses; your biology text orders animals according to whether they are mammals, birds, reptiles, and so on; your local supermarket arranges items in aisles according to whether they are fruits, vegetables, meats, canned goods, cleaning products, and so on. Classification and division are common because they help us order items or pieces of information to study them easier, retrieve them faster, or deal with them more efficiently. Imagine, for a moment, a world without groupings. How hard would it be to find what you need in the grocery store or to locate a book in the library?

THE PURPOSES OF CLASSIFICATION-DIVISION

A writer can classify or divide in order to *inform* the reader. Sometimes a writer wants to inform the reader of the relative merits of the items grouped so the reader can choose one wisely. For example, you might group various CD and tape clubs according to expense and variety of selections so the reader can decide which club to join. Sometimes a writer classifies or divides to give the reader a fresh appreciation of the familiar. In "White Lies" (page 458), Sissela Bok groups white lies, something we all know about, in order to help us better understand them and their significance. Sometimes a classification-division helps the reader understand something he or she is not familiar with. For example, "Territorial Behaviour" (page 488) groups the kinds of human territory. A reader who knows little about anthropology is likely to find this information highly informative.

A classification-division can also allow the writer to *express feelings and relate experience.* This would be the case if you classified various ways to celebrate Halloween in order to relate your own childhood experiences with the holiday or if you classified kinds of professors to express how you feel about each type.

Very often, a classification-division has a *persuasive purpose,* as is the case with "The Ways of Meeting Oppression" (page 463). In this essay, Dr. Martin Luther King, Jr., groups the ways to deal with oppression in order to convince the reader that one of those ways is better than the rest and should be employed.

Finally, classification-division can *entertain* the reader. For example, to amuse your audience, you could group all your eccentric relatives according to their amusing traits and behaviors.

Classification-division is often the sole method of development in essays, but it can also be combined with other patterns as well. For example, in "Shades of Black" (page 469), Mary Mebane explains color discrimination among African-Americans and its effects on young females. To help make her point, she combines this cause-and-effect analysis with the classification of people by social class and the classification of African-American women according to how they find a place for themselves.

Classification-Division in College Writing

You are likely to have many occasions to employ classification-division in your college classes. For example, in an education class, you may need to explain the components of a successful lesson plan to demonstrate that you can write such a plan. Similarly, a business class might require you to note the components of a sound business plan to demonstrate that you could develop a plan, and a communications class may require you to give the components of an effective survey to show that you know how to construct one.

At times, you will write classification-division to show that you understand the relative merits and uses of various categories of something. For example, in an advertising class, you could write a paper that classifies the kinds of direct mail campaigns, noting what kind of audience each approach appeals to and what kind of product each approach is best suited for. Such a paper would demonstrate that you knew when to use each kind of campaign.

Perhaps most frequently, you will write classification-division to demonstrate your comprehension of information. This would be the case in a biology class that required you to classify the mating behavior of birds or in a communications class that required you to explain the types of political rhetoric.

SELECTING A PRINCIPLE FOR CLASSIFICATION-DIVISION

Most things can be classified or divided more than one way, depending on the ordering principle used. For example, you could group colleges according to their cost, their location, the degrees they offer, their faculty, or prestige. Cost, location, degrees offered, faculty, prestige—each of these is an *ordering principle*.

Obviously, you must decide which principle you will use to group the items under consideration. When you do so, keep your purpose in mind and choose a principle compatible with that

purpose. For example, if you were classifying white lies to entertain your reader, your ordering principle would not be the degree of hurtfulness of the lies; however, it might be the degree of
inventiveness of the lies. If your purpose were to inform, then degree of hurtfulness would be an acceptable ordering principle.

When you establish your ordering principle, be sure to
pick something that allows for at least three groups. If you have
only two groups, then you are really comparing and contrasting,
rather than classifying or dividing.

SELECTING DETAILS

When you select detail, do not omit any groupings, or your classification-division will be incomplete. Say, for example, that you
are grouping the forms of financial aid to inform students of ways
to get help paying for college. You could include these groupings:
loans, grants, and scholarships. However, by omitting work-
study programs, your essay is less helpful than it could—and
should—be.

On the other hand, you should avoid including groups that
are not compatible with your ordering principle. For example, if
you are classifying coaches according to how important winning
is to them, you might have these groupings: coaches who think
winning is everything; coaches who think winning is less important than learning and having fun; coaches who think winning is
completely unimportant. In such a classification, you could not
include coaches who are inexperienced, because that group is
unrelated to the ordering principle.

In general, classification-division will include an explanation of what the groupings are and what elements are in each. Beyond that, your supporting detail can include a wide range of
patterns of development meant to explain the characteristics of
each grouping. Say, for example, that you are classifying Halloween celebrations into three types: the sedate, the jolly, and the
scary. You could use *examples* to illustrate the kinds of harmless
pranks people play for a jolly celebration; you could *describe* the

frightening costumes people wear for a scary celebration; you could *narrate* the story of your last Halloween celebration, which was sedate. In addition, you could use *process analysis* to tell how to prepare for a scary Halloween celebration; you could use *cause-and-effect analysis* to explain the effects of the pranks played during the jolly celebration; you could use *definition* to explain the meaning of a sedate celebration; you could use *comparison-contrast* to show the similarities and differences among the three kinds of celebrations. Of course, you will not use all these patterns in a single essay, but they are all available for your consideration as ways to develop your details.

STRUCTURING CLASSIFICATION-DIVISION

The thesis for classification-division can be handled a variety of ways. First, you can indicate what you are classifying or dividing and the ordering principle you will use, like this:

> **The current crop of television talk shows can be classified according to the kinds of guests that appear.** (Television talk shows will be classified; the ordering principle is the guests that appear.)

Another way to handle the thesis is to indicate what you are classifying or dividing, without mentioning the ordering principle. Here's an example:

> **Although more talk shows are on television than ever before, all of these shows are one of three types.** (The thesis makes it clear that television talk shows will be grouped, but the ordering principle is not given.)

A third way to handle the thesis is to indicate what will be classified or divided, along with the specific groupings that will be discussed, like this:

> **Television talk shows can be distinguished according to whether the guests are primarily entertainers, politicians, or oddballs.** (The thesis indicates that television talk shows will be grouped, and the groupings will be those with guests who are entertainers, those with guests who are politicians, and those who are oddballs.)

Organizing a classification-division essay can be easier when topic sentences introduce the discussion of each grouping. For example, the classification of talk shows might have topic sentences like these:

The most common variety of talk show has entertainers for guests. (A discussion of talk shows with entertainers as guests would follow.)

Although more intellectual than the first type, another frequently seen talk show has politicians for guests. (A discussion of talk shows with politicians as guests would follow.)

Increasingly popular is the talk show that showcases oddballs. (A discussion of talk shows with oddballs as guests would follow.)

To move smoothly from one grouping to another, you can include transitional phrases in your topic sentences, phrases like these:

Another category . . .

A more significant group . . .

A more common kind . . .

A second division of . . .

When you order your details, consider your thesis. If it notes your groupings, then you should present those groupings in the same order they appear in the thesis. Otherwise, order is not much of an issue, unless your purpose is persuasive. Then you are likely to present the recommended grouping last. This is the case in "The Ways of Meeting Oppression," when Dr. Martin Luther King, Jr., presents last the method he wants people to adopt.

When you are discussing the same characteristics for each grouping, you should present those characteristics in the same order each time. Thus, if you group Halloween celebrations and discuss decorations, costumes, and degree of scariness for each kind of celebration, then you should discuss these features in the same order for each grouping.

SUGGESTIONS FOR WRITING CLASSIFICATION-DIVISION

1. To help order your draft, try writing your ordering principle at the top of a page. Then below that, write each of your groupings or divisions at the top of a column. Three groupings or divisions will give you three columns, four will give you four columns, and so on. Under each column write out the elements in the grouping or division. Number the columns in the order you want to treat them. You now have a form of outline for your draft.

2. To discover methods for developing your points, ask yourself the following questions of every element in your columns. You can make notes on your outline, if you like.

    a. Can I narrate a story to develop this point?

    b. Can I describe something to develop this point?

    c. Can I analyze a process to develop this point?

    d. Can I analyze causes and/or effects to develop this point?

    e. Can I provide an example to develop this point?

    f. Can I define something to develop this point?

    g. Can I compare and/or contrast something to develop this point?

3. Using your outline as a guide, write your draft in one sitting without worrying about grammar, spelling, punctuation, or anything else.

Checklist for Revising Classification-Division

1. Do you have at least three groupings?
2. Have you included all relevant groupings?
3. Have you omitted groups unrelated to your ordering principle?
4. Does your thesis indicate that you are classifying or dividing? Should it indicate your ordering principle?
5. Have you used transitional words to move from grouping to grouping?
6. If you have discussed the same characteristics for each grouping, do they appear in the same order each time?

ANNOTATED STUDENT ESSAY

Student-author David Wolfe uses classification to inform his reader about the origins of some common expressions. As you read, notice how the author uses examples to help make his point.

Strictly Speaking

1   Expressions derived from outdoor life are so ingrained in everyday English that we fail to notice them or consider their origins. However, it is interesting to pause and think about these terms, and one way to do that is to look at three basic categories of expressions: those derived from the use of firearms, those derived from hunting, and those derived from the characteristics of wildlife or game.

Paragraph 1
This is the introduction. The thesis (the last sentence) indicates that classification will occur, and it gives the categories that will be used.

2   Some common sayings come directly from the use of firearms. For example, if we buy something "lock, stock, and barrel," we have purchased the whole object or believed the whole story. This expression originally meant to buy the whole gun by purchasing its three parts: the "lock" as in the flintlock, the wooden "stock," and the metal "barrel." We also talk about "going off half-cocked," which means taking action or setting out without being fully prepared. This expression goes back to having a gun on "half-cock." In the half-cocked position, the hammer is between the relaxed position and the fully cocked position, which means the gun is halfway between unready and fully ready for firing. Often we say we had our "sights set on" something or had a goal "in our sights." Both of these expressions refer to aiming a gun at something. Also, we can be "primed and ready," or fully prepared, as when a flintlock rifle is fully primed or prepared and ready to fire.

Paragraph 2
The first sentence is the topic sentence. It presents the first category. The supporting detail is examples of expressions in the category.

3   A second group of expressions is derived from hunting. For example, the word "hello" has its origins there. It comes from hunters calling out "hulloa" or "haloo" when they saw other hunters in the woods in order to attract attention and avoid being accidentally hurt. "Stop beating around the bush" is another example of a hunting expression. It comes from the European practice of using "beaters" or people to drive game out of the brush for the hunter to shoot at. To do the job properly, beaters had to get into the middle of the bush where the game was. Otherwise, they were

Paragraph 3
The topic sentence is the first sentence. It presents the second category. Supporting details are examples. Note the transition provided by *a second group, for example, another example,* and *similarly.*

not getting the job done because they were beating around the bush. If we "make tracks," we hurry. Originally, this expression referred to an animal going in a hurry and thus leaving behind a set of tracks that were easy to follow. Being on "the right trail" refers to doing something properly or going in the right direction, but its original meaning referred to a hunter being on the right trail while tracking game. Similarly, if we are "barking up the wrong tree," we are as mistaken as the hunting dogs that are howling up one tree when the raccoon is out on the limb of a different tree.

4   Sayings related to wildlife or game are also interesting. We brag about saving money when we are "feathering our nests" or "building up our nest eggs," the way a bird does in the spring. We may be called "owl-eyed" for wearing glasses or be "wise as an owl" for knowing the right answers. If we are "blind as a bat," we can't see very well, just as a bat has poor vision. If we have a bad disposition, we are "grouchy as a bear" or told "don't be such a bear," since bears have angry temperaments. In addition, there are two ways we can get "skunked." We can actually get sprayed by a skunk, or we can lose a game of some kind very badly—in either case, we lose.

Paragraph 4
The first sentence is the topic sentence. It includes the transition *also* and presents the next category. The supporting details are examples.

5   Expressions from the outdoors are so common that even those of us who never hunt, shoot, or get close to animals will find ourselves drawing on vocabulary derived from these sources, a fact you may be more aware of from now on.

Paragraph 5
The conclusion repeats the idea in the introduction that these expressions are ingrained in English.

WAIT DIVISIONS
Tom Bodett

Born in 1955 in Champaign, Illinois, and raised in Sturgis, Michigan, Tom Bodett attended Michigan State University. He worked as a logger, contractor, and deckhand in Oregon and Alaska. A well-known humorist, Bodett has been heard locally on Alaskan radio and nationally on National Public Radio. His humorous essays are collected in As Far as You Can Go Without a Passport *(1985),* Small Comforts *(1987), and* The End of the Road *(1989). In the following essay, taken from* Small Comforts, *Bodett classifies for only one reason—to amuse his audience. As you read, notice how Bodett achieves his humorous effects.*

THE PATTERN	THE PURPOSE
classification-division	*to entertain*

1   I read somewhere that we spend a full third of our lives waiting. I've also read where we spend a third of our lives sleeping, a third working, and a third at our leisure. Now either somebody's lying, or we're spending all our leisure time waiting to go to work or sleep. That can't be true or league softball and Winnebagos never would have caught on.

2   So where are we doing all of this waiting and what does it mean to an impatient society like ours? Could this unseen waiting be the source of all our problems? A shrinking economy? The staggering deficit? Declining mental health and moral apathy? Probably not, but let's take a look at some of the more classic "waits" anyway.

3   The very purest form of waiting is what we'll call the *Watched-Pot Wait.* This type of wait is without a doubt the most annoying of all. Take filling up the kitchen sink. There is absolutely nothing you can do while this is going on but keep both eyes glued to the sink until it's full. If you try to cram in some extracurricular activity, you're asking for it. So you stand there, your hands on the faucets, and wait. A temporary suspension of duties. During these waits it's common for your eyes to lapse out of focus. The brain disengages from the body and wanders around the imagination in search of distraction. It finds none and

springs back into action only when the water runs over the edge of the counter and onto your socks.

4   The phrase "A watched pot never boils" comes of this experience. Pots don't care whether they are watched or not; the problem is that nobody has ever seen a pot actually come to a boil. While they are waiting, their brains turn off.

5   Other forms of the Watched-Pot Wait would include waiting for your drier to quit at the laundromat, waiting for your toast to pop out of the toaster, or waiting for a decent idea to come to mind at a typewriter. What they all have in common is that they render the waiter helpless and mindless.

6   A cousin to the Watched-Pot Wait is the *Forced Wait*. Not for the weak of will, this one requires a bit of discipline. The classic Forced Wait is starting your car in the winter and letting it slowly idle up to temperature before engaging the clutch. This is every bit as uninteresting as watching a pot, but with one big difference. You have a choice. There is nothing keeping you from racing to work behind a stone-cold engine save the thought of the early demise of several thousand dollars' worth of equipment you haven't paid for yet. Thoughts like that will help you get through a Forced Wait.

7   Properly preparing packaged soup mixes also requires a Forced Wait. Directions are very specific on these mixes. "Bring three cups water to boil, add mix, simmer three minutes, remove from heat, let stand five minutes." I have my doubts that anyone has ever actually done this. I'm fairly spineless when it comes to instant soups and usually just boil the bejeezus out of them until the noodles sink. Some things just aren't worth a Forced Wait.

8   All in all Forced Waiting requires a lot of a thing call *patience,* which is a virtue. Once we get into virtues I'm out of my element, and can't expound on the virtues of virtue, or even lie about them. So let's move on to some of the more far-reaching varieties of waiting.

9   The *Payday Wait* is certainly a leader in the long-term anticipation field. The problem with waits that last more than a few minutes is that you have to actually do other things in the meantime. Like go to work. By far the most aggravating feature of the Payday Wait is that even though you must keep functioning in the interludes, there is less and less you are able to do as the big day draws near. For some of us the last few days are best spent alone in a dark room for fear we'll ac-

cidentally do something that costs money. With the Payday Wait comes a certain amount of hope that we'll make it, and faith that everything will be all right once we do.

10   With the introduction of faith and hope, I've ushered in the most potent wait class of all, the *Lucky-Break Wait,* or the *Wait for One's Ship to Come In.* This type of wait is unusual in that it is for the most part voluntary. Unlike the Forced Wait, which is also voluntary, waiting for your lucky break does not necessarily mean that it will happen.

11   Turning one's life into a waiting game of these proportions requires gobs of the aforementioned faith and hope, and is strictly for the optimists among us. For these people life is the thing that happens to them while they're waiting for something to happen to them. On the surface it seems as ridiculous as following the directions on soup mixes, but the Lucky-Break Wait performs an outstanding service to those who take it upon themselves to do it. As long as one doesn't come to rely on it, wishing for a few good things to happen never hurt anybody.

12   In the end it is obvious that we certainly do spend a good deal of our time waiting. The person who said we do it a third of the time may have been going easy on us. It makes a guy wonder how anything at all gets done around here. But things do get done, people grow old, and time boils on whether you watch it or not.

13   The next time you're standing at the sink waiting for it to fill while cooking soup mix that you'll have to eat until payday or until a large bag of cash falls out of the sky, don't despair. You're probably just as busy as the next guy.

Reading Closely and Thinking Critically

1. Bodett does not specifically state his ordering principle; yet there is a logic to his groupings. What do you think his ordering principle is?

2. According to Bodett, why is his classification important?

3. What kind of reader do you think "Wait Divisions" would appeal to? How do you know?

4. How does the Watched-Pot Wait differ from the Forced Wait? How does the Forced Wait differ from the Lucky-Break Wait?

5. Why do you think we find waiting so annoying?

Examining Structure and Strategy

1. Which sentence is the thesis of "Wait Divisions"?

2. Bodett introduces each of his groupings in a topic sentence. What are these topic sentences?

3. In what kind of order does Bodett present his groupings?

4. Bodett uses examples in paragraphs 3, 6, and 7. How do these examples help him develop his classification?

5. How does Bodett relate his conclusion (paragraphs 12 and 13) to the rest of his essay?

Considering Language and Style

1. Bodett's tone is relaxed, informal, conversational, and familiar. How does he achieve that tone?

2. How do the rhetorical questions in paragraph 2 contribute to the essay's humor?

3. Consult a dictionary if you are unsure of the meaning of any of these words: *Winnebagos* (paragraph 1), *render* (paragraph 5), *demise* (paragraph 6), *potent* (paragraph 10).

For Group Discussion or Writing

With some classmates, identify the aspects of the essay that you find the most amusing. What techniques does Bodett employ to create the humor?

Writing Assignments

1. *In your journal.* Think back to recent times when you were forced to wait (in a traffic jam, in a checkout line, in a doctor's office, and so on). Explain how you felt while you were waiting and what you did to pass the time. Do you need to alter what you think, feel, and do when you must wait?

2. *Using the pattern.* Like Bodett, write a humorous classification of some annoying aspect of life: poor driving practices, annoying shoppers in supermarkets, annoying telephone calls, frustrating salesclerks, and so on. If you like, use some of the humorous techniques in "Wait Divisions."

3. *Using the pattern.* Just as there are many times when we find ourselves waiting, there are many times when we find ourselves hurrying up. With that in mind, write a humorous classification called "Rush Divisions."

4. *Using the pattern.* Using a different ordering principle and therefore different groupings, write your own classification of the kinds of waiting people engage in.

5. *Considering a theme.* For many people, stress is a troublesome fact of life, and waiting can contribute to that stress. Discuss other sources of stress that people must cope with on a routine basis. If you like, you can consider these questions: What are the effects of that stress? How does it affect the quality of life? Is stress the inevitable price we pay for certain lifestyles? Is the price worth it?

6. *Connecting the readings.* Read "University Days" (page 211) and write a humorous classification of some aspect of college life: teachers, students, study techniques, ways to take examinations, roommates, advisors, and so on.

WHITE LIES
Sissela Bok

Born in 1934, Sissela Bok earned her Ph.D. from Harvard University. She is a frequent writer on ethics in medicine and government and has lectured on medical ethics at Harvard and MIT. Bok won the Orwell Award for her book Lying: Moral Choice in Private and Public Life *(1978), from which "White Lies" is taken. In the selection, Bok informs her reader of the kinds of white lies, and she makes a persuasive point about the harm these lies cause. As you read, consider how often you tell white lies.*

THE PATTERN	THE PURPOSES
classification-division	*to inform and to persuade*

1   White lies are at the other end of the spectrum of deception from lies in a serious crisis. They are the most common and the most trivial forms that duplicity can take. The fact that they are so common provides their protective coloring. And their very triviality, when compared to more threatening lies, makes it seem unnecessary or even absurd to condemn them. Some consider *all* well-intentioned lies, however momentous, to be white; in this book, I shall adhere to the narrower usage: a white lie, in this sense, is a falsehood not meant to injure anyone, and of little moral import. I want to ask whether there *are* such lies; and if there are, whether their cumulative consequences are still without harm; and, finally whether many lies are not defended as "white" which are in fact harmful in their own right.

2   Many small subterfuges may not even be intended to mislead. They are only "white lies" in the most marginal sense. Take, for example, the many social exchanges: "How nice to see you!" or "Cordially Yours." These and a thousand other polite expressions are so much taken for granted that if someone decided, in the name of total honesty, not to employ them, he might well give the impression of an indifference he did not possess. The justification for continuing to use such accepted formulations is that they deceive no one, except possibly those unfamiliar with the language.

3   A social practice more clearly deceptive is that of giving a false excuse so as not to hurt the feelings of someone making an invitation or request: to say one "can't" do what in reality one may not *want* to do. Once again, the false excuse may prevent unwarranted inferences of greater hostility to the undertaking than one may well feel. Merely to say that one can't do something, moreover, is not deceptive in the sense that an elaborately concocted story can be.

4   Still other white lies are told in an effort to flatter, to throw a cheerful interpretation on depressing circumstances, or to show gratitude for unwanted gifts. In the eyes of many, such white lies do not harm, provide needed support and cheer, and help dispel gloom and boredom. They preserve the equilibrium and often the humaneness of social relationships, and are usually accepted as excusable so long as they do not become excessive. Many argue, moreover, that such deception is so helpful and at times so necessary that it must be tolerated as an exception to a general policy against lying. Thus Bacon observed:

> Doth any man doubt, that if there were taken out of men's minds vain opinions, flattering hopes, false valuations, imaginations as one would, and the like, but it would leave the minds of a number of men poor shrunken things, full of melancholy and indisposition, and unpleasing to themselves?

5   Another kind of lie may actually be advocated as bringing a more substantial benefit, or avoiding a real harm, while seeming quite innocuous to those who tell the lies. Such are the placebos given for innumerable common ailments, and the pervasive use of inflated grades and recommendations for employment and promotion.

6   A large number of lies without such redeeming features are nevertheless often regarded as so trivial that they should be grouped with white lies. They are the lies told on the spur of the moment, for want of reflection, or to get out of a scrape, or even simply to pass the time. Such are the lies told to boast or exaggerate, or on the contrary to deprecate and understate; the many lies told or repeated in gossip; Rousseau's[1] lies told simply "in order to say something"; the embroidering on facts that seem too tedious in their own right; and the substitution of a quick lie for the lengthy explanations one might otherwise have to provide for something not worth spending time on.

---

[1]Jean-Jacques Rousseau (1712 – 1778) — a French philosopher and author.

7   Utilitarians often cite white lies as the *kind* of deception where their theory shows the benefits of common sense and clear thinking. A white lie, they hold, is trivial; it is either completely harmless, or so marginally harmful that the cost of detecting and evaluating the harm is much greater than the minute harm itself. In addition, the white lie can often actually be beneficial, thus further tipping the scales of utility. In a world with so many difficult problems, utilitarians might ask: Why take the time to weigh the minute pros and cons in telling someone that his tie is attractive when it is an abomination, or of saying to a guest that a broken vase was worthless? Why bother even to define such insignificant distortions or make mountains out of molehills by seeking to justify them?

8   Triviality surely does set limits to when moral inquiry is reasonable. But when we look more closely at practices such as placebo-giving, it becomes clear that all lies defended as "white" cannot be so easily dismissed. In the first place, the harmlessness of lies is notoriously disputable. What the liar perceives as harmless or even beneficial may not be so in the eyes of the deceived. Second, the failure to look at an entire practice rather than at their own isolated case often blinds liars to cumulative harm and expanding deceptive activities. Those who begin with white lies can come to resort to more frequent and more serious ones. Where some tell a few white lies, others may tell more. Because lines are so hard to draw, the indiscriminate use of such lies can lead to other deceptive practices. The aggregate harm from a large number of marginally harmful instances may, therefore, be highly undesirable in the end—for liars, those deceived, and honesty and trust more generally.

Reading Closely and Thinking Critically

1. What do you think Bok means when she says in paragraph 1, "The fact that [white lies] are so common provides their protective coloring"?

2. What kinds of white lies does Bok classify? What are the justifications for each of these kinds of white lies?

3. Who are the utilitarians that Bok refers to in paragraph 7? What is their view of white lies?

4. What is Bok's view of the white lie?

5. Is there any kind of white lie that Bok might find acceptable? Cite evidence from the selection to support your view.

Examining Structure and Strategy

1. What is Bok's ordering principle?

2. In what kind of order does Bok arrange her groupings?

3. Bok introduces her groupings with topic sentences. What are those topic sentences? What transitions appear in the topic sentences in paragraphs 4 and 5? What purpose do these transitions serve?

4. What approach does Bok take to the introduction? What approach does she take to the conclusion?

5. In paragraph 2, Bok gives examples of items in one of her groupings. What purpose do these examples serve? Would any other paragraphs benefit from the addition of examples? Explain.

6. How does Bok use cause-and-effect analysis? (Cause-and-effect analysis, discussed in Chapter 8, explains the causes and/or effects of something.)

Considering Language and Style

1. What is a *placebo* (paragraphs 5 and 8) and how is it a form of lie?

2. Consult a dictionary if you are unsure of the meaning of any of these words: *spectrum* (paragraph 1), *duplicity* (paragraph 1), *innocuous* (paragraph 5), *utilitarians* (paragraph 7), *aggregate* (paragraph 8).

For Group Discussion or Writing

Describe what day-to-day living would be like if people never told white lies. After considering your description, decide if some kinds of lies would be missed more than others. Also decide whether or not white lies are largely a positive or negative force in communication and interpersonal relationships.

Writing Assignments

1. *In your journal.* In a page or two, respond to these questions: How often do you tell white lies? What kinds of white lies do you usually tell? Have you ever told a white lie that has hurt someone? Have you ever been hurt by a white lie?

2. *Using the pattern.* Rather than focus on white lies as Bok does, write a classification of all lies. Explain the causes and effects of the lies. As an alternative, use division to break down the lie into its components. Then evaluate its causes and effects.

3. *Using the pattern.* Classify the lies told in some specific context: in school, on a date, at family gatherings, in the workplace, and so on. Evaluate the degree of harm that the lies cause.

4. *Using the pattern.* Classify the lies parents tell their children or the lies that teenagers tell their parents. Explain the causes and effects of these lies.

5. *Using the pattern.* Write a classification of the types of some form of undesirable behavior: cheating, procrastination, disloyalty, and so on. Evaluate the degree of harm that the behaviors cause. As an alternative, use division to break down one form of undesirable behavior into its components and evaluate its degree of harm.

6. *Considering a theme.* Overall, do you agree with the utilitarian evaluation of white lies, or do you agree with Bok's evaluation? Write an essay that supports your view.

7. *Connecting the readings.* Read "Talk in the Intimate Relationship: His and Hers" (page 354), which describes the ways men and women communicate with each other. Drawing on your own experience and observation, explain what role white lies play in the communication between men and women.

THE WAYS OF MEETING OPPRESSION
Martin Luther King, Jr.

Dr. Martin Luther King, Jr. (1929–1968) was a Baptist minister and the most prominent civil rights leader of the 1950s and 1960s. He founded the Southern Christian Leadership Conference in 1957 and worked tirelessly to achieve racial integration through nonviolent means. Named Time *magazine's Man of the Year in 1963 and winner of the Nobel Peace Prize in 1964, King organized numerous peaceful civil rights demonstrations. His writings include* Letter from Birmingham City Jail *(1963) and* Where Do We Go from Here: Chaos or Community? *(1967). In "The Ways of Meeting Oppression," taken from* Stride toward Freedom *(1958), King classifies ways to respond to oppression in order to inform his reader of the options oppressed people have. He then works to persuade his reader that nonviolent resistance is the best way to oppose oppression. As you read, notice that the thesis and topic sentences provide a clear organizational framework for the classification.*

THE PATTERN	THE PURPOSES
classification-division	*to inform and to persuade*

---

1   Oppressed people deal with their oppression in three characteristic ways. One way is acquiescence: the oppressed resign themselves to their doom. They tacitly adjust themselves to oppression, and thereby become conditioned to it. In every movement toward freedom some of the oppressed prefer to remain oppressed. Almost 2800 years ago Moses set out to lead the children of Israel from the slavery of Egypt to the freedom of the promised land. He soon discovered that slaves do not always welcome their deliverers. They become accustomed to being slaves. They would rather bear those ills they have, as Shakespeare pointed out, than flee to others that they know not of. They prefer the "fleshpots of Egypt" to the ordeals of emancipation.

2   There is such a thing as the freedom of exhaustion. Some people are so worn down by the yoke of oppression that they give up. A few years ago in the slum areas of Atlanta, a Negro guitarist used to sing almost daily: "Been down so long that down don't bother me." This is the type of negative freedom and resignation that often engulfs the life of the oppressed.

3   But this is not the way out. To accept passively an unjust system
is to cooperate with that system; thereby the oppressed become as evil
as the oppressor. Noncooperation with evil is as much a moral obligation as is cooperation with good. The oppressed must never allow the
conscience of the oppressor to slumber. Religion reminds every man
that he is his brother's keeper. To accept injustice or segregation passively is to say to the oppressor that his actions are morally right. It is
a way of allowing his conscience to fall asleep. At this moment the oppressed fails to be his brother's keeper. So acquiescence—while often
the easier way—is not the moral way. It is the way of the coward. The
Negro cannot win the respect of his oppressor by acquiescing; he merely
increases the oppressor's arrogance and contempt. Acquiescence is interpreted as proof of the Negro's inferiority. The Negro cannot win the
respect of the white people of the South or the peoples of the world if
he is willing to sell the future of his children for his personal and immediate comfort and safety.

4   A second way that oppressed people sometimes deal with oppression is to resort to physical violence and corroding hatred. Violence
often brings about momentary results. Nations have frequently won
their independence in battle. But in spite of temporary victories, violence never brings permanent peace. It solves no social problem; it
merely creates new and more complicated ones.

5   Violence as a way of achieving racial justice is both impractical
and immoral. It is impractical because it is a descending spiral ending
in destruction for all. The old law of an eye for an eye leaves everybody
blind. It is immoral because it seeks to humiliate the opponent rather
than win his understanding; it seeks to annihilate rather than to convert. Violence is immoral because it thrives on hatred rather than love.
It destroys community and makes brotherhood impossible. It leaves society in monologue rather than dialogue. Violence ends by defeating itself. It creates bitterness in the survivors and brutality in the destroy-
ers. A voice echoes through time saying to every potential Peter, "Put
up your sword."[1] History is cluttered with the wreckage of nations that
failed to follow this command.

6   If the American Negro and other victims of oppression succumb
to the temptation of using violence in the struggle for freedom, future

---

[1]The apostle Peter had drawn his sword to defend Christ from arrest. The voice was Christ's, who
    surrendered himself for trial and crucifixion (John 18:11).

generations will be the recipients of a desolate night of bitterness, and our chief legacy to them will be an endless reign of meaningless chaos. Violence is not the way.

7   The third way open to oppressed people in their quest for freedom is the way of nonviolent resistance. Like the synthesis in Hegelian philosophy, the principle of nonviolent resistance seeks to reconcile the truths of two opposites—the acquiescence and violence—while avoiding the extremes and immoralities of both. The nonviolent resister agrees with the person who acquiesces that one should not be physically aggressive toward his opponent; but he balances the equation by agreeing with the person of violence that evil must be resisted. He avoids the nonresistance of the former and the violent resistance of the latter. With nonviolent resistance, no individual or group need submit to any wrong, nor need anyone resort to violence in order to right a wrong.

8   It seems to me that this is the method that must guide the actions of the Negro in the present crisis in race relations. Through nonviolent resistance the Negro will be able to rise to the noble height of opposing the unjust system while loving the perpetrators of the system. The Negro must work passionately and unrelentingly for full stature as a citizen, but he must not use inferior methods to gain it. He must never come to terms with falsehood, malice, hate, or destruction.

9   Nonviolent resistance makes it possible for the Negro to remain in the South and struggle for his rights. The Negro's problem will not be solved by running away. He cannot listen to the glib suggestion of those who would urge him to migrate en masse to other sections of the country. By grasping his great opportunity in the South he can make a lasting contribution to the moral strength of the nation and set a sublime example of courage for generations yet unborn.

10   By nonviolent resistance, the Negro can also enlist all men of good will in his struggle for equality. The problem is not a purely racial one, with Negroes set against whites. In the end, it is not a struggle between people at all, but a tension between justice and injustice. Nonviolent resistance is not aimed against oppressors but against oppression. Under its banner consciences, not racial groups, are enlisted.

Reading Closely and Thinking Critically

1. According to King, what are the problems with acquiescence? With physical violence?

2. In paragraph 2, King refers to the "freedom of exhaustion." What does this phrase mean?

3. In paragraph 1, King says that some "would rather bear those ills they have . . . than flee to others they know not of." What does King mean by this? Why do you think that he makes this point?

4. According to King, how does nonviolent resistance balance the approaches of those who acquiesce and those who engage in physical violence?

5. Why does King advocate nonviolent resistance?

Examining Structure and Strategy

1. What ordering principle does King use? What are his groupings?

2. Which sentence is the thesis of "The Ways of Meeting Oppression"?

3. King presents his groupings in topic sentences. What are those topic sentences?

4. Cause-and-effect analysis appears in paragraphs 5 and 6 and 8 through 10. (Cause-and-effect analysis, the explanation of the causes or the effects of something, is discussed in Chapter 8.) How does the analysis help advance the classification?

5. Which paragraph includes definition? (Definition, an explanation of what something means, is discussed in Chapter 10.) What purpose does that definition serve? What paragraphs include examples? What purpose do those examples serve?

6. Where in the essay does King make his persuasive purpose clear? Why do you think he waits so long to establish his persuasive point?

7. In what order does King arrange his details?

Considering Language and Style

1. Paragraph 5 includes two biblical references: the mention of "an eye for an eye" and the mention of Peter. Explain these references and evaluate their appropriateness.

2. "The Ways of Meeting Oppression" comes from King's 1958 book *Stride toward Freedom*. What elements of King's language are clues to the selection's age? Do these dated elements in any way detract from the piece? Explain.

3.   Consult a dictionary if you are unsure of the meaning of any of these words: *tacitly* (paragraph 1), *fleshpots* (paragraph 1), *desolate* (paragraph 6), *legacy* (paragraph 6), *perpetrators* (paragraph 8), *glib* (paragraph 9), *en masse* (paragraph 9).

For Group Discussion or Writing

How much oppression exists in contemporary life? With two or three classmates, make a list of all the examples of oppression that you can think of, drawing on what you read in newspapers and magazines, what you see on television, and what you know from your own experience and observation. Then select one of the examples and decide how effective nonviolent resistance would be in combating that oppression.

Writing Assignments

1. *In your journal.* Write about a time when you witnessed, experienced, or heard about some form of oppression or discrimination. Tell what the incident was and how it made you feel.

2. *Using the pattern.* Classify the ways to deal with a bully, being sure to present the chief advantages and/or disadvantages of each way. Explain the effects of each technique.

3. *Using the pattern.* Classify the ways to respond to snobs, being sure to present the chief advantages and/or disadvantages of each way. Also, explain the effects of each technique.

4. *Using the pattern.* Classify the ways to deal with either stress or depression, being sure to present the chief advantages and/or disadvantages of each way. Also, explain the effects of each technique.

5. *Using the pattern.* Classify the ways to deal with sex discrimination or sexual harassment. Indicate which of the ways is best and work to persuade your reader of that fact.

6. *Considering a theme.* Tell about a time when you witnessed, experienced, or heard about an instance of discrimination or oppression. Explain what happened and how you reacted. Also explain whether or not you have changed your thinking or behavior as a result of the incident. (Your journal entry may help you with ideas for this essay.)

7. **Connecting the readings.** Read "Untouchables" on page 236 and write an essay that explains to what extent the homeless are victims of oppression. Indicate whether or not you think King's policy of nonviolent resistance would help the homeless and explain why you believe as you do.

SHADES OF BLACK
Mary E. Mebane

Born in Durham, North Carolina, Mary Mebane (1933–1992) earned a Ph.D. in English from the University of North Carolina. She was first a public school teacher and then an English professor at the University of South Carolina. Mebane wrote mostly about the lives of Southern blacks after 1960. She is also the author of two autobiographical works: Mary *(1981) and* Mary, Wayfarer *(1983). In the following selection, taken from* Mary, *Mebane informs her reader about color discrimination among blacks and its effects on black women. The piece also allows Mebane to relate her experiences as a victim of discrimination. As you read, notice that the author establishes two classifications.*

THE PATTERNS	THE PURPOSES
classification-division with exemplification, narration, definition, and cause-and-effect analysis	*to express feelings and relate experience and to inform*

1   During my first week of classes as a freshman, I was stopped one day in the hall by the chairman's wife, who was indistinguishable in color from a white woman. She wanted to see me, she said.

2   This woman had no official position on the faculty, except that she was an instructor in English; nevertheless, her summons had to be obeyed. In the segregated world there were (and remain) gross abuses of authority because those at the pinnacle, and even their spouses, felt that the people "under" them had no recourse except to submit—and they were right except that sometimes a black who got sick and tired of it would go to the whites and complain. This course of action was severely condemned by the blacks, but an interesting thing happened— such action always got positive results. Power was thought of in negative terms: I can deny someone something, I can strike at someone who can't strike back, I can ride someone down; that proves I am powerful. The concept of power as a force for good, for affirmative response to people or situations, was not in evidence.

3   When I went to her office, she greeted me with a big smile. "You know," she said, "you made the highest mark on the verbal part of the examination." She was referring to the examination that the entire fresh- man class took upon entering the college. I looked at her but I didn't feel warmth, for in spite of her smile her eyes and tone of voice were saying, "How could this black-skinned girl score higher on the verbal than some of the students who've had more advantages than she? It must be some sort of fluke. Let me talk to her." I felt it, but I managed to smile my thanks and back off. For here at North Carolina College at Durham, as it had been since the beginning, social class and color were the primary criteria used in determining status on the campus.

4   First came the children of doctors, lawyers, and college teachers. Next came the children of public-school teachers, businessmen, and anybody else who had access to more money than the poor black work- ing class. After that came the bulk of the student population, the chil- dren of the working class, most of whom were the first in their families to go beyond high school. The attitude toward them was: You're here be- cause we need the numbers, but in all other things defer to your betters.

5   The faculty assumed that light-skinned students were more in- telligent, and they were always a bit nonplussed when a dark-skinned student did well, especially if she was a girl. They had reason to be ap- palled when they discovered that I planned to do not only well but bet- ter than my light-skinned peers.

6   I don't know whether African men recently transported to the New World considered themselves handsome or, more important, whether they considered African women beautiful in comparison with Native American Indian women or immigrant European women. It is a question that I have never heard raised or seen research on. If African men considered African women beautiful, just when their shift in in- terest away from black black women occurred might prove to be an in- teresting topic for researchers. But one thing I know for sure: by the twentieth century, really black skin on a woman was considered ugly in this country. This was particularly true among those who were exposed to college.

7   Hazel, who was light brown, used to say to me, "You are *dark,* but not *too* dark." The saved commiserating with the damned. I had the feeling that if nature had painted one more brushstroke on me, I'd have had to kill myself.

8   Black skin was to be disguised at all costs. Since a black face is rather hard to disguise, many women took refuge in ludicrous makeup. Mrs. Burry, one of my teachers in elementary school, used white face powder. But she neglected to powder her neck and arms, and even the black on her face gleamed through the white, giving her an eerie appearance. But she did the best she could.

9   I observed all through elementary and high school that for various entertainments the girls were placed on the stage in order of color. And very black ones didn't get into the front row. If they were past caramel-brown, to the back row they would go. And nobody questioned the justice of these decisions—neither the students nor the teachers.

10   One of the teachers at Wildwood School, who was from the Deep South and was just as black as she could be, had been a strict enforcer of these standards. That was another irony—that someone who had been judged outside the realm of beauty herself because of her skin tones should have adopted them so wholeheartedly and applied them herself without question.

11   One girl stymied that teacher, though. Ruby, a black cherry of a girl, not only got off the back row but off the front row as well, to stand alone at stage center. She could outsing, outdance, and outdeclaim everyone else, and talent proved triumphant over pigmentation. But the May Queen and her Court (and in high school, Miss Wildwood) were always chosen from among the lighter ones.

12   When I was a freshman in high school, it became clear that a light-skinned sophomore girl named Rose was going to get the "best girl scholar" prize for the next three years, and there was nothing I could do about it, even though I knew I was the better. Rose was caramel-colored and had shoulder-length hair. She was highly favored by the science and math teacher, who figured the averages. I wasn't. There was only one prize. Therefore, Rose would get it until she graduated. I was one year behind her, and I would not get it until after she graduated.

13   To be held in such low esteem was painful. It was difficult not to feel that I had been cheated out of the medal, which I felt that, in a fair competition, I perhaps would have won. Being unable to protest or do anything about it was a traumatic experience for me. From then on I instinctively tended to avoid the college-exposed dark-skinned male, knowing that when he looked at me he saw himself and, most of the time, his mother and sister as well, and since he rejected his blackness, he had rejected theirs and mine.

14   Oddly enough, the lighter-skinned black male did not seem to feel so much prejudice toward the black black woman. It was no accident, I felt, that Mr. Harrison, the eighth-grade teacher, who was reddish-yellow himself, once protested to the science and math teacher about the fact that he always assigned sweeping duties to Doris and Ruby Lee, two black black girls. Mr. Harrison said to them one day, right in the other teacher's presence, "You must be some bad girls. Every day I come down here ya'll are sweeping." The science and math teacher got the point and didn't ask them to sweep anymore.

15   Uneducated black males, too, sometimes related very well to the black black woman. They had been less firmly indoctrinated by the white society around them and were more securely rooted in their own culture.

16   Because of the stigma attached to having dark skin, a black black woman had to do many things to find a place for herself. One possibility was to attach herself to a light-skinned woman, hoping that some of the magic would rub off on her. A second was to make herself sexually available, hoping to attract a mate. Third, she could resign herself to a more chaste life-style—either (for the professional woman) teaching and work in established churches or (for the uneducated woman) domestic work and zealous service in the Holy and Sanctified churches.

17   Even as a young girl, Lucy had chosen the first route. Lucy was short, skinny, short-haired, and black black, and thus unacceptable. So she made her choice. She selected Patricia, the lightest-skinned girl in the school, as her friend, and followed her around. Patricia and her friends barely tolerated Lucy, but Lucy smiled and doggedly hung on, hoping that some who noticed Patricia might notice her, too. Though I felt shame for her behavior, even then I understood.

18   As is often the case of the victim agreeing with and adopting the attitudes of oppressor, so I have seen it with black black women. I have seen them adopt the oppressor's attitude that they are nothing but "sex machines," and their supposedly superior sexual performance becomes their sole reason for being and for esteeming themselves. Such women learn early that in order to make themselves attractive to men they have somehow to shift the emphasis from physical beauty to some other area—usually sexual performance. Their constant talk is of their desirability and their ability to gratify a man sexually.

19   I knew two such women well—both of them black black. To hear their endless talk of sexual conquests was very sad. I have never

seen the category that these women fall into described anywhere. It is not that of promiscuity or nymphomania. It is the category of total self-rejection: "Since I am black, I am ugly, I am nobody. I will perform on the level that they have assigned to me." Such women are the pitiful results of what not only white America but also, and more important, black America has done to them.

20   Some, not taking the sexuality route but still accepting black society's view of their worthlessness, swing all the way across to intense religiosity. Some are staunch, fervent workers in the more traditional Southern churches—Baptist and Methodist—and others are leaders and ministers in the lower status, more evangelical Holiness sects.

21   Another avenue open to the black black woman is excellence in a career. Since in the South the field most accessible to such women is education, a great many of them prepared to become teachers. But here, too, the black black woman had problems. Grades weren't given to her lightly in school, nor were promotions on the job. Consequently, she had to prepare especially well. She had to pass examinations with flying colors or be left behind; she knew that she would receive no special consideration. She had to be overqualified for a job because otherwise she didn't stand a chance of getting it—and she was competing only with other blacks. She had to have something to back her up: not charm, not personality—but training.

22   The black black woman's training would pay off in the 1970s. With the arrival of integration the black black woman would find, paradoxically enough, that her skin color in an integrated situation was not the handicap it had been in an all-black situation. But it wasn't until the middle and late 1960s, when the post-1945 generation of black males arrived on college campuses, that I noticed any change in the situation at all. *He* wore an afro and *she* wore an afro, and sometimes the only way you could tell them apart was when his afro was taller than hers. Black had become beautiful, and the really black girl was often selected as queen of various campus activities. It was then that the dread I felt at dealing with the college-educated black male began to ease. Even now, though, when I have occasion to engage in any type of transaction with a college-educated black man, I gauge his age. If I guess he was born after 1945, I feel confident that the transaction will turn out all right. If he probably was born before 1945, my stomach tightens, I find myself taking shallow breaths, and I try to state my business and escape as soon as possible.

Reading Closely and Thinking Critically

1. What is the primary point about discrimination that Mebane makes in "Shades of Black"?

2. Why is Mebane careful to note that she was challenged by a woman "who was indistinguishable in color from a white woman" (paragraph 1)?

3. How does Mebane define power in the segregated world?

4. Why did uneducated black men relate better to black black women than did educated black men?

5. How did the mid-1960s and 1970s mark a turning point for the black black woman?

6. Explain what you think Mebane's attitude is toward the light- and dark-skinned blacks she writes about and the discrimination she describes.

Examining Structure and Strategy

1. Which sentence best presents the thesis of "Shades of Black"?

2. Paragraphs 1 through 3 present a narration. What point does that narration make? What does it contribute to the essay?

3. "Shades of Black" has two distinct classifications. In each case, what is classified and what is the ordering principle?

4. Mebane uses a number of examples. What do the examples in paragraphs 10 and 11, 12, 14, and 17 contribute to the essay?

5. What elements of cause-and-effect analysis appear? (Cause-and-effect analysis, discussed in Chapter 8, explains the causes or effects of something.) What does this cause-and-effect analysis contribute to the essay?

Considering Language and Style

1. Mebane labels some African-American women as "black black." Explain what the phrase means and why Mebane uses the word *black* twice.

2. In paragraph 3, Mebane uses direct quotation to present both the speech and thought of the chairman's wife. What does the direct quotation contribute?

3. Consult a dictionary if you are unsure of the meaning of any of these words: *pinnacle* (paragraph 2), *fluke* (paragraph 3), *nonplussed* (paragraph 5), *commiserating* (paragraph 7), *stymied* (paragraph 11), *declaim* (paragraph 11), *stigma* (paragraph 16), *doggedly* (paragraph 17), *nymphomania* (paragraph 19), *staunch* (paragraph 20).

For Group Discussion or Writing

Were you surprised to learn that members of a group are capable of discriminating against other members of that same group? Explain why or why not. What do you think accounted for the discrimination of lighter-skinned blacks against darker-skinned blacks?

Writing Assignments

1. In your journal. Mebane tells about times in school when she was treated unfairly. If you have been treated unfairly in school (by a teacher, by a coach, or by a student), or if you have witnessed unfair treatment, tell what happened in a page or two.

2. Using the pattern. Mebane explains that black women were classified according to the shade of their skin color. Write a classification that shows another way that we group people (by attractiveness, intelligence, wealth, and so on). Indicate whether or not the tendency to classify in this way is discriminatory and why or why not. If you like, you can also indicate the effects the classification has on the people in the groupings.

3. Using the pattern. Mebane classifies the way black black women made their way in the world. Select another group of people who are stigmatized (for example, the disabled, the overweight, the very tall or very short, or the unattractive) and classify the ways they make their way in the world and/or the ways they respond to their stigma.

4. Using the pattern. Students in high school are often classified into groups, with members of some groups treated better than members of others. Write an essay that presents the ways students in your high school were grouped, as well as the discrimination members of one or more of these groups experienced.

5. Considering a theme. Write an essay that notes what our most frequently occurring prejudices are. Explain why you think we have these prejudices and what we can do to counteract them.

6. *Connecting the readings.* Compare and contrast the attitudes toward skin color in "Shades of Black" and "Complexion" (page 401). (Comparison-contrast is discussed in Chapter 7). Also consider to what extent our appearance affects the way others judge us and to what extent it shapes our perception of ourselves.

COLLEGE PRESSURES
William Zinsser

*William Zinsser was born in 1922 in New York City. A 1944 graduate of
Princeton University, he has been a writer, drama editor, and film critic for the
New York* Herald Tribune *and a writer for the* New York Times *and* Life
*magazine. He has also been an English teacher at Yale University and editor of
the Book-of-the Month Club. His books on writing and American culture include* Writing to Learn *(1988) and* American Places: A Writer's Pilgrimage
to 15 of This Country's Most Visited and Cherished Sites *(1992). In "College Pressures" (1979), Zinsser combines classification-division, exemplification,
and cause-and-effect analysis to inform his reader of the nature and extent of
the pressures Yale students face. In addition, he has a persuasive purpose: He
argues that students, themselves, must eliminate the college pressures.*

THE PATTERNS	THE PURPOSES
classification-division with	*to inform and to persuade*
exemplification, and	
cause-and-effect analysis	

1   Dear Carlos: I desperately need a dean's excuse for my chem
midterm which will begin in about 1 hour. All I can say is that I totally
blew it this week. I've fallen incredibly, inconceivably behind.

2   Carlos: Help! I'm anxious to hear from you. I'll be in my room
and won't leave it until I hear from you. Tomorrow is the last day
for. . . .

3   Carlos: I left town because I started bugging out again. I stayed
up all night to finish a take home make-up exam & am typing it to
hand in on the 10th. It was due on the 5th. P.S. I'm going to the dentist. Pain is pretty bad.

4   Carlos: Probably by Friday I'll be able to get back to my studies.
Right now I'm going to take a long walk. This whole thing has taken a
lot out of me.

5   Carlos: I'm really up the proverbial creek. The problem is I really *bombed* the history final. Since I need that course for my
major. . . .

6   Carlos: Here follows a tale of woe. I went home this weekend, had to help my Mom, & caught a fever so didn't have much time to study. My professor. . . .

7   Carlos: Aargh! Nothing original but everything's piling up at once. To be brief, my job interview. . . .

8   Hey Carlos, good news! I've got mononucleosis.

9   Who are these wretched supplicants, scribbling notes so laden with anxiety, seeking such miracles of postponement and balm? They are men and women who belong to Bradford College, one of the twelve residential colleges at Yale University, and the messages are just a few of the hundreds that they left for their dean, Carlos Hortas—often slipped under his door at 4 A.M.—last year.

10   But students like the ones who wrote those notes can also be found on campuses from coast to coast—especially in New England and at many other private colleges across the country that have high academic standards and highly motivated students. Nobody could doubt that the notes are real. In their urgency and their gallows humor they are authentic voices of a generation that is panicky to succeed.

11   My own connection with the message writers is that I am master of Branford College. I live in its Gothic quadrangle and know the students well. (We have 485 of them.) I am privy to their hopes and fears—and also to their stereo music and their piercing cries in the dead of night ("Does anybody *ca-a-are?*"). If they went to Carlos to ask how to get through tomorrow, they come to me to ask how to get through the rest of their lives.

12   Mainly I try to remind them that the road ahead is a long one and that it will have more unexpected turns than they think. There will be plenty of time to change jobs, change careers, change whole attitudes and approaches. They don't want to hear such liberating news. They want a map—right now—that they can follow unswervingly to career security, financial security, Social Security and, presumably, a prepaid grave.

13   What I wish for all students is some release from the clammy grip of the future. I wish them a chance to savor each segment of their education as an experience in itself and not as a grim preparation for the next step. I wish them the right to experiment, to trip and fall, to learn that defeat is as instructive as victory and is not the end of the world.

14   My wish, of course, is naive. One of the few rights that America does not proclaim is the right to fail. Achievement is the national god, venerated in our media—the million-dollar athlete, the wealthy executive—and glorified in our praise of possessions. In the presence of such a potent state religion, the young are growing up old.

15   I see four kinds of pressure working on college students today: economic pressure, parental pressure, peer pressure, and self-induced pressure. It is easy to look around for villains—to blame the colleges for charging too much money, the professors for assigning too much work, the parents for pushing their children too far, the students for driving themselves too hard. But there are no villains, only victims.

16   "In the late 1960s," one dean told me, "the typical question that I got from students was 'Why is there so much suffering in the world?' or 'How can I make a contribution?' Today it's 'Do you think it would look better for getting into law school if I did a double major in history and political science, or just majored in one of them?'" Many other deans confirmed this pattern. One said: "They're trying to find an edge—the intangible something that will look better on paper if two students are about equal."

17   Note the emphasis on looking better. The transcript has become a sacred document, the passport to security. How one appears on paper is more important than how one appears in person. *A* is for Admirable and *B* is for Borderline, even though, in Yale's official system of grading, *A* means "excellent" and *B* means "very good." Today, looking very good is no longer good enough, especially for students who hope to go on to law school or medical school. They know that entrance into the better schools will be an entrance into the better law firms and better medical practices where they will make a lot of money. They also know that the odds are harsh. Yale Law School for instance, matriculates 170 students from an applicant pool of 3,700; Harvard enrolls 550 from a pool of 7,000.

18   It's all very well for those of us who write letters of recommendation for our students to stress the qualities of humanity that will make them good lawyers or doctors. And it's nice to think that admission officers are really reading our letters and looking for the extra dimension of commitment or concern. Still, it would be hard for a student not to visualize these officers shuffling so many transcripts studded with *As* that they regard a *B* as positively shameful.

19   The pressure is almost as heavy on students who just want to graduate and get a job. Long gone are the days of the "gentleman's C," when students journeyed through college with a certain relaxation, sampling a wide variety of courses—music, art, philosophy, classics, anthropology, poetry, religion—that would send them out as liberally educated men and women. If I were an employer I would rather employ graduates who have this range and curiosity than those who narrowly pursued safe subjects and high grades. I know countless students whose inquiring minds exhilarate me. I like to hear the play of their ideas. I don't know if they are getting As or Cs, and I don't care. I also like them as people. The country needs them, and they will find satisfying jobs. I tell them to relax. They can't.

20   Nor can I blame them. They live in a brutal economy. Tuition, room, and board at most private colleges now comes to at least $7,000, not counting books and fees. This might seem to suggest that the colleges are getting rich. But they are equally battered by inflation. Tuition covers only 60 percent of what it costs to educate a student, and ordinarily the remainder comes from what colleges receive in endowments, grants, and gifts. Now the remainder keeps being swallowed by the cruel costs—higher every year—of just opening the doors. Heating oil is up. Insurance is up. Postage is up. Health-premium costs are up. Everything is up. Deficits are up. We are witnessing in America the creation of a brotherhood of paupers—colleges, parents, and students, joined by the common bond of debt.

21   Today it is not unusual for a student, even if he works part time at college and full time during the summer, to accrue $5,000 in loans after four years—loans that he must start to repay within one year after graduation. Exhorted at commencement to go forth into the world, he is already behind as he goes forth. How could he not feel under pressure throughout college to prepare for this day of reckoning? I have used "he," incidentally, only for brevity. Women at Yale are under no less pressure to justify their expensive education to themselves, their parents, and society. In fact, they are probably under more pressure. For although they leave college superbly equipped to bring fresh leadership to traditionally male jobs, society hasn't yet caught up with this fact.

22   Along with economic pressure goes parental pressure. Inevitably, the two are deeply intertwined.

23   I see many student taking pre-medical courses with joyless tenacity. They go off to their labs as if they were going to the dentist. It sad-

dens me because I know them in other corners of their life as cheerful people.

24   "Do you want to go to medical school?" I ask them.

25   "I guess so," they say, without conviction, or "Not really."

26   "Then why are you going?"

27   "Well, my parents want me to be a doctor. They're paying all this money and . . ."

28   Poor students, poor parents. They are caught in one of the oldest webs of love and duty and guilt. The parents mean well; they are trying to steer their sons and daughters toward a secure future. But the sons and daughters want to major in history or classics or philosophy— subjects with no "practical" value. Where's the payoff on the humanities? It's not easy to persuade such loving parents that the humanities do indeed pay off. The intellectual faculties developed by studying subjects like history and classics—an ability to synthesize and relate, to weigh cause and effect, to see events in perspective—are just the faculties that make creative leaders in business or almost any general field. Still, many fathers would rather put their money on courses that point toward a specific profession—courses that are pre-law, pre-medical, pre-business, or, as I sometimes heard it put, "pre-rich."

29   But the pressure on students is severe. They are truly torn. One part of them feels obligated to fulfill their parents' expectations, after all, their parents are older and presumably wiser. Another part tells them that the expectations that are right for their parents are not right for them.

30   I know a student who wants to be an artist. She is very obviously an artist and will be a good one—she has already had several modest exhibits. Meanwhile she is growing as a well-rounded person and taking humanistic subjects that will enrich the inner resources out of which her art will grow. But her father is strongly opposed. He thinks that an artist is a "dumb" thing to be. The student vacillates and tries to please everybody. She keeps up with her art somewhat furtively and takes some of the "dumb" courses her father wants her to take—at least they are dumb courses for her. She is a free spirit on a campus of tense students—no small achievement in itself—and she deserves to follow her muse.

31   Peer pressure and self-induced pressure are also intertwined, and they begin almost at the beginning of freshman year.

32   "I had a freshman student I'll call Linda," one dean told me, "who came in and said she was under terrible pressure because her room-

mate, Barbara, was much brighter and studied all the time. I couldn't tell her that Barbara had come in two hours earlier to say the same thing about Linda."

33   The story is almost funny—except that it's not. It's symptomatic of all the pressure put together. When every student thinks every other student is working harder and doing better, the only solution is to study harder still. I see students going off to the library every night after dinner and coming back when it closes at midnight. I wish they could sometimes forget about their peers and go to a movie. I hear the clacking of typewriters in the hours before dawn. I see the tension in their eyes when exams are approaching and papers are due: *"Will I get everything done?"*

34   Probably they won't. They will get sick. They will get "blocked." They will sleep. They will oversleep. They will bug out. *Hey Carlos, help!*

35   Part of the problem is that they do more than they are expected to do. A professor will assign five-page papers. Several students will start writing ten-page papers to impress him. Then more students will write ten-page papers, and a few will raise the ante to fifteen. Pity the poor student who is still just doing the assignment.

36   "Once you have twenty or thirty percent of the student population deliberately overexerting," one dean points out, "it's bad for everybody. When a teacher gets more and more effort from his class, the student who is doing normal work can be perceived as not doing well. The tactic works, psychologically."

37   Why can't the professor just cut back and not accept longer papers? He can, and he probably will. But by then the term will be half over and the damage done. Grade fever is highly contagious and not easily reversed. Besides, the professor's main concern is with his course. He knows his students only in relation to the course and doesn't know that they are also overexerting in their other courses. Nor is it really his business. He didn't sign up for dealing with the student as a whole person and with all the emotional baggage the student brought along from home. That's what deans, masters, chaplains, and psychiatrists are for.

38   To some extent this is nothing new: a certain number of professors have always been self-contained islands of scholarship and shyness, more comfortable with books than with people. But the new pauperism has widened the gap still further, for professors who actually like to spend time with students don't have as much time to spend. They also are overexerting. If they are young, they are busy trying to publish in

order not to perish, hanging by their fingernails onto a shrinking profession. If they are old and tenured, they are buried under the duties of administering departments—as departmental chairmen or members of committees—that have been thinned out by the budgetary axe.

39   Ultimately it will be the students' own business to break the circles in which they are trapped. They are too young to be prisoners of their parents' dreams and their classmates' fears. They must be jolted into believing in themselves as unique men and women who have the power to shape their own future.

40   "Violence is being done to the undergraduate experience," says Carlos Hortas. "College should be open-ended: at the end it should open many, many roads. Instead, students are choosing their goal in advance, and their choices narrow as they go along. It's almost as if they think that the country has been codified in the type of jobs that exist— that they've got to fit into certain slots. Therefore, fit into the best-paying slot.

41   "They ought to take chances. Not taking chances will lead to a life of colorless mediocrity. They'll be comfortable. But something in the spirit will be missing."

42   I have painted too drab a portrait of today's students, making them seem a solemn lot. That is only half of their story; if they were so dreary I wouldn't so thoroughly enjoy their company. The other half is that they are easy to like. They are quick to laugh and to offer friendship. They are not introverts. They are usually kind and are more considerate of one another than any student generation I have known.

43   Nor are they so obsessed with their studies that they avoid sports and extracurricular activities. On the contrary, they juggle their crowded hours to play on a variety of teams, perform with musical and dramatic groups, and write for campus publications. But this in turn is one more cause of anxiety. There are too many choices. Academically, they have 1,300 courses to select from; outside class they have to decide how much spare time they can spare and how to spend it.

44   This means that they engage in fewer extracurricular pursuits than their predecessors did. If they want to row on the crew and play in the symphony they will eliminate one; in the '60s they would have done both. They also tend to choose activities that are self-limiting. Drama, for instance, is flourishing in all twelve of Yale's residential colleges as it never has before. Students hurl themselves into these productions—as actors, directors, carpenters, and technicians—with a

dedication to create the best possible play, knowing that the day will come when the run will end and they can get back to their studies.

45   They also can't afford to be the willing slave of organizations like the *Yale Daily News*. Last spring at the one-hundredth anniversary banquet of that paper—whose past chairmen include such once and future kings as Potter Stewart, Kingman Brewster, and William F. Buckley, Jr.[1]—much was made of the fact that the editorial staff used to be small and totally committed and that "newsies" routinely worked fifty hours a week. In effect they belonged to a club; Newsies is how they defined themselves at Yale. Today's student will write one or two articles a week, when he can, and he defines himself as a student. I've never heard the word Newsie except at the banquet.

46   If I have described the modern undergraduate primarily as a driven creature who is largely ignoring the blithe spirit inside who keeps trying to come out and play, it's because that's where the crunch is, not only at Yale but throughout American education. It's why I think we should all be worried about the values that are nurturing a generation so fearful of risk and so goal-obsessed at such an early age.

47   I tell students that there is no one "right" way to get ahead—that each of them is a different person, starting from a different point and bound for a different destination. I tell them that change is a tonic and that all the slots are not codified nor the frontiers closed. One of my ways of telling them is to invite men and women who have achieved success outside the academic world to come and talk informally with my students during the year. They are heads of companies or ad agencies, editors of magazines, politicians, public officials, television magnates, labor leaders, business executives, Broadway producers, artists, writers, economists, photographers, scientists, historians—a mixed bag of achievers.

48   I ask them to say a few words about how they got started. The students assume that they started in their present profession and knew all along that is was what they wanted to do. Luckily for me, most of them got into their field by a circuitous route, to their surprise, after many detours. The students are startled. They can hardly conceive of a career that was not pre-planned. They can hardly imagine allowing the hand of God or chance to nudge them down some unforeseen trail.

---

[1] Ed. Note: Stewart was a U.S. Supreme Court Justice; Brewster was a president of Yale; and Buckley is a conservative editor and columnist.

Reading Closely and Thinking Critically

1. According to Zinsser, what factors cause the pressure that college students experience?

2. Make a list of at least five words or phrases that describe the college student Zinsser writes about.

3. In a sentence or two, summarize Zinsser's advice to college students. What do you think of this advice?

4. According to Zinsser, how can college pressures be eliminated?

5. Do you think that the author's description of Yale students and his classification of the pressures they face is representative of students and their pressures in general? Explain.

6. In paragraph 39, Zinsser tells of inviting people to speak to his students. Do you think these classroom visits changed the attitudes of many students? Why or why not?

Examining Structure and Strategy

1. In your own words, write out Zinsser's thesis.

2. In which paragraph does Zinsser's classification begin and in which paragraph does it end? What is he classifying? What does the classification contribute to the essay?

3. What element of cause-and-effect analysis appears in the essay? (Cause-and-effect analysis, discussed in Chapter 8, presents the causes and/or effects of something.) What does the analysis contribute to the essay?

4. What is the purpose of the opening examples of notes written to Carlos Hortas?

Considering Language and Style

1. Zinsser uses *he* to refer to college students and professors. He says, however, in paragraph 21 that he uses this pronoun for "brevity"; he recognizes that women, too, are under pressure. Do you think Zinsser should have been more careful to use language that includes women? Explain.

2. What metaphor appears in paragraph 9? Do you find the metaphor appropriate? Explain. (Metaphors are explained on page 73.)

3. Consult a dictionary if you are unsure of the meaning of any of these words: *supplicants* (paragraph 9), *gallows humor* (paragraph 10), *privy* (paragraph 11), *venerated* (paragraph 14), *matriculates* (paragraph 17), *accrue* (paragraph 21), *exhorted* (paragraph 21), *muse* (paragraph 30), *blithe* (paragraph 46), *circuitous* (paragraph 48).

For Group Discussion or Writing
In paragraph 13, Zinsser expresses his wish for students. Do you share his wish? How likely is it that his wish can come true? What changes would have to occur in order for it to come true? Consider these questions with two or three classmates.

Writing Assignments
1. *In your journal.* In two or three pages, describe the kinds and amount of pressure you experience as a college student. Then explain the effects this pressure has on you.

2. *Using the pattern.* In paragraph 12, Zinsser says that students "want a map—right now—that they can follow unswervingly to career security, financial security, Social Security and, presumably, a prepaid grave." If you disagree with Zinsser, or if you think students want more than a map, classify the things that students want and explain why they want what they do.

3. *Using the pattern.* If you disagree with Zinsser's assertion that college students in general are pressured, stressed, and overly competitive, write a classification that informs your reader of what you think the various kinds of college students are. Try to use examples from your own experience and observation to illustrate your groupings. As an alternative, use division to explain the aspects of a typical college student.

4. *Using the pattern.* Write an essay that classifies the pressures in some nonacademic setting. You could classify the pressures of parenthood, being an only child, working as a table server, being a housewife or househusband, or being a lifeguard. Like Zinsser, offer some advice for overcoming the pressures and/or explain the cause and effect of those pressures.

5. *Using the pattern.* If you disagree with Zinsser's classification of college pressures, write your own classification of these pressures. Like Zinsser, explain the causes and effects of the pressures and use examples to illustrate their nature.

6. *Considering a theme.* In paragraph 14, Zinsser says, "One of the few rights that America does not proclaim is the right to fail." Do you think that Americans fear failure and therefore feel pressured to succeed? Cite examples to support your view.

7. *Connecting the readings.* "University Days" (page 211) was published in 1933, and "College Pressures" was published in 1979. Study these essays, then write about what has changed and what has stayed the same from 1933 to 1979 to the present.

TERRITORIAL BEHAVIOUR
Desmond Morris

Born in England in 1929, Desmond Morris earned his Ph.D. from Oxford University. After graduation, he was first an animal behavior researcher in Oxford's zoology department and then a curator of mammals at the Zoological Society of London. Morris popularized his findings about human behavior in his well-received books The Naked Ape *(1967),* The Human Zoo *(1970),* Manwatching *(1977), and* Bodywatching *(1985). In "Territorial Behaviour," an excerpt from* Manwatching, *Morris classifies the kinds of human territory and uses cause-and-effect analysis and exemplification to inform the reader that we often act the way we do as a result of our efforts to mark or protect our space.*

THE PATTERNS	THE PURPOSE
classification-division with cause-and-effect analysis, and exemplification	*to inform*

1   A territory is a defended space. In the broadcast sense, there are three kinds of human territory: tribal, family and personal.

2   It is rare for people to be driven to physical fighting in defence of these "owned" spaces, but fight they will, if pushed to the limit. The invading army encroaching on national territory, the gang moving into a rival district, the trespasser climbing into an orchard, the burglar breaking into a house, the bully pushing to the front of a queue, the driver trying to steal a parking space, all of these intruders are liable to be met with resistance varying from the vigorous to the savagely violent. Even if the law is on the side of the intruder, the urge to protect a territory may be so strong that otherwise peaceful citizens abandon all their usual controls and inhibitions. Attempts to evict families from their homes, no matter how socially valid the reasons, can lead to siege conditions reminiscent of the defence of a medieval fortress.

3   The fact that these upheavals are so rare is a measure of the success of Territorial Signals as a system of dispute prevention. It is sometimes cynically stated that "all property is theft," but in reality it is the

opposite. Property, as owned space which is *displayed* as owned space, is a special kind of sharing system which reduces fighting much more than it causes it. Man is a co-operative species, but he is also competitive, and his struggle for dominance has to be structured in some way if chaos is to be avoided. The establishment of territorial rights is one such structure. It limits dominance geographically. I am dominant in my territory and you are dominant in yours. In other words, dominance is shared out spatially, and we all have some. Even if I am weak and unintelligent and you can dominate me when we meet on neutral ground, I can still enjoy a thoroughly dominant role as soon as I retreat to my private base. Be it ever so humble, there is no place like a home territory.

4   Of course, I can still be intimidated by a particularly dominant individual who enters my home base, but his encroachment will be dangerous for him and he will think twice about it, because he will know that here my urge to resist will be dramatically magnified and my usual subservience banished. Insulted at the heart of my own territory, I may easily explode into battle—either symbolic or real—with a result that may be damaging to both of us.

5   In order for this to work, each territory has to be plainly advertised as such. Just as a dog cocks its leg to deposit its personal scent on the trees in its locality, so the human animal cocks its leg symbolically all over his home base. But because we are predominantly visual animals, we employ mostly visual signals, and it is worth asking how we do this at the three levels: tribal, family and personal.

6   First, the Tribal Territory. We evolved as tribal animals, living in comparatively small groups, probably of less than a hundred, and we existed like that for millions of years. It is our basic social unit, a group in which everyone knows everyone else. Essentially the tribal territory consisted of a home base surrounded by extended hunting grounds. Any neighbouring tribe intruding on our social space would be repelled and driven away. As these early tribes swelled into agricultural super-tribes, and eventually into industrial nations, their territorial defence systems became increasingly elaborate. The tiny, ancient home base of the hunting tribe became the great capital city, the primitive war-paint became the flags, emblems, uniforms and regalia of the specialized military, and the war-chants became national anthems, marching songs and bugle calls. Territorial boundary-lines hardened into fixed borders, often conspicuously patrolled and punctuated with defensive structures—

forts and look-out posts, checkpoints and great walls, and, today, customs barriers.

7   Today each nation flies its own flag, a symbolic embodiment of its territorial status. But patriotism is not enough. The ancient tribal hunter lurking inside each citizen finds himself unsatisfied by membership in such a vast conglomeration of individuals, most of whom are totally unknown to him personally. He does his best to feel that he shares a common territorial defence with them all, but the scale of the operation has become inhuman. It is hard to feel a sense of belonging with a tribe of fifty million or more. His answer is to form sub-groups, nearer to his ancient pattern, smaller and more personally known to him—the local club, the teenage gang, the union, the specialist society, the sports association, the political party, the college fraternity, the social clique, the protest group, and the rest. Rare indeed is the individual who does not belong to at least one of these splinter groups, and take from it a sense of tribal allegiance and brotherhood. Typical of all these groups is the development of Territorial Signals—badges, costumes, headquarters, banners, slogans, and all the other displays of group identity. This is where the action is, in terms of tribal territorialism, and only when a major war breaks out does the emphasis shift upwards to the higher group level of the nation.

8   Each of these modern pseudo-tribes sets up its own special kind of home base. In extreme cases non-members are totally excluded, in others they are allowed in as visitors with limited rights and under a control system of special rules. In many ways they are like miniature nations, with their own flags and emblems and their own border guards. The exclusive club has its own "customs barrier": the doorman who checks your "passport" (your membership card) and prevents strangers from passing in unchallenged. There is a government: the club committee; and often special displays of the tribal elders: the photographs or portraits of previous officials on the walls. At the heart of the specialized territories there is a powerful feeling of security and importance, a sense of shared defence against the outside world. Much of the club chatter, both serious and joking, directs itself against the rottenness of everything outside the club boundaries—in that "other world" beyond the protected portals.

9   In social organizations which embody a strong class system, such as military units and large business concerns, there are many territorial rules, often unspoken, which interfere with the official hierarchy. High-

status individuals, such as officers or managers, could in theory enter any of the regions occupied by the lower levels in the pecking order, but they limit this power in a striking way. An officer seldom enters a sergeant's mess or a barrack room unless it is for a formal inspection. He respects those regions as alien territories even though he has the power to go there by virtue of his dominant role. And in businesses, part of the appeal of unions, over and above their obvious functions, is that with their officials, headquarters and meetings they add a sense of territorial power for the staff workers. It is almost as if each military organization and business concern consists of two warring tribes, the officers versus the other ranks, and the management versus the workers. Each has its special home base within the system, and the territorial defence pattern thrusts itself into what, on the surface, is a pure social hierarchy. Negotiations between managements and unions are tribal battles fought out over the neutral ground of a boardroom table, and are as much concerned with territorial displays as they are with resolving problems of wages and conditions. Indeed, if one side gives in too quickly and accepts the other's demands, the victors feel strangely cheated and deeply suspicious that it may be a trick. What they are missing is the protracted sequence of ritual and counter-ritual that keeps alive their group territorial identity.

10   Likewise, many of the hostile displays of sports fans and teenage gangs are primarily concerned with displaying their group image to rival fan-clubs and gangs. Except in rare cases, they do not attack one another's headquarters, drive out the occupants, and reduce them to a submissive, subordinate condition. It is enough to have scuffles on the borderlands between the two rival territories. This is particularly clear at football matches, where the fan-club headquarters becomes temporarily shifted from the club-house to a section of the stands, and where minor fighting breaks out at the unofficial boundary line between the massed groups of rival supporters. Newspaper reports play up the few accidents and injuries which do occur on such occasions, but when they are studied in relation to the total numbers of displaying fans involved, it is clear that the serious incidents represent only a tiny fraction of the overall group behaviour. For every actual punch or kick there are a thousand war-cries, war-dances, chants and gestures.

11   Second: the Family Territory. Essentially, the family is a breeding unit and the family territory is a breeding ground. At the centre of this space, there is the nest—the bedroom—where, tucked up in bed, we

feel at our most territorially secure. In a typical house the bedroom is upstairs, where a safe nest should be. This puts it farther away from the entrance hall, the area where contact is made, intermittently, with the outside world. The less private reception rooms, where intruders are allowed access, are the next line of defence. Beyond them, outside the walls of the building, there is often a symbolic remnant of the ancient feeding grounds—a garden. Its symbolism often extends to the plants and animals it contains, which cease to be nutritional and become merely decorative—flowers and pets. But like a true territorial space it has a conspicuously displayed boundary-line, the garden fence, wall, or railings. Often no more than a token barrier, this is the outer territorial demarcation, separating the private world of the family from the public world beyond. To cross it puts any visitor or intruder at an immediate disadvantage. As he crosses the threshold, his dominance wanes, slightly but unmistakably. He is entering an area where he senses that he must ask permission to do simple things that he would consider a right elsewhere. Without lifting a finger, the territorial owners exert their dominance. This is done by all the hundreds of small ownership "markers" they have deposited on their family territory: the ornaments, the "possessed" objects positioned in the rooms and on the walls; the furnishings, the furniture, the colours, the patterns, all owner-chosen and all making this particular home base unique to them.

12   It is one of the tragedies of modern architecture that there has been a standardization of these vital territorial living units. One of the most important aspects of a home is that it should be similar to other homes only in a general way, and that in detail it should have many differences, making it a *particular* home. Unfortunately, it is cheaper to build a row of houses, or a block of flats, so that all the family living-units are identical, but the territorial urge rebels against this trend and house-owners struggle as best they can to make their mark on their mass-produced properties. They do this with garden-design, with front-door colours, with curtain patterns, with wallpaper and all the other decorative elements that together create a unique and different family environment. Only when they have completed this nest-building do they feel truly "at home" and secure.

13   When they venture forth as a family unit, they repeat the process in a minor way. On a day-trip to the seaside, they load the car with personal belongings and it becomes their temporary, portable territory. Arriving at the beach, they stake out a small territorial claim, marking it

with rugs, towels, baskets and other belongings to which they can return from their seaboard wanderings. Even if they all leave it at once to
bathe, it retains a characteristic territorial quality and other family
groups arriving will recognize this by setting up their own "home" bases
at a respectful distance. Only when the whole beach has filled up with
these marked spaces will newcomers start to position themselves in
such a way that the inter-base distance becomes reduced. Forced to
pitch between several existing beach territories, they will feel a momentary sensation of intrusion, and the established "owners" will feel a
similar sensation of invasion, even though they are not being directly
inconvenienced.

14   The same territorial scene is being played out in parks and fields
and on riverbanks, wherever family groups gather in their clustered
units. But if rivalry for spaces creates mild feelings of hostility, it is true
to say that without the territorial system of sharing and space-limited
dominance, there would be chaotic disorder.

15   Third: the Personal Space. If a man enters a waiting-room and
sits at one end of a long row of empty chairs, it is possible to predict
where the next man to enter will seat himself. He will not sit next to
the first man, nor will he sit at the far end, right away from him. He
will choose a position about halfway between these two points. The
next man to enter will take the largest gap left, and sit roughly in the
middle of that, and so on, until eventually the latest newcomer will be
forced to select a seat that places him right next to one of the already
seated men. Similar patterns can be observed in cinemas, public uri-
nals, airplanes, trains and buses. This is a reflection of the fact that we
all carry with us, everywhere we go, a portable territory called a Personal Space. If people move inside this space, we feel threatened. If they
keep too far outside it, we feel rejected. The result is a subtle series of
spatial adjustments, usually operating quite unconsciously and producing ideal compromises as far as this is possible. If a situation becomes
too crowded, then we adjust our reactions accordingly and allow our
personal space to shrink. Jammed into an elevator, a rush-hour com-
partment, or a packed room, we give up altogether and allow body-to-
body contact, but when we relinquish our Personal Space in this way,
we adopt certain special techniques. In essence, what we do is to convert these other bodies into "nonpersons." We studiously ignore them,
and they us. We try not to face them if we can possibly avoid it. We
wipe all expressiveness from our faces, letting them go blank. We may

look up at the ceiling or down at the floor, and we reduce body movements to a minimum. Packed together like sardines in a tin, we stand
dumbly still, sending out as few social signals as possible.

16   Even if the crowding is less severe, we still tend to cut down our
social interactions in the presence of large numbers. Careful observations of children in play groups revealed that if they are high-density
groupings there is less social interaction between the individual children, even though there is theoretically more opportunity for such contacts. At the same time, the high-density groups show a higher frequency of aggressive and destructive behaviour patterns in their play.
Personal Space—"elbow room"—is a vital commodity for the human
animal, and one that cannot be ignored without risking serious trouble.

17   Of course, we all enjoy the excitement of being in a crowd, and
this reaction cannot be ignored. But there are crowds and crowds. It is
pleasant enough to be in a "spectator crowd," but not also appealing to
find yourself in the middle of a rush-hour crush. The difference between the two is that the spectator crowd is all facing in the same direction and concentrating on a distant point of interest. Attending a the-
atre, there are twinges of rising hostility towards the stranger who sits
down immediately in front of you or the one who squeezes into the seat
next to you. The shared armrest can become a polite, but distinct, territorial boundary-dispute region. However, as soon as the show begins,
these invasions of Personal Space are forgotten and the attention is focused beyond the small space where the crowding is taking place. Now,
each member of the audience feels himself spatially related, not to his
cramped neighbours, but to the actor on the stage, and this distance is,
if anything, too great. In the rush-hour crowd, by contrast, each member of the pushing throng is competing with his neighbours all the time.
There is no escape to a spatial relation with a distant actor, only the
pushing, shoving bodies all around.

18   Those of us who have to spend a great deal of time in crowded
conditions become gradually better able to adjust, but no one can ever
become completely immune to invasions of Personal Space. This is because they remain forever associated with either powerful hostile or
equally powerful loving feelings. All through our childhood we will
have been held to be loved and held to be hurt, and anyone who invades our Personal Space when we are adults is, in effect, threatening
to extend this behaviour into one of these two highly charged areas of
human interaction. Even if his motives are clearly neither hostile nor

sexual, we still find it hard to suppress our reactions to his close approach. Unfortunately, different countries have different ideas about exactly how close is close. It is easy enough to test your own "space reaction": when you are talking to someone in the street or in any open space, reach out with your arm and see where the nearest point on his body comes. If you hail from western Europe, you will find that he is at roughly fingertip distance from you. In other words, as you reach out, your fingertips will just about make contact with his shoulder. If you come from eastern Europe, you will find you are standing at "wrist distance." If you come from the Mediterranean region, you will find that you are much closer to your companion, a little more than "elbow distance."

19   Trouble begins when a member of one of these cultures meets and talks to one from another. Say a British diplomat meets an Italian or an Arab diplomat at an embassy function. They start talking in a friendly way, but soon the fingertips man begins to feel uneasy. Without knowing quite why, he starts to back away gently from his companion. The companion edges forward again. Each tries in his way to set up a Personal Space relationship that suits his own background. But it is impossible to do. Every time the Mediterranean diplomat advances to a distance that feels comfortable for him, the British diplomat feels threatened. Every time the Briton moves back, the other feels rejected. Attempts to adjust this situation often lead to a talking pair shifting slowly across a room, and many an embassy reception is dotted with western-European fingertip-distance men pinned against the walls by eager elbow-distance men. Until such differences are fully understood and allowances made, these minor differences in "body territories" will continue to act as an alienation factor which may interfere in a subtle way with diplomatic harmony and other forms of international transaction.

20   If there are distance problems when engaged in conversation, then there are clearly going to be even bigger difficulties where people must work privately in a shared space. Close proximity of others, pressing against the invisible boundaries of our personal body-territory, makes it difficult to concentrate on non-social matters. Flat-mates, students sharing a study, sailors in the cramped quarters of a ship, and office staff in crowded work-places, all have to face this problem. They solve it by "cocooning." They use a variety of devices to shut themselves off from the others present. The best possible cocoon, of course, is a

small private room—a den, a private office, a study or a studio—which physically obscures the presence of other nearby territory-owners. This is the ideal situation for non-social work, but the space-sharer cannot enjoy this luxury. Their cocooning must be symbolic. They may, in certain cases, be able to erect small physical barriers, such as screens and partitions, which give substance to their invisible Personal Space boundaries, but when this cannot be done, other means must be sought. One of these is the "favoured object." Each space-sharer develops a preference, repeatedly expressed until it becomes a fixed pattern, for a particular chair, or table, or alcove. Others come to respect this, and friction is reduced. This system is often formally arranged (this is my desk, that is yours), but even where it is not, favoured places soon develop. Professor Smith has a favourite chair in the library. It is not formally his, but he always uses it and others avoid it. Seats around a messroom table, or a boardroom table, become almost personal property for specific individuals. Even in the home, father has his favourite chair for reading the newspaper or watching television. Another device is the blinkers-posture. Just as a horse that over-reacts to other horses and the distractions of the noisy race-course is given a pair of blinkers to shield its eyes, so people studying privately in a public place put on pseudo-blinkers in the form of shielding hands. Resting their elbows on the table, they sit with their hands screening their eyes from the scene on either side.

21   A third method of reinforcing the body-territory is to use personal markers. Books, papers and other personal belongings are scattered around the favoured site to render it more privately owned in the eyes of companions. Spreading out one's belongings is a well-known trick in public-transport situations, where a traveller tries to give the impression that seats next to him are taken. In many contexts carefully arranged personal markers can act as an effective territorial display, even in the absence of the territory owner. Experiments in a library revealed that placing a pile of magazines on the table in one seating position successfully reserved that place for an average of 77 minutes. If a sports-jacket was added, draped over the chair, then the "reservation effect" lasted for over two hours.

22   In these ways, we strengthen the defences of our Personal Spaces, keeping out intruders with the minimum of open hostility. As with all territorial behaviour, the object is to defend space with signals rather than with fists and at all three levels—the tribal, the family and the per-

sonal—it is a remarkably efficient system of space-sharing. It does not always seem so, because newspapers and newscasts inevitably magnify the exceptions and dwell on those cases where the signals have failed and wars have broken out, gangs have fought, neighbouring families have feuded, or colleagues have clashed, but for every territorial signal that has failed, there are millions of others that have not. They do not rate a mention in the news, but they nevertheless constitute a dominant feature of human society—the society of a remarkably territorial animal.

Reading Closely and Thinking Critically

1. In paragraph 2, Morris says that "it is rare for people to be driven to physical fighting in defense of these 'owned' spaces, but fight they will, if pushed to the limit." Agree or disagree with this statement and explain why you think the way you do.

2. How does territorial behavior reconcile the seemingly conflicting cooperative and competitive aspects of human beings?

3. Why are people uncomfortable with membership in large tribal groups and what do they do to alleviate that discomfort?

4. Why does Morris define family as a "breeding unit" and family territory as a "breeding ground"? Do you find these definitions insulting or inappropriate? Explain.

5. What happens when people have their personal space invaded? What happened the last time your own personal space was invaded?

6. What does Morris explain is the purpose of territorial behavior? That is, why do we need a territorial system of dominance?

Examining Structure and Strategy

1. In what place or combination of places is the thesis best expressed?

2. Morris does not begin the classification until paragraph 6. What purpose do the first five paragraphs serve?

3. Morris's third category is personal space. Within that category, he includes two other classifications. What are those classifications, and what categories do they include?

4. Morris uses many examples throughout the selection. Which paragraphs are particularly well served by examples? What would be lost if those examples were not there?

5. What elements of cause-and-effect analysis appear? (Cause-and-effect analysis, which gives the reasons for or the results of something, is explained in Chapter 8.)

6. What transitions does Morris use to move from one category to another? Evaluate the effectiveness of these transitions.

Considering Language and Style

1. Why does Morris spell the following words the way he does: *behaviour, defence, centre, colours, favoured?*

2. The tone of "Territorial Behaviour" is formal and academic, yet it is not stuffy or stiff. In fact, you likely found the selection very readable. What strategies does Morris use to keep his writing accessible to an average reader?

3. Consult a dictionary if you are unsure of the meaning of any of these words: *encroachment* (paragraph 4), *regalia* (paragraph 6), *clique* (paragraph 7), *pseudo* (paragraph 8), *portals* (paragraph 8), *peck order* (paragraph 9), *demarcation* (paragraph 11), *render* (paragraph 21).

For Group Discussion or Writing

With some classmates, identify the kinds of territorial behavior evident on college campuses. Also consider what purposes these behaviors serve.

Writing Assignments

1. *In your journal.* In paragraph 7, Morris discusses subgroups and why people belong to them. List the subgroups that you belong to and note what you get out of each of these groups.

2. *Using the pattern.* In paragraph 4, Morris refers to the "home base." Classify the kinds of home bases and give examples of each.

3. *Using the pattern.* Classify the "specialized territories" that create "a powerful feeling of security and importance" (paragraph 8) for you or for people in general.

4. *Using the pattern.* In paragraph 11, Morris says that "we feel at our most territorially secure" in the bedroom. Where else do we feel territorially secure? Classify these places and explain why we feel secure there.

5. *Using the pattern.* Define *cocooning* and classify the kinds of cocooning that you and your family engage in. As an alternative, classify the kinds of cocooning that you and your co-workers engage in.

6. *Considering a theme.* Morris presents territorial behavior as an important force for minimizing conflict among people. Do you agree that territorial behavior is a positive social force, or do you think it is actually a source of conflict and tension? Explain and illustrate your view.

7. *Connecting the readings.* Read "Just Walk on By: A Black Man Ponders His Power to Alter Public Space" (page 413) and explain what principles of territorial behavior the author illustrates. Then go on to suggest how the author can deal with his problem using some of the sociological principles pointed out in "Territorial Behaviour."

ADDITIONAL ESSAY ASSIGNMENTS

See pages 449 and 450 for suggestions for writing classification-division and for a revision checklist.

   1. Write a classification of popular music to inform people who do not know much about this variety of music.

   2. Write a classification of either television talk shows or situation comedies to explain the nature of these forms of entertainment. As an alternative, use division to break down one of these shows into its various parts.

   3. Classify teachers you have had.

   4. Classify baseball pitchers, football quarterbacks, basketball forwards, or others who play a particular position on an athletic team.

5. Classify movie superstars to explain what their appeal is. As an alternative, use division to break down the typical superstar into his or her components.

6. Classify your friends, past and present.

7. Classify either radio disc jockeys or television newscasters.

8. Classify babysitters or divide them into their components. If you like, you can make this one humorous.

9. To inform or entertain, classify fast-food restaurants.

10. Classify types of inner strength or types of courage.

11. To help explain their appeal, classify horror movies or break them down into their various parts.

12. Classify parenting styles. If you wish, your purpose can be to persuade your reader that a particular style is the best.

13. Classify types of drivers. If you like, your purpose can be to entertain.

14. Classify beer advertisements on television or cigarette advertisements in magazines to inform your reader of the persuasive strategies that are employed.

15. Classify the kinds of parties college students attend. As an alternative, use division to present the various aspects of a college party.

16. Classify football, baseball, or basketball fans.

17. Classify the kinds of neighbors people can have.

18. Write a classification of the kinds of good luck or bad luck.

19. Classify the different kinds of theme parks or roller coasters.

20. *Classification-division in context:* Assume you are the entertainment editor for your campus newspaper. For the first issue of the fall term, write an article that classifies the kinds of entertainment available to students at your school. Your purpose is to inform new freshmen of the options available to them and the chief features of each kind of entertainment in order to help them adjust to your campus.

THE PATTERN

A dictionary will tell you what a word means. However, sometimes you want to go beyond a word's literal dictionary meaning
to explain the significance, associations, private meanings, and
personal experiences associated with the word. This information
can only come from an *extended definition,* the kind of essay this
chapter treats. For example, consider the word *sled.* A dictionary
will tell a reader that it is a vehicle on runners used for coasting
on snow. However, an extended definition can tell the reader that
a sled contributed to the happiest times you shared with your
brother and father. Now consider the word *prejudice,* which can
mean different things to different people. An extended definition
allows you to explain the meaning and significance *you* ascribe to
the word. Thus, an extended definition affords a writer the opportunity to go beyond literal meaning to express feelings, opinions, knowledge, unusual views, and personal experiences associated with a word.

THE PURPOSES OF DEFINITION

More often than not, an extended definition informs. Sometimes
you inform by clarifying something that is complex. For example, an essay that defines *freedom* can help the reader understand
this very difficult concept. A definition can also inform by bringing the reader to a fresh appreciation of something familiar or
taken for granted. For example, if you think that Americans do
not sufficiently appreciate free speech, you could define *free
speech* to help readers renew their appreciation for this important
liberty. A definition can also bring a reader to an understanding
of something unfamiliar. In "What Is Poverty?" (page 515), for
example, the author defines poverty for an audience who has not
experienced it and hence does not fully understand what it means.

In addition to informing, an extended definition can allow
you to express feelings and relate experience. For example, you

could define *teenager* by explaining what your own teenage years were like and in this way relate part of your experience with adolescence. Similarly, in "The View from 80" (page 543) author Malcolm Cowley relates his experience as an octogenarian to clarify his definition of aging.

A definition can also entertain, as when you write a humorous definition of *freshman*, to amuse your reader. John Leo's "Journalese" (page 530) is an example of a definition that entertains.

Finally, an extended definition can serve a persuasive purpose. This is particularly true when the definition points to a conclusion about a controversial issue. For example, Jo Goodwin Parker presents a powerful, graphic definition of *poverty* in "What Is Poverty?" in order to move the reader to take steps to end this social condition. Similarly, Judy Brady defines *wife* in "I Want a Wife" (page 510) to convince the reader that the traditional wifely role is unfair to women.

In addition to using definition to develop entire essays, you will often use this pattern with other methods of development. For example, if you classify kinds of folk art, you might first define what folk art is; if you provide examples of courage, you might begin with your personal definition of courage; and if you explain the causes and effects of anorexia nervosa, you will probably define anorexia nervosa early on.

Definition in College Writing

College work often involves learning the meaning of terms and concepts, and a good way to demonstrate your understanding of these terms and concepts is to write definitions. Sometimes these definitions will be extended, as when you define *existentialism* in a paper for a philosophy class or when you define *naturalism* for an essay for an American literature class. You might also write an extended definition of *natural selection* for a biology class, of *the enclosure movement* for an economics class, or *cultural relativity* for an anthropology class.

Many times, you will incorporate definition with other patterns of development. For example, a history paper might require you to define the *chivalric code* and then go on to explain its effects. Similarly, an introduction to psychology course might require you to define and classify *defense mechanisms* and then go on to give examples of each kind.

SUPPORTING DETAILS

In general, an extended definition presents the characteristics of what is being defined. Thus, to define *courage,* you might note that its characteristics include doing what needs to be done without regard to personal cost and doing what needs to be done even when afraid.

Often when you present the characteristics, you rely on other patterns. For example, if you define *sinus headache* to relate your own experiences with this misery, you could *describe* the pain. To define *math anxiety* to inform the reader of what this condition is like, part of your essay could *narrate* an account of a time you experienced this anxiety. To define a *good teacher* to inform your reader of what a teacher should be like, you could include examples of good teachers from your past. To define *maturity* to clarify this concept, you could include a *contrast* of maturity with immaturity. To define *sexual harassment* to convince people to take action against this practice, part of your piece could *analyze the causes and effects* of sexual harassment to show why it is such a problem.

Sometimes it makes sense to explain what your subject is not, especially if you need to correct a misconception. For example, if you were defining *poverty,* you could note that poverty is not always something that people can escape if they just try hard enough.

When you write your definition, you should avoid stating the obvious, and you should avoid using a dictionary style. If you state the obvious, you will bore your reader. Thus, if you are defining *mother*, you need not state that a mother is a female parent. Similarly, a dictionary style is likely to bore a reader because it is stiff and unlike your own natural style. Thus, avoid defining *teenager* as "a person in that developmental period of hormonal and social change marking the transition from childhood to adulthood"—unless, of course, you want to put your reader to sleep.

Another problem to avoid is the "is when" construction, which is ungrammatical.

> no: Depression is when a person feels sad although his or her life is going well.

> yes: Depression causes a person to feel sad although his or her life is going well.

> yes: With depression, a person feels sad although his or her life is going well.

Finally, be careful to avoid circular definitions because they communicate very little. Instead, they merely repeat words and ideas.

> circular: Male liberation is the liberation of men.

> circular: Male liberation involves freeing men.

> better: Male liberation allows men to relinquish their historical roles to assume roles formerly held only by women.

STRUCTURING DEFINITION

The thesis for an extended definition can state what will be defined and your view of what will be defined, like this:

> Adolescence is not the happy time many people remember it to be.

This thesis allows you to define *adolescence* and show that it can be a difficult period.

You can also shape a thesis by noting what will be defined and why it is important to understand the term, like this:

> If we do not understand the meaning of free speech, we will be in danger of losing it.

To create interest in your essay, your introduction can explain the significance of the definition. Thus, if you are defining *homelessness,* you can note the extent of homelessness in this country to show why an understanding is important. You can also tell a story related to what you are defining. In addition, if the meaning of your term has changed over the years, you can explain what your term used to mean before going on to give a current definition. For example, if you are defining *dating,* you could open by noting that dating used to mean sitting in the parlor with a girl's parents or attending a church social.

Since definition often includes other patterns, the order of details will be influenced by these patterns. Thus, narrations will use chronological order, cause-and-effect analysis will reproduce causal chains, and so on. Purpose, too, can influence order. Thus, if your purpose is persuasive, you may want to place the characteristics of what you are defining in a progressive order to save the most important points for last.

SUGGESTIONS FOR WRITING DEFINITION

1. If you need help with topic selection, consider the roles you play in your life and the aspects of those roles. For example, if you are an athlete, you can define *student athlete* or *competition.* If you select a topic this way, you can draw on your own experience for detail. Another way to find a topic is to consider the emotions and moods you have been experiencing lately. In this way, you might settle on defining something like *anger, anxiety, jealousy, anticipation,* or *satisfaction,* using recent personal experience as detail.

2. To generate details, make a list of all the characteristics of what you are defining. Then go back and circle the ones you want to treat.

3. For each characteristic you circled, ask yourself the following to come up with ideas for development:

a. Is there a story I can tell to reveal or illustrate the characteristic?

b. Are there examples I can provide to illustrate the characteristics?

c. Can I describe the characteristic?

d. Can I compare the characteristic with something?

e. Can I contrast the characteristic with something?

f. What causes the characteristic?

g. What are the effects of the characteristic?

4. Decide if you need to clear up any misconceptions by explaining what your subject is *not.*

5. Write out a statement of the significance of your term and why it is important to define it. You can use a version of this for your introduction, thesis, or conclusion.

6. Using the ideas you generated, develop an outline.

7. In one sitting, write a draft from your outline. Just get your ideas down the best way you can without worrying about grammar, punctuation, spelling, or anything else.

Checklist for Revising Definition

1. Have you avoided stating the obvious?
2. Have you avoided a dictionary style?
3. Have you avoided "is when" constructions?
4. Have you avoided circular definitions?
5. Do all your details help you achieve your purpose?
6. Are all the relevant characteristics of your term developed?
7. As needed, have you explained what your term is not?
8. Is the significance of your definition clearly stated or strongly implied?

ANNOTATED STUDENT ESSAY

You will probably appreciate the following definition of a chocoholic, even if you find chocolate eminently resistable. Notice, in particular, the specific word choice and relaxed, informal style.

Prison Bars of Chocolate

1   Who is that embarrassed woman hovering over the five-foot solid chocolate Easter bunny in the candy store every spring? Who is that slightly overweight daddy eagerly volunteering every Halloween to take his children trick or treating? And what about that lovesick teenager whose heart-shaped box of candy for the love of his life is somehow mysteriously empty each February 14th? Their names are not significant; what is important is the addictive habit they have in common. These poor souls are hard-core chocoholics. I speak of them with sympathy as well as authority, for I, too, am a chocoholic.

Paragraph 1
The introduction creates interest with rhetorical questions. The thesis is the last sentence. It notes that chocoholics will be the focus and it gives the author's credentials. Both the subject matter and the style reflect the informal, light-hearted tone and that the purpose is to entertain.

2   Now, I'm not talking about your everyday candy lover, the one who would just as soon have a handful of Skittles as a handful of M&M's. I'm not talking, either, about your casually indulging, once-a-year-at-Christmas chocolate fancier. No, I'm talking about the true chocoholics of the world, those whose cravings for the stuff require daily gratification. We are the ones heading straight for the solid chocolate chunks in the gourmet candy store. None of those sissy mints or truffles for us, as least not until we have inhaled several chunks of plain, thick, rich, soul-satisfying chocolate, enough to ease the craving and permit us to then savor the more refined chocolate delicacies surrounding us.

Paragraph 2
The paragraph notes what the chocoholic is not. It also gives the first characteristic: the need for daily gratification. Note the specific nouns (*M&M's, Skittles*) and modifiers (*sissy, soul-searching*).

3   We pay dearly, of course, for our habit. The last pound of chocolate chunks I purchased cost me over seven dollars; it lasted two days. Even a simple chocolate candy bar can cost anywhere from fifty cents to a dollar. The neighborhood kids just love me—I'm good for every case of chocolate they have to sell for every school, little league, girl scout, or church fundraiser that comes along, no matter what the cost. And the machines! At least once or twice a week, my secret supply at work is depleted, and I find myself in front of a candy machine, shelling out eighty-five cents for a thin brown bar so stale and waxy that is does not even deserve the name of chocolate. I have even tried buying the big economy bags and boxes of candy and cookie bars, but— like the hopeful, cost-conscious smoker who buys

Paragraph 3
Paragraph begins with a topic sentence that presents the second characteristic of what is being defined (paying for the habit). The supporting details are examples and cause-and-effect analysis.

a carton of cigarettes instead of a pack every day—I found myself giving in to the habit at least twice as often and not saving a single penny as a result. What's worse, I gained twelve pounds in three weeks of my "economy" plan.

4   Like every other unhappily plumpish chocoholic I know, I have tried giving the habit up. I have tried tapering off, cutting consumption back slowly. I have tried substituting fake chocolate and low-cal "chocolate" desserts. I have tried using chocolate only as a reward. None of it worked. Finally I gave it up completely, cut off my supply, and went cold turkey. The result? Instant caffeine withdrawal. By the end of the first week, I was unbearable, snapping and snarling at anyone within striking distance. I had a migraine that would not quit, and *everything* reminded me of chocolate. Co-workers were begging me to please, please, take just one little bite of this nice chocolate, and my small son sacrificed his even smaller allowance on chocolate kisses, tearfully offering them up to me. I was an ogre. Eventually, of course, the caffeine craving wore off. I could deal with the little traumas of daily life without chocolate and without resorting to violence. I was free!

5   But the freedom was only temporary. Just the other day, I realized that I was right back where I had started, hiding in the bathrooms with my stash of Milky Ways, picking out the walnuts from the brownies before wolfing them down for breakfast. Today, I will be stopping in at that gourmet shop. You will know me if you see me; I'm the woman making a beeline straight for those chocolate chunks of heaven. Try not to get in my way.

Paragraph 4
The paragraph begins with a topic sentence that presents the next characteristic (what happens when trying to give up chocolate). The informal tone and style continue. Supporting details include narration and cause-and-effect analysis.

Paragraph 5
The conclusion provides closure by finishing the narration and with the author placing herself in a store where candy is sold, which harkens to the introduction. Specific words include *Mars bar, wolfing, chocolate chunks of heaven.*

I WANT A WIFE
Judy Brady

Born in San Francisco in 1937, Judy Brady earned a degree in painting from the University of Iowa in 1962. She is a freelance writer, feminist, and political activist. She has edited Women and Cancer *(1990) and* One in Three: Women with Cancer Confront an Epidemic *(1991). Involved in women's issues since 1969, Brady published "I Want a Wife" in 1972 for the first issue of* Ms. *magazine, and it quickly became a classic of feminist literature. In the essay, Brady informs the reader of the servile nature of the traditional wifely role, and she works to persuade the reader of the fundamental injustice of that role. As you read, decide how much of what the author says is still true today.*

THE PATTERN	THE PURPOSES
definition	*to inform and to persuade*

1   I belong to that classification of people known as wives. I am A Wife. And, not altogether incidentally, I am a mother.

2   Not too long ago a male friend appeared on the scene from the Midwest fresh from a recent divorce. He had one child, who is, of course, with his ex-wife. He is obviously looking for another wife. As I thought about him while I was ironing one evening, it suddenly occurred to me that I, too, would like to have a wife. Why do I want a wife?

3   I would like to go back to school so that I can become economically independent, support myself, and, if need be, support those dependent upon me. I want a wife who will work and send me to school. And while I am going to school I want a wife to take care of my children. I want a wife to keep track of the children's doctor and dentist appointments. And to keep track of mine, too. I want a wife to make sure my children eat properly and are kept clean. I want a wife who will wash the children's clothes and keep them mended. I want a wife who is a good nurturant attendant to my children, arranges for their schooling, makes sure that they have an adequate social life with their peers, takes them to the park, the zoo, etc. I want a wife who takes care of the children when they are sick, a wife who arranges to be around when

the children need special care, because, of course, I cannot miss classes at school. My wife must arrange to lose time at work and not lose the job. It may mean a small cut in my wife's income from time to time, but I guess I can tolerate that. Needless to say, my wife will arrange and pay for the care of the children while my wife is working.

4   I want a wife who will take care of *my* physical needs. I want a wife who will keep my house clean. A wife who will pick up after my children, a wife who will pick up after me. I want a wife who will keep my clothes clean, ironed, mended, replaced when need be, and who will see to it that my personal things are kept in their proper place so that I can find what I need the minute I need it. I want a wife who cooks the meals, a wife who is a *good* cook. I want a wife who will plan the menus, do the necessary grocery shopping, prepare the meals, serve them pleasantly, and then do the cleaning up while I do my studying. I want a wife who will care for me when I am sick and sympathize with my pain and loss of time from school. I want a wife to go along when our family takes a vacation so that someone can continue to care for me and my children when I need a rest and a change of scene.

5   I want a wife who will not bother me with rambling complaints about a wife's duties. But I want a wife who will listen to me when I feel the need to explain a rather difficult point I have come across in my course of studies. And I want a wife who will type my papers for me when I have written them.

6   I want a wife who will take care of the details of my social life. When my wife and I are invited out by my friends, I want a wife who will take care of the babysitting arrangements. When I meet people at school that I like and want to entertain, I want a wife who will have the house clean, will prepare a special meal, serve it to me and my friends, and not interrupt when I talk about the things that interest me and my friends. I want a wife who will have arranged that the children are fed and ready for bed before my guests arrive so that the children do not bother us. I want a wife who takes care of the needs of my guests so that they feel comfortable, who makes sure that they have an ashtray, that they are passed the hors d'oeuvres, that they are offered a second helping of the food, that their wine glasses are replenished when necessary, that their coffee is served to them as they like it. And I want a wife who knows that sometimes I need a night out by myself.

7   I want a wife who is sensitive to my sexual needs, a wife who makes love passionately and eagerly when I feel like it, a wife who

makes sure that I am satisfied. And, of course, I want a wife who will not demand sexual attention when I am not in the mood for it. I want a wife who assumes the complete responsibility for birth control, because I do not want more children. I want a wife who will remain sexually faithful to me so that I do not have to clutter up my intellectual life with jealousies. And I want a wife who understands that *my* sexual needs may entail more than strict adherence to monogamy. I must, after all, be able to relate to people as fully as possible.

8   If, by chance, I find another person more suitable as a wife than the wife I already have, I want the liberty to replace my present wife with another one. Naturally, I will expect a fresh, new life; my wife will take the children and be solely responsible for them so that I am left free.

9   When I am through with school and have acquired a job, I want my wife to quit working and remain at home so that my wife can more fully and completely take care of a wife's duties.

10   My God, who *wouldn't* want a wife?

Reading Closely and Thinking Critically

1. What is Brady's attitude toward the wifely role she depicts in the essay?

2. What view of men does Brady present in her essay? Do you think she is being fair to men? Explain.

3. Why does Brady say she wants a wife? Do you think there is more to it than what she says? Explain.

4. What kind of woman would enjoy being the wife Brady describes?

5. Is "I Want a Wife" as pertinent today as it was when it was first published in 1972? Explain.

Examining Structure and Strategy

1. Paragraphs 1 and 2 form the introduction of "I Want a Wife." What approach does Brady take to that introduction?

2. In your own words, write out the thesis of "I Want a Wife."

3. Brady uses classification-division to help develop her definition. (Classification-division, discussed in Chapter 9, sorts items into categories.) What categories does Brady establish for the wife's duties?

4. A *rhetorical question* is one for which no answer is expected. Brady closes "I Want a Wife" with a rhetorical question. Do you think this creates an effective conclusion? Explain.

5. Why does Brady open with a statement that she is a wife and mother?

Considering Language and Style

1. Brady frequently repeats the words "I want." What does this repetition contribute?

2. Can Brady be taken literally? That is, does she mean *exactly* what she says? Explain.

3. Consult a dictionary if you are unsure of the meaning of any of these words: *nurturant* (paragraph 3), *hors d'oeuvres* (paragraph 6), *entail* (paragraph 7), *monogamy* (paragraph 7).

For Group Discussion or Writing

"I Want a Wife" originally appeared in *Ms.* in 1972. If the essay were published today, in what magazines could it appropriately appear? Develop a list with two or three classmates, and explain why you have chosen the magazines on your list.

Writing Assignments

1. *In your journal.* Write a description of the ideal spouse. To what extent does your description conform to the stereotype of the ideal wife or husband?

2. *Using the pattern.* Write an essay entitled "I Want a _____." Fill in the blank with some family role (husband, child, older brother, younger sister, mother, father, grandmother, grandfather, and so on.) Define the role and point out its difficulty and/or unfairness. If you like, you can borrow Brady's technique and repeat the words "I want a _____ who . . ."

3. *Using the pattern.* Write an essay that defines what you think the role of *wife* should be. As an alternative, define what you think the role of *husband* should be.

4. *Using the pattern.* Write a definition of one of the roles you currently play or have played in the past: wife, husband, mother, father, child, friend, soldier, student, track star, musician, younger brother, older sister, student athlete, nontraditional student, international student, coach, and so on. Like Brady, let your definition convey how you feel about the role.

5. *Using the pattern.* Define the role of someone who has traditionally been exploited: a table server, a nurse, a babysitter, a cleaning person, and so on.

6. *Considering a theme.* Brady presents the stereotype of the ideal wife, as it existed in 1972. What is the current stereotype of the ideal wife or husband? Describe that stereotype and explain what factors are responsible for that stereotype (television, movies, the women's movement, advertisements, and so on).

7. *Connecting the readings.* Describe the traditional view of women. Then using women you know as examples, explain to what extent women today conform to or depart from that view. The information in "I Want a Wife" and "What I've Learned from Men" (page 229) may give you some ideas.

WHAT IS POVERTY?
Jo Goodwin Parker

When University of Oklahoma professor George Henderson was gathering material for his book America's Other Children: Public Schools Outside Suburbia *(1971), the following essay was mailed to him from West Virginia with the name Jo Goodwin Parker on it. We do not know for sure whether Ms. Parker is writing of herself or others. Either way, unless you have experienced poverty yourself, her definition will be an eye-opener for you. In addition to informing her audience about the nature of poverty, the definition attempts to persuade the reader to help solve the problem. As you read, consider how Parker's description helps her fulfill her purposes.*

THE PATTERN	THE PURPOSES
definition	*to inform and to persuade*

1   You ask me what is poverty? Listen to me. Here I am, dirty, smelly, and with no "proper" underwear on and the stench of my rotting teeth near you. I will tell you. Listen to me. Listen without pity. I cannot use your pity. Listen with understanding. Put yourself in my dirty, worn out, ill-fitting shoes, and hear me.

2   Poverty is getting up every morning from a dirt- and illness-stained mattress. The sheets have long since been used for diapers. Poverty is living in a smell that never leaves. This is a smell of urine, sour milk, and spoiling food sometimes joined with the strong smell of long-cooked onions. Onions are cheap. If you have smelled this smell, you did not know how it came. It is the smell of the outdoor privy. It is the smell of young children who cannot walk the long dark way in the night. It is the smell of the mattresses where years of "accidents" have happened. It is the smell of the milk which has gone sour because the refrigerator long has not worked, and it costs money to get it fixed. It is the smell of rotting garbage. I could bury it, but where is the shovel? Shovels cost money.

3   Poverty is being tired. I have always been tired. They told me at the hospital when the baby came that I had chronic anemia caused from poor diet, a bad case of worms, and that I needed a corrective opera-

tion. I listened politely—the poor are always polite. The poor always listen. They don't say that there is no money for iron pills, or better food, or worm medicine. The idea of an operation is frightening and costs so much that, if I had dared, I would have laughed. Who takes care of my children? Recovery from an operation takes a long time. I have three children. When I left them with "Granny" the last time I had a job, I came home to find the baby covered with fly specks, and a diaper that had not been changed since I left. When the dried diaper came off, bits of my baby's flesh came with it. My other child was playing with a sharp bit of broken glass, and my oldest was playing alone at the edge of a lake. I made twenty-two dollars a week, and a good nursery school costs twenty dollars a week for my three children. I quit my job.

4   Poverty is dirt. You say in your clean clothes coming from your clean house, "Anybody can be clean." Let me explain about housekeeping with no money. For breakfast I give my children grits with no oleo or cornbread without eggs and oleo. This does not use up many dishes. What dishes there are, I wash in cold water and with no soap. Even the cheapest soap has to be saved for the baby's diapers. Look at my hands, so cracked and red. Once I save for two months to buy a jar of Vaseline for my hands and the baby's diaper rash. When I had saved enough, I went to buy it and the price had gone up two cents. The baby and I suffered on. I have to decide every day if I can bear to put my cracked, sore hands into the cold water and strong soap. But you ask, why not hot water? Fuel costs money. If you have a wood fire it costs money. If you burn electricity, it costs money. Hot water is a luxury. I do not have luxuries. I know you will be surprised when I tell you how young I am. I look so much older. My back has been bent over the wash tubs for so long, I cannot remember when I ever did anything else. Every night I wash every stitch my school-age child has on and just hope her clothes will be dry by morning.

5   Poverty is staying up all night on cold nights to watch the fire, knowing one spark on the newspaper covering the walls means your sleeping children die in flames. In summer poverty is watching gnats and flies devour your baby's tears when he cries. The screens are torn and you pay so little rent you know they will never be fixed. Poverty means insects in your food, in your nose, in your eyes, and crawling over you when you sleep. Poverty is hoping it never rains because diapers won't dry when it rains and soon you are using newspapers.

Poverty is seeing your children forever with runny noses. Paper hand-kerchiefs cost money and all your rags you need for other things. Even more costly are antihistamines. Poverty is cooking without food and cleaning without soap.

6   Poverty is asking for help. Have you ever had to ask for help, knowing your children will suffer unless you get it? Think about ask-ing for a loan from a relative, if this is the only way you can imagine asking for help. I will tell you how it feels. You find out where the of-fice is that you are supposed to visit. You circle that block four or five times. Thinking of your children, you go in. Everybody is very busy. Fi-nally, someone comes out and you tell her that you need help. That never is the person you need to see. You go see another person, and af-ter spilling the whole shame of your poverty all over the desk between you, you find that this isn't the right office after all—you must repeat the whole process, and it never is any easier at the next place.

7   You have asked for help, and after all it has a cost. You are again told to wait. You are told why, but you don't really hear because of the red cloud of shame and the rising black cloud of despair.

8   Poverty is remembering. It is remembering quitting school in ju-nior high because "nice" children had been so cruel about my clothes and and my smell. The attendance officer came. My mother told him I was pregnant. I wasn't but she thought that I could get a job and help out. I had jobs off and on, but never long enough to learn anything. Mostly I remember being married. I was so young then. I am still young. For a time, we had all the things you have. There was a little house in another town, with hot water and everything. Then my hus-band lost his job. There was unemployment insurance for a while and what few jobs I could get. Soon, all our nice things were repossessed and we moved back here. I was pregnant then. This house didn't look so bad when we first moved in. Every week it gets worse. Nothing is ever fixed. We now had no money. There were a few odd jobs for my husband, but everything went for food then, as it does now. I don't know how we lived through three years and three babies, but we did. I'll tell you something, after the last baby I destroyed my marriage. It had been a good one, but could you keep on bringing children in this dirt? Did you ever think how much it costs for any kind of birth con-trol? I knew my husband was leaving the day he left, but there were no good-byes between us. I hope he has been able to climb out of this mess somewhere. He never could hope with us to drag him down.

9   That's when I asked for help. When I got it, you know how much it was? It was, and is, seventy-eight dollars a month for the four of us; that is all I ever can get. Now you know why there is no soap, no needles and thread, no hot water, no aspirin, no worm medicine, no hand cream, no shampoo. None of these things forever and ever and ever. So that you can see clearly, I pay twenty dollars a month rent, and most of the rest goes for food. For grits and cornmeal, and rice and milk and beans. I try my best to use only the minimum electricity. If I use more, there is that much less for food.

10   Poverty is looking into a black future. Your children won't play with my boys. They will turn to other boys who steal to get what they want. I can already see them behind the bars of their prison instead of behind the bars of my poverty. Or they will turn to the freedom of alcohol or drugs, and find themselves enslaved. And my daughter? At best, there is for her life like mine.

11   But you say to me, there are schools. Yes, there are schools. My children have no extra books, no magazines, no extra pencils, or crayons, or paper and the most important of all, they do not have health. They have worms, they have infections, they have pink-eye all summer. They do not sleep well on the floor, or with me in my one bed. They do not suffer from hunger, my seventy-eight dollars keeps us alive, but they do suffer malnutrition. Oh yes, I do remember what I was taught about health in school. It doesn't do much good. In some places there is a surplus commodities program. Not here. The county said it cost too much. There is a school lunch program. But I have two children who will already be damaged by the time they get to school.

12   But, you say to me, there are health clinics. Yes, there are health clinics and they are in the towns. I live out here eight miles from town. I can walk that far (even if it is sixteen miles both ways), but can my little children? My neighbor will take me when he goes; but he expects to get paid, *one way or another.* I bet you know my neighbor. He is that large man who spends his time at the gas station, the barbershop, and the corner store complaining about the government spending money on the immoral mothers of illegitimate children.

13   Poverty is an acid that drips on pride until all pride is worn away. Poverty is a chisel that chips on honor until honor is worn away. Some of you say that you would do *something* in my situation, and maybe you would, for the first week or the first month, but for year after year?

14   Even the poor can dream. A dream of a time when there is money. Money for the right kinds of food, for worm medicine, for iron

pills, for toothbrushes, for hand cream, for a hammer and nails and a bit of screening, for a shovel, for a bit of paint, for some sheeting, for needles and thread. Money to pay *in money* for a trip to town. And, oh, money for hot water and money for soap. A dream of when asking for help does not eat away the last bit of pride. When the office you visit is as nice as the offices of other governmental agencies, when there are enough workers to help you quickly, when workers do not quit in defeat and despair. When you have to tell your story to only one person, and that person can send you for other help and you don't have to prove your poverty over and over and over again.

15   I have come out of my despair to tell you this. Remember I did not come from another place or another time. Others like me are all around you. Look at us with an angry heart, anger that will help you help me. Anger that will let you tell of me. The poor are always silent. Can you be silent too?

Reading Closely and Thinking Critically

1. According to Parker, what are the chief characteristics of poverty?

2. What are the effects of poverty on children?

3. According to the author, why doesn't education provide a way out of poverty for children?

4. In paragraphs 11, 12, and 13, Parker addresses people who say that schools, health clinics, and the poor themselves can help alleviate poverty. How does she counter the argument these people make? Why does she bother to address this argument?

5. Paragraph 8 describes a vicious cycle that is part of poverty. What other vicious cycles can you detect as a result of reading the essay?

6. What kind of audience do you think is appropriate for "What Is Poverty?"

Examining Structure and Strategy

1. Parker uses a great deal of description in her essay. Is this description objective or expressive? (See page 70 on objective and expressive details.) What does the descriptive detail contribute to the essay?

2. In which paragraph does Parker use examples? What do these examples contribute?

3. In which paragraph does Parker use cause-and-effect analysis? (Cause-and-effect analysis, discussed in Chapter 8, explains the causes and/or effects of something.) What does the analysis contribute to the essay?

4. What approach does Parker take to the introduction?

5. What approach does Parker take to the conclusion?

Considering Language and Style

1. Many of Parker's paragraphs begin with the words "Poverty is . . ." Do you think that this technique is effective? Explain.

2. Consult a dictionary if you are unsure of the meaning of any of these words: *privy* (paragraph 2), *oleo* (paragraph 4), *antihistamines* (paragraph 5), *repossessed* (paragraph 8).

For Group Discussion or Writing

With two or three classmates, decide which of Parker's descriptions best help her fulfill her purpose. Then explain why the description functions so effectively.

Writing Assignments

1. *In your journal.* Compare and contrast your understanding of poverty before and after you read "What Is Poverty?" What, if anything, did you learn as a result of reading the essay?

2. *Using the pattern.* Define a problem that you have firsthand knowledge of (drug use, alcohol use, peer pressure, pressure faced by adolescents, sexual experimentation, materialism, sexism, racism, apathy, sexual harassment, and so on). Like Parker, try to arouse your audience to take action to solve the problem.

3. *Using the pattern.* Define a school problem (for example, pressure for grades, competition, cheating, exam anxiety, or math anxiety). Like Parker, use description and/or exemplification.

4. *Using the pattern.* Define one of the following: fear, ambition, pride, jealousy, hunger, or depression. Draw on personal experience for clarifying examples.

5. *Considering a theme.* Compare and contrast the stereotype of the poor with the description of the poor in "What Is Poverty?" (See Chapter 7 on comparison-contrast.)

6. *Connecting the readings.* Using information from "What Is Poverty?" and "Untouchables" (page 236), write an essay to persuade legislators to increase their effort to aid the poor and homeless. If you like, you can also include information gathered from newspapers and magazines like *Time, Newsweek,* and *U.S. News and World Report,* along with your own ideas. (See the appendix for information on how to handle material borrowed from sources.)

LISTS
Jeanine Larmoth

Are you a list maker? If so, the following essay, from Town and Country *(Nov. 1989), may give you a fresh view of those lists you make. Even if you are not a list maker, you will probably enjoy "Lists" because it entertains at the same time it relates something of the role lists play in the author's life. As you read, notice what a skillful wordsmith Jeanine Larmoth is.*

THE PATTERN	THE PURPOSES
definition	*to express feelings and relate experience, to entertain, and to inform*

1   My mother's way of reviewing a movie, in the days when we often went, was simple. If she found she was going over her lists in her head while Gable nibbled on Colbert's ear, the movie was poor. A good movie could make you forget even your lists.

2   Oh, the pleasure of lists, endless, ongoing lists. Lists of things that must be done, places to go, people to see, wines to try, courses to take, plays to applaud, restaurants to avoid, hotels to discover, books to read on a desert island. Shopping lists, laundry lists, Christmas card lists, lists of resolutions, lists scratched on the back of old envelopes, lists scrawled on a chalkboard in the kitchen. Lists no bigger than a postage stamp, stuck in a wallet. Lists like a friend of mine's, which unroll from his pocket like the Dead Sea Scrolls. Lists of lists.

3   Lists offer a wonderful way to confine the nearly insuperable demands of the chaotic, freewheeling world to the possible, of turning abstracts into specifics, cutting experience into bite sizes. I can do it. Only three more to go. With every scoring of the pen, a sense of achievement. Like Ariadne's thread, lists unwind to show us the way out of the maze of everyday life. They are maps of the earthworks of ennui—the duties, responsibilities, appointments and chores so ready to suffocate us in the mundane. Lists are a strategy, a declaration of intent to overtake rather than be overtaken; to clump and conquer. They even make it possible to go to the dentist in a neat, orderly fashion, as if it were a reasonable thing to do. Something more to be crossed off. Another triumph.

4   The danger, of course, is that, like many other labor-saving devices, the lists may enslave the list maker. The mob of waiting exigencies is kept at bay, to be sure, but suddenly a small scrap of paper, not the things to be done, becomes the despot. You're so busy checking your list, you don't notice life going by on the streets outside the bus or train window. Rather than enjoying the view from the Bridge of Sighs, what's more important is ticking it off the list of sights. The mere pleasure of going down the list, eliminating things done, becomes more rewarding than doing even agreeable things. Instead of leading you out of the maze, the thread is actually entangling your feet.

5   The best way around a list is to lose it; or drop it in a puddle, splatter it with olive oil or glob it with butter (because you're going over it during lunch), and thus have to toss it away; to use it, when no other scrap of paper is handy, to mash a threatening mosquito on the bedroom wall; or just to throw the still-current one out under the delusion that it's an old, superseded list.

6   Somewhat craftier ways to avoid a list are to mislay your glasses so you can't read it, leave it in another pocket or pocketbook, or just plain forget to look at it. Such omissions strike at the very heart of the problem, since forgetfulness is a great reason lists exist. The failure of memory, so frightening and frequent in these days of overloaded minds, is part of why you keep them (or so lists would have you believe). Often, however, what we're afraid of overlooking might *well* be overlooked.

7   Any assurance from the cocky non-list keeper (with a knowing wink at Freud) that we will remember only what we want to remember causes the list keeper to pause briefly, like a startled hare, then go on scribbling. The true list maker is well aware that knowing what one wants is a matter of such complexity that quite a few people spend a lifetime pondering it without arriving at clear-cut answers. Such an assurance teeters on the twin fallacies that we know what we want, from moment to moment, and that we can act on this knowledge—when, in fact, we will forget the ice cream but remember the toothpaste, buy a special birthday card for a dear friend a year in advance, and then forget to send it in time for the actual birth date.

8   But, generally, lists are indestructible. You're more likely to let a dollar bill fall in the gutter than a list, spill drops of olive oil on a silk shirt or linen trousers, throw away a divine love letter, let travelers' checks go through the wash, mash the mosquito with a long-awaited

rare book just received from the bookseller. The list will keep on being there, insisting, like the mosquito—missed—on the bedroom wall after you've turned out the light and are trying to suffocate yourself beneath the sheet (by God, he won't get you alive!).

9   In their tenacity, lists are like one of my favorites from the symbol-making days of childhood: the toy with a weighted bottom. Made of papier-mâché and standing about a foot high, the toy was introduced to me as a London bobby. Properly pear-shaped, he had a blue uniform, black belt and black helmet, rather prominent eyes and a bushy black mustache. As with all such toys whose mission is to give early lessons in frustration, he had the rebounding power of a rubber ball, and bounced back up with an irritatingly cheerful jingle. I disliked the toy intensely, as I was surely meant to do, and probably tried a variety of strategies to get him down, once and for all: sneaking up behind him, and then alternating a slow shove and a fast push, for example. Useless. He is still going strong.

10   Even were one to forgo the tyranny of a personal list, lists are like an ever-encroaching dragnet. There are lists of best-dressed men and women, worst-dressed men and women, lists of bestsellers, leading stocks, the richest men in America, the most wanted criminals in America, the world's endangered species, the wonders of the ancient world, world's records. Real estate pages are lists, as are want ads. Television guides are lists. The Academy Award ceremonies televised every spring are nothing but illustrated lists; the running of the Kentucky Derby, a list in motion.

11   Whole industries have sprung up around lists. To jolly up the lists covering the refrigerator door, there are the cunning magnets shaped like lollipops, daises, teddy bears in paper bags. 3M cleverly sells small pads of stick-'em-backed bits of yellow paper so that lists may be scattered with the profligacy of autumn leaves—everywhere, at all times and for all reasons. They might be called notes, but add them together and they are lists. What do computers do, basically, but make lists, lists that talk to lists, lists that answer lists with lists of their own?

12   From time to time, as well, attempts have been made to formulate ready-made lists to cash in on the compulsion. I once discovered a chic set of back-to-back lists, one simply headed "Town" and the other "Country," useful for those whose real reason for having a weekend house is to carry things back and forth. The laundry lists that are found in hotel rooms must be fairly satisfactory, since they are supplied as cus-

tomarily as little soaps, shampoos and bath hats. Room-service order lists, on the other hand, hint at one reason ready-made lists never quite make it. The blank space on the order for special instructions doesn't stay blank. Not with me, in any case. Take ordering breakfast in Italy: a relatively straightforward procedure, it would seem. The choices could hardly be simpler: type of fruit juice, way the coffee should be prepared, time the breakfast should be brought. The pastry goes without saying, unless there's a blank. If there is, I jot down my preference for plain Italian bread rolls, not the Italian, sweet-doughed variations on a French theme. If there's not, room service has to be called. It would be simpler to call in the first place.

13   Occasionally, someone comes out with a ready-made shopping list for groceries. All well and good for the egg-milk-butter-and-bread person. But then, hardly necessary, since the stops for such persons would be automatic. For people who need grocery lists, what should be on them are the items not regularly stocked in the kitchen and liable to be overlooked in the store: the anchovy paste in a tube that's half hidden by tins of salmon, the artichoke hearts that are kept on a shelf well above eye level. Yet no printed list that aspired to be shorter than my friend's scrolls could include all the possibilities. Grocery stores would have to provide rest stops where people could consult their lists and chart their next moves.

14   Undoubtedly, the theory behind ready-made lists is that people will be enormously relieved only to have to check the appropriate boxes. Not a bit of it. Lists, at the simplest level, give us an opportunity to use one of our first real skills: writing. Few of us, even those with indifferent-to-illegible handwriting, are immune to a childlike sense of satisfaction at seeing black ink impress white paper. More important, the composition of the list—headings, subheadings, order in which the must-do's appear, underlinings, exclamation points, asterisks, different colored inks—is part of the art. It requires a measure of clarity to compose a list, a sorting out of importances. There is even a sense that a well-assembled list might almost take care of itself; that by recognizing what has to be done, you're partway to getting it done. In making the list, you have foreseen the problems that can arise, with the result that some items may seem ripe for immediate crossing off, others must be attacked at a run, and still others you may dozily decide to put off—which very often proves the best resolution of all.

15   Perhaps it's due to this dependence on composition that lists are often seen as a substitute for poetry or prose—with mixed results. A

public speaker, having gotten off the requisite, feeble joke, can launch immediately into lists—thus slips the hour away. I have listened, trying not to, more than once to a priest whose sermons are nothing but lists, lists of stirring adjectives, superbly modulated, resonantly recited, which give the effect of something having been said, when nothing has been. Books, too, may be largely compilations of lists and statistics—space-sopping, page-gnawing lists—lists that, like the priest's, convince the reader he is acquiring something of substance or, at the very least, additional material for lists of his own.

16   A reliance on lists is not, however, automatically a sign of intellectual poverty. Just as a telephone directory recited by a well-schooled actor is said to be riveting, so the list flowing from the pen of an artist is a splendid tool. Lists, such as those quoted from an anonymous recorder by Vita Sackville-West in the introduction to the diary of Lady Anne Clifford, pile up images that bring a scene to exotic life. Before our eyes, a harbor's rim expands, piled high with the revealing magnificence of plunder brought back from the Azores for Queen Elizabeth I.

17   As Sackville-West quotes the unidentified scribe, "They unladed and discharged about five millions of silver all in pieces of eight or ten pound great, so that the whole quay lay covered with plates and chests of silver. . . . Elephants teeth, porcelain, vessels of china, coconuts, hides, ebon wood as black as jet, bedsteads of the same; cloth of the rinds of trees very strange for the matter and artificial in workmanship."

18   Sackville-West concludes: "All this and more was trundled out on to English quays, together with ropes, corn, bacon, copper, all in great store, Negroes, monkeys, and Spanish prisoners, dark seamen with silver rings in their ears, herded together, sullen and aloof."

19   Used to quite different purpose is a list of Montaigne's cataloging the polarities in his own soul. "All contradictions are to be found in me in some shape or manner," he wrote. "Bashful, insolent; chaste, lustful; talkative, taciturn; tough, delicate; ingenious, stupid; morose, affable; lying, truthful; learned, ignorant; and liberal, and miserly, and prodigal: I find all this in myself, more or less, as I turn myself about; and whoever studies himself very attentively finds in himself, yes, even in his judgment, this mutability and discord."

20   Though the ordinary list cannot aspire to these literary heights, it nonetheless plays its part in the dream of eternity, for not only does a list control life, it prolongs it. However goaded by his lists the list maker is, he is comforted by the confidence that he can never die: his

list isn't finished. There will always be petunias that need planting, a let-ter-to-the-editor to be dashed off, the birdbath to be waterproofed, stamps to be bought, a friend who's not been telephoned for a while. In short, the list maker is just too busy—though thanks awfully for the invitation.

21   Delighted as I am by the prospect of poetic lists, or failing that, immortality, I am, however, convinced that the only way to approach the simplification of life and true freedom that lists delude us into sup-posing they promote is to destroy them.

22   Unfortunately, mine don't allow me a moment to figure out how.

Reading Closely and Thinking Critically

1. According to Larmoth, what purpose do lists serve?

2. How is it that lists, meant to help the list maker, can actually enslave him or her?

3. According to Larmoth, what are the chief characteristics of lists?

4. Why does list making appeal to people?

5. Using the information in the essay for clues, explain what you think Larmoth's view of list making is. Is there a paragraph that best expresses that view? If so, which one?

6. How serious do you think Larmoth is in her essay?

Examining Structure and Strategy

1. Larmoth's essay on lists includes lists of its own. For example, paragraph 2 includes a list of different kinds of lists. Cite one other example of lists in the essay. What do you think these lists contribute?

2. Larmoth uses many examples in her essay. Cite two such examples. What do the examples contribute to the definition?

3. Part of the pleasure of reading "Lists" comes from Larmoth's specific word choice. For example, in paragraph 15, she refers to "space-sopping, page-gnawing lists." Cite two examples of phrases or sentences that appeal to you because of the specific word choice. (See page 72 on specific word choice.)

4. Which paragraph makes use of comparison to explain a characteristic? (Comparison, discussed in Chapter 7, notes similarities.) Which paragraphs make use of cause-and-effect analysis? (Cause-and-effect analysis, discussed in Chapter 8, notes the causes and/or effects of something.)

5. Paragraphs 21 and 22 form the conclusion of the essay. Do those paragraphs bring the essay to a satisfying close? Explain.

Considering Language and Style

1. In paragraph 3, Larmoth uses a simile to compare lists to Ariadne's thread, and in paragraph 4 the thread image appears again. (See page 73 for an explanation of similes.) What is Ariadne's thread? Does it work as an appropriate image? Explain. Cite one other simile in the essay and evaluate its appropriateness.

2. In paragraph 4, Larmoth refers to the Bridge of Sighs. Explain the meaning of this reference.

3. Consult a dictionary if you are unsure of the meaning of any of these words: *Dead Sea Scrolls* (paragraph 2), *insuperable* (paragraph 3), *earthworks* (paragraph 3), *ennui* (paragraph 3), *exigencies* (paragraph 4), *tenacity* (paragraph 9), *encroaching* (paragraph 10), *dragnet* (paragraph 10), *profligacy* (paragraph 11), *quays* (paragraph 18).

For Group Discussion or Writing
Using the information and clues in "Lists," give the chief characteristics of the list maker.

Writing Assignments

1. *In your journal.* Are you a list maker? If so, explain why you make lists and their advantages and/or disadvantages. If not, explain why not and how you keep your life ordered without them.

2. *Using the pattern.* Write a definition of something that helps you simplify your life: an answering machine, a microwave oven, a computer, and so on.

3. *Using the pattern.* Define something that tyrannizes or enslaves you, the way lists tyrannize and enslave Larmoth (for example, aerobics, running, weight training, vegetarianism, making the dean's list, dressing for success, video games, or a hobby). Try to show how you are enslaved by what you define.

4. *Using the pattern.* Write a definition of *list maker* or *lists* based on your own experience and understanding. Feel free to disagree with Larmoth's definition. (The preceding group activity may help you.)

5. *Considering a theme.* Summarize the kinds of lists and their purposes, using the information in "Lists" (and your own ideas, if you wish). Then go on to explain what the need to make lists says about modern life.

6. *Connecting the readings.* In paragraph 4, Larmoth explains that although the purpose of lists is ostensibly to order life and keep it manageable, lists may really interfere with the full enjoyment of life. Discuss what else is ostensibly meant to facilitate things but really has the potential to hinder in some way. Some of the ideas in "Talk in the Intimate Relationship" (page 354) and "White Lies" (page 458) may help you.

JOURNALESE, OR WHY ENGLISH IS THE SECOND LANGUAGE OF THE FOURTH ESTATE
John Leo

Born in 1935, John Leo has extensive experience as a journalist. He was a senior writer at U.S. News and World Report *before becoming a contributing editor. He was also a reporter for the* New York Times *and associate editor and senior writer at* Time *magazine. In addition, Leo has also held positions at* Commonweal *and* Village Voice. *"Journalese, or Why English Is the Second Language of the Fourth Estate" is from* How the Russians Invented Baseball **and** Other Essays of Enlightenment. *In the essay, Leo combines definition with exemplification and classification to explain the characteristics of journalese, the variety of English reporters use to say one thing and mean another. While very informative, the essay has many entertaining, humorous aspects. In addition, you may notice a persuasive purpose lurking in Leo's ironic tone.*

THE PATTERNS	THE PURPOSES
definition with exemplification and classification	*to inform, to entertain, and to persuade*

1   As a cub reporter, columnist Richard Cohen of *The Washington Post* trudged out one day to interview a lawyer who had been described in many newspaper reports as "ruddy-faced." The man was woozily abusive and lurched about with such abandon that young Cohen instantly realized that the real meaning of *ruddy-faced* is drunk. This was his introduction to journalese, the fascinating second tongue acquired by most reporters as effortlessly as an Iranian toddler learns Farsi or a Marin County child learns psychobabble.

2   Fluency in journalese means learning all about "the right stuff," "life in the fast lane," and the vexing dilemma of being caught "between a rock and a hard place," the current Scylla-Charybdis image. The Middle East is "war-torn" or "strife-torn," except during those inexplicable moments when peace briefly breaks out. Then it is simply "much-troubled." Kuwait is located just east of the adjective *oil-rich,* and the Irish Republican Army lurks right behind the word *outlawed.*

3   Much of the difficulty of mastering journalese stems from its slight overlap with English. *Imposing,* for instance, when used to describe a male, retains its customary English meaning, but when used in reference to a female, it means "battle-axe." In journalese the word *chilling* has the very solemn task of modifying *scenario* (in nuclear weapons stories), *reminder* (in crime stories) and *effect* (any story on AIDS or the imminent repeal of the First Amendment), whereas in English it is merely something one does with white wine.

4   Some English words mean exactly the opposite in journalese. *Multitalented,* for example, means untalented, and is used to identify applause-starved entertainers who prance about with amazing pep and perspiration, but do nothing particularly well. *Community* means noncommunity, as in the intelligence community, the gay community, or the journalese-speaking community. Under this usage, everyone shooting everyone else in and around Beirut, say, could be fairly described as the Lebanese community.

5   *Feisty* refers to a person whom the journalist deems too short and too easily enraged, though many in the journalese-speaking fraternity believe it is simply the adjective of choice for any male under five feet six who is not legally dead. This usage reflects the continual surprise among tall journalists that short people have any energy at all. Women are rarely feisty, although they usually meet the height restriction. No journalist in America has ever referred to a six-foot male as feisty. At that height, men are "outspoken" (i.e., abusive).

6   In general, adjectives in journalese are as misleading as olive sizes. Most news consumers know enough to translate *developing nations* and *disadvantaged nations* back into English, but far smaller numbers know that *militant* means "fanatic," *steadfast* means "pigheaded," and *self-made* means "crooked." *Controversial* introduces someone or something the writer finds appalling, as in "the controversial Miss Fonda," and *prestigious* heralds the imminent arrival of a noun nobody cares about, as in "the prestigious Jean Hersholt Humanitarian Award."

7   Journalese is rich in mystic nouns: *gentrification, quichification, greenmail, watershed elections, the sleaze factor, Japan-bashing, level playing fields,* the dread *T-word* (taxes), and the equally dread *L-word* (liberal). Though these nouns are patently glorious, students of the language agree that adjectives do most of the work, smuggling in actual information under the guise of normal journalism. Thus the use of *soft-spoken* (mousy), *loyal* (dumb), *high-minded* (inept), *ageless* (old), *hard-*

working (plodding), *irrepressible* (insanely giddy), and *pragmatic* (morally appalling, felonious). A person who is truly dangerous as well as immoral can be described as a fierce competitor or gut fighter, and a meddling boss is a hands-on executive.

8   When strung together properly, innocuous modifiers can acquire megaton force. For instance, a journalist may write, "A private, deliberate man, Frobisher dislikes small talk, but can be charming when he wants to." In translation, this means "An antisocial and sullen plodder, Frobisher is outstandingly obnoxious and about as articulate as a cantaloupe." The familiar phrase "can be charming" is as central to good journalese as "affordable" is to automobile ads and "excellence" is to education reports. It indicates smoothly that Frobisher's charm production is the rare and meager result of mighty exertion, yet it manages to end the revelation about his dismal character on a plausibly upbeat note.

9   In journalese, folks are not grim but "grim-faced," not just plain upset but "visibly upset." *Spry* and *sprightly* refer to any senior citizen who is not in a wheelchair or a coma. Other useful adjectives include *crusty* (obnoxious), *unpredictable* (bonkers), *experienced* (over the hill), *earnest* (boring), and *authentic* (fake). The noun *stereotype* introduces the discussion of something entirely obvious which the writer intends to disparage, as in "the stereotype that little boys like to play with trucks and little girls like to play with dolls." *Life-style* has made the transition from psychobabble to journalese. Though often used incorrectly to indicate homosexuals, joggers, wheat-germ consumers, and other defiant minorities, it actually refers to any practice that makes the normal citizen's hair stand on end. The fellow who tortures iguanas in his basement has a life-style. The rest of us merely have lives.

10   The hyphenated modifier is the meat and potatoes of journalese. Who can forget "scandal-plagued Wedtech," "concession-prone Gorbachev," "the mop-top quartet (the mandatory second reference to the Beatles), and the many "ill-fated" airliners, not to be confused with the "ill-fitting red wig" of Watergate fame. Murderers on death row are often saved by "eleventh-hour" reprieves, which would be somewhere between ten and eleven o'clock in English, but shortly before midnight in journalese.

11   Many sociologists have speculated (widely) about the love affair between journalese-users and their hyphens. The gist of all this cerebration seems to be that the rhythm of a hyphenated modifier is soothing, like a mother's heartbeat to a babe in arms. Besides, research shows

that readers cannot stand the shock of an unmodified noun, at least on first reference, any more than viewers of TV news can bear to hear Peter Jennings or Dan Rather reveal that World War III is under way without a comforting lead-in that will enable dinner to continue, though the world may not. Thus we have "Libyan-sponsored terrorism," "earthquake-ravaged Armenia," "debt-laden Brazil," and the two most popular hyphenated modifiers of the nineteen eighties, *financially-troubled* and *financially-plagued,* which can fairly be used to describe many banks, the indoor football league, the United States of America, and the entire world economy.

12   Many such hyphenated constructions come and go with blinding speed. "Syrian-backed PLO," once a serious contender for the hyphenation hall of fame, had to be retired when the Syrian backers began shooting at the PLO backs. Any dictator who leaves his homeland hastily, with or without his bullion and wife's shoe collection, is not running away; he is merely traveling into that famed journalistic nirvana, "self-imposed exile." In real life nobody talks that way ("Hey, Madge, did you hear? Embattled dictator Ferdinand Marcos has fled his turmoil-ridden island nation and taken up self-imposed exile on a tree-lined street in multiracial Hawaii!"), but in journalese such hyphenated chatter is considered normal.

13   Many meaningless adjectives, most of them hyphenated for mesmerizing effect, are permanently welded to certain nouns: *blue-ribbon panel, fact-finding mission, devout Catholic,* and *rock-ribbed Republican.* In journalese, for some reason, there are no devout Protestants or Jews, and no Democrats with strong or stony ribs. Similarly, Republicans but not Democrats may be described as staunch, which means "stiff-necked, unbending."

14   Like *clinically tested* and *doctor-recommended* in headache-remedy advertising, hyphenated journalese is not weakened in the slightest by the lack of any known meaning. *Wide-ranging discussions* refers to any talks at all, and *award-winning journalist* refers to any reporter, employed three or more years, who still has his own chair in a city room. A totally disappointing report, containing nothing but yawn-inducing truisms, can always be described as a "ground-breaking new study." The most exciting news on the hyphen front is that adventurous journalese-users, like late medieval theologians, are experimenting with new forms, to wit, multihyphen modifiers. So far *actor-turned-politician,* which can be found just to the left of Clint Eastwood's name in any story about

Carmel, is the most beloved two-hyphen term, while *state-of-the-art* (i.e., new) is the only approved three-hyphen entry since the memorable introduction of *dyed-in-the-wool* two generations back. It is regarded as such a successful breakthrough that it may be used several times each week without reproof from any living editor.

15   Unbeknownst to an unsuspecting public, Boy George's[1] drug troubles touched off a severe crisis in hyphenated journalese. How should reporters and pundits refer to the suddenly woozy singer? *Much-troubled* seemed apropos, but that adjective, like *war-torn,* is reserved for stories about the Middle East. One tabloid, apparently eager to dismiss multiproblemed George as a wanton hussy, called him "gender-confused rock star Boy George." This was a clear violation of journalese's most cherished tenet: one must, of course, do in the rich and famous, but never appear huffy in the process. *Newsweek* settled for "cross-dressing crooner," while many newspapers daringly abandoned the hyphenated tradition to label George "flamboyant," a familiar journalese word meaning "kinky" or "a person who does not have all of his or her paddles in the water."

16   In general, personal attacks in journalese should be accompanied by large quantities of feigned sympathy, the more unctuous the better. Thus any journalist wishing to reveal that Representative Frobisher has not been sober for ten years, will do so by respectfully hailing the poor fellow's "decade-long battle against alcohol addiction." One imaginative magazine, dishing new dirt about wife-beating in Hollywood, sadly cited one leading man's "lonely struggle against wife abuse."

17   Historians of journalese will agree that the first flowering of the language occurred in the description of women by splashy tabloids during the nineteen thirties and forties. In contrast to Pentagonese, which favors oxymorons *(Peacekeeper missiles, build-down),* the tabloids relied on synecdoche *(leggy brunette, bosomy blonde, full-figured redhead). Full-figured,* of course, meant "fat," and *well-endowed* meant "big-breasted," a signal to all concerned that a photo must accompany the story. *Statuesque* (too large, mooselike) and *petite* (too small, mouselike) were adjectives of last resort, meaning that the woman under discussion had no bodily parts that interested the writer. The only adjective feebler than *statuesque* and *petite* was *pert,* which indicated a plain, short woman whom the writer devoutly wished would disappear from the story.

---

[1]Boy George, a pop singer, was very popular in the 1980s.

18   Since it is no longer considered proper to draw the reader's attention to various protuberances and organs of the female body, journalese-users have been reduced to numbingly tame references such as *an attractive woman* (any female over fifty with no obvious facial scars) and *a handsome woman* (any woman at all). *Pert* is falling out of favor, but a formerly pert women who is overactive or too loud as well as too short can fairly be called "perky." And of course, women are no longer blond, brunette, redheaded, or gray-haired. Any reference at all to a woman's hair color will induce a blizzard of angry feminist letters asking, in effect, why President Reagan was never described as a Clairol brunette.

19   Like Latin, journalese is primarily a written language, prized for its incantatory powers, and is best learned early while the mind is still supple. Every cub reporter, for instance, knows that fires rage out of control, minor mischief is perpetrated by vandals (never Visigoths, Franks, or one Vandal working alone), and key labor accords are hammered out by weary negotiators in marathon, round-the-clock bargaining sessions, thus narrowly averting threatened walkouts. The discipline required for a winter storm report is awesome. The first reference to seasonal precipitation is "snow," followed by "the white stuff," then either "it" or "the flakes," but not both. The word *snow* may be used once again toward the end of the report, directly after discussion of ice-slicked roads and the grim highway toll.

20   One perennial challenge in journalese is the constant need to manufacture new euphemisms for *fat*. Words such as *jolly* and *Rubenesque* have long since been understood by the public and therefore discarded. One promising recent entry, "He has a heart as big as all outdoors," while not totally successful, did manage to imply that all the rest of the gentleman's organs and limbs are quite too bulky as well. A *Washington Post* writer did better by praising a prominent woman's "Wagnerian good looks," which is far more delicate than saying, "She is not bad-looking for a massive Brunhild." This is also a sturdy example of negative journalese, which works by combining a complimentary word with an apparently innocent but actually murderous modifier. "She is still pretty," for instance, means "She is amazingly long in the tooth." The favorite female companion of a recent presidential appointee was described in the *Washington Post* as having a "blushed, taut face," which means she uses too much makeup and has had at least one face-lift.

21   In general, detraction in journalese must be indirect. To indicate subtle distaste for the suburbs, A *New York Times* reporter once deftly called attention to the "array of carefully trimmed lawns and neat flower beds," thus artfully suggesting compulsiveness, conformity, and a high level of intolerance for life in its hearty untrimmed state.

22   For years the masters of this prose cast about for a nonlibelous euphemism for *mistress*. The winning entry, *great and good friend*, was invented by *Time* magazine to describe Marion Davies's relationship to William Randolph Hearst. *Constant companion* evolved later and gave way to such clunking modernisms as *roommate* and *live-in lover*. Nowadays the only sexuality about which journalese is coy tends to be homosexuality, and that is adequately covered by "He has no close female friends" or "He is not about to settle down."

23   Many terms in journalese come from sportswriting. *A complex, sensitive man* (lunatic) and *ebullient* (hyperactive space cadet) were developed by baseball writers confronted by a new breed of overpaid and therefore totally unpredictable jocks. *Great natural ability* is the current catchphrase for the new incompetent superstars who hit a lot of home runs but can't seem to catch a simple fly ball, throw to the right base, or correctly remember the score, the number of outs, or what day it is. Darryl Strawberry is often hailed for his great natural ability.

24   When ballplayers of the nineteen forties and fifties were fined for the usual excesses with women and booze, the writers dutifully reported that the penalties were for "nightclubbing." Presumably everyone knew what that meant except the nightclubbers' wives. Nowadays the vast consumption of controlled and uncontrolled substances would be covered by such time-tested circumlocutions as "He works hard and he plays hard." In sports, it is understood that all rapid declines are drug-related, and sportswriters, the original masters of journalese, are constantly casting about for nonlibelous ways of suggesting that Johnny Jumpshot is deeply in love with complex chemical compounds. The current code words are *listlessness* and *lack of concentration*. Recently, the writers have developed another unfailing indicator of drug abuse: the information that Johnny has been known to miss the team bus. This informs the astute fan that Jumpshot no longer knows where or who he is, though his body may still turn up occasionally for games. Drunken jocks, incidentally, are not listless, merely "red-eyed."

25   Sportswriters also taught journalese-users how to recast a boring story with exciting verbiage. Hence all the crucial issues, dramatic con-

frontations, and stunning breakthroughs, which stir and trigger almost daily. *Arguably* is the most useful adverb on the excitement frontier, because it introduces a sweeping factoid that no one will be able to check: "Frobisher is arguably the richest Rotarian living west of the Susquehanna." The runner-up adverb is *literally,* which always means "figuratively." Reforms and changes can only be "sweeping," and investigations are forever "widening," especially on days when the investigators have nothing to report, but would like a headline anyway. All arrays are bewildering, whereas contrasts are striking, except when the journalese-speaker is aware that his story is a crushingly dull one, in which case the contrast is allowed to be startling. Mounting is always followed by pressures, deficits, or concern. Slopes are slippery, precision is surgical, anyone tossed out of a job is "ousted unceremoniously," and nearly all references are "thinly veiled," unless, of course, they are "thinly disguised." Thickly disguised references are genuinely rare.

26   Television anchorpersons add interest to their monologues by accenting a few syllables chosen at random. Since print journalists cannot do this, except when reading aloud to spouse and family, they strive for a similar effect by using words like *crisis* and *revolution. Crisis* means any kind of trouble at all, and *revolution* means any kind of change at all, as in "the revolution in meat-packing." *Street value* lends dash to any drug-bust story without bearing any financial relationship to the actual value of the drugs being busted. In stories mentioning the street value of such contraband, it is generally wise to divide by ten or twelve to get the real, or nonstreet, value.

27   In political journalese, an officeholder who has no idea what is going on can best be described as one who "prefers to leave details to his staff." Or he can be described as having a hands-off or disengaged management style (i.e., his computer is down; he is out to lunch). Any Noriega-style gangster who runs a foreign country will usually be referred to as "strongman" until his death, and "dictator" thereafter. *Strongman,* unlike many terms in journalese, has no correlative. In the nineteen sixties, "Nicaraguan strongman Somoza" was never balanced with "Cambodian weakman Prince Sihanouk."

28   What to say about a public figure who is clearly bonkers? Since it is unsporting and possibly libelous to write, "Representative Frobisher, the well-known psychopath," journalese has evolved the helpful code words *difficult, intense,* and *driven.* If an article says, "Like most of us, Frobisher has his ups and downs," we are being told that Frobisher

is manic-depressive. Any politician described as "suffering from exhaustion" has gone completely around the bend and is now having his mail opened for him at a discreet institution.

29   *Middle America* has disappeared from political journalese, for the simple reason that after eight Reagan years, America seems to be all middle with no edges. Similarly, yesterday's "radical right-winger" is today's mainstream Republican, while *unabashed* (i.e., abashed) now modifies *liberal* instead of *conservative*. Yet most political journalese is timeless. A "savvy political pro" is anyone who has lived through two or more administrations and can still get a decent table in a Washington restaurant. An elder statesman is an out-of-office politician who is senile. All seasoned reporters (old-timers) know that when two or more political appointees are fired on the same day, they need only check their calendars before tapping out "Bloody Wednesday" or "the early-Thursday-afternoon massacre." Unless, of course, *-scam* or *-gate* can be affixed to yet another noun. Each major daily has an official scam-gate editor who remains ever alert for possible new coinages. A scandal involving Madison Square Garden, for instance, would be Garden-gate and the illegal skimming of revenues could be labeled Skim-scam. *Tail-gate* has been officially considered for various scandals, not all of them automotive.

30   Political journalese also has a number of famed option plays. One man's squealer is another's whistle-blower, and Frobisher's magnificent five-point agenda can always be described as a shopping list, or worse, a wish list. My new political action group is a dedicated band of volunteers, while yours is "small but well financed" (sinister).

31   Political journalese, of course, requires a knowledge of sources. An unnamed analyst or observer can safely be presumed to be the writer of the article. The popular plurals *observers* and *analysts* refer to the writer and his cronies. Insiders, unlike observer-analysts, sometimes exist in the real world outside the newsroom. This, however, is never true of quotable chestnut vendors in Paris, Greenwich Village bartenders, and other colorful folk conjured up on deadline to lend a badly needed flourish to drab stories.

32   Almost all sources, like most trial balloonists, live in or around Washington. In order of ascending rectitude, they are: informants, usually reliable sources, informed sources, authoritative sources, sources in high places, and unimpeachable sources. Informants are low-level operatives, whose beans are normally spilled to police rather than to reporters. Informed sources, because of their informed nature, are con-

sulted most often by sophisticated journalists. An unimpeachable source is almost always the President, with the obvious exception of Richard Nixon, who was not unimpeachable.

33   One of the many stressing problems in the field is writing serious articles about celebrities who recall serving in Joan of Arc's army or strolling through Iran with Jesus Christ. *Free spirit, flamboyant,* and *controversial* are not really up to the task. The journalist must avoid probing questions, such as "What does Jesus think of the Vatican's Middle East policy?" and stick to sober, respectful observations. This is best done by keeping matters vague. One *People* magazine writer, for instance, while profiling a well-known woman who has lived several times before, struck a proper tone this way: "More than most people on this earth, she has found spiritual answers."

34   In crime journalese, any youngster done in by a gang will turn out to be either an honor student or an altar boy. Otherwise the story will be spiked as unconventional. In any urban area, the top thug is always referred to as a "reputed mafia chieftain," or "reputed mob boss," and is generally depicted as an untutored but charismatic leader of a surprisingly efficient business operation. Except in tabloids, the chieftain's apprentice thugs are his "associates." This sort of coverage reflects the automatic respect and dignity accorded organized crime figures who know where reporters live and recognize the understandable desire of journalists everywhere to keep their kneecaps in good working order.

35   One inflexible rule of journalese is that American assassins must have three names: John Wilkes Booth, Lee Harvey Oswald, James Earl Ray, Mark David Chapman. This courtesy of a resonant three-part moniker is also applied to other dangerous folk. This is why the subway gunman, for the first two months of coverage, was "Bernhard Hugo Goetz" to reporters who considered him a monster. Later these same scribes stripped Goetz of his Hugo, apparently on grounds that he seemed more like a malevolent wimp than an authentic three-named villain.

36   One subcategory of journalese, which may yet develop into a true dialect, involves the language used to indicate a powerful or celebrated person who is about to self-destruct or walk the plank. In politics, two or more stories in the same week referring to a power person as "clever," or worse, "brilliant," indicate that the end is near. Soon Mr. Scintillation will be labeled a "loose cannon" and transmute himself into a consultant, the Washington version of self-imposed exile. In business

journalism, the phrase *one of the most respected managers in his field* informs knowing readers that envy is unnecessary—the respected manager is on the way out. Before long, there will be hints that his managerial ferocity is insufficient, perhaps a profile mentioning that he drinks decaffeinated coffee, loves San Francisco, or collects porcelain miniatures. This means we are less than a week from an announcement that the executive is "leaving to pursue outside interests," just like Ferdinand Marcos.

37   In sum, journalese is a truly vital language, the last bulwark against libel, candor, and fresh utterance. Its prestigious, ground-breaking, state-of-the-art lingo makes it arguably the most useful of tongues, and its untimely demise would have a chilling effect, especially on us award-winning journalists.

Reading Closely and Thinking Critically

1. Define *journalese* in your own words.

2. Why is journalese difficult to learn?

3. The essay notes and explains the characteristics of journalese. What are those characteristics?

4. What is Leo's chief complaint about hyphenated journalese?

5. Leo explains that the origins of journalese rest in tabloid descriptions of women (paragraph 17) and sportswriting (paragraphs 23 and 24). Why do you think that journalese originated in these places?

6. What is Leo's opinion about the way journalists use English?

7. Of what is Leo trying to persuade the reader? Where is his persuasive purpose best expressed?

Examining Structure and Strategy

1. Paragraph 1 is the introduction. What approach does Leo take to his introduction?

2. Comment on the frequency and purpose of Leo's use of examples.

3. Why does Leo discuss hyphenated journalese (paragraphs 10 through 15) in such detail?

4. What elements of classification are apparent in the essay?

5. Leo uses a considerable amount of humor in "Journalese." Cite two or three examples of that humor. What purpose does the humor serve?

6. What approach does Leo take to his conclusion? Do you find the conclusion effective? Explain.

Considering Language and Style

1. In paragraph 17, Leo refers to *synecdoche* and *oxymorons*. Define these terms and give two examples of each that do not appear in the essay.

2. How would you describe the tone of the essay? (See page 37 for an explanation of tone.)

3. Consult your dictionary if you are unsure of the meaning of any of these words: *fourth estate* (title); *cub reporter* (paragraph 1); *psychobabble* (paragraph 1); *Scylla-Charybdis image* (paragraph 2); *nirvana* (paragraph 12); *to wit* (paragraph 14); *pundits* (paragraph 15); *unctuous* (paragraph 16); *circumlocutions* (paragraph 24); *moniker* (paragraph 35).

For Group Discussion or Writing

With some classmates, examine four or five newspapers. Note examples of journalese, the literal meaning conveyed in that journalese, and what you think is the intended meaning.

Writing Assignments

1. *In your journal.* As a result of reading "Journalese," will your reaction to newspaper and magazine articles change? Explain why or why not.

2. *Using the pattern.* Define and illustrate the variety of language used by academics. You can call this language *academese*.

3. *Using the pattern.* Define and illustrate the variety of language used by politicians. You can call this language *politicalese*.

4. *Using the pattern.* Define and illustrate the variety of language used by bureaucrats. You can call this language *bureaucratese*.

5. *Using the pattern.* Define and illustrate the variety of language used by medical personnel. You can call this language *medicalese*. As an alternative, define and illustrate *psychobabble* (paragraph 1).

6. *Considering a theme.* What responsibilities do journalists have to the public? Explain one or more of those responsibilities and go on to note to what extent journalists are fulfilling their responsibility or responsibilities. Feel free to examine publications and cite examples to support your view. (See the appendix on how to document borrowed material.)

7. *Connecting the readings.* Compare and contrast journalese and politically correct language. "Journalese" and "Excuuuse Me" (page 407) may give you some ideas.

THE VIEW FROM 80
Malcolm Cowley

A graduate of Harvard University who served in the American Ambulance Corps during World War I, Malcolm Cowley (1898–1989) was a distinguished literary historian, critic, and poet. He was also a translator and visiting professor at many universities. In 1929, he began 15 years as a literary editor at the New Republic. *His book,* Exile's Return *(1934), is an important book of literary criticism. His other books include* The Literary Situation *(1954) and* The Flower and the Leaf *(1984). In "The View from 80," taken from his book of the same name (1981), Cowley blends description, pointed examples, cause-and-effect analysis, and narration to define old age and thereby inform the reader of what it is really like to be old. As he tells of his journey to the "country of age," the author also expresses the joy and the sadness of this stage of life.*

THE PATTERNS	THE PURPOSES
definition with exemplification, description, cause-and-effect analysis, and narration	*to inform and to express feelings and relate experience*

1   They gave me a party on my 80th birthday in August 1978. First there were cards, letters, telegrams, even a cable of congratulation or condolence; then there were gifts, mostly bottles; there was catered food and finally a big cake with, for some reason, two candles (had I gone back to very early childhood?). I blew the candles out a little unsteadily. Amid the applause and clatter I thought about a former custom of the Northern Ojibwas when they lived on the shores of Lake Winnipeg. They were kind to their old people, who remembered and enforced the ancient customs of the tribe, but when an old person became decrepit, it was time for him to go. Sometimes he was simply abandoned, with a little food, on an island in the lake. If he deserved special honor, they held a tribal feast for him. The old man sang a death song and danced, if he could. While he was still singing, his son came from behind and brained him with a tomahawk.

2   That was quick, it was dignified, and I wonder whether it was any more cruel, essentially, than some of our civilized customs or inadvertencies in disposing of the aged. I believe in rites and ceremonies. I believe in big parties for special occasions such as an 80th birthday. It was a sort of belated bar mitzvah, since the 80-year-old, like a Jewish adolescent, is entering a new stage of life; let him (or her) undergo a *rite de passage,* with toasts and a cantor. Seventy-year-olds, or septuas, have the illusion of being middle-aged, even if they have been pushed on a shelf. The 80-year-old, the octo, looks at the double-dumpling figure and admits that he is old. The last act has begun, and it will be the test of the play.

3   To enter the country of age is a new experience, different from what you supposed it to be. Nobody, man or woman, knows the country until he has lived in it and has taken out his citizenship papers. Here is my own report, submitted as a road map and guide to some of the principal monuments.

4   The new octogenarian feels as strong as ever when he is sitting back in a comfortable chair. He ruminates, he dreams, he remembers. He doesn't want to be disturbed by others. It seems to him that old age is only a costume assumed for those others; the true, the essential self is ageless. In a moment he will rise and go for a ramble in the woods, taking a gun along, or a fishing rod, if it is spring. Then he creaks to his feet, bending forward to keep his balance, and realizes that he will do nothing of the sort. The body and its surroundings have their messages for him, or only one message: "You are old." Here are some of the occasions on which he receives the message:

- when it becomes an achievement to do thoughtfully, step by step, what he once did instinctively

- when his bones ache

- when there are more and more little bottles in the medicine cabinet, with instructions for taking four times a day

- when he fumbles and drops his toothbrush (butterfingers)

- when his face has bumps and wrinkles, so that he cuts himself while shaving (blood on the towel)

- when year by year his feet seem farther from his hands

- when he can't stand on one leg and has trouble pulling on his pants

- when he hesitates on the landing before walking down a flight of stairs

- when he spends more time looking for things misplaced than he spends using them after he (or more often his wife) has found them

- when he falls asleep in the afternoon

- when it becomes harder to bear in mind two things at once

- when a pretty girl passes him in the street and he doesn't turn his head

- when he forgets names, even of people he saw last month ("Now I'm beginning to forget nouns," the poet Conrad Aiken said at 80)

- when he listens hard to jokes and catches everything but the snapper

- when he decides not to drive at night anymore

- when everything takes longer to do—bathing, shaving, getting dressed or undressed—but when time passes quickly, as if he were gathering speed while coasting downhill. The year from 79 to 80 is like a week when he was a boy.

5   Those are some of the intimate messages. "Put cotton in your ears and pebbles in your shoes," said a gerontologist, a member of that new profession dedicated to alleviating all maladies of old people except the passage of years. "Pull on rubber gloves. Smear Vaseline over your glasses, and there you have it: instant aging." Not quite. His formula omits the messages from the social world, which are louder, in most cases, than those from within. We start by growing old in other people's eyes, then slowly we come to share their judgment.

6   I remember a morning many years ago when I was backing out of the parking lot near the railroad station in Brewster, New York. There was a near collision. The driver of the other car jumped out and started to abuse me; He had his fists ready. Then he looked at me and said, "Why, you're an old man." He got back into his car, slammed the door, and drove away, while I stood there fuming. "I'm only 65," I thought. "He wasn't driving carefully. I can still take care of myself in a car, or in a fight, for that matter."

7   My hair was whiter—it may have been in 1974—when a young woman rose and offered me a seat in a Madison Avenue bus. That mes-

sage was kind and also devastating. "Can't I even stand up?" I thought
as I thanked her and declined the seat. But the same thing happened
twice the following year, and the second time I gratefully accepted the
offer, though with a sense of having diminished myself. "People are
right about me," I thought while wondering why all those kind gestures
were made by women. Do men now regard themselves as the weaker
sex, not called upon to show consideration? All the same it was a relief
to sit down and relax.

8   A few days later I wrote a poem, "The Red Wagon," that belongs
in the record of aging:

For his birthday they gave him a red express wagon
with a driver's high seat and a handle that steered.
His mother pulled him around the yard.
"Giddyap," he said, but she laughed and went off
to wash the breakfast dishes.

"I wanta ride too," his sister said,
and he pulled her to the edge of a hill.
"Now, sister, go home and wait for me,
but first give a push to the wagon."
He climbed again to the high seat,
this time grasping that handle-that-steered.
The red wagon rolled slowly down the slope,
then faster as it passed the schoolhouse
and faster as it passed the store,
the road still dropping away.
Oh, it was fun.

But would it ever stop?
Would the road always go downhill?

The red wagon rolled faster.
Now it was in strange country.
It passed a white house he must have dreamed about,
deep woods he had never seen,
a graveyard where, something told him, his sister
was buried.

Far below
the sun was sinking into a broad plain.

The red wagon rolled faster.
Now he was clutching the seat, not even trying to steer.
Sweat clouded his heavy spectacles.
His white hair streamed in the wind.

9   Even before he or she is 80, the aging person may undergo another identity crisis like that of adolescence. Perhaps there had also
been a middle-aged crisis, the male or the female menopause, but the
rest of adult life he had taken himself for granted, with his capabilities
and failings. Now, when he looks in the mirror, he asks himself, "Is this
really me?"—or he avoids the mirror out of distress at what it reveals,
those bags and wrinkles. In his new makeup he is called upon to play
a new role in a play that must be improvised. André Gide, that long-
lived man of letters, wrote in his journal, "My heart has remained so
young that I have the continual feeling of playing a part, the part of the
70-year-old that I certainly am; and the infirmities and weaknesses that
remind me of my age act like a prompter, reminding me of my lines
when I tend to stray. Then, like the good actor I want to be, I go back
into my role, and I pride myself on playing it well."
10   In his new role the old person will find that he is tempted by
new vices, that he receives new compensations (not so widely known),
and that he may possibly achieve new virtues. Chief among these is the
heroic or merely obstinate refusal to surrender in the face of time. One
admires the ships that go down with all flags flying and the captain on
the bridge.
11   Among the vices of age are avarice, untidiness, and vanity, which
last takes the form of a craving to be loved or simply admired. Avarice
is the worst of those three. Why do so many old persons, men and
women alike, insist on hoarding money when they have no prospect of
using it and even when they have no heirs? They eat the cheapest food,
buy no clothes, and live in a single room when they could afford better lodging. It may be that they regard money as a form of power; there
is a comfort in watching it accumulate while other powers are dwin-
dling away. How often we read of an old person found dead in a hovel,
on a mattress partly stuffed with bankbooks and stock certificates! The
bankbook syndrome, we call it in our family, which has never succumbed.
12   Untidiness we call the Langley Collyer syndrome. To explain,
Langley Collyer was a former concert pianist who lived alone with his

70-year-old brother in a brownstone house on upper Fifth Avenue. The once fashionable neighborhood had become part of Harlem. Homer, the brother, had been an admiralty lawyer, but was now blind and partly paralyzed; Langley played for him and fed him on buns and oranges, which he thought would restore Homer's sight. He never threw away a daily paper because Homer, he said, might want to read them all. He saved other things as well and the house became filled with rubbish from roof to basement. The halls were lined on both sides with bundled newspapers, leaving narrow passageways in which Langley had devised booby traps to catch intruders.

13   On March 21, 1947, some unnamed person telephoned the police to report there was a dead body in the Collyer house. The police broke down the front door and found the hall impassable; then they hoisted a ladder to a second-story window. Behind it Homer was lying on the floor in a bathrobe; he had starved to death. Langley had disappeared. After some delay, the police broke into the basement, chopped a hole in the roof, and began throwing junk out of the house, top and bottom. It was 18 days before they found Langley's body, gnawed by rats. Caught in one of his own booby traps, he had died in a hallway just outside Homer's door. By that time the police had collected, and the Department of Sanitation had hauled away, 120 tons of rubbish, including, besides the newspapers, 14 grand pianos and the parts of a dismantled Model T Ford.

14   Why do so many old people accumulate junk, not on the scale of Langley Collyer, but still in a dismaying fashion? Their tables are piled high with it, their bureau drawers are stuffed with it, their closet rods bend with the weight of clothes not worn for years. I suppose that the piling up is partly from lethargy and partly from feeling that everything once useful, including their own bodies, should be preserved. Others, though not so many, have such a fear of becoming Langley Collyers that they strive to be painfully neat. Every tool they own is in its place, though it will never be used again; every scrap of paper is filed away in alphabetical order. At least their immoderate neatness becomes another vice of age, if a milder one.

15   The vanity of older people is an easier weakness to explain, and to condone. With less to look forward to, they yearn for recognition of what they have been: the reigning beauty, the athlete, the soldier, the scholar. It is the beauties who have the hardest time. A portrait of themselves at twenty hangs on the wall, and they try to resemble it by mak-

ing an extravagant use of creams, powders, and dyes. Being young at heart, they think they are merely revealing their essential persons. The athletes find shelves for their silver trophies, which are polished once a year. Perhaps a letter sweater lies wrapped in a bureau drawer. I remember one evening when a no-longer athlete had guests for dinner and tried to find his sweater. "Oh, that old thing," his wife said, "The moths got into it and I threw it away." The athlete sulked and his guests went home early.

16   But there are also pleasures of the body, or the mind, that are enjoyed by a greater number of older persons. Those pleasures include some that younger people find hard to appreciate. One of them is simply sitting still, like a snake on a sun-warmed stone, with a delicious feeling of indolence that was seldom attained in earlier years. A leaf flutters down; a cloud moves by inches across the horizon. At such moments the older person, completely relaxed, has become a part of nature—and a living part, with blood coursing through his veins. The future does not exist for him. He thinks, if he thinks at all, that life for younger persons is still a battle royal of each against each, but that now he has nothing more to win or lose. He is not so much above as outside the battle, as if he had assumed the uniform of some small neutral country, perhaps Liechtenstein or Andorra. From a distance he notes that some of the combatants, men or women, are jostling ahead—but why do they fight so hard when the most they can hope for is a longer obituary? He can watch the scrounging and gouging, he can hear the shouts of exultation, the moans of the gravely wounded, and meanwhile he feels secure; nobody will attack him from ambush.

17   Age has other physical compensations besides the nirvana of dozing in the sun. A few of the simplest needs become a pleasure to satisfy. When an old woman in a nursing home was asked what she really liked to do, she answered in one word: "Eat." She might have been speaking for many of her fellows. Meals in a nursing home, however badly cooked, serve as climactic moments of the day. The physical essence of the pensioners is being renewed at an appointed hour; now they can go back to meditating or to watching TV while looking forward to the next meal. They can also look forward to sleep, which has become a definite pleasure, not the mere interruption it once had been.

18   Here I am thinking of old persons under nursing care. Others ferociously guard their independence, and some of them suffer less than one might expect from being lonely and impoverished. They can be re-

joiced by visits and meetings, but they also have company inside their heads. Some of them are busiest when their hands are still. What passes through the minds of many is a stream of persons, images, phrases, and familiar tunes. For some that stream has continued since childhood, but now it is deeper; it is their present and their past combined. At times they conduct silent dialogues with a vanished friend, and these are less tiring—often more rewarding—than spoken conversations. If inner resources are lacking, old persons living alone may seek comfort and a kind of companionship in the bottle. I should judge from the gossip of various neighborhoods that the outer suburbs from Boston to San Diego are full of secretly alcoholic widows. One of these widows, an old friend, was moved from her apartment into a retirement home. She left behind her a closet in which the floor was covered wall to wall with whiskey bottles. "Oh, those empty bottles!" she explained. "They were left by a former tenant!"

19   Not whiskey or cooking sherry but simply giving up is the greatest temptation of age. It is something different from a stoical acceptance of infirmities, which is something to be admired.

20   The givers-up see no reason for working. Sometimes they lie in bed all day when moving about would still be possible, if difficult. I had a friend, a distinguished poet, who surrendered in that fashion. The doctors tried to stir him to action, but he refused to leave his room. Another friend, once a successful artist, stopped painting when his eyes began to fail. His doctor made the mistake of telling him that he suffered from a fatal disease. He then lost interest in everything except the splendid Rolls-Royce, acquired in his prosperous days, that stood in the garage. Daily he wiped the dust from its hood. He couldn't drive it on the road any longer, but he used to sit in the driver's seat, start the motor, then back the Rolls out of the garage and drive it in again, back twenty feet and forward twenty feet; that was his only distraction.

21   I haven't the right to blame those who surrender, not being able to put myself inside their minds or bodies. Often they must have compelling reasons, physical or moral. Not only do they suffer from a variety of ailments, but also they are made to feel that they no longer have a function in the community. Their families and neighbors don't ask them for advice, don't really listen when they speak, don't call on them for efforts. One notes that there are not a few recoveries from apparent senility when that situation changes. If it doesn't change, old persons

may decide that efforts are useless. I sympathize with their problems, but the men and women I envy are those who accept old age as a series of challenges.

22   For such persons, every new infirmity is an enemy to be outwitted, an obstacle to be overcome by force of will. They enjoy each little victory over themselves, and sometimes they win a major success. Renoir was one of them. He continued painting, and magnificently, for years after he was crippled by arthritis; the brush had to be strapped to his arm. "You don't need your hand to paint," he said. Goya was another of the unvanquished. At 72 he retired as an official painter of the Spanish court and decided to work only for himself. His later years were those of the famous "black paintings" in which he let his imagination run (and also of the lithographs, then a new technique). At 78 he escaped a reign of terror in Spain by fleeing to Bordeaux. He was deaf and his eyes were failing; in order to work he had to wear several pairs of spectacles, one over another, and then use a magnifying glass; but he was producing splendid work in a totally new style. At 80 he drew an ancient man propped on two sticks, with a mass of white hair and beard hiding his face and with the inscription "I am still learning."

23   "Eighty years old!" the great Catholic poet Paul Claudel wrote in his journal. "No eyes left, no ears, no teeth, no legs, no wind! And when all is said and done, how astonishingly well one does without them!"

Reading Closely and Thinking Critically

1. How would you describe Cowley's attitude toward old age and the elderly? Overall, would you say that his attitude toward old age is positive or negative? Explain.

2. Why does Cowley tell about the Ojibwa's customs for dealing with their aged (paragraph 1)? Does he find the customs cruel, or does he think they have something to recommend them? Explain.

3. According to Cowley, what are some of the positive characteristics of being old? What are the negative characteristics?

4. According to Cowley, what causes each of the vices of old age: avarice, untidiness, and vanity?

5. According to Cowley, why do some of the elderly just give up? Do you blame these people for not trying any longer? Explain.

Examining Structure and Strategy

1. Where in the essay does Cowley present his thesis?

2. Cowley uses a considerable number of examples as part of his definition. Cite three paragraphs that include examples, and explain what the examples contribute to the definition.

3. Cause-and-effect analysis explains the causes and/or effects of something (see Chapter 8 for a full discussion). What elements of cause-and-effect analysis appear in paragraphs 11 through 15? In paragraphs 20 and 21?

4. Narration is storytelling (see Chapter 4 for a full discussion). What is the purpose of the narration in paragraphs 12 and 13?

5. In paragraph 4, Cowley includes a lengthy list of evidence of old age. Do you think listing is a suitable technique here?

Considering Language and Style

1. In literature, a *symbol* is a situation, character, or thing that stands for something else. In Cowley's poem "The Red Wagon," what do you think the red wagon symbolizes? What is the strange country that the wagon rolls through? Why does the wagon roll faster and faster?

2. Cowley often uses *metaphors* (see page 73). Mention two metaphors that are part of the definition. What purpose do these metaphors serve?

3. Consult a dictionary if you are unsure of the meaning of any of these words: *Ojibwas* (paragraph 1), *inadvertencies* (paragraph 2), *rite de passage* (paragraph 2), *cantor* (paragraph 2), *ruminates* (paragraph 4), *gerontologist* (paragraph 5), *hovel* (paragraph 11), *lethargy* (paragraph 14), *indolence* (paragraph 16), *nirvana* (paragraph 17), *lithographs* (paragraph 22).

For Group Discussion or Writing
With two or three classmates, answer these questions:

1. How do we treat the elderly in this country?

2. Is our treatment of the elderly more or less dignified and cruel than the practices of the Ojibwas mentioned in paragraph 1?

Writing Assignments

1. *In your journal.* What do you think old age will be like for you? Are there aspects you dread? Are there aspects you look forward to? Have any of your feelings been influenced by Cowley's essay?

2. *Using the pattern.* Write an essay called "The View from
_____." (Fill in the blank with your age.) Using definition and any other patterns you wish, explain what is like to be your age. If you like, you may include a list, as Cowley does in paragraph 4.

3. *Using the pattern.* In paragraph 9, Cowley refers to identity crises and mentions that a person may have one during adolescence, one during middle age, and one during old age. If you have ever had an identity crisis, write a definition of this phenomenon and explain the causes and/or effects of the crisis.

4. *Using the pattern.* Cowley explains that three of the vices of old age are avarice, untidiness, and vanity. Write a definition of one of these vices. If you like, use examples and/or narration to illustrate your points. Also, try to explain the causes and/or effects of the vice.

5. *Using the pattern.* If you are familiar with old age as a result of spending time with an elderly friend, relative, or neighbor, write your own definition of *old age*.

6. *Considering a theme.* At what point do you think you will be old? Answer that question and go on to explain in detail what you think old age will be like for you. Consider such things as your health, social life, activities, place of residence, or anything else you think is pertinent. If you already consider yourself old, compare and contrast the reality of your old age with what you thought it would be like. As an alternative, describe the vices of adolescence the way Cowley describes the vices of old age (beginning in paragraph 11).

7. *Connecting the readings.* Compare and contrast the joys and difficulties of adolescence with those of old age. (Comparison-contrast is discussed in Chapter 7.) Some of the ideas in "Complexion" (page 401) and "The View from 80" may help you.

TO BE A JEW
Elie Wiesel

Born near the Ukranian border in 1928, Elie Wiesel is a survivor of the Holo-
caust, which claimed the lives of his parents and youngest sister. He was at
both Auschwitz and Buchenwald concentration camps, experiences he has
both written about and lectured on. His writings, although ultimately very
successful, were initially met with skepticism because people resisted hearing
the dark truths he tells. His frequent efforts to examine human suffering and
injustice associated with the Holocaust so we do not forget our capacity to
commit atrocities won Wiesel the Nobel Peace Prize in 1986 and the Ellis Is-
land Medal of Honor in 1992. In "To Be a Jew," which is taken from A Jew
Today (1979), Wiesel combines definition with narration and cause-and-
effect analysis to inform the reader of what it means to be a Jew and to
relate his experiences and express his feelings as a Jew before and during the
Holocaust.

THE PATTERNS	THE PURPOSES
definition with cause-and-effect	*to inform and to relate experiences*
analysis and narration	*and express feelings*

1   Once upon a time, in a distant town surrounded by mountains,
there lived a small Jewish boy who believed himself capable of seeing
good in evil, of discovering dawn within dusk and, in general, of deci-
phering the symbols, both visible and invisible, lavished upon him by
destiny.

2   To him, all things seemed simple and miraculous: life and death,
love and hatred. On one side were the righteous, on the other the
wicked. The just were always handsome and generous, the miscreants
always ugly and cruel. And God in His heaven kept the accounts in a
book only He could consult. In that book each people had its own page,
and the Jewish people had the most beautiful page of all.

3   Naturally, this little boy felt at ease only among his own people,
his own setting. Everything alien frightened me. And alien meant not
Moslem or Hindu, but Christian. The priest dressed in black, the wood-
cutter and his ax, the teacher and his ruler, old peasant women cross-

ing themselves as their husbands uttered oath upon oath, constables looking gruff and merely preoccupied—all of them exuded a hostility I understood and considered normal, and therefore without remedy.

4   I *understood* that all these people, young and old, rich and poor, powerful and oppressed, exploiters and exploited, should want my undoing, even my death. True, we inhabited the same landscape, but that was yet another reason for them to hate me. Such is man's nature: he hates what disturbs him, what eludes him. We depended on the more or less unselfish tolerance of the "others," yet our life followed its own course independently of theirs, a fact they clearly resented. Our determination to maintain and enrich our separate history, our separate society, confused them as much as did that history itself. A living Jew, a believing Jew, proud of his faith, was for them a contradiction, a denial, an aberration. According to their calculations, this chosen and accursed people should long ago have ceased to haunt a mankind whose salvation was linked to the bloodstained symbol of the cross. They could not accept the idea of a Jew celebrating his Holy Days with song, just as they celebrated their own. That was inadmissible, illogical, even unjust. And the less they understood us, the more I understood them.

5   I felt no animosity. I did not even hate them at Christmas or Easter time when they imposed a climate of terror upon our frightened community. I told myself: They envy us, they persecute us because they envy us, and rightly so; surely *they* were the ones to be pitied. Their tormenting us was but an admission of weakness, of inner insecurity. If God's truth subsists on earth in the hearts of mortals, it is our doing. It is through us that God has chosen to manifest His will and outline His designs, and it is through us that He has chosen to sanctify His name. Were I in their place I, too, would feel rejected. How could they not be envious? In an odd way, the more they hunted me, the more I rationalized their behavior. Today I recognize my feelings for what they were: a mixture of pride, distrust and pity.

6   Yet I felt no curiosity. Not of any kind, or at any moment. We seemed to intrigue them, but they left me indifferent. I knew nothing of their catechism, and cared less. I made no attempt to comprehend the rites and canons of their faith. Their rituals held no interest for me; quite the contrary, I turned away from them. Whenever I met a priest I would avert my gaze and think of something else. Rather than walk in front of a church with its pointed and threatening belfry, I would cross the street. To see was as frightening as to be seen; I worried that

a visual, physical link might somehow be created between us. So ignorant was I of their world that I had no idea that Judaism and Christianity claimed the same roots. Nor did I know that Christians who believe in the eternity and in the divinity of Christ also believe in those
of God, *our* God. Though our universes existed side by side, I avoided
penetrating theirs, whereas they sought to dominate ours by force. I had
heard enough tales about the Crusades and the pogroms, and I had repeated enough litanies dedicated to their victims, to know where I
stood. I had read and reread descriptions of what inquisitors, grand and
small, had inflicted on Jews in Catholic kingdoms; how they had
preached God's love to them even as they were leading them to the
stake. All I knew of Christianity was its hate for my people. Christians
were more present in my imagination than in my life. What did a Christian do when he was alone? What were his dreams made of? How did
he use his time when he was not engaged in plotting against us? But
none of this really troubled me. Beyond our immediate contacts, our
public and hereditary confrontations, he simply did not exist.

7   My knowledge of the Jew, on the other hand, sprang from an in-
exhaustible source: the more I learned, the more I wanted to know.
There was inside me a thirst for knowledge that was all-enveloping, all-
pervasive, a veritable obsession.
8   I knew what it meant to be a Jew in day-to-day life as well as in
the absolute. What was required was to obey the Law; thus one needed
first to learn it, then to remember it. What was required was to love
God and that which in His creation bears His seal. And His will would
be done.
9   Abraham's covenant, Isaac's suspended sacrifice, Jacob's fiery
dreams, the revelation at Sinai, the long march through the desert,
Moses' blessings, the conquest of Canaan, the pilgrimages to the Temple
in Jerusalem, Isaiah's and Habakkuk's beautiful but harsh words, Jere-
miah's lamentations, the Talmudic legends: my head was abuzz with ancient memories and debates, with tales teeming with kings and prophets,
tragedies and miracles. Every story contained victims, always victims,
and survivors, always survivors. To be a Jew meant to live with memory.
10   Nothing could have been easier. One needed only to follow tradition, to reproduce the gestures and sounds transmitted through generations whose end product I was. On the morning of Shavuoth there
I was with Moses receiving the Law. On the eve of Tishah b'Av, seated

on the floor, my head covered with ashes, I wept, together with Rabbi Yohanan Ben-Zakkai, over the destruction of the city that had been thought indestructible. During the week of Hanukkah, I rushed to the aid of the Maccabees; and on Purim, I laughed, how I laughed, with Mordecai, celebrating his victory over Haman. And week after week, as we blessed the wine during Shabbat meals, I accompanied the Jews out of Egypt—yes, I was forever leaving Egypt, freeing myself from bondage. To be a Jew meant creating links, a network of continuity.

11   With the years I learned a more "sophisticated," more modern vocabulary. I was told that to be a Jew means to place the accent simultaneously and equally on verb and noun, on the secular and the eternal, to prevent the one from excluding the other or succeeding at the expense of the other. That it means to serve God by espousing man's cause, to plead for man while recognizing his need of God. And to opt for the Creator *and* His creation, refusing to pit one against the other.

12   Of course, man must interrogate God, as did Abraham; articulate his anger, as did Moses; and shout his sorrow, as did Job. But only the Jew opts for Abraham—who questions—*and* for God—who is questioned. He claims every role and assumes every destiny: he is both sum and synthesis.

13   I shall long, perhaps forever, remember my Master, the one with the yellowish beard, telling me, "Only the Jew knows that he may oppose God as long as he does so in defense of His creation." Another time he told me, "God gave the Law, but it is up to man to interpret it—and his interpretation is binding on God and commits Him."

14   Surely this is an idealized concept of the Jew. And of man. And yet it is one that is tested every day, at every moment, in every circumstance.

15   At school I read in the Talmud: Why did God create only one man? The answer: All men have the same ancestor. So that no man, later, could claim superiority over another.

16   And also: A criminal who sets fire to the Temple, the most sacred, the most revered edifice in the world, is punishable with only thirty-nine lashes of the whip; let a fanatic kill him and *his* punishment would be death. For all the temples and all the sanctuaries are not worth the life of a single human being, be he arsonist, profanator, enemy of God and shame of God.

17   Painful irony: We were chased from country to country, our Houses of Study were burned, our sages assassinated, our schoolchild-

ren massacred, and still we went on tirelessly, fiercely, praising the inviolate sanctity of life and proclaiming faith in man, any man.

18   An extraordinary contradiction? Perhaps. But to be a Jew is precisely to reveal oneself within one's contradictions by accepting them. It means safeguarding one's past at a time when mankind aspires only to conquer the future; it means observing Shabbat when the official day of rest is Sunday or Friday; it means fervently exploring the Talmud, with its seemingly antiquated laws and discussions, while outside, not two steps away from the heder or the yeshiva, one's friends and parents are rounded up or beaten in a pogrom; it means asserting the right of spirituality in a world that denies spirituality; it means singing and singing again, louder and louder, when all around everything heralds the end of the world, the end of man.

19   All this was really so. The small Jewish boy is telling only what he heard and saw, what he lived himself, long ago. He vouches for its truth.

20   Yes, long ago in distant places it all seemed so simple to me, so real, so throbbing with truth. Like God, I looked at the world and found it good, fertile, full of meaning. Even in exile, every creature was in its place and every encounter was charged with promise. And with the advent of Shabbat, the town changed into a kingdom whose madmen and beggars became the princes of Shabbat.

21   I shall never forget Shabbat in my town. When I shall have forgotten everything else, my memory will still retain the atmosphere of holiday, of serenity pervading even the poorest houses: the white tablecloth, the candles, the meticulously combed little girls, the men on their way to synagogue. When my town shall fade into the abyss of time, I will continue to remember the light and the warmth it radiated on Shabbat. The exalting prayers, the wordless songs of the Hasidim, the fire and radiance of their Masters.

22   On that day of days, past and future suffering and anguish faded into the distance. Appeased man called on the divine presence to express his gratitude.

23   The jealousies and grudges, the petty rancors between neighbors could wait. As could the debts and worries, the dangers. Everything could wait. As it enveloped the universe, the Shabbat conferred on it a dimension of peace, and aura of love.

24   Those who were hungry came and ate; and those who felt abandoned seized the outstretched hand; and those who were alone, and

those who were sad, the strangers, the refugees, the wanderers, as they left the synagogue were invited to share the meal in any home; and the grieving were urged to contain their tears and come draw on the collective joy of Shabbat.

25   The difference between us and the others? The others, how I pitied them. They did not even know what they were missing; they were unmoved by the beauty, the eternal splendor of Shabbat.

26   And then came the Holocaust, which shook history and by its dimensions and goals marked the end of a civilization. Concentration-camp man discovered the anti-savior.

27   We became witnesses to a huge simplification. On the one side there were the executioners and on the other the victims. What about the onlookers, those who remained neutral, those who served the executioner simply by not interfering? To be a Jew then meant to fight both the complacency of the neutral and the hate of the killers. And to resist—in any way, with any means. And not only with weapons. The Jew who refused death, who refused to believe in death, who chose to marry in the ghetto, to circumcise his son, to teach him the sacred language, to bind him to the threatened and weakened lineage of Israel—that Jew was resisting. The professor or shopkeeper who disregarded facts and warnings and clung to illusion, refusing to admit that people could so succumb to degradation—he, too, was resisting. There was no essential difference between the Warsaw ghetto fighters and the old men getting off the train in Treblinka: because they were Jewish, they were all doomed to hate, and death.

28   In those days, more than ever, to be Jewish signified *refusal*. Above all, it was a refusal to see reality and life through the enemy's eyes—a refusal to resemble him, to grant him that victory, too.

29   Yet his victory seemed solid and, in the beginning, definitive. All those uprooted communities, ravaged and dissolved in smoke; all those trains that crisscrossed the nocturnal Polish landscapes; all those men, all those women, stripped of their language, their names, their faces, compelled to live and die according to the laws of the enemy, in anonymity and darkness. All those kingdoms of barbed wire where everyone looked alike and all words carried the same weight. Day followed day and hour followed hour, while thoughts, numb and bleak, groped their way among the corpses, through the mire and the blood.

30   And the adolescent in me, yearning for faith, questioned: Where was God in all this? Was this another test, one more? Or a punishment?

And if so, for what sins? What crimes were being punished? Was there a misdeed that deserved so many mass graves? Would it ever again be possible to speak of justice, of truth, of divine charity, after the murder of one million Jewish children?

31   I did not understand, I was afraid to understand. Was this the end of the Jewish people, or the end perhaps of the human adventure? Surely it was the end of an era, the end of a world. That I knew, that was all I knew.

32   As for the rest, I accumulated uncertainties. The faith of some, the lack of faith of others added to my perplexity. How could one believe, how could one not believe, in God as one faced those mountains of ashes? Who would symbolize the concentration-camp experience— the killer or the victim? Their confrontation was so striking, so gigantic that it had to include a metaphysical, ontological aspect: would we ever penetrate its mystery?

33   Questions, doubts. I moved through the fog like a sleepwalker. Why did the God of Israel manifest such hostility toward the descendants of Israel? I did not know. Why did free men, liberals and humanists, remain untouched by Jewish suffering? I did not know.

34   I remember the midnight arrival at Birkenau. Shouts. Dogs barking. Families together for the last time, families about to be torn asunder. A young Jewish boy walks at his father's side in the convoy of men; they walk and they walk and night walks with them toward a place spewing monstrous flames, flames devouring the sky. Suddenly an inmate crosses the ranks and explains to the men what they are seeing, the truth of the night: the future, the absence of future; the key to the secret, the power of evil. As he speaks, the young boy touches his father's arm as though to reassure him, and whispers, "This is impossible, isn't it? Don't listen to what he is telling us, he only wants to frighten us. What he says is impossible, unthinkable, it is all part of another age, the Middle Ages, not the twentieth century, not modern history. The world, Father, the civilized world would not allow such things to happen."

35   And yet the civilized world did know, and remained silent. Where was man in all this? And culture, how did it reach this nadir? All those spiritual leaders, those thinkers, those philosophers enamored of truth, those moralists drunk with justice—how was one to reconcile their teachings with Josef Mengele, the great master of selections in Auschwitz? I told myself that a grave, a horrible error had been com-

mitted somewhere—only, I knew neither its nature nor its author. When and where had history taken so bad a turn?

36   I remember the words of a young Talmudist whose face was that of an old man. He and I worked as a team, carrying boulders weighing more than the two of us.

37   "Let us suppose," he whispered, "let us suppose that our people had not transmitted the Law to other nations. Let us forget Abraham and his example, Moses and his justice, the prophets and their message. Let us suppose that our contributions to philosophy, to science, to literature are negligible or even nonexistent. Maimonides, Nahmanides, Rashi: nothing. Spinoza, Bergson, Einstein, Freud: nothing. Let us suppose that we have in no way added to progress, to the well-being of mankind. One thing cannot be contested: the great killers, history's great assassins—Pharaoh, Nero, Chmelnitzky, Hitler—not one was formed in our midst."

38   Which brings us back to where we started: to the relations between Jews and Christians, which, of course, we had been forced to revise.   For we have been struck by a harsh truth: in Auschwitz all the Jews were victims, all the killers were Christian.

39   I mention this here neither to score points nor to embarrass anyone. I believe that no religion, people or nation is inferior or superior to another; I dislike facile triumphalism, for us and for others. I dislike self-righteousness. And I feel closer to certain Christians—as long as they do not try to convert me to their faith—than to certain Jews. I felt closer to John XXIII and to François Mauriac than to self-hating Jews. I have more in common with an authentic and tolerant Christian than with a Jew who is neither authentic nor tolerant. I stress this because what I am about to say will surely hurt my Christian friends. Yet I have no right to hold back.

40   How is one to explain that neither Hitler nor Himmler was ever excommunicated by the church? That Pius XII never thought it necessary, not to say indispensable, to condemn Auschwitz and Treblinka? That among the S.S. a large proportion were believers who remained faithful to their Christian ties to the end? That there were killers who went to confession between massacres? And that they all came from Christian families and had received a Christian education?

41   In Poland, a stronghold of Christianity, it often happened that Jews who had escaped from the ghettos returned inside their walls, so hostile did they find the outside world; they feared the Poles as much

as the Germans. This was also true in Lithuania, in the Ukraine, in White Russia and in Hungary. How is one to explain the passivity of the population as it watched the persecution of its Jews? How explain the cruelty of the killers? How explain that the Christian in them did not make their arms tremble as they shot at children or their conscience bridle as they shoved their naked, beaten victims into the factories of death? Of course, here and there, brave Christians came to the aid of Jews, but they were few: several dozen bishops and priests, a few hundred men and women in all of Europe.

42   It is a painful statement to make, but we cannot ignore it: as surely as the victims are a problem for the Jews, the killers are a problem for the Christians.

43   Yes, the victims remain a serious and troubling problem for us. No use covering it up. What was there about the Jew that he could be reduced so quickly, so easily to the status of victim? I have read all the answers, all the explanations. They are all inadequate. It is difficult to imagine the silent processions marching toward the pits. And the crowds that let themselves be duped. And the condemned who, inside the sealed wagons and sometimes on the very ramp at Birkenau, continued not to see. I do not understand. I understand neither the killers nor the victims.

44   To be a Jew during the Holocaust may have meant not to understand. Having rejected murder as a means of survival and death as a solution, men and women agreed to live and die without understanding.

45   For the survivor, the question presented itself differently: to remain or not to remain a Jew. I remember our tumultuous, anguished debates in France after the liberation. Should one leave for Palestine and fight in the name of Jewish nationalism, or should one, on the contrary, join the Communist movement and promulgate the ideal of internationalism? Should one delve deeper into tradition, or turn one's back on it? The options were extreme: total commitment or total alienation, unconditional loyalty or repudiation. There was no returning to the earlier ways and principles. The Jew could say: I have suffered, I have been made to suffer, all I can do is draw closer to my own people. And that was understandable. Or else: I have suffered too much, I have no strength left, I withdraw, I do not wish my children to inherit this suffering. And that, too, was understandable.

46   And yet, as in the past, the ordeal brought not a decline but a renascence of Jewish consciousness and a flourishing of Jewish history. Rather than break his ties, the Jew strengthened them. Auschwitz made him stronger. Even he among us who espouses so-called universal causes outside his community is motivated by the Jew in him trying to reform man even as he despairs of mankind. Though he may be in a position to become something else, the Jew remains a Jew.

47   Throughout a world in flux, young Jews, speaking every tongue, products of every social class, join in the adventure that Judaism represents for them, a phenomenon that reached its apex in Israel and Soviet Russia. Following different roads, these pilgrims take part in the same project and express the same defiance: "They want us to founder, but we will let our joy explode; they want to make us hard, closed to solidarity and love, well, we will be obstinate but filled with compassion." This is the challenge that justifies the hopes the Jew places in Judaism and explains the singular marks he leaves on his destiny.

48   Thus there would seem to be more than one way for the Jew to assume his condition. There is a time to question oneself and a time to act; there is a time to tell stories and a time to pray; there is a time to build and a time to rebuild. Whatever he chooses to do, the Jew becomes a spokesman for all Jews, dead and yet to be born, for all the beings who live through him and inside him.

49   His mission was never to make the world Jewish but, rather, to make it more human.

Reading Closely and Thinking Critically

   1. Make a list of modifiers that describe Wiesel as a boy.

   2. How does Wiesel say his non-Jewish neighbors viewed him? Why did they view him that way? Was Wiesel troubled by the view? Explain.

   3. According to Wiesel's definition, what are the characteristics of a Jew?

   4. Wiesel says that to be a Jew is "to live with memory" (paragraph 9). What do you think Wiesel means?

   5. Why was Shabbat (Sabbath) so important to Wiesel when he was a boy?

6. For what kind of audience is "To Be a Jew" well suited? Do you think the intended audience is non-Jewish? Explain.

7. Using the evidence in the essay, explain how Wiesel feels about being Jewish.

Examining Structure and Strategy

1. Wiesel narrates an account of his childhood, he provides a definition of a Jew, and he gives an account of the Holocaust. How do these elements relate to each other? That is, how is it possible to include all three in the same essay?

2. What is the effect of the conversation in paragraph 34?

3. Like transitional words and phrases, transitional paragraphs connect ideas to move the reader smoothly from the discussion of one point to a discussion of the next. Which paragraphs are transitional paragraphs, and what ideas to they connect?

4. What cause-and-effect analysis does Wiesel include in the essay?

5. Wiesel often asks questions in the essay. What purposes do these questions serve? Are they an effective strategy? Explain.

Considering Language and Style

1. Why does Wiesel switch from the third person pronouns *he/him* in paragraphs 1 and 2 to the first person pronouns *I/me* in paragraph 3? Is the switch a problem for you? Explain.

2. "To Be a Jew" includes many historical and religious references some readers may not be familiar with. Are these references a problem? Explain.

3. Consult a dictionary if you are unfamiliar with any of these words: *miscreants* (paragraph 2), *catechism* (paragraph 6), *canons* (paragraph 6), *pogroms* (paragraphs 6, 18), *inquisitors* (paragraph 6), *Talmud* (paragraphs 9, 15), *espousing* (paragraph 11), *heder* (paragraph 18), *yeshiva* (paragraphs 18, 20), *Shabbat* (paragraphs 18, 21, 23), *Hasidim* (paragraph 21), *metaphysical* (paragraph 32), *ontological* (paragraph 32), *nadir* (paragraph 35), *excommunicated* (paragraph 40), *promulgate* (paragraph 45), *renascence* (paragraph 46).

For Group Discussion or Writing

Wiesel points out a number of contradictions. For example, he notes that Christians and Jews of his childhood believed in the same God, but they lacked knowledge of each other. What other contradictions are noted, and what are their significance?

Writing Assignments

1. *In your journal.* In a page or two, tell what you know about the Holocaust and how you came to know it.

2. *Using the pattern.* Write an essay with the title "To Be a _____." (Fill in the blank with a noun that indicates your religious affiliation: Protestant, Moslem, Jehovah's Witness, Catholic, and so forth.) Like Wiesel, use definition to explain the chief characteristics of a person with the affiliation. As an alternative, write an essay with the title "To Be an Atheist" or "To Be an Agnostic."

3. *Using the pattern.* Write a definition of *Sabbath* or another religious day or ceremony: confirmation, Easter, Ramadan, Holy Communion, Kwanzaa, Chanukah, and so forth. Include the chief characteristics of the event, including how it is celebrated and its significance for you.

4. *Using the pattern.* In paragraph 32, Wiesel writes about faith. Write a definition of *faith.*

5. *Using the pattern.* In paragraph 49, Wiesel says that the Jew's mission is "to make [the world] more human." Write a definition of *human* that explains what it means to be "human."

6. *Considering a theme.* Write an essay that explains what a single individual can do on a day-to-day basis to help make the world "more human" (paragraph 49).

7. *Connecting the readings.* Each year Jews commemorate the Holocaust, its victims and survivors, with an observance called Yom Hashoah, which is a day of remembrance. If a Holocaust remembrance were to become a national day of observance, how do you think it should be celebrated? Both "To Be a Jew" and "On Holidays and How to Make Them Work" (page 207) may give you ideas for this essay.

ADDITIONAL ESSAY ASSIGNMENTS

See pages 506 and 507 for suggestions for writing definition and for a revision checklist.

1. To help your reader understand something complex, define one of the following: *fear, beauty,* or *loyalty.*

2. To give your reader a fresh appreciation for the familiar, define one of the following: *friend, family,* or *the ideal teacher.*

3. To help your reader appreciate its value, define *freedom of the press* or *freedom of religion.*

4. To persuade your reader that it is either good or bad, define *censorship.*

5. Define *racism, sexism,* or *homophobia.*

6. Define *horror movie* to help your reader appreciate the genre more.

7. Define *situation comedy* in a way that indicates your view of the quality of the genre.

8. Define *leisure* in a way that entertains your reader.

9. Define and illustrate *politically correct* to help your reader better understand its significance.

10. Define one of the following: *police officer, lifeguard, camp counselor, doctor,* or *nurse.*

11. To help your reader understand something complex, define *integrity.*

12. Define *peer pressure* to help your reader understand what a potent force it is.

13. Define *gossip* to inform and/or entertain.

14. To clarify something not well understood, define *creativity.*

15. To entertain and/or to inform, define *style.*

16. To entertain and/or to inform, define *tacky.*

17. To express your own thoughts and feelings, define *Christmas spirit.*

18. Define *frustration.* If you want to make the piece amusing, your purpose can be to entertain.

19. If you are a member of an ethnic group, define some ethnic term (*chutzpah, gringo,* and so on) so someone who is not a member of your group will understand it.

20. *Definition in context:* Assume you are a tutor in your campus writing center and the director has asked you to develop a pamphlet on writer's block to be given to students who come to the center. Write a definition of *writer's block* and its effects, suitable for inclusion in the pamphlet. You may also include narrations about experiencing writer's block if those narrations help illustrate its characteristics.

11

⑥ ADDITIONAL READINGS: A CASEBOOK FOR ARGUMENTATION-PERSUASION

Both *argumentation* and *persuasion* work to convince the reader to adopt a particular view or to take a particular action. In the purest sense, argumentation relies on sound reasoning and logic to move the reader, while persuasion employs appeals to emotions, values, and beliefs. In practice, however, reason and logic are usually combined with appeals to emotions, values, and beliefs. The difference in any given case is which is emphasized more: argumentation or persuasion.

Already in this book, you have dealt with a number of essays with a persuasive purpose because each chapter of readings so far has included one or more selections meant to move the reader to think or act a particular way. In this chapter, however, you will work with individual, pairs, and trios of readings to study argumentative-persuasive technique in greater detail. In addition, the readings will provide ideas for your own argumentation-persuasion essays.

PURPOSE AND AUDIENCE

Argumentation-persuasion works to convince the reader to think or act a particular way. For example, a newspaper editorial argues that the city's layoff of municipal employees is unnecessary in order to convince readers to think a particular way. Campaign literature extols the virtues of a candidate to convince people to vote a particular way.

Sometimes you have no hope of convincing your reader, so you must establish a less ambitious goal, such as softening your reader's objection or convincing your reader that your view has some merit. Say, for example, that you are arguing that the governor should increase the sales tax to support public education. If your reader has children in school, you can reasonably aim to convince your audience to agree with you. However, if your reader is a retired person on a fixed income, expecting agreement may be unreasonable. In this case, a more suitable goal is to convince your reader that there are some good reasons to raise the sales tax—even if he or she does not fully support the idea.

Perhaps you are wondering what good it is to soften a reader's objection or convince that person that your view has some merit. The answer is that if you can lessen a reader's resistance to your view, he or she may come around to your thinking eventually or work less hard to oppose you.

As you have probably figured out, audience assessment is particularly important in argumentation-persuasion. Not only must you size up your reader in order to establish a reasonable purpose for your writing, you must also understand the characteristics of your audience so you know which points need to be stated and proven, what kind of evidence will be the most effective, how hard you must work to convince your reader, and how your audience will respond to emotional appeals.

Argumentation in College Writing

Argumentation will be a considerable part of your college writing. While many times you will be tested on your ability to recall information, other times you will need to do more than restate what you have read in a text or heard in a lecture. To show that you have thoughtfully considered that information, you will be asked to analyze it, consider points of view, and then draw your own conclusions, which your instructors will ask you to present and defend in logical, argumentative pieces that rely mostly on reason and very little (if at all) on emotion.

For example, in a political science or American studies class, you may be asked to do more that just explain affirmative action initiatives and their history; you may also have to argue whether or not such initiatives have hurt or helped minority populations. In an ethics class, you may need to do more than explain what is possible with genetic engineering; you may have to develop guidelines governing cloning and argue for their acceptance. In a history class, you may need to explain why the atomic bomb was dropped during World War II and then argue that it should or should not have been used to end the war with Japan; in a business course, you may need to define inflation, explain how to combat it, and then go on to argue which combative strategy is the best. In an environmental science course, you may need to argue that the government should or should not sponsor legislation to control global warming.

THE PARTS OF ARGUMENTATION-PERSUASION

In his book *The Uses of Argument* (1958), Stephen Toulmin identifies three parts of an argument. An adaptation of his division is given here.

You can think of argumentation-persuasion as having three parts: the claim, the support, and the assumption.

The *claim* is the point you are arguing; it is what you are trying to convince your reader of. Here are some examples of claims.

claim: This university should switch from its current quarter system to the semester system.

claim: Teachers should not be permitted to engage in labor strikes.

claim: The United States's immigration policy creates many problems.

In an argumentation-persuasion essay, the claim appears in the thesis.

The *support* is the ideas and information you include to convince the reader. The support can be evidence based on logical reasoning—statistics and facts, for example—or it can be appeals to emotions, values, and beliefs. Here are examples of both kinds of support.

claim:	This university should switch from its current quarter system to the semester system.
support (based on reason):	The administration says that the switch would save the university money because fewer terms would reduce the cost of registration and advisement.
support (appeal to belief):	Semesters allow students to study subjects at a more leisurely pace. (An appeal to the belief that it is better to study something for 15 weeks than for 10.)

In an argumentation-persuasion essay, the support will be the supporting details.

The third part of argumentation-persuasion is the *assumption*, which is the inference or belief that connects the claim and the support. To see how the assumption connects the claim and support, study this example.

claim: This university should switch from its current quarter system to the semester system.

support (reason): The administration says that the switch would save the university money because fewer terms would reduce the cost of registration and advisement.

unstated assumption: The administration is trustworthy, so it can be believed when it says that money will be saved.

If the reader trusts the administration, the assumption is accepted and the support is convincing. However, if the reader does not trust the administration, then the assumption is not accepted and the support fails to convince. When a reader might not accept an assumption automatically, you must support the assumption to make it convincing.

stated assumption with support: The administration says that the switch would save the university money because fewer terms would reduce the cost of registration and advisement. They arrived at this conclusion after surveying 200 schools that have switched from the quarter to the semester system.

Sometimes an assumption is a value or belief.

claim: Teachers should not be allowed to engage in labor strikes.

support: When teachers strike, they cause a great deal of harm.

assumption: Teachers are different from other workers who engage in strikes that create problems.

This example shows that the assumption is very much at the heart of an argument because it is what will or will not incline the reader to move from the support to accepting the claim. To prove that teachers should not strike, you would have to prove the assumption and show how teachers are different from others who strike: steel workers, truck drivers, television writers, and so forth.

Sometimes the assumption is self-evident, so it need not be written out. Say, for example, that you want to argue that we should censor the Internet to protect children from predatory adults. The assumption that we do not want children harmed is so obvious that it need not be stated. Now say that you want to argue that teenagers who commit murder should be tried as adults. In this case, the assumption that some teenagers are emotionally and intellectually mature needs to be stated and proven. Otherwise, your reader may have difficulty moving from your support to accepting your claim.

ARGUMENTATIVE DETAIL

For the most part, your argumentative detail will be the reasons you hold your view. Thus, if you want to convince your reader that the federal government should pay day care expenses for working parents, you would give all the reasons this is a good idea. However, supplying reasons for your stand is not enough; you must also back up those reasons with support. Say you argue that the family unit is in trouble and you give the high divorce rate as one reason to support your view. You must then go on to back up this reason, perhaps by giving a statistic about how high the divorce rate is and by explaining the specific negative effects of divorce on the family.

To back up your reasons, you can rely on a number of sources and strategies, including personal experience and observation, facts and statistics, quotations and paraphrases, interviews, speculation about the effects of adopting or not adopting your view, and the patterns of development. These are discussed next.

Draw on Personal Experience and Observation

Say that you are in favor of federally funded day care, and you cite as one reason the fact that children of working parents do not always get satisfactory care without it. To back up this claim, you could rely on observation by telling about your neighbor, who cannot afford decent care for her child while she is at work. If your own experience as a working parent supports the point, you could also write about that experience to back up your claim.

Use Facts and Statistics

Say that you want to convince your reader to become a vegetarian and that you make the point that eating meat causes the death of huge numbers of living things. You could support that point by citing Joy Williams's claim (page 653) that 130,000 cattle, 7,000 calves, 360,000 pigs, and 24 million chickens are slaughtered each day in the United States. If you do use facts and statistics taken from sources, be sure to document this information according to the conventions explained in the appendix.

Use Quotations and Paraphrases

If you want to argue that the animal rights movement interferes with medical research, you could quote or paraphrase John Hubbell, who says on page 667, "If we want to defeat the killer diseases that still confront us—AIDS, Alzheimer's, cancer, heart disease and many others, the misguided fanatics of the animal-rights movement must be stopped." If you do use quotations or paraphrases, be sure to follow the guidelines given in the appendix.

Conduct Interviews

Say that to argue for federally funded day care you note that the day care fees are too high for some individuals. To support this reason, you can interview the owners of local day care centers to learn the cost of enrollment. If the figures are high, you could report them and note that many people cannot afford the tuition.

Speculate about What Would Happen If Your View Were or Were not Adopted

Sometimes you can argue your case by explaining the good that would result if your view were adopted or the bad that would result if your view were not adopted. Say, for example, that you want to argue for the elimination of the foreign language requirement for mathematics and science majors. You could argue that if your view is adopted, science and math majors will have more time to participate in valuable internship programs. As an alternative, you could argue that if the requirement is not abolished, many prospective math and science students will attend school at the nearby colleges that do not require a foreign language.

Use the Patterns of Development

To explain and back up the reasons for your stand, you can use any of the patterns discussed in this book. If, for instance, you want to convince your reader that couples should marry rather than just live together, you can *narrate* an account of what happened when your brother and his girlfriend lived together. You can also *provide examples* of the problems couples face when they do not marry. You can *contrast* the benefits of marriage with the drawbacks of living together. You can *classify* the benefits of marriage, you can *describe* the embarrassment of older relatives of the unmarried couple, and so on.

PERSUASIVE DETAIL

In addition to appealing to your reader's intellect with sound reasons, you can be convincing by appealing to your reader's emotions, needs, values, beliefs, and concerns. For example, to convince your reader to support assisted suicide, you can move the reader to compassion by describing the agony of a patient who must linger in pain with no hope of recovery. Similarly, to convince your reader that the federal government should fund day care, you can stir up the reader's emotions with a graphic explanation of the substandard care the child next door is getting. Persuasive detail, then, uses emotionally charged language to move a reader to a particular view or action.

While appealing to your reader's emotions is a valid technique, you must be careful not to overdo. Emotional appeal should be restrained. It is fine to move your reader's emotions by arousing compassion for a homosexual couple who wants to marry, but it is unfair to charge that tens of thousands of people are despondent and totally unfulfilled because they cannot marry. Further, the number of emotional appeals should be reasonable. They should appear *in addition to* logical reasons—not *instead of* them. Thus, rely mostly on sound reasons, and supplement those reasons with emotional appeal when appropriate.

Another caution to keep in mind concerns uses of clauses such as "most knowledgeable people realize," and "as anyone can see." Wording like this will annoy a seasoned reader. You are expected to prove your point by providing evidence—not by announcing what others (knowledgeable or not) believe.

INDUCTIVE AND DEDUCTIVE REASONING

Induction and deduction are two methods of reasoning especially helpful in argumentation-persuasion.

Induction

Induction is a form of reasoning that moves from specific evidence to a general conclusion. That is, when you reason inductively, you examine specific facts, cases, examples, and other available evidence and then draw a reasonable conclusion based on that information. If you look around, you will see that induction is used all the time: A doctor ponders a patient's symptoms and test results and reasons inductively to reach a diagnosis; a jury considers the evidence presented at the trial and reasons inductively to reach a verdict; a police officer studies the crime scene, examines clues, and reasons inductively to establish a list of suspects; your writing instructor reads your essays, weighs out the evidence of its strengths and weaknesses, reasons inductively, and records a grade.

When you write argumentation-persuasion, induction can serve you well. Assume, for example, that you wish to argue the need for a traffic light at the corner of First Street and Third Avenue. You can first present your specific evidence: In the last year, traffic accidents at that intersection have increased 80 percent; five people have died there, including two children; traffic at that intersection has increased since the shopping mall opened a mile away; the State Highway Patrol has said a traffic light there could reduce the number of accidents. After offering this evidence, you can present your view in the form of a generalization that follows from the evidence: We need a traffic light installed at the corner of First Street and Third Avenue. This generalization would be your thesis.

No matter how compelling your evidence seems to be, you cannot always be certain of the reliability of the generalization you conclude from it. Thus, it may well be true that a traffic light would solve the problem at First Street and Third Avenue, but it could also be true that the real problem is the speed limit and a better solution is to reduce the speed from 55 mph to 35 mph. Because the conclusion drawn in inductive reasoning is rarely accurate beyond a doubt, that conclusion is called an *inference*. To increase the likelihood that your inferences are accurate, be sure that your evidence is sound. Be careful that you supply enough evidence and that the evidence is accurate, recent, specific, and representative. For help with supplying sound evidence, review the information on avoiding errors in logic on page 55.

Deduction

In a broad sense, deduction involves reasoning from the general to the specific, but you should not think of deduction as the opposite of induction. Instead, *deduction* moves from a generalization (called a *major premise*) to a specific case (called a *minor premise*) and on to a conclusion, like this:

major premise (generalization):	Because of compulsory attendance laws, a number of students who do not want to be in school disrupt the educational process.
minor premise (specific case):	Many students in this state do not want to be in school, and they disrupt the educational process for those who do want to learn.
conclusion:	If we abolish compulsory attendance laws in this state, students who do not want to be in school can leave and make it easier for others to learn.

Recall that with inductive reasoning, the conclusion is an inference rather than a certainty. In deductive reasoning, however, if the two premises are accurate, then the conclusion will follow inescapably. If one or both of the premises are wrong, then the conclusion will not follow, as is the case in this example:

major premise:	All college students drink beer.
minor premise:	Chris is a college student.
conclusion:	Chris drinks beer.

In this example, the conclusion cannot be accepted because the major premise is an overgeneralization. (See page 55). Not all college students drink beer; therefore, we cannot conclude inescapably that college-student Chris drinks beer. To be sure your major and minor premises meet the test of logic, refer to page 55 on avoiding errors in logic.

When you write argumentation-persuasion, deductive reasoning can provide a very useful framework. You can set up your essay so that your supporting details present the evidence demonstrating the truth of each premise. With the premises proven, your reader will accept your conclusion, which is the point you are arguing—your thesis.

RAISING AND COUNTERING OBJECTIONS

No matter what stand you take on an issue, some reasonable people will disagree with you, and those people will have valid points to support their view. While it is tempting to ignore this opposition, doing so will weaken your argumentation or persuasion because you will not come across as someone who has carefully examined both sides before arriving at a position. Furthermore, even if you ignore the opposition, your reader will not. Your audience will be thinking about the points that work against your view, and if you do not deal with those points, you may fail to convince your reader. Thus, you must recognize the opposing arguments and find a way to diffuse them. Recognizing and diffusing opposition points is called *raising and countering objections*.

To raise and counter objections, you first acknowledge the objection to your stand by stating it. This is *raising the objection*. Then you make the objection less compelling. This is *countering the objection*. In general, you can raise and counter objections three ways, as illustrated below.

1. State that the opposition has a point, but so do you.

Many people are concerned because federally funded day care will raise taxes [objection raised]. However, children who are currently given substandard care because we lack a comprehensive, federally funded program will not thrive. Children who do not thrive fail to realize their potential or they develop problems, both of which end up costing society more money than day care [objection countered].

2. State that the opposition has a point, but your point is better.

Although some are concerned about the cost of federally funded day care [objection raised], we cannot put a price tag on the well-being of our children because they are our hope for a better future [objection countered].

3. State that the opposition's point is untrue.

There are those who maintain that we do not need federally funded day care [objection raised]. However, the number of mothers who must work outside the home is very high, and many of these working mothers are the sole support of their children and could not stay home even if they wanted

to. As a result, many parents are forced into substandard, or even down-
right dangerous, child care arrangements [objection countered].

Raising and countering objections helps strengthen your argumentation-persuasion, but you need not deal with every opposition view. Instead, identify the most compelling objections and
deal with those.

ORGANIZING ARGUMENTATION-PERSUASION

The introduction of argumentation-persuasion can be handled
many ways. Explaining why the issue is important can be effective because it helps the reader understand the seriousness of
your purpose. Thus, if you are arguing that high schools should
have day care centers for teenage mothers, your introduction can
note the large number of teen mothers who drop out of school
because they have no child care. This figure should help your
reader appreciate the urgency of the issue. If your reader needs
certain background information in order to appreciate your argument, the introduction can be a good place to provide that information. Thus, if you are arguing the need to return to homogeneous groupings in classrooms, you should explain what a
homogeneous grouping is if your reader is not likely to know.

Your thesis, whether it appears in the opening paragraphs
or elsewhere, should state the issue and your stand on that issue,
like one of the following:

The United States desperately needs federally funded day care. (*issue:* federally funded day care; *stand:* in favor of it)

Federally funded day care would create more problems than it solves.
(*issue:* federally funded day care; *stand:* against it)

Be sure that the issue you are arguing is genuinely debatable. There is no reason to argue that parents should love their
children because no one will disagree with you. Similarly, avoid
matters of taste. For example, arguing that basketball is a better
sport than football is not productive because the issue is a matter of personal preference.

In general, arranging your points in a progressive order (from least to most compelling) is effective. This way, you can save your most convincing arguments for the end so your reader leaves your essay with them fresh in mind. Or you can place your strongest arguments first and last for a big opening and finish. Remember, the points at the end of an essay are in the most emphatic position and therefore likely to have the biggest impact.

If you are reasoning inductively, you can place your thesis at the end of your essay, after you have presented all the specific evidence pointing to the inference that stands as your thesis. If you are reasoning deductively, you can first present the evidence to support your major premise, and then present the evidence to support your minor premise.

You will probably find topic sentences helpful when you structure argumentation-persuasion. You can place each reason for your view in its own topic sentence and follow each topic sentence with the appropriate support. Thus, an essay arguing that we should pay college athletes rather than give them scholarships could have these topic sentences:

> If we pay college athletes, the players can use the money for whatever they like—including tuition and books.

> If we pay college athletes, we can finally dispel the myth that the players are always students first.

> Finally, once we pay college athletes, we can allow colleges to openly stand as farm clubs for professional teams.

If you raise and counter objections, you can do this throughout the essay, wherever a point to be countered logically emerges. However, if you are dealing with very few objections, you can raise and counter them together in one or two paragraphs at the beginning or end of the essay.

To conclude argumentation-persuasion, you can reaffirm your position for emphasis, summarize your chief arguments if your reader is likely to appreciate the reminder, or present your most persuasive point. In addition, you can call your audience to action by explaining what you want your reader to do. Or you can recommend a particular solution to a problem. Finally, explaining what would happen if your view were or were not adopted can be an effective closing.

SUGGESTIONS FOR WRITING
ARGUMENTATION-PERSUASION

1. If you have trouble thinking of a topic, review the essays in this book for ideas. You can also review local and campus newspapers to learn about issues of current importance.

2. Another way to come up with a topic is to fill in the blank in one of these sentences:

   a. It is unfair that _____.
   b. It makes me angry that _____.
   c. I disagree with people who believe that _____.

3. List every reason you think of to support your view.

4. If any readings in this book deal with your issue, check them for facts, statistics, paraphrases, and quotations you can use.

5. For additional details, answer these questions:

   a. Why is the issue important?
   b. What would happen if my view were adopted?
   c. What would happen if my view were not adopted?
   d. What are the chief objections to my view?
   e. How can these objections be countered?
   f. Who can I interview for information?
   g. How can I appeal to my reader's emotions?

6. Draft a thesis that presents the issue and your stand.

7. Write an outline and then a first draft.

Checklist for Revising Argumentation-Persuasion

1. Is your topic genuinely debatable?
2. Does your introduction provide background, explain why your topic is important, or otherwise engage interest?

3. Does your thesis note the issue and your stand on the issue?

4. Are all your points clarified and supported?

5. Have you avoided statements like "as anyone can see" or "most informed people realize"?

6. If necessary for your reader, have you stated and supported the assumptions that connect your claims and support?

7. Have you used appeals to emotion, values, and beliefs with the appropriate restraint?

8. Have you avoided problems with logic?

9. Have you raised and countered compelling objections?

10. Are paraphrases and quotations documented according to the conventions given in the appendix?

11. Are your details in a progressive or other suitable order?

12. Does your conclusion bring the essay to a satisfying close?

ANNOTATED STUDENT ESSAY

Student-author Laurel Mahoney uses techniques of both argumentation and persuasion to convince the reader that the unwed teenage mother should decide the fate of her child.

Who Should Decide?

1   Sherry was sixteen, and she thought she was in love. Her boyfriend, a smooth talker, used every line imaginable to get what he wanted from Sherry. He promised to love and care for her forever, and so one night in the back seat of his car, Sherry became pregnant. Soon the guy who promised to love and care for her was gone, and Sherry's life was forever altered.

2   Should Sherry have known better? Of course. Was she to blame? Certainly. However, this is not a new story. In fact, teen pregnancy is more of a problem than ever, despite all the sex education in schools. The problem and its solutions are well publicized, so everyone knows the pregnant teen's options: adoption, abortion, or motherhood at a ridiculously early age. What most people have not considered, however, is who

Paragraphs 1 and 2

This section forms the introduction. Paragraph 1 is a narration with emotional content. Paragraph 2 provides background information. The last sentence of paragraph 2 is the thesis, which presents the issue (who decides the fate of the teen's baby) and the writer's stand (the teen should).

should make the decision: the teenage girl or her parents. By law, the teen is entitled to make the decision, and that is just how it should be.

3   The most obvious reason that the teenage mother should decide is that she is the biological parent and hence the responsible party. In the purest physiological sense, the decision is hers to make. Many parents argue, however, that while the girl may make the decision, it is the parents who will bear the responsibility because they will have to house the girl and her child, as well as provide financial support. Parents looking forward to the end of the bulk of their own parenting responsibilities may feel particularly burdened by continued support of their daughter and grandchild. That is certainly unfortunate, but two things must be remembered. Parenthood has no ending date, so the daughter—pregnant or not—remains the parents' responsibility. They are thus obligated to care for the girl and her child. Also, the financial burden and crowded house will be temporary. Once the girl graduates from school and gets a job, she can move out and be more self-supporting. True, she may still need some help, but her need should gradually lessen.

4   In addition to the financial aspect, the emotional aspect must be considered. If parents force their daughter to give up or abort her child when she does not want to, the decision will haunt her the rest of her life, filling her with pain and regret from which she may never recover. Imagine the poor girl spending her life wondering about the child she never knew and hating herself and her parents. What kind of life would that be?

5   Many parents would argue that the teenager lacks sufficient maturity to make such a decision. No one will argue that a teenager is mature enough to fully appreciate the ramifications of her decisions. However, parents, her doctor, and counselors can provide her with information, and she will have to make the best decision she can with that information. Then she will have to live with that decision. Even adults are forced to make important decisions before they are ready, and they do the same thing: They get information, make the best decision they can at the time, and

Paragraph 3
The topic sentence (the first sentence) presents the first reason to support the writer's view (biological responsibility). An objection is raised (parents will be financially responsible) and countered (the pregnant teen is her parents' responsibility and the burden will be temporary).

Paragraph 4
The topic sentence (the first sentence) presents the next reason supporting the writer's view (the emotional aspect). The paragraph makes an emotional appeal. Detail is cause-and-effect analysis.

Paragraph 5
The topic sentence (the first sentence) presents an objection, and the rest of the paragraph counters that objection.

live with it. That part of life never changes, regardless of age.

6   Finally, the most important reason the teenage girl should be allowed to make the decision is that she probably knows in her heart what is best for her and the child. Her parents may *think* they know, but the girl is the better judge. Furthermore, the parents may decide according to what is best for them rather than their daughter.

Paragraph 6
The topic sentence (the first sentence) presents the last reason. The transition, the most important reason, indicates a progressive order.

7   Teenage pregnancy is a serious, ongoing problem for both the girl and her parents. The best way to deal with the decision about the baby is to provide the girl with all the information possible about her options and their consequences. Counseling by social workers, religious leaders, and psychologists can help. During this process, the parents should provide love, support, and acceptance. Then they must stand back and let their daughter make the decision.

Paragraph 7
The conclusion provides closure by suggesting a course of action.

PERILS OF PROHIBITION
Elizabeth M. Whelan

President of the American Council of Science and Health, Elizabeth Whelan earned a master's degree in public health from Yale School of Medicine and a doctoral degree from Harvard School of Public Health. A prolific writer, Whelan has authored and co-authored over 20 books. She has been honored with the Walter Alvarez Award from the American Writers Association and an Early Career Award from the Public Health Association. In "Perils of Prohibition," which first appeared in Newsweek *(1995), Whelan uses cause-and-effect analysis, exemplification, and contrast to persuade the reader that the legal drinking age of 21 contributes to alcohol abuse among young people.*

THE PATTERNS	THE PURPOSE
cause-and-effect analysis, exemplification, and contrast	*to persuade*

1   My colleagues at the Harvard School of Public Health, where I studied preventive medicine, deserve high praise for their recent study on teenage drinking. What they found in their survey of college students was that they drink "early and . . . often," frequently to the point of getting ill.

2   As a public-health scientist with a daughter, Christine, heading to college this fall, I have professional and personal concerns about teen binge drinking. It is imperative that we explore why so many young people abuse alcohol. From my own study of the effects of alcohol restrictions and my observations of Christine and her friends' predicament about drinking, I believe that today's laws are unrealistic. Prohibiting the sale of liquor to responsible young adults creates an atmosphere where binge drinking and alcohol abuse have become a problem. American teens, unlike their European peers, don't learn how to drink gradually, safely and in moderation.

3   Alcohol is widely accepted and enjoyed in our culture. Studies show that moderate drinking can be good for you. But we legally proscribe alcohol until the age of 21 (why not 30 or 45?). Christine and her classmates can drive cars, fly planes, marry, vote, pay taxes, take out

loans and risk their lives as members of the U.S. armed forces. But laws in all 50 states say that no alcoholic beverages may be sold to anyone until that magic 21st birthday. We didn't always have a national "21" rule. When I was in college, in the mid-'60s, the drinking age varied from state to state. This posed its own risks, with underage students crossing state lines to get a legal drink.

4   In parts of the Western world, moderate drinking by teenagers and even children under their parents' supervision is a given. Though the per capita consumption of alcohol in France, Spain and Portugal is higher than in the United States, the rate of alcoholism and alcohol abuse is lower. A glass of wine at dinner is normal practice. Kids learn to regard moderate drinking as an enjoyable family activity rather than as something they have to sneak away to do. Banning drinking by young people makes it a badge of adulthood—a tantalizing forbidden fruit.

5   Christine and her teenage friends like to go out with a group to a club, comedy show or sports bar to watch the game. But teens today have to go on the sly with fake IDs and the fear of getting caught. Otherwise, they're denied admittance to most places and left to hang out on the street. That's hardly a safer alternative. Christine and her classmates now find themselves in a legal no man's land. At 18, they're considered adults. Yet when they want to enjoy a drink like other adults, they are, as they put it, "disenfranchised."

6   Comparing my daughter's dilemma with my own as an "underage" college student, I see a difference—and one that I think has exacerbated the current dilemma. Today's teens are far more sophisticated than we were. They're treated less like children and have more responsibilities than we did. This makes the 21 restriction seem anachronistic.

7   For the past few years, my husband and I have been preparing Christine for college life and the inevitable partying—read keg of beer— that goes with it. Last year, a young friend with no drinking experience was violently ill for days after he was introduced to "clear liquids in small glasses" during freshman orientation. We want our daughter to learn how to drink sensibly and avoid this pitfall. Starting at the age of 14, we invited her to join us for a glass of champagne with dinner. She'd tried it once before, thought it was "yucky" and declined. A year later, she enjoyed sampling wine at family meals.

8   When, at 16, she asked for a Mudslide (a bottled chocolate-milk-and-rum concoction), we used the opportunity to discuss it with her. We explained the alcohol content, told her the alcohol level is lower

when the drink is blended with ice and compared it with a glass of wine. Since the drink of choice on campus is beer, we contrasted its potency with wine and hard liquor and stressed the importance of not drinking on an empty stomach.

9   Our purpose was to encourage her to know the alcohol content of what she is served. We want her to experience the effects of liquor in her own home, not on the highway and not for the first time during a college orientation week with free-flowing suds. Although Christine doesn't drive yet, we regularly reinforce the concept of choosing a designated driver. Happily, that already seems a widely accepted practice among our daughter's friends who drink.

10   We recently visited the Ivy League school Christine will attend in the fall. While we were there, we read a story in the college paper about a student who was nearly electrocuted when, in a drunken state, he climbed on top of a moving train at a railroad station near the campus. The student survived, but three of his limbs were later amputated. This incident reminded me of a tragic death on another campus. An intoxicated student maneuvered himself into a chimney. He was found three days later when frat brothers tried to light a fire in the fireplace. By then he was dead.

11   These tragedies are just two examples of our failure to teach young people how to use alcohol prudently. If 18-year-olds don't have legal access to even a beer at a public place, they have no experience handling liquor on their own. They feel "liberated" when they arrive on campus. With no parents to stop them, they have a "let's make up for lost time" attitude. The result: binge drinking.

12   We should make access to alcohol legal at 18. At the same time, we should come down much harder on alcohol abusers and drunk drivers of all ages. We should intensify our efforts at alcohol education for adolescents. We want them to understand that it is perfectly OK not to drink. But if they do, alcohol should be consumed in moderation.

13   After all, we choose to teach our children about safe sex, including the benefits of teen abstinence. Why, then, can't we—schools and parents alike—teach them about safe drinking?

Reading Closely and Thinking Critically

1. What argument to support her view does Whelan present in paragraph 3? Is that argument logical and persuasive? Explain.

2. What reasons does Whelan give to support her stand? Which of those reasons do you find the most convincing? Do any of her reasons go unsupported? Explain.

3. How does Whelan explain the binge drinking on college campuses? Do you agree with her explanation? Explain.

4. Do you find "Perils of Prohibition" to be a convincing argument? Why or why not?

Examining Structure and Strategy

1. Which sentence in the essay is Whelan's thesis?

2. In paragraph 2, Whelan cites her credentials. Why does she do this? Does this information contribute to the persuasive quality of the essay? Explain.

3. How does Whelan use examples? Do the examples serve Whelan's persuasive purpose? Explain.

4. What elements of contrast appear in the essay? What elements of cause-and-effect analysis appear?

5. Where in the essay does Whelan appeal to the reader's emotions?

Considering Language and Style

1. In paragraph 4, Whelan says that when we ban drinking by young people, we make alcohol a forbidden fruit. Explain the reference to *forbidden fruit*. Is the reference a good one? Explain.

2. Consult a dictionary if you are unfamiliar with any of these words: *proscribe* (paragraph 3), *on the sly* (paragraph 5), *disenfranchised* (paragraph 5), *exacerbated* (paragraph 6), *anachronistic* (paragraph 6).

For Group Discussion or Writing
Whelan says that teens today are more sophisticated than they were when she was young (paragraph 6). With some classmates decide whether or not this statement is true. Be sure to cite examples to support your view.

Writing Assignments

1. *In your journal.* In a page or so, tell about your own experience with alcohol or that of someone close to you.

2. Using the pattern. Write an argument for or against banning alcohol on your college campus.

3. Using the pattern. Argue that the current legal drinking age of 21 should not be lowered. Be sure to raise and counter the points presented by Whelan.

4. Using the pattern. Write an argument for or against banning beer advertisements on television.

5. Using the pattern. Devise a plan for dealing with alcohol or drug abuse on college campuses and then write an essay arguing for implementing the plan on your campus.

6. Considering a theme. What alcohol-related problems exist on your campus? (If necessary, check with your student services office and campus police for this information.) Then write a paper that explains what problems exist, how your college is dealing with them, and whether or not these measures are sufficient. If there is little or no problem on your campus, explain why not and what other schools can learn from your college.

7. Connecting the readings. What risks do today's young people face, and how can they protect themselves from these risks? Explore these questions in an essay. The ideas in "Perils of Prohibition," "College Pressures" (page 477), "What Is Behind the Growth of Violence on College Campuses?" (page 420), and "It's Just Too Late" (page 429) may give you some ideas.

I WISH THEY'D DO IT RIGHT
Jane Doe

Nothing is known of the author of "I Wish They'd Do It Right" because she wished to remain anonymous. Hence the piece was attributed to Jane Doe when it first appeared in the New York Times *in 1977. In the essay, the author expresses her feelings about the fact that her son and the mother of his child live out of wedlock, and she argues that they should marry. As you read, notice the combination of reasoned argument and emotional appeal. Also, ask yourself why "Jane Doe" wanted to keep her identity a secret.*

THE PATTERN	THE PURPOSES
cause-and-effect analysis	*to persuade and to express feelings and relate experience*

1   My son and his wife are not married. They have lived together for seven years without benefit of license. Though occasionally marriage has been a subject of conjecture, it did not seem important until the day they announced, jubilantly, that they were going to have a child. It was happy news. I was ready and eager to become a grandmother. Now, I thought, they will take the final step and make their relationship legal.

2   I was apprised of the Lamaze method of natural childbirth. I was prepared by Leboyer for birth without violence. I admired the expectant mother's discipline. She ate only organic foods, abstained from alcohol, avoided insecticides, smog and trauma. Every precaution was taken to insure the arrival of a healthy, happy infant. No royal birth had been prepared for more auspiciously. All that was lacking was legitimacy.

3   Finally, when my grandson was two weeks old, I dared to question their intentions.

4   "We don't believe in marriage," was all that was volunteered.

5   "Not even for your son's sake?" I asked. "Maybe he will."

6   Their eyes were impenetrable, their faces stiffened to masks. "You wouldn't understand," I was told.

7   And I don't. Surely they cannot believe they are pioneering, making revolutionary changes in society. That frontier has long been tamed.

Today marriage offers all the options. Books and talk shows have surfeited us with the freedom offered in open marriage. Lawyers, psychologists and marriage counselors are growing rich executing marriage contracts. And divorce, should it come to that, is in most states easy and inexpensive.

8   On the other hand, living together out of wedlock can be economically impractical as well as socially awkward. How do I present her—as my son's roommate? his spouse? his spice, as one facetious friend suggested? Even my son flounders in these waters. Recently, I heard him refer to her as his girlfriend. I cannot believe that that description will be endearing to their son when he is able to understand.

9   I have resolved that problem for myself, bypassing their omission, introducing her as she is, as my daughter-in-law. But my son, in militant support of his ideology, refutes any assumptions, however casual, that they have taken vows.

10   There are economic benefits which they are denying themselves. When they applied for housing in the married students dormitory of the university where he is seeking his doctorate, they were asked for their marriage certificate. Not having one, they were forced to find other, more expensive quarters off campus. Her medical insurance, provided by the company where she was employed, was denied him. He is not her husband. There have been and will be other inconveniences they have elected to endure.

11   Their son will not enjoy the luxury of choice about the inconveniences and scurrility to which he will be subject from those of his peers and elders who dislike and fear society's nonconformists.

12   And if in the future, his parents should decide to separate, will he not suffer greater damage than the child of divorce, who may find comfort in the knowledge that his parents once believed they could live happily ever after, and committed themselves to that idea? The child of unwed parents has no sanctuary. His mother and father have assiduously avoided a pledge of permanency, leaving him drifting and insecure.

13   I know my son is motivated by idealism and honesty in his reluctance to concede to what he considers mere ceremony. But he is wise enough to know that no one individual can fight all of society's foibles and frauds. Why does he persist in this, a battle already lost? Because though he rejects marriage, California, his residence, has declared that while couples living together in imitation of marriage are no longer under the jurisdiction of the family court, their relationship is viewed by

the state as an implicit contract somewhat like a business agreement. This position was mandated when equal property rights were granted a woman who had been abandoned by the man she had lived with for a number of years.

14   Finally, the couple's adamancy has been depriving to all the rest of the family. There has been no celebration of wedding or anniversaries. There has been concealment from certain family elders who could not cope with the situation. Its irregularity has put constraint on the grandparents, who are stifled by one another's possible embarrassment or hurt.

15   I hope that one day very soon my son and his wife will acknowledge their cohabitation with a license. The rest of us will not love them any more for it. We love and support them as much as possible now. But it will be easier and happier for us knowing that our grandson will be spared the continued explanation and harassment, the doubts and anxieties of being a child of unmarried parents.

Reading Closely and Thinking Critically

1. What issue is the author treating, and what is her stand on that issue?

2. In the opening sentence, the author refers to her grandchild's mother as her son's "wife." Why do you think she uses "wife"?

3. In paragraph 7, the author argues in favor of marriage by saying that "today marriage offers all the options." What do you think she means?

4. What reasons does Jane Doe give to support her view that her son should marry the mother of his child? Do you find these reasons convincing? Why or why not?

5. What objections to her view does Jane Doe raise? How does she counter them?

6. Why do you think the author did not want to reveal her identity?

Examining Structure and Strategy

1. Paragraphs 1 through 6 form the introduction of "I Wish They'd Do It Right." What approach does the author take to the introduction?

2. To what extent does the author speculate on what will happen if her view is not adopted? Where does she speculate on what will happen if her view *is* adopted?

3. What elements of emotional appeal appear in the essay? Are they sufficiently fair and restrained? Do they add to the convincing quality of the essay?

4. What reasons for her view does the author back up with examples?

5. What approach does Jane Doe take to her conclusion?

Considering Language and Style

1. In paragraphs 12 and 13, Jane Doe uses *rhetorical questions* (questions for which no answers are expected because the answers are obvious). What purpose do Doe's rhetorical questions serve?

2. Consult a dictionary if you are unsure of the meaning of any of these words: *conjecture* (paragraph 1), *apprised* (paragraph 2), *Lamaze* (paragraph 2), *Leboyer* (paragraph 2), *auspiciously* (paragraph 2), *surfeited* (paragraph 7), *facetious* (paragraph 8), *scurrility* (paragraph 11), *assiduously* (paragraph 12), *foibles* (paragraph 13).

For Group Discussion or Writing

With some classmates, decide how you think Jane Doe should refer to the mother of her grandchild and explain why you think as you do.

Writing Assignments

1. *In your journal.* Consider the reasons Jane Doe gives for her view, along with her emotional appeals and counters to objections. What facet of her argumentation-persuasion is the most convincing and why?

2. *Using the pattern.* Use argumentation-persuasion to convince Jane Doe that her son's living arrangement has its advantages. Try to counter one or more of the points Doe makes in her essay.

3. *Using the pattern.* Paragraph 7 refers to a number of relatively recent innovations in the marriage institution: open marriage (which does not require spouses to be monogamous), marriage contracts, and easy, cheap divorces. Select one of these innovations and argue that it is or is not an improvement in marriage.

4. *Using the pattern.* In paragraph 10, the author notes two economic drawbacks her son faced because he was not married to his partner: denial of admission to married students' housing and denial of coverage by his partner's medical insurance. Do you think these denials were a form of discrimination? Argue your view, being sure to raise and counter compelling objections.

5. *Considering a theme.* The divorce rate in the United States is very high, as high as 50 percent. Write an essay that considers what can be done to strengthen or redefine the institution of marriage so that it meets the needs of today's couples and reduces the rate of divorce.

6. *Connecting the readings.* Write an essay that examines to what extent the changing roles of men and women are altering the institution of marriage. In addition to your own experience and observation, you might want to consider the ideas in "I Want a Wife" (page 510) and "I Wish They'd Do It Right."

RACISM HAS ITS PRIVILEGES: THE CASE FOR AFFIRMATIVE ACTION

Roger Wilkins

Roger Wilkins is on the editorial board of the Nation *and a history professor at George Mason University. He earned his law degree from the University of Michigan and went on to serve as assistant attorney general for Lyndon Johnson. A journalist as well, Wilkins has written for the* New York Times, *the* Washington Post, *and the* Washington Star. *In 1972, he earned a Pulitzer Prize for his part in the Watergate coverage. Wilkins's publications include* A Man's Life *(1982) and* Quiet Riots: Race and Poverty in the United States, *for which he was an editor with former senator Fred R. Harris. In "Racism Has Its Privileges," which first appeared in the* Nation *in 1995, Wilkens argues that affirmative action is responsible for "enlarging opportunity and developing and utilizing a far broader array of the skills available in the American population." It also, he argues, works to counter the effects of past and current racism.*

THE PATTERNS	THE PURPOSE
cause-and-effect analysis,	*to persuade*
classification-division,	
comparison-contrast, narration,	
and process analysis	

1   The storm that has been gathering over affirmative action for the past few years has burst. Two conservative California professors are leading a drive to place an initiative on the state ballot in 1996 that will ask Californians to vote affirmative action up or down. Since the state is beloved in political circles for its electoral votes, advance talk of the initiative has put the issue high on the national agenda. Three Republican presidential contenders—Bob Dole, Phil Gramm and Lamar Alexander—have already begun taking shots at various equal opportunity programs. Congressional review of the Clinton Administration's enforcement of these programs has begun. The President has started his own review, promising adherence to principles of nondiscrimination and full opportunity while asserting the need to prune those programs that are unfair or malfunctioning.

2   It is almost an article of political faith that one of the major influences in last November's election was the backlash against affirmative action among "angry white men," who are convinced it has stacked the deck against them. Their attitudes are shaped and their anger heightened by unquestioned and virtually uncheckable anecdotes about victimized whites flooding the culture. For example, *Washington Post* columnist Richard Cohen recently began what purported to be a serious analysis and attack on affirmative action by recounting that he had once missed out on a job someplace because they "needed a woman."

3   Well, I have an anecdote too, and it, together with Cohen's, offers some important insights about the debate that has flared recently around the issues of race, gender, and justice. Some years ago, after watching me teach as a visiting professor for two semesters, members of the history department at George Mason University invited me to compete for a full professorship and endowed chair. Mason, like other institutions in Virginia's higher education system, was under a court order to desegregate. I went through the appropriate application and review process and, in due course, was appointed. A few years later, not long after I had been honored as one of the university's distinguished professors, I was shown an article by a white historian asserting that he had been a candidate for that chair but that at the last moment the job had been whisked away and handed to an unqualified black. I checked the story and discovered that this fellow had, in fact, applied but had not even passed the first threshold. But his "reverse discrimination" story is out there polluting the atmosphere in which this debate is taking place.

4   Affirmative action, as I understand it, was not designed to punish anyone; it was, rather—as a result of a clear-eyed look at how America actually works—an attempt to enlarge opportunity for *everybody*. As amply documented in the 1968 Kerner Commission report on racial disorders, when left to their own devices, American institutions in such areas as college admissions, hiring decisions and loan approvals had been making choices that discriminated against blacks. That discrimination, which flowed from doing what came naturally, hurt more than blacks: It hurt the entire nation, as the riots of the late 1960s demonstrated. Though the Kerner report focused on blacks, similar findings could have been made about other minorities and women.

5   Affirmative action required institutions to develop plans enabling them to go beyond business as usual and search for qualified people in places where they did not ordinarily conduct their searches or their

business. Affirmative action programs generally require some proof that there has been a good-faith effort to follow the plan and numerical guidelines against which to judge the sincerity and the success of the effort. The idea of affirmative action is *not* to force people into positions for which they are unqualified but to encourage institutions to develop realistic criteria for the enterprise at hand and then to find a reasonably diverse mix of people qualified to be engaged in it. Without the requirements calling for plans, good-faith efforts and the setting of broad numerical goals, many institutions would do what they had always done: assert that they had looked but "couldn't find anyone qualified," and then go out and hire the white man they wanted to hire in the first place.

6   Affirmative action has done wonderful things for the United States by enlarging opportunity and developing and utilizing a far broader array of the skills available in the American population than in the past. It has not outlived its usefulness. It was never designed to be a program to eliminate poverty. It has not always been used wisely, and some of its permutations do have to be reconsidered, refined or, in some cases, abandoned. It is not a quota program, and those cases where rigid numbers are used (except under a court or administrative order after a specific finding of discrimination) are a bastardization of an otherwise highly beneficial set of public policies.

7   President Clinton is right to review what is being done under present laws and to express a willingness to eliminate activities that either don't work or are unfair. Any program that has been in place for thirty years should be reviewed. Getting rid of what doesn't work is both good government and good politics. Gross abuses of affirmative action provide ammunition for its opponents and undercut the moral authority of the entire effort. But the President should retain—and strengthen where required—those programs necessary to enlarge social justice.

8   What makes the affirmative action issue so difficult is that it engages blacks and whites exactly at those points where they differ the most. There are some areas, such as rooting for the local football team, where their experiences and views are virtually identical. There are others—sometimes including work and school—where their experiences and views both overlap and diverge. And finally, there are areas such as affirmative action and inextricably related notions about the presence of racism in society where the divergences draw out almost all the points of difference between the races.

THIS LAND IS MY LAND

9   Blacks and whites experience America very differently. Though we often inhabit the same space, we operate in very disparate psychic spheres.

10   Whites have an easy sense of ownership of the country; they feel they are entitled to receive all that is best in it. Many of them believe that their country—though it may have some failure—is superior to all others and that, as Americans, they are superior as well. Many of them think of this as a white country and some of them even experience it that way. They think of it as a land of opportunity—a good place with a lot of good people in it. Some suspect (others *know*) that the presence of blacks messes everything up.

11   To blacks there's nothing very easy about life in America, and any sense of ownership comes hard because we encounter so much resistance in making our way through the ordinary occurrences of life. And I'm not even talking here about overt acts of discrimination but simply about the way whites intrude on and disturb our physic space without even thinking about it.

12   A telling example of this was given to me by a black college student in Oklahoma. He said whites give him looks that say: "What are *you* doing here?"

13   "When do they give you that look?" I asked.

14   "Every time I walk in a door," he replied.

15   When he said that, every black person in the room nodded and smiled in a way that indicated recognition based on thousands of such moments in their own lives.

16   For most blacks, America is either a land of denied opportunity or one in which the opportunities are still grudgingly extended and extremely limited. For some—that one-third who are mired in poverty, many of them isolated in dangerous ghettos—America is a land of desperadoes and desperation. In places where whites see a lot of idealism, blacks see, at best, idealism mixed heavily with hypocrisy. Blacks accept America's greatness, but are unable to ignore ugly warts that many whites seem to need not to see. I am reminded here of James Baldwin's searing observation from *The Fire Next Time:*

> The American Negro has the great advantage of having never believed that collection of myths to which white Americans cling: that their ancestors were all freedom-loving heroes, that they were

born in the greatest country the world has ever seen, or that Americans are invincible in battle and wise in peace, that Americans have always dealt honorably with Mexicans and Indians and all other neighbors or inferiors, that American men are the world's most direct and virile, that American women are pure.

17   It goes without saying, then, that blacks and whites remember America differently. The past is hugely important since we argue a lot about who we are on the basis of who we think we have been, and we derive much of our sense of the future from how we think we've done in the past. In a nation in which few people know much history these are perilous arguments, because in such a vacuum, people tend to weave historical fables tailored to their political or psychic needs.

18   Blacks are still recovering the story of their role in America, which so many white historians simply ignored or told in ways that made black people ashamed. But in a culture that batters us, learning the real history is vital in helping blacks feel fully human. It also helps us understand just how deeply American we are, how richly we have given, how much has been taken from us and how much has yet to be restored. Supporters of affirmative action believe that broad and deep damage has been done to American culture by racism and sexism over the whole course of American history and that they are still powerful forces today. We believe that minorities and women are still disadvantaged in our highly competitive society and that affirmative action is absolutely necessary to level the playing field.

19   Not all white Americans oppose this view and not all black Americans support it. There are a substantial number of whites in this country who have been able to escape our racist and sexist past and to enter fully into the quest for equal justice. There are other white Americans who are not racists but who more or less passively accept the powerful suggestions coming at them from all points in the culture that whites are entitled to privilege and to freedom from competition with blacks. And then there are racists who just don't like blacks or who actively despise us. There are still others who may or may not feel deep antipathy, but who know how to manipulate racism and white anxiety for their own ends. Virtually all the people in the last category oppose affirmative action and some of them make a practice of preying upon those in the second category who are not paying attention or who, like the *Post's* Richard Cohen, are simply confused.

THE POLITICS OF DENIAL

20   One of these political predators is Senate majority leader Bob
Dole. In his offhandedly lethal way, Dole delivered a benediction of "let
me now forgive us" on *Meet the Press* recently. After crediting affirmative action for the 62 percent of the white male vote garnered by the
Republicans, he remarked that slavery was "before we were born" and
wondered whether future generations ought to have to continue "paying a price" for those ancient wrongs.

21   Such a view holds that whatever racial problems we once may
have had have been solved over the course of the past thirty years and
that most of our current racial friction is caused by racial and gender
preferences that almost invariably work to displace some "qualified"
white male. Words and phrases like *punish* or *preference* or *reverse discrimination* or *quota* are dropped into the discourse to buttress this view,
as are those anecdotes about injustice to whites. Proponents of affirmative action see these arguments as disingenuous but ingenious because
they reduce serious and complex social, political, economic, historical
and psychological issues to bumper-sticker slogans designed to elicit
Pavlovian responses.

22   The fact is that the successful public relations assault on affirmative action flows on a river of racism that is as broad, powerful and
American as the Mississippi. And, like the Mississippi, racism can be violent and deadly and is a permanent feature of American Life. But while
nobody who is sane denies the reality of the Mississippi, millions of
Americans who are deemed sane—some of whom are powerful and
some even thought wise—deny, wholly or in part, that racism exists.

23   It is critical to understand the workings of denial in this debate
because it is used to obliterate the facts that created the need for the
remedy in the first place. One of the best examples of denial was provided recently by the nation's most famous former history professor,
House Speaker Newt Gingrich. According to *The Washington Post*, "Gingrich dismissed the argument that the beneficiaries of affirmative action, commonly African Americans, have been subjected to discrimination over a period of centuries. 'That is true of virtually every American,'
Gingrich said, noting that the Irish were discriminated against by the
English, for example."

24   That is breathtaking stuff coming from somebody who should
know that blacks have been on this North American continent for 375

years and that for 245 the country permitted slavery. Gingrich should also know that for the next hundred years we had legalized subordination of blacks, under a suffocating blanket of condescension and frequently enforced by nightriding terrorists. We've had only thirty years of something else.

25   That something else is a nation trying to lift its ideals out of a thick, often impenetrable slough of racism. Racism is a hard word for what over the centuries became second nature in America—preferences across the board for white men and, following in their wake, white women. Many of these men seem to feel that it is un-American to ask them to share anything with blacks—particularly their work, their neighborhoods or "their" women. To protect these things—apparently essential to their identity—they engage in all forms of denial. For a historian to assert that "virtually every American" shares the history I have just outlined comes very close to lying.

26   Denial of racism is much like the denials that accompany addictions to alcohol, drugs or gambling. It is probably not stretching the analogy too much to suggest that many racist whites are so addicted to their unwanted privileges and so threatened by the prospect of losing them that all kinds of defenses become acceptable, including insistent distortions of reality in the form of hypocrisy, lying or the most outrageous political demagogy.

"THOSE PEOPLE" DON'T DESERVE HELP

27   The demagogues have reverted to a new version of quite an old trick. Before the 1950s, whites who were busy denying that the nation was unfair to blacks would simply assert that we didn't deserve equal treatment because we were *inferior.* These days it is not permissible in most public circles to say that blacks are inferior, but it is perfectly acceptable to target the *behavior* of blacks, specifically poor blacks. The argument then follows a fairly predictable line: The behavior of poor blacks requires a severe rethinking of national social policy, it is said. Advantaged blacks really don't need affirmative action anymore, and when they are the objects of such programs, some qualified white person (unqualified white people don't show up in these arguments) is (as Dole might put it) "punished." While it is possible that color-blind affirmative action programs benefiting all disadvantaged Americans are needed, those (i.e., blacks) whose behavior is so distressing must be

punished by restricting welfare, shriveling the safety net and expanding the prison opportunity. All of that would presumably give us, in William Bennett's words, "what we want—a color-blind society," for which the white American psyche is presumably fully prepared.

28   There are at least three layers of unreality in these precepts. The first is that the United States is not now and probably never will be a color-blind society. It is the most color-conscious society on earth. Over the course of 375 years, whites have given blacks absolutely no reason to believe that they can behave in a color-blind manner. In many areas of our lives—particularly in employment, housing and education—affirmative action is required to counter deeply ingrained racist patterns of behavior.

29   Second, while I don't hold the view that all blacks who behave badly are blameless victims of a brutal system, I do believe that many poor blacks have, indeed, been brutalized by our culture, and I know of no blacks, rich or poor, who haven't been hurt in some measure by the racism in this country. The current mood (and, in some cases like the Speaker's, the cultivated ignorance) completely ignores the fact that some blacks never escaped the straight line of oppression that ran from slavery through the semislavery of sharecropping to the late mid-century migration from Southern farms into isolated pockets of urban poverty. Their families have always been excluded, poor and without skills, and so they were utterly defenseless when the enormous American economic dislocations that began in the mid-1970s slammed into their communities, followed closely by deadly waves of crack cocaine. One would think that the double-digit unemployment suffered consistently over the past two decades by blacks who were *looking for work* would be a permanent feature of the discussions about race, responsibility, welfare, and rights.

30   But a discussion of the huge numbers of black workers who are becoming economically redundant would raise difficult questions about the efficiency of the economy at a time when millions of white men feel insecure. Any honest appraisal of unemployment would reveal that millions of low-skilled white men were being severely damaged by corporate and Federal Reserve decisions; it might also refocus the anger of those whites in the middles ranks whose careers have been shattered by the corporate downsizing fad.

31   But people's attention is kept trained on the behavior of some poor blacks by politicians and television news shows, reinforcing the

stereotypes of blacks as dangerous, as threats, as unqualified. Frightened whites direct their rage at pushy blacks rather than at the corporations that export manufacturing operations to low-wage countries, or at the Federal Reserve, which imposes interest rate hikes that slow down the economy.

WHO BENEFITS? WE ALL DO

32   There is one final denial that blankets all the rest. It is that only society's "victims"—blacks, other minorities and women (who should, for God's sake, renounce their victimological outlooks)—have been injured by white male supremacy. Viewed in this light, affirmative action remedies are a kind of zero-sum game in which only the "victims" benefit. But racist and sexist whites who are not able to accept the full humanity of other people are themselves badly damaged—morally stunted—people. The principal product of a racist and sexist society is damaged people and institutions—victims and victimizers alike. Journalism and education, two enterprises with which I am familiar, provide two good examples.

33   Journalistic institutions often view the nation through a lens that bends reality to support white privilege. A recent issue of *U.S. News & World Report* introduced a package of articles on these issues with a question on its cover: "Does affirmative action mean NO WHITE MEN NEED APPLY?" The words "No white men need apply" were printed in red against a white background and were at least four times larger than the other words in the question. Inside, the lead story was illustrated by a painting that carries out the cover theme, with a wan white man separated from the opportunity ladders eagerly being scaled by women and dark men. And the story yielded up the following sentence: "Affirmative action poses a conflict between two cherished American principles: the belief that all Americans deserve equal opportunities and the idea that hard work and merit, not race or religion or gender or birthright, should determine who prospers and who does not."

34   Whoever wrote that sentence was in the thrall of one of the myths that Baldwin was talking about. The sentence suggests—as many people do when talking about affirmative action—that America is a meritocratic society. But what kind of meritocracy excludes women and blacks and other minorities from all meaningful competition? And even in the competition among white men, money, family and connections

often count for much more than merit, test results (for whatever they're worth) and hard work.

35   The *U.S. News* story perpetuates and strengthens the view that many of my white students absorb from their parents: that white men now have few chances in this society. The fact is that white men still control virtually everything in America except the wealth held by widows. According to the Urban Institute, 53 percent of black men aged 25–34 are either unemployed or earn too little to lift a family of four from poverty.

36   Educational institutions that don't teach accurately about why America looks the way it does and why the distribution of winners and losers is as it is also injure our society. Here is another anecdote.

37   A warm, brilliant young white male student of mine came in just before he was to graduate and said that my course in race, law and culture, which he had just finished, had been the most valuable and the most disturbing he had ever taken. I asked how it had been disturbing.

38   "I learned that my two heroes are racists," he said.

39   "Who are your heroes and how are they racists?" I asked.

40   "My mom and dad," he said. "After thinking about what I was learning, I understood that they had spent all my life making me into the same kind of racists they were."

41   Affirmative action had brought me together with him when he was 22. Affirmative action puts people together in ways that make that kind of revelation possible. Nobody is a loser when that happens. The country gains.

42   And that, in the end, is the case for affirmative action. The arguments supporting it should be made on the basis of its broad contributions to the entire American community. It is insufficient to vilify white males and to skewer them as the whiners that journalism of the kind practiced by *U.S. News* invites us to do. These are people who, from the beginning of the Republic, have been taught that skin color is destiny and that whiteness is to be revered. Listen to Jefferson, writing in the year the Constitution was drafted:

> The first difference that strikes us is that of colour. . . . And is the difference of no importance? Is it not the foundation of a greater or less share of beauty in the two races? Are not the fine mixtures of red and white . . . in the one, preferable to that eternal monotony, which reigns in the countenances, that immovable veil of

black which covers all the emotions of the other race? Add to these, flowing hair, a more elegant symmetry of form, their own judgment in favor of the whites, declared by their preference for them, as uniformly as is the preference of the Oran-ootan for the black women over those of his own species. The circumstance of superior beauty, is thought worthy attention in the propagation of our horses, dogs, and other domestic animals; why not in that of man?

In a society so convinced and so dedicated, it is understandable that white males would take their preferences as a matter of natural right and consider any alteration of that a primal offense. But a nation that operates in that way abandons its soul and its economic strength, and will remain mired in ugliness and moral squalor because so many people are excluded from the possibility of decent lives and from forming any sense of community with the rest of society.

43   Seen only as a corrective for ancient wrongs, affirmative action may be dismissed by the likes of Gingrich, Gramm and Dole, just as attempts to federalize decent treatment of the freed slaves were dismissed after Reconstruction more than a century ago. Then, striking down the Civil Rights Act of 1875, Justice Joseph Bradley wrote of blacks that "there must be some stage in the progress of his elevation when he takes the rank of a mere citizen, and ceases to be the special favorite of the laws, and when his rights, as a citizen or a man, are to be protected in the ordinary modes by which other men's rights are protected."

44   But white skin has made some citizens—particularly white males—*the special favorites of the culture.* It may be that we will need affirmative action until most white males are really ready for a color-blind society—that is, when they are ready to assume "the rank of a mere citizen." As a nation we took a hard look at that special favoritism thirty years ago. Though the centuries of cultural preference enjoyed by white males still overwhelmingly skew power and wealth their way, we have in fact achieved a more meritocratic society as a result of affirmative action than we have ever previously enjoyed in this country.

45   If we want to continue making things better in this society, we'd better figure out ways to protect and defend affirmative action against the confused, the frightened, the manipulators and, yes, the liars in politics, journalism, education and wherever else they may be found. In the name of longstanding American prejudice and myths and in the service of their own narrow interests, power-lusts or blindness, they are

truly victimizing the rest of us, perverting the ideals they claim to stand for and destroying the nation they pretend to serve.

Reading Closely and Thinking Critically

1. According to Wilkins, why is affirmative action needed?

2. Wilkins does not just believe that affirmative action is needed; he also believes that it has done a great deal of good. What good does he think affirmative action has done?

3. In paragraph 17, Wilkins says that blacks and whites have different views of the past. Why is that difference important, and what significance does it have to a discussion of affirmative action?

4. Wilkins believes that politicians have hurt the cause of equal opportunity for blacks a number of ways. What are they?

5. Wilkins also believes that the media have hurt the cause of affirmative action. Explain how.

6. How do the "psychic spheres" of blacks and whites differ? Why do you think this difference is important to a discussion of affirmative action?

7. In paragraph 19, Wilkins notes several categories of Americans. Which of these do you think makes the best audience for the essay? Why? How likely is Wilkins to convince this audience to support affirmative action?

Examining Structure and Strategy

1. What is Wilkins's thesis, and where in the essay is it located?

2. Why does Wilkins open by noting the political opposition to affirmative action?

3. Does Wilkins arrange his argument in a deductive or inductive pattern?

4. What elements of narration appear in the essay? Process analysis? Cause-and-effect analysis? Classification? Comparison-contrast?

5. What objections does Wilkins raise, and how does he counter them? Are the counters effective? Are there any objections he should have raised but did not? Explain.

6. In paragraph 42, Wilkins quotes Thomas Jefferson at some length. How does this quotation advance Wilkins's persuasive purpose?

Considering Language and Style

1. In paragraph 9, Wilkins refers to the different "psychic spheres" of blacks and whites. Explain what you think he means by *psychic spheres.*

2. In paragraph 22, Wilkins uses a metaphor to compare racism to a river, and in paragraph 25, he uses another metaphor to compare racism to a slough. Do you find these metaphors equally apt? Explain. (*Metaphors* are explained on page 73.)

3. Consult a dictionary if you are unfamiliar with any of these words: *article of faith* (paragraph 2), *permutations* (paragraph 6), *bastardization* (paragraph 6), *buttress* (paragraph 21), *disingenuous* (paragraph 21), *Pavlovian responses* (paragraph 21), *demagogy* (paragraph 26), *meritocracy* (paragraph 34), *in the thrall of* (paragraph 34).

For Group Discussion or Writing
With some of your classmates, consider what would happen if all affirmative action laws were eliminated.

Writing Assignments

1. *In your journal.* How do you "remember America" (paragraph 17) and how does that view affect your perception of yourself and your vision of your future?

2. *Using the pattern.* In paragraph 20, Wilkins notes Robert Dole's position. Agree or disagree with that position.

3. *Using the pattern.* In paragraph 32, Wilkins says that women should "renounce their victimilogical outlooks." Agree or disagree with this view.

4. *Using the pattern.* Select one point that Wilkins makes and write a persuasive essay to defend or attack that point.

5. *Considering a theme.* Wilkins says, "Journalistic institutions often view the nation through a lens that bends reality to support white privilege" (paragraph 33). Examine magazines and newspapers and use examples you find there either to attack or to defend Wilkins's view.

6. *Connecting the readings.* Define *psychic spheres* (paragraph 9) and explain how they influence the behavior of different groups of people. "Racism Has Its Privileges," "Untouchables" (page 236), "The View from 80," (page 543), "Once More to the Lake," (page 110), and "The Water-Faucet Vision" (page 184) may give you some ideas.

A NEGATIVE VOTE ON AFFIRMATIVE ACTION
Shelby Steele

Shelby Steele was born in Chicago in 1946. He earned his Ph.D. from the University of Utah in 1974 and became an English professor at San Jose State University. A prolific essayist who has published in Harper's, *the* American Scholar, *the* Washington Post, *the* New Republic, *and the* New York Times Book Review, *Steele won the National Magazine Award in 1989. In 1990, Steele published his best-selling collection of controversial essays called* The Content of Our Character: A New Vision of Race in America, *which won the National Book Critics Circle Award. In "A Negative Vote on Affirmative Action," first published in the* New York Times Magazine *(1990), Steele uses cause-and-effect analysis to argue that affirmative action, although well-intentioned, hurts the cause of racial equality by stigmatizing blacks with the perception of incompetence. In addition, he expresses his own conflict about allowing preferential college admissions policies to help his children.*

THE PATTERN	THE PURPOSES
cause-and-effect analysis	*to persuade and to express feelings and relate experience*

1   In a few short years, when my two children will be applying to college, the affirmative-action policies by which most universities offer black students some form of preferential treatment will present me with a dilemma. I am a middle-class black, a college professor, far from wealthy, but also well removed from the kind of deprivation that would qualify my children for the label "disadvantaged." Both of them have endured racial insensitivity from whites. They have been called names, have suffered slights and have experienced firsthand the peculiar malevolence that racism brings out of people. Yet they have never experienced racial discrimination, have never been stopped by their race on any path they have chosen to follow. Still, their society now tells them that if they will only designate themselves as black on their college applications, they will probably do better in the college lottery than if they conceal this fact. I think there is something of a Faustian bargain in this.

2   Of course many blacks and a considerable number of whites would say that I was sanctimoniously making affirmative action into a test of character. They would say that this small preference is the meagerest recompense for centuries of unrelieved oppression. And to these arguments other very obvious facts must be added. In America, many marginally competent or flatly incompetent whites are hired every day—some because their white skin suits the conscious or unconscious racial preference of their employers. The white children of alumni are often grandfathered into elite universities in what can only be seen as a residual benefit of historic white privilege. Worse, white incompetence is always an individual matter, but for blacks it is often confirmation of ugly stereotypes. Given that unfairness cuts both ways, doesn't it only balance the scales of history, doesn't this repay, in a small way, the systematic denial under which my children's grandfather lived out his days?

3   In theory, affirmative action certainly has all the moral symmetry that fairness requires. It is reformist and corrective, even repentent and redemptive. And I would never sneer at these good intentions. Born in the late 1940's in Chicago, I started my education (a charitable term, in this case) in a segregated school, and suffered all the indignities that come to blacks in a segregated society. My father, born in the South, made it only to the third grade before the white man's fields took permanent priority over his formal education. And though he educated himself into an advanced reader with an almost professorial authority, he could only drive a truck for a living, and never earned more than $90 a week in his entire life. So yes, it is crucial to my sense of citizenship, to my ability to identify with the spirit and the interests of America, to know that this country, however imperfectly, recognizes its past sins and wishes to correct them.

4   Yet good intentions can blind us to the effects they generate when implemented. In our society affirmative action is, among other things, a testament to white good will and to black power, and in the midst of these heavy investments its effects can be hard to see. But after 20 years of implementation I think that affirmative action has shown itself to be more bad than good and that blacks—whom I will focus on in this essay—now stand to lose more from it than they gain.

5   In talking with affirmative-action administrators and with blacks and whites in general, I found that supporters of affirmative action focus on its good intentions and detractors emphasize its negative effects.

It was virtually impossible to find people outside either camp. The closest I came was a white male manager at a large computer company who said, "I think it amounts to reverse discrimination, but I'll put up with a little of that for a little more diversity." But this only makes him a halfhearted supporter of affirmative action. I think many people who don't really like affirmative action support it to one degree or another anyway.

6   I believe they do this because of what happened to white and black Americans in the crucible of the 1960's, when whites were confronted with their racial guilt and blacks tasted their first real power. In that stormy time white absolution and black power coalesced into virtual mandates for society. Affirmative action became a meeting ground for those mandates in the law. At first, this meant insuring equal opportunity. The 1964 civil-rights bill was passed on the understanding that equal opportunity would not mean racial preference. But in the late 60's and early 70's, affirmative action underwent a remarkable escalation of its mission from simple anti-discrimination enforcement to social engineering by means of quotas, goals, timetables, set-asides and other forms of preferential treatment.

7   Legally, this was achieved through a series of executive orders and Equal Employment Opportunity Commission guidelines that allowed racial imbalances in the workplace to stand as proof of racial discrimination. Once it could be assumed that discrimination explained racial imbalances, it became easy to justify group remedies to presumed discrimination rather than the normal case-by-case redress.

8   Even though blacks had made great advances during the 60's without quotas, the white mandate to achieve a new racial innocence and the black mandate to gain power, which came to a head in the very late 60's, could no longer be satisfied by anything less than racial preferences. I don't think these mandates, in themselves, were wrong, because whites clearly needed to do better by blacks and blacks needed more real power in society. But as they came together in affirmative action, their effect was to distort our understanding of racial discrimination. By making black the color of preference, these mandates have reburdened society with the very marriage of color and preference (in reverse) that we set out to eradicate.

9   When affirmative action grew into social engineering, diversity became a golden word. Diversity is a term that applies democratic principles to races and cultures rather than to citizens, despite the fact that

there is nothing to indicate that real diversity is the same thing as pro-
portionate representation. Too often the result of this, on campuses for
example, has been a democracy of colors rather than of people, an artificial diversity that gives the appearance of an educational parity between black and white students that has not yet been achieved in reality. Here again, racial preferences allow society to leapfrog over the
difficult problem of developing blacks to parity with whites and into a
cosmetic diversity that covers the blemish of disparity—a full six years
after admission, only 26 to 28 percent of blacks graduate from college.

10   Racial representation is not the same thing as racial development.
Representation can be manufactured; development is always hard
earned. But it is the music of innocence and power that we hear in affirmative action that causes us to cling to it and to its distracting emphasis on representation. The fact is that after 20 years of racial preferences the gap between median incomes of black and white families is
greater than it was in the 1970's. None of this is to say that blacks don't
need policies that insure our right to equal opportunity, but what we
need more of is the development that will let us take advantage of society's efforts to include us.

11   I think one of the most troubling effects of racial preferences for
blacks is a kind of demoralization. Under affirmative action, the quality that earns us preferential treatment is an implied inferiority. However this inferiority is explained—and it is easily enough explained by
the myriad deprivations that grew out of our oppression—it is still inferiority. There are explanations and then there is the fact. And the fact
must be borne by the individual as a condition apart from the explanation, apart even from the fact that others like himself also bear this
condition. In integrated situations in which blacks must compete with
whites who may be better prepared, these explanations may quickly
wear thin and expose the individual to racial as well as personal self-
doubt. (Of course whites also feel doubt, but only personally, not
racially.)

12   What this means in practical terms is that when blacks deliver
themselves into integrated situations they encounter a nasty little reflex
in whites, a mindless, atavistic reflex that responds to the color black
with negative stereotypes, such as intellectual ineptness. I think this
reflex embarrasses most whites today and thus it is usually quickly re-
pressed. On an equally atavistic level, the black will be aware of the reflex his color triggers and will feel a stab of horror at seeing himself

reflected in this way. He, too, will do a quick repression, but a lifetime of such stabbings is what constitutes his inner realm of racial doubt. Even when the black sees no implication of inferiority in racial preferences, he knows that whites do, so that—consciously or unconsciously—the result is virtually the same. The effect of preferential treatment—the lowering of normal standards to increase black representation—puts blacks at war with an expanded realm of debilitating doubt, so that the doubt itself becomes an unrecognized preoccupation that undermines their ability to perform, especially in integrated situations.

13   I believe another liability of affirmative action comes from the fact that it indirectly encourages blacks to exploit their own past victimization. Like implied inferiority, victimization is what justifies preference, so that to receive the benefits of preferential treatment one must, to some extent, become invested in the view of one's self as a victim. In this way, affirmative action nurtures a victim-focused identity in blacks and sends us the message that there is more power in our past suffering than in our present achievements.

14   When power itself grows out of suffering, blacks are encouraged to expand the boundaries of what qualifies as racial oppression, a situation that can lead us to paint our victimization in vivid colors even as we receive the benefits of preference. The same corporations and institutions that give us preference are also seen as our oppressors. At Stanford University, minority-group students—who receive at least the same financial aid as whites with the same need—recently took over the president's office demanding, among other things, more financial aid.

15   But I think one of the worst prices that blacks pay for preference has to do with an illusion. I saw this illusion at work recently in the mother of a middle-class black student who was going off to his first semester of college: "They owe us this, so don't think for a minute that you don't belong there." This is the logic by which many blacks, and some whites, justify affirmative action—it is something "owed," a form of reparation. But this logic overlooks a much harder and less digestible reality, that it is impossible to repay blacks living today for the historic suffering of the race. If all blacks were given a million dollars tomorrow it would not amount to a dime on the dollar for three centuries of oppression, nor would it dissolve the residues of that oppression that we still carry today. The concept of historic reparation grows out of man's need to impose on the world a degree of justice that simply does not

exist. Suffering can be endured and overcome, it cannot be repaid. To think otherwise is to prolong the suffering.

16   Several blacks I spoke with said they were still in favor of affirmative action because of the "subtle" discrimination blacks were subject to once they were on the job. One photojournalist said, "They have ways of ignoring you." A black female television producer said: "You can't file a lawsuit when your boss doesn't invite you to the insider meetings without ruining your career. So we still need affirmative action." Others mentioned the infamous "glass ceiling" through which blacks can see the top positions of authority but never reach them. But I don't think racial preferences are a protection against this subtle discrimination; I think they contribute to it.

17   In any workplace, racial preferences will always create two-tiered populations composed of preferreds and unpreferred. In the case of blacks and whites, for instance, racial preferences imply that whites are superior just as they imply that blacks are inferior. They not only reinforce America's oldest racial myth but, for blacks, they have the effect of stigmatizing the already stigmatized.

18   I think that much of the "subtle" discrimination that blacks talk about is often (not always) discrimination against the stigma of questionable competence that affirmative action marks blacks with. In this sense, preferences make scapegoats of the very people they seek to help. And it may be that at a certain level employers impose a glass ceiling, but this may not be against the race so much as against the race's reputation for having advanced by color as much as by competence. This ceiling is the point at which corporations shift the emphasis from color to competency and stop playing the affirmative-action game. Here preference backfires for blacks and becomes a taint that holds them back. Of course one could argue that this taint, which is after all in the minds of whites, becomes nothing more than an excuse to discriminate against blacks. And certainly the result is the same in either case—blacks don't get past the glass ceiling. But this argument does not get around the fact that racial preferences now taint this color with a new theme of suspicion that makes blacks even more vulnerable to discrimination. In this crucial yet gray area of perceived competence, preferences make whites look better than they are and blacks worse, while doing nothing whatever to stop the very real discrimination that blacks may encounter. I don't wish to justify the glass ceiling here, but only suggest the very subtle ways that affirmative action revives rather than extinguishes the old rationalizations for racial discrimination.

19   I believe affirmative action is problematic in our society because we have demanded that it create parity between the races rather than insure equal opportunity. Preferential treatment does not teach skills, or educate, or instill motivation. It only passes out entitlement by color, a situation that in my profession has created an unrealistically high demand for black professors. The social engineer's assumption is that this high demand will inspire more blacks to earn Ph.D.'s and join the profession. In fact, the number of blacks earning Ph.D.'s has declined in recent years. Ph.D.'s must be developed from preschool on. They require family and community support. They must acquire an entire system of values that enables them to work hard while delaying gratification.

20   It now seems clear that the Supreme Court, in a series of recent decisions, is moving away from racial preferences. It has disallowed preferences except in instances of "identified discrimination," eroded the precedent that statistical racial imbalances are prima facie evidence of discrimination, and, in effect, granted white males the right to challenge consent degrees that use preference to achieve racial balances in the workplace. Referring to this and other Supreme Court decisions, one civil-rights leader said, "Night has fallen . . . as far as civil rights are concerned." But I am not so sure. The effect of these decisions is to protect the constitutional rights of everyone, rather than to take rights away from blacks. Night has fallen on racial preferences, not on the fundamental rights of black Americans. The reason for this shift, I believe, is that the white mandate for absolution from past sins has weakened considerably in the 1980's. Whites are now less willing to endure unfairness to themselves in order to grant special entitlements to blacks, even when those entitlements are justified in the name of past suffering. Yet the black mandate for more power in society has remained unchanged. And I think part of the anxiety many blacks feel over these decisions has to do with the loss of black power that they may signal.

21   But the power we've lost by these decisions is really only the power that grows out of our victimization. This is not a very substantial or reliable power, and it is important that we know this so we can focus more exclusively on the kind of development that will bring enduring power. There is talk now that Congress may pass new legislation to compensate for these new limits on affirmative action. If this happens, I hope the focus will be on development and anti-discrimination, rather than entitlement, on achieving racial parity rather than jerry-building racial diversity.

22   But if not preferences, what? The impulse to discriminate *is* subtle and cannot be ferreted out unless its many guises are made clear to people. I think we need social policies that are committed to two goals: the educational and economic development of disadvantaged people regardless of race and the eradication from our society—through close monitoring and severe sanctions—of racial, ethnic, or gender discrimination. Preferences will not get us to either of these goals, because they tend to benefit those who are not disadvantaged—middle-class white women and middle-class blacks—and attack one form of discrimination with another. Preferences are inexpensive and carry the glamour of good intentions—change the numbers and the good deed is done. To be against them is to be unkind. But I think the unkindest cut is to bestow on children like my own an undeserved advantage while neglecting the development of those disadvantaged children in the poorer sections of my city who will most likely never be in a position to benefit from a preference. Give my children fairness; give disadvantaged children a better shot at development—better elementary and secondary schools, job training, safer neighborhoods, better financial assistance for college and so on. A smaller percentage of black high school graduates go to college today than 15 years ago; more black males are in prison, jail or in some other way under the control of the criminal-justice system than in college. This despite racial preferences.

23   The mandates of black power and white absolution out of which preferences emerged were not wrong in themselves. What was wrong was that both races focused more on the goals of those mandates than on the means to the goals. Blacks can have no real power without taking responsibility for their own education and economic development. Whites can have no racial innocence without earning it by eradicating discrimination and helping the disadvantaged to develop. Because we ignored the means, the goals have not been reached and the real work remains to be done.

Reading Closely and Thinking Critically

1. Explain the dilemma college affirmative action policies present for Steele.

2. What does Steele see as the positive aspects of affirmative action?

3. For what reasons does Steele believe affirmative action policies are harmful and counterproductive?

4. Some people think that affirmative action is one way to repay African-Americans for past repression. What does Steele think of this view? Do you agree with him? Explain.

5. Steele refers to affirmative action as a form of social engineering. What does he mean by *social engineering?* How is affirmative action a form of social engineering?

6. Refer to Toulmin's parts of an argument (page 573) to answer these questions: What generalization is presented in paragraph 14? What evidence does that paragraph give to support the generalization? What assumption links the generalization and support?

7. What audience do you think Steele was addressing in "A Negative Vote on Affirmative Action"?

Examining Structure and Strategy

1. Is paragraph 1 an effective opening? Why or why not?

2. Why does Steele raise so many objections to his view so early in the essay (in paragraph 2)?

3. Steele's thesis does not appear in paragraph 1. Where is the thesis? Why does Steele delay presenting it?

4. In paragraphs 6 through 9, Steele explains the history of civil-rights legislation and its effects on society. How does this material help Steele achieve his persuasive purpose?

5. In paragraph 22, Steele offers an alternative to affirmative action and racial preferences. How does this material help Steele achieve his persuasive purpose?

Considering Language and Style

1. Steele says that if his children were to take advantage of affirmative action policies when they apply to college, they would be engaging in "something of a Faustian bargain" (paragraph 1). Explain this reference and discuss its appropriateness.

2. Consult a dictionary if you are unfamiliar with any of these words: *malevolence* (paragraph 1), *sanctimoniously* (paragraph 2), *recompense* (paragraph 2), *grandfathered* (paragraph 2), *crucible*

(paragraph 6), *eradicate* (paragraph 8), *atavistic* (paragraph 12), *prima facie* (paragraph 20), *jerry-building* (paragraph 21), *ferreted out* (paragraph 22).

For Group Discussion or Writing

In paragraph 9, Steele defines *diversity* and explains its effect. Describe the amount of diversity on your campus. (If necessary, check with your admissions or student services office to find out.) Also, explain the effects of the diversity (or lack of it) on your college community, whether or not you think more diversity is needed on your campus, and why or why not.

Writing Assignments

1. *In your journal.* In a page or so, explain to what extent you are affected by affirmative action policies and whether those effects are positive or negative.

2. *Using the pattern.* Select one of the points Steele makes about affirmative action, racial preferences, or diversity and argue the opposite point of view.

3. *Using the pattern.* In paragraph 15, Steele says that "it is impossible to repay blacks living today for the historic suffering of the race." Agree or disagree with this view.

4. *Using the pattern.* Argue for affirmative action by citing its benefits.

5. *Considering a theme.* In paragraph 22, Steele says that "we need social policies that are committed to two goals: the educational and economic development of disadvantaged people regardless of race and the eradication from our society . . . of racial, ethnic, or gender discrimination." Design one such policy and explain how it would help. Consider keeping your focus narrow by dealing with something like how to encourage whites to patronize businesses owned by African-Americans, how to teach economically disadvantaged children the value of education, how to reduce the college drop-out rate among minorities, and so forth.

6. *Connecting the readings.* Describe the current state of race relations in the United States. Explain how much progress we have

made, what more needs to be done, and how we can go about improving. The ideas in "A Negative Vote on Affirmative Action," "On Being the Target of Discrimination" (page 219), and "Just Walk on By" (page 413) may help you.

FREE SPEECH ON CAMPUS
Nat Hentoff

Born in 1925 in Boston, Nat Hentoff has been a columnist for the Village Voice, *the* New Yorker, *and the* Washington Post. *A prolific author of both fiction and nonfiction, Hentoff's books include his autobiography* Boston Boy *(1987),* The First Freedom: The Tumultuous History of Free Speech in America *(1989) and* Speech for Me—But Not for Thee *(1993). Although Hentoff usually defends the political left, in "Free Speech on Campus," first published in* Progressive *(1989), he argues that the left's commitment to politically correct language comes at the expense of free speech on college campuses.*

THE PATTERNS	THE PURPOSE
cause-and-effect analysis and exemplification	*to persuade*

1   A flier distributed at the University of Michigan some months ago proclaimed that blacks "don't belong in classrooms, they belong hanging from trees."

2   At other campuses around the country, manifestations of racism are becoming commonplace. At Yale, a swastika and the words WHITE POWER! were painted on the building housing the University's Afro-American Cultural Center. At Temple University, a White Students Union has been formed with some 130 members.

3   Swastikas are not directed only at black students. The Nazi symbol has been spray-painted on the Jewish Student Union at Memphis State University. And on a number of campuses, women have been singled out as targets of wounding and sometimes frightening speech. At the law school of the State University of New York at Buffalo, several women students have received anonymous letters characterized by one professor as venomously sexist.

4   These and many more such signs of the resurgence of bigotry and know-nothingism throughout the society—as well as on campus—have to do solely with speech, including symbolic speech. There have also been physical assaults on black students and on black, white, and

Asian women students, but the way to deal with physical attacks is clear: call the police and file a criminal complaint. What is to be done, however, about speech alone—however disgusting, inflammatory, and rawly divisive that speech may be?

5   At more and more colleges, administrators—with the enthusiastic support of black students, women students, and liberal students— have been answering that question by preventing or punishing speech. In public universities, this is a clear violation of the First Amendment. In private colleges and universities, suppression of speech mocks the secular religion of academic freedom and free inquiry.

6   The Student Press Law Center in Washington, D.C.—a vital source of legal support for student editors around the country—reports, for example, that at the University of Kansas, the student host and producer of a radio news program was forbidden by school officials from interviewing a leader of the Ku Klux Klan. So much for free inquiry on that campus.

7   In Madison, Wisconsin, the *Capital Times* ran a story in January about Chancellor Sheila Kaplan of the University of Wisconsin branch at Parkside, who ordered her campus to be scoured of "some anonymously placed white supremacist hate literature." Sounding like the legendary Mayor Frank ("I am the law") Hague of Jersey City, who booted "bad speech" out of town, Chancellor Kaplan said, "This institution is not a lamppost standing on the street corner. It doesn't belong to everyone."

8   Who decides what speech can be heard or read by everyone? Why, the Chancellor, of course. That's what George III used to say, too.

9   University of Wisconsin political science professor Carol Tebben thinks otherwise. She believes university administrators "are getting confused when they are acting as censors and trying to protect students from bad ideas. I don't think students need to be protected from bad ideas. I think they can determine for themselves what ideas are bad."

10   After all, if students are to be "protected" from bad ideas, how are they going to learn to identify and cope with them? Sending such ideas underground simply makes them stronger and more dangerous.

11   Professor Tebben's conviction that free speech means just that has become a decidedly minority view on many campuses. At the University of Buffalo Law School, the faculty unanimously adopted a "Statement Regarding Intellectual Freedom, Tolerance, and Political Harass-

ment." Its title implies support of intellectual freedom, but the statement warned students that once they enter "this legal community," their right to free speech must become tempered "by the responsibility to promote equality and justice."

12   Accordingly, swift condemnation will befall anyone who engages in "remarks directed at another's race, sex, religion, national origin, age, or sex preference." Also forbidden are "other remarks based on prejudice and group stereotype."

13   This ukase is so broad that enforcement has to be alarmingly subjective. Yet the University of Buffalo Law School provides no due-process procedures for a student booked for making any of these prohibited remarks. Conceivably, a student caught playing a Lenny Bruce, Richard Pryor, or Sam Kinison album in this room could be tried for aggravated insensitivity by association.

14   When I looked into this wholesale cleansing of bad speech at Buffalo, I found it had encountered scant opposition. One protester was David Gerald Jay, a graduate of the law school and a cooperating attorney for the New York Civil Liberties Union. Said the appalled graduate: "Content-based prohibitions constitute prior restraint and should not be tolerated."

15   You would think that the law professors and administration at this public university might have known that. But hardly any professors dissented, and among the students only members of the conservative Federalist Society spoke up for free speech. The fifty-strong chapter of the National Lawyers Guild was on the other side. After all, it was more important to go on record as vigorously opposing racism and sexism than to expose oneself to charges of insensitivity to these malignancies.

16   The pressures to have the "right" attitude—as proved by having the "right" language in and out of class—can be stifling. A student who opposes affirmative action, for instance, can be branded a racist.

17   At the University of California at Los Angeles, the student newspaper ran an editorial cartoon satirizing affirmative action. (A student stops a rooster on campus and asks how the rooster got into UCLA. "Affirmative action," is the answer.) After outraged complaints from various minority groups, the editor was suspended for violating a publication policy against running "articles that perpetuate derogatory or cultural stereotypes." The art director was also suspended.

18   When the opinion editor of the student newspaper at California State University at Northridge wrote an article asserting that the

sanctions against the editor and art director at UCLA amounted to censorship, he was suspended too.

19   At New York University Law School, a student was so disturbed by the pall of orthodoxy at that prestigious institution that he wrote to the school newspaper even though, as he said, he expected his letter to make him a pariah among his fellow students.

20   Barry Endick described the atmosphere at NYU created by "a host of watchdog committees and a generally hostile classroom reception regarding any student comment right of center." This "can be arguably viewed as symptomatic of a prevailing spirit of academic and social intolerance of . . . any idea which is not 'politically correct.'"

21   He went on to say something that might well be posted on campus bulletin boards around the country, though it would probably be torn down at many of them: "We ought to examine why students, so anxious to wield the Fourteenth Amendment, give short shrift to the First. Yes, Virginia, there are racist assholes. And you know what, the Constitution protects them, too."

22   Not when they engage in violence or vandalism. But when they speak or write, racist assholes fall right into this Oliver Wendell Holmes definition—highly unpopular among bigots, liberals, radicals, feminists, sexists, and college administrators: "If there is any principle of the Constitution that more imperatively calls for attachment than any other, it is the principle of free thought—not free only for those who agree with us, but freedom for the thought we hate."

23   The language sounds like a pietistic Sunday sermon, but if it ever falls wholly into disuse, neither this publication nor any other journal of opinion—right or left—will survive.

24   Sometimes, college presidents and administrators sound as if they fully understand what Holmes was saying. Last year, for example, when the *Daily Pennsylvanian*—speaking for many at the University of Pennsylvania—urged that a speaking invitation to Louis Farrakhan be withdrawn, University President Sheldon Hackney disagreed.

25   "Open expression," said Hackney, "is the fundamental principle of a university." Yet consider what the same Sheldon Hackney did to the free-speech rights of a teacher at his own university. If any story distills the essence of the current decline of free speech on college campuses, it is the Ballad of Murray Dolfman.

26   For twenty-two years, Dolfman, a practicing lawyer in Philadelphia, had been a part-time lecturer in the Legal Studies Department of
the University of Pennsylvania's Wharton School. For twenty-two years,
no complaint had ever been made against him; indeed his student
course evaluations had been outstanding. Each year students competed
to get into his class.

27   On a November afternoon in 1984, Dolfman was lecturing about
personal-service contracts. His style somewhat resembles that of Professor Charles Kingsfield in *The Paper Chase.*[1] Dolfman insists that students he calls on be prepared—or suffer the consequences. He treats all
students this way—regardless of race, creed, or sex.

28   This day, Dolfman was pointing out that no one can be forced to
work against his or her will—even if a contract has been signed. A
court may prevent the resister from working for someone else so long
as the contract is in effect but, Dolfman said, there can "be nothing that
smacks of involuntary servitude."

29   Where does this concept come from? Dolfman looked around the
room. Finally, a cautious hand was raised: "The Constitution?"

30   "Where in the Constitution?" No hands. "The Thirteenth Amendment," said the teacher. So, what does *it* say? The students were looking everywhere but at Dolfman.

31   "We will lose our liberties," Dolfman often told his classes, "if we
don't know what they are."

32   On this occasion, he told them that he and other Jews, as ex-
slaves, spoke at Passover of the time when they were slaves under the
Pharaohs so that they would remember every year what it was like not
to be free.

33   "We have ex-slaves here," Dolfman continued, "who should know
about the Thirteenth Amendment." He asked black students in the class
if they could tell him what was in that amendment.

34   "I wanted them to really think about it," Dolfman told me recently, "and know its history. You're better equipped to fight racism if
you know all about those post–Civil War amendments and civil rights
laws."

35   The Thirteenth Amendment provides that "neither slavery nor
involuntary servitude . . . shall exist within the United States."

---

[1] A popular 1974 film starring John Houseman as a stern Harvard law professor.

36   The black students in his class did not know what was in the amendment, and Dolfman had them read it aloud. Later, they complained to university officials that they had been hurt and humiliated by having been referred to as ex-slaves. Moreover, they said, they had no reason to be grateful for a constitutional amendment which gave them rights which should never have been denied them—and gave them precious little else. They had not made these points in class, although Dolfman—unlike Professor Kingsfield—encourages rebuttal.

37   Informed of the complaint, Dolfman told the black students he had intended no offense, and he apologized if they had been offended.

38   That would not do—either for the black students or for the administration. Furthermore, there were mounting black-Jewish tensions on campus, and someone had to be sacrificed. Who better than a part-time Jewish teacher with no contract and no union? He was sentenced by—George Orwell would have loved this—the Committee on Academic Freedom and Responsibility.

39   On his way to the stocks, Dolfman told President Sheldon Hackney that if a part-time instructor "can be punished on this kind of charge, a tenured professor can eventually be booted out, then a dean, and then a president."

40   Hackney was unmoved. Dolfman was banished from the campus for what came to be a year. But first he was forced to make a public apology to the entire university and then he was compelled to attend a "sensitivity and racial awareness" session. Sort of like a Vietnamese reeducation camp.

41   A few conservative professors objected to the stigmatization of Murray Dolfman. I know of no student dissent. Indeed, those students most concerned with making the campus more "sensitive" to diversity exulted in Dolfman's humiliation. So did most liberals on the faculty.

42   If my children were still of college age and wanted to attend the University of Pennsylvania, I would tell them this story. But where else could I encourage them to go?

Reading Closely and Thinking Critically

1. What issue is Hentoff arguing, and what is his stand on the issue?

2. According to Hentoff, how have college administrators been reacting to hate speech? What does Hentoff think of this reaction?

3. Do you think that students should be protected from bad ideas (paragraph 9)? Explain.

4. Why do you think there was so little opposition to the University of Buffalo's "Statement Regarding Intellectual Freedom, Tolerance, and Political Harassment"?

5. Explain the double meaning of the essay's title.

6. What assumptions connect Hentoff's claim and support? (See page 573 on claims, support, and assumptions.)

Examining Structure and Strategy

1. Which paragraphs form the introduction? What approach does Hentroff take to this introduction? Do you find it effective? Explain.

2. Where does Hentoff state the issue and his stand?

3. Hentoff uses quite a few examples in the essay. Do these examples add to the persuasive quality of the piece? Explain.

4. What specific evidence does Hentoff give to support his stand? Is this evidence adequate and convincing? Explain.

5. Does Hentoff use emotional appeal as a persuasive strategy? Explain.

6. To what extent does Hentoff raise and counter objections? Are there any compelling objections he did not deal with but should have? Explain.

7. Why is the example of Murray Dolfman developed in such detail?

Considering Language and Style

1. In paragraph 5, Hentoff refers to "the secular religion of academic freedom and free inquiry." How can a religion be secular? How can academic freedom and free inquiry be a religion? Explain this use of language and its meaning.

2. Hentoff refers to George Orwell in paragraph 38. Explain the significance of this reference.

3. Consult a dictionary if you are unfamiliar with any of these words: *know-nothingism* (paragraph 4), *ukase* (paragraph 13), *pall* (paragraph 19), *pariah* (paragraph 19), *rebuttal* (paragraph 36), *stocks* (paragraph 39).

For Group Discussion or Writing
Administrators on college campuses must respond to many, sometimes conflicting, groups: teachers, students, parents, the general public, alumni, boards of directors, financial contributors, and so forth. Explain what you think a university president must take into consideration when deciding on a policy for handling hate speech.

Writing Assignments

1. *In your journal.* Do you think a member of the Ku Klux Klan or a member of the Nazi party should be allowed to speak to the student body of your school? Explain why or why not in a page or so.

2. *Using the pattern.* Do you think the sanctions against Professor Dolfman were appropriate? Argue your view, being sure to raise and counter compelling objections.

3. *Using the pattern.* Write a publication policy for your campus newspaper that gives guidelines for handling articles, advertisements, and reporting that includes hate speech. Then argue for the adoption of these guidelines on your campus.

4. *Using the pattern.* Write an essay that argues for or against free speech in high school.

5. *Using the pattern.* Hentoff believes there is a difference between bigoted, hateful speech and bigoted, hateful physical actions (paragraph 4). The first should be protected, but the second should be punished. Do you agree with this distinction? State and defend your view.

6. *Considering a theme.* In paragraph 16, Hentoff refers to "the pressures to have the 'right' attitude." Explain what the "right attitude" is, what pressures are brought to bear, and how society is affected as a result.

7. *Connecting the readings.* Should humor about race, gender, and ethnicity be protected, encouraged, discouraged, punished, or ignored? State and defend your view, drawing on your own ideas, those in "Free Speech on Campus," and those in "Don't Just Stand There" (page 288).

THE DEBATE OVER PLACING LIMITS ON RACIST SPEECH MUST NOT IGNORE THE DAMAGE IT DOES TO ITS VICTIMS
Charles R. Lawrence III

A professor at Stanford University, Charles R. Lawrence adapted the follow-ing essay from a speech he delivered to the American Civil Liberties Union. The written version was first published in the Chronicle of Higher Educa-tion *(1989), which is read primarily by college faculty and administrators. In the essay, Lawrence argues that hate speech on college campuses should not be protected. As you read, ask yourself how the American Civil Liberties Union was likely to respond to Lawrence's speech version.*

THE PATTERN	THE PURPOSE
cause-and-effect analysis	*to persuade*

1   I have spent the better part of my life as a dissenter. As a high school student, I was threatened with suspension for my refusal to par-ticipate in a civil-defense drill, and I have been a conspicuous consumer of my First Amendment liberties ever since. There are very strong rea-sons for protecting even racist speech. Perhaps the most important of these is that such protection reinforces our society's commitment to tol-erance as a value, and that by protecting bad speech from government regulation, we will be forced to combat it as a community.

2   But I also have a deeply felt apprehension about the resurgence of racial violence and the corresponding rise in the incidence of verbal and symbolic assault and harassment to which blacks and other tradi-tionally subjugated and excluded groups are subjected. I am troubled by the way the debate has been framed in response to the recent surge of racist incidents on college and university campuses and in response to some universities' attempts to regulate harassing speech. The prob-lem has been framed as one in which the liberty of free speech is in conflict with the elimination of racism. I believe this has placed the bigot on the moral high ground and fanned the rising flames of racism.

3   Above all, I am troubled that we have not listened to the real vic-tims, that we have shown so little understanding of their injury, and that

we have abandoned those whose race, gender, or sexual preference continues to make them second-class citizens. It seems to me a very sad irony that the first instinct of civil libertarians has been to challenge even the smallest, most narrowly framed efforts by universities to provide black and other minority students with the protection the Constitution guarantees them.

4   The landmark case of *Brown* v. *Board of Education* is not a case that we normally think of as a case about speech. But *Brown* can be broadly read as articulating the principle of equal citizenship. *Brown* held that segregated schools were inherently unequal because of the *message* that segregation conveyed—that black children were an untouchable caste, unfit to go to school with white children. If we understand the necessity of eliminating the system of signs and symbols that signal the inferiority of blacks, then we should hesitate before proclaiming that all racist speech that stops short of physical violence must be defended.

5   University officials who have formulated policies to respond to incidents of racial harassment have been characterized in the press as "thought police," but such policies generally do nothing more than impose sanctions against intentional face-to-face insults. When racist speech takes the form of face-to-face insults, catcalls, or other assaultive speech aimed at an individual or small group of persons, it falls directly within the "fighting words" exception to First Amendment protection. The Supreme Court has held that words which "by their very utterance inflict injury or tend to incite an immediate breach of the peace" are not protected by the First Amendment.

6   If the purpose of the First Amendment is to foster the greatest amount of speech, racial insults disserve that purpose. Assaultive racist speech functions as a preemptive strike. The invective is experienced as a blow, not as a proffered idea, and once the blow is struck, it is unlikely that a dialogue will follow. Racial insults are particularly undeserving of First Amendment protection because the perpetuator's intention is not to discover truth or initiate dialogue but to injure the victim. In most situations, members of minority groups realize that they are likely to lose if they respond to epithets by fighting and are forced to remain silent and submissive.

7   Courts have held that offensive speech may not be regulated in public forums such as streets where the listener may avoid the speech by moving on, but the regulation of otherwise protected speech has

been permitted when the speech invades the privacy of the unwilling listener's home or when the unwilling listener cannot avoid the speech. Racist posters, fliers, and graffiti in dormitories, bathrooms, and other common living spaces would seem to clearly fall within the reasoning of these cases. Minority students should not be required to remain in their rooms in order to avoid racial assault. Minimally, they should find a safe haven in their dorms and in all other common rooms that are a part of their daily routine.

8   I would also argue that the university's responsibility for ensuring that these students receive an equal educational opportunity provides a compelling justification for regulations that ensure them safe passage in all common areas. A minority student should not have to risk becoming the target of racially assaulting speech every time he or she chooses to walk across campus. Regulating vilifying speech that cannot be anticipated or avoided would not preclude announced speeches and rallies—situations that would give minority-group members and their allies the chance to organize counterdemonstrations or avoid the speech altogether.

9   The most commonly advanced argument against the regulation of racist speech proceeds something like this: We recognize that minority groups suffer pain and injury as the result of racist speech, but we must allow this hate mongering for the benefit of society as a whole. Freedom of speech is the lifeblood of our democratic system. It is especially important for minorities because often it is their only vehicle for rallying support for the redress of their grievances. It will be impossible to formulate a prohibition so precise that it will prevent the racist speech you want to suppress without catching in the same net all kinds of speech that it would be unconscionable for a democratic society to suppress.

10   Whenever we make such arguments, we are striking a balance on the one hand between our concern for the continued free flow of ideas and the democratic process dependent on that flow, and, on the other, our desire to further the cause of equality. There can be no meaningful discussion of how we should reconcile our commitment to equality and our commitment to free speech until it is acknowledged that there is real harm inflicted by racist speech and that this harm is far from trivial.

11   To engage in a debate about the First Amendment and racist speech without a full understanding of the nature and extent of that

harm is to risk making the First Amendment an instrument of domination rather than a vehicle of liberation. We have not all known the experience of victimization by racist, misogynist, and homophobic speech, nor do we equally share the burden of the societal harm it inflicts. We are often quick to say that we have heard the cry of the victims when we have not.

12   The *Brown* case is again instructive because it speaks directly to the psychic injury inflicted by racist speech by noting that the symbolic message of segregation affected "the hearts and minds" of negro children "in a way unlikely ever to be undone." Racial epithets and harassment often cause deep emotional scarring and feelings of anxiety and fear that pervade every aspect of a victim's life.

13   *Brown* also recognized that black children did not have an equal opportunity to learn and participate in the school community if they bore the additional burden of being subjected to the humiliation and psychic assault contained in the message of segregation. University students bear an analogous burden when they are forced to live and work in an environment where at any moment they may be subjected to denigrating verbal harassment and assault. The same injury was addressed by the Supreme Court when it held that sexual harassment that creates a hostile or abusive work environment violates the ban on sex discrimination in employment of Title VII of the Civil Rights Act of 1964.

14   Carefully drafted university regulations would bar the use of words as assault weapons and leave unregulated even the most heinous of ideas when those ideas are presented at times and places and in manners that provide an opportunity for reasoned rebuttal or escape from immediate injury. The history of the development of the right to free speech has been one of carefully evaluating the importance of free expression and its effects on other important societal interests. We have drawn the line between protected and unprotected speech before without dire results. (Courts have, for example, exempted from the protection of the First Amendment obscene speech and speech that disseminates official secrets, that defames or libels another person, or that is used to form a conspiracy or monopoly.)

15   Blacks and other people of color are skeptical about the argument that even the most injurious speech must remain unregulated because, in an unregulated marketplace of ideas, the best ones will rise to the top and gain acceptance. Our experience tells us quite the opposite. We have seen too many demagogues elected by appealing to America's

racism. We have seen too many good liberal politicians shy away from the issues that might brand them as being too closely allied with us.

16   Whenever we decide that racist speech must be tolerated because of the importance of maintaining societal tolerance for all unpopular speech, we are asking blacks and other subordinated groups to bear the burden for the good of all. We must be careful that the ease with which we strike the balance against the regulation of racist speech is in no way influenced by the fact that the cost will be borne by others. We must be certain that those who will pay that price are fairly represented in our deliberations and that they are heard.

17   At the core of the argument that we should resist all government regulation of speech is the ideal that the best cure for bad speech is good, that ideas that affirm equality and the worth of all individuals will ultimately prevail. This is an empty ideal unless those of us who would fight racism are vigilant and unequivocal in that fight. We must look for ways to offer assistance and support to students whose speech and political participation are chilled in a climate of racial harassment.

18   Civil-rights lawyers might consider suing on behalf of blacks whose right to an equal education is denied by a university's failure to ensure a nondiscriminatory educational climate or conditions of employment. We must embark upon the development of a First Amendment jurisprudence grounded in the reality of our history and our contemporary experience. We must think hard about how best to launch legal attacks against the most indefensible forms of hate speech. Good lawyers can create exceptions and narrow interpretations that limit the harm of hate speech without opening the floodgates of censorship.

19   Everyone concerned with these issues must find ways to engage actively in actions that resist and counter the racist ideas that we would have the First Amendment protect. If we fail in this, the victims of hate speech must rightly assume that we are on the oppressors' side.

Reading Closely and Thinking Critically

1. Lawrence expresses discomfort with the way the debate over hate speech has been framed. What problems does he see?

2. What irony does Lawrence identify in the debate over hate speech?

3. Lawrence offers the landmark Supreme Court decision in *Brown v The Board of Education* as one reason to punish hate speech.

Explain his reasoning. Do you agree with his reasoning? Why or why not?

4. Why does Lawrence believe that racial insults do not deserve first amendment protection?

5. What support and assumption does Lawrence use for his argument in paragraph 12? (See page 573 on support and assumptions.)

Examining Structure and Strategy

1. Lawrence opens by noting that he has been a long-time dissenter. Why does he make this opening remark? What does this statement suggest about Lawrence's view of his audience?

2. What objections does Lawrence raise, and how does he counter them?

3. Does Lawrence rely more on logical reasoning or emotional appeal to persuade his reader?

4. In paragraph 14, Lawrence notes historical exemptions to free speech. Does that information contribute to the persuasive quality of the essay? Explain.

5. Lawrence uses deductive reasoning to present his argument. What are his major and minor premises? (See page 579 on deductive reasoning.)

6. Which paragraphs form the conclusion? What approach does Lawrence take to that conclusion?

Considering Language and Style

1. In paragraph 2, Lawrence mentions symbolic assaults. Cite examples of symbolic (nonverbal) language that is threatening to some people.

2. Consult a dictionary if you are unfamiliar with any of these words: *catcalls* (paragraph 5), *preemptive strike* (paragraph 6), *invective* (paragraph 6), *epithets* (paragraphs 6, 11), *vilifying* (paragraph 8), *hate mongering* (paragraph 9), *unconscionable* (paragraph 9), *misogynist* (paragraph 11), *heinous* (paragraph 14), *demagogues* (paragraph 15).

For Group Discussion or Writing

Lawrence says that the most important reason to protect hate speech is that "such protection reinforces our society's commitment to tolerance as a value" (paragraph 1). Consider other ways we can make a commitment to tolerance. Would any of these ways compensate for punishing hate speech?

Writing Assignments

1. *In your journal.* Lawrence delivered an earlier version of the essay as a speech before members of the American Civil Liberties Union. Characterize the audience for the speech and consider how that audience was likely to react to Lawrence's thesis. What kind of persuasive goal do you think Lawrence could reasonably have established for the speech?

2. *Using the pattern.* Lawrence believes that hate speech does not deserve first amendment protection, largely because "the perpetrator's intention is not to . . . initiate dialogue but to injure the victim" (paragraph 6). Agree or disagree with this reasoning.

3. *Using the pattern.* Do college instructors have the right to express their opinions, even if those opinions are hurtful to others? For example, can they publicly express the view that homosexuals are sinful or that women are inferior to men or that African-Americans are less intelligent than whites or that Jews are responsible for society's ills? Argue your view, being sure to counter the compelling objections.

4. *Using the pattern.* Do you think that punishing racist language will improve race relations in this country? Argue your view, being sure to counter the compelling objections.

5. *Considering a theme.* Write a definition of *hate speech.* Explain its characteristics so that your reader will understand exactly what kind of language is at the heart of the debate about free speech on campus. (See Chapter 10 on definition.)

6. *Connecting the readings.* Compare and contrast the views of Lawrence and Nat Hentoff in "Free Speech on Campus" (page 623). Then note whether any points have been overlooked, overemphasized, or underemphasized by either author.

PROTECTING FREEDOM OF EXPRESSION AT HARVARD

Derek Bok

Born in 1930 in Bryn Mawr, Pennsylvania, Derek Bok attended Stanford and Harvard, earning a law degree at the latter school. A professor of labor and antitrust law and dean of Harvard Law School, Bok also served as that university's president from 1971 to 1991. Bok's books include Beyond the Ivory Tower *(1982) and* Universities and the Future of America *(1990). "Protecting Freedom of Expression at Harvard" first appeared in the* Boston Globe *in 1991. In it, Bok argues a position more moderate than that seen in the previous two essays.*

THE PATTERN	THE PURPOSE
cause-and-effect analysis	*to persuade*

1   For several years, universities have been struggling with the problem of trying to reconcile the rights of free speech with the desire to avoid racial tension. In recent weeks, such a controversy has sprung up at Harvard. Two students hung Confederate flags in public view, upsetting students who equate the Confederacy with slavery. A third student tried to protest the flags by displaying a swastika.

2   These incidents have provoked much discussion and disagreement. Some students have urged that Harvard require the removal of symbols that offend many members of the community. Others reply that such symbols are a form of free speech and should be protected.

3   Different universities have resolved similar conflicts in different ways. Some have enacted codes to protect their communities from forms of speech that are deemed to be insensitive to the feelings of other groups. Some have refused to impose such restrictions.

4   It is important to distinguish between the appropriateness of such communications and their status under the First Amendment. The fact that speech is protected by the First Amendment does not necessarily mean that it is right, proper, or civil. I am sure that the vast majority of Harvard students believe that hanging a Confederate flag in public view—or displaying a swastika in response—is insensitive and

unwise because any satisfaction it gives to the students who display these symbols is far outweighed by the discomfort it causes to many others.

5   I share this view and regret that the students involved saw fit to behave in this fashion. Whether or not they merely wished to manifest their pride in the South—or to demonstrate the insensitivity of hanging Confederate flags by mounting another offensive symbol in return—they must have known that they would upset many fellow students and ignore the decent regard for the feelings of others so essential to building and preserving a strong and harmonious community.

6   To disapprove of a particular form of communication, however, is not enough to justify prohibiting it. We are faced with a clear example of the conflict between our commitment to free speech and our desire to foster a community founded on mutual respect. Our society has wrestled with this problem for many years. Interpreting the First Amendment, the Supreme Court has clearly struck the balance in favor of free speech.

7   While communities do have the right to regulate speech in order to uphold aesthetic standards (avoiding defacement of buildings) or to protect the public from disturbing noise, rules of this kind must be applied across the board and cannot be enforced selectively to prohibit certain kinds of messages but not others.

8   Under the Supreme Court's rulings, as I read them, the display of swastikas or Confederate flags clearly falls within the protection of the free-speech clause of the First Amendment and cannot be forbidden simply because it offends the feelings of many members of the community. These rulings apply to all agencies of government, including public universities.

9   Although it is unclear to what extent the First Amendment is enforceable against private institutions, I have difficulty understanding why a university such as Harvard should have less free speech than the surrounding society—or than a public university.

10   One reason why the power of censorship is so dangerous is that it is extremely difficult to decide when a particular communication is offensive enough to warrant prohibition or to weigh the degree of offensiveness against the potential value of the communication. If we begin to forbid flags, it is only a short step to prohibiting offensive speakers.

11   I suspect that no community will become humane and caring by restricting what its members can say. The worst offenders will simply find other ways to irritate and insult.

12   In addition, once we start to declare certain things "offensive," with all the excitement and attention that will follow, I fear that much ingenuity will be exerted trying to test the limits, much time will be expanded trying to draw tenuous distinctions, and the resulting publicity will eventually attract more attention to the offensive material than would ever have occurred otherwise.

13   Rather than prohibit such communications, with all the resulting risks, it would be better to ignore them, since students would then have little reason to create such displays and would soon abandon them. If this response is not possible—and one can understand why—the wisest course is to speak with those who perform insensitive acts and try to help them understand the effects of their actions on others.

14   Appropriate officials and faculty members should take the lead, as the Harvard House Masters have already done in this case. In talking with students, they should seek to educate and persuade, rather than resort to ridicule or intimidation, recognizing that only persuasion is likely to produce a lasting, beneficial effect. Through such effects, I believe that we act in the manner most consistent with our ideals as an educational institution and most calculated to help us create a truly understanding, supportive community.

Reading Closely and Thinking Critically

1. In your own words, state the thesis of the essay.

2. When he considers the issue of speech limitations, what important distinction does Bok make?

3. Bok says that offensive speech enjoys first amendment protection, but he never tries to prove this point. Why not? Is the lack of proof a problem? Explain.

4. What does Bok see as a primary danger of censorship?

5. Do you think Bok's views are influenced by the fact that he is an attorney and former president of Harvard University? Explain.

Examining Structure and Strategy

1. Bok's argumentation begins in paragraph 6. What purposes do the first five paragraphs serve?

2. Does Bok reason inductively or deductively? Explain.

3. Which objections does Bok raise, and how does he counter them?

4. Are all of Bok's points adequately supported? Are there any points that need more development? If so, note which ones.

5. Does Bok rely more on emotional appeal or on reasons?

Considering Language and Style

1. Bok notes that Confederate flags and swastikas are forms of symbolic language. What do these symbols communicate?

2. Consult a dictionary if you are unfamiliar with either of these words: *aesthetic* (paragraph 7), *tenuous* (paragraph 12).

For Group Discussion or Writing
Agree or disagree with what Bok says in paragraph 11, citing reasons for your view.

Writing Assignments

1. *In your journal.* Bok recommends that college officials and faculty members "educate and persuade" the perpetrators of hate speech. How successful do you think this solution would be?

2. *Using the pattern.* Assume the role of the director of student services on your campus, and write a letter to a student who has displayed the Confederate flag from the window of his or her apartment. Try to "educate and persuade" the student, as Bok suggests in paragraph 14.

3. *Using the pattern.* Limiting speech—even hate speech—is a form of censorship. Is there any form of censorship (of pornography, violence in television programs, profanity in books for teenagers, and so forth) that you favor? If so, state and defend your view. If you are against all forms of censorship, explain why.

4. *Considering a theme.* Develop a course for college freshmen that will promote understanding among different racial, ethnic, and religious groups. Describe the components of the course and explain how they will promote understanding.

5. *Connecting the readings.* Explain what you as an individual can do on your campus to help eliminate hurtful communication and promote understanding. You may find the ideas in "Protecting Freedom of Expression at Harvard," "Don't Just Stand There" (page 288), and "The Ways of Meeting Oppression" (page 463) helpful.

THE INHUMANITY OF THE ANIMAL PEOPLE
Joy Williams

A short-story writer, essayist, novelist, and animal-rights advocate, Joy Williams wrote "The Inhumanity of the Animal People" for Harper's Maga-zine *(1997). In the essay, Williams combines cause-and-effect analysis, ex-emplification, and descriptive language to inform the reader about the cru-elty to animals and to argue for a change in the way we treat them. As you read, notice how Williams appeals to emotions, values, and beliefs.*

THE PATTERNS	THE PURPOSES
cause-and-effect analysis, *exemplification, and description*	*to persuade and to inform*

1   St. Francis once converted a wolf to reason. The wolf of Gubbio promised to stop terrorizing an Italian town; he made pledges and as-surances and pacts, and he kept his part of the bargains. But St. Fran-cis only performed this miracle once, and as miracles go, it didn't seem to capture the public's fancy. Humans don't want animals to reason. It would be an unnerving experience. It would bring about all manner of awkwardness and guilt. It would make our treatment of them seem, well, unreasonable. The fact that animals are voiceless is a relief to us, it frees us from feeling much empathy or sorrow. If animals did have voices, if they could speak with the tongues of angels—at the very least with the tongues of angels—it is unlikely that they could save them-selves from mankind. Their mysterious otherness has not saved them, nor have their beautiful songs and coats and skins and shells, nor have their strengths, their skills, their swiftness, the beauty of their flights. We discover the remarkable intelligence of the whale, the wolf, the ele-phant—it does not save them, nor does our awareness of the com-plexity of their lives. It matters not, it seems, whether they nurse their young or brood patiently on eggs. If they eat meat, we decry their vi-ciousness; if they eat grass and seeds, we dismiss them as weak. We know that they care for their young and teach them, that they play and grieve, that they have memories and a sense of the future for which they sometimes plan. We know about their habits, their migrations, that

they have a sense of home, of finding, seeking, returning to home. We know that when they face death, they fear it. We know all these things and it has not saved them from us.

2   Anything that is animal, that is not *us*, can be slaughtered as a pest or sucked dry as a memento or reduced to a trophy or eaten, eaten, eaten. For reasons of need or preference or availability. Or it's culture, it's a way to feed the poor, it's different, it's plentiful, it's not plentiful, which makes it more intriguing, it arouses the palate, it amuses the palate, it makes your dick bigger, it's healthy, it's somebody's way of life, it's somebody's livelihood, it's somebody's business.

3   Agriculture has become agribusiness, after all. So the creatures that have been under our "stewardship" the longest, that have been codified by habit for our use, that have always suffered a special place in our regard—the farm animals—have never been as cruelly kept or confined or slaughtered in such numbers in all of history. Aldo Leopold, in his naturalist classic *A Sand Country Almanac,* argues that wild animals and domesticated animals have different moral statuses—domestic animals are not free and therefore are unworthy of our regard. Catholic moral textbooks instruct that we have no duties of justice or charity toward animals; our only duties concerning them are the proper use we make of them. But large-scale corporate agribusinesses, enjoying fat federal tax breaks, don't need to have their interests defended by effete ethical rationalizations. Factory farmers are all Cartesians. Animals are no more than machines—milk machines, piglet machines, egg machines— production units converting themselves into profits. They are explicitly excluded from any protection offered by the federal Animal Welfare Act, an act that is casually and lightly enforced, if at all, by the Department of Agriculture: "Normal agricultural operation" precludes "humane" treatment, and anticruelty laws do not apply to that which is raised for food.

4   The factory farm today is a crowded, stinking bedlam, filled with suffering animals that are quite literally insane, sprayed with pesticides and fattened on a diet of growth stimulants, antibiotics, and drugs. Two hundred and fifty thousand laying hens are confined within a single building. (The high mortality rate caused by overcrowding is economically acceptable; nothing is more worthless than an individual chicken.) Pigs are raised in bare concrete cages in windowless metal buildings or tightly restrained in foul pens and gestation boxes. Cows are kept pregnant to produce an abnormal amount of milk, which is further artifi-

cially increased with hormone injections. The by-products of the dairy industry, calves, are chained in crates twenty-two inches wide and no longer than their bodies, and raised on a diet of drug-laced liquid feed for a few months until they're slaughtered for the "delicacy" veal. (Yet some people say, *Well, apparently they're raised in the darkness, in crates or something, but the taste is creamy, sort of refined, a very nice taste . . .*) People will stop eating veal only if they think they will get a killer disease if they don't. In England, the beef industry had a setback when a link was found between bovine spongiform encephalopathy, a fatal disease of cattle, and Creutzfeldt-Jakob disease, a fatal neurological virus in humans. The cows became ill because they were fed the rendered remains of sick sheep. Of course, in this country we are assured that our cows aren't being fed sick sheep and that no BSE-infected cattle have been found here. We do have many "downer" animals, though, about 100,000 of them a year, that collapse from stress or something, heaven knows, and end up dead prior to the slaughtering process. They are rendered and ground up and become pet food and animal feed. Cattle do eat cattle here. They are fed the ground offal of those that have succumbed to unknown causes, and this has been the practice for many years. If BSE were ever confirmed in this country, which is not at all unlikely, people would stop eating meat for a while for the same reasons the English did. Not because they'd had a sudden telepathic vision of the horrors of the abattoir, or because they'd all been subjected to a reading of James Agee's remarkable fable about a Christlike steer, "A Mother's Tale," but because they thought that eating steak would make their brains go funny. Once assured by the government that there was no need for alarm, they would be back in the spotless supermarkets, making their selections among the sliced, cubed, and shrink-wrapped remains, which have borne no resemblance to living things in our minds for some time now. They are merely some things, in a different department from the toilet-bowl cleanser. The supermarket has never been a place where one thinks—Animal.

5   Now genetic manipulation is becoming a commonplace as well. One of the problems in poultry production is that bacteria-laden feces fly all over the carcasses in the slaughtering process. It's just always been a problem. Awaiting government approval is a proposed product called Rectite, a sort of superglue that seals the rectal cavities of poultry so all that salmonella contamination can be avoided. But Rectite already

sounds a little old-fashioned. Genetic engineers might want to create a turkey, say, that had no vent at all, possibly no feet, and even a smaller head to save space. This would likely be hailed as quite an advantage over the traditionally constructed bird. Researchers probably dream about this nightly (when they're not dreaming about genetically identical sheep). Researchers are, in fact, creating entire new orders of creatures—specifically designed, transgenic, xenograph-ready. Around the world in labs with names such as Genpharm International Inc., Genzyme Corporation, and Pharmaceutical Proteins, biotechnocrats are inserting human genes in livestock to form animals that can produce human proteins and hormones: drugstores on the hoof. Pigs, long attractive to the farmer, not because of any Babe- or Miss Piggy–like charm but because they have short pregnancies and big litters, have become a favorite of researchers who are altering them to make the perfect organ donors. Doctors, awaiting the eventual blessing of the FDA, are eagerly anticipating placing genetically altered pig livers in just about everybody. (The drunks will probably get them to start.) Humans are requiring and demanding fresh new organs all the time (employing animals in this way seems so much more sophisticated than merely eating them), and the ethics of raising or breeding animals for body parts to replace our own failing ones seems to give people pause only when combined with warnings of dangers to human health. A person might not want that little monkey's heart, not because he wanted the monkey to keep it but because he'd worry that he might contract the Ebola virus and that his skin would get pulpy, he'd vomit black blood, and his eyeballs would burst.

6   We distance ourselves more and more from animals as we use them in increasingly bizarre ways. Animals are being subsumed in a weird unnaturalness. Indeed, technology, which is forever pressing to remove animals from nature, to muddy and morph the remaining integrity of the animal kingdom, has rendered the word "natural" obsolete. A side benefit of the new and developing technologies is that soon we won't have to feel guilty about the suffering and denigration of the animals because we will have made them up. (That's not an animal, it's a donor . . .) Any sentience they posses will have been invented by man or eliminated altogether. An animal will have no more real "life" than a lightbulb.

7   In the laboratory, animals have already been reclassified. They are tools, they're part of the scientific apparatus, they undergo transforma-

tions, they are metamorphosed into data. Rats and mice are already excluded from the very definition of "animal" by the Department of Agriculture. The offspring of these un-animals are then genetically reinvented. There are countless variations of mutant "knock-out" mice, creatures whose genetic code has been grotesquely altered, who lack particular genes crucial to learning or to instinctual behavior and self-destruct in novel ways, or who develop terrible diseases or deformities. As for the cats and dogs and rabbits and primates other than man in the laboratory, although not deemed un-animals, they are transformed semantically into "research animals." These animals, like "food" animals, qualify for very little protection under the Animal Welfare Act. At present this act does not prohibit any experiment or procedure that might be performed on animals in labs, and makes clear that the government cannot interfere with the conduct or design of any experiment. Blinding has long been a popular procedure in the lab, as are any and all "deprivology" studies. Of endless interest is the study of an animal's reaction to unrelieved, inescapable pain. The procedures, of course, are never cruelty but science—they may result in data that might be of some use to us sometime. So dogs are decerebrated or mutilated or poisoned or burned to provide grist for a learned thesis; other dogs are tormented into states of trauma, into states of "learned helplessness," into "psychological death," to see if their observed decline can give any insights into human depression. Some experiments merely satisfy scientific "curiosity." (*Wow, this stuff took that puppy's skin right down to the bone. I wonder if it will take the rust off the lawn furniture with no mess.*) Other experiments serve to confirm prior conclusions—to verify previously known LD (lethal dose) levels, for example. LD tests, used by industry to determine the toxicity of floor waxes and detergents, end when half the animals in a test group die. Animals never leave laboratories. They keep undergoing more and more corrosive tests until they expire, or until their bodies, unable to provide even the most utterly senseless data, are "humanely destroyed."

8   But dogs and cats and rabbits are as nothing to the researcher when compared with what can be extrapolated from the most desirable lab animal of them all—the chimpanzee. The chimpanzee, humankind's closest relative, has been infected and maimed and killed for over fifty years now, for us, for the possible advantage to us, because they're so much like us; they possess 98 percent of the same DNA, the same

genetic material, as humans. That missing 2 percent allows them to be vivisected on our behalf. If it weren't for that lucky-for-us 2, they wouldn't be able to be used as experimental surrogates because they'd be *just* like us, and medical advancement would come to a standstill. Or at best it would, in the words of a doctor writing in *The New Physician,* slow to a "snail's pace."

9   So in our country's finest universities (as well as in some of our just so-so ones), researchers, not to be likened to snails, are still making chimpanzees "hot" with deadly diseases and screwing bolts into their heads. They're still removing infants from their mothers and "containerizing" them in solitary so that their psychological and emotional suffering and decline can be observed. They're still performing cataract surgery on healthy chimps, then giving them different rehabilitative treatments, then killing them and dissecting their brains to see which treatment produced the best result within the visual cortex. And they're still trying to give chimps AIDS. Scientists have been frustrated because chimps just won't get this disease, though their own simian immune systems can be destroyed in the lab. Over 100 chimps have been dosed with the human AIDS virus, but none have developed human AIDS. In 1995, researchers from the Yerkes Regional Primate Research Center at Emory University in Atlanta were able to announce that one chimp, infected with the virus ten years earlier, had come down with AIDS, or, rather, had come down with the opportunistic diseases associated with AIDS. Managing to give one chimp the symptoms of AIDS was certainly not science's finest hour.

10   In any case, what is all this "research" for? Artificially induced diseases in animals practically never result in a cure that can be applicable to humans. Even scientists have begun to recognize the ambiguity of their work to the extent that it is common now, after the announcement of any discovery wrung from animal research, for the researchers to caution publicly using the findings to draw conclusions about human disease or behavior. Still, researchers work hard at public relations. Parents' terrors of the mysterious sudden infant death syndrome were manipulated shamelessly with the *cure dependent upon animal research* mantra—until the precipitous recent drop in infant deaths was attributed to the simple act of putting babies to bed on their backs instead of their stomachs. (Prevention may be worth a pound of cure, but it's not something the drug companies are interested in.) Misleading monkey experiments delayed an effective polio vaccine for decades. (As for

insight into the cancer problem, 46 percent of substances deemed carcinogenic in mice are found not to be carcinogenic in rats.) Successes
in human kidney transplants, blood transfusions, and heart-bypass
surgery all resulted only when doctors ignored the baleful results of experiments on dogs and used human material. Animal tests, in fact, do
not predict side effects in humans up to 52 percent of the time. Guinea
pigs die when injected with penicillin. Thalidomide was found safe for
rodents; so was Opren, an arthritis drug that caused fatal liver toxicity
in a number of human patients before it was taken off the market. Animals are sacrificed in laboratories to show the safety of products too;
they are not all employed to test the dangerous side effects. The tobacco
industry was able to deny a link between cigarette smoking and lung
cancer for decades because many thousands of dogs, monkeys, rabbits,
and rats, fitted with masks and placed in "smoking chambers," or immobilized in stereotaxic chairs with tubes blowing smoke down their
windpipes, could not be encouraged to develop carcinomas.

11   *The horror! The horror!* if I may be so bold as to quote Conrad.
12   Yet most people believe they like animals, are kind to them, and,
by accepting any new "uses" that can be found for them, have sensible
attitudes regarding them. *Normal* people are fond of animals and disapprove of wanton cruelty, but keep their priorities in order. That is,
they seem to want to be kinder to animals even as they continue to use
them and eat them and expect them to relocate themselves when it's
time to build a vacation home. But they certainly don't want to run the
risk of being denigrated as *animal people* by regarding animals too highly
or caring too much.
13   When a dog was found bound and hanged with electrical cord
and set on fire in Miami in April 1996, people contributed money to a
reward fund for the apprehension of his killer. A few people contributing a little money would have been normal, but hundreds of people
contributed a considerable amount of money, which made them peculiar, which makes them animal people. The *Miami Herald* was puzzled:
"[The collected money] exceeds the $11,000 offered by law enforce-
ment agencies for the capture of a serial killer who beats and burns
homeless women in Miami."
14   When a seventeen-year-old with cancer wanted to go to Alaska
and kill a Kodiak bear, and was sent to do just that thanks to the gen-
erosity of the Make-A-Wish Foundation, it set off what the papers

referred to as an "animal-rights furor." The extent of that furor caused others to be more "objective" about the situation, saying things like, *Hey, it'll make the poor kid happy, and it's something he can do with his dad.*
15   When boys on a high school team in Texas battered a cat with their baseball bats, put it in a bag, and ran over it with their pickup truck, killing it, because it had taken to hanging around and soiling the pitcher's mound, the animal people were outraged and demanded that the players be kicked off the team. Such intense disapproval "bewildered" the youths and caused a backlash. *We all did things to cats when we were young. This is just ridiculous. Some people think a cat is more important than a boy.* Although such arguments are not up to the debating dazzle, say, of Dostoevsky's Grand Inquisitor, a humanist argument in any form defends normal thinking against the misanthropic nuts—the animal people or, worst of all, *the animal-rights people*—who seek to question it.
16   "A rat is a pig is a dog is a boy," the statement made by People for the Ethical Treatment of Animals (PETA) some years ago, has been used with considerable success to discredit the animal-rights movement (though a rat does seem to be a boy when it suits science's purposes). PETA's actual remark was, "When it comes to having a nervous system and the ability to feel pain, hunger, and thirst, a rat is a pig is a dog is a boy." Even addressing the statement as intended has resulted in a not so edifying debate about suffering. Do animals suffer or don't they? And if they do (they certainly seem to), does that *ability*, rather than the ability to speak or reason, give them the rights of life, liberty, and freedom from torture? "Rights" has become practically the only ethical language we speak in this country, and to the animal-rights activist, it means *equal consideration of interests.* But to normal people, rights for animals is ridiculous, and much merriment is had by placing the concept in the most ludicrous light possible. What kind of rights exactly? The right to vote? The right to a good education? The right of a doggy not to be nutted at the vet's? Not only are the animal-rights people considered annoying because of their boycotts and protests and extremely politically incorrect use of Holocaust and slavery references regarding the status of animals; they're considered antihuman, even monstrous, in their misguidedness. (Hitler was a vegetarian, you know, and he adored his German shepherds.) An animal-rights activist is perceived to be the kind of person who would sneak into a school cafeteria and whisper to the innocent, impressionable children there, *You know that sandwich Mommy*

packed for you? Well, I know you love your mommy very much, but you know that substance in your sandwich once had a mommy and a life too, and it wanted to live that life just as much as you want to live yours.

17   The animal-rights people are widely thought to be—well, crazy.

18   There are thousands of animal-advocacy organizations in the United States, with millions of members. Feral cats, wild horses, greyhounds, fowls, bats, as well as the more dramatic gorillas, pandas, and dolphins, all have their devoted protectors, and various methods are used to win public sympathy for them. But many advocates are working for the humane treatment of animals and would prefer not to argue the rights issue at all. To argue that an animal has the right not to have its arms cut off in an experiment is far different than arguing that a pig should be treated more kindly before being converted into a Heavenly Ham. It is one thing to show up as a carrot at the county fair, toting a placard that reads "Eat Your Veggies, Not Your Friends," and quite another to find a convincing language with an irrefutable philosophical base for the concept of animal dignity. It's easier to have a yard sale to benefit your local wildlife rehabilitation center than to wade into real rights talk and tempt flake status. An animal-welfare advocate can feel quietly victorious convincing someone to adopt a pet from the pound rather than buy one from a pet store, but a rights person is always plunging into the eschatological dark. ("You actually believe that animals have souls?" "Yes, I do. I do believe that. Their natures are their souls.")

19   Welfare groups have been laboring on behalf of the animals for some time—the American Society for the Prevention of Cruelty to Animals and the American Anti-Vivisection Society are both over a hundred years old—but the rights movement took off only in 1973, when *The New York Review of Books* published an unsolicited review of a book about animals, men, and morals. The reviewer was the Australian philosopher Peter Singer, who quickly expanded his article into the rights bible, *Animal Liberation.* PETA, founded by Ingrid Newkirk and Alex Pacheco in 1980, is the group that perhaps best personifies the rights movement, because it broke tactical ground in 1981 with a daring legal action that attempted to prosecute a researcher for animal cruelty. Pacheco volunteered as an assistant to a Dr. Edward Taub at the Institute of Behavioral Research in Silver Spring, Maryland, with the intention of secretly documenting conditions in an "ordinary" lab. Taub

had been surgically crippling primates to monitor the rehabilitation of impaired limbs for many years, apparently suspending his efforts only long enough to write proposals for federal grants that would, and did, allow him to continue his labors. Pacheco and PETA got a precedent-setting search warrant from a circuit judge, and police raided the filthy lab and confiscated seventeen monkeys, as well as Taub's files and a monkey's severed hand that the less than charismatic researcher kept on his desk as a paperweight. Although the rights of the mutilated primates could not be argued, as those rights had never been established, Taub was found guilty by a jury of cruelty to animals. The conviction was overturned on appeal when the court ruled that state statutes did not apply to research conducted under a federal program. Taub, supported by the animal-experimentation industry, seemed to have unlimited funds for defense at his disposal. Still, PETA's persistence and style brought publicity and respect for animal advocates.

20   Today, pharmaceutical companies, agribusinesses, the National Association for Biomedical Research, and the American Medical Association (all of which have only our best interests at heart) revile as extremists such groups as PETA, Last Chance for Animals, Friends of Animals, and the Animal Liberation Front. These rights groups can argue rights with all solemnity but prefer vivid direct action. After a letter-writing campaign and a tourist boycott led by the Fund for Animals made no impression on the governor of Alaska, the group was assisted by Friends of Animals, which aired, on national television, an undercover video of Alaskan officials tirelessly exterminating wolves. The ALF breaks into labs, damages equipment, and frees animals, all to great notoriety and accusations of terrorism, but its raids often provide irrefutable proof of researchers' barbarism. The ALF stole films from the University of Pennsylvania's head injury lab that showed baboons in vises getting their heads smashed while researchers chortled. The National Institutes of Health had called the Pennsylvania lab "one of the best in the world," but the federal government cut off funding after the improperly acquired film was made public. (What does the Animal Rights Direct Action Coalition do to relax? They drive up to McDonald's in a pickup truck with a dead cow in the back and a sign reading, "Here's Your Lunch.")

21   Moderates in the movement—the ones who have struggled quietly for reform—are tolerated by society as long as they can be considered harmless do-gooders. Activists, of course, put this toleration at

risk. But even moderate groups are taking responsibility for a more meaningful ethic regarding the animals. The Humane Society of the United States, founded in 1954, has five million members and is considered a reasonable group working in a mannerly way within the system, lobbying governments and promoting ballot initiatives on behalf of the animals. Still, although the HSUS studiously avoids using rights language, its position that animals should not be treated more cruelly than humans is a view quite revolutionary in its implications. It is, in fact, a rights position, an animal-rights extremist position.

22   Amid controversies and organizational politicking, the animal people never stop thinking about animals. And they never stop thinking about the ways they can make the rest of us think about animals, for we've grown awfully comfortable with animals' erasure from our lives. (If we don't erase them, we absorb them.) The animal people are vegetarians. They'd better be if they don't want to be accused of being hypocritical. (Of course, by not being hypocritical, they can be accused of being self-righteous.) But people don't admire them overmuch for living lightly on the planet, and their "Meat Is Murder" chirping seems to be an irritant right up there with a leaf blower or a jet ski. Their wishful hope that by their example animals will be saved and the slaughterhouses will fall silent is dismissed as absurd, because on an average day in America, 130,000 cattle, 7,000 calves, 360,000 pigs, and 24 million chickens are killed, and you can't just shut down a show like that overnight. Besides, the argument goes, a vegetarian, unless he is a zealot, practically a Jain, is culpable in the death of animals from the moment he wakes up in the morning. Modern slaughterhouses find a use for everything but the squeal, the cluck, and the moo, as the ag spokesmen like to say. As well as being turned into the more obvious sofas, shoes, wallets, and "tough chic" jackets and skirts, animals are transmogrified into antiaging creams and glue and paint and antifreeze. Gelatin—benign gelatin, formerly known as hooves—constitutes Jell-O, of course, and is also in ice cream and the increasing number of "fat free" products we consume. Animals are turned into all manner of drugs, mood enhancers, and mood stabilizers. Premarin, an estrogen drug for menopausal women, comes from the urine of pregnant mares. This is a whole new industry that results in the births of approximately 75,000 unwanted foals each year. Off to the slaughterhouse the little ones go, to be turned into . . . something else. Animals are everywhere in our lives; we just

can't look into their eyes. We'd prefer not to think about their eyes at all, actually.

23   Vegetarians do their best, but they seem to lack influence. A recent article in *The New York Times Magazine* marveled over a meeting between environmentalists and ranchers that took place at a steakhouse in Orofino, Idaho, a restaurant described as "a shrine to red meat and raw timber." As the two groups "sparred and joked over steak," they realized they had a great deal in common. They both wanted wolves, grizzlies, and open spaces. They forged a new and potentially powerful bond as they literally chewed the fat. A vegetarian could never come to such an understanding with the Big Dogs. Never! (Particularly if he tried to break the ice with George Bernard Shaw's witticism that "meat eating is cannibalism with the heroic dish omitted." The ranchers and environmentalists together would throw him out on his ass into the parking lot.)

24   The animal people have never been embraced by the increasingly corporate environmental community. Mainstream enviro groups, with their compromises and retreats, have lost the moral background on the American scene in less than thirty years. They've become ecowimps. Even the far from ecowimpy Earth First! has never entangled itself in the briar patch that is animal rights. To this group, farm animals are the problem. *Shoot Cows Not Bears,* Earth First! exhorts in its Dada way. As for the environmental philosophers, the Deep Ecologists, they have never fully acknowledged the reality of the animals, preferring to deal in the abstractions of biodiversity and species instead. Although they call for a less human-centered ethic, our ugly and troubled relationship with the nonhuman animal is a problem they do not care to address.

25   Only the animal people struggle to address this problem, and there is no limit to the horrible things they can worry about or the disappointments they must endure. Public awareness and revulsion at our treatment of animals is often raised only to fade or be circumvented. Two successes for the movement involved the fur and cosmetics industries. The wearing of fur was discredited for a time through the tactic of howling insult. "Corpse Coat!" activists would scream at any opportunity, or they would solicitously ask of some fur wearer, "How did you get the blood off that?" Then they'd go out and paint "Shame" and "Death" all over furriers' windows. Most cosmetics companies eliminated animal testing after the word got out to the kids (*Mommy, is it true that they blinded hundreds of white bunnies to make this pretty soap?*)

and consumers were organized to boycott. But the fur industry is still around, hoping for government subsidies to boost export sales and counting on a new wave of designers—there's always a new wave—who believe the trend gurus' predictions of a "fur renaissance fueled by a growing interest in luxury investments" and are churning out the beaver capes, the burgundy pony-skin jackets, and the acid-green sable barn jackets. And some of the big names in the beauty industry—Helene Curtis, Chesebrough Pond's—continue to test on animals. Overall, the use of animals in research could very well be increasing—who knows? Corporate monoliths such as Procter & Gamble and Bausch & Lomb never stopped animal testing; the Department of Defense could still be cutting the vocal cords of beagles and testing nerve gas on them. The DOD doesn't have to release any figures at all, and research facilities in general enjoy institutionalized secrecy and seldom have to provide real numbers to the public.

26   No, there's little cause for real happiness among the animal people and scant opportunity for self-congratulation. Commercial whaling has never really been outlawed, trade in exotic species is brisk, trophy hunting is back. Whenever a victory is claimed for the animals, it doesn't stay a victory for long: it's either not definitive or it's superseded by something worse. Cases continue to be won only to be lost on appeal, and the cases that remain won involve animal cruelty or welfare, never the rights of an animal to an equal consideration of interests, for an animal has no standing in a court of law. Injuries to a person's "aesthetic interests" can be judicially recognized (*I am offended by seeing spotted owls mounted on the hoods of logging trucks*), but an animal's interest in continuing to exist cannot.

27   The animal people need their day in court on the rights issue, and groups such as the Animal Legal Defense Fund are seeking to find, try, and win the perfect case—the case that will take animals out of the realm of property and grant them legal status of their own. The plaintiff will undoubtedly be a chimp. The chimpanzee's ability to be trained in sign language, and their further ability to use that language to express their fears and needs, could provide the scientific basis for the argument that they deserve the same freedom from enslavement that humans now enjoy. Peter Singer's latest philosophical effort is the Great Ape Project, a rhetorical demand for the extension of the "community of equals" to include all the great apes: human beings and "our disquieting doubles"—chimpanzees, gorillas, and orangutans. The rights of

life and freedom from torture and imprisonment would be granted to these animals, and then, possibly, would trickle down to those that are less our disquieting doubles.

28   Sometimes a number of the animal people gather together, as they did last year for a "World Congress" at the cavernous USAir Arena in Landover, Maryland, just outside Washington, D.C. The arena can hold 18,000 people and it was far from full. There were no lovely animals there, of course. Animals can never be called upon to do a star turn on the movement's behalf—that would be using the animals. So only people were there, and only about 3,000 of them. The arena itself, so vast and impersonal, so disconcertingly inert, seemed to emphasize the gargantuan task the little group had taken on, and the gaunt specter of hopeless helplessness appeared more than once. Unspeakably wretched images were projected on immense screens: gruesome videos of steel leg-hold traps going off and nailing a remarkable array of creatures, videos of moribund lab animals and terrified stockyard animals, videos of berserk zoo and circus animals being shot. The animal people sat silently watching, watching simian horror, avian and equine horror, hunting and puppy-mill and pound horror—witnessing things a normal person would never want to know about. There were three days of speeches. The speakers were impassioned but calm, well-spoken, well-dressed, well-prepared; they politely restricted themselves to the time allotted. Nobody screamed, "We've got to stop dressing up as carrots!" or, "Whose idea was it to petition the town of Fishkill to change its name. It made us look like morons!" The importance of unity was stressed, the importance if being perceived as a single-interest political group that could effect change. Between speeches, people would wander out to the encircling satellite area and line up for the beyond-veggie, no-dairy vegan food that the arena's concessionaires were serving up with a certain amount of puzzlement. The Franks A Lot stand was sensibly shuttered. On the fourth day there was a March for Animals, from the Ellipse up Constitution Avenue to the Capitol. It was a nice march, orderly. Bystanders seemed a little baffled by it. Perhaps because there were no animals.

29   After the march, the animal people went home—to continue to work, work, work for the animals so that they might be saved from our barbarism. Has any primarily middle-class group in this country ever had such an extremist agenda, based utterly on non-self-fulfillment and

non-self-interest? The animal people are calling for a moral attitude toward a great and mysterious and mute nation, which can't, by our stern reckoning, act morally back. Their quest is quixotic; their reasoning, assailable; their intentions, almost inarticulate. The implementation of their vision would seem madness. But the future world is not this one. Our treatment of animals and our attitude toward them is crucial not only to any pretensions we have to ethical behavior but to humankind's intellectual and moral evolution. Which is how the human animal is meant to evolve, isn't it?

Reading Closely and Thinking Critically

1. In your own words, state the thesis of "The Inhumanity of the Animal People."

2. How does Williams characterize the "animal people"?

3. In paragraphs 4 and 7, italicized words appear in parentheses. What is the significance of those words?

4. What reasons does Williams supply to support her contention that the animal people are inhumane?

5. How does Williams feel about using animal organs for transplant into humans? Do you agree with her view? Explain.

6. Williams says that technology is removing animals from nature. What does she mean?

7. Do you find Williams's argument convincing? Explain why or why not.

Examining Structure and Strategy

1. To what extent does Williams rely on emotional appeal as a persuasive strategy? Give examples of emotional appeal in the essay.

2. Describe the tone of the essay. (See page 37 for an explanation of tone.)

3. How does Williams use examples? How do the examples contribute to the persuasive quality of the essay?

4. In paragraph 7, what strategy does Williams use to persuade the reader that using animals for research is wrong?

5. Cite three or four examples of specific word choice in the essay. What is the effect of this word choice?

6. Williams does little to raise and counter objections. Is this a problem? Explain.

Considering Language and Style

1. Williams says that farm animals "have always suffered a special place in our regard" (paragraph 3). Explain the use of *suffered*.

2. In paragraph 4, Williams refers to "shrink-wrapped remains." What does this phrase mean? What effect is it meant to have on the reader?

3. Consult a dictionary if you are unfamiliar with any other these words: *effete* (paragraph 3), *Cartesians* (paragraph 3), *bedlam* (paragraph 4), *offal* (paragraph 4), *abattoir* (paragraph 4), *transgenic* (paragraph 5), *sentience* (paragraph 6), *vivisected* (paragraph 8), *mantra* (paragraph 10), *misanthropic* (paragraph 15), *eschatological* (paragraph 18), *Jain* (paragraph 22), *Dada* (paragraph 24), *quixotic* (paragraph 29).

For Group Discussion or Writing

Devise a slogan or statement for PETA to replace "A rat is a pig is a dog is a boy" (paragraph 16) and explain how it would advance PETA's cause.

Writing Assignments

1. *In your journal.* How would you characterize your treatment of animals? After reading "The Inhumanity of the Animal People," do you plan to alter your behavior toward animals in any way? Explain.

2. *Using the pattern.* In paragraph 5, Williams says that researchers alter animals "to make the perfect organ donors." Argue for or against breeding animals exclusively for harvesting organs for human beings who need them.

3. *Using the pattern.* In paragraph 14, Williams refers to a 17-year-old cancer victim whose wish was to hunt and kill a Kodiak bear. Do you think this wish should have been granted by the Make-A-Wish Foundation (a nonprofit organization that grants the wishes of children with cancer)? State and defend your view.

4. *Using the pattern.* Argue for or against one of the following: vegetarianism, deer hunting, trapping, wearing fur, using animals for cosmetics testing.

5. *Using the pattern.* Argue that animals do or do not have rights.

6. *Considering a theme.* Write an essay that explains what we can do to treat animals "more humanely" without dramatically altering our lifestyles. What would be gained and lost with these changes?

7. *Connecting the readings.* Explain the role of suffering in life. Consider the nature of suffering, its extent, and whether or not it has any value. You may get some ideas from "The Inhumanity of the Animal People," "The Deer at Providencia" (page 94), and "Am I Blue?" (page 374).

THE "ANIMAL RIGHTS" WAR ON MEDICINE
John G. Hubbell

*John Hubbell, a graduate of the University of Minnesota, was a public rela-
tions specialist at Honeywell, Inc., before beginning work at Reader's Digest
in 1955. In 1960, he became a roving editor for the magazine. He has also
written for the* Saturday Evening Post *and* Catholic Digest. *In "The 'Animal Rights' War on Medicine," which first appeared in Reader's Digest in
1990, Hubbell uses cause-and-effect analysis and exemplification to inform
the reader of the tactics of animal-rights activists and to argue that these tactics jeopardize important medical research—research that helps both humans
and animals.*

THE PATTERNS	THE PURPOSES
cause-and-effect analysis and exemplification	*to inform and to persuade*

1   In the predawn hours of July 4, 1989, members of the Animal
Liberation Front (ALF), an "animal rights" organization, broke into a
laboratory at Texas Tech University in Lubbock. Their target: Prof. John
Orem, a leading expert on sleep-disordered breathing.

2   The invaders vandalized Orem's equipment, breaking recorders,
oscilloscopes and other instruments valued at some $70,000. They also
stole five cats, halting his work in progress—work that could lead to
an understanding of disorders such as Sudden Infant Death Syndrome
(SIDS), or crib death, which kills over 5000 infants every year.

3   An organization known as People for the Ethical Treatment of
Animals (PETA), which routinely issues press releases on ALF activities,
quoted ALF claims that biomedical scientists are "animal-Nazis" and
that Orem "abuses, mutilates and kills animals as part of the federal
grant gravy train."

4   That was only the beginning of the campaign. A month later, on
August 18, animal-rights activists held statewide demonstrations against
Orem, picketing federal buildings in several Texas cities. The result: a
flood of hate mail to the scientist and angry letters to the National Institutes of Health (NIH), which had awarded Orem more than $800,000

in grants. Finally PETA, quoting 16 "experts," filed a formal complaint with the NIH which called Orem's work "cruel" and without "scientific significance." The public had no way of knowing that none of the 16 had any expertise in sleep–disordered breathing or had ever been in Orem's lab.

5   NIH dispatched a team of authorities in physiology, neuroscience and pulmonary and veterinary medicine who, on September 18, reported back. Not only did they find the charges against Orem to be unfounded, but they judged him an exemplary researcher and his work "important and of the highest scientific quality."

MONKEY BUSINESS

6   PETA first intruded on the public consciousness in 1981, during a notorious episode in Silver Spring, Md. That May, a personable college student named Alex Pacheco went to research psychologist Edward Taub for a job. Taub was studying monkeys under an NIH grant, searching for ways to help stroke victims regain use of paralyzed limbs. Pacheco said he was interested in gaining laboratory experience. Taub offered him a position as a volunteer, which Pacheco accepted.

7   Late that summer, Taub took a vacation, leaving his lab in the care of his assistants. As he was about to return to work on September 11, an assistant called. Police, armed with a search warrant, were confiscating the monkeys; there was also a crowd of reporters on hand.

8   To his amazement, Taub was charged with 119 counts of cruelty to animals—most based on information provided to the police by Alex Pacheco, who, it turned out, was one of the PETA's founders.

9   After five years in the courts, Taub was finally cleared of all charges. Yet the animal-rights movement never ceased vilifying him, producing hate mail and death threats. Amid the controversy the NIH suspended and later terminated Taub's grant (essentially for not buying new cages, altering the ventilation system or providing regular visits by a veterinarian). Thorough investigations by the American Physiological Society and the Society for Neuroscience determined that, in the words of the latter, the NIH decision was "incommensurate with the deficiencies cited." Yet a program that could have benefited many of the 2.5 million Americans now living with the debilitating consequences of stroke came to a screeching halt.

10   Wiped out financially, Taub lost his laboratory, though the work of this gifted researcher had already helped rewrite accepted beliefs about the nervous system.

DRAMATIC PROGRESS

11   The animal rights movement has its roots in Europe, where anti-vivisectionists have held the biomedical research community under siege for years. In 1875, Britain's Sir George Duckett of the Society for the Abolition of Vivisection declared: "Vivisection is monstrous. Medical science has little to learn, and nothing can be gained by repetition of experiments on living animals."

12   This sentiment is endlessly parroted by contemporary "activists." It is patently false. Since Duckett's time, animal research has led to vaccines against diphtheria, polio, measles, mumps, whooping cough, rubella. It has meant eradication of smallpox, effective treatment for diabetes and control of infection with powerful antibiotics.

13   The cardiac pacemaker, micro-surgery to reattach severed limbs, and heart, kidney, lung, liver and other transplants are all possible because of animal research. In the early 1960s, the cure rate for acute lymphocytic leukemia in a child was four percent. Today, because of animal research, the cure rate exceeds 70 percent. Since the turn of the century, animal research has helped increase our life-span by nearly 28 years. And now animal research is leading to dramatic progress against AIDS and Alzheimer's disease.

14   Animals themselves have benefited. We are now able to extend and improve the lives of our pets and farm animals through cataract surgery, open-heart surgery and cardiac pacemakers, and can immunize them against rabies, distemper, anthrax, tetanus and feline leukemia. Animal research is an unqualified success story.

15   We should see even more spectacular medical breakthroughs in the coming decades. But not if today's animal-rights movement has its way.

ANIT-HUMAN ABSURDITIES

16   In the United States, the movement is spearheaded by PETA, whose leadership insists that animals are the moral equivalent of human beings. Any differentiation between people and animals constitutes "speciesism," as unethical as racism. Says PETA co-founder and director Ingrid Newkirk, "There really is no rational reason for saying a hu-

man being has special rights. . . . A rat is a pig is a dog is a boy." She compares the killing of chickens with the Nazi Holocaust. "Six million people died in concentration camps," she told the *Washington Post,* "but six billion broiler chickens will die this year in slaughterhouses."

17   Newkirk has been quoted as saying that meat-eating is "primitive, barbaric, arrogant," that humans have "grown like a cancer. We're the biggest blight on the face of the earth," and that if her father had a heart attack, "it would give me no solace at all to know his treatment was first tried on a dog."

18   The movement insists that animal research is irrelevant, that researchers simply refuse to move on to modern techniques. "The movement's big buzzword is 'alternatives,' meaning animals can now be replaced by computers and tissue cultures," says Bessie Borwein, associate dean for research-medicine at the University of Western Ontario. "That is nonsense. You cannot study kidney transplantation or diarrhea or high blood pressure on a computer screen."

19   "A tissue culture cannot replicate a complex organ," echoes Frederick Goodwin, head of the U.S. Alcohol, Drug Abuse and Mental Health Administration (ADAMHA).

20   What do the nation's 570,000 physicians feel about animal research? A 1988 American Medical Association survey found that 97 percent of doctors support it, despite the animal-rights movement's propaganda to the contrary.

21   "Without animal research, medical science would come to a total stand-still," says Dr. Lewis Thomas, best-selling author and scholar-in-residence at New York's Cornell University Medical College.

22   "As a human being and physician, I cannot conceive of telling parents their sick child will die because we cannot use all the tools at our disposal," says pioneering heart surgeon Dr. Michael E. DeBakey of Houston's Baylor College of Medicine. "How will they feel about a society that legislates the rights of animals above those of humans?"

23   "The power of today's medical practice is based on research—and that includes crucial research involving animals," adds Dr. Louis W. Sullivan, Secretary of the U.S. Department of Health and Human Services.

RADICAL INFILTRATION

24   How then have the animal-rights activists achieved respectability? By exploiting the public's rightful concern for humane treatment

of animals. ADAMHA's Goodwin explains: "They have gradually taken over highly respectable humane societies by using classic radical techniques: packing memberships and steering committees and electing directors. They have insidiously gained control of one group after another."

25   The average supporter has no idea that societies which traditionally promoted better treatment for animals, taught pet care, built shelters and cared for strays are now dedicated to ending the most effective kind of medical research. For example, the Humane Society of the United States (HSUS) insists it is not anti-vivisectionist; yet it has persistently stated that animal research is often unnecessary. It published an editorial by animal-rights proponent Tom Regan endorsing civil disobedience for the cause. Says Frederick A. King, director of the Yerkes Regional Primate Center of Emory University, "HSUS flies a false flag. It is part of the same group that has attempted to do severe damage to research."

26   PETA's chairman, Alex Pacheco, says that it is best to be "strategically assertive" in seeking reforms while never losing sight of the ultimate goal: "total abolition" of "animal exploitation." This strategy has worked. It has taken the research community about ten years to realize that it is not dealing with moderates. It is dealing with organizations like ALF, which since 1988 has been on the FBI's list of domestic terrorist organizations. And with Trans-Species Unlimited, which trumpets: "The liberation of animal life can only be achieved through the radical transformation of human consciousness and the overthrow of the existing power structures in which human and animal abuse are entrenched."

27   Consider some of the movement's "liberation activities":

28   • In the early hours of April 3, 1989, hooded animal-rights activists broke into four buildings at the University of Arizona at Tucson. They smashed expensive equipment, spray-painted messages such as "Scum" and "Nazis" and stole 1231 animals. They set fire to two of the four buildings.

29   ALF took credit for the destruction, the cost of which amounted to more than $200,000. Fifteen projects were disrupted. One example: 30 of the 1160 mice taken by ALF were infected with Cryptosporidium, a parasite that can cause severe intestinal disease in humans. The project's aim was to develop an effective disinfectant for Cryptosporidium-contaminated water. Now, not only is the work halted but researchers

warn that, with less than expert handling, the stolen mice could spread cryptosporidiosis, which remains untreatable.

30   • On October 26, 1986, an ALF contingent broke into two facilities at the University of Oregon at Eugene. The equipment the intruders smashed and soaked with red paint included a $10,000 microscope, an electrocardiogram machine, an X-ray machine, an incubator and a sterilizer. At least 150 research animals were taken. As a result, more than a dozen projects were seriously delayed, including research by neuroscientist Barbara Gordon-Lickey on visual defects in newborns. An ALF statement called the neuroscientist a "butcher" and claimed that the animals had found new homes through "an intricate underground railroad network, much like the one used to transport fugitive slaves to the free states of the North in the last century."

31   Police caught up with one of the thieves: Roger Troen, 56, of Portland, Ore., a member of PETA. He was tried and convicted. PETA denied complicity, but Ingrid Newkirk said that PETA would pay Troen's legal expenses, including an appeal of his conviction. PETA then alleged to the NIH that the university was guilty of 12 counts of noncompliance with Public Health Service policy on humane care and use of laboratory animals.

32   Following a lengthy investigation, investigators found all PETA's charges groundless. "To the contrary," their report to the NIH stated, "evidence suggests a firm commitment to the appropriate care and use of laboratory animals."

33   But animal-rights extremists continued their campaign against Gordon-Lickey. They posted placards urging students not to take her courses because she tortured animals. As Nobel Laureate Dr. David H. Hubel of Harvard University, a pioneer in Gordon-Lickey's field, says, "Their tactics are clear. Work to increase the costs of research and stop its progress with red tape and lawsuits."

34   • Dr. Herbert Pardes, president of the American Psychiatric Association, arrived in New York City in 1984 to take over as chairman of psychiatry at Columbia University. His office was in the New York State Psychiatric Institute, part of the Columbia Presbyterian Medical Center complex. Soon after, he noticed that people were handing out leaflets challenging the value of animal research. They picketed Dr. Pardes's home and sent him envelopes containing human feces.

35   Another Columbia scientist received a phone call on December 1, 1988, from someone who said, "We know where you live. How much insurance do you have?" A few mornings later, he found a pool of red paint in front of his house. On January 4, 1989, a guest cottage at his country home burned down.

DEVASTATING RESULTS

36   How effective has the animal-rights movement been? Very. Although recent polls reveal that more than 70 percent of Americans support animal research, about the same number believe the lie that medical researchers torture their animals.

37   According to ADAMHA's Frederick Goodwin, the movement has at its disposal at least $50 million annually, millions of which it dedicates to stopping biomedical research. It has been especially successful in pressuring state legislatures, as well as Congress, which in turn has pressured the federal health establishment. As a result, new regulations are demoralizing many scientists and driving up the cost of research. (For fiscal 1990, an estimated $1.5 billion—approximately 20 percent of the entire federal biomedical-research budget—may be needed to cover the costs of proposed regulation changes and increased security.)

38   At Stanford University, a costly security system has had to be installed and 24-hour guards hired to protect the animal-research facilities. As a consequence of the April 1989 raid at the University of Arizona at Tucson, the school must now spend $10,000 per week on security, money that otherwise could have been used for biomedical research.

39   Threats of violence to researchers and their families are having an effect as well. "It's hard to measure," says Charles R. McCarthy, director of the Office for Protection from Research Risks at the NIH. "But all of a sudden there is a hole in the kind of research being done."

40   In the past two years, for instance, there has been a 50- to 60-percent drop in the number of reports published by scientists using primates to study drug abuse. Reports on the use of primates to learn about severe depression have ended altogether.

41   And what of our future researchers? Between 1977 and 1987 there was a 28-percent drop in the number of college students graduating with degrees in biomedical science, and the growing influence of the animal-rights movement may add to that decline.

STOP THE FANATICS

42   How are we to ensure that the animal-rights movement does not put an end to progress in medical research?

1. Don't swallow whole what the movement says about horrors in our biomedical-research laboratories. With rare exceptions, experimental animals are treated humanely. Biomedical researchers know that an animal in distress is simply not a good research subject. Researchers are embarked on an effort to alleviate misery, not cause it.

2. There are many humane societies that are truly concerned with animal welfare and oppose the animal-rights movement. They deserve your support. But before you contribute, make sure the society has not been taken over by animal-rights extremists. If you are not sure, contact iiFAR (incurably ill For Animal Research), P.O. Box 1873, Bridgeview, Ill. 60455. This organization is one of medical research's most effective allies.

3. Oppose legislation at local, state and federal levels that is designed to hamper biomedical research or price it out of business. Your representatives in government are lobbied by the animal-rights movement all the time. Let them know how *you* feel.

4. Support HR 3270, the "Farm Animal and Research Animal Facilities Protection Act of 1989," introduced by Rep. Charles Stenholm (D., Texas). This bill would make the kinds of break-ins and vandalism ALF has been perpetrating a federal offense subject to a maximum of three years in prison and/or fine of up to $10,000. Also support HR 3349, the "Health Facilities Protection and Primate Center Rehabilitation Act of 1989," introduced by Rep. Henry A. Waxman (D., Calif.). This bill makes criminal assaults on federally funded facilities a federal offense.

If we want to defeat the killer diseases that still confront us— AIDS, Alzheimer's, cancer, heart disease and many others—the misguided fanatics of the animal-rights movement must be stopped.

Reading Closely and Thinking Critically

1. Where does Hubbell state his thesis?

2. How does Hubbell characterize animal-rights activists?

3. What kinds of tactics does Hubbell say that animal-rights activists use? What do you think of these tactics?

4. According to Hubbell, have the tactics of animal-rights activists been successful? Explain.

5. What does Hubbell consider to be the effect of animal-rights activists' infiltration of humane societies?

Examining Structure and Strategy

1. What approach does Hubbell take to the opening of his essay? Is this opening effective? Explain.

2. Hubbell quotes statements made by people on both sides of the issue. What purpose do these quotations serve? How do they contribute to the persuasive quality of the piece?

3. Which objections does Hubbell raise, and how does he counter them?

4. Hubbell gives examples of the tactics of animal-rights activists. How do these examples contribute to the persuasive quality of the piece?

5. Hubbell uses both reason and emotional appeal. Cite an example of each.

6. Does Hubbell arrange his argument in an inductive or deductive pattern?

Considering Language and Style

1. What do animal-rights activists gain when they invoke Nazi images with language like *animal-Nazis* (paragraph 3), and when they compare the killing of chickens to the Nazi Holocaust (paragraph 16)?

2. Consult a dictionary if you are unfamiliar with any of these words: *gravy train* (paragraph 3), *vilifying* (paragraph 9), *incommensurate* (paragraph 9), *vivisection* (paragraph 11), *insidiously* (paragraph 24).

For Group Discussion or Writing

Compare and contrast the versions of what happened to Edward Taub that appear in "The 'Animal Rights' War on Medicine" (paragraphs

6–10) and in "The Inhumanity of the Animal People" (paragraph 19). How does each version serve the thesis of the essay it appears in?

Writing Assignments

1. *In your journal.* What do you think of Ingrid Newkirk's likening of killing chickens to the Nazi Holocaust (paragraph 16)? Is the comparison a valid one?

2. *Using the pattern.* Defend or attack the tactics used by animal-rights activists, as they are described in Hubbell's essay.

3. *Using the pattern.* Define *speciesism* (paragraph 16) and attack or defend it.

4. *Considering a theme.* Argue for or against using animals in biomedical research. The ideas in "The Inhumanity of the Animal People" (page 643) may be helpful.

5. *Connecting the readings.* Explain which essay presents the more convincing argument: "The Inhumanity of the Animal People" (page 643) or "The 'Animal Rights' War on Medicine." You are not explaining which argument you agree with but which one is more convincingly presented.

IN DEFENSE OF THE ANIMALS
Meg Greenfield

A native of Seattle, Washington, Meg Greenfield graduated from Smith College and was a Fulbright scholar at Cambridge University. She is the Washington Post *editorial page editor, and she also writes a regular column for* Newsweek, *which is mostly about life in Washington, D.C. In 1978, Greenfield won a Pulitzer Prize for editorial writing. "In Defense of the Animals" first appeared in* Newsweek *in 1989. Somewhat embarrassed by the stand she takes in the essay, Greenfield admits that the animal-rights people have convinced her to moderate her view. Some might think her stand indefensible, but Greenfield argues a case for some animal cruelty while drawing the line at "wanton" and "frivolous" experimentation. As she does so, Greenfield expresses her feelings about both sides of the issue and her own change of heart.*

THE PATTERNS	THE PURPOSES
cause-and-effect analysis and exemplification	*to persuade and to express feelings and relate experience*

1   I might as well come right out with it: Contrary to some of my most cherished prejudices, the animal-rights people have begun to get to me. I think that in some part of what they say they are right.

2   I never thought it would come to this. As distinct from the old-style animal rescue, protection, and shelter organizations, the more aggressive newcomers, with their "liberation" of laboratory animals and periodic championship of the claims of animal well-being over human well-being when a choice must be made, have earned a reputation in the world I live in as fanatics and just plain kooks. And even with my own recently (relatively) raised consciousness, there remains a good deal in both their critique and their prescription for the virtuous life that I reject, being not just a practicing carnivore, a wearer of shoe leather, and so forth, but also a supporter of certain indisputably agonizing procedures visited upon innocent animals in the furtherance of human welfare, especially experiments undertaken to improve human health.

3   So, viewed from the pure position, I am probably only marginally better than the worst of my kind, if that: I don't buy the complete "speciesist" analysis or even the fundamental language of animal "rights" and continue to find a large part of what is done in the name of that cause harmful and extreme. But I also think, patronizing as it must sound, that the zealots are required early on in any movement if it is to succeed in altering the sensibility of the leaden masses, such as me. Eventually they get your attention. And eventually you at least feel obliged to weigh their arguments and think about whether there may not be something there.

4   It is true that this end has often been achieved—as in my case—by means of vivid, cringe-inducing photographs, not by an appeal to reason or values so much as by an assault on squeamishness. From the famous 1970s photo of the newly skinned baby seal to the videos of animals being raised in the most dark, miserable, stunting environments as they are readied for their life's sole fulfillment as frozen patties and cutlets, these sights have had their effect. But we live in a world where the animal protein we eat comes discreetly prebutchered and prepacked so the original beast and his slaughtering are remote from our consideration, just as our furs come on coat hangers in salons, not on their original proprietors; and I see nothing wrong with our having to contemplate the often unsettling reality of how we came by the animal products we make use of. Then we can choose what we want to do.

5   The objection to our being confronted with these dramatic, disturbing pictures is first that they tend to provoke a misplaced, uncritical and highly emotional concern for animal life at the direct expense of a more suitable concern for human suffering. What goes into the animals' account, the reasoning goes, necessarily comes out of ours. But I think it is possible to remain stalwart in your view that the human claim comes first and in your acceptance of the use of animals for human betterment and *still* to believe that there are some human interests that should not take precedence. For we have become far too self-indulgent, hardened, careless, and cruel in the pain we routinely inflict upon these creatures for the most frivolous, unworthy purposes. And I also think that the more justifiable purposes, such as medical research, are shamelessly used as cover for other activities that are wanton.

6   For instance, not all of the painful and crippling experimentation that is undertaken in the lab is being conducted for the sake of medical knowledge or other purposes related to basic human well-being and

health. Much of it is being conducted for the sake of superrefinements in the cosmetic and other frill industries, the noble goal being to contrive yet another fragrance or hair tint or commercially competitive variation on all the daft, fizzy, multicolored "personal care" products for the medicine cabinet and dressing table, a firmer-holding hair spray, that sort of thing. In other words, the conscripted, immobilized rabbits and other terrified creatures, who have been locked in boxes from the neck down, only their heads on view, are being sprayed in the eyes with different burning, stinging substances for the sake of adding to our already obscene store of luxuries and utterly superfluous vanity items.

PHONY KINSHIP

7   Oddly, we tend to be very sentimental about animals in their idealized, fictional form and largely indifferent to them in realms where our lives actually touch. From time immemorial, humans have romantically attributed to animals their own sensibilities—from Balaam's biblical ass who providently could speak and who got his owner out of harm's way right down to Lassie and the other Hollywood pups who would invariably tip off the good guys that the bad guys were up to something. So we simulate phony cross-species kinship, pretty well drown in the cuteness of it all—Mickey and Minnie and Porky—and ignore, if we don't actually countenance, the brutish things done in the name of Almighty Hair Spray.

8   This strikes me as decadent. My problem is that is also causes me to reach a position that is, on its face, philosophically vulnerable, if not absurd—the muddled, middling, inconsistent place where finally you are saying it's all right to kill them for some purposes, but not to hurt them gratuitously in doing it or to make them suffer horribly for one's own trivial whims.

9   I would feel more humiliated to have fetched up on this exposed rock, if I didn't suspect I had so much company. When you see pictures of people laboriously trying to clean the Exxon gunk off of sea otters even knowing that they will only be able to help out a very few, you see this same outlook in action. And I think it *can* be defended. For to me the biggest cop-out is the one that says that if you don't buy the whole absolutist, extreme position it is pointless and even hypocritical to concern yourself with lesser mercies and ameliorations. The pressure of the animal-protection groups has already had some impact in im-

proving the way various creatures are treated by researchers, trainers, and food producers. There is much more in this vein to be done. We are talking about rejecting wanton, pointless cruelty here. The position may be philosophically absurd, but the outcome is the right one.

Reading Closely and Thinking Critically

1. Where does Greenfield state her thesis?

2. Explain Greenfield's position on the treatment of animals.

3. What does Greenfield see as the role of zealots? Do you agree with her? Explain.

4. What assumption connects Greenfield's claim with her support? (See page 573 on claim, support, and assumptions.) Does that assumption need to be proven? If so, has Greenfield provided that proof? Explain.

5. Does Greenfield convince you of the virtue of her moderate position? Explain.

Examining Structure and Strategy

1. In paragraph 4, Greenfield admits that she has altered her position in response to the emotional appeals of the animal-rights activists. Does the fact that her position was reached in response to emotional appeal weaken her argument? Explain.

2. What objections does Greenfield raise, and how does she counter them? Are there any objections that she should have raised but did not? If so, which ones?

3. What element of emotional appeal does Greenfield include? How does that appeal contribute to her persuasive purpose?

4. In paragraph 9, Greenfield notes that she is not alone in her view. Evaluate the persuasive quality of that statement.

5. What approach does Greenfield take to her conclusion? Is it effective? Explain.

Considering Language and Style

1. Describe the tone of the essay. (See page 37 for an explanation of tone.)

2. Consult a dictionary if you are unfamiliar with any of these words: *carnivore* (paragraph 2), *patronizing* (paragraph 3), *zealots* (paragraph 9), *wanton* (paragraph 5), *immemorial* (paragraph 7), *gratuitously* (paragraph 8), *cop-out* (paragraph 9), *ameliorations* (paragraph 9).

For Group Discussion or Writing
Is there a difference between using animals that resemble us, like chimpanzees, in research and using animals more distant from us, like rats? Explore this issue with several classmates.

Writing Assignments

1. ***In your journal.*** If you could save the lives of thousands of people by conducting painful, lethal experiments on dogs, cats, and chimpanzees, would you do it? Explain why or why not in a page or so.

2. ***Using the pattern.*** Greenfield is opposed to some, but not all, animal experimentation and suffering. Is her position a convenient but indefensible solution, or is it a solid, defensible response? State and support your view.

3. ***Using the pattern.*** Greenfield says we are "sentimental about animals in their idealized, fictional form" (paragraph 7). Agree or disagree with this contention by citing examples to support your view. Your examples may come from literature, the media, and advertising.

4. ***Using the pattern.*** Assume a person is on trial for destroying the laboratory of a researcher who uses animals to test cosmetics. Write closing arguments to the jury, arguing either to convict or not to convict the defendant.

5. ***Considering a theme.*** Greenfield accepts some forms of animal cruelty but rejects "wanton, pointless cruelty" (paragraph 9). Write a set of guidelines that clarify the difference between acceptable and unacceptable levels of cruelty. Think of the guidelines as being used in university research laboratories.

6. ***Connecting the readings.*** Explain what you believe is the relationship between human beings and animals. Some of the ideas in "The Deer at Providencia" (page 94), "The Stone Horse" (page 119), and "In Defense of the Animals" may help you.

ADDITIONAL ESSAY ASSIGNMENTS

See pages 584 and 585 for suggestions for writing argumentation-persuasion and for a revision checklist.

1. Summarize the views of Shelby Steele (page 612) and Roger Wilkins (page 598) on affirmative action. Then state and defend your own position.

2. Find out what your school's policy is on limiting speech and argue whether or not that policy is a good one. As an alternative, argue for a specific change in your school's policy. (See "Free Speech on Campus" (page 623) and "The Debate over Placing Limits on Racist Speech Must Not Ignore the Damage It Does to Its Victims" (page 631) for ideas.)

3. What tactics are acceptable when people fight for causes they believe in? Can property be damaged? Can lies be told? Does the end justify the means? Consider these questions and the ideas in "The Inhumanity of the Animal People" (page 643) and "The 'Animal Rights' War on Medicine" (page 660) when you argue for your position.

4. Elizabeth Whelan suggests a remedy for alcohol abuse on college campuses. Pick another problem on college campuses and argue for the implementation of a particular solution.

5. Use the information in "The Water-Faucet Vision" (page 184) and "I Wish They'd Do It Right" (page 593), along with your own experience and observation, to attack or defend the idea that couples should make decisions about whether to marry or divorce based on what is best for their children.

6. Write an argumentation-persuasion essay on any of the following topics:
  a. Assisted suicide.
  b. Distributing condoms in high schools.
  c. Eliminating athletic scholarships.
  d. Paying student athletes.
  e. Dress codes for high school students.
  f. Limiting immigration into the United States.
  g. Bilingual education.
  h. Censoring rock lyrics.

7. *Argumentation-persuasion in context:* By now, you have probably identified some aspects of student life that could be improved upon. You may desire changes in grading policies, housing conditions, examination practices, parking regulations, advising procedures, scheduling practices, and so forth. Select one change you would like to see on your campus and write an argumentation-persuasion essay to be published in the opinion section of your campus newspaper. Your goal is to garner both student and administrative support for the change you are recommending.

Writing Paraphrases, Quotations, Summaries, and Syntheses

Writers frequently draw on the work of other writers. For example, you may use an idea from someone's essay to back up one of your points, or another writer's idea may prompt you to write an essay of your own. That is one of the exciting things about writing—writers engage in an ongoing conversation by responding to each other's ideas and using them for support or departure points. However, to be a part of this conversation, you must learn its rules, and that is what this appendix is all about. Here you will learn how writers can fairly and responsibly draw on the work of others.

PARAPHRASING

To *paraphrase,* you restate another author's ideas, using your own writing style and wording. Paraphrasing is helpful because it allows you to incorporate brief excerpts from different sources into your essays to support your own ideas. (The sample synthesis on page 693 shows how paraphrases of different sources can be brought together.)

When you paraphrase, you must follow specific rules. These rules are illustrated with paraphrases of the following excerpt from paragraph 8 of "Protecting Freedom of Expression at Harvard" (page 638):

> Under the Supreme Court's rulings, as I read them, the display of swastikas or Confederate flags clearly falls within the protection of the free-speech clause of the First Amendment and cannot be forbidden simply because it offends the feelings of many members of the community. These rulings apply to all agencies of government, including public universities.

1. Introduce the paraphrase with the author and/or source and a present tense verb; after the paraphrase, place in parentheses the page number the paraphrase was taken from.

source   author
↑   ↑

yes: In "Protecting Freedom of Expression at Harvard," Derek Bok
present tense→ expresses his belief that past Supreme Court decisions allow the display of swastikas and Confederate flags in public universities, even if the displays are offensive, because such displays are protected by the First Amendment's guarantee of free speech (639). ← page number

2. Do not add or alter meaning.

no: According to Derek Bok in "Protecting Freedom of Expression at Harvard," the Supreme Court's past decisions allow the display of swastikas and Confederate flags at all universities and colleges (639).

explanation: Bok says the Supreme Court rulings apply to government agencies, including *public* universities. He does not include private universities and colleges.

3. Alter style and wording so they are yours rather than the author's.

no: Derek Bok says in "Protecting Freedom of Expression at Harvard" that people can display swastikas and Confederate flags because these displays clearly fall under the protection of the free-speech clause of the First Amendment of the Constitution (639).

explanation: *Clearly fall under the protection of the free-speech clause of the First Amendment* is almost identical to the source.

4. Do not paraphrase by substituting synonyms, or you will have something that sounds stilted and unnatural.

no: In "Protecting Freedom of Expression at Harvard," Derek Bok says that according to Supreme Court decisions, the presentation of the Nazi symbol or flag of the South from the Civil War obviously comes within the safeguarding of the freedom of speech provision of the First Amendment (639).

explanation: Although technically accurate, the paraphrase reads poorly. Rather than plug in synonyms, explain the material in your own words to achieve a more natural style.

QUOTING

To *quote*, you reproduce an author's exact words. Like paraphrasing, quoting is useful for bringing together ideas from one or more sources and for using another author's ideas to support your own point. However, you should limit the amount of quoting you do because if you quote too much, your writing will lack your distinctive style. As a general guide, limit your quoting to those times when paraphrase proves difficult or when something is so well expressed that you want to preserve the original wording.

A number or conventions govern the use of quotations. Several of these are illustrated below; all but the last example uses material from "Protecting Freedom of Expression at Harvard" (page 638).

1. Introduce the quotation with a statement of the author and/or source and a present tense verb. After the quotation, place in parentheses the page number the quotation was taken from. Be sure to preserve the words and punctuation in the original, and punctuate and capitalize correctly.

source: The fact that speech is protected by the First Amendment does not necessarily mean that it is right, proper, or civil.

quotation: Derek Bok says, "The fact that speech is protected by the First Amendment does not necessarily mean that it is right, proper, or civil" (638).← page number

The words "author" (with arrow) and "present tense" (with arrow) label "Derek Bok" and "says" respectively.

2. When the introduction to the quotation has a direct object, use a colon instead of a comma before the quotation.

source: See number 1.

quotation: Derek Bok makes an important observation: "The fact that speech is protected by the First Amendment does not necessarily mean that it is right, proper, or civil" (638).

3. Omit the comma and capital letter when the quotation follows an introduction with *that* in it.

source: See number 1.

quotation: Derek Bok explains that "the fact that speech is protected by the First Amendment does not necessarily mean that it is right, proper, or civil" (638).

4. Use ellipses (three spaced periods) within brackets to indicate that something has been left out.

source: Under the Supreme Court's rulings, as I read them, the display of swastikas or Confederate flags clearly falls within the protection of the free-speech clause of the First Amendment and cannot be forbidden simply because it offends the feelings of many members of the community.

quotation: Bok notes, "Under the Supreme Court's rulings [. . .] the display of swastikas or Confederate flags clearly falls within the protection of the free-speech clause of the First Amendment and cannot be forbidden simply because it offends the feelings of many members of the community" (639).

5. Use brackets to add clarification or to make changes to work the quotation into your sentence.

source: I share this view and regret that the students involved saw fit to behave in this fashion.

quotation: Bok says that he "share[s] this view [that displaying hate symbols is insensitive and unwise] and regret[s] that the students involved saw fit to behave in this fashion" (639).

6. For a quotation within a quotation, use single quotation marks where double quotation marks appear in the source.

source: In addition, once we start to declare certain things "offensive," with all the excitement and attention that will follow, I fear that much ingenuity will be exerted trying to test the limits. . . ."

quotation: Bok says that "once we start to declare certain things 'offensive,' with all the excitement and attention that will follow, I fear that much ingenuity will be exerted trying to test the limits . . ." (640).

7. If your typewriter or printer cannot reproduce italics, underline to indicate that something appeared in italics in the source.

source: Parents' terror of the mysterious sudden infant death syn- drome were manipulated shamelessly with the *cure depen- dent upon animal research* mantra—until the precipitous re- cent drop in infant deaths was attributed to the simple act of putting babies to bed on their backs instead of their stom- achs.

quotation: Joy Williams points out that "parents' terrors of the mysteri- ous sudden infant death syndrome were manipulated shame- lessly with the cure dependent upon animal research man- tra—until the precipitous recent drop in infant deaths was attributed to the simple act of putting babies to bed on their backs instead of their stomachs" (648).

DOCUMENTING BORROWED MATERIAL

You probably know that taking another person's work and pass- ing it off as your own is a form of academic dishonesty called *pla- giarism.* However, another form of plagiarism, which is often un- intentional but nonetheless serious, occurs when you paraphrase or quote and neglect to *document* the material by crediting its source.

If you use the words or ideas from sources in this text, you can document the borrowed material according to the conven- tions of the Modern Language Association (MLA). These con- ventions will be described below. However, different disciplines and different instructors will favor different conventions. In the social sciences, for example, the conventions of the American Psychological Association (APA) are often preferred. When in doubt, check with your instructor to learn which conventions you should follow.

When you paraphrase or quote, MLA documentation dic- tates that you credit the source material. To do so, provide an in- troduction, a parenthetical citation, and Works Cited entry. The introduction states to whom the borrowing should be attributed, the parenthetical citation gives the page number where the borrowing can be found, and the Works Cited entry provides complete bibliographic information about the source. Here are examples of the possibilities.

1. The first time you use a source, introduce it with the author's full name and the title of the source:

For example, in "A Negative Vote on Affirmative Action," Shelby Steele admits that affirmative action is well-intentioned (613), but he objects to the fact that the policies are the product of the "racial guilt" of whites (614).

Note: The page number where the borrowed idea can be found appears in parentheses; the period goes outside those parentheses.

2. After the first time you use a source, you can introduce with either the author's last name or the title of the source; you do not need both.

As Wilkins points out, left to our own devices, we discriminate, so affirmative action is needed until "most white males are really ready for a color-blind society" (608).

Note: Exact words appear in quotation marks; the page number appears in parentheses; the period goes outside those parentheses. Notice that the verb in the introduction is in the present tense.

3. If you quote or paraphrase a source that is cited in a second source, you should note the secondhand nature of the borrowing with *qtd.in* in the parenthetical citation, which stands for "as quoted in."

What we do know for sure is what the Urban Institute of America reports: 53 percent of the male blacks in this country who are 25–34 years old are either unemployed or failing to earn enough to move their families out of poverty (qtd. in Wilkins 607).

Note: The borrowing is introduced with the name of primary source; the secondary source is noted in the parenthetical citation.

4. Proper documentation requires you to follow your writing with an alphabetical listing of your sources. This listing appears on a page with the heading *Works Cited,* and it includes full bibliographic information on each source you quoted or paraphrased from. Sample citations appear below. If you use sources that do not fit the following models, consult a handbook or research paper guide for the correct format.

Book with One Author

Johnson, Paul. <u>Birth of the Modern: World Society 1815–1830</u>.
    New York: Harper, 1991.

Book with Two or Three Authors

Silverstein, Olga, and Beth Rashbaum.
    <u>The Courage to Raise Good Men</u>. New York:
    Viking, 1994.

Book with More than Three Authors

Shafer, Raymond P., et al. <u>Marijuana: A Signal of</u>
    <u>Misunderstanding</u>. New York: NAL, 1972.

Revised Edition of a Book

Miller, Casey, and Kate Swift. <u>The Handbook of</u>
    <u>Nonsexist Writing</u>. 2nd ed. New York:
    Harper, 1988.

A Book with an Editor

Arnold, Matthew. <u>Culture and Anarchy</u>. Ed. J. Dover
    Wilson. Cambridge: Cambridge UP, 1961.

Marshall, Sam A., ed. <u>1990 Photographer's Market</u>.
    Cincinnati: Writer's Digest, 1989.

More than One Book by the Same Author

Tannen, Deborah. That's Not What I Meant! New York:
Ballantine, 1986.

---. You Just Don't Understand: Women and
Men in Conversation. New York: Ballantine,
1990.

Selection from an Anthology

Larmoth, Jeanine. "Lists." Patterns for a Purpose: A
Rhetorical Reader. Ed. Barbara Fine Clouse. 2nd ed.
New York: McGraw, 1999. 522–527.

Article from a Weekly or Biweekly Magazine

Hamilton, Kendall. "Louder and Prouder." Newsweek 10
Nov. 1997: 68.

"How Recession Happens." Newsweek 10 Nov. 1997: 42.

Article from a Monthly or Bimonthly Magazine

Arnold, Marilyn. "Willa Cather's Nostalgia: A Study
in Ambivalence." Research Studies Mar. 1981:
23–24.

Newspaper Article

Farrell, William E. "Ex-Soviet Scientist, Now in Israel,
Tells of Nuclear Disaster." New York Times 9 Dec.
1976 late ed.: A8.

Article from a Scholarly Journal with Continuous Pagination

Crumley, E. Frank. "The Adolescent Suicide Attempt:
A Cardinal Symptom of a Serious Psychiatric

Disorder." <u>American Journal of Psychotherapy</u> 26
(1982): 158–65.

Article from Scholarly Journal with Separate Pagination

Tong, T.K. "Temporary Absolutisms Versus Hereditary
Autocracy." <u>Chinese Studies in History</u> 21.3 (1988):
3–22.

Radio or Television Program

Moyers, Bill, and Robert Bly. <u>A Gathering of Men.</u>
PBS. WNET, New York. 8 Jan. 1990.

Personal Interview

DeSalvo, Joy. Personal interview. 30 Sept. 1996.

Material from a Portable Database (CD-ROM, Diskette, Magnetic Tape)

"Nuclear Energy: How Protons and Neutrons Change."
<u>Compton's Interactive Encyclopedia</u>. 1995 ed.
CD-ROM. New York: Softkey Multimedia, 1996.

Material from a Professional Site

<u>Hemorrhagic Stroke</u>. National Stroke Association.
10 Oct. 1997 <http://www.stroke.org/HEM_ol.html>.
Note: The date refers to the date of access.

Article in a Reference Database

"Abbott, Berenice." <u>Women in American History</u>.
Encyclopaedia Britannica. 9 April 1998 <http://
women.eb.com/women/articles/abbott_bernice.html>.
Note: The date refers to the date of access.

Magazine Article

Fromatz, Samuel. "Groovin' with Scofield, Medeski,
Martin, and Wood." <u>All about Jazz</u>. April 1998. 10
April 1998 <http://www.allaboutjazz.com/Bios/
jxsbio.htm>.

Journal Article

Krueger, Ellen. "Media Literacy Does Work." <u>English
Journal</u> Jan. 1998. 5 Feb. 1998 <http://digit.soe.vcu.
edu/ej/krueger.htm>.

Material from an Electronic Source That Has Also Appeared in Print

"The End of Life." <u>The Atlantic Unbound</u>. 12 Nov. 1997.
14 Nov. 1997 <http://www.theatlantic.com/
unbound/citation/wc971112.htm>.

Note: The second date is the date the material was accessed.

Material from a Scholarly Site

<u>The Labyrinth</u>: <u>Resources for Medieval Studies</u>. 1977.
Georgetown. 30 Apr. 1998 <http://www.
georgetown.edu/labyrinth/labyrinth-home.html>.

Online Posting

Quinlan, Rob. "Biocultural Evolution." Online posting.
19 Sept. 1995. Anthro-I: The General Anthropology
Bulletin Board. 30 Apr. 1998 <http://www.anatomy.
usyd.edu.au/danny/anthropology/anthro-1/>.

SUMMARIZING

To *summarize,* you restate the main ideas of a piece, using your own style and wording. You may not interpret the author's ideas, evaluate them, or in any way add points that did not appear in the original. Thus, a summary is the distillation of what you see as the author's most important points. Because a summary includes only the highlights, it will be shorter than the original.

The Purpose of Summaries

College provides many opportunities to summarize. For one thing, summarizing is a valuable study technique because writing out the main points of material gives you a study guide and helps you learn information.

You may also write summaries for a grade. For example, instructors may ask you to summarize material so they can determine if you have read and understood assignments. On midterms and finals, they may also ask you to summarize reading assignments so they can check your comprehension and retention.

In addition, summaries are frequent components of other kinds of writing. If you are writing a research paper, for example, you will summarize information you discover in the library. If you are writing an argumentation-persuasion essay, you can summarize the main points in something you have read and go on to disagree with those points. If you read something that helps explain a point you want to make in an essay, you can summarize what you read and use it as part of your supporting detail.

Suggestions for Writing a Summary

Step 1. Read the material over as many times as necessary in order to understand it. Look up unfamiliar words and get help with anything you do not understand. (You cannot summarize material you do not understand.)

Step 2. Identify the main points and underline them in the text or list them on a piece of paper. You can omit examples, description, repetition, or explanation that supports main points.

Step 3. Draft an opening sentence that mentions the author's name, the title of the piece you are summarizing, and one, two, or three of the following: the thesis, the author's purpose, the author's point of view. Here are some examples:

author, title, and thesis:	In "I Wish They'd Do It Right," Jane Doe expresses her belief that her son is wrong not to marry the mother of his child.
author, title, and purpose:	"I Wish They'd Do It Right" is Jane Doe's attempt to convince people, including her son, that marriage is preferable to living together.
author, title, point of view:	In "I Wish They'd Do It Right," Jane Doe examines the issue of cohabitation from a parent's perspective.

Note: Use a present tense verb with the author's name because the words "live on" into the present: Jane Doe *says, notes, expresses, believes* (not *said, noted, expressed, believed*).

Step 4. Following your opening statement, draft your summary by writing out the main points you underlined or listed. Be sure to express these points in your own distinctive style by using your own wording and sentence structure. If you have trouble rewording a phrase or sentence, you can use the original if you place the borrowed words in quotation marks. Just be careful to use quotations sparingly.

Note: If you have trouble expressing the author's ideas in a different way, imagine yourself explaining each idea to a friend. Then write each point the way you would explain it.

Note: To keep your summary flowing smoothly, use transitions to show how ideas relate to each other. In addition, repeat the author's name with a present tense verb as a transitional device, like this:

Smith explains
Smith further believes
The author goes on to note

Step 5. Revise by checking every point to be sure you have not added or altered meaning in any way. Also be sure that you have used your own wording and style and that you have placed borrowed words and phrases in quotation marks. Then read your summary out loud and listen for any gaps or abrupt shifts that signal the need to add transitions.

A Sample Summary

The following is a summary of "I Wish They'd Do It Right," which appears on page 593. The annotations in the margin call your attention to some of the summary's key features.

Summary of "I Wish They'd Do It Right"
by Jane Doe

[1.]In "I Wish They'd Do It Right," the anonymous author (Jane Doe) [2.]argues· that her son and his companion (who is the mother of his child) should get married. She has several reasons for her position.

[3.]First, Doe points out that the two young people are mistaken if they think that living together is a form of [4.]"pioneering," for there is nothing new about their arrangement. [5.]Further, she explains, [6.]marriage offers the couple more advantages, and divorce, should it be called for, is no longer difficult to obtain.

[7.]Doe goes on to explain that [8.] [9.]"living together out of wedlock can be economically impractical, as well as socially awkward." As examples she notes the problem of what to call the mother of her grandchild, the fact that the couple cannot live in inexpensive married student housing, and the fact that her son cannot be carried on his companion's insurance policy.

[10.]The author is particularly concerned about the effects of the couple's arrangement on their son, who may be teased by people and traumatized if his parents separate without ever having legally committed to each other. Although she recognizes that her son's failure to marry is motivated by idealism and honesty, [11.]Doe points out

[1] Summary opens with a statement that gives the author, title, and thesis of material summarized.

[2] Verb is in the present tense.

[3] First main point is given.

[4] Borrowed word appears in quotation marks.

[5] Transition is achieved with *further* and pronoun. Note present tense.

[6] Next main point is given.

[7] Transition is achieved with repetition of the author's name. Note the present tense.

[8] Borrowed words appear in quotation marks.

[9] Next main point is given.

[10] *The author* provides transition. Next main points appear.

[11] Transition is achieved with repetition of the author's name. Note the present tense.

that the issue should be moot for him, since the state recognizes the couple's union as a legal agreement.

 [12.]Finally, the author points out that [13.]the family is diminished by their inability to celebrate her son's wedding and anniversaries. It is further strained by the need to conceal the arrangement from those family members who would be upset by the truth.

[14.]Work Cited

Doe, Jane. "I Wish They'd Do It Right." Patterns

   for a Purpose: A Rhetorical Reader. Ed. Bar-

   bara Fine Clouse. 2nd ed. New York: McGraw,

   1998. 593–595.

[12] Transitional word eases the flow.

[13] The last main points are given.

[14] In *your* summary, the "Works Cited" page should begin on a separate page.

SYNTHESIZING

Synthesizing involves bringing material from two or more sources together in one essay. When you synthesize, you may evaluate the material you are working with and form judgments about it; you may draw conclusions from the material; you may use the material to support the thesis of your essay; or you may use the material to back up one or more of your points.

The Purposes of Synthesis

Synthesis can have an informational purpose. For example, to inform your reader about the effects of televised violence on children, you could mention all the effects discussed in a number of essays and books on the subject. Synthesis can also allow a writer to inform by presenting an overview of a topic. For example, if authorities disagree on how children are affected by televised violence, you could synthesize these views to inform your reader of current thinking on the subject.

Writers can use information from two or more sources to back up points in support of a thesis. In this case, the synthesis often serves a persuasive purpose. For example, to argue that televised violence is harmful to children, you could bring together the statements made in different sources about the ways televised violence is thought to hurt younger viewers.

Detail in a Synthesis

Sometimes a synthesis includes only the information from your sources. For example, you could present an overview of the controversy surrounding animal rights by drawing on the information in the essays in Chapter 11. Other times, a synthesis blends source material and your own ideas. Thus, you could present an overview of the controversy surrounding animal rights by drawing on your own thoughts, experiences, and observations, as well as the information in Chapter 11's essays.

Sometimes you evaluate your synthesized material and draw a conclusion. For example, you could present all the issues surrounding animal rights from the essays in Chapter 11; then you could conclude that it is acceptable to use animals in medical research and explain why. Other times, you can use synthesized material to support your own points. For example, you could argue that people should become vegetarians by referring to points in the essays in Chapter 11 for support.

An essay with synthesized material can take a number of forms. You can agree or disagree with information in sources. You can also show areas of agreement and disagreement between different sources, or you can show how the ideas in one source prove or disprove the ideas in another. You can even show how the ideas in one source serve as an example of points in another. Even these do not exhaust all the possibilities, for what you do with the material from sources is limited only by the conclusion you draw and the relationships you see among ideas.

Suggestions for Synthesizing Information

Step 1. Be sure you understand everything in all the sources you are dealing with. If necessary, look up words and ask your instructor for clarification.

Step 2. Underline or list the main ideas in each source.

Step 3. Review the main ideas and determine how they relate to each other. Answering these five questions can help:

1. Do the ideas in the sources support each other or contradict each other?

2. Do the ideas in the sources form a cause-and-effect relationship?

3. Do the ideas in one source explain or exemplify the ideas in another source?

4. Do the ideas in one source pick up where the ideas in another source end?

5. Do the sources examine the same topic from different perspectives?

Step 4. Decide how you want to use the material in the sources. Answering these five questions can help:

1. Can I use the information to explain something?

2. Can I use the information to prove something?

3. Can I show how the sources contradict each other or present different perspectives?

4. Can I explain the significance of the information?

5. Can I use the information to suport my own experience or observation?

Step 5. Write some form of outline and a thesis that makes clear what point your essay makes.

Step 6. Write a draft from your outline.

Step 7. When you revise, check the accuracy of your paraphrases and quotations, and be sure you have properly documented your sources with introductions and parenthetical citations. (See page 681 on documentation.)

A Sample Synthesis

The following essay shows one way ideas from two sources ("Racism Has Its Privileges: The Case for Affirmative Action" on page 598 and "A Negative Vote on Affirmative Action" on page 612) can be synthesized. The notes in the margin call your attention to some of the key features of the synthesis.

Reconsidering Affirmative Action:
Stay the Course

[1]The debate over affirmative action has escalated. No longer are affirmative action practices taken for granted, for more states are reconsidering their policies, and some, like California, are wiping affirmative action regulations off the books. While some people are alarmed by the current trend, others see it as an opportunity to correct our course. Convincing arguments have been presented on both sides, and neither side is without its troublesome issues. [2]Nonetheless, those who favor affirmative action hold the better position.

People of all races have questioned the effectiveness of affirmative action. Even [3]Roger Wilkins, a proponent of affirmative action, notes in "Racism Has Its Privileges: The Case for Affirmative Action" that affirmative action [4]"has not always been used wisely" [5](600). He [6]further admits that some affirmative action regulations should be revised or eliminated (600). Despite that, [7]Wilkins believes that affirmative action "has done wonderful things for the United States" (600). To [8]me, one of those wonderful things is the promotion of minorities into visible positions

[1] The writer's own background and evaluation lead in to the synthesis.

[2] The thesis.

[3] The introduction credits source. It includes the author's full name and the title of the essay, since this is the first use of the source.

[4] Direct quotation from paragraph 6.

[5] Parenthetical citation to credit the source.

[6–7] Paraphrase and quotation from paragraph 6. Note transition, present tense introductions, and parenthetical citations.

[8] Writer's ideas.

of responsibility. As a result, a whole generation is growing up with the understanding that bright, capable people exist in all ethnic groups.

[9]The fact that affirmative action has created opportunities for minorities is not enough to persuade everyone of the virtues of the program. For example, in "A Negative Vote on Affirmative Action," [10]Shelby Steele admits that affirmative action is well-intentioned (613), [11]but he objects to the fact that the policies are the product of the "racial guilt" of whites (614). Thus, [12]Steele creates an odd contradiction: he sees the policies as well-intentioned at the same time he faults them for being impurely motivated. Frankly, whites have good reason to feel guilty for over 300 years of mistreatment of blacks, and if affirmative action helps right the wrongs, then the policies should be maintained. As [13]Wilkins points out, left to our own devices, we discriminate, so affirmative action is needed until "most white males are really ready for a color-blind society" (608). We are not at that point yet.

[14]Some people oppose affirmative action policies because they think these policies cause discrimination against whites, white males in particular. Other people share the view that affirmative action policies discriminate against whites, but these people support the policies anyway. They take a position similar to the white male manager that [15]Steele quotes: "'I think it [affirmative action] amounts to reverse discrimination, but I'll put up with a little of that for a little more diversity'" (614). [16]While the increased diversity that affirmative action promotes is one good reason to support it, reverse discrimination is not a reason to oppose affirmative action because there is no substantial evidence that significant reverse discrimination exists. Yes, we hear people complain that they lost jobs or promotions as a result of affirmative action regulations, but these stories are just that—stories. Rarely is proof offered. What we do know for sure is what the Urban Institute of America reports: 53 percent of the male blacks in this country who are 25 to 34 years old are either unemployed or failing to earn enough to move their families out of poverty

[9] Writer's analysis.

[10] Paraphrase from paragraph 3.

[11] Paraphrase from paragraph 6; key words quoted.

[12] Writer's conclusion.

[13] Only last name is used because full name used previously. Note that writer synthesizes opposing viewpoints and draws a conclusion.

[14] The topic sentence is the writer's evaluation.

[15] Quotation from paragraph 5. Note brackets, single quotation marks, and parenthetical citation.

[16] Writer's ideas.

(qtd.in [17]Wilkins 607). [18]This figure does not suggest that black males are being hired and promoted with some kind of discriminatory abandon.

[19]Steele has reservations about affirmative action because he believes it "does not teach skills, or educate, or instill motivation" (618). [20]On the contrary, once people are employed and paid meaningfully, their standard of living increases, and they are better able to educate their children. The higher standard of living and increased level of education translate to what the American dream has always been about—the ability to move up. Affirmative action grants blacks the same access to that dream and means to make it come true that whites have always had. [21]Without affirmative action, the United States will fail, as Wilkins puts it, to "lift its ideals out of a thick, often impenetrable slough of racism" (604).

[17] Secondary source is given in parentheses; paraphrase is from paragraph 35.

[18] Writer's conclusion.

[19] Introduction with the author's last name because full name given previously. Note the present tense. Quotation is from paragraph 19.

[20] Writer counters the objection.

[21] Writer achieves closure with quotation from paragraph 25.

[22]Works Cited

[22] In *your* synthesis, the "Works Cited" page should begin on a new page.

Steele, Shelby. "A Negative Vote on Affirmative Action." Patterns for a Purpose: A Rhetorical Reader. Ed. Barbara Fine Clouse. 2nd ed. New York: McGraw, 1998. 612 – 619.

Wilkins, Roger. "Racism Has Its Privileges: The Case for Affirmative Action." Patterns for a Purpose: A Rhetorical Reader. Ed. Barbara Fine Clouse. 2nd ed. New York: McGraw, 1998. 598 – 609.

ACKNOWLEDGMENTS

Barry, Dave. "America Has Gone on a Trip Out of Tune" by Dave Barry from *Miami Herald*, July 14, 1991. © Tribune Media Services, Inc. All Rights Reserved. Reprinted with permission.

Bodett, Tom. From *Small Comforts* by Tom Bodett. © 1987 by Tom Bodett. Reprinted by permission of Addison Wesley Longman.

Bok, Derek. "Protecting Freedom of Expression at Harvard" by Derek Bok. Copyright © 1991 by Derek Bok. Reprinted by permission of Georges Borchardt, Inc. for the author. Originally appeared in *The Boston Globe*.

Bok, Sissela. "White Lies" from *Lying* by Sissela Bok. Copyright © 1978 by Sissela Bok. Reprinted by permission of Pantheon Books, a division of Random House, Inc.

Brady, Judy. "Why I Want a Wife" by Judy Brady, as appeared in *Ms. Magazine*, December, 1971. Copyright © 1970 by Judy Brady. Reprinted by permission of the author.

Britt, Suzanne. "Neat People vs. Sloppy People" from *Show and Tell* by Suzanne Britt. Reprinted by permission of the author.

Campa, Arthur. "Anglo vs Chicano: Why?" by Arthur Campa from *Western Review*, Vol. IX, Spring 1972. Reprinted by permission of Western Review: A Journal of the Humanities, Western New Mexico University, Silver City, New Mexico.

Cole, Diane. "Don't Just Stand There" by Diane Cole originally published in *The New York Times*, April 16, 1989. Reprinted by permission of the author.

Satter, Robert. "Whom to Believe?" from *Doing Justice* by Robert Satter 1990. Reprinted by permission of the author.

Segal, David. "Excuuuse Me" by David Segal, *The New Republic*, May 11, 1992. Reprinted by permission of The New Republic © 1992 The New Republic, Inc.

Shepherd, Jean. "Lost at C," copyright © 1973 by Playboy Enterprises, Inc. First appeared in *Playboy* Magazine, from *A Fistful of Fig Newtons* by Jean Shepherd. Used by permission of Doubleday, a division of Bantam Doubleday Dell Publishing Group, Inc.

Siegel, Dorothy. "What Is Behind the Growth of Violence on College Campuses?" by Dorothy Siegel, *USA Today*, May 1994. Reprinted from USA Today magazine, May. Copyright 1994 by the Society for the Advancement of Education.

Staples, Brent. "Just Walk On By: A Black Man Ponders His Power to Alter Public Space" by Brent Staples published in *Ms.* Magazine. Reprinted by permission of the author.

Steele, Shelby. "A Negative Vote on Affirmative Action" by Shelby Steele as appeared in *The New York Times* May 13, 1995. Reprinted by permission of the author.

Tannen, Deborah. "Talk in the Intimate Relationship: His and Hers" from *That's Not What I Meant* by Deborah Tannen. Copyright © 1986 by Deborah Tannen. Reprinted by permission of William Morrow & Company, Inc.

Thurber, James. "University Days" from *My Life and Hard Times* by James Thurber. Copyright © 1933 by James Thurber. Copyright © renewed 1961 by Helen Thurber and Rosemary A. Thurber. Reprinted by arrangement with Rosemary A. Thurber and the Barbara Hogenson Agency.

Trillin, Calvin. "It's Just Too Late" by Calvin Trillin. Copyright © 1984 by Calvin Trillin. Originally appeared in *The New Yorker*. This usage granted by permission.

Vámos, Miklós. "How I'll Become an American" by Miklós Vámos, *The New York Times*, April 17, 1989. Copyright © 1989 by The New York Times Co. Reprinted by permission.

Walker, Alice. "Am I Blue?" from *Living By The Word: Selected Writings 1973–1987,* copyright © 1986 by Alice Walker, reprinted by permission of Harcourt Brace & Company.

Whelan, Elizabeth. "Perils of Prohibition" by Elizabeth Whelan. From *Newsweek,* May 29, 1995. All rights reserved. Reprinted by permission.

White, E.B. "Once More to the Lake" from *One Man's Meat* by E.B. White. Text copyright © 1941 by E.B. White, renewed 1998 by Joel White. Reprinted by permission of Tilbury House, Publishers, Gardiner, Maine.

Wiesel, Elie. "To Be A Jew" from *A Jew Today* by Elie Wiesel translated from the French by Marion Wiesel. Copyright © 1978 by Elirion Associates, Inc. Reprinted by permission of Random House, Inc.

Wilkins, Roger. "Racism Has Its Privileges: The Case for Affirmative Action" by Roger Wilkins. Reprinted with permission from the March 27, 1995 issue of *The Nation*. © 1995.

Williams, Joy. "The Inhumanity of the Animal People" by Joy Williams. Copyright © 1997 by Joy Williams. Reprinted by permission of International Creative Management. Originally appeared in *Harper's Magazine*.

INDEX